LEIPOLDT'S FOOD & WINE

LEIPOLDT'S FOOD & WINE

by

C LOUIS LEIPOLDT

Leipoldt's Cape Cookery

Culinary Treasures

Three Hundred Years of Cape Wine

EDITED BY T S EMSLIE *AND* P L MURRAY

STONEWALL BOOKS

'Look! There is Jackson's brigade standing behind you like a stone wall!'

2003

Leipoldt's Cape Cookery was published by W J Flesch & Partners in 1976
The articles in *Culinary Treasures* were published in *Die Huisgenoot* from 1942
to 1947, and by Tafelberg Publishers as *Polfyntjies vir die Proe* in 1963
Culinary Treasures was translated from the original Afrikaans
by Dr W L Liebenberg
Three Hundred Years of Cape Wine was published by Tafelberg Publishers
in 1952

ISBN 0-620-30617-3

INDEX BY T S EMSLIE
COVER BY FLAME DESIGN
CONTEMPORARY PHOTOGRAPHY BY ANNE EMSLIE
SET, PRINTED AND BOUND IN THE REPUBLIC OF SOUTH AFRICA
BY CREDA COMMUNICATIONS

STONEWALL BOOKS

52 MAIN ROAD • ST JAMES • CAPE TOWN • 8000 • SOUTH AFRICA

Distributed in Southern Africa by Book Promotions
P O Box 5 • Plumstead • 7800 • South Africa
Tel: 021-706-0949 • Fax: 021-706-0940
email: orders@bookpro.co.za
and in the United Kingdom by Central Books
99 Wallis Road • London • E9 5LN • England
Tel: 020-8986-4854 • Fax: 020-8533-5821
email: orders@centralbooks.com

For Charles Yeats Louw

Historical Photographs

With the exception of the photographs of Leipoldt (held by the Manuscripts and Archives Library at the University of Cape Town), the historical photographs listed below are from the Elliot Collection (and in the case of *Big Game Hunting in Transvaal* the Jeffreys Collection) at the South African Archives in Cape Town.

Contents

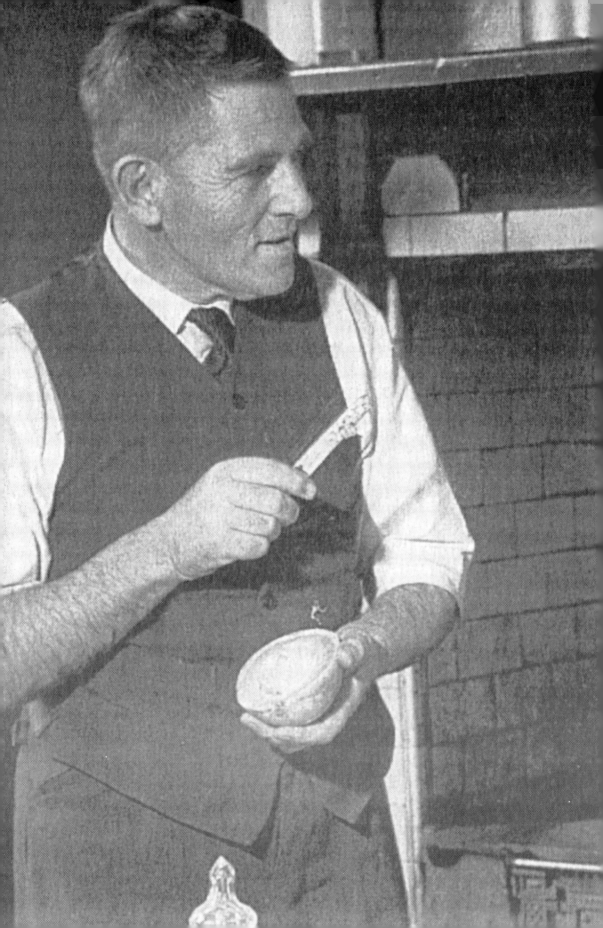

Leipoldt and friends with Peter Shields

Foreword

This is more properly a recollection of my years in Dr C Louis Leipoldt's household than a foreword to this trilogy, but I nevertheless hope that my remembrances will give the reader an insight into the domestic side of the author and in this way enhance his or her enjoyment of the three wonderful books that follow.

I was twelve years of age when, in 1930, I went to live with Leipoldt at his house, *Arbury*, in the Cape Town suburb of Kenilworth. 'Doc', as we called him, had an adopted son, Jeff, a few years younger than me, and the three of us lived together until Jeff and I went off to fight as volunteers in World War II.

Although I have now lived for the past twenty-five years in England, where I was born, my impression is that most South Africans think of Leipoldt as an Afrikaans poet, but do not know enough to appreciate the many other sides of this versatile man.

Doc was very liberal for his time. He was also great fun and was very, very mischievous. You never quite knew whether he was pulling your leg — it was always a problem to know whether or not to take him seriously. For instance, I remember him telling us that in China it was considered a delicacy to take a live baby mouse by the tail, dip it in honey, put it in your mouth, and let it scamper down your throat!

Doc claimed to be a Buddhist. I think he needed to break free of the dictates of his strict Protestant upbringing, remembering that his father had been the *dominee* of the Dutch Reformed Church in Clanwilliam and that he never went to school — he was taught by his father, and could recite long extracts from the Bible. We didn't go to church. Doc wasn't against organised religion – he just wasn't interested in it.

Doc played a lot of tennis. I remember that Mr Justice Van Zyl often came to tennis on Sundays (we had a court at *Arbury*) and that his daughter was a very good tennis player. Doc did no running on court, but was nevertheless an effective and dangerous player: he would stand there and place his lobs with great skill.

He was a brilliant billiards player; and played a great deal of bridge, often with Mrs Bolus – I think the Boluses were like family to him. He must have been a very good bridge player as he had a formidable memory.

Doc had no dress-sense whatsoever. I remember going swimming with him at St James pool, and his swimwear was so ghastly that Jeff and I didn't want to be seen near him. He probably didn't care. One Saturday evening he ventured forth in a dinner jacket with his bowtie so unbelievably skew that I instinctively went up to him to straighten it. He stopped me, saying: 'Don't! They won't recognise me if you do that.'

For many years we didn't have a wireless at *Arbury* – Doc wouldn't allow it. But in 1937 he suddenly went out and bought a very large one. He would sit and listen to Adolf Hitler's speeches, getting very angry. Of course he could understand German, whereas the rest of us couldn't.

We spoke mainly English at home, and Doc actually did a lot of his writing in English. He wrote several poems in English that were published under the pseudonym Pheidippides. I would say that about half of Doc's friends who visited the house were English-speaking, and the other half Afrikaans.

We used to go for wonderful trips in the countryside, and one always met lots of interesting people in his company. I remember visiting General Smuts on his farm at Irene, outside Pretoria, and thinking that his wife, *Ouma* Smuts, was the maid, so unpretentious was she. We often visited General Smuts.

Doc loved Clanwilliam and the Cederberg, and went there fairly often. They were his spiritual home. He knew a terrific number of people in that part of the world, and wherever he went he would call on friends.

Doc would always sing while he drove. He would tease me about the Irish Republican song, the one about hanging men and women for wearing the green, and he would often sing this song while driving. He wasn't really musical, but he loved church music and would go to church to listen to musical performances.

After the war Doc didn't drive much, and he gave me his car when I was demobilised and returned to Cape Town. Occasionally he would borrow it to go off botanising, and it was always filthy when he returned it!

Doc used to tell wonderful ghost stories, especially when we were out camping. Of course he would tell them at night, just before we went to bed. They were always made up on the spot. I particularly remember one about people being poisoned by mushrooms, and about the horrible deaths they died. (Needless to say, Doc used to collect mushrooms himself when the opportunity arose!)

Doc did not cook on an everyday basis. He employed a cook for this purpose. One cook he employed just before the war was a German woman, and I remember that we gave her quite a hard time. I didn't then give much thought to the food we ate; and while I can say that we always ate extremely well, I cannot say that it was particularly exotic.

Doc himself cooked when he gave a dinner party, which he did fairly often. There were always interesting people at his dinner parties, and Jeff and I were always included.

Doc loved arguing. He would have made a great lawyer. He was also a great talker, continually asking questions — usually pulling your leg. He would suddenly decide to give you a hard time, and then the temporary verbal assault would begin! He loved to present you with an alternative view of whatever point you were making, even if you were merely stating a fact.

There were rules in the house, but Jeff and I were never afraid of Doc. He instituted a sort of 'prefect' system with older boys, usually medical students, looking after us, as he was often away lecturing at the University of Cape Town Medical School in the evenings. He instituted a 'black book' system, something I think he had picked up at Rubgy School in England. Five black marks meant a hiding — but Doc wasn't really a disciplinarian and the hiding never materialised. Where he was strict was on one's attitudes to *people*. If Jeff or I commented disparagingly on other people, he would always say: 'Don't be such a snob.'

Doc had worked as a medical inspector of schools in England and he held a high opinion of English public schools. He approved of them. He would say to Jeff and me that we really ought to be at school at Rugby in England.

He did get fed up with us at times, for instance if one of us trod on one of his best flowers. Then he would storm off in anger, but generally he was very even tempered.

Doc would set Jeff and I 'exams' approximately once a month. He didn't test what we knew, but set us tasks to find out and discover things before the next 'exam'. In retrospect I think this was very worthwhile.

I think Doc was reasonably comfortably off, but not wealthy. He left cash of about £20 000 in his estate, and Jeff and I each inherited some £10 000. (I was the executor of his literary estate, and in this capacity I assigned the copyrights owned by his estate to the University of Cape Town when I left South Africa in 1978.)

Doc always had wine with his meals, and Jeff and I were also always given wine. Doc used to make us describe it, something I wasn't much good at. He considered wine to be a good thing, and we all enjoyed it. My recollection is that Doc's preference was for red wine. He was never snobbish about wine, or about anything else for that matter. I never saw him 'tight'. He seldom had more than two glasses of wine.

Doc would have loved to see the current state of development of South African wine, which was still very ordinary in the 1940s, and he would no doubt be pleased to know that in the twenty-first century I remain very fond of wine.

Doc used to come home with his medical bag stuffed full of books, having stopped off at the library on his way. He was a very fast reader and would borrow about five books at a time, often reading all five in one night. Sometimes he would toss one at me, saying as it flew through the air: 'Here, this might interest you.'

He had many books. One wall of his study was lined with them. These he bequeathed to the South African Library.

Many people seem to think that Doc was, or might have been, homosexual. I must say that I cannot see that it matters; but if he was, we never saw anything of it at all. Not a hint. Of course one didn't discuss such things in those days, at any rate not in the way people do nowadays, but quite frankly the possibility never crossed our minds, and I am absolutely certain that there was nothing like that at all in our household. There is no question of it being otherwise.

It is true that he didn't have much to do with women, except women friends of long standing. And he didn't have women in the house, except our German cook. I remember him kicking up a fuss when her daughter came to stay, but I imagine that that had more to do with us — he was afraid one of us might get her into trouble.

Doc had a Hugo Naude portrait of a French woman hanging on his wall at *Arbury*. He found it stuffed behind a couch at Naude's house, said to Naude: 'Don't you want this?' and Naude asked him whether he would like it! It now hangs on my wall, and I love it.

On the subject of the Anglo-Boer War, my impression is that towards the end of the war Doc had blotted his copybook, so to speak, in the eyes of the British. He was reporting on the war from the Afrikaner side, and he had annoyed the military authorities. I think it was important for him to leave Cape Town when he did, or he would have landed in trouble.

Oom Gert Vertel and other poems dealing with the war were, I think, based on real incidents.

I imagine that living in England must have changed Doc's attitude to the English whom, until then, during the war, he had had every reason for regarding as the enemy.

A lot of things Doc said were taken up the wrong way, for example the controversy over his statement that it would be better for schoolchildren to be given wine than milk. At that time milk was dished out to schoolchildren in mugs, and it was often contaminated. This was the context of his remarks about wine being better for schoolchildren than milk.

I was at Medical School, after my return from the war, when they called me out of a lecture with the news that Doc had had a heart attack. I went straight to see him, and visited him every day until his death about five days later. I used to take him books. I think he sensed that the end was nigh for he said to me: 'I see the little goblins. They've come to get me.' (He always used to joke about goblins or little somethings-or-other.)

'Oh, nonsense,' I replied, but he died during the night.

I greatly enjoyed living in Doc's home, and I learned an immense amount from him. Thinking back, I was exceedingly fortunate — I had lost my own father, also a doctor, who died in 1925 and whom I adored; but Doc stepped in and provided me with a good, wholesome, easy childhood.

And yes, I loved him. He was like a big bear, with a somewhat gruff voice. I always think of him as a big bear.

Doc was happiest, I think, when he was out on the veld botanising.

Dr Peter Shields
Berkhamsted

August 2003

Preface

In 2000 we began editing and preparing for publication the typed manuscript of *The Valley*, Leipoldt's trilogy of historical novels which spans the period 1820 to 1930 and is set in the Cederberg — that wonderful, evocative, beloved region of the Cape where Christie (as Leipoldt was known to his family) spent his formative years and where his ashes now lie buried on the Pakhuis Pass. For us this was the beginning of an abiding fascination with Christian Frederik Louis Leipoldt (1880-1947), stimulated further by Dr J C Kannemeyer's meticulous and scholarly *Leipoldt 'n Lewensverhaal* and by Leipoldt's own wide-ranging intellect and presence, expressed in his poetry and other publications. It was inevitable that we would re-read, with greater appreciation, *Leipoldt's Cape Cookery* and *Three Hundred Years of Cape Wine*, and that we should discover the admirable *Polfyntjies vir die Proe*, now skilfully translated from the original Afrikaans by Dr W L Liebenberg and adapted by T S Emslie into its final form as *Culinary Treasures*.

Leipoldt was without exaggeration a poet, playwright, novelist, journalist, chef, botanist, medical doctor — *l'uomo universale* — and in our view his many talents combine perfectly in the works now inspanned as *Leipoldt's Food & Wine*.

In 1902, at the age of twenty-one, Leipoldt left Cape Town — where he had worked as a journalist — for London. There he studied medicine at Guy's Hospital (where he won gold medals for both medicine and surgery) and, after qualifying as a doctor, headed across the Atlantic to the United States of America, spending an interlude as medical adviser to Joseph Pulitzer, after whom the literary prize was named. He travelled widely in Europe and the East, worked as a medical inspector of schools in London, and returned to South Africa in 1914.

As a student in London, Leipoldt often worked on Sunday evenings at hotels such as the Carlton, the Ritz and the Savoy, where he washed dishes to supplement his income. At the Carlton he met the master chef Auguste Escoffier, whom he described as 'that . . . inventor of new dishes, the most celebrated artist of all time in his chosen profession'. When Escoffier moved to the Savoy, Leipoldt made it his business to be employed there so that he could learn as much as possible from this master of the culinary art, under whose guidance he enrolled for and obtained a diploma in international cuisine.

Leipoldt's nostalgia and respect for the traditions of his forefathers, his keen interest in the historical origins of things, and his rigorous, no-nonsense approach to food and to old manuscript recipes are wonderfully balanced by his subversive and revolutionary quest for culinary ingenuity.

Only Leipoldt could describe the outstanding characteristics of Malay cookery as 'the free, almost heroic, use of spices and aromatic flavourings, the prolonged steady, but slow, application of moist heat to all meat dishes, and the skilful blending of many diverse constituents into a combination that still holds the essential goodness of each'.

Who else could, or would, recommend that an *oleroso* sherry 'be taken at about eleven in the morning, especially on a beautiful sunny day when the figs are blossoming and the sheaves of wheat are being brought in from the lands'? Virgil perhaps, although sherry did not exist in his day – but the sensibility did!

And which other son of a Dutch Reformed Church minister would refer to the Dutch East India Company as 'that most profitable combination of unblushing piracy and commercialised Protestantism'?

The pieces contained in *Culinary Treasures* were first published as articles in *Die Huisgenoot* from 1942 to 1947, under the pseudonym K A R Bonade — in which guise the author laments the lack of an index in Leipoldt's *Kos Vir Die Kenner*. It is clear from the date of publication of each article that references in *Culinary Treasures* to wartime restrictions are to those resulting from South Africa's participation in World War II. The last article was published on 21 March 1947, shortly before Leipoldt's death on 12 April 1947. *Three Hundred Years of Cape Wine* and *Leipoldt's Cape Cookery* were published posthumously, in 1952 and 1976 respectively.

We have asked ourselves whether it makes sense to publish a history of Cape winemaking alongside two books dealing with the preparation and enjoyment of food and wine. Our answer to this question is that all three works are suffused with a strong element of nostalgia, of savouring what is best from the past in the most delectable way, and that Leipoldt of all people would have enjoyed a glass of 'natural, unadulterated farm wine' all the more for knowing the travails and tribulations entailed in the production of its predecessors. For Leipoldt, an appreciation of the past was an integral part of the present.

The suggestion has also been made that we should consider bringing the story of Cape wine up to date with an appendix on winemaking over the past half-century and more. Of course winemaking has developed considerably since 1946, and of course many of the views and criticisms expressed in *Three Hundred Years of Cape Wine* are no longer valid. Of this there can be no doubt. But our overarching objective has been to publish *Leipoldt's* views on food and wine, for it is in the words of this talented man that the commonplace becomes extraordinary and our cultural heritage almost tangible. Leipoldt's books are about food and wine; our compilation is about Leipoldt the connoisseur — and herein lies its 'timeless' quality.

We are indebted to Barbara Knox-Shaw for her skilled proofreading of the text and for much else besides — her botanical, culinary and linguistic expertise enabled her to make valuable editorial contributions.

Last year we spent a wonderful evening at *Ochterlony*, the Newlands home of Ian and Karin Woods, where the dinner described by Leipoldt in chapter 5 of *The Mask*, published as part of *The Valley* trilogy by Stormberg Publishers in 2001, was prepared by Jessica Setterberg and enjoyed at the cedarwood table that used to belong to Leipoldt in the house where he once lived. We enjoyed a magnificent dinner as well as a fun-filled photo opportunity.

On 16 August 2003 Trevor Emslie spent a delightful English summer's afternoon chatting to Dr Peter Shields at his home in Berkhamsted, gleaning insights into the colourful character of 'Doc'. This discussion fructified into the foreword to this book, and we are honoured and grateful to Dr Shields for his contribution.

Some readers may gain the impression from his willingness to exercise his culinary skills on all manner of game that Leipoldt was 'anti-conservation'. That this was not the case is clear from what he said in *Bushveld Doctor*, published in 1937:

> 'I have no taste for shooting and no desire to collect trophies. . . . More often I wandered away by myself with field glasses and a shotgun, to lie in some glade near the river and watch the blue monkeys playing in the thorn trees.'

But Leipoldt was never slow to discern a potentially tasty meal, as the following episode, also from *Bushveld Doctor*, illustrates:

> 'She showed me the water tortoises. Three of them, each as large as a dinner plate, lay wallowing in the mud. I remarked that they were good eating. "Eating?" she said, scornfully. "Who'd eat a water tortoise? You must think we are uncivilised here, Doctor, if you imagine that we would eat such rubbish."'

The answer to the question posed is, of course: Leipoldt would!

Such is the enthusiasm for food and wine expressed in this trilogy that it almost seems that 'Doc' recalls his anecdotes, thoughts and recipes for his own enjoyment as much as for that of his readers. But what a wonderful legacy he has bequeathed us in the works now gathered under the rubric of *Leipoldt's Food & Wine*.

It has been suggested that food and language are important repositories of history and culture. This is certainly true of Leipoldt's combined mastery of the culinary and the linguistic arts — the poetry is in the eating, the flavour in the words.

Trevor Emslie
Paul Murray
Editors

Cape Town
October 2003

Leipoldt's Cape Cookery

by

C Louis Leipoldt

Contents

Introduction

My interest in cookery dates from the time when, as a little boy in the late eighties of the last century,[1] I assisted, in a very minor and suppressed capacity, at the culinary operations of a very expert Coloured woman cook who bore the reputation of being one of the best in the Cape Colony. Fat to the verge of obesity, she presided over a kitchen whose cleanliness could have served as a model for an operating theatre of a modern hospital, largely because she insisted that punctilious, painstaking ablution was an indispensable preliminary in the preparation of food. Her inculcation of these elementary principles, often accompanied by a good-natured but nevertheless painful prodding of my juvenile person with the large wooden spoon that was her sceptre, helped me — in later days when I learned to better my taste and broaden my experience — to realise how any infringement of them inevitably impairs the excellence of all cookery.

The Ayah's art was the result of many years of instruction and experience in the traditional methods of Malay cookery, whose outstanding characteristics are the free, almost heroic, use of spices and aromatic flavourings, the prolonged steady, but slow, application of moist heat to all meat dishes, and the skilful blending of many diverse constituents into a combination that still holds the essential goodness of each. Her dishes, that were eaten by Governors, Prime Ministers and Very Important Persons, were made from old recipes that were firmly enshrined in her memory, for she never referred to written or printed directives. Nearly every one of these recipes is to be found in cookery books that were then already well known — without, however, the little modifications that her own ingenuity and experience had enabled her to add for their improvement. All of them had already been written down, in manuscripts for domestic use for those who had to rely on such aids when preparing food.

When I returned from Europe in 1914, it was a labour of love to collect such cookery manuscripts, and to compare what they contained with the printed collections of directives that date from the year 1483. That entailed the acquisition of representative cookbooks, and although I had, at the time, no intention of emulating Viel or any other great collector of books on food and drink, I found the task of comparing and collating so entrancing, the search for recipes in manuscript so exciting, and the pride of possessing interesting rarities so uplifting, that what had begun as a passing fancy remained as a serious and not altogether unproductive study.

Some of the results I have tried to epitomise in this book. It does not claim to be exhaustive. There are thousands of recipes for preparing food;

---

1 The nineteenth century.

but those that may presume to merit the prefix of a regional adjective, by reason of their insistence on some local method of blending or cooking, are far fewer than is commonly supposed. The art of the cook is international in its general application, and only in particulars, and more especially in the use of local ingredients, does the cookery of one nation or country differ from that of its neighbours. The recipes that I have included here are those that have been in vogue in South Africa from the earliest times, and are nearly all variations of similar ones that were popular in Europe and the East. But most of them have been modified, and many of them have been immensely improved, by the skill and experience of Cape cooks, while there are some that have been adapted to local foodstuffs that are found nowhere else. In the majority of cases the original text has been followed as closely as possible, and where it has been necessary to translate from the Dutch the interpretation has been textual.

No attempt has been made to transcribe the great number of recipes for cakes and confectionery, of which there are many in manuscript and quite enough in print. With few exceptions they are merely replicas of familiar European directives, possibly with some slight modification to which a new name has been given. A good example of such plagiarism is the number of fruit or spice cakes that figure under the names of some local celebrity, but that are not justified in claiming any merit for originality. Where a particular kind of cake or confectionery is required to be served as an accompaniment to a sweet or a meat dish, directions for its preparation are given.

Similarly nothing has been said about aboriginal cookery. Undoubtedly the Africans have modified some methods of preparing food, but so far as I know, no one has as yet attempted to collect their recipes or describe their methods. There is undoubtedly sufficient material to warrant such a compilation, but its collecting and editing must be left to the industrious inquiry of a student fully conversant with African languages and customs.

Nor has it seemed necessary to attach a bibliography, or to indicate, by footnotes, the source of some of the references. It may, however, be mentioned that all the 'literature' from which this book has been compiled is to be found in the collection of cookery books in the South African Public Library at Cape Town, which also contains most of the manuscripts from which the recipes have been extracted. Most of the latter have already been published, in Afrikaans, in my own cookery book, *Kos vir die Kenner*, that was issued in 1933.

C Louis Leipoldt

Cape Town
December 1946

Chapter 1

Origins of Cape Cookery

The settlement at the Cape of Good Hope was started in 1652 as a revictualing station for the ships of the East India Company of Holland trading between the mother country and the East. In the course of time it became the halfway house on the great 6 000 mile sea route from the Texel, the Thames and the Tagus in the north, to Colombo and Calcutta, Tandjong Priok and Tonkin in the south. Its few hundred inhabitants increased to several thousands, augmented by immigrants from Europe, Chinese convicts and state prisoners from Java and slaves from Mozambique, with the result that the straggling town, under the shadow of its imposing mountain, acquired an almost cosmopolitan character that was to have its influence on the habits and customs of its citizens.

Nowhere was this influence to be more recognisable, even though its effects were insidious and not immediately apparent, than in the methods and ways of preparing food for the table. What we may today call 'Cape cookery' is characterised, not by a wholly original, intrinsically national character, but by a subtle combination of various and diverse fashions in cooking, adapted and modified from many different countries, to which the use of certain locally-grown ingredients has given a new and peculiar tinge. As the patient Mentzel[1] has told us, the Chinese cooks at the Cape were celebrated, even in their rude and vulgar little chop shops, for their extreme cleanliness and the fastidiousness with which they prepared their succulent dishes. Mrs Kindersley, some years later, commented on the variety of spices that were considered necessary in a Cape kitchen, while many other visitors testified at times to the strangeness but more often to the savouriness of the viands that they tasted at private houses or at public eating-places.

While there is no dish, with the exception of those for the preparation of which the main ingredient must be something that can be procured only in South Africa, that can be considered peculiar to the Cape, in so far as its replica cannot be found elsewhere, there are many Cape cookery recipes that have been evolved from prototypes in old European cookery books. But they have been so changed — and possibly improved — by local methods, that the dishes prepared from them can be said to possess a distinctive and peculiarly local excellence.

The foundations of Cape cookery, like those of the cookery of all western nations, are the methods that have descended to us from the Greek and Roman civilisation, which through the centuries have been altered, elaborated and bettered by cooks in various European countries, whose

---

1 O.F. Mentzel's account of life at the Cape (published in Germany in 1785) was translated into English by the Van Riebeeck Society as *Geographical and Topographical Description of the Cape of Good Hope* (1921, 1925).

originality and ingenuity, imagination and expert skill have evolved systems that are of national significance. It is impossible today to adjudicate on the claims for priority made by these varied systems. After all, the oldest cookery book with a right to be considered as an exposition of the art of cooking is the early Chinese compilation, far antedating any Greek papyrus, that gives admirable recipes for cooking rice and making stews. However, Atheaeus tells us that Agis, the Rhodian cook, first discovered how to roast fish; Charides, the Athenian, to make forcemeat; Aphthonetus to broil sausages; and Lamprias to concoct a palatable soup. But there is no evidence that any of his pre-eminent chefs created a special system of Greek cookery.

The truth of the matter is that the cookery of every nation has borrowed freely, often with unblushing audacity, from that of every other nation, and that only where it has succeeded in impressing its own stamp on its cooking technique, by the practice of local methods and the employment of local foodstuffs, can it be said to have reached the level that merits a distinctive territorial adjective.

Bearing this truth in mind, we can readily understand how much Cape cookery owes to Dutch, Flemish, English, German, French, Italian, Portuguese and especially Oriental cookery. Its indebtedness to Russian, Swedish, Danish or American cookery is negligible, has been incurred only in recent years, and cannot be said to have benefited it. What is good in American cookery, for instance, derives from practically the same sources as Cape cookery and there is in some respects a cousinship between the two, for both owe much to Dutch and Flemish influence.

As the early settlers at the Cape came from Holland, it is not surprising that Dutch influence in Cape cookery should be considerable, although it does not overshadow that of Oriental cookery. At the time when Van Riebeeck landed — that is, in the middle of the seventeenth century — there was no defined system of Dutch cookery, but domestic cookery in the lowlands had already developed methods and dishes that were different from those in neighbouring countries. The art of cookery in Holland, as indeed in every country in Europe, was largely influenced by Italian cooks, for in the Middle Ages Italian cooks were considered masters of the craft and the Vatican cooks were ranked as the best in the world. Later French cuisine increased in estimation, and to a large extent supplanted Italian cookery. In Flanders and in Holland, at the time when European civilisation was best exemplified by the cultural and economic expansion of these countries, cookery, as an art, had rapidly developed and had assimilated the best that was to be found in the cookery of neighbouring nations.

The first cookery books in South Africa, as also in Europe, were manuscript collections of domestic recipes, of traditional methods of preparing food, and of household directions, home remedies and rules of health. One of the best-known European manuscripts is that of William Tirel, called Taillevent, copies of which are now in the Vatican Library and in the National Library at Paris. Taillevent was cook to King Charles V from 1373 to 1387, and his recipes were edited and republished by Baron Pichon and Georges Vicaire in 1891. Another contemporary collection of culinary recipes is that of the Master Cook of Richard II of England, compiled in 1390, known to cooks under the title of *The Forme of Cury*. Many other such collections of recipes are known to exist in various forms.

In South Africa there are several manuscript cookery books, the earliest, in the South African Public Library at Cape Town, dating to the fifteenth century, with copious additions, in various handwritings, extending into the sixteenth and seventeenth centuries. These manuscripts were undoubtedly brought into the country as family treasures, carefully preserved and judiciously expanded by their owners. Similar manuscript collections were started in the eighteenth and the early part of the nineteenth century by local housewives, containing original recipes and copies of those already published. In the latter part of the seventeenth century the number of printed cookery books in Europe greatly increased, while their prices were low enough to win them a wide and deserved popularity. Every housewife could buy one, and thus it was scarcely necessary to compile a private collection of recipes for each household.

At the Cape, however, such printed works were always relatively scarce, and it is interesting to note that among the books in the largest private collections at the time when the Cape was still in the possession of the Dutch, there is not a single copy of a printed cookery book.

The South African Public Library does possess a varied collection of cookery books, but few of its finest volumes were procured from local sources. The oldest book in the collection was printed in 1517 at the Strassburg press of Johannes Knoblouch. It is a later edition of the first cookery book ever printed, the *De Honesta Voluptate et Valetudine* of Baptista Platina, of which the first edition appeared in 1479. It was exceedingly popular and went through many editions and, in 1528, a French translation was published at Lyons. Compiled by a practical cook, who was an artist and no mean scholar, it was a useful, readable and interesting epitome of the art of cookery in the fourteenth century and contained more than 300 recipes. As the earliest printed cookery book it merits the attention of every student of the art, for in it is enshrined the original conception of everything that is good in modern cookery.

South African cooks are unlikely ever to have read it. Nor is it reasonable to believe that they had any acquaintance with the works of Platina's many successors that came tumbling from European printing presses in the next 200 years. But in the eighteenth century Dutch, German and French books on cookery were to be found at the Cape. Among these, Christian Sachsstadter's treatise on the cookery of fish undoubtedly gave many suggestions to our cooks, as the manuscript collections of recipes prove, while the works of Dankwerth, Eger, Cocceius and especially the

standard *Le Cuisinier Modern* of the famous Vincent le Chapelle, cook in the Prince of Orange's household, were frequently and usefully consulted. This last book, with the anonymous but extremely practical *Verstandighe Kock* which, published at the end of the seventeenth century, gave a clear account of Flemish and Dutch cookery, served for many years as a reservoir from which all subsequent compilers freely watered their culinary nurseries.

Much later writers in Holland and England drew on the knowledge of visitors to the East, who brought back with them directions for making dishes that were not included in the older inventories. English cookery books of the early eighteenth century gave directions for preparing Indian dishes, but only in the first half of the nineteenth century do we come across recipes that are of purely local origin, although even here there is some doubt about the matter. We must bear in mind the fact that the contact between West and East dates back to far beyond the time of Platina and Scappi. The Crusades had already introduced oriental spices and eastern ways of preparing food for the table into occidental kitchens.

Hashed meat, baked with a curried sauce, spiced with red pepper and sweetened with blanched almonds, exactly similar to the modern *bobotie* of Cape cookery, was well known to the old Italian cooks. Savoury dried meat, the South African *biltong*, or, in its more primitive form, the Dutch *tassal*, was prepared by the peasants in the Ardour valley when that part of France was still regarded as an English possession — and is still so made in Switzerland. The vegetable and meat stews, known as *bredies* to Cape cooks, were old favourites of the Greek chefs, whose name for them is so totally unpronounceable that I have never yet come across a modern Greek who can say it without stuttering.

The two recipes quoted in a late edition of Mrs Rundle's *Domestic Economy and Cookery*, first published in 1827 and later edited and amplified by Miss Morris, who had visited the Cape, are, however, so distinctly South African and entail the use of ingredients hardly likely to be popular, or even procurable, in England, that one can safely assume that they were directly transcribed from manuscript recipes consulted at Cape Town. This assumption is strengthened by the names given to the dishes, which include a word not to be found in an ordinary English dictionary though perfectly well known to every English-speaking housewife then living at the Cape.

It may be added, in passing, that no printed book on Cape cookery has included these recipes, although they are to be found, with variations not mentioned by Miss Morris, in several manuscript collections, and are almost traditional at the Cape.

Undoubtedly the most potent influence on Cape cookery has been the methods, tastes and culinary customs of the Malay cooks brought directly from Java in the early part of the eighteenth century. Mr Spencer St John, in his entertaining book *Life in the Forests of the Far East*, published in the latter part of the last century, has paid a well-deserved compliment to his Malay cook:

Malay cookery is sometimes very tasty; I remember spending a fortnight in the Sultan's palace, and we were fed daily from his kitchen; sometimes the stewed fowls were admirable and there was a particular kind of rice-cake, sent in very hot, which was delicious. But the triumph of Malay cookery is to send in the sambals in perfection, particularly the one called *blachang*; the best is composed of the very finest prawns, caught, I imagine, soon after the little ones have burst from their eggs, and pounded up with chillies and a little ginger. Coarser kinds are made from the larger prawn, or even from the smallest fish caught on the river's banks. Sometimes the material is first exposed to the sun in order to be completely dried, or it would not keep or mix very well, though it is often soaked till nearly decomposed, and that is perhaps the favourite way when it emits a rather powerful scent, but it is very tasty. Prawns and fish are cooked in a great variety of ways, but roasting them over a fire as kebabs is an excellent fashion if you first sprinkle them with curry mixture . . .

I have mentioned the admirable curry which Ahtan put before me; perhaps I ought to explain how we make that dish in the Far East; it appears a very different thing from what I have tasted in England under the name of curry. A fowl is cut up into small pieces, and four dried and two green onions, five chillies, half a turmeric, one teaspoonful of coriander seed, one of white cumin, and one of sweet cumin, are provided. You must well pound the seeds, turmeric and chillies, and slice the onions fine; then take the saucepan and, after buttering it, slightly brown the onions, then add the pounded ingredients with just sufficient water to reduce them to a paste, and throw in the fowl and well mix them up, till the meat has a yellow tint, and lastly, add the cocoa-nut milk, and boil till the curry be thoroughly cooked . . . The cocoa-nut milk is made by scraping the meat of half an old nut very fine, then soaking it in warm water, and after squeezing out the milk, throw the fibre away.

These directions are identical with those of some of our earliest manuscript recipes, and show how closely East Indian methods were followed at the Cape, even though the *blachang* referred to is obviously a mistake for the much more pungent *trassi* condiment that never became naturalised anywhere outside the Malay archipelago. At first nearly all the necessary ingredients for preparing Indian dishes had to be imported; later on the settlement grew its own rice, chillies, ginger, cumin, coriander and garlic, but it still had to get its tamarind, turmeric, black pepper, mace, nutmeg, saffron, cinnamon and coconuts from the East. It was customary for Cape housewives to commission captains of ships going to Batavia to buy and bring back modest quantities of these spices and delicacies. A domestic account book of the early part of the past century gives a list of the prices paid for such things, and includes among them 'candy sugar; black moist sugar; birds-nests; dried prawns; dessicated sea urchins.'

The Malay community at the Cape has always had a reputation for its good cookery and even now the best women cooks are to be found among the Coloured people who have been trained to appreciate all that is best in both eastern and western culinary fashions. In the old days a Malay cook was regarded as indispensable for the household that wished to entertain; slaves who had knowledge of this kind of cookery commanded a far higher price than other domestic chattels. Thus a local advertisement stated that 'Malani, a good cook, exceptionally skilled and not wasteful in the kitchen', was one of five slaves to be sold on behalf of the estate of a deceased owner; while an account of a slave auction related that 'there was spirited competition for Emerentia, who is an acknowledged artist of the pot'. At the hospitable house where the young officer, later on to be Lord Wellington, the conqueror of Napoleon, but at that time rusticating on his way to India, was frequently entertained by the richest man in Cape Town, the cook was a Coloured woman, skilled in the preparation of oriental dishes and ably supported by her husband who acted as butler.

Oriental influence, indeed, was predominant in Cape cookery, and its importance can easily be judged by the value attached to eastern spices and condiments in the old-fashioned recipes.

The first printed collection of such recipes published at the Cape is today perhaps one of the rarest items of Africana known to exist, for only one copy, that in the South African Public Library, has survived the tribulations that seem to make the life of the average cookery book much shorter than that of its owner. It is a small octavo pamphlet, printed by a Pietermaritzburg firm in Natal, in the early seventies of the past century.[1] It gives, in English, a series of recipes none of which can be said to be peculiarly South African, as their originals are all to be found in works published in Europe before that date. It is possible that an earlier collection of recipes was published, also in pamphlet form, at Cape Town, some years before the Natal publication, but no specimen of this has survived.[2] From the beginning of the nineteenth century, newspapers and periodicals in English and Dutch, and later in Afrikaans, had printed family and domestic recipes, but no one had thought it worthwhile to collect them for reprinting in book form, probably because there was no demand for a volume on local cookery as every housewife possessed her own collection of manuscript recipes, or relied on her training and memory for her cooking. The publication of the obscure and incomplete compilation in Natal must have aroused some interest for, although it was never reprinted, it was soon followed by a much more authoritative little book which even today may be consulted with advantage as it is a thoroughly trustworthy, clear and concise epitome of Cape cookery.

---

1 The nineteenth century.
2 There is mention of such a collection in the headnote to a recipe 'Taken from Messrs Cleghorn's book'. [L]

This was Miss A G Hewitt's *Cape Cookery*, a small octavo, 88 page volume, published by Darter Bros and Walton of Cape Town in 1889, of which a second and final edition was published in the following year. Although it included several recipes that were extracted from overseas cookery books, it gave the first accurate account of many local recipes, assembled under five headings. The first chapter was devoted to fish, and gave directions for the preparation of such dishes as *smoored kreef*; stewed *klipkous*; *ingelegde* fish; *snoek pekelaar*; *smoored snoek*; and *kreef* salad. These are generally correct, although it may be pointed out that bones are used to enrich the pearl mussel[1] stew, which is quite unnecessary, and that water is added, which makes the meat tough; while the braised snoek is made without potatoes and the crayfish salad omits the savoury portions to be found under the carapace as well as the coral.

The second chapter deals with meat and poultry, and gives recipes for preparing roast meat or poultry in the baking pot; *hoender pastei*; *zout ribbetjie*; *bobotee*; *sassaties*; *ingelegde kop en pootjes*; tomato, quince, bean, pumpkin, cauliflower and cabbage *bredies*; porcupine skin; Cape curry and *biltong*.

By following Miss Hewitt's directions most of these dishes can be made without difficulty, but some of them will lack the savoury excellence to which they are entitled.

In the third chapter sweet dishes are discussed; in the fourth, preserves, and in the fifth a number of miscellaneous recipes are given, among them being *sambal*; *blatjang*; Cape chutney; sea-weed blancmange; apricot vinegar; peach pickle; penguin eggs; and Van der Hum liqueur. The little book is a model of conciseness, but entirely lacking in character and distinction, while it errs on the side of frugality and plainness, eschewing the use of wine and spices in places where these are regarded as indispensable in the older manuscript recipes. It is, however, a useful compilation and was deservedly popular in its day, although it could not claim that it was an exhaustive collection of Cape recipes, nor that it gave the reader copies of the best to be found in the old family manuscript cookbooks.

Contemporaneously with it appeared Mrs A R Barnes's *Colonial Household Guide*, by ARB, published by the same firm as an octavo volume of 150 pages. It contained, besides many cookery recipes, most of which are taken from printed works, farming and household hints, home remedies and directions for preparing, cleaning and polishing materials. The only recipes that can be said to be of local origin were those that dealt with *Keokuk* toast; cabbage *bredie*; *sosaties*; *baba* or barbel fish; wild buck; green *mielies* and sweet potatoes. Even these are poor, and if scrupulously followed will hardly prepare dishes that are worthy of their titles. As a guide to Cape cookery, Mrs Barnes's book is much inferior to Miss Hewitt's.

Both were soon afterwards followed, and altogether displaced, by an

---

1 Venus ear or *perlemoen*. [L]

authoritative and comprehensive work on Cape cookery that for a long time remained the standard book on the subject and may even now be consulted with advantage as a thoroughly trustworthy and excellently written and annotated collection of Cape cookery recipes.

This was *Hilda's Where is It?* published by Chapman and Hall of London in 1891, and which before 1908 had sold 24 000 copies and had reached its nineteenth edition. Its authoress was Miss Hildagonda Johanna Duckitt, who assured her readers that the book contained 'amongst other practical and tried recipes, many old Cape, Indian and Malay Dishes and Preserves; also Directions for polishing furniture, cleaning Silk etc, and a Collection of Home Remedies in case of Sickness', all in rigid accordance with the then prevailing fashion in cookery books. The volume was interleaved with blank pages for manuscript recipes and had attached to it a neat little lead pencil for the convenience of transcribers.

Miss Duckitt, in her *Diary of a Cape Housekeeper* — published in 1902, and in some ways a more interesting and original work than her first book — gave details about her background that proved her to be fully justified in undertaking to speak on behalf of Cape cooks. Her grandfather, William Duckitt, of the Treasurer-General's Department in London, accepted an offer from the Cape administration to come out and supervise the establishment of model farms under the newly formed Department of Agriculture in the early part of the past century. He brought with him his family, a staff of 30 servants and pedigree sheep and cattle, together with various agricultural gadgets that he had invented for the better cultivation of hard soils. The wine farmers in the western districts of the Cape are indebted to him for much good advice and many practical demonstrations, but in 1839 he tired of government service, and settled on his own farm, *Groot Pos*, in the Malmesbury district, an estate that had been developed and improved by Lord Charles Somerset. His sons married into colonial families. Miss Duckitt's father espoused Hildagonda Versfeld, and so became allied to several of the oldest and best Dutch families at the Cape — for the most part wealthy wine and wheat farmers, who lived in comfortable affluence, served by many slaves and priding themselves on their unstinted hospitality and the quality of their fare. On the farm where Miss Duckitt spent her childhood, the cook was an East Indian, an adept at making curry and Malay dishes, who had also learned to prepare food in accordance with traditional Dutch methods. From her relations and friends she learned many household secrets, had access to the family collections of recipes that were then the substitutes for printed cookery books, and received, as was customary in those days, a sound education in housekeeping and domestic economy. She was thus admirably fitted to write what for a long time was to remain the soundest and most authoritative manual on Cape cookery.

Her *Hilda's Where is It?* contains about 150 recipes that are characteristically South African, inasmuch as they are modifications, improvements or adaptations of European recipes. About 50 others are

exclusively South African in so far as the preparation of the ingredients is totally different from that recommended in then existing cookery books. These latter show the influence of Oriental cooking methods, combined with local ingenuity in blending flavours and enhancing the savour of the dish. Unfortunately the book contains no recipes for the peculiarly South African dishes manufactured from ingredients that are essentially local — such as water hawthorn stew and the purées made from veld plants — and omits some of the recipes to be found in manuscript collections. She made no pretence to catholicity, and her directions are everywhere so clear and precise — as for example where she deals with the preparation of *Haliotis* mussel[1] and emphasises the necessity to avoid adding water to the dish — that her cookbook may be accepted as an authoritative practical guide to Cape cookery.

The first Afrikaans cookery book was published about the same time as Miss Duckitt's manual, by the *Patriot* publishers at the Paarl. It was a compilation by Mrs E J Dijkman of the Orange Free State, and was translated, badly, into English in 1905. It went into several editions, and enjoyed a large measure of popularity, not so much on account of its cookery recipes but because it contained many hints on first aid and household remedies, some of the latter being strange but harmless. In comparison with Miss Duckitt's book it is greatly inferior; most of its recipes are merely transcriptions from familiar Dutch cookery books, and the few really South African ones are of minor importance. One misses in it any reference to the popular 'veld food' dishes, while the chapter on fish is singularly incomplete. The book is a mere compilation by one who had had some experience of plain domestic cookery, but who had not been accustomed to any great variety and is not an expert in the true sense of the term. Mrs Dijkman gives fancy names to some of her concoctions. There are, for instance, *Afrikander Bond*, *President Kruger*, *President Steyn*, *General de la Rey* and *General Botha* cakes, which are nothing more than variations of ordinary fruit cakes. If some of her directions are to be followed precisely, as for example in the recipe for stewing pearl mussel, the resulting dish is likely to be far from satisfactory. Her cookery is economical, even parsimonious, and she is frugal in her employment of wine and spices, with the result that her dishes, if not insipid, sometimes lack the fragrant pungency that they ought to have.

From the beginning of the twentieth century the number of books on Cape cookery steadily increased. There are today many well-known manuals. Most of these are merely compilations, while in some modern American methods are adapted to South African ingredients, not always with the best results.

Perhaps the most striking feature about these newer books on Cape cookery is the total omission of wine in the recipes, and the neglect to

---

1 Venus ear or pearl mussel. [L]

produce something that is original, either in blending or in using local ingredients that will give a distinct flavour to the dishes. Domestic cookery is taught in girls' schools, but it is indoctrinated in accordance with a syllabus that does not in the slightest degree arouse the interest of the cook or the lover of good food. Moreover, old methods of cooking are neglected in favour of the pestilential but handy and convenient electric stove; the open fireplace is almost a thing of the past. Another cause of the decay of Cape cookery is the popularity of tinned and dehydrated food and of the ready-made bottled sauce and salad dressing. But undoubtedly the most important reason for the lack of development and the absence of originality is the ignorance of the professional as well as domestic cooks of the old and tried methods and recipes that in the past century made Cape cookery an art that was justified in claiming a technique and a merit of its own.

Chapter 2
Methods of Cooking

Properly speaking, the art of cookery is the art of preparing food for eating by cooking it, that is to say, by rendering it more palatable through the application of heat. In practice, however, the art of cookery includes much more than that, for it embraces all methods of preparing food for the table, even those in which no attempt is made to vary the character of the crude ingredients except by the addition of flavouring or the subtraction of what interferes with the palatability.

Nevertheless heat, in its various forms, is the chief means whereby raw natural food can be suitably modified to serve human needs by making it more eatable, digestible and nourishing. It may be applied in various forms, directly or indirectly, and a predilection for one or more of these different ways of using it may perhaps be a distinguishing feature between two systems of national cookery. Among peoples who lack the amenities provided by a more sophisticated domestic culture, such as stoves and ovens, the open fire, on a flat hearth or in some sheltered spot of the garth, is the main (and sometimes the only) means of cooking. The result is that roasting, broiling and grilling have been more highly developed in these communities than other methods of cooking.

In Cape cookery, which developed when the settlement was still primitive and was largely influenced by Oriental methods and to some extent by the rough technique employed in the ship's caboose, all forms of heat are used — though there is a preference for direct application of heat, especially to meats and to edibles that have a resistant covering. The three principal ways of applying such heat are roasting, baking and grilling or broiling, in all of which the food is subjected to the direct action of fire or to such action communicated through the intermediary of a pot or pan or oven.

In *boiling*, which is another essential way of cooking, the heat is communicated to the foodstuff through the intermediary of water that has been raised to a high, or boiling, temperature; in *frying*, oil is substituted for water, but the principle remains the same. In both boiling and frying a part of the flavour and nutritive quality of the food may be lost, because it is taken up by the water or the oil. It is therefore necessary to stop for a moment to consider what actually occurs when either of these methods is used, to compare their advantages with other methods in which direct heat is employed.

When a foodstuff is placed in water and that water is brought to the boil, some part of the soluble ingredients in the food is dissolved in the water. The result is that when the food has been cooked it has lost that portion of its contents which is now to be found in the water in which it has been boiled. In frying, this is less often of importance, because oil is not a good solvent and the heat of the oil usually coats the foodstuff with an impermeable film through which its soluble content cannot percolate. We take advantage of this when we make soup or extracts. The foodstuff is placed in water which is brought to the boil, and then slowly simmered, so as to extract from the food as much of its soluble content as possible.

In that way we obtain a soup, which is in reality a decoction of foodstuffs.

If, however, we wish to have the foodstuff boiled for itself, it is necessary to plunge it into boiling water, the heat of which at once solidifies the surface into a protective film behind which the soluble contents may be allowed to cook steadily until the food itself is tender. The old cooks understood this perfectly and in Cape recipes a clear distinction is always drawn between boiling to extract the soluble content of the food — in which it is always recommended that cold or lukewarm water should be used and generally heated — and boiling to make the food itself more palatable.

By *roasting*, the Cape cook did not mean spit roasting, although this method was sometimes employed, especially in the kitchens of the large town houses where the hearths were big enough to permit the installation of a turning jack or spit. Properly speaking, roasting is by exposure of the foodstuff to the direct action of fire, which is tempered, to prevent scorching, by the basting juice with which the food is constantly wetted. This method gives admirable results, and has been a favourite with English cooks, whose roasts have been extolled by all who have tasted them. But it is a laborious and expensive method, which demands constant attention on the part of the cook, and the excellence of the results obtained by it depends to a large extent on the quality of the meat. At the Cape beef has never been of prime excellence, and the domestic cook had much more to attend to than to waste time turning the jack and painstakingly dripping basting juice over the joint.

With meat that was indifferent in quality, an equally good result was obtainable by *pot-roasting*, in which the food was placed in an iron pot with a heavy iron lid. All this was put on the fire and live coals or embers were heaped on the lid. Occasionally the lid was lifted and the food was basted, but as its exuding juice remained in the pot, there was no necessity for a roasting pan and no reason to fear that it would scorch. It was subjected to a steady, equable heat, that cooked it nicely and made even the toughest goat-mutton tender. Pot-roasting was a popular method of cooking, and was indeed the only method generally used, although oven roasts, in which the meat was baked, were later on more fashionable and seem to be preferred today.

The pot roast was economical, time saving and satisfactory. In course of time its principle was extended to other methods, of which *smooring* (literally, smothering) or *smoorbraai* (stew-roasting) was the chief modification. This is the old-fashioned braising, in which the food was stewed or braised by heat applied from above and below, and was used chiefly for combinations of meat and vegetables. *Bredies*, for instance, are always carefully and slowly smothered — and the longer this gentle and persuasive manner of cooking is applied the better and more savoury will be the result of the stew, provided care is taken, by frequently shaking the pot, to prevent the contents from burning.

Stewing and *steaming* were further modifications of applying indirect heat, and both were much employed by Cape cooks; fish, for instance, was generally steamed, usually with a spoonful of white wine to hasten the cooking and give piquancy to the dish.

For meats, fish and some vegetables, a favourite method of preparation was *grilling* directly over the hot embers, either on a spit or on a grid. Nothing can exceed in savouriness a tender mutton chop grilled over the embers of a rhinoceros-bush fire. The aromatic flavour of the smoke imparts to the meat a peculiar and altogether original taste, and if a good camp cook is in charge of the business the 'carbonade' is as delicious as it is tender and succulent.

All *kabobs* should be grilled, but nowadays when one has to depend on a coal fire, it is not easy to resist the temptation to cook them in the oven in a pan, or fry them on the stove. Old Cape cooks never used coal, a fuel that was exclusively reserved for blacksmiths and never became popular in domestic kitchens before the arrival of steamships. They used firewood, of which the supply never failed or, when they could get it, charcoal that still provides the finest heat for grilling.

Almost as important as braising was *simmering*, a slow, prolonged process in which the food is subjected, sometimes for many hours, to a quiet, steady and continuous gentle heat — not sufficient to solidify, in meat, its gelatinous constituents or to harden, in vegetables, their cellulose fibres. The perfection of simmering depends on the equability of the temperature, and that again on the care which is taken to avoid sudden changes in the quality of the heat that is applied to the foodstuffs. Generally an iron pot was used that, after a preliminary boiling or braising of the contents, was drawn aside to a cooler position on the hearth and allowed to continue at the same temperature for varying periods. Simmering was especially effective with vegetable and meat stews. A *bredie*, for instance, can never be exactly what it ought to be unless it has been slowly simmered for several hours to give all the constituents a proper chance to become intimately blended into a composite whole that possesses all the good qualities of its several ingredients.

Simmering, which is after all merely a variant of *stewing*, is economical and scientific. Properly done, it transforms the foodstuff into its most

appetising, palatable and therefore nourishing form, developing, by this slow, steady and prolonged action of moist heat, chemical changes in the food of whose nature and effect on digestion we still do not know enough to dogmatise.

Baking, roasting, frying, sautéing and other methods of direct application of heat did not differ in any degree from those used by other cooks. Bread and cakes were usually baked in brick or clay ovens — on some of the farms in ant heaps excavated into suitable receptacles for the purpose — the heat being wood or brushwood and never coal or coke. Oven roasting, which is properly baking, was rarely used for meat, but very often for vegetables such as sweet potatoes, pumpkins and ordinary potatoes, and also for some made dishes such as *bobotie*, toad-in-the-hole, fruit and meat pies, and of course all kinds of cakes and baked puddings.

Frying in deep fat was generally confined to town kitchens; on the farms and as a rule, frying, or more properly sautéing, was done in a shallow frying pan with just enough fat, lard or butter to give the necessary sharp moist heat to brown the substance fried. Batter was invariably used, but some of the old recipes distinctly state that bananas, pineapples, squashes, cucumbers and some other fruits and vegetables must not be fried in batter but by themselves — a directive that needs considerable skill and dexterity to carry out in such a way as to obtain a perfect result.

Steaming foodstuffs, either in their natural moisture, or in very little liquid of some other kind than their own juice (the *water-sootjie* business that is familiar enough to all cooks) was a popular method, particularly valuable when dealing with fish. It brought out the fine flavour of delicate foodstuffs, aided, when desired, by appropriate combinations of spices or herbs. A modification of this method, adopted in camp cookery, was to swathe the foodstuff in thick leaves, usually vine leaves or large dock leaves, in which they really simmered gently. Steaming needs a really low temperature, a gentle heat that percolates rather than concentrates its intensity on any particular section of the substance cooked.

In skilled hands it is one of the best methods of preparing food, but if the cook is inexperienced it usually produces something that is very much underdone, tough and insipid.

Much depends, in good cookery, on the preparation of the good foodstuffs before they are subjected to one or other method of cooking. At the Cape beef has always been stringy, tough and tasteless; veal has been slightly better, though it has never reached the European or American standard of excellence. Both, therefore, require good larding and all the old recipes are emphatic in their insistence that beef and game should be well larded. The larding was done, not with a needle, but by inserting good pork fat with the point of the knife an inch or two below the surface of the meat. Wild fowl were larded in the usual way and some kinds of fish, like the bonito, were larded with strips of bacon.

Larding has now died out of fashion, and is very rarely seen, although some old-fashioned cooks still use it, with the result that their dishes are far more savoury and succulent than anything that can be obtained in hotels or restaurants.

Preliminary *marinading* of meats was also popular; it is essential for *sosaties*, and for some kinds of *boboties*, although it is nowadays never used for the latter. It is also useful in dealing with certain kinds of fish, especially freshwater fish. The marinade usually employed is a mixture of natural wine and wine vinegar, in which has been steeped various kinds of herbs, and sometimes wormwood (*wilde als*)[1] that is particularly admirable for game and waterfowl.

Old-time custom was to have two principal meals in the day. There was no real breakfast. On arising in the early morning, coffee and biscuits were taken. The first meal of the day was about nine o'clock or later in the morning, and was fairly substantial; the principal meal was after noon and, later on, coffee and cake or preserves were partaken of, with a supper in the evening.

In the middle of the eighteenth century, although the chief meal was still at midday, fashionable circles provided a substantial collation between six and seven in the afternoon, and towards the end of the century some families tended, under English influence, to concentrate dinner in the evening as the chief meal of the day. During the time of Lord Charles Somerset, when Government House set the fashion, at least as far as Cape Town and its immediate neighbourhood were concerned, the correct dining-hour was between five and six in the later afternoon, the dinners sometimes lasting till late in the night.

The Duke of Wellington, then a plain and unimportant major, used to leave his lodgings at Maitland at four o'clock to ride to the hospitable house at Newlands, where he (as Cheap Jack has recorded the matter) was usually 'the only officer who hadn't to be helped to get on his horse when he left', to attend the six o'clock dinner that was reckoned the best in the Peninsula. The cook there was a Coloured woman, the daughter of a Malay slave, who had been trained by a Mozambique cook. Her pastries, curries, *boboties*, *sosaties* and fish dishes were renowned, and there is a legend that on occasion she was invited to show her skill at Government House, which had a White cook and stuck to French cookery.

Mrs Kindersley noted that Cape Town breakfasts were, even in her day, pretty substantial. That, however, was a later innovation.

Fifty years ago all the good Cape Town hotels provided a breakfast that today would be regarded as sumptuous in the extreme. I have, as a boy, sat

---

1 *Artemisia afra.*

down at Haylett's White House in the Strand at nine o'clock of a morning to consume, not cereals and Melba toast (for these did not figure on the bill of fare, though those who wanted it could have old-fashioned oatmeal porridge served with salt instead of sugar) but turmeric scones, *sosaties* with *fried* bananas and fried eggs, long, much-spiced sausages deliciously fried over wood coals, and a buffet of cold game and fowl and gammon ham.

At Poole's in New Street — formerly Garden Street and nowadays Queen Victoria Street — one could get partridge pie, batter chops and yellow rice for breakfast, which indeed differed from the midday meal only in not having soup on the bill. Dinner, at midday, was a fuller and coarser matter. There was always soup, generally a full-flavoured, appetising, thick soup, though sometimes, in summer, a clear vegetable or herb soup was provided. Two kinds of fish came next, and thereafter stews, roasts and vegetables, with a couple of sweets to follow. Wine was always served at this meal, in a carafe for the resident boarders, in bottles for the chance comers who paid for it, and it was generally a sound, wholesome natural wine. At dessert a sweet wine, usually fortified, was handed round, followed by coffee and preserves.

At private houses, both in town and on the farms, the ritual at dinner was much more elaborate and there, as is generally the case all over the world, one got far better and more skilfully prepared dishes than at any hotel. Some dishes were almost heirlooms; they could be tasted only at particular family houses and then only on special occasions. Others, more particularly those which figured ingredients that could not be grown in gardens or cultivated but were obtained from the veld, could be tasted only on farms.

There was from the earliest times a good market at Cape Town, which persisted till the end of the past century[1] when, like the beautiful foreshore between Mouille Point and Bantry Bay, it was sacrificed to the utilitarian gods that abhor whatever is beautiful and artistic. In that cool, inviting colonnade, one could get almost anything that one could think of for the kitchen — out-of-the-way herbs; tortoises and turtles; the tasty little *klip* fish; the aromatic berries that came from bushes growing on the edge of the Green Point Common lake; the succulent fennel roots that made such delicious preserve; the delightful, but rather vulgar, rose apples that some folk liked to mingle in their sweet dishes; the immense crayfish (the like of which one no longer sees, since Government has taken them under its protection and tried to teach us to call them crawfish); *malagas*[2] eggs (more tasty than those of the penguin); and even that most delectable of all delicacies, the prepared skin of an adolescent porcupine.

In those circumstances it was comparatively easy to follow implicitly the

---

1 The nineteenth century.
2 Ganet.

directions in the old recipes, as there was no great difficulty in obtaining the necessary ingredients. Now it is sometimes impossible and generally very difficult to adhere faithfully to the directives.

Some travellers have complained that old Cape cookery was too greasy, too generous altogether in fats and tit-bits. The same charge has been laid against Italian cookery, German cookery and Creole cookery. It is true that certain dishes, notably the very fat, Karoo-fed mutton when pot-roasted, are decidedly greasy, but a good cook can easily eliminate the oiliness. *Bredies* and stews insufficiently simmered and inexpertly prepared may have a film of grease, but here too a good cook will know how to deal with it. Possibly the frequent use of wine in Cape cookery was an attempt to counteract the abundance of lard and sheep's tail fat so commonly used in farm cookery. Crisp frying, with adequate drainage when the fried portions are properly cooked, should also eliminate greasiness in most cases.

Chapter 3

Spices, Herbs and Flavourings

The art of making food palatable consists in skilfully improving the taste and quality of the foodstuffs by combining with their original flavour something that enhances and blends with it to bring out its full perfection. For that purpose we make use of various materials, generally those that possess a distinctive and sometimes a strong taste. Of these the most important are spices, herbs and extracts.

What are known as spices are, generally speaking, the mature or immature seeds of different species of plants, usually dried and prepared for the market. Only two kinds of spice, ginger and chillies were grown in South Africa. From the earliest times most spices have been imported from the East Indies, nearly all in the ordinary commercial forms — though one kind, mace, was sometimes procured, privately, preserved in a thin syrup, a form in which it is no longer obtainable.

Of these various spices the chief were ginger, cinnamon and cassia, nutmeg and mace, pimento or allspice, cloves, black and white pepper, turmeric, chillies, saffron and garlic. Aromatic seeds such as poppy seed, cardamon seed, coriander seed, cumin seed, fennel seed and dill were also popular; but a few of the spicy seeds that figure in European recipes, such as fenugreek, capers and star aniseed and flavourings such as calamus, angelica, gentian, juniper berries and valerian are not ingredients in Cape cookery. A rare Oriental flavouring, zedoary, is mentioned in a few old recipes, but was never commonly used, and its neglect in modern days is no loss because it can easily be dispensed with, as can also that other culinary absurdity, assafoetida, that is sometimes used in the preparation of Asiatic dishes.

Ginger is the underground stem of *Zingiber officinale*, now locally grown to a large extent, although not in sufficient quantity to obviate importation. When fresh it is unpeeled and, like nearly all spices, contains starch and a volatile oil that gives to it its characteristic ginger taste, which is aromatic, biting and slightly sweet. The dried ginger, in which form it is usually sold on the market, is white or brown in colour and has lost its peel. It is more fibrous, less aromatic, but a bit more pungent, can be powdered easily and retains its spicy flavour for a long time. It is indispensable for making curries, and is used as a flavouring in sweet dishes, condiments and some meat dishes and, to a slighter extent, in puddings and cakes.

Allspice, or *pimento*, is the fruit of *Eugenia acris pimento*, a West Indian tree. It is exported in the dried form which, however, contains a large amount of the essential oil that gives it its characteristic clovelike flavour, known to chemists as *eugenol*. It is commonly used in all dishes in which cloves or pepper are likely to be admixed. In practice it is of little value when compared with these two spices and, as it easily loses its pungency when exposed to the air, it has never been popular in Cape cookery.

Cinnamon, on the other hand, is perhaps, next to pepper and nutmeg, the spice most commonly used at the Cape. Some old manuscript cookery books give precise and clear directions for distinguishing it from *cassia*, which today has almost supplanted it. Both are barks of an Oriental laurel tree; cinnamon being derived from *Cinnamomum zeylanicum*, and cassia from *C. cassia*. Both have a pleasant, cinnamon scent and a warm, aromatic and slightly sweet taste that are characteristics of cinnamon oil, a highly volatile liquid whose chief constituent is cinnamic aldehyde.

Cassia is a coarser, more stringy bark, less fragrant but slightly sweeter than cinnamon, and it has a sharp pungency that in some specimens is almost acrid and appears to be strengthened in the presence of sugar. For that reason there is a real difference in the quality of dishes prepared with cinnamon and that in which the cheaper and coarser cassia quills are used — a fact perfectly well known to old Cape cooks who were careful to use 'the thinnest and finest Colombo cinnamon, soft enough to take the impress of one's nail'. Such cinnamon was never bought in powdered form, for it was known that cinnamon powder lent itself easily to adulteration; it was always purchased as quills or 'featherings', which were slightly cheaper — for Ceylon cinnamon was always a highly priced spice on the market — and when it was wanted in powder form it was pounded in a mortar and sieved through a fine-meshed sieve. Generally, however, it was used whole, a small bit being broken off the quill and added to the dish.

For flavouring much less cinnamon had to be used than cassia but, as the latter was much the cheaper, it gradually replaced the pure cinnamon and today, unfortunately, most cooks do not know the difference between the two. To the initiated, however, that difference is profound and may greatly influence the taste of a particular dish, especially when other flavourings are used at the same time. Cassia does not combine particularly well with some flavourings, whereas cinnamon blends blandly and kindly with most, even with the vulgar and pervasive vanilla.

Nutmeg and *mace*, although apparently so utterly different, are integral parts of one another, for the nutmeg is the seed of *Myristica fragrans*;[1] while mace is the beautiful red covering of that seed, which when dried is of a yellow or brownish red hue. It was formerly imported exclusively from Java, for its home is in the Moluccas, but the tree has for generations been cultivated in the West Indies and today the best nutmegs are said to come

---

1 Various spices, indigenous and exotic, are grown. The Santa Fé nutmeg, pungent and coarse, is from *M. stobra*, which gives white mace. The Madagascar nutmeg is usually from *M. acuminata*. [L]

from Grenada. With cinnamon and pepper, nutmeg and mace may be said to be the most important spices employed in Cape cookery, for they figure in the oldest recipes and are still extensively used. One form in which they were formerly occasionally used, as a preserve of the ripe fruit in thin syrup, can no longer be obtained. This is a pity, for the syrup extracted much of the essential oil of both the covering and the kernel and served admirably as a concentrated flavouring for puddings and sweet dishes. Grated nutmeg goes with practically all steamed vegetables, while mace is incorporated in vegetable and meat stews. Both blend well with other flavourings and neither, when properly used, is overpowering.

The same cannot be said of cloves, which are the dried, unopened buds of *Caryophyllus aromaticus*, another native tree of the Spice Islands. The commercial article has a pronounced aromatic scent and a strong, almost bitingly sharp, spicy taste. Zanzibar cloves are more mellow and less pungent. The aroma and taste they get from their essential oil, which is cousin-german to that contained in allspice. Cloves are used, somewhat arbitrarily, to flavour many sweet and unsweetened dishes and are an ingredient in all the standard recipes for the manufacture of Van der Hum liqueur. They should, however, be cautiously used and can easily be dispensed with in most cases, even when the recipe favours them. Their flavour blends indifferently well with other flavours and generally stifles the delicate taste of some vegetables and fruits.

Pepper is another typically eastern spice of which there are several commercial varieties, technically called by the name of the particular town that exports them. In its official form it is the dried fruit capsule of *Piper nigrum*, a climbing plant of the East Indian forests, now extensively cultivated. Black pepper is the fruit still complete in its dark, black husk; white pepper is the berry from which the dark outer covering has been removed by soaking and bruising it in warm water. The burning hot taste and aromatic pungent odour of both are from the essential oil contained in the whole berry and its covering. The so-called long pepper, the berry of another species of *Piper*, is less pungent and, like other kinds of pepper, comparatively rarely used in cookery. Substitutes for pepper, some containing the same essential oil and therefore to all intents and purposes equally fit for all purposes for which black pepper is employed, are found in all tropical countries. South Africa, too, possesses a wild pepper, the seeds of which on occasion serve as a makeshift.[1]

Pepper has always been the chief and most important condiment spice; without it many dishes would lose the sharp, pleasingly warm taste that is a peculiarity of this flavouring. Practically all meat, and most vegetable dishes and soups, call for its addition, as it blends admirably with all. Even with sugar it may be made to agree, although it is not usually added to any sweet

1 Presumably *Piper capense*, found from Swellendam eastwards.

dish. The black variety is more pungent and more economical than the white, but the latter is required for dishes in which the intense black colour of the former is a disadvantage. The berries should always be added whole or, if desired in powder form, should be freshly ground in a pepper mill. Powdered pepper should always be preserved in closely-sealed jars, for the essential oil is volatile and easily dissipates, especially when the powder has been allowed to get wet.

When the East Indiaman *Haarlem*, with a cargo of spice on board, was wrecked on the shores of Table Bay some years before the settlement was started, the reek from the bags of pepper washed ashore lingered for many months in the vicinity and was even noted by some of the old travellers who visited the scene two years later.

Chillies, also known as red peppers, capsicum paprika, Cayenne pepper, pimiento, Mexican pepper, tabasco and hot pepper are in Cape recipes invariably referred to as *rissies*, although sometimes the Malay word *lombok* is used and occasionally the Dutch *Spaansche peper*. They are, curiously enough, the fruit pods of a plant of the potato family and there are now many cultivated varieties, different from each other in their shape, colour and pungency. The immature pod is bright green, turning yellow or red when it ripens; its shape is elongated, oval or irregularly or smoothly round, sometimes as small as a cherry or a small pea pod, sometimes the size of a cucumber or a small squash. It may be used as a vegetable, in which case one of the larger and less pungent varieties — sweet peppers — must be chosen, but its main value in cookery lies in the peculiar flavour of the pod itself and, more especially, of the seeds. It is stated to contain no volatile oil, and all cooks know that the pods can be preserved in the open for many years without losing their intensely sharp, fiercely biting taste, a peculiarity that makes its dust most irritating to the eyes and nostrils of anyone handling it.

Whatever it is that imparts this extraordinarily sharp, stimulating quality to chillies, also imbues them with distinctively individual merits that have long been appreciated and valued by South African cooks, who use them to an extent and in ways that are characteristic of much of their best cookery. Indeed, the test of the excellence of some South African soups and *bredies* is the manner in which the chilli flavour has been made to blend with, enhance and modify that of the other ingredients. Great skill and experience are needed in using this spice; it is so powerful, sharp and acrid that it cannot possibly be made to harmonise with some dishes, but it is also stimulating, so valuable as a contrasting flavour, and so delicious when properly used, that other dishes, without it, are insipid and altogether lack distinction.

While care is necessary in the use of all spices, none will repay patient and meticulous study and experiment better than chillies. Although there are probably more than fifty varieties in cultivation, only one — the ordinary small, attenuated, intensely sharp-tasting herb-garden variety that grows on a little bush half a foot high and flowers and fruits all the year round — need be stocked for kitchen use, and it does not greatly matter whether its pods are fresh or dried. When its full strength is required, the whole pod is used; when it is wished to have its flavour more mild, the seeds are first removed. The immature pod, which is bright green, is regarded as slightly milder than the full-grown, ripe, brilliantly red seed vessel.

Turmeric, like ginger, is the rootstock of an East Indian plant and is usually obtained only in powdered form. I have seen it growing in old gardens at the Cape, but have never heard of the fresh rootstock being used in a Cape kitchen, although formerly the dried, or partly-dried, root was easily bought on the vegetable market. Its Dutch name, *kurkumana wortel*, is no longer used, having been replaced by the old term *borrie* that is used in the first recipes. It has a slightly bitter, and not a very pronounced aromatic taste, caused by a mild volatile oil. It contains much starch, and a colouring extractive that imparts a bright yellow tint to cellulose and albumin. Nowadays it is chiefly used in curries and in yellow rice dishes.

Saffron always has been the most expensive spice on the market and has, in consequence, been so much adulterated that most cooks have managed to do without it. It is, however, an extremely valuable spice, with a distinctive, individual flavour — slightly bitter, moderately pungent, and exceedingly penetrating — so that a very little goes a very long way in cookery. It readily gives up its bright yellow-red colouring matter, which is soluble in water and wine, and can be used to colour soups and sweet dishes. Real saffron is the dried stigma of the crocus, which is carefully plucked out when the flower is beginning to fade, spread on muslin and sun-dried. When dry, only the finest red stigmas are collected and sold by the ounce or gram. They were usually retailed to cooks by the pennyweight.

Today there is almost no real saffron to be obtained; what passes for it is a substitute, the florets of a composite American plant, with a much less aromatic taste and a more yellow colour. It does very well for cakes and biscuits, but hardly can replace the real article in soups and fish dishes.

Garlic is extensively grown at the Cape and no longer imported, so that it is possible to get fresh bulbs. The commercial powder, which is a mixture of pounded bulb, starch and salt, never need be used. As a flavouring, garlic has always been popular with Cape cooks, who used it more sparingly than their Oriental contemporaries, and combined it, perhaps more skilfully, with other spices. They sometimes used a native garlic (*Tulbaghia sp.*), a common garden plant with lilac blue flowers, whose leaves are excellent as a substitute for true garlic but whose bulbs are much too strongly aromatic for culinary use.[1]

---

1 Probably *Tulbaghia violacea*.

The Cape cook relied greatly, so far as his spicy seeds were concerned, on *coriander* seed, that was formerly extensively imported from Asia but is now home-grown. It is derived from a plant of the carrot family, which has a pretty, feathery white flower and small, ridged seeds that are supposed to resemble a bedbug. To this fancied resemblance the plant owes its name, which is from the Greek for one of these disgusting little *goggas*. The seed, however, is far from disgusting. It has a clean aromatic odour and taste, and imparts an agreeable flavour to all meats and starches, while it can be preserved for some time without losing its good qualities. A little bruising generally brings out these much better.

Mustard seed is too well known to need comment; it is now always used in its powdered, commercial form. A very little of it may on occasion be advantageous in a dish, but it contains so outrageously active an intestinal irritant (known to chemists as isothiocyanate of allyl) that it should be employed with the utmost caution. All the piquancy that it is supposed, in the advertisements, to give to whatever we eat, can be more healthily and artistically given by other condiments.

Poppy seed, on the other hand, has no deleterious qualities. They are slightly nutty in taste and are prescribed in some old recipes for adorning cakes. They contain no opium, and the good lady traveller who states that she 'fell asleep too readily after eating of the poppy-cakes' somewhere in Strand Street was most certainly drawing on a saltatory imagination.

Cardamon, celery and *dill seed* are sparingly used in their current commercial forms. *Fennel seed* is less commonly used than fennel leaves or, in some old-fashioned kitchens, the root of the plant. *Caraway, aniseed* and *cumin* are much more popular.

They may be said to be the chief spice seeds in daily use and all three have distinctive odours and tastes, though when subjected to heat there is not much difference between any two of them. Aniseed, perhaps, imparts more of its peculiar flavour to farinaceous dishes than does either cumin or caraway, while the two latter also give a less pronounced flavour and taste to any liquid in which they are steeped or boiled. The so-called star aniseed is not a seed at all, and although it is often used in Oriental cookery, I have never seen it mentioned in any authentic Cape recipe, though it has lately made its appearance (obviously derived from second-hand American sources) in popular cookery hints by someone who apparently has vague ideas of what kind of spice it is.

More than on spicy seeds, the Cape cook relies on flavouring extracts that he obtains from fresh herbs and leaves. Formerly every house that had a garden had a corner of it reserved for the growing of pot and kitchen herbs. How varied and extensive these collections were in some cases is

spices, herbs and flavourings

exemplified by the jottings, in one manuscript book, of a Cape lady writing at the beginning of the last century:[1]

> In the little garden there are now: mint, thyme, mignonette, Spanish peppers, rosemary, endive, wild garlic, pepperroot, nasturtiums, tarragon, mountain sage, marjoram, celery, anise, sorrel, and scented verbena . . . the bean-herb (savory) has died and so has the balsam herb (basil) which cannot be replaced . . .

All these are still used and all are referred to, somewhere or other, in old Cape recipes; but some, like savory and basil, tarragon and pepperroot, sweet thyme and catmint, are now exceedingly scarce and hardly to be obtained, even from the nurserymen. As most of them are well known, we need say little about them here, but sorrel and scented verbena are fully worth an annotation.

Sorrel is of two kinds. There is the common or garden sorrel, also known as French or Belgian sorrel, that is easily cultivated in the garden and is the sort that is mentioned in all cookery books. The other kind is the indigenous 'Cape sorrel', to pick which the mariners landed on the Peninsula nearly a hundred years before Van Riebeeck established his refreshment station here. It is a true *Oxalis*, flourishes extensively all through winter, spring and early summer, and sometimes makes splendid splashes of chrome yellow on the hills.

Its history cannot be told here, for it is too long and intricate a tale. In the kitchen it serves to soften and improve nearly all vegetable stews; makes an excellent soup; and may even be served up as vegetable puree or in its uncooked form added to a vegetable salad. It is pleasantly sub-acid and probably (if that is of the least interest to any cook) has quite a considerable amount of vitamin, but for all that it is an excellent food adjunct without which Cape cookery would not be what it should be.

Scented verbena (and to some extent also the various sweet-scented indigenous pelargoniums) may be used for flavouring, for blending with other herbs in vegetable and meat stews and in soups, and as an addition to sweet drinks. Their essential oils are soft and fragrant, combine admirably with various spices, and are perfectly harmless.

So too are *laurel leaves*, the foliage of the sweet bay tree (*Laurus nobilis*), native to southern Europe but fairly common in Cape gardens. The leaves have a characteristic scent of oil of laurel and an aromatic, slightly bitter and astringent taste. They are used alone or in combination with other flavouring materials, generally in cold dishes, such as brawns and marinated fish or meats. Some caution must be observed in their use, for a decoction of the leaves is decidedly poisonous. Probably for this reason they are

---

1 The nineteenth century.

usually replaced in Cape cooking recipes by *lemon leaves*, whose flavour, odour and taste are very similar and whose use is devoid of danger.

There are several other kinds of leaves, such as those of the peach, the pittosporum, and orange or tangerine, that are used for flavouring, while young fig leaves are sometimes added to soups or stews to give a bright green colour.

In a country with such vast botanical wealth it is not surprising to find many different kinds of wild plants that can with advantage be added to the already long list of spices and flavourings. Some of these will be mentioned when we discuss camp cooking, but most of them have not yet been fairly tried. Much remains to be done in this wide and fallow field, where the ingenuity and artistry of the expert cook may find scope for unlimited combination and experiment. One need refer only to one of the most fragrant and distinctive South African seeds, that of the *Gethyllis*, whose pods are now used solely to scent domestic linen, but whose possibilities as a food flavouring appear to be vast.

There remains one other flavouring that does not fall into any of the categories that have so far been dealt with. This is *tamarind*, the pasty dried fruit of an Indian tree that was at one period deemed indispensable in the preparation of many Cape dishes, particularly curries. For several years good tamarind has been practically unobtainable; now it is again on the market, and it should be used wherever it is prescribed in the recipes. An infusion of the fruit is more aromatic and spicier than *vinegar*, which in modern days has almost supplanted it. It need scarcely be said that the vinegar used in Cape cookery is always good wine vinegar; wood or malt vinegar is never used by any cook who has the slightest respect for his art or his dishes.

Extracts of herbs or spices in vinegar are useful to have at hand when the fresh or dried flavourings cannot be obtained.

In conclusion I may briefly refer to one or two other flavourings that are mentioned in many recipes. One is *tangerine peel* (*naartjieskil*), the dried rind of the tangerine or mandarin orange commonly found throughout South Africa. It is used in small pieces, for it is a strong and distinctive flavouring, and nearly always for sweet dishes. Lemon and orange, citron and kumquat peel or zests are also used according to taste; each has its own, slightly different, taste and flavour, and all are pleasingly and warmly aromatic.

Several kinds of nuts are also flavoured. Among these are pistachio, almonds, both the sweet and the bitter kind, peach and apricot kernels, and pine kernels — all ingredients in old recipes. Of these pistachio alone is imported; all the others are home-grown.

For colouring, powdered ochre, saffron and turmeric were relied on, although much use was made of caramel, molasses and *moskonfyt*. Perfumes were used in the early eighteenth century, but fell into disfavour. Their place was taken by the essential oils of almonds and lemon. Rose water and orange flower-water are mentioned in some recipes; musk in one only.

Chapter 4

Soups

Following the west-European custom of starting the principal meal with a soup course, Cape colonists did not know, or if they knew did not use, *hors d'oeuvres* as a preparatory relish at lunch or dinner. *Vorspeise* of this sort were introduced from Russia and the Scandinavian countries, and recipes for their preparation are not found in the old Colonial manuscript books. Soups, on the other hand, were always popular, and the humblest kitchen relied on a good soup to start a meal. The result was that most of the Cape soups were considered as an integral part of the meal, rather than as a relish to stimulate appetite. They were almost without exception highly nutritious, satisfying concoctions, well flavoured and rich — varying in consistency from the thin liquid vegetable consommés to the almost porridge-like consistency of the heavy purées and game soups with their added thickening of farinaceous material.

They were usually carefully prepared, for to a large extent the skill of the cook was tested by the soup. Artificial colouring was rarely used; when necessary, burnt sugar or a brown roux, the preparation of which differed in no way from that prescribed in printed cookery books, was used. For a red colour, beetroot leaves; for green, spinach or fig leaves; and for a bright yellow, turmeric or curry powder could be employed. In one recipe for fish soup, saffron is mentioned, which gives a pale apricot tint. For the richer soups a zest of egg yolks beaten up with a glass of wine and a grating of nutmeg was nearly always prescribed. It was placed in the soup tureen and the boiling soup was poured on it immediately before serving.

With such rich soups, snippets of bread, fried in fat, were handed round; with curry soups, white rice, cooked dry, was served in some households; and salt-dried fish, *bokkoms* or 'Indian duck' as old East Indians preferred to call it, in others.

The soup was ladled out by the hostess into deep china or earthenware plates, and handed round to the guests, each being served with a liberal portion. It was not the custom to hand round cream or any made-up condiment with the soup; all spice or flavouring that was necessary was put in before it reached the table. I have known a guest's name deleted from his hostess's dining list because he had added salt and pepper to his soup, thereby inferentially questioning the cook's skill.

Nowadays we are not so strong minded, and it is not uncommon to see some 'bright young thing' lighting a cigarette at table between the soup and the fish course, unwithered by an appositely scathing remark from her hostess.

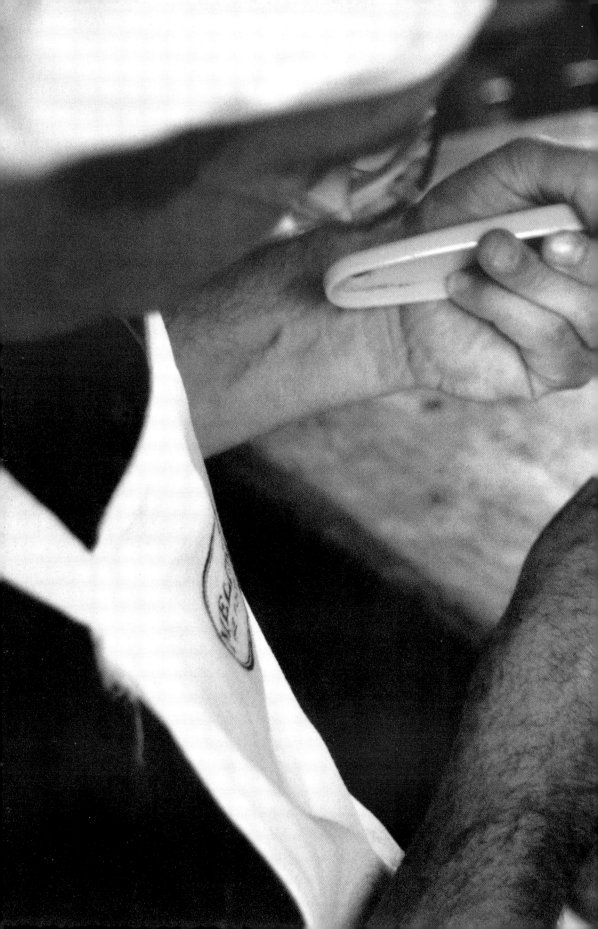

The basic constituent of most soups is a meat extract in water, such as a beef bouillon, a consommé in the manufacture of which two different kinds of meat, usually beef and mutton, have been used, and a veal consommé. When these are used instead of water, the soup is of course richer and contains an additional amount of nourishment. It is seldom, however, that the old recipes prescribe these basic liquids. They usually direct that, if meat of any kind is to be used, such meat should be boiled with the other ingredients. In a number of soups no meat whatever is used, and the substitutes for a meat extract are then milk, wine, beer, fruit juice, and especially coconut milk.

The last is prepared by scraping the flesh of a ripe coconut, adding to it the original fluid contained in the nut, and then pouring boiling water over it. As soon as the water cools, the mixture is compressed and all the moisture forced out. Such coconut milk is a thin, whitish-grey fluid, slightly sweet and glutinous to the taste; it serves admirably as a diluent and has many other uses in Cape cookery. What remains after the moisture has been extracted, the dry, white scrapings, still has a certain amount of flavour and considerable food value, and may be used for puddings, cakes and some entrées.

It is not my intention to write down the recipes for the several hundred different kinds of soups. All are to be found in printed cookery books, and most of them are variations of directives that appear in the oldest. There are, however, recipes that have been modified at the Cape and a few others that, on account of the purely local character of some of their constituents, may be said to be peculiar to South Africa. In a post-war[1] Afrikaans cookery book, 110 kinds of soups are described; of these probably a fourth may claim to differ in some way from similar kinds enumerated in European cookery books published before the middle of the last century.[2] There is ample scope for the ingenuity of the South African cook to concoct new kinds by slightly modifying these age-old recipes and by blending the ingredients with some of the distinctive local herbs and flavourings.

One of the best soups of which mention is made in the older recipes was undoubtedly developed on the lines laid down by the wandering demobbed soldier in Grimm's folk-tale. When the first mariners walked on the shores of Table Bay, they found round them almost a meadowland sprinkled with all sorts of edible herbs that to sailormen, yearning for fresh vegetables to counteract the persistent tendency to scurvy that endangered all long voyages, promised immediate relief. It was easy enough to gather armloads of these greens, boil them in the caboose with the addition of scraps of salt pork, consume the resultant liquid as a health-giving soup, and serve up the remaining mess as a vegetable stew.

Later there was opportunity to be more selective, discriminating and

----

1 Probably the Anglo-Boer War of 1899-1902.
2 The nineteenth century.

artistic, and the varieties of this vegetable soup show a progressive aptitude for studying flavour and blending tastes. A comprehensive synopsis of these different recipes is afforded by the following directions in one of the oldest manuscripts.

> *Garden Soup.* Take of thyme, marjoram, young leaves of the beetroot, sorrel, dock and lettuce enough for your purpose; chop up a handful of green beans, a couple of young onions, with their leaves, a slice of green pumpkin, a couple of soft, young turnips, and a medium-sized green chilli. Put all into the soup pot and cover with cold water. Bring to the boil and skim; then let slowly simmer for four hours, adding lukewarm water to make up for what evaporates. Add a bit of mace, a few slices of green ginger and a few peppercorns, and allow to simmer for half an hour longer. Strain through muslin and serve after salting.

The result should be a thin, reddish-brown liquid, deliciously and pungently aromatic, which, if it is too sharp for ordinary tastes, may be diluted advantageously with a dash of cream, a few tablespoons of coconut milk, or a glass of wine. Almost anything in the garden may be used in preparing this soup; in fact, the more varied the mixture of herbs and vegetables is, the better will be the result. What remains after straining may be mashed with butter and a dash of wine into a tasty puree, after removing the remnants of the mace, peppercorns and chilli.

The soup is as good if it is served cold after a short spell in the refrigerator.

Crayfish soup. Select for this the female of the species, which you will know by the double-toed claw or, better still, by the hispidity under the tail.

Select, if you can get them, living crayfish, dark brown and crawling, and eschew the cardinal-coloured, commercially-boiled ones that lack all delicacy, whose flesh is sodden and stringy. Proceed according to the old-fashioned recipe, compiled by cooks who knew how to get the best out of these tasty crustaceans.

> Take two young carrots, two onions, two shallots, two lemon leaves, a teaspoonful of thyme, a clove of garlic bruised, a few scented verbena leaves; a slither of lemon rind, a slice of fat bacon, and half a pound of raw ham; chop these fine, and simmer lightly with butter. Season with pepper and salt; pour over a bottle of wine and let the whole boil up. Boil your crayfish in this *mirepoix*, and let it cool down in it when cooked.
>
> Now take out your crayfish, and remove from it all the flesh, especially the soft white and green substance found under the carapace, and the meat from the larger claws. Crush the remains of the crayfish in a mortar, and put it back, together with part of the tail flesh, in the *mirepoix*, to which you add a few cups of good fish or mutton stock, and let it slowly simmer for a couple of hours. Strain, and set the liquor aside for the moment.

soups

53

Pound the flesh, together with the coral and green meat, in a mortar with some butter, a morsel of mace, and a pinch of ginger powder, and add it to the liquor; simmer slowly taking care that no lumps are formed and add, finally, half a cupful of boiled rice, and some of the tail flesh cut into dice.

Beat up a couple of egg yolks in the soup tureen with a glassful of sherry, pour in the soup, and serve immediately with croutons of fried bread.

A crayfish *bisque*, prepared in this way, is a rich, delicately flavoured soup, far different from that ordinarily made from commercially-boiled crayfish or cold-storage tails. Some folk put in a handful of green seaweed; others add cream, which makes a smoother but heavier soup. By adding curry or turmeric powder it becomes a crayfish *mulligatawny*; with tomatoes and potatoes mixed in it, it becomes a crayfish *chowder*. Experts garnish it with marble-sized dumplings made from the soft carapace flesh and the coral, mixed with egg white and boiled in the soup.

The test of its excellence is the exquisite flavour given to it by the soft parts found under the carapace, which is usually lost when the tail flesh alone is used. Old recipes warn against the reputedly dangerous intestinal tract in the animal which, as a matter of fact, easily comes away and has really no poisonous properties.

Fish soup, made from the firmer varieties such as bonito or yellowtail and Cape salmon (*geelbek*) is prepared in much the same way, by first making a strong and well-flavoured fish stock from the bones, adding portions of the fish (sometimes first lightly fried in butter or lard) and pouring the boiling liquid over a zest of beaten yolk of egg mixed with cream and a glass of wine.

A curry fish soup, and one in which saffron is used, are merely variations of this method, which lends itself to innumerable modifications.

A fish chowder and a *bouillabaisse* need for their proper preparation a variety of fish, cooked in a rich stock with the addition of potatoes and tomatoes, ochra or green beans for the one, and saffron, garlic and green ginger for the other. All fish soups are improved by boiling some green seaweed with them; few by the addition of chillies (a notable exception is curried fish, which is eaten cold). They are thickened, if desired, by rice flour, tapioca or maizena, and can be made extravagantly glutinous by ochra or seaweed.

Bean soup. There are many kinds of beans and all, when dried, make excellent soup — though some, like the small black-and-white sort, have a peculiar flavour. Perhaps the best of all is the large, almost inch long and proportionately broad, beautifully marbled *governor's beans* that could formerly be obtained cheaply but nowadays are quite costly.

As an example of the general recipe for bean soup the following recipe for a dish made from *hereboontjies*, as these big marbled beans were formerly called, will serve:

> Soak two pounds of beans in cold water; peel them, rejecting all that float. Braise some sliced onions, a small green chilli, a slice of green ginger, and some green herbs in butter or fat; pour over cold water, add the beans, a slice of fat pork and a mutton bone and let the whole simmer carefully for several hours, stirring the pot frequently and skimming carefully to remove the fat. Pour through the tammy, and separate the beans, keeping a few of them whole; mash the rest and return to the liquid. Salt and pepper to taste and boil for a quarter of an hour; add a glass of wine and serve.

It should be a smooth, white, moderately thick soup, which some people enrich by adding cream and egg yolk, although it requires neither, being by itself a nourishing and exceedingly palatable broth.

All fried pulses may be used for soup in the same way. A strong, harshly flavoured dried pea, lentil or bean soup is made with salt pork and is served garnished with croutons of fried bread. This is a favourite caboose dish and was formerly, under the name of *snert*, exceedingly popular; but is perhaps too powerfully flavoured for ordinary palates. A thin bean *consommé*, made from *bouillon* in which dried beans have been boiled, is a delicately flavoured soup that fulfils all the requirements for a preliminary dinner relish. For garnish, the whole beans that have escaped the mashing process are to be used. Some recipes prescribe a sprinkling of fennel leaves, and all white soups are supposed to be improved by the addition of grated nutmeg.

Limpet soup. Limpets, periwinkles and mussels were formerly easily obtainable; they flourished within hand grasp in the waters washing the shores of Table Bay. Now one must go far afield to get specimens that are not sullied by sewage, and as they are no longer sold on the fish market, one must gather them laboriously with personal effort. Limpet soup, as made by the old Malay cooks, was a distinctive and highly fragrant, appetising dish, and was prepared as follows:

> Collect as many limpets off the rocks as your backache allows you; put them in a bucket of fresh water and clean them as well as you are able to. A coarse scrubbing brush helps, but do not be too pernickety as long as you get rid of most of the sand. Put them into a mortar and crush their shells and then, without washing them again, place them in the soup pot, with some sliced onions, a garlic clove, a handful of green seaweed and some peppercorns; it does not matter if you are slightly extravagant with the pepper. Boil them up, and then let them simmer gently for a couple of hours. Strain through cloth, and put the liquid back into the pot. Add some burnt roux or burnt sugar mixed with a little flour, some salt (very little is

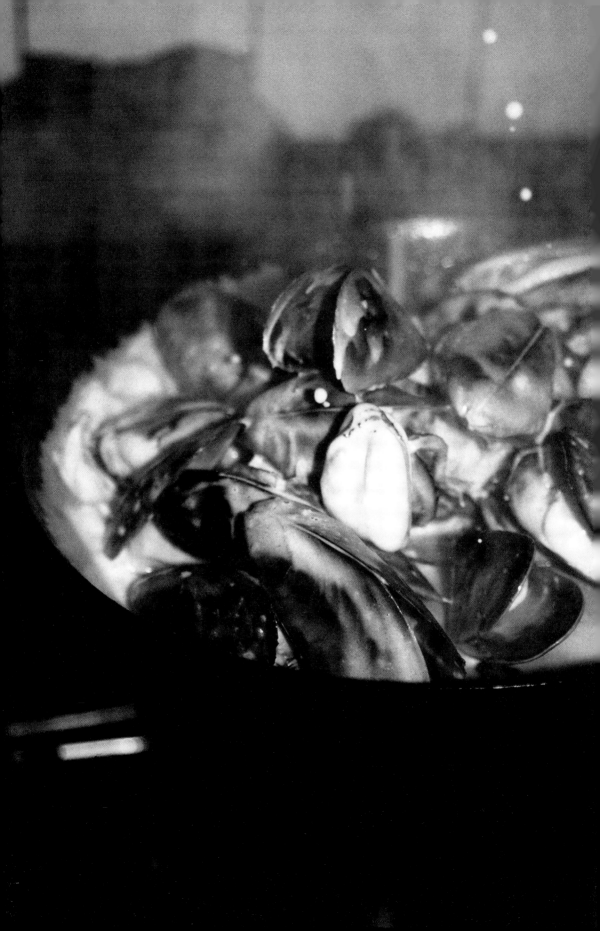

needed) and, if you like, a tablespoonful of ketchup or Worcester sauce, and boil up once more. Finally add a couple of glasses of sherry and serve.

Mussel soup can be made in the same way, but a far better method for mussels, especially the white variety, is to stew them lightly with herbs and butter and then pass them through a mincing machine or pound them in a mortar before simmering them in a good fish-stock or *bouillon*. This mussel soup really needs no thickening, but it is improved by adding cream. Another delicious soup is *klipkous soup*, which is made from the flesh of the large pearl mussel (*Haliotis capensis*) after it has been prepared for the table (see the recipe for pearl mussel). Into a rich fish stock, adequately spiced and herb flavoured, the pounded and cooked flesh is stirred slowly, to avoid forming lumps, and then simmered gently for a quarter of an hour.

Some people add saffron to this soup, but that is a mistake, for the flavour of the *Haliotis* is distinctive, delicate, and easily overpowered. Blending must therefore be skilfully done, and no soup needs more tasting on the part of the cook than this. When properly made, it should be smooth, greyish-white in colour, fragrant and full of rich suavity of taste that is the hallmark of the shellfish itself. I have never been quite satisfied that the addition of wine or cream add greatly to either its taste or its subtleness, but most recipes advise one or other of these adjuncts.

Turtle soup was well known to Cape cooks and at one time dried turtle, and on occasion fresh bits of the creature, were easily procurable at the fish market; but now it is a rarity and proportionately expensive. The manner in which it was prepared differed in no way from that prescribed in the printed manuals on cookery and ranged from Carême's elaborate recipe to the simpler ones in which far fewer ingredients were used.[1] Cape cooks specified a conglomeration of spices — the more, apparently, the better — and favoured large pieces of the flesh, so succulently fat, for garnishing.

Tortoise soup, made from the native tortoise that prowled all over the Cape Peninsula and is now protected inside and outside its borders, was esteemed a particularly efficacious tonic. The water tortoise, that is admirable eating, was rarely used for soup, probably because of its obnoxious odour. To make the soup the tortoise was killed, thoroughly scrubbed in warm water, and then boiled in a slightly salted water to which herbs and spices had been added according to taste, the boiling lasting until the animal had practically fallen to pieces. The liquid was then strained off and, for medicinal purposes, was left to get jellied. If wanted immediately, it was thickened with some tapioca. A little lemon juice and a cupful of wine were added and it was sent to table garnished with titbits of the flesh, preferably also of the liver, previously fried in butter.

---

1 A. Carême's 5-volume *L'Art de la cuisine française aux XIXe siècle* was published in Paris in 1835.

It made an admirable clear soup, with a distinctive but not too strong flavour, and was quite equal to the clear turtle soup made from dried meat.

Another soup that was reputed to possess medicinal value was *fish-roe soup*, of which the method was a variation of one of the oldest recipes in existence, and one of these that owed more to Occidental than to Eastern tradition:

> Soak the roes in water and remove all membrane. Simmer them slowly in a *mirepoix* made with vinegar, onions, green ginger and herbs; take them out and cut them up into small pieces, which you then place, with a cupful of green peas, in some good bouillon; simmer gently; add a glassful of white wine, grate nutmeg over (some cooks prefer powdered fennel) and serve with toasted bread.

Game soup was generally made from several kinds of game and wild fowl, usually with the addition of fat pork. It was always heavily herbed and spiced, thickened with brown roux, and strengthened by the addition of a moderately sweet wine. Sometimes it was preferred slightly sour, in which case the brown roux was mixed with vinegar or lemon juice.

Sour cream was never served with it; indeed, sour cream is rarely mentioned in the old recipes, and is even today scarcely ever used. Which is a pity, for with clear vegetable soups, especially those like garden soup, its addition is often an improvement.

Other meat soups, such as *veal soup, oxtail soup, calf's-head soup, calf's-foot soup, tripe soup, liver soup* and *kidney soup* were made in accordance with the usual recipes given in printed cookery books, though here and there one notices slight modifications that individual cooks have made. These are not always improvements on the orthodox directives. With meat soups, dumplings or small meatballs were sometimes served.

An interesting paraphrase of the old-fashioned *blancmange* or *potage a la reine* is the following:

> *Cream chicken soup.* Lightly brown a cooking fowl in fat or butter; simmer it in *bouillon* with a couple of sliced onions, a couple of carrots and a bunch of mixed herbs. When tender, take out and remove all the white flesh; replace the carcass and brown flesh in the soup pot and allow it to simmer. Pound the white flesh in a mortar with half a pound of cooked rice, a lump of butter, and a morsel of mace; add this to the soup pot and allow to simmer slowly for half an hour; now add a cupful of coconut milk (some recipes prescribe almond milk) and let it come to the boil. Pour through a tammy, and then into the soup tureen in which you have mixed a couple of egg yolks with a cupful of cream. Grate nutmeg over and serve immediately.

This soup should be a fairly thick puree, smooth and without lumps. It needs no pepper, but salt should be added, though the old recipe which I quote here does not mention it, probably because salted butter was used for browning the chicken. The taste should be delicate and would be spoiled by the addition of wine.

Mulligatawny soup. There are many recipes for this, which is essentially an eastern soup. It may be a thin clear curry-spiced *consommé*, or it may be a thick *potage*. The best cooks used to make it with fresh spices, but today it is far easier to use any good curry powder. The basis of the soup is a rich, strong double stock, made principally of chicken meat with a small amount of beef added to give 'body'. One recipe runs as follows:

> Cut into pieces a good sized fowl and lightly brown in fat; place them in the soup pot with four peeled and sliced mealy apples, four onions, a clove of garlic, previously bruised and slightly browned in butter, the bone from a roast leg of mutton from which most of the meat has been removed and, tied in a bit of muslin, a sprig of mint, thyme and marjoram, a bruised red chilli, some peppercorns and a morsel of mace. Allow to come to the boil and simmer slowly for a couple of hours.

> Remove the mutton bone and the herbs. Take an ounce of tamarind, previously steeped in water; pound it in a mortar with the water in which it has been steeped; pour through a wire sieve, and mix the liquid smoothly with two tablespoonsful of curry powder with an equal amount of fine rice flour. Let the soup come to the boil and stir in this mixture, taking care to allow no lumps to form; continue stirring for some minutes while it boils. Pour through a sieve or tammy, adding salt; put some of the chicken meat, boned, into the soup tureen; pour over a glass of white wine, add the soup and serve at once, handing round hot boiled rice or, if you like, pounded dried fish with it.

In all meat soups and generally, too, in others, it is significant that the old recipes prefer that salt should be added at the last moment. This is correct, provided it is permitted to dissolve completely and become intimately mixed with the liquid. Its addition at an earlier stage may harden some ingredients and undoubtedly does interfere with the proper blending of some of the spices and herbs, perhaps because of the chemical action of the salt solution on the essential oils.

Of the vegetable soups that have a particular local significance there are some that are prepared from plants that are indigenous, but their preparation differs in no way from that of any other vegetable soup. Their basis is a good stock; it may be a prepared meat stock, a vegetable stock, or a composite stock made by boiling the vegetable itself with meat and bones or with another vegetable. If the vegetable is mashed in the soup, it becomes a thick puree; if portions alone are retained and the soup consists merely of the juice and extractives from the vegetables used, it is a thin, clear or clouded *consommé*. Sometimes the vegetables are put into the cold bouillon or water without any preparation; sometimes they are first lightly braised in butter or fat, or dusted with flour before the water is poured on them. In all vegetable soups herbs and spices figure, according to most South African formularies.

As examples of vegetable soups made from ingredients peculiar to South Africa the following may be cited.

Uintjie soup. Uintjies are the edible corms of certain species of an iris (*Moraea edulis*) or of an oxalis (*Oxalis lupinifolia*), both of which are in season in the early spring (July to September). The corms are first boiled in salted water, peeled, and then made into a soup precisely in the manner in which governor's beans are done. The taste is like that of chestnuts. The soup, when well prepared, is rich, creamy-white, nourishing and highly appetising.

Water hawthorn soup is made from a puree of the buds of the wild water hawthorn or *wateruintjie* (*Aponogeton distachyos*) a common plant that grows on most inland ponds and shallow-river reaches, and is in season in winter and spring.

Sorrel soup is made from the leaves of the wild, yellow-flowered sorrel (*Oxalis pes-caprae*) that may be gathered almost all the year round. *Wild cabbage soup* is made from the buds of a veld plant, an anthericum, that blossoms in winter.[1] In addition the buds of one kind of aloe, the white part of the thick leaves of a river plant (*Prionium palmita*), the fronds of the bracken fern, and one or two kinds of seaweed provide ingredients for making soups that have a distinctive taste. Their preparation is simple like that of a spinach or lettuce soup. The cook prepares a good stock, in which the vegetable is boiled, with or without the addition of spices. In most cases, where the veld plant has a particularly delicate flavour, spices should be used with caution to enhance and not overpower the distinctive flavour of the principal ingredient.

Cape cooks also favoured sweet soups, which in winter were usually served hot and in summer chilled. Most of them are wine soups; a few, like *loquat soup*, are fruit soups, and are simply a mixture of fruit juices with a wine stock, thickened with rice flour or cream, or in some cases with coconut milk. The oldest recipe for a wine soup in my collection is the following:

Wine soup (*wynsoep*). Boil four cups of unskimmed milk with a morsel of tangerine peel, a blade of mace, a slither of cinnamon and four allspice; stir in a tablespoonful of butter and two ounces of candy sugar. Boil separately three pints of red wine with a slice of green ginger and a pinch of aniseed, and as soon as it comes to the boil stir it in the boiling milk; add a pinch of salt; let it stand where it remains hot, but do not let it boil

---

1 Probably *Trachyandra falcata* or *T. ciliata*, members of the asphodel family, which is closely related to the anthericums.

again. Beat up two fresh eggs in the soup tureen and pour the hot soup over them, beating continuously so that the eggs are thoroughly mixed with the soup. Grate nutmeg over, and serve with thin, sweet biscuits.

Another simpler and equally good recipe:

Cut a lemon in slices and sprinkle it with powdered candy sugar. Take a cupful of white breadcrumbs, and toss them in a pan in melted butter until they have absorbed it all; place the slices of lemon on top and let them remain there while the pan is kept hot on the side of the stove. Boil up four cups of a good red or white wine with some candy sugar, a feathering of cinnamon, and a couple of cloves. Put the soaked crumbs and the slices of lemon in the soup tureen and pour over them the boiling wine. Put on the cover and let the soup stand for ten minutes; stir, grate some nutmeg on the top, and serve with toasted bread.

Both kinds may be served cold, if desired. Wine and beer soups are sometimes thickened with sago or tapioca and garnished with raisins or preserved citron. A peculiarly fragrant — and it must be added, rather an insipid — wine soup is made with rose apples.

A few more recipes:

Green mielie soup. Cut the mielies from the cob, and cook them in a mixture of four parts water and one part white wine, to which you have added a bunch of herbs, a blade of mace, and some peppercorns. When tender, take out the corn, mash it, and return it to the soup pot with a cupful of strong meat stock, properly salted. Let it simmer for half an hour; then stir in a teaspoonful of candy sugar and serve.

Sometimes this soup is thickened by adding a white sauce, but it is better without that addition.

Garlic soup. Braise some sliced onions in butter with a clove of bruised garlic and a small bit of onion leaf. Add 24 cloves[1] and as many black peppercorns. Mix a teaspoonful of good curry powder in half a cupful of tamarind water, and stir this into the braise; add ten cups of good stock (or of coconut milk) and let it boil; then add a pound of ripe tomatoes, peeled and cut into quarters, a bay leaf and a lemon leaf, and salt to taste. Let it simmer slowly; pour through a coarse sieve, and serve with fried bread.

The recipe states: 'This soup has a decidedly sharp taste, and many prefer to dilute it with sour cream'.

---

1 Of garlic.

Blood soup. Take the fresh blood of a fowl and mix it with sifted flour, vinegar, powdered white pepper and salt. Stir this mixture slowly into a boiling chicken stock. Serve with meatballs made by mixing finely-minced chicken meat with white of egg, spiced with mace, ginger powder, and salt and pepper, and boiled in the soup.

Bread soup. Take slices of stale white bread; remove the crust and boil the slices in a good, well-spiced, chicken *consommé*. Take out and press through a wire sieve; mix with butter, grated nutmeg, salt and white pepper; return to the soup pot and let it boil, stirring carefully to prevent lumping. Serve in plates and garnish each plate with a poached egg dusted with nutmeg.

A similar soup is made with onions and bread, and is one of the variations of the many *onion soup* recipes.

Pawpaw soup. This is made from green pawpaws, boiled in a highly-spiced and herb-flavoured *bouillon*, mashed and then passed through the tammy. A glass of sherry improves it, and it is one of the few vegetable soups in which a suspicion of chilli enhances the flavour. An equally smooth soup can be made from avocado pears.

Chapter 5

Fish and Sea Food

The seas that wash the African continent are extraordinarily rich in things that are not merely edible but appetisingly eatable. They range from algae or seaweed to the many varieties of fish, shellfish and other invertebrates, and cetaceans that are really salt-water mammals and should, properly speaking, be considered in the following chapter, which deals with meat.

There was a time when the Cape Town fish market was the repository of practically all fish in season; when, on the little sandy cove at the bottom of Adderley Street, when the fishing boats came in, one could cheaply buy them freshly caught; and when, at Kalk Bay, one could even get a bunch of mullets for the asking, so plentiful was the catch. The raucous horn of the fish cart was heard every morning in the centre and suburbs of the town; a large *snoek* changed owners for a modest four pennies; and an immense crayfish cost a penny. Today we have changed all that and fish, that can and should be among the cheapest of foodstuffs, is prodigiously dear, hardly ever fresh, and never in sufficient supply to meet the demand.

With some patience and a knowledge of local conditions, however, most of the different kinds can still be obtained when in season, though some of the best, like butterfish, klipfish and klip sole, are rarely to be seen.

More than 100 years ago, an enthusiastic district surgeon published a list of 40 different kinds of edible fish to be obtained in the Cape Town fish market. His pamphlet is now a rare bit of Africana and contains some interesting particulars about the better-known varieties. Among these are the following:

Banksteenbras (*Palunolepis grandis* Gunth), Baardman (*Umbrina capensis* Pappe), Bonito (*Sarda sarda* Bloch), Bontrok (*Sargus cervinus* Iowe), Bishop (*Sparus sp.*), Dassie (*Sargus rondeletti*), Daybreak or Dageraad (*Pagrus laticeps*), Galjoen (*Dipteron capensis*), Geelbek (*Atractoscion aequideris*), Albacore or Yellowtail (*Seriola lalandii*), Hottentot (*Gymnocrolaphus curvidens* Gunth), Leatherfish (*Lichia amia* L.), Kabeljou (*Sciaena holopelidota*), Katonkel (*Scomberomorus commersonii*), Mackerel (*Scomber colias*), Maasbanker (*Trachurus trachurus*), Snoek (*Thyrsites atun*), Red steenbras (*Dentex rupestris*), White steenbras (*Pagellus lithognatus*), Red stumpnose (*Pagrus gibbiceps*), White stumpnose (*Sparus globiceps*), Red Roman (*Pagrus laticeps*), Stock fish, Klipfish, Haarder or Mullet, Springer, Butterfish, Pilchard, Skate, Sole, Klipsole, King Klipfish, Elf, Jacopiewer or Gurnard, Kalk or Chalk fish, and Silverfish.

Of these the sorts that are still easily obtainable in season are galjoen, geelbek, yellowtail, hottentot, kabeljou, mackerel, maasbanker, kingklip, snoek, the two kinds of steenbras, red and white, red and white stumpnose, red roman, stockfish, harder, sole, skate, silverfish, elf and gurnard. Katonkel, a delicious game fish, is rarely seen though it is more common on the fish markets at Port Elizabeth and East London. Pilchards or sardines are rarely to be had fresh, but are mainly used for canning; butterfish, perhaps the most tasty of all, is a deep-sea species only occasionally seen on the fish stalls.

There are many kinds of freshwater fish, among them being the mackerel, yellowfish, carp, barbel and trout, but they can seldom be bought.

Cape cooks dealt with all fish in various ways that were all modifications of traditional recipes. Large fish were cut up; we have no recipe for preparing for the table a 14 or 15 lb fish. Moderate sized specimens might on occasion be brought to table in their entirety, plain steamed or water *sootjied*, and served with butter sauce. But most recipes direct that the fish should be cut into small square pieces, known as *mootjies*, or filleted; skins and bones were used for making fish stock. Very little water was used for boiling, and the best recipes always prescribe boiling in a *coulis*, prepared with sliced onions, spice, herbs and a glass of wine or vinegar; sometimes a *court bouillon* is to be used.

Grilled fish was plainly cooked on the gridiron over the coals; for frying, lard or sheeptail fat was used; and deep-frying, in which the food was plunged into boiling oil or fat, was not favoured. Baking was not commonly used, but stewing, braising and slow simmering were popular methods of dealing with dried fish. Marinades of various kinds were employed, and batter was occasionally used when frying.

Fish was usually cooked as fresh as possible, although expert cooks declared that they should not 'come fresh from the water' but should be allowed to lie for some hours before being subjected to heat. Out of season they were regarded as indifferent, some kinds even as unwholesome. The roes and livers of a few kinds were esteemed as delicacies.

One of the best-known fish dishes at the Cape is also one of the oldest and is undoubtedly of Eastern origin. It is known as *ingelegde vis*, which is commonly 'Englished' into 'curried fish', although it should properly be called a pickled fish curry. It is never eaten hot but always cold, and must be allowed to stand for a week or a fortnight before it is served. It may be packed in jars with a layer of fat on top, and will in that way keep for several months.

Ingelegde vis. Choose a fairly firm-fleshed fish, such as geelbek or yellowtail; softer kinds, such as stock or kabeljou, will not keep as long.

Clean and cut up[1] the fish into equal sized pieces about three inches square; fry them in lard without previously dusting them with flour or covering them with batter; strew some salt on them and let them drain while you are making the pickle.

For this you lightly brown sliced onions and a bruised garlic clove, a couple of crushed chillies, a dozen black peppercorns, a tablespoonful of moist brown sugar, and one or two lemon or bay leaves, stirring them constantly till they are well braised. Then add half a cupful of good curry powder, mixed with two cups of good vinegar, and let it simmer for a quarter of an hour. Now add enough vinegar to make the pickle into a fairly thick liquid. Put some of this at the bottom of the dish in which you intend to keep the fish, and put on it a layer of fried fish; cover with more pickle and proceed in the same way till the dish is full.

Mix what remains of the sauce with more curry powder, boil it up with two cups of vinegar, and pour this thin sauce over the fish. Put aside in a cool place for several days and serve when required with thin bread and butter.

This recipe, which is the oldest that I have been able to find, is perhaps not definite enough. The onion 'rings' should remain whole, although properly cooked, and the dish is really a series of curried fried fish layers embedded in layers of fried onion, and saturated with a sour-sweet, spiced pickle. It is also greatly improved by the addition of a little tamarind juice and is, of course, much more fragrant when it is made with freshly-prepared curry paste.

A variant of this dish is the *penang vis*, prepared as follows:

Make a good fish stock from fish bones, herbs, sliced green ginger, peppercorns and a couple of lemon leaves. Strain, then brown in butter or fat a couple of sliced onions, with a tiny morsel of garlic, a teaspoonful of brown sugar, one of salt and a large tablespoonful of curry powder, mixing all with sufficient vinegar or lemon juice to make a paste. Pour on this the fish stock, and let it slowly simmer for a few minutes. Add to it fillets of raw fish; let them boil for ten or fifteen minutes, and serve hot, with boiled rice and potatoes.

Less watery, but hardly less appetising, are the *penangs* in which no fish stock is used but the fillets are gently braised in the curry sauce. These are really fish curries, and are immensely improved by the addition of coconut milk and chillies. The *penangs* made with fish stock are variations of *bouillabaisse*, and there are many recipes for them, in some of which saffron is used.

---

1 Note that the fish is not boned. In properly made *ingelegde vis*, the bones are so soft that they can be eaten without harm, thereby much increasing the nourishing qualities of the dish! [L]

Fish cakes, variously styled *fish balls*, *fish frikkadels*, and *fish dumplings*, are things quite different from the dry, tasteless namesakes that figure on so many bills of fare and are nowadays usually concocted from tinned fish. According to the old recipes, they are all made from raw or cooked fish, carefully boned and vigorously pounded in the mortar, always in fellowship with butter or cream, wine, spices and herbs; sometimes too with the addition of blanched almonds and chutney. This paste, sweetly smooth and soft and exquisitely flavoured, was then rolled into tiny balls, patted into neat little cakes, or shaped as small rolls, boiled in fish stock or carefully fried in fat, and served always with the accompaniment of a moderately sharp sauce. Sometimes the fish paste was pounded with bread soaked in milk and the fish cakes were dusted with breadcrumbs before being fried. The result was generally a soft, well-cooked and appetising dish, which could stand on its own merits or suffer the company of some neutral vegetable such as boiled rice. When eaten cold, it went admirably with a simple salad. Similar cakes were made from fish's roe or fish liver, but in these eggs were generally used to bind the ingredients.

Fish with eggs. The ordinary fish omelette was well known, but a more interesting dish was made in accordance with the recipes that are taken from a late eighteenth century manuscript book:

Clean and carefully bone some pieces of raw fish and lightly fry them in fat or butter, with a crushed chilli, a blade of mace, some onion rings, a pinch of ginger, a sprig of thyme, a sprig of rosemary, and salt and pepper to taste. When nicely braised, stir in your eggs, which you have beaten up with a teaspoonful of old wine or brandy. Cook till the eggs are set and serve at once.

Take pieces of dried fish (snoek or herring). Soak in water, bone, and braise with onions, spices and herbs, in plenty of butter. When properly braised, add a spoonful of cream and one of wine or brandy and simmer; stir in beaten eggs, and serve.

In both these dishes the result should be of the consistency of buttered eggs, light, rich and succulent. The colour is always improved by adding a little saffron (which should be steeped in wine for a few minutes before being added). The chilli may be omitted, but it does add to the piquancy of the dish. Crayfish flesh may be substituted for the fish and makes an excellent variant.

Fish bobotie is simply a *bobotie* in which fish has been substituted for meat and may be called a baked fish pudding. The oldest recipe for it is the following:

Pound raw or cooked fish, after having carefully removed all bones, with a couple of slices of white bread soaked in milk, a blade of mace, a few sprigs of parsley, marjoram and thyme, a pinch of black pepper, a pinch of powdered ginger, a teaspoonful of salt and a tablespoonful of brown sugar. Brown some slices of onion in fat with, if you care to add them, a clove of garlic and a crushed red chilli. Add to it two teaspoonsful of curry powder stirred into a cupful of tamarind water, or vinegar if you have no tamarind in the pantry. Let this sauce simmer for a few minutes, and then stir into it your fish paste. Work it smoothly with a wooden spoon and add coconut water or cream. Cook for ten minutes. Place it into a pie dish, coated inside with butter; put blanched almonds on top, pour over all a couple of eggs beaten up with salt, nutmeg and a few spoonsful of unskimmed milk and bake it in the oven 'until a knife blade comes out of it clean'. Serve with boiled rice.

For an old *fish pudding* there are these directions:

What is left over of your boiled elf, you may, if you are frugal (*sic*), use for a made dish which the good man will like as much as the children. You must take of the flesh three-quarters of a pound, and free it from bones, skin and gristle; then you must beat it to a smooth paste, adding salt, pepper, mace and ginger. When it is smooth you must add to it, gradually, so as to mix thoroughly with the paste, half a cup of onion that you have chopped up very fine and previously scalded, and then you must stir the paste into half a gill of cream with which you have beaten up the yolks of six eggs and put it all in your buttered pudding form which you must cover with a cloth and place in a pot of water to boil steadily. It is good to eat, either hot immediately when cooked or, better still, cold with pickles the day after you have made it. Aunt G— always adds a quarter of a pound of butter to the paste, but that tends to make it too heavy.

Experimentally, I have found that a little butter added improves this dish, which is made still better if the despised whites of the eggs are lightly whipped and incorporated with the paste before it is boiled. A melted butter sauce, soured with a little lemon juice, is the proper thing to serve it with.

The *kedgerees*, of which there are several varieties, are fish pilaffs — that is to say more or less dry risottos with fish as the principal protein ingredient. The generic recipe for them is the following:

Another way to use what is left over from your boiled fish is to make of it a kitshiri such as they prepare in the Indies. For this you must boil a cupful of rice and set it aside to swell and dry. Your fish you must chop fine, removing from it all bones and mixing it with hard-boiled eggs which you have also chopped up, in the proportion of two eggs to every cupful of fish. Put into a flat pan a few onion rings, a chilli, some pepper, nutmeg and salt, and fry lightly in butter. Then add a large lump of butter and when it is melted stir in the rice, fish and chopped egg, and let it simmer, shaking the pan until everything has been well soaked and blended. You may eat it with chutney as they do in the Indies.

It should be quite dry and not the least greasy. All sorts of experimental

fish and sea food

69

modifications may be made of this dish. Some incorporated grated cheese with it; some a little curry powder; and some, to give it more piquancy, chopped anchovies. An interesting kedgeree is made with the claw flesh of the crayfish and hard-boiled penguin egg, but the taste is perhaps a bit too pronounced for most palates. Crab meat makes an excellent kedgeree and so does the flesh of the pearl mussel. Instead of being fried in the way indicated, the mixture may be packed into shells or pannikins and baked in the oven.

Allied to the kedgerees, but more strongly flavoured, are the varieties of *gesmoorde vis*, which is 'smothered fish' in literal translation, but in practice is usually dried fish, salted and wind-dried, braised with onions and potatoes. The typical recipe is for *gesmoorde snoek*:

> Put the pieces of fish in fresh water for an hour; throw the water off and boil the pieces in fresh water for 15 minutes. Take them out, remove all bones, and break up into small pieces. Braise sliced onions in a little fat or butter; add a crushed chilli, pepper, salt, a sprinkling of powdered ginger and a teaspoonful of brown sugar and floury, cooked potatoes cut into slices. Put the fish into this and let it slowly simmer, adding butter if it is too dry. Serve with rice.

This dish should be pungent, spicy, and satisfying, and neither too dry nor too moist. Care is necessary to strike the true mean, but is well repaid by the excellent result.

Somewhat similar is a *vis bredie* or fish stew:

> Cut up raw or cooked fish into small, neat pieces, from which the bones should be removed. Put them into a saucepan with butter, a cupful of chopped celery, a similar quantity of peeled and diced potatoes, a couple of sliced onions, half a clove of garlic, a crushed chilli, a teaspoonful of brown sugar, a sprinkling of powdered ginger, half a teaspoonful of white pepper, and salt to taste; add a small cupful of fish or meat stock. Put on the fire with the lid on the saucepan, and let simmer, shaking carefully to prevent burning. The longer and more slowly it stews, the better will be the result. When the stew is ready, stir in a cupful of boiled rice and a tablespoonful of soya sauce. Let it simmer for another quarter of an hour and serve.

Fish simply prepared is sometimes, especially where the more delicate kinds are concerned, the best way in which to cook it. Elf is one of the best Cape fishes, and the recipe for dealing with it may serve as a model for other sorts:

> Clean the fish, and rub it with mint leaves. Lay it in a fish pan and strew over it some shallots, a sprig of rosemary, a blade of mace, some peppercorns and a little salt. Pour over all enough white wine to cover it.

Put the lid on and bring to the boil. Let it boil gently for some minutes; remove and drain and serve at once with a sour butter sauce.

The same method may be followed in the case of stockfish (hake) which is now obtainable, thanks to cold storage, practically all the year round, although it is essentially a summer fish (like elf) and practically all kinds of soft-fleshed fish. There are innumerable recipes for boiling such kinds, especially sole. Filleted, they may be steamed, simply or stuffed, garnished with various vegetables and fruits — such as peeled fresh grapes, stewed aubergines, loquats or carrots, fried bananas, pineapple slices, or vegetable chips — and sophisticated with accompaniments of various purees.

A few notes on particular kinds of fish may be added.

Galjoen is supposed to be at its best in the early summer months. It is a coarse fish, its flesh singularly marbled by the large blood vessels, and is usually, in season, excessively fat. It is best grilled or broiled over the coals of a wood fire; second best when stuffed and baked in the oven; excellent when planked and served with pickled walnuts; not so good when boiled or piece-fried.

Haarders or *mullets* are admirable when grilled and served with a butter sauce; boiled or fried, they are insipid and need the encouragement of a good, savoury sauce. Dried, as *bokkoms*, they are very tasty when, after a preliminary soaking to get rid of the excess salt, they are butter-steamed (not fried) in a covered pan and served with a dusting of fried parsley.

Snoek, in season from April to June, is best served grilled or fried in fat or butter in moderate-sized pieces. The belly portion is reckoned the most savoury and it is certainly, when the fish is fat, the most delicate part; other parts are, even when carefully cooked, apt to be stringy and dry. It needs the accompaniment of much melted butter. Boiled, it is coarse and flavourless, but when sun-dried it makes excellent and tasty dishes braised, stewed or marinated.

Panger, now rarely obtainable, is in season in June, and most excellent when fried. *Kabeljou* or cod, reputed to be at its best in March, is best plain-boiled, with a butter sauce. *Roman*, in August, is one of the choicest fishes and should be steamed in wine, like elf, which is a mid-summer fish, and served with an appropriate sauce. *Hottentot*, in season in September, is best fried. So, too, are the delicate, now alas very rare, *klipfish*. The *kingklip*, *geelbek* and *katonkel* are all firm-fleshed, none particularly delicate in flavour, and all capable of improvement with appropriate treatment with spices and herbs. All three make excellent pickled curried fish and are much in demand for this.

Sole and *skate* are now usually obtained from cold storage and can be prepared in accordance with the innumerable recipes in all cookery books. There are, so far as I know, no specially local recipes for serving either of

fish and sea food

them. *Pilchards* or *sardines* are no longer obtainable fresh; formerly they were, and we then served them crisply fried in fat and found them delicious.

Little need be said about the freshwater fish. Procedures for their tasty preparation are mostly slight variations of the age-old European recipes with the stuffing generally omitted.

Yellowfish, which is found in practically all the rivers in the Cape Province and may attain several pounds in weight, is soft-fleshed, bony, delicately-flavoured, and one of the best freshwater fish for the table. It is generally simply split, salted and peppered, and grilled or broiled over the hot coals, or shallow fried in fat or butter.

An excellent variation is to marinade it as follows:

Mix half a pint of vinegar with the same quantity of red wine, and boil the liquid with a few bay leaves, a couple of shallots, an onion sliced, a dozen allspice, a blade of mace, a dozen black peppercorns, a pinch of powdered or a slice of green ginger, a sprig of rosemary, half a dozen cloves, a crushed chilli, and salt to taste, adding gradually a cup of boiling water in which you have mixed a tablespoonful of chutney sauce (*blatjang*). Put the whole yellowfish, carefully scraped and gutted and rubbed with a morsel of garlic, into the boiling liquid; add a large lump of butter, and allow to boil gently for half an hour; draw the pot aside and allow the fish to get cold in the marinade. Serve with any salad sauce.

Any soft-fleshed sea fish may be prepared in a similar way; the marinade may be used several times, provided fresh vinegar and wine are added.

From yellowfish a good *fish sambal* or cold relish can be made:

Pound the cooked fish, from which the bone has been removed, with some raw onion, a tiny scrap of garlic, a pinch of ginger powder, and as much green or red chillies as suits your taste; moisten with lemon juice and incorporate into the paste enough coconut milk to make it moderately soft. Salt to taste and serve on thin bread and butter with some grated carrot over.

Instead of the carrot, crayfish coral may be used, which adds immeasurably to the piquancy of the paste. All sambals must be chilled, and ought not to be over-salted.

Besides fish many other foodstuffs come out of the sea, and of these many are used in Cape cookery. Indeed, it is with this variety of seafood that the Cape cook, following the old recipes, sometimes creates dishes that have the merit of being original — not merely because some of the ingredients are essentially local, but also because they have been benignly blended to produce some marvellously exhilarating combinations. Various crustaceans, shellfish and seaweeds are used, with cuttlefish. Something has already been said about the way in which these may be made use of in preparing soups; it remains to detail other methods of preparing them for the table.

Crayfish, now often and quite mistakenly referred to as crawfish, are delectable eating, especially when you can procure them live. Ordinarily crayfish are exposed for sale when they have already been boiled, and that indeed is nowadays the only way in which the average cook can get hold of them. Boiled crayfish claws are also sold by the pound. The fastidious cook will make a point of securing a live crayfish, and preparing it for all dishes that are to be made from it by first boiling it lightly in a thin, well-spiced and herbed stock. This gives it a mellowness and preserves its soft, delicate taste and fine flavour, both of which are irretrievably lost by quick boiling in salt water. From the flesh of crayfish cooked in such a *coulis* many dishes may be prepared in accordance with the old recipes. Here are a few:

Crayfish salad. Take the flesh from the large and small claws and break it into neat pieces; add to it some of the flesh from the tail, diced, and all the soft white and green meat from the inside of the carapace. Mix all this well with salt, pepper, powdered ginger, some finely chopped onion, and a few crushed coriander seeds. Beat up three yolks of eggs in a cupful of vinegar with a teaspoonful of lemon juice, salt and pepper to taste, so as to make a smooth cream, and mix with it a few tablespoonsful of pounded blanched almonds. Pour over the fish and let it stand in a cool place for half an hour. Mix thoroughly and serve on lettuce leaves, garnished with slices of hard-boiled eggs and fresh cucumber, and with grated coral all over.

This salad is altogether more piquant and tasty than that usually provided which is simply boiled and served with a mayonnaise or oil and vinegar dressing. Some old cooks made it with the sauce so liberally added that it was almost a gruel, to be eaten with a spoon, but the more conservative way is to have the meat well coated with the sauce. There is a school that prescribes powdered red chilli with it, but I do not subscribe to it, for too much sharpness deprives the flesh of that delicate flavour that the salad should have. When crayfish flesh, already cooked, is reheated in some way, the addition of chillies is sometimes a vast improvement.

Baked crayfish. The meat is pounded with whatever spices, herbs and nuts your fancy may fix on (one of the oldest recipes mentions among the herbs, lavender, among the spices, cardamons, and among the nuts, pistachio), butter and soaked bread. It is salted to taste, mixed with cream and put back into the shell, which is then adorned with a few lumps of butter and put into the oven to bake.

There are many variations of this. The pounded flesh is mixed with a white sauce; with grated cheese; with (in recipes that are comparatively modern) tomatoes, avocado pear, mashed potatoes or aubergines; brandy is added, or chopped anchovies — your own imagination will enable you to experiment to your heart's content. You will find that, unless you absolutely drown the crayfish in one particular spice, its flesh blends admirably with nearly everything you can think of; no matter how unskilful your technique is, you can never quite ruin this dish.

Crayfish soufflé, on the contrary, demands the most scrupulous care in preparing and cooking. It is made by stirring into a good soufflé mixture a white sauce thickened with yolk of egg, the carapace flesh pounded with nutmeg, salt, pepper and a little grated lemon peel, adding a teaspoonful of brandy and whipping in the beaten egg white. After this it is baked in a quick oven and served at once. It should be feathery light, but with enough stamina to make it succulent and tasty.

Crayfish curry is simply the tail flesh diced, stewed in white wine and then braised in butter with curry powder, which should have a good pinch of powdered red chilli added to it. It should be served with boiled rice, lightly-fried eggs and fried bananas.

Crayfish with pineapple was never a common dish, as the fruit was by no means easy to obtain in the old days. The pineapple was peeled and cored, thinly sliced, and a layer of it was placed in an earthenware dish, powdered with salt, ginger, red pepper and a little rice flour. On this a layer of the fish was placed, after having been lightly braised with some onion rings. Over this came a layer of apple slices, followed by another layer of fish, covered finally by a top layer of pineapple slices. A cup of wine was poured over and the dish was baked in the oven.

The combination of sweet, spicy pungency and the characteristic crayfish taste is interesting and attractive.

There are similar recipes for ordinary fish, with or without the addition of mussels or oysters.

Crabs are seldom obtainable in sizes that allow them to be treated like crayfish, but when they are available the same recipes will serve for them.

Mussels, of which there are two chief kinds, the large oval white-shelled and the elongated dark blue sort, were generally boiled with a little white wine (after having been washed in fresh water), strained and served in their shells. Sometimes spices and herbs were added to the wine, but usually the mussels were eaten with an appropriate sauce, made by adding vinegar or lemon juice to melted butter beaten up with an egg yolk. Sometimes they were stewed in white wine, braised with leeks or onions, curried or fried in batter. More elaborate dishes were made by mincing them, cooked, mixing with cream, spices and pot herbs, and steaming the mince as a pudding or baking it in the oven.

Limpets, essentially the poor man's dish, needed a little more elaborate treatment:

Take them from their shells, wash them thoroughly in water, remove their fringes and beat them with a wooden mallet or flat stone; after which wash them again, and then dry them in a cloth. In a flat iron stewpot put a large lump of fat and melt; then slice into it a couple of onions, and let them brown; now add the limpets, with a crushed chilli, a dozen peppercorns, a blade of mace, and a handful of small shallots. Put on the lid and let the contents slowly simmer, shaking the pot frequently. After stewing for half an hour, add a cupful of wine, a pinch of salt and a teaspoonful of brown sugar; mix all together, and let it simmer till the stew is well combined and the limpets are tender. Serve after thickening the gravy with a little tapioca.

This limpet stew is a most satisfying dish and was a great favourite when limpets were easily procurable. Now one seldom sees it, and even more rarely does one get it well prepared. The secret of success with it (and it is a dish that easily can be ruined) is prolonged, steady, but slow and mild simmering.

The best of all seafood dishes at the Cape is undoubtedly that made from the flesh of the perlemoen or pearl mussel (*Haliotis sp.*) which is found below highwater mark on most of the rock ledges along the eastern coast. It varies in size from a couple to twelve inches in diameter, and is a univalve that attaches itself strongly to the rock. It must be first removed from its shell, for which a sharp, strong knife is required, and must then be trimmed of its 'beard' or fringe, and cleaned vigorously with a scrubbing brush. We now have a cartilaginously hard substance, ugly looking and unattractive, that must be beaten with a mallet until its rigidity has changed to a texture not unlike that of a raw steak. This is now carefully dried in a clean cloth, and is ready for use.

The mussel, it is pertinent to remark, must be quite fresh; the least taint about it ruins its flavour and makes it tough. However, care taken in this preliminary preparation will be well repaid by the excellence of the cooked result.

Stewed pearl mussel (gestoofde klipkous, perlemoen). Cut the mussels up into equal-sized pieces about two inches square. Take care that no water remains on them. Put them in the pot with a large lump of fat or butter, a blade of mace, a couple of cloves, and a little white pepper, but no salt. Put on the lid and place the pot on the fire, where let the contents simmer, shaking occasionally. The mussel flesh is done when a fork easily sinks in and usually ten minutes simmering will cook them; more may make them stringy. Now add salt, a wineglassful of brandy and a cupful of cream, and let the pieces stew in that for a few minutes. Take them out and put them in the serving dish; thicken the gravy with a little rice flour and serve immediately, grating nutmeg over it.

This superb dish will be spoiled if — as some printed modern recipes

fish and sea food

direct — any water is used in the process of cooking. Likewise if salt is added before the cooking has made the flesh tender; hence the directive to add the salt, cream and brandy at a later stage. The flesh should be as soft as marrow and yet firm, creamy white, with a peculiar, wholly pleasant, seaweed-like aroma, and a delicate, original taste about which the epicure may rave.

This virgin delicacy should not be marred by over-spicing; the mace and the cloves, and later on the zest of the brandy, are all that it needs for its enhancement. However, there are many who think differently, as the variety of recipes for sophisticating *klipkous* shows. Some would add to it all kinds of spices — including chillies, which do not blend at all with it, and Worcester sauce, which quite spoils its flavour — and festoon it with potato chips, fried aubergine, aye, and even cauliflower saturated in white sauce. One recipe simmers it with onion. Another mixes it with tomatoes, after boiling it in *bouillon* — obviously a comparatively modern recipe, echoes from some American cookbook. A third would have you believe that it is improved with a mornay or cheese sauce; a fourth makes curry of it. Perhaps the only recipe that a conscientious cook can recommend, and that on account of its originality and because it does bring into juxtaposition on one's tongue two agreeable tastes at the same time, is that which states that you may, when you have removed the cooked pieces, thicken the gravy, not with tapioca, but with a mixture of white breadcrumb and grated ripe, raw quince. Boil this up and pour it over the klipkous before serving.

But this mussel is altogether too delicate and too noble to be cooked in any other style than that described in the first recipe. It is of all South African dishes indubitably the finest when prepared in this way. If any portion of the dish is left over (something that, in my experience, has never happened) you may mince it and make fish cakes of it, or a fine bisque or, best of all, metamorphose it into a *klipkous* kedgeree that is really a revelation of what such things can be.

Far more strongly flavoured than perlemoen, and thus not to everyone's liking, are *cuttlefish* and *octopus*, both in great demand by Malay cooks who are connoisseurs and know the good things that come out of the sea. Alive both cephalopods are ugly, unappetising-looking objects; properly cooked they are, for those who like a full-flavoured dish with a dash of the bizarre in it, highly succulent, surprisingly eatable, and wonderfully rich foods. The octopus is known as *fiskat* or fishcat, and the smaller cuttlefish as *tjokka*. The former is regularly used by fishermen for bait, and moderately-sized specimens are not difficult to obtain.

The tentacles are skinned, beaten with a wooden mallet, and cut into medium-sized pieces as a preliminary to any method by which they may be cooked. The *tjokka*, sometimes still to be found exposed for sale at the fish market, is skinned, the dark-coloured fluid in its 'bag' is retained, and its flesh, too, is softened by beating before it is cut up.

The older recipes for both state that the flesh must be cooked in fat or butter, with the addition of a host of spices, herbs and nuts, a glass of brandy and, in the case of the *tjokka*, the coloured fluid from the head of the beast into which a little rice flour has been stirred. Then it must be allowed to simmer gently for several hours, being frequently shaken to prevent burning. Before serving, a couple of egg yolks, beaten up with a tablespoonful of lemon juice, must be quickly stirred into the gravy and the dish sent to table at once, to be eaten with boiled rice.

More modern recipes favour a treatment in which the flesh is simmered with the flavourings, with tomatoes, and gets a final addition of blanched almonds, pistachios and seeded raisins. It can be braised also into a curry sauce, or stewed with cheese and potatoes.

The main characteristic of a dish made from it must be its full, rich, over-spiced and extraordinarily fragrant quality. For that reason you must not be sparing with the chillies, nor with the herbs; practically every garden herb blends with it, and the greater the variety of flavours the better is the result. Here, too, the flesh must not be water-boiled, else it will get tough and stringy; it should be gently simmered in fat or butter, and only when it is duly soft must the other fluid concomitants of the stew be added.

Oysters and *clams*, both of which are easily procurable as they are to be found in both the Indian Ocean and the Atlantic, were not greatly esteemed. The recipes for their preparation are not older than the early part of the nineteenth century and are all obviously copied from printed cookery books. Some old recipes, however, mention them as additions to meat or fish dishes; for instance, one old recipe for fish *bobotie* says that 'a few oysters will improve this dish'.

Eels, too, both the conger and the freshwater variety, although formerly common enough on the market, do not seem to have exercised the special ingenuity of Cape cooks. There are old recipes for their cooking, but I have not been able to find any that differ in essentials from those printed in European books before 1750. Later on, obviously under the Oriental influence, an 'eel stew' was directed to be made with the addition of 'chillies, garden sage, green ginger, verbena and allspice and peppercorns'. There is also a recipe for an eel sambal which is merely a variant of that for the fish sambal already mentioned.

I have once eaten, at the old White House Hotel in Strand Street, where the Coloured cook — my most proficient instructress in the art of making pancakes — used fish and eel flesh for the dish, a delectable *eel pancake*, made as follows:

> Pound the flesh of a grilled eel in a mortar, separating the bones; add to it melted butter, cream, grated nutmeg, a drop of anchovy sauce, pepper and salt, and a few drops of rum. Make paper-thin pancakes from a batter of eggs, sifted flour and salt; cover them with the paste and roll them up. Place in a dish, grate over a little nutmeg, place in the oven to keep warm, and serve with chutney.

Any fish or meat paste can be used; the pancakes should be light, very thin, and succulent, and the warmth of the oven must be only enough to heat the paste without making its covering tough.

Seaweed dishes may, perhaps, more appropriately be dealt with in the chapter on vegetables. It may be said that old Cape cooks liked on occasion to put a handful of seaweed in the *court bouillon* in which they cooked fish, and sometimes permitted a few shreds to share in the flavouring of fish stews. The variety favoured for making jellies was also employed in soup-making and in fact replaced, round about 1825, the expensive birds nests from Java that were deemed indispensable for a jellied *consommé*.

Chapter 6

Meat and Meat Dishes

Meat has always been man's chief food. For all that faddists may say, meat and wine and oil and wheat make a diet that can sustain the human body in perfect health, and for this reason meat has always ranked first among the available foodstuffs in both civilised and barbarian communities. It is therefore reasonable to expect that more care and attention have been bestowed on its culinary improvement than on other foodstuffs, and that the variations in recipes for its preparation for consumption exceed in number those for any other class of food.

At the Cape the earliest settlers found an abundance of meat, chiefly beef, that was, and remains, of inferior quality, lacking that close intermixture of fat with muscle fibre that distinguishes stall-fed beef. The mutton, however, was beautifully tender, deliciously fat, and unusually, on account of the aromatic veld bush on which the sheep fed, exceedingly well flavoured. Pork and poultry meat were introduced, but there were many different kinds of wild animals that yielded good meat, and from the earliest times these were killed and eaten. In general, the recipes for meat dishes were copied from instructions in printed books, but there were many local adaptations and improvements, both in methods of cooking and in the use of accessories to improve the flavour and succulence of the dishes.

Beef was nearly always pot-roasted, boiled, pickled or dried to form *biltong* or *tassal*. Minced or pounded it was used for sausages and frikkadels. The best cooks larded it with fat pork and it was rarely grilled or fried, though on occasion one comes across a recipe for a 'fried steak' or 'beef chops'. Only when no other meat was obtainable was it used for stews or *bredies*, for which mutton was much preferred. With pork, it was the meat most often salted or pickled for long sea voyages, and in its dried form it was the main item in the commissariat of those who undertook inland trips, for there are few more satisfying and nutritious snacks than a thick slice of bread and butter overlaid with snippets of homemade biltong.

Many kinds of dishes were prepared from the internal organs of the ox — the brains, liver, heart, kidneys, sweetbreads, tongue and tripe being used — while stock was made from the bones, and a strong, jellied *consommé* from the gelatinous parts. Farcing was rarely used for beef, but was extensively employed with other meats, and a few words may here be interpolated about farces that play an important part in meat cookery.

Properly speaking a farce is a filling or stuffing round which the meat is wrapped so that its flavouring can permeate the meat from within outwards. Larding is, after all, merely a variant of farcing in this sense, although its primary intention is not to flavour but to fatten the meat. Finicky cooks divide farces into two main kinds, but in practice no such demarcation line need be drawn. The principal farces used in Cape cookery are the following.

Vetvulsel (fatty stuffing) used for any meat dish. Mince six ounces of kidney suet with breadcrumbs, chopped shallots, parsley, thyme, nutmeg, salt and pepper, and mix with two tablespoonsful of unskimmed milk and the yolks of two eggs, till the mixture is smooth and stiff. To this can be added the minced cooked liver of a hare, a Muscovy duck, a goose or a calf, when the mixture is known as a liver stuffing.

Onion farce (*uie vulsel*). Braise four minced onions with a handful of minced sage leaves and six ounces of breadcrumbs in a little butter or fat; season with salt and pepper. This is used for poultry and pork dishes.

Oyster farce (*oester vulsel*). Chop a dozen fresh oysters or clams, and mix with four ounces of breadcrumbs, an ounce and a half of salted butter, a pinch of grated nutmeg, some finely-chopped marjoram and parsley leaves, a small fragment of chilli, the juice of one large lemon, and the yolk of an egg; add some of the native liquid of the oysters; form the mixture into small patties or balls (this needs some skill; most cooks therefore make it easier, but no better, by adding more breadcrumbs and butter) and use immediately for stuffing fish or poultry.

Almond farce (*amandel vulsel*). Beat three egg yolks with a cupful of cream and a pinch of grated nutmeg. Pound three ounces of blanched almonds in a mortar with a little of the white of egg, and stir into the beaten egg yolk, with six ounces of fine breadcrumbs and two ounces of fresh butter diced. Beat quickly and add the rest of the whites, whipped to a stiff froth, and continue beating till it is smooth and moderately stiff. Use as a stuffing for poultry.

Baked farce (*gebakte vulsel*). Mix suet, finely chopped, with breadcrumbs, grated lemon rind, pepper, salt and nutmeg, and incorporate in it enough yolk of egg to make into a stiff paste. Shape into small balls, roll in sifted flour and bake lightly in the oven. Use for stuffing poultry. By mixing minced ham with this paste we get *ham farce*, which need not be baked previously.

Brain farce (*harsingvulsel*). Lightly cook sheep's or calf's brains in butter or white wine, and pound in a mortar with pepper, salt, parsley, a little onion juice and a few drops of rum. Make into a stiff paste with egg yolk and white bread soaked in milk from which all the milk has been squeezed out; shape into small balls, roll in sifted flour and bake lightly. Stuff poultry with this.

Curry stuffing (*kerrievulsel*), *egg stuffing* (*eiervulsel*), *crayfish stuffing* (*kreefvulsel*), *avocado-pear stuffing* (*avocadopeer vulsel*) and *tomato stuffing* (*tamatievulsel*) are all made in the same way, using respectively curry powder, pounded hard-boiled egg yolks, the pounded flesh of crayfish, mashed raw avocado pear, and tomato purée, instead of brain paste.

> *Stuffing for a sucking pig* (*speenvarkvulsel*). Mince, but do not pound, sliced onion, sage leaves, thyme, marjoram, green ginger, mace and plenty of green chillies. Mix with breadcrumbs and salt, and make into a stiff paste with egg yolk and a little brandy. Stuff the pig tightly with this mixture, and sew up well.

I have learned by experiment that this farce may be improved by the addition of a couple of pittosporum leaves.

> *Dried fruit stuffing* (*droëvrugtevulsel*). Soak dried apricots, prunes and peaches, equal quantities of each, in wine or water; remove stones from the prunes and place the soaked fruit in a saucepan with some tamarind, sugar, tangerine peel, ginger, a few cloves and a feather of cinnamon; cover with wine, and boil gently. Remove from the liquid and place in a dry saucepan, with a large lump of butter. Let the butter melt and shake the pot so that the fruit becomes well coated with the butter. Use as a filling for poultry or sucking pig. Handle carefully so that the fruit remains whole.

Fresh fruit is used in the same way to make a farce. Stewed fruit is often served, whole or as a purée, with roasted meat. A well-known, though not often used, recipe is that for baking a lamb with a fruit stuffing. The lamb is coated inside with butter or fat, and then filled with pomegranate seeds, pistachio nuts, preserved dates, citron and a few chopped rose apples mixed with a little dried ginger and tangerine peel. It is then slowly roasted or baked, being frequently basted with a mixture of wine and vinegar. The result is excellent. Many modifications of this essentially Persian recipe exist.

> *Green mielie stuffing* (*groenmielievulsel*). This is simply fresh, young mielies, cut off the cob, mixed with spices and herbs, some cream and the yolk of eggs, and stiffened with breadcrumbs. Some cooks add a few drops of rum.

There is, of course, no end to the variations in the composition of farces. The main consideration is that the flavour of whatever combination is used should not be so strong and definite as to impair the flavour of the meat; therefore garlic and chillies are infrequently mentioned among the ingredients, preference being given to spices and herbs that blend more easily.

There are old-fashioned recipes that tell of a stuffing within a stuffing; one of the most curious of these is the recipe that directs that a large sucking pig should be coated inside with its proper farce, and then be filled with partridges stuffed with a liver paste. My own experience is that the

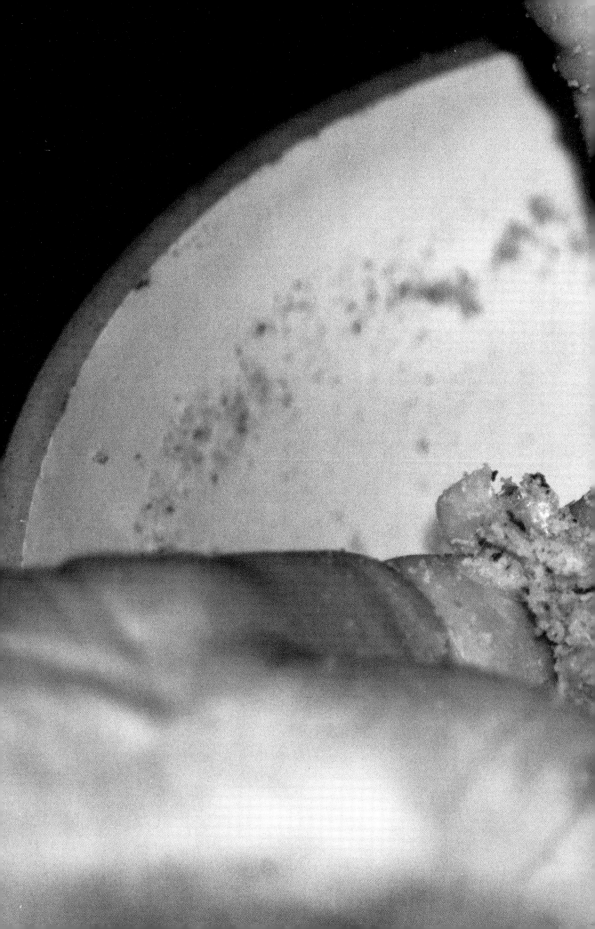

partridges are most excellent, but that the pig differs in no manner from one that has been roasted in a less elaborate manner.

All kinds of vegetables are used for farcing, sometimes whole but more often in the shape of a fairly thick purée, adequately seasoned, and properly used these fillings greatly improve the taste of wild birds and some domestic fowl. But be careful with celery; if you want your meat to have a distinctive but not too strong taste of celery, feed the fowl on the chopped leaves some weeks before it is killed. Nuts, too, are often useful as a paste for farcing, as their sweetish taste is generally agreeable; an exception is groundnuts whose flavour, when heated, is apt to be too strong.

No useful purpose would be served, and much room would be taken up, by describing the various ways in which different kinds of meat can be cooked. Let me therefore confine my remarks to a few recipes which may be considered traditional in South Africa, although none of them can be claimed to be strictly speaking original, as each has its counterpart in the cookery of other lands.

Mutton. Cape mutton is generally excellent. The best comes from the Karoo farms or from the grasslands of Natal or the Free State, but a particularly fine quality stems from the Sandveld of the South Western districts of the Cape Province where the sheep browse on halophytic shrubs. In the butchers' shops one obtains cold storage mutton or mutton from sheep that have been over-driven; this sort of mutton does not do justice to the excellence that characterises the flesh of the farm-fed sheep. Lamb is commonly slaughtered too old, and is not of the same quality, though it can be very good indeed. Well-fed farm sheep are always fat and mutton from them sometimes needs considerable trimming, and certainly never needs larding. It is always succulent, delicately flavoured, and tender.

Mutton chops made from Karoo sheep are a joy. They are trimmed, lightly beaten, dusted with fine breadcrumbs and grilled on the gridiron. In the open air they can be wrapped in vine or lettuce leaves and grilled over the fire made with the *rhenoster* bush (*Elytropappus rhinocerotis*), the smoke of which imparts to the meat a distinct and attractive flavour. They are also fried in thin batter, or braised with onions and spices and herbs, dashed with a little wine, dusted with pepper and served with boiled rice.

Boiled mutton according to the old recipes was something different from the tasteless, stringy meat, served with caper sauce, that is commonly dished up in restaurants:

Trim a leg of mutton; wash it and wrap in a wet cloth. In a large saucepan, which you have filled with water and white wine, half and half, slice a handful of carrots, an onion, two shallots, a dozen cloves, a crushed chilli, half a dozen black peppercorns and a tablespoonful of coarse salt. Let it come to the boil and when it properly bubbles, unwrap your mutton and plunge it into the pot; let it boil quickly for ten minutes; then draw the pot aside and allow it to boil gently till the meat is cooked down to the bone. Take out the meat and put it in a dish in the oven, leaving the oven door open. Braise some young carrots in butter, whole, and arrange them around the meat. Make a white sauce with flour, the water in which the mutton has been boiled and the yolk of an egg; salt and pepper it, and thin it with white wine and lemon juice. Pour over the mutton and serve.

Goat's meat was, and still is, extensively eaten. While it is commonly supposed to be tougher, stringier, and leaner than mutton, it need not therefore be despised, for it can be obtained, on occasion, of a quality that, after making allowance for the coarser taste, compares very favourably with ordinary butcher's mutton. Goat's meat of such a quality makes excellent grilled chops; indeed in all the recipes for mutton, goat's meat can be substituted for the mutton, although the result will not be quite the same as when good mutton is used. Where salt mutton is prescribed, as for example in the recipe for *sout ribbetjie*, goat's flesh serves equally well.

It is usually far stronger in flavour, and in some cases, where the animals have fed on highly aromatic shrubs, its taste may be repugnant and must be overcome by using strong spices. In that case it is best served as a curry or as a 'black sour stew'. A goat's head and trotters make excellent brawn, and its tripe is not to be distinguished from that of the sheep.

Sosaties (curried *kabobs*). There are many recipes for this Indian dish. The generic one is the following:

Take two pounds of fillet of pork, a quarter of a pound of pork fat from which you have removed the rind, and two pounds of loin of mutton, from which you have removed all bone, gristle and membrane. Cut the meat into neat two-inch square pieces. Mix them and powder them with ginger, white pepper and salt. Put a layer of them at the bottom of an earthenware jar and cover it with a thin layer of very lightly braised onion; strew coriander seeds and some minced chilli over; add similar layers till the jar is nearly full, placing a few dried apricots, seeded raisins, a couple of bay leaves and some slices of green ginger in the middle layers. Now braise some sliced onions in a deep saucepan, with four tablespoonsful of good curry powder, a large tablespoonful of moist brown sugar, adding butter or fat till you have a rich curry sauce. Pour on it a bottle of good vinegar mixed with half a bottle of wine, and let it boil up. As soon as it comes to the boil, pour the liquid over the meat.

Let it stand in a cool place for three or four days, shaking well occasionally, so as to let the marinade percolate through. For cooking, string the bits of meat on bamboo skewers, putting a piece of mutton alternately with a piece of pork and a piece of the pork fat in the middle and at the end of each skewer. Grill on the gridiron. Boil up the pickle, till it is a thick sauce. Pour over the cooked skewered meat and serve with rice, fried bananas and fried eggs.

Variations: add a cupful of milk to the marinade when it has stood for

24 hours; instead of wine and vinegar, use half a pound of tamarind steeped in white wine; use raw, instead of lightly braised onions between the layers; omit the raisins and apricots and substitute a handful of blanched almonds. A few blanched almonds in the sauce, and the use of tamarind instead of vinegar certainly adds greatly to the piquancy of the dish, while the addition of milk imparts to it a blandness that contrasts well with the extreme pungency that the chillies give to it.

Sosaties, when properly made, should be tender and tasty, yet with a crispness that rivals a grilled chop, and bitingly spicy yet with a suavity that rivals the best-made curry. At a pinch they may be made wholly of mutton, but in that case pork fat must be used more prodigally. They should be grilled to a turn and no more, and the curry sauce should be pipingly hot. If they are properly spiced, the fried bananas and the lightly fried eggs that should accompany them are very welcome to moderate the aromatic fierceness of the sauce.

A variant of them is *kabobs*, which are simply bits of meat, previously marinaded in spiced wine and vinegar, skewered on bits of bamboo alternately with sections of tomatoes and onions, fried in a shallow saucepan with mutton fat, and served with a chutney sauce, no curry being used. With them, as well as with *sosaties*, it is customary to serve fresh *sambals* and chutney.

A *sosatie* course is in reality a mild imitation of the familiar *rystafel* of Java, in which a number of dishes, always including at least two meat, one fish, and a curry dish and several vegetables, fried potatoes, fried bananas, fried eggs, fried aubergines and crumbled dried fish, are served on a plateful of rice and mixed with a strong curry soup or sauce, to be eaten with a spoon.

Another modification is *penangvleis*, which is made in the same way as penang fish, already mentioned.

There are various *curries* (*kerrievleis*) made from mutton, pork, or poultry. In all of them the meat, braised with some onions and a tinge of garlic, with the addition of various fragrant herbs, is finally simmered in a rich curry sauce. If a wet curry is wanted, coconut milk is added and stirred into the brew, which is allowed to continue simmering till it has to be served. If a dry curry is preferred, the cooking is done in an open saucepan, to allow much of the liquid to evaporate, and it must then be frequently shaken to prevent burning, the slightest sign of which spoils any curry.

A mild curry is made without chillies or much pepper and the addition of more sugar and plenty of coconut milk; a hot curry is surcharged with chillies, ginger and pepper, and has much tamarind in it; a black curry which is superlatively pungent is made by adding burnt sugar to the tamarind juice and using much black pepper in powder. Expert cooks always preferred to make their curry powder fresh, by pounding green ginger, cardamons, chillies, peppercorns, cloves, mace, fennel, cumin and aniseed, coriander, garlic and turmeric into a paste, which is mixed with tamarind juice before it is stirred into the braise. Such a curry paste makes a much more delicious curry than most of the commercial curry powders, and even now can be made at home quite easily.

While pork and mutton were preferred for making curries, poultry flesh was sometimes used. A good recipe for a *chicken curry* runs as follows:

> Let me implore you not to choose any old rooster for your curry; select a youngster, or two or three of them if you have many guests. Singe it well, and cut it up nicely, but take pains not to crush the bones, for a splinter (as I have myself observed) may cause great discomfort and annoyance to the eater. Lay the pieces on a pan and brown them in butter. Braise your onions, which you must cut up into thin slices, in butter or fat, with a couple of sour apples sliced, a spoonful of brown sugar, and a teaspoonful of salt. Mix a couple of spoonfuls of curry powder with some tamarind water or vinegar and add to the onions; let it simmer and then add the pieces of chicken. Cover the pot, and let all simmer quietly for a couple of hours, shaking the pot frequently; add a few tablespoonsful of coconut milk and let the curry brew gently on the side of the stove until you serve it up with boiled rice and chutney.

Boerewors (farm sausage) is now a thing of the past, although it often appears on the table — a travesty of what it should be and a disgrace to the modern cook. Formerly it was made principally of pork, with a small amount of mutton and beef added. The meat was chosen with care, all gristle being rejected, and was always pounded in the mortar as there were no mincing machines in the olden days, but it is really better to mince it finely by passing it through the machine two or three times. The mince was mixed with finely diced pork fat, powdered ginger, mace, cloves, nutmeg, fennel, coriander, thyme, rosemary and mint, pepper and salt, and a mixture of equal parts of wine and vinegar was worked into it. Then it was stuffed into long skins, suspended for a few days in a cool place and fried in a pan or, better still, grilled over the coals. No fat was used; the diced pork gave sufficient fatty substance to the sausage and prevented it from burning.

Such *boerewors* was a treat to eat when fried, and it was almost as good when it was dried and eaten raw, in slices spread on buttered brown farm bread fresh from the oven. The substitute that we get for it nowadays is a tasteless, anaemic thing, compounded chiefly of gristle and stale bread, generally without any blending of spices within it, and always without any savouriness.

Meat frikkadels, meat cakes, patties or mince, were compounded of minced meat, spices, herbs, cream and wine or vinegar, made into various shapes, and generally shallow-fried in fat, alone or in company with sliced onions. Such meat pastes were sometimes boiled or baked in shallow dishes,

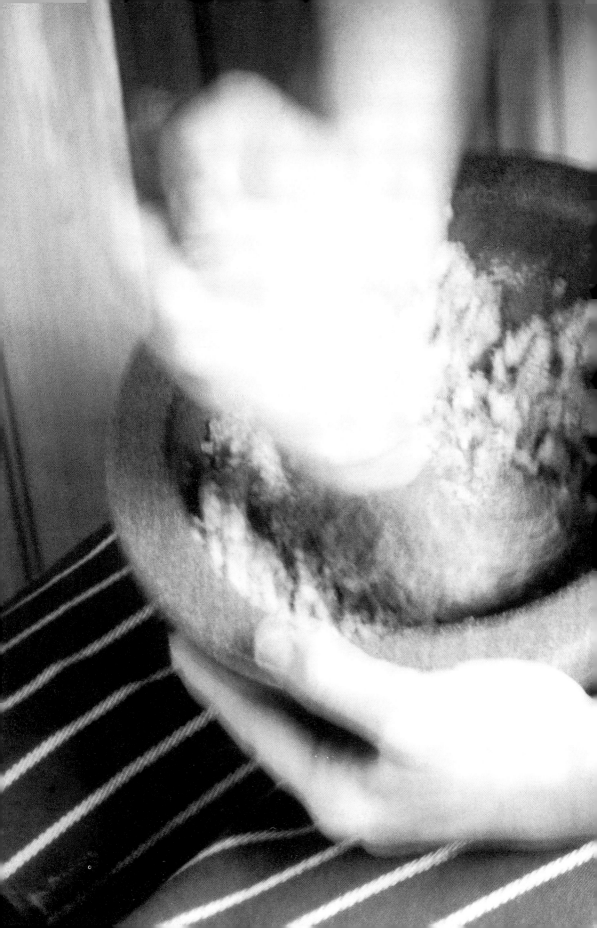

with various ingredients added to them — indeed the recipes for them abound, for they were favourite ways of dealing with leftovers from the joint or boiled meat.

An almost indigenous minced meat dish is *bobotie*, which was, however, known in Europe in the Middle Ages when the Crusaders brought turmeric from the East. The oldest recipe I have is one of the seventeenth century:

> To make a Bobootie it is necessary to have clean hands, for you must knead the meat as you do a dough. Take, then, of tender mutton and the backstring (fillet) of pork, of each a pound in weight, and that without fat or hard part; pound it vigorously in your mortar, with a handful of blanched almonds, 12 peppercorns, a slice of green ginger, a chilli, a leaf of the herb marjoram, some coriander seeds, a very small piece of fresh garlic, or if you have none of it, half a leaf of an onion, and the grated rind of a lemon, and work into it half a cupful of wine in which you have soaked an ounce of tamarind. Let it stand overnight. Then beat into it half a cupful of cream and two tablespoonsful of good butter, not too much salt, and knead it well. Shape it into a round loaf and put it into an earthenware pie-dish that you have well smeared inside with butter and sprinkled with a few cumin seeds.
>
> Put it in the oven and when it gets hot and expands, but not before, pour over it two cups of milk in which you have beaten up the yolks of three eggs and a tablespoonful of curry powder such as you may get at the Malay store. Let it bake till it is well set, and then put upon it a few blanched almonds and a grating of nutmeg. Before you send it to table you may, if you are not pleased with its top colour, pass a hot salamander over it.

Another recipe says that the curry powder should be mixed with the mince, and the custard added before the baking; another advises that a couple of bay leaves should be added. I cannot honestly affirm that either modification improves the dish, and have found lemon or pittosporum leaves to blend better with the mixture, although it can do very well without them. A *bobotie* should be marrow-soft, melting on the tongue, and is best eaten with white, not yellow, rice, with a moderately sharp chutney as accompaniment.

> *Smoorvleis* or stewed (smothered) meat. Cut the meat — which should preferably be mutton or veal or pork — into small, equal sized pieces, rejecting all gristly bits, and dry and coat them with sifted flour. Put into a pot with onion slices, salt and pepper, a little brown sugar, a bruised chilli, a few cloves, a blade of mace and some powdered ginger; add a large lump of sheeptail fat. Cover the pot and place on the fire and as soon as the fat has melted, add a cupful of wine, or stock. Put the lid on and allow the meat to simmer gently for several hours, shaking frequently; finally add a glass of sherry, and thicken the gravy with a little brown roux.

A *white smoorvleis*, which is really a blanquette, is made in the same way, but the braising is allowed to go on just long enough to slightly brown the meat, when a thin white sauce is added and the cooking is continued till the stew is ready. Here the secret is to cook gently, but continuously, and there is little chance of overdoing it if the heat is steady. Both dishes are excellent and not too strongly spiced, but the chillies may be left out if desired.

Sout ribbetjie (salted rib of mutton). Choose the whole rib of a lamb or part of that of a full-grown sheep. Trim it, and rub it well with a mixture of one part salt and one part saltpetre, coriander seed, pepper and ginger mixed. Lay it on a layer of this mixture in a cool place, and continue rubbing in the salt the next day. Allow it to hang in a draught, and rub in more of the mixture each day for several days, adding to the salt mixture on the second day an equal part of moist brown sugar. In a week's time it will be ready for cooking. You can then grill it whole on the gridiron or, if you prefer it, you can remove the rib bones, cut the meat into pieces and, after parboiling it in wine, shallow-fry it in a pan or again roast it. The meat should have a fine pink colour, and should be salty and spicy, without being too much so. It is preferably served with 'wet rice', which is rice that has been boiled to a mushy softness.

Swart suur (black sour braised meat). Take ribs of mutton, cut them into convenient pieces, without removing the bone; two pounds of the meat is convenient. Braise them in a pot with some onions and a little fat; add a cup of wine, and let simmer; skim off the fat; stir in salt and pepper, a cupful of tamarind water, a teaspoonful of grated nutmeg and one of powdered cloves, and a bruised chilli. Simmer for an hour, add a cupful of red wine, and let it boil; then add some small dumplings, made of sifted flour, whipped white of egg and a little melted butter. As soon as the dumplings are cooked serve with boiled rice and potatoes.

Some cooks add blood to this braise, and others prefer to thicken it with brown roux.

An old-fashioned, extremely savoury, *toad-in-the-hole* (*padda in die gat*) is made as follows:

Make a batter with two cups of sifted flour, a teaspoonful of salt, a little bicarbonate of soda, half a cupful of soft chicken fat, and two cupsful of buttermilk. Cut up a couple of pounds of tender mutton without any bones into small pieces, each the size of a half-crown[1] and about an inch thick; flour them and put them in a pie dish, preferably a very deep one, and sprinkle over them salt, pepper, grated nutmeg, a blade of mace rubbed fine, and a few coriander seeds. Add a glass of wine and another of orange and lemon juice mixed. Pour the batter over, and bake in the oven for a couple of hours.

---

1 About 2 cm across.

meat and meat dishes

The bredies. These are combinations of meat with vegetables so intimately stewed that the flesh is thoroughly impregnated with the vegetable flavour while the vegetables have benefited from the meat juices. Almost any vegetable, and several fruits, can be used for *bredies*, but the only meat that is really suitable is a mutton rib cut up into appropriate sizes, care being taken that no slivers of bone are allowed to enter the stew. The essential steps are that the meat is first braised in butter or fat, with spices, herbs and onions. The vegetables, always raw (except in a very few cases where parboiling is necessary to get rid of some constituent) and generally sliced or minced, are then added, with salt and a cup of water, wine or stock, and the whole is allowed to simmer gently for several hours, the pot being kept closed but frequently shaken and great care being taken that the contents do not burn. *Bredies*, whether made with chillies or not, must always be smooth, bland and uniform in taste; they ought never to be greasy, lumpy or too liquid; the meat constituent should be deliciously tender and wholly in sympathy with the main vegetable ally so that neither dominates but both combine to make a delectable whole that is a triumph of co-operative achievement. A *bredie* tests the cook's skill not only in blending, but also regarding that subtle aptitude that experience alone can make perfect – to decide when the margin between perfection and over-cooking has been reached.

While all *bredies* are generically similar, there is a subtle difference in each that accounts for the wide discrepancy in popularity. Some, of course, can be had only when the particular vegetable or fruit which is their basic ingredient is in season; others, again, can be made all the year round. The following are perhaps the most generally known, and all of them are to be found in the oldest recipes: cabbage *bredie*, green bean *bredie*, dried bean *bredie*, lentil *bredie*, quince *bredie*, potato *bredie*, pumpkin *bredie*, squash *bredie*, *wateruintjie bredie*, sweet-potato *bredie*, wild cabbage *bredies*, carrot, parsnip and turnip *bredies*, rice *bredie*, spinach *bredie*, mielie *bredie*, turnip or broad bean tops *bredie*, cauliflower *bredie*, brussels sprouts *bredie*, endive or lettuce *bredie*, and tomato *bredie*.

A couple of recipes will show the general technique to be followed in making them.

Potato bredie. Braise in a shallow pot sliced onions, a fragment of garlic, a few coriander seeds, and pepper and salt to taste, with some butter or fat. Add a pound of rib of mutton chopped into pieces about three inches square; the bone must be well trimmed to remove all splinters and the meat must be moderately fat. Add also a small piece of pork or ham, cut into pieces, and let all simmer till nicely browned. Then stir in a pound and a half of parboiled potatoes, cut into slices, a crushed chilli, if the bredie is to be pungent, or a little lemon juice and a cupful of good stock or white wine. Let the *bredie* simmer for two to three hours, very slowly, with the lid off the pot. Add stock or water if it becomes too dry. It must be moist without being watery, and all the ingredients must be properly blended.

Tomato bredie. Peel two pounds of ripe tomatoes by plunging them into boiling water and removing the thin skin, and cut them into quarters; add a couple of green ones. Take two pounds of thick rib of mutton, as fat as you can get it; cut it up into neat slices; dry and dust with flour; put into a shallow saucepan with a pound of sliced onions, three sliced leeks or shallots, half an ounce of green ginger, a few cardamons, coriander seeds, peppercorns and fennel seeds, and crushed thyme, marjoram and garlic leaves. If you like the *bredie* to be hot, add a crushed chilli and plenty of black pepper. Braise all this with sheep fat and when the meat is nicely browned, add the tomatoes; cover closely and let it simmer for several hours, very slowly, shaking frequently. Then add salt to taste, a teaspoonful of chutney sauce and a tablespoonful of moist sugar, and let it simmer for another couple of hours, with the lid off, till it is thickened. Finally add a glass of wine and serve.

Tomato *bredie* must be a well-spiced tomato purée, surrounding tender bits of meat magnificently impregnated with its flavour. It must not be too watery, and it must never, *never* be greasy, so when the lid is taken off the pot for the open, evaporation cooking for the last couple of hours, all the superabundant fat should be artfully skimmed off, without removing any of the essential gravy. When properly made it is a magnificent dish, always to be served with white rice and boiled potatoes.

Any vegetable can be substituted for potatoes or tomatoes in these recipes; green leaf vegetables, like spinach, are usually puréed before being added to the braised meat. A *bredie* that is both slightly sweet and sour is made by adding sorrel leaves and a little extra moist sugar to any vegetable *bredie*. An interestingly quaint dish, as Nash would have described it, is *quince bredie*, made as follows:

Half a dozen ripe quinces; one pound of ribs of mutton cut into small pieces and as fat as you can get it; three large onions; two cloves; a teaspoonful of powdered ginger, a blade of mace, two teaspoonsful of salt, a sprig of rosemary; a little white pepper; half a teacupful of wine; half an ounce of moist sugar. Braise the meat, with all the other ingredients except the quinces (the onions finely sliced) in a little sheep fat; peel the quinces and cut them up into slices without removing the seeds or core; add to the braise and simmer very slowly for three hours or more. Serve with rice and potatoes.

The old-fashioned *borrie* quince, with a highly aromatic flesh, was used for this. A similar *bredie* was made from apples, pears (especially the monstrous kind that now seems to be extinct) and just-ripe yellow peaches. The combination of meat with a fruit flavour is decidedly attractive.

Sometimes a combination of vegetables and fruit was attempted, but such very mixed *bredies* were not favoured, and the best *bredies* are unquestionably those in which one principal ingredient is used with the meat. *Bredies* occupy an anomalous position between vegetable and meat dishes, but are to be regarded as entrées, and are always served with boiled white rice, though some cooks on occasion serve yellow rice with them, a change which is welcome when the *bredie* is very pungent and contains much chilli.

Stuffed or *farced meat* (*gevulde vleis*) is mentioned in the earliest manuscript recipes. Beef was very rarely treated in this way; mutton, pork and game more often, while for poultry it was considered indispensable. A leg or shoulder was taken, the bone removed, the cavity stuffed with one of the farces already described, stitched or skewered up, and the whole was pot-roasted, being basted with its own gravy mixed with wine.

This was also a favourite method of cooking ox or sheep's heart, the organ being first boiled in wine, the stuffed whole cut into slices and braised in fat.

Salt or pickled meat. The recipes for this are among the oldest we possess, and are relics of the rough domestic cookery of the homelands, gradually modified as taste became more selective. Whatever meat is used, it is first well rubbed with a mixture of salt, saltpetre, pepper and coriander seed, and is then immersed in a sharp salt-water brine, where it may be left for any length of time. When required for use, it is taken out, well washed and placed in cold fresh water for 24 hours and then boiled — first quickly in water to which a little vinegar has been added, and then more slowly in fresh water with the addition of a bunch of sweet herbs. A few minutes before serving small carrots and turnips are added, and these are served with it. Cold cooked salt or pickled meat may be sliced and fried or grilled or minced according to the various recipes for ham that are given in all the cookery books.

Pork has always been a common and popular meat in South Africa and there are innumerable recipes for preparing it for the table, but few differ in any important point from those with which all European cooks were familiar long before there were any cooks at the Cape. When home-killed it is generally excellent, fat and tender. The sucking-pig — which was never of that ideal youth which Lamb would have preferred and was considered in season in spring and not at Christmas — was always baked or pot-roasted, stuffed and served whole. Pork chops were usually cut thick and the best showed a bit of kidney substance; they were grilled, shallow-fried, and braised; fillets were always braised or fried, but were held to be ideal when pork was required for any made dish such as a meat pie.

The following is from an old directive:

How to make a good *pork pie*. You must first make the dough for it, for which you want a cupful of fine flour, a lump of butter the size of an egg, two tablespoonsful of the marrow from the bone of an ox, a whole egg and enough fermented must of grape, to which you have added a thimbleful of salt to make a firm paste when you mix it with all the other ingredients. Roll this out several times and then crumple it up and let it stand in a cool place. Then line your dish with a layer of it, keeping some over to cover the meat. For your pie, you take enough pieces of nice pork, not too fat nor yet too lean, and half their number of pieces of some other meat, which you must put in milk and let lie in it for half an hour. Take them out and braise them very lightly in a pan with butter, mace, pepper and salt; then put them in your pie dish with a few hard-boiled eggs cut into slices, a few onion rings, some cloves, a bay leaf and a sprig of lavender; pour over a cupful of wine, cover with the dough, and bake for an hour (or more if you like) in the oven. If you wish it to be coloured outside, rub egg yolk on the dough.

Nowadays one uses baking-powder instead of half-fermented must. A spoonful of tapioca added improves the pie which is, however, quite eatable without it.

Poultry, as far as the early cooks were concerned, comprised barnyard fowls, mostly superfluous cocks, ducks and ducklings, of which the Muscovy duck was reckoned the choicest, geese, tame pigeons and, more rarely, turkeys that were never common as they were difficult to rear and when fully-grown were usually tough and tasteless. All these were preferably pot-roasted, with spices and herbs and a dash of wine to add to their savour, sometimes larded with pork fat and nearly always appropriately stuffed. Spatchcock grilling was rare; old chickens were usually boiled or stewed, sometimes with elaborate additions.

A few typical recipes will suffice.

Roasted Muscovy duck. Truss, trim and rub the carcass inside and out with a clove of garlic. Fill the inside with any stuffing you prefer and sew up tightly. Skewer thin strips of pork fat over the breast and back. Dust with pepper and salt. Put in a pot with sliced onions, pot herbs, a blade of mace and butter or fat. Place on the fire and let it slowly braise, turning the meat over once or twice; then add a cupful of wine, put the lid on, and continue the simmering, putting hot coals on top of the lid; shake the pot, but do not lift the lid. The simmering must be gentle; so must the shaking for the bird must be firm and whole when it is served. When it is quite tender, which takes a couple of hours at least, put it on the dish in which it is to be served and drip lemon juice over it. Thicken the gravy with a little brown roux, adding salt if required, and serve separately in a sauce boat.

Stewed fowl. If the fowl is old, let it hang for a couple of days after it has been cleaned. Cut it into neat pieces; flour them and put them into a fireproof dish with a well-fitting cover; add a bunch of pot herbs, a blade of mace, peppercorns, and a handful of small onions, peeled and cut in halves, and a cup of white wine. Cover the dish and place it in the oven for a few hours; then let it get cold, add some more wine, salt to taste, and replace it in the oven for another slow stewing for at least three hours. Take out the pieces, and put them on the serving dish; beat up the yolk of a fresh egg with a tablespoonful of tamarind water (or lemon juice); stir it into the gravy and let it thicken but not boil; pour over the fowl and serve.

Some old recipes add vermicelli or tapioca; some allspice, and one even mentions chillies; but poultry does not take kindly, when boiled, to the sharp pungency of Spanish pepper. Pigeons stewed in this way are delicious, but they need larding; so does a turkey. A goose, on the other hand, is generally fat enough to do without additional lubrication and is best pot-roasted, with an appropriate stuffing. Both it and the Muscovy duck, when so roasted, are sent to the table accompanied by their livers, fried in butter with a little salt and pepper, of which each guest receives a small portion as a special tit-bit.

Chapter 7

More Meat Dishes

On the farms, when domestic animals were slaughtered, no part of the animal was discarded; what could not be used for food was useful in some other way. The old recipes paid due attention to the preparation of *afval*, which literally means 'cast offings', but include not only tripe but organs such as the heart, kidneys, liver, sweetbreads and certain other glands, as well as 'butcher's pieces' like trotters, feet, heads, tongues and ears. As it was a common custom to kill more than one animal at a time, there was ample opportunity to combine different meats and convert all the scraps from the different carcasses into wholesome food.

One of the best known and most popular, as well as one of the most tasty dishes, was:

Pig's Brawn (*vark sult*). Take a pig's head and split it; take also the feet and tail; clean them all thoroughly; strew salt over and let them stand in a cool place overnight. The next day rub them lightly with a mixture of salt and saltpetre and let them again abide for a night in a cool place. Then place them in a saucepan with cold water and let them remain in it for a couple of hours; take them out and put them in another saucepan with enough water to cover them; boil till the flesh easily strips from the bone; pour through a sieve, and let the liquid remain warm on the stove; sort the meat from the bones; put the bones back in the liquid; skin the tongue and put the skin, with the pig's ears, also back into the liquid, which must slowly simmer. Cut up the tongue and all the meat into small pieces. Strain the soup and reject what remains in the sieve. Put the liquid back in the saucepan, add the tongue and meat, mace, a couple of laurel leaves, grated nutmeg, pepper and salt; boil till it begins to thicken; then add a cup of good vinegar or of tamarind water; pour into moulds. Serve cold.

Some recipes recommend the addition of turmeric or curry powder; some add saffron, which agreeably varies both the taste and the colour. The brawn should be moderately stiff, variegated in appearance, piquantly sour and with the flavour of a strong jellied *consommé*.

Pannas,[1] that like *tassal* really has no English name, is a modification of a dish that was known to the Avignon cooks in the fifteenth century. It is referred to by old travellers as 'a greasy blood pudding, or haggis, badly fried', but when well made is nothing of the sort, although its taste may have to be acquired. Here it is:

---

1 See also pp 245–247.

The liver and kidneys of the pig to be cleaned of all skin and gristle, cut into bits and lightly fried; then to be pounded in the mortar, with breadcrumbs, pepper and salt and a teaspoonful of fennel seed; then to be mixed thoroughly with enough blood to make a paste, to which you add enough tamarind water to sour it slightly, and put it in a flat pan, smeared with fat, and bake it in the oven. When it is baked, pour butter, melted, over it, and you can keep it for several weeks. To use it, you take it out of the pan, slice it and fry the slices in fat. If you like, you may strew parsley over it before it goes to the table.

An excellent breakfast dish, but the recipe omits something it should have mentioned — tiny bits of pork fat that should be incorporated in the paste; they add greatly to its savouriness.

An old recipe for *marrow pudding*:

Put in a lubricated pudding dish a layer of white crumbs previously soaked in milk, from which the moisture has been pressed; put on it the marrow from the bone of an ox, a few chopped almonds, blanched, and a few walnuts and flavour with salt, pepper, nutmeg and a scraping of lemon peel. Fill the mould in this way with two or three layers, with a bread layer on top. Make a sauce with egg yolk, butter and milk; salt it and pour it over the pudding. Tie a cloth over it, place the mould in a large saucepan and steam it for an hour. Turn out and serve with a sour sauce.[1]

Here is one for *kidneys in potatoes*:

Take a couple of calf's kidneys and four pig's kidneys; clean them and remove all membrane vessels and hard bits; chop them up and braise them in butter with some parsley, grated nutmeg, lemon rind, pepper and salt; bake large potatoes in their skin in the oven, and when they are soft, divide each carefully, without breaking them, lengthwise; scoop out a hollow in each half and fill with the braised kidney; put the two halves together and tie with a thread; put in the oven to get thoroughly hot and serve.

Liver was always a highly popular part of the animal and was supposed to have health-giving qualities, a presumption that is thoroughly warranted. There are many ways of preparing it, most of them simply variants of recognised European recipes. It was grilled over the coals, larded and braised with tomatoes (a comparatively late recipe), onions or aubergines, made into patties and puddings, steamed or fried, stewed with or without additions, and served with curry sauce. One recipe is peculiar in that it mentions a particular kind of liver, and may be quoted, although it properly belongs to the next chapter:

---

1 See p 109.

Creamed liver. Take of the liver of a Muscovy duck, or of a goose or fowl or, which is best of all, of a flamingo, half a pound; wash and dry it, and strew salt and pepper over it. Put in a deep pie dish, buttered, a layer of sliced onions and parsnips; lay the liver on top of this and cover it with a layer of breadcrumbs; pour over a cupful of thin, sour cream; put in the oven and let it bake. Take boiled rice and mix it with chopped parsley, cloves, pepper and salt. Put it in a pan with plenty of butter and heat it till the rice has absorbed all the butter, adding some strong stock to keep it moist; put the rice in a dish, pile the stewed liver on it and cover with the cream sauce.

Ham figures extensively in the recipes. It was cured according to the age-old methods employed in Europe, but was rarely eaten raw and more often boiled or baked and, as a breakfast dish, fried with eggs.

Baked ham. Place it in cold water for several hours, and then plunge it into boiling water; as soon as the water again boils, take it out and place it in another saucepan. Cover it with a mixture of wine and vinegar, and whatever spice and herbs you fancy, and boil it slowly until it is done. Then take it out; wipe it dry, and cover with a paste made of honey and flour, after you have first skinned it neatly. Stick into it as many cloves as you wish, and bake it in a shallow pan in the oven, pouring over it wine, and basting it frequently with the gravy. Serve hot or cold as you please.

Tongue, both sheep's and ox-tongue, was always boiled or parboiled before being served; it was never dried, but frequently pickled or salted and was always regarded as a delicate dish. A fresh boiled ox-tongue was not usually skinned, but when served cold or pickled, skinning was a usual preliminary, and the meat was allowed to jelly in the liquid in which it had been boiled.

Stewed tongue. Cut a cooked fresh or salt tongue into thick slices; rub into them sage, marjoram, pounded coriander seed, salt and pepper; braise a few onion slices in butter; put in the tongue and pour over it a little rum. Let it simmer gently, shaking the pan frequently so that the meat absorbs as much of the juice as possible; serve on fried bread, with a dusting of parsley.

Sheep's tongue with celery. Take half a dozen sheep tongues; clean and trim them. Put them in a stewpot with a cup of wine, the white part of six young celery shoots, a few young onions chopped up, a blade of mace, grated nutmeg and pepper and salt. Cover closely and simmer, shaking frequently. When the tongues are soft, add a large lump of butter, a tablespoonful of lemon juice and a handful of young carrots; stew for not longer than ten minutes and serve.

The carrots should be just parboiled, retaining all their crispness; a chilled *sambal* is served with the dish, which is really a combination of braised celery and stewed tongue.

Tongue bobotie. Take cooked pig's and sheep tongues; skin and pound them to a paste; mix with it the yolks of two eggs, a crushed chilli, a bay leaf, half a dozen allspice, a few coriander seeds, a teaspoonful of rum, a tablespoonful of tamarind water in which you have mixed some turmeric powder, and half a cupful of coconut milk, with salt and pepper to taste. Pour over this a mixture of egg yolk and cream, mixed with a little turmeric powder; stick a few blanched almonds on top and bake in the oven.

This is much improved if pounded almonds are incorporated in the paste. It is served with boiled rice, *sambals* and chutney.

Ox and sheep's hearts were always stuffed, parboiled and then braised with onions, spices, herbs and a little rum or wine, after having been cut in moderately thin slices. An interesting, and to strangers impressive, modification was to stuff them with an almond farce, stew them lightly in white wine, and serve with a white sauce, appropriately spiced. Another variation was to fry the slices, previously stuffed, in batter. A third was to mince the cooked hearts and to braise the mince with onions, spices and herbs and fill small pancakes with them, serving these with a sour white sauce. A later recipe directs that they be stewed in white wine, with grated pineapple, with the usual spice flavourings, covered with tart dough and baked in the oven — a modified kind of *dariole* that was popular about the middle of the past century, but is now no longer fashionable although it is well worth eating.

Brains and sweetbreads were lightly parboiled, and then stewed, with spices, herbs, a few drops of rum, or fried by themselves or with the addition of spices, breadcrumbs and herbs. Sometimes they were fried in batter; less often they were braised with vegetables into a ragout. Gently steamed in white wine, with the addition of salt, pepper and nutmeg, they were esteemed as a dish for invalids.

A dish which although not peculiar to the Cape — as it is mentioned in the early Italian cookery books that date from the sixteenth century — is one that was common enough a hundred years ago but is nowadays never mentioned. When young rams were castrated, the genital glands were available for culinary use and were prepared for the table in exactly the same way as were sweetbreads. They were shallow-fried, braised with garlic and onion and herbs and spices, stewed in butter and wine, or fried in batter, and were regarded as a great delicacy. Two recipes for the preparation of 'A ragout of lamb's stones' and 'A lamb-stone stew' are given in Mrs Rundle's *Domestic Cookery* published in 1827, and are obviously transcripts from a manuscript Cape cookery book. As it is now practically impossible to obtain the material for this dish, except for those who live on a farm, it is not necessary to give directions for its preparation, and the curious are referred to the printed work mentioned.

It may be said that the ragout is a delicate and intriguing dish that certainly merits a gourmet's attention.

Trotters, that apparently consist merely of tough sinews and bone, were extensively used — not only for brawn, for which both pig's and sheep's trotters were employed, and for jelly, for which sheep's and calf's feet served, but also for several attractive dishes in which the cook had an opportunity to show skill and artistry. The old recipes laid great emphasis on the desirability of keeping the 'oil' that came from boiling the tendons and bones; it was skimmed off and preserved in jars, and was in great demand as a salad and toilet oil.

> *Stewed trotters.* For this you want half a dozen pig's or sheep's feet, which you must carefully clean, scrape and wash well in salt water. Cut them up into pieces and boil them in salt water till the flesh comes off the bone; skim off the fat which you may use in other ways. Take the flesh and put it into a shallow pot with three large onions sliced, a blade of mace, a sprig of rosemary or the top leaves of a sprig of mint, some pepper and some salt and a few tablespoonsful of wine; stew gently for half an hour and add some breadcrumbs; stir well and let it stand for a few moments; then whisk in a couple of egg yolks beaten up with the juice of a large lemon; serve at once with a grating of nutmeg over all.

An attractive dish; the addition of a pittosporum leaf is an important improvement; so is the help of a few tablespoonsful of cream.

There are recipes for currying trotters, serving them with a cheese sauce or in a batter, pickling them and simply sautéing them in butter. They may even be stuffed by a skilled cook, though the result is not always what it should be. Cold they make an excellent salad and in a pie they lend an enticing blandness to the contents.

There is perhaps no foodstuff that in English cookery books is treated so scurvily as *tripe*. Its nutritive value is high and, properly prepared, it makes a delicate and tender dish. Most of the recipes at the Cape are undoubtedly echoes from the cookery of the south of France, where the methods of cooking tripe are almost as numerous as the sauces that may be served with it. They have, of course, undergone modifications here, as the following recipes show:

> *Stewed tripe.* Soak it in salt water; then clean it thoroughly; wash in fresh water and beat it with a wooden mallet, but not enough to wound it. Cut up into small pieces; put these in a stew pot with some bits of fat pork, a couple of lemon leaves, a large piece of mace, some sliced onions, white pepper and salt; cover with white wine, and let it boil slowly for several hours till the meat is quite tender, adding wine to make up for what

evaporates. When tender, let it simmer till the liquid has been reduced to half, taking care that the meat does not burn. Add a cup of cream mixed with a tablespoonful of lemon juice; thicken with rice flour and serve with grated nutmeg.

Baked tripe with tangerine peel. Boil the tripe, cut in small strips, in white wine or stock. When tender, take out the pieces and put them in a buttered pie dish. Take some of the liquid in which it has been boiled; add to it a large lump of butter, a teaspoonful of grated nutmeg, a teaspoonful of pounded tangerine peel, a teaspoonful of Chinese (soya) sauce, the juice of half a lemon, a little pepper and salt to savour, boil it up, mix it with some breadcrumbs, and pour it over the tripe. Stew breadcrumbs over, dot with bits of butter, and bake in the oven.

Buttermilk tripe. Cook the tripe in buttermilk till it is quite tender (a good way to do this is to place it with the milk in a jar with a closely fitting lid, and put the jar in a saucepan of boiling water, where it must remain for the whole night boiling slowly). It will need at least several hours to boil perfectly tender, and you must add milk from time to time, bringing it to the boil again after each addition. When done, add some parsley, grated lemon peel, pepper, salt and either some blades of mace or cloves, whichever you prefer. Boil again for half an hour, and then take out the tripe, put it in your dish, and pour over what remains of the buttermilk — to which you have added a large lump of butter and a cupful of good thick cream beaten up with the yolk of an egg and a glass of rum or brandy. Serve with a little grated nutmeg over.

Quince tripe. Cook the tripe, cut into pieces, in wine with a little salt and pepper till it is quite tender; take out the pieces and put them in a fireproof dish, with sliced ripe quinces, a powdering of ginger, a few cloves, and some salt; moisten with some wine and lemon juice mixed and put in the oven till the quinces are soft; beat up a couple of egg yolks with thin cream and melted butter, add a little rice flour and salt, stir into the dish and bake till it has set. Grate a little nutmeg over it, and serve.

Fried tripe. Take pieces of cooked tripe, selecting the thickest; dip them in a thin batter made by mixing an egg yolk with sifted flour and a little milk, to which you have added salt and a pinch of powdered chilli (cayenne pepper) and fry them in fat or butter. Pile the pieces on a dish and strew parsley over and serve.

Tripe and sheep's head (kop en pootjies). For this you want not only sheep's tripe, but also the head of the sheep and the trotters. Clean all three well and cut up the tripe into small pieces. Put the head and trotters in a saucepan,[1] with some onions, a bunch of herbs, salt and pepper, and

---

1 And presumably the tripe as well.

boil till the flesh easily separates from the bones. Take the flesh and the pieces of tripe and place in a stewpot with pepper and salt, a blade of mace, a lemon leaf, a little grated nutmeg, a wineglassful of lemon juice and two cups of strong stock; let it boil up, then simmer gently till the liquid part is thickened. Serve with chopped parsley. This dish is varied by adding curry powder, in which case it becomes a jellied curry, or by thickening with cream, tapioca, or vermicelli.

Oxtail is generally stewed or braised, always with a good wine and spices and herbs as an appropriate addition. *Ox marrow* is baked in the oven, the bone being cut into short lengths and both ends closed with a pat of dough. It is served with bread and eaten with a little salt and pepper or, more rarely, with a sweet mustard, made with plenty of sugar and cream and butter.

South African *biltong*, which is really spiced dried meat, is made from beef or from game meat. In the former case it is always cut into exceedingly thin slices and eaten on bread and butter; in the latter it is generally grated or pounded and is always dry, whereas beef biltong should be moist with a modicum of fat attached to it. Beef biltong, cut slightly thicker, is also fried like a bacon rasher or grilled, and is then served with fried eggs. Another name for biltong, often used in the older recipes, is *tassal*, in which, however, the meat was generally cut into small strips as is now done with game biltong.

Beef biltong. Take a good-sized piece (18 or 24 inches long) of the inner back muscle, or of the thigh muscle, selecting a nicely rounded strip, about six inches in diameter. It must not have any tendon, but should have some fat, though not too much. Trim it into an even, elongated oval. Make a mixture of salt, pepper, saltpetre, crushed coriander and fennel seed and moisten it with vinegar; rub this into the meat, and cover the meat with it for a few days, rubbing the mixture in every day. Hang the biltong in a draught and continue the rubbing with the spicy mixture till the outside is wind-dry. Tie a cheese cloth round it and hang it in a chimney for a couple of weeks to get thoroughly smoked. Keep it in a cool place, and use it when you have need for it.

Some makers put the biltong in a brine for a couple of days, and then start the rubbing process. Whichever method is used, the result should be a dark-coloured, firm, elongated piece of dried meat, which cuts easily and when sliced is a tender, garnet-red segment, surrounded by a thin, more darkly covered integument that need never be pared off before eating. Its taste is deliciously spicy, and whatever bits of fat remain in or on it are agreeably soft, without any suspicion of rancidity. If it has been hung in the smoke of a wood fire, it has that added aromatic flavour that is so difficult to describe yet so characteristic of smoked meat.

Game biltong as made in the field is quite another thing. It is simply game meat, cut into thin strips, rubbed with salt and perhaps a little crushed

more meat dishes

105

coriander seed, and sun-dried in the open air till it is as hard as a board. Bits of it are cut off with a pocketknife and chewed by those whose teeth are strong enough for such manducation, or are roughly pounded to a loose, grey mass that can be mastered even by those who have to rely on their dentures. The best way of serving game biltong is to grate it on a grater or rasp it with a broad rasp; the resultant powder, which should be greyish red, is spread on thin bread and butter. Biltong is an extremely nutritious and a most easily digested food, and can be given safely to invalids, while it is a deliciously savoury filling for sandwiches. As it is always made from lean meat, it should be eaten with butter. Practically any game meat can be used for it, but the best kind is reputed to be that made from the flesh of the eland or *riet* buck. I have tasted good biltong made from lion's meat and, most excellent of all, from zebra meat. All game biltong, however, can be much improved if it is made with the addition of some aromatic spices to the salt with which it is rubbed before being dried.

It is so excellent by itself that it needs no embellishment. Nevertheless it makes an excellent sandwich filling, mixed with butter and a few drops of onion or lemon juice. It is also a food companion to certain egg dishes, like shirred,[1] scrambled and poached eggs. A little-known way of using it is to incorporate it in an egg and milk and cream custard which is baked in the oven.

---

1 Baked in a dish.

Chapter 8

Sauces and Salad Dressings

The dictionaries define sauce as 'a liquid relish for food'; etymologists derive the word from the Latin word *salsa* which is supposed to mean a saltish fluid, but Von Vaerst thinks that it is of Eastern derivation. What can be stated as a fact is that the old Roman cooks never called their sauce a *salsa*. Apicius, one of the first writers on cookery, speaks of *salso* by which, apparently, he means a salty addition to a wine, for in his time it was customary to dilute table wine with sea water. Pliny and Cato refer to *salsugo*, and as the latter states that it may be thickened with *amylum*, which is ordinary starch, it is likely that it corresponded to a made sauce. Roman cooks used as a relish for all their meat and fish dishes something they called *jus*, which was the juice or gravy in which the foodstuff was prepared. The French cooks gave us the word sauce for the combinations of such juices with cream, oil and various other ingredients. In old Cape recipes the word *sous* is used indiscriminately for such made-up sauce, for gravy (for which Dutch cooks use the word *jus*) and for whatever remains liquid in the stewpan, while uncooked juice of fruit or vegetables is termed *sap*.

Obviously the preparation of an elaborate sauce represents a sophistication of the art of cookery to which the early Cape cooks had not attained. Their first examples of such sauces were made from Oriental recipes, and were cooked sauces. Raw sauces, which are more correctly speaking dressings, were used — but there were few, the principal one being *sour sauce*, made by beating up an egg with vinegar, salt and pepper. One reason for this was the scarcity of vegetable oil, which had to be brought from Europe or Java. Even today South Africa, which has many indigenous oil-holding plants, does not produce enough vegetable oil for domestic use, although a small quantity of excellent cold-drawn olive oil is seasonally made in the Cape Province.

Oil for sauce-making purposes was usually extracted from fats. A favourite oil for such use was that skimmed off in the first boiling of trotters or meat containing tendons or fat; this was clarified, put into bottles and used when required. Coconut oil, brought from the East, was also sometimes used and, after the eighteenth century, various seed oils, also imported.

According to Kettner there are two basic sauces, one white and the other brown, that masquerade under various names, but are generically known as white sauce and Spanish sauce. The difference between them is that the first is essentially a cooked sauce, while in the second the flour has been braised. Both were known to the old Cape cooks, and recipes for them are indeed to be found in the oldest cookery books. The Cape method of preparation directs that a very strong broth should be made, mainly of veal and chicken, boiled in good *bouillon* to which has been added a sliced onion, a bunch of carrots, a bouquet of pot herbs, pepper, salt and a little sugar. The fat should be carefully skimmed off. The broth is then strained through a cloth, and replaced in the saucepan. In another saucepan a cup of butter is melted and half a cup of sifted flour is stirred into it, till it is a smooth paste, which is then stirred into the broth, which is boiled under constant stirring. As soon as this boils, it is drawn to a cooler place on the stove, and allowed to simmer gently till it is smooth and thick. It is then poured through a fine sieve, and is ready to be used either as a sauce by itself, or as the basis for other sauces.

Thus, beaten up with an equal quantity of nearly boiling cream, it becomes béchamel sauce which again, when mixed with a jellied chicken broth and allowed to cool, becomes cold béchamel sauce. The gamut of variations is almost endless, as may be seen from consulting any good modern cookery book. None of these sauces, made with such basic velvet sauce, is original in Cape cookery. The earliest variant of the brown variety is the following:

> *Brown sauce* (*bruin sous*). Place in a saucepan a layer of sliced onions, with a tablespoonful of sheep's-tail fat; put on it a pound each of beef and veal, cut up into sizeable pieces. Pour on two cups of water and let it boil till most of the water has boiled away and the broth is thick enough 'to cling to the side of the pot.' Take great care that it does not burn. Now add four cups of boiling water and put the pot on a cooler part of the stove where it can simmer gently; add a little salt, and skim; then add carrots, parsley, a bunch of celery, a few cloves, a blade of mace and a pinch of black pepper. Let it simmer gently for four hours or more; then pour through a sieve and mix with brown roux to the required consistency.

This is not different from the usual recipes in European cookery books, except for the addition of the mace and cloves that impart to the sauce a spicy piquancy. Like the velvet sauce, it is used both as a basis for other sauces and by itself. The most common addition, in early times, was a teaspoonful of China (soya) sauce, or of a sharp chilli sauce. The following made-sauces required no foundation sauce but were complete in themselves:

> *Quince sauce*. Bake the quinces; peel them when they are soft and remove the seeds. Beat them with a wooden spoon to a purée; add salt, a little powdered ginger, tangerine peel and white pepper; rub through a fine sieve, and dilute with a little lemon juice.

Apple and pear sauce was made in the same way, but usually a few drops of rum were added.

> *Oil sauce* (used for brawn and salt meat). Mix oil and vinegar in equal

proportions, with salt, pepper, a little moist brown sugar and the expressed juice of an orange; beat well and serve cold.

Celery sauce. Braise white celery shoots cut into small pieces in butter with a little onion, pepper, salt and sugar; when tender, stir in some sifted flour, add a cupful of milk and let it simmer till thick; pour through a sieve and serve very hot.

Cape gooseberry sauce (appelliefiesous). Boil the gooseberries in water; when tender take them out and press through a sieve; add to the purée a large lump of butter, a little sugar and, if you like, a pinch of powdered ginger and a teaspoonful of salt; put on the fire and beat constantly, adding a little white wine while you are whipping it, but do not let it boil. It may be coloured yellow by adding a little turmeric. It should be sour-sweet; if you wish it to be sharply sour, cook some unripe grapes with the berries.

Several kinds of fruit — loquats, green grapes, cherries and strawberries — were similarly treated to make a fruit sauce. A very pleasant-tasting and smooth fruit sauce was made from the berries of the *duinbessie* (*Nylandtia spinosa*) that grew abundantly on Green Point Common and could be obtained, when in season, on the market for a penny a pound. *Duneberry sauce* had a sharp, sweet-sour taste and an intriguing, aromatic flavour, and was excellent with all meat dishes.

Pork fat sauce (speksous) was made from slightly salted, but not cured, pork fat, which was cut into tiny pieces, and braised with pepper and salt, a pinch of powdered chilli and a few crushed sage leaves. A tablespoonful of sifted flour was mixed to a paste with wine or water, and stirred into a cup of water mixed with vinegar in which the yolks of three eggs had been whipped. When the pork was nicely browned, the mixture of flour, egg yolk and vinegar was stirred into it, and was allowed to simmer gently till the sauce was smoothly thickened. It was used both hot and cold.

Old-fashioned sauce. This was the *ousous* of some recipes; *rissiesous* of others. It was made as follows:

Pound two peeled onions in the mortar with three green chillies, salt and a couple of tablespoonsful of the flesh of a braised *bokkom* (dried herring or mullet). Braise this purée with plenty of butter; add a few tablespoonsful of a mild *blatjang* (fruit chilli sauce; later recipes substitute for it tomato sauce) and thin, if required, with stock or white sauce.

Sour sauce. Melt an ounce of salt butter and whip into it the yolks of two eggs, the sap of a large lemon, a pinch of white pepper and a cup of boiled cream. Put on the fire, whipping constantly, and let it thicken, but take care that it does not boil. Some recipes add vinegar or tamarind water, but the lemon juice should sour it sufficiently; it should never be a sharp sauce.

Burnt almond sauce. Burnt almonds are pounded and mixed with a butter sauce, with sugar, lemon juice, and enough red ochre (*rooi bolus*)[1] to colour the sauce bright red. Finally a glass of very sweet wine or of homemade liqueur is added. It is a favourite sauce for steamed puddings, but can be served also with meat dishes.

Moskonfytsous has for its main ingredients the boiled, partly-fermented wine must known as *moskonfyt*, which is simply grape juice in which the sugar has been largely, though not wholly, caramelised. By itself *moskonfyt*, which was well known to the ancient Romans, who also used it as a sweet sauce, is a dark mahogany-coloured thin syrup, with a vinous yet aromatic flavour combined with the distinct, characteristic taste of burnt sugar. It is commonly used by itself as a syrup with bread and butter at breakfast and, commercially, as a sweetening agent for fortified wines of the port type. As a sauce principally for puddings and sweet dishes and, more rarely, for meat dishes, it is thickened with arrowroot, rice flour, or sifted wheat flour, mixed with well-chopped seeded raisins, dates and some chilli sauce to give it additional pungency. In that way it becomes one of the many sweet sauces, of which there are innumerable varieties that need not be detailed here. Reference will be made in a later chapter to some of them.

Klipkoussous, made by mixing finely pounded braised or stewed flesh of the pearl mussel[2] with a basic white or velvet sauce, always needs the addition of lemon juice, egg yolk and spices. It is a delicately flavoured sauce which, like all sauces that contain fish, has a distinct and rather an esoteric taste. Like crayfish sauce, in which the principal ingredient is the coral and the very soft parts found under the carapace, and oyster sauce, it is usually served with fish dishes.

Herb sauces, of which the best known to European cooks are mint and sage sauce, are made either plainly by boiling the chief constituent in vinegar, with sugar and some spice that will not overpower the characteristic flavour of the herb, or by combining the herbs with other ingredients. As an example of an old-fashioned sauce of this kind the following recipe will serve:

Fennel sauce. Take a handful of young fennel leaves and chop them up fine, with a little parsley, salt and pepper, and the yolk of a hard-boiled egg pressed through a sieve. Make an emulsion of oil, lemon juice and vinegar, and whip it up with the fennel mixture, adding a little ground

---

1 Red bole: a powder derived from red clay, used at the Cape for colouring food, such as biscuit dough, red.
2 *Perlemoen*, abalone.

ginger if desired. Serve with fish. It was regarded as the sauce for an eel pie, and was also favoured as a relish for all firm-fleshed fish.

A sauce that is of ancient date but is now rarely encountered is:

Saffron sauce. Braise sliced onions, shallots, and a tiny morsel of garlic in butter; add to it the pounded flesh of a baked quince or apple, a pinch of powdered saffron, a large lump of salt butter and a little white stock; let it slowly simmer; press through a sieve, add another lump of butter, and let it get thoroughly hot again, without boiling. It should be uniformly bright yellow in colour and quite smooth. Some recipes thicken it with a little rice flour.

The Malay cooks were adepts at making the exceedingly pungent, sharp, well-spiced sauces that are so much favoured in the East. They vary in consistency from the thick, jammy chutneys to the thinner, more liquid combinations of spices and other ingredients with tamarind or vinegar, professionally known as *blatjangs*. Sometimes the latter were made with a fish paste and with partly fermented, even decomposed, materials that gave a very strong, and often, to Occidental taste at least, a repulsive odour. An example of such a strongly flavoured and odoriferous sauce is the Malay *trassie*, a variant of which was apparently regarded as a delicacy by the early Romans who made it from decomposed anchovies. More in keeping with modern palates are the following recipes:

Fish trassie. Pound to a paste in a mortar six anchovies, a dried salt mullet, three red chillies, a slice of ginger, half a dozen peppercorns, a teaspoonful of coriander and the same amount of aniseed. Braise in butter half a cupful of chopped onion and a small clove of garlic; pour over it a cupful of tamarind water, mix it with the fish paste, and let it slowly simmer, keeping the lid on the saucepan till all ingredients have been well cooked, adding more tamarind water or vinegar to make a pasty fluid. Put in bottles and cork.

This is a fiery sauce, which keeps well, and is without the nauseating odour of the true *trassie* that is made from decomposed fish.

Hot blatjang. Take a pound of dried apricots and soak them in vinegar till they are soft enough to be mashed. Peel two pounds of onions, bake them, and pound them, with the mashed apricots, to a smooth purée, in which you incorporate a quarter of a pound of salt, half an ounce of coriander seed, half a pound of chopped green chillies, two large cloves of garlic, a teaspoonful of powdered ginger, and half a pound of blanched almonds previously well pounded. Put in a saucepan six pints of vinegar and bring it to the boil; add your paste, stirring constantly, and let it simmer till it reaches the thickness you wish to have. Put in bottles or jars and cork. It will keep indefinitely.

Blatjang should be a uniform red colour, and it is better to use red, that is mature, chillies, but the green ones make a more pungent relish. This recipe gives a *blatjang* that is scaldingly hot and should be used cautiously by those who are unfamiliar with its properties. By adding sugar, or apricot jam, to it, decreasing the amount of chillies or omitting them altogether and substituting ordinary pepper, a sweet *blatjang* can be made according to this recipe. There are many other recipes for making this favourite condiment, but the essentials are that it should be bitingly spicy, pungently aromatic, moderately smooth and a very intimately mixed association of all the ingredients.

Atjar, another favourite relish, is simply a variety of vegetables and fruits, boiled and preserved in a very strong chilli pickle. The more varieties of vegetables in it, the better it is supposed to be. An old recipe states:

> For *atjar* you must take small onions, shallots, cauliflower, very young *mielie* (corn) cobs, green beans, half-ripe apricots, very small immature cucumbers, squashes and pumpkins, not more than two inches in length, and not thicker than your little finger, ripe loquats from which you have removed the seeds, one or two half-ripe rose apples (*djam boes*), dried peeled peaches, a few green and red chillies, some lemon leaves, some green ginger diced, peppercorns, curry powder, moist sugar, salt and vinegar. After cleaning your vegetables and fruit, you must put them in the vinegar and boil them till they are soft; then you must make a paste with the sugar, salt and curry powder, and stir it into the boiling vinegar, adding the peppercorns, chillies and lemon leaves, and let it all boil sweetly till the liquid begins to thicken. Now put it in jars and tie a vinegar-wetted cloth over, and let it stand for a week or two when you can eat it as a pickle with meat.

A well-made *atjar* is an enthralling relish, for you never know, when you are fishing in the jar, what you may come across — and every bit is as enticing as a good vegetable pickle can be. Some cooks add too much sugar and make it too sweet; it should be pleasantly sour, with a sweetish aftertaste, and every constituent should be deliciously tender. Perhaps the titbit in it is the young mielie cobs, each encrusted with its serried rows of unripened grain, but there is really no end to the variety of things you can incorporate in it.

Chutneys are sour-sweet, hot-sweet, or simply sweet concoctions of fruits or vegetables with spices and vinegar; their sweetness depends on the amount of sugar (formerly honey) that was added to them; their fieriness they owe to the pepper and chillies that go into them. Formerly they were all made at home; now they are usually bought ready-made by mass production, and are far from being what they ought to be.

There are many recipes for making them, but it would obviously be monotonous to transcribe so many whose generic similarity is obvious. I have been served with apricot chutney, almond chutney made from green almonds, bean chutney, mango chutney, pineapple chutney, rose apple chutney, cucumber chutney, melon chutney, apple chutney, quince chutney (perhaps the best of all), peach chutney, plum chutney, pumpkin chutney, *mielie* chutney made from small, immature cobs, pear chutney, grape chutney, kei apple chutney, kaffir plum chutney (both made from indigenous fruits), raisin chutney, mixed dried fruit chutney and last, and very definitely least, the modern tomato chutney, which is not really a chutney, but a sauce. For chutney should be essentially a preserve, in which the consistency of the main ingredient, that gives a name to it, should be maintained and something of its original form should remain. Tomatoes do not figure in the old recipes, for they were a comparatively late introduction, but when they were freely grown a tomato chutney was made and it is a delicious chutney. It was prepared from young, unripe tomatoes, stewed with sugar, spice and tamarind juice, and was quite unlike the modern watery red concoction that consists of ripe tomato mash, boiled up with sugar, raisins and what passes for vinegar.

The following two recipes describe how, generally speaking, a chutney should be made:

Quince chutney. Take two dozen borrie quinces,[1] just ripe; peel and slice but do not core them, for the gelatinous seeds add much to the flavour of the chutney. Cook them till soft in white wine. Now add to them six or seven cloves of garlic, bruised, and two pounds of moist sugar, and let them simmer. Pound in a mortar a pound of young onions, peeled and sliced, half a pound of dried chillies, a pound of seeded hanepoot raisins, a quarter of a pound of green ginger, a teaspoonful of cardamons, allspice, and pepper, and a tablespoonful of tangerine peel, and add this to the quinces; pour over three bottles of good wine vinegar or tamarind water, and let it come to the boil, stirring constantly. Let the chutney simmer till it is of the right consistency, taking care that the quince slices retain their shape. Put in wide-mouthed jars. It will keep indefinitely.

Rose apple chutney. Boil the rose apples[2] in wine till they are soft; remove their seeds. Make a paste of onion, fennel seed, coriander seed, garlic, cloves, moist sugar and ginger powder, and stir this into boiling vinegar; let it simmer, and add pounded raisins and dates, chillies enough to make the chutney very hot, and half a cupful of salt; put into it your boiled rose apples, and let all simmer slowly for three hours, taking care that it does not burn.

This is a delicious chutney, for the strong flavour of the rose apples is predominant. It was usually far too strong, however, for delicate palates, but its fieriness can of course be moderated by using little or no chillies. Let me again emphasise that a real chutney is not a sauce but a sour-sweet preserve, in which the main ingredient retains its pristine shape, or as much of it as

1 'Borrie' is an old quince cultivar found at the Cape with especially yellow flesh.
2 The fruit of *Syzigium jambos*.

sauces and salad dressings

possible, for in one or two recipes — for apple and pumpkin chutney and, more especially, for the many mixed fruit chutneys — it is directed that the fruit or the vegetable should be mashed. Such chutneys are, however, more properly described as thick fruit or vegetable sauces and are more in the nature of a *blatjang* than a real chutney.

We now come to *salads*. Here again there is considerable difference of opinion about the derivation of the word and its original meaning, matters with which we need not concern ourselves at the moment. The word *slaai*, which is Dutch, and the word *sambal*, which is Malay, are interchangeably used in the old recipes to denote a cold meat, vegetable or fruit dish, garnished with a cold dressing, and served sometimes by itself but more often as an accompaniment of some other dish. The meat and fish salads were copied from recipes that occur in the oldest cookery books and, as far as I have been able to ascertain, none of them shows any modification (apart from the inclusion of some ingredients that are indigenous to the country) that can be considered an original improvement. Any cold meat or fish could be served up as a salad. The meat was simply sliced into small, convenient pieces, mixed with sliced onions and fresh herbs or salad vegetables, dressed with a sour sauce, and served with appropriate decorative garnishes.

At the Cape, the dressing was generally the yolk of an egg beaten with vinegar or sour cream, with salt, pepper and perhaps some powdered chilli added. A mayonnaise sauce was a late introduction, for oil, as has been mentioned, was rare; on the farms one very seldom came across an oil dressing for a salad. For the decorative garnishing, hard-boiled eggs, cut into thin slices (I have seen hard-boiled ostrich eggs used for this purpose), boiled beetroot, and pickles were generally used. In more fashionable homes in the towns, nuts, anchovies and, for sweet salads, preserved ginger, citron, shaddock and *naartje* or rose apple preserve were used to dress them up.

No recipes for meat and fish salads need be given; they are to be found in all cookery books. The only noticeable hint I have discovered in the old Cape recipes is that in hussar salad, if made in the early summer, the inclusion of a few slices of ripe figs is a decided improvement. An interesting, though not novel, modification in chicken salad (which all the best recipes insist should be made from the breast flesh only) is the addition of a few drops of rum, the directive being: 'Before adding the sauce, put a few drops of a good rum on the pieces of chicken and toss them about so that each piece gets a touch of it'. Rum as a flavouring for meat is nothing new, but its use in so delicate a dish as a chicken salad is to be carefully controlled, and I cannot say that my own experience with it has convinced me that it improves the dish.

Crayfish, crab and shellfish salad have already been dealt with in the chapter on fish; it may be added that no Cape cook would have dreamed of making a crayfish salad from the tail flesh alone; the indispensable parts were supposed to be the soft flesh immediately under the carapace, the meat from the claws, and the green 'mush' that is found near the coral.

Before we finish with sauce, it is desirable to say something about a sauce that is rarely used by itself but is indispensable for the making of many dishes. This is *kerrie sous* or *curry sauce*, in whose preparation the Malay cook demonstrated the highest skill of his craft. It was essentially a braise of many different spices, with herbs, vegetables, salt and sugar, in butter or fat, to which was added, as a thinning, tamarind water or vinegar and coconut milk. The most elaborate recipe is also one of the oldest, and although half of the ingredients mentioned in it may be omitted, it is here given as a curiosity to show how the old cooks proceeded when they had no means of obtaining ready-made curry powder.

> *To make a good curry sauce.* Pound separately in your mortar (which you must wipe out after each pounding with a little coconut milk) green ginger, fennel seed, aniseed, allspice, coriander seed, cardamon seed, a peach kernel and three blanched almonds, green and red chillies, mace, nutmeg, black pepper, cloves and fresh lemon peel. Cut up very finely an onion and a few cloves of garlic, with some thyme, basil, celery, sage and rosemary; and braise them in a little sheep's fat. When brown, add a few cumin seeds. Take all that you have pounded and mix it intimately with powdered turmeric, till it has a fine yellow colour; moisten it with tamarind water and stir it into the braised onion and garlic; add more tamarind water to make a thick sauce. This you can use for making any curry, by frying your meat in it. If you think it burns the tongue too much, you may mellow it by adding sugar or by reducing the amount of chillies.

Sometimes such a curry sauce, made in a far less elaborate fashion, was prepared for home use and stored in a bottle or jar. Very soon (it seems as early as 1670) a curry powder composed of all the necessary ingredients was imported from China. A convicted Chinaman, who was sent out as a prisoner to the Cape, is said to have first used it. Tradition also has it that he was the first to keep a restaurant, somewhere on the shore of Rogge Bay, which was where the war monument now stands. Later, so tradition avers, he was sent for on occasion to the Castle to cook special dinners for Governor Simon van der Stel who was a gentleman of good taste and liked to eat a well-cooked dish.

From the beginning of the eighteenth century, curry powder was invariably employed in making curry sauce; in my young days I knew of only one cook who still made the old-fashioned and almost obsolete curry paste – the old artist who ruled the kitchen (and menagerie in the backyard) at the White House Hotel in Strand Street, then the recognised Mecca of all who wished to taste good Malay cookery.

The *sambals* were Oriental relishes that were highly popular at the Cape, but somehow do not appear to have appealed to English taste. Miss Morris, who edited Mrs Rundle's cookery book, and who had visited the Cape where she doubtless copied the recipe for her '*Ragout of Lambstones*', does not mention them; neither does Mrs Kindersley who came later. According to the Coloured butler who, many years later when 'Major Wellesley' had reached fame, gave his recollection of the Duke of Wellington, the Duke liked 'quince *sambal*' and asked for it whenever he came to dine at the hospitable Newlands house of the richest man in the Colony.

Sambals are in theory very easy to make: they are simply finely chopped fresh fruit or vegetables, dressed with simple spices or herbs and a little vinegar or lemon juice. In practice, however, a great deal of skill is necessary to serve them smooth, fresh and virgin in their colouring, for within a couple of hours they lose their crispness and turn brown. They must therefore be made immediately before they are to be used and the several kinds, each in its own little glass dish, are presented on a salver from which the guest may help himself to a few spoonfuls at a time. They are served as a rule with all curries, sometimes with meat or fish dishes. The favourites are:

Apple sambal. Peel and grate a sour apple and half a sweet one; mix with a little salt, red pepper, grated nutmeg and lemon juice.

Quince sambal. Peel and grate a ripe quince; if it is a borrie or turmeric quince, the sambal will be a pale yellow colour; ordinary quince sambal, like apple sambal, should be snowy white. Mix the grated flesh with lemon juice, powdered chilli and white pepper and a little salt.

Cucumber sambal. Take a young cucumber, peel it and remove the seeds; mince it finely, and strew salt on it; let it stand for a quarter of an hour; pour off the water that has drained from it, and lightly dry the mince in a thin cloth. Mix well with a little vinegar, white pepper and lemon juice.

Apricot sambal. Peel and seed firm, not quite ripe, apricots, and chop them fine; mix with a little lemon juice, salt, and white pepper.

Onion sambal. Scald a large white onion and chop it up; mix with salt, pepper, a pinch of chillies, some chopped marjoram and a little vinegar.

Radish sambal. Clean and grate raw unpeeled radish; mix with red pepper, salt, a little minced onion and some vinegar.

Banana sambal. Pare a firm, not too ripe, banana and chop it into small dice; mix with red pepper, salt, minced marjoram and a little lemon juice.

Carrot sambal. Grate young raw carrots; mix with salt, grated nutmeg, very little white pepper and vinegar or lemon juice.

Mixed herbs sambal. Chop up finely marjoram, fennel, thyme, mint, parsley, scented verbena, celery and young sorrel leaves with a green chilli; mix them to a paste with a little tamarind water, salt and sugar.

Loquat and spring onion sambal. Take large ripe loquats; plunge them into boiling water and peel them; take out, seed and dry. Chop them into very small pieces, with some spring onions, a pinch of red pepper, ginger and salt; mix intimately with lemon juice in which a little vinegar has been stirred.

Any vegetable or fruit that is capable of being grated or minced without losing its crispness is suitable for a *sambal*. It is this 'crunchiness' that, combined with the sharp pungency of the chillies, gives the *sambal* its appetising taste and that makes it so valuable as a relish for a hot curry.

Salad materials are plentiful in South Africa, but the old cooks favoured for their vegetable salads lettuce and cabbage. Both were usually, and unfortunately, shredded, mixed with a boiled beetroot, raw onions and a dressing either of simple vinegar, salt and pepper, or vinegar in which these condiments were beaten up with egg yolk and an oil in the form of melted butter or the clarified oil obtained from sheep's trotters.

The garnishing was hard-boiled eggs cut in slices, as for the meat and fish salads.

With the exception of salads made from certain indigenous plants, all the recipes follow the ordinary rules of the European cookbooks and it is unnecessary to give any examples. Fruit salads, in which some modifications were introduced, will be dealt with in a later chapter.

Chapter 9

Vegetables

The settlers started by planting vegetables from seeds brought with them from Holland. These flourished exceedingly well as Van Riebeeck, an enthusiastic gardener, noted in his Log. For several years the settlement was supplied with vegetables from the Company's garden; then from the farm in the neighbourhood of Green Point Common. But when the Free Burghers were granted allotments, vegetables were extensively grown and were sold in what became the first general market. Since then vegetables, including all the varieties known to European cooks, were easily procurable. There is no reason why vegetable foodstuffs should ever be scarce in the country, for it has excellent garden soil and all that is wanted is intensive cultivation and an absence of bureaucratic control.

Early Cape cooks followed the Continental method of preparing vegetables for the table, with the result that cooked vegetables retained their flavour and sometimes much of their succulence. They were never plainly boiled in water; soda was never used in cooking them; they were discarded if not fresh and untainted; and when they were combined with other foodstuffs care was taken not to destroy their individual taste. The cooking of vegetables at the Cape was favourably commented on by several writers. While epicures like Baron von Boechenroeder, an 'Indian Officer', complained that meat dishes in the Colony were always greasy and sometimes overstewed − neither of which accusations is substantiated by the recipes − they agreed that so far as the vegetable cookery was concerned 'it compared favourably with the best Italian'.

That was deserved praise.

English cooks, as Wharton and others have testified, have always ill-treated their vegetables; even today, when they have learned a great deal, they seem to be more concerned about retaining the vitamins, that are of no importance whatever in a properly balanced diet, than about preserving the original individuality of the vegetable or felicitously improving its palatability by blending it with an alien spicy or aromatic flavour.

Such old manuscript cookery books as give what may be regarded as general hints for the cook state that vegetables preferably must be steamed; at any rate they should all be cooked very slowly, especially when they are past their prime. For some young vegetables the Malay cooks recommended a quick, short immersion in boiling water; all are agreed that plain boiled vegetable is not a dish to set before anyone. The directives for 'finishing' a vegetable are thus many and varied and it is interesting to see how closely they follow the recipes contained in Dutch, Flemish, German and Italian cookery books of the seventeenth century. They speak of 'dry-cooking' (*droogkook*) which is really sautéing in butter or fat, with the difference that the vegetable is not allowed, as in a true sauté, to become slightly impregnated with the oil; of mashing or making a purée of the vegetable; of creaming, which means slow simmering in cream; and of glazing, in which the vegetable was stewed in a jelly-*bouillon* with a little butter and sugar. They hardly ever prepared a true *frittura*, in which the vegetable was plunged into boiling oil or fat; a frying-basket rarely figured among their kitchen utensils, for they preferred to deal with their vegetables by shallow-frying or by frying in batter.

Great care was taken in cleaning the vegetables, and usually the first paragraphs of the recipes are devoted to instructions how this should be done. These are omitted, and in the examples here given it is presupposed that the ingredients have been properly shorn of whatever is extraneous.

We may now describe some of the ways in which the various vegetables were dealt with, referring the reader who wishes to know about the preparation of indigenous vegetables to the later chapter on Veld Food. Only such recipes as exhibit some modification that may reasonably be regarded as of local invention are given.

Potatoes. A popular method was to steam them in their skins, with a little salt, thyme leaves and green ginger in the pot, and to send them to table with melted butter served in a sauceboat. For made-dishes, they were treated like this, the skins drawn off, and the potatoes used as directed. Otherwise they were thinly peeled before being cooked. Fried, boiled, buttered, roast, sautéd and baked potatoes were made exactly in accordance with European recipes; the only difference is that peeled boiled potatoes were never sent to the table without first being 'tossed' in a little butter and having nutmeg grated over them.

Herbs were most frequently used in flavouring them; when spice was used it was generally nutmeg, pepper or allspice, chillies being considered incompatible except in a potato *bredie*. Mashed potatoes were creamed by adding butter, cream and egg yolk and a seasoning of nutmeg.

> *Potatoes with wine.* Beat up two large boiled mealy potatoes with some grated nutmeg, an ounce of salt butter and a glass of sherry; add the yolks of two eggs. Shape it into a loaf; paint it with egg yolk beaten up with a little of the white, dust it with breadcrumbs and bake it in a buttered dish in the oven. When it is golden brown all over, drench it with a sauce made of egg yolk, wine, sugar and nutmeg, with a little salt, that you have allowed to simmer till moderately thick. Serve at once with any meat dish.

> *Hot potato snow.* Steam large, mealy potatoes in their skins with a little ginger, herbs and a bit of lemon rind. Peel them and press them through a sieve, so that the flakes fall lightly on the dish. Dust with powdered nutmeg and salt and a little pepper mixed, and serve as hot as possible.

Potato rice. Make a rather stiff potato purée, and press it through a colander on a hot dish, holding the colander some distance above the dish, so that the little balls of potato form a pyramid. Dust with pepper and salt, place in a quick oven for a few minutes and serve.

Potato dumplings. Make a purée with some mealy potatoes, butter, salt, pepper, grated nutmeg and egg yolk; thicken if necessary with a little rice flour; form into small round balls and boil in *bouillon*. A variation of this directs that the whites of eggs should be stiffly whipped and incorporated in the dumpling mixture, which must then be scooped up in a spoon which is dipped into the boiling soup or *bouillon*; this is certainly an easier method to make the dumplings which have an unfortunate propensity to disintegrate.

Potatoes with tail fat. Put peeled potatoes in a flat pot with sufficient sheep's tail fat to cover the bottom; strew salt and a little marjoram over the potatoes. Put on the lid and let the potatoes stew till they are well done, shaking the pot occasionally. Another, and better, way is: braise diced pork fat with some chopped parsley, a bay leaf, salt, pepper and nutmeg; stir in a cup of strong broth or *bouillon* and put in your potatoes, which must be already boiled and mealy. Put on the lid and allow to stew slowly for 20 minutes.

Potato curry. Cut boiled potatoes in slices and stew these lightly in sharp curry sauce, taking care that they are not broken.

Vinegar potatoes. Melt two ounces of butter in a pan and mix it smoothly with one ounce of sifted flour; when it begins to get brown, stir into it a tablespoonful of vinegar, a tablespoonful of brown sugar, pepper and salt and a cupful of broth (or wine). Boil it till it has the consistency of cream, and slice into it four large peeled potatoes. Let it simmer gently till the potatoes are quite tender and serve with some minced onion strewn over.

Potato cheese. Boil four pounds of potatoes in their skins with onions, ginger, salt and pepper; peel them, and mash them well; put the mash in a jar with a pound's weight of new milk and a teaspoonful of rennet, a teaspoonful of caraway and aniseed mixed, and a few coriander seeds; knead the mixture well, and put it aside, covered with a damp cloth, in a cool place for four or five days; knead it again, press out all the moisture, and put the mixture in a mould, and let it stand till it begins to show cracks on its surface; paint these over with a mixture of sour milk and cream. When the cheese is hard on its outside, which will be in about a month's time, you may use it like any ordinary cheese.

One recipe advised that the cheese should be coloured with saffron. It is by no means bad eating and is comparatively easy to make.

Asparagus. There are several indigenous varieties, though the cultivated kind has been a favourite from very early days. Up to the end of the past century,[1] one could buy large bunches of the local 'wild' asparagus from the hawkers in Cape Town streets, generally at a penny a bunch. It was then a very cheap vegetable, although it was regarded as a delicacy of which Rhodes was known to be very fond. The local product was thin, long, very green and exquisitely flavoured; nowadays it is almost impossible to get, and the thick, often woody, etiolated cultivated fronds have taken its place. It was always steamed, with a little salt, and served with melted butter, its flavour being regarded as too delicate to be benefited by any spice or herb. It was also used for soups, and a purée of the boiled plant was sometimes sophisticated with spices and breadcrumbs and baked in the oven.

Mushrooms were never popular, and there are few recipes that are not copied from Dutch or English books for their preparation, although many varieties of edible mushrooms are to be found on the veld. So far as my investigations go, there is no special South African modification for preparing them, and all recipes that mention them, as constituents of dishes, are merely copies of already published directives.

Endive was stewed, made into a *bredie*, or served as a purée, always with nutmeg, pepper, plenty of butter and sometimes with a meat gravy. *Lettuce* was similarly treated, and both vegetables were, like *spinach*, thought to have considerable tonic value.

Aubergine or *egg-plant*, of which there are several varieties, was known as *brinjal*. It was excellently served by itself, stewed, braised, sautéed and even grilled, or in combination with other vegetables and meats. It was also stuffed with one of the farces mentioned in a former chapter, or served with poached eggs. A curious recipe is the following, which produces, as I can testify from personal experience, a most tasty dish:

> *Aubergine with pine kernels.* Select your brinjals with care, choosing a moderate-sized one, with firm and thick flesh; peel it thinly and cut it in slices, on which you strew salt; let the brinjal lie till most of the water has been extracted; then wipe the slices and dust them with fine flour which you have previously mixed with powdered white pepper, ginger and nutmeg; slice and brown some onions with fat; lay on them the brinjal slices and strew over them plenty of pine kernels; then add enough sherry to cover them and stew with the lid closed, till everything is well blended. A little chilli and a teaspoonful of *blatjang* added much improves it.

Artichoke. Both kinds, the *girasole* or Jerusalem and the globe variety, are mentioned in the recipes, but neither has interested the Cape cook sufficiently to stimulate his inventive ingenuity, although the former is responsible for the following two recipes:

> *Banana artichokes.* Dice some artichokes that have been steamed in

---

1   The nineteenth century.

wine; put the pieces of artichoke in a saucepan, slice on them the bananas; add a lump of butter, a little salt, pepper and parsley; let them simmer for a few minutes; add a glass of sherry, and a little flour to thicken; shake well and add some more salt if required, and finally a cup of boiling thin cream. Serve with nutmeg grated over.

Artichokes with penguin eggs. Make a purée of cooked artichokes and mix it with the mashed yolks of hard-boiled penguin eggs. Add salt, pepper, a little powdered chilli, a blade of mace, a glass of sherry; let it simmer on the fire, stirring constantly, till it no longer cleaves to the side of the saucepan. Take out and serve on a dish with the jellied white of the eggs as a decoration.

Beetroot. One of the oldest recipes is also one of the best, even though it has no other title than:

How to prepare beetroot. A dozen young beetroots, none larger than a bantam's egg; two large, flat white onions; six shallots; a tablespoonful of honey; a tablespoonful of sifted wheat flour; leaves of the herb marjoram; two tablespoonsful fat; a teaspoonful of vinegar; as much salt as will savour. Scrape the beets and cut them into quarters; smother (braise) the onions and shallots, herb and salt in the fat, add the beets and let them slowly simmer till they are soft, which will take only a few minutes. Add the flour, honey and vinegar, beaten up, and let it all stew for half an hour, when you can serve it with rice.

This was obviously a bourgeois recipe; it is much improved by adding spices, substituting sugar for the honey and tamarind water for the vinegar. But even without these improvements, it makes a very nice dish, either hot or cold.

Beans. There are so many varieties of beans that few, outside the bureaucrats of an Agricultural Department, can classify them. For the cook, however, they may all be lumped into two simple categories — green beans and dried beans. Both were standard foodstuffs at the Cape from the earliest times. From the East came those magnificent dried beans that were known as *katjang boontjies* and many others, some as small as a peppercorn, others nearly an inch and a half oval. The method of preparing them was invariably the same. Soak your beans overnight in cold water, rejecting those that float; stew them gently in fat, with a glass of wine as zest, and season them with braised onions, herbs, spices and chillies.

You ate them hot with their own sauce, or cold with a sour sauce. You made them into *bredie* with some pieces of fat neck, or rib of lamb or mutton. You dealt similarly with dried peas and broad beans. A 'recipe for the less affluent', as the old cookbooks quaintly put it, dictated a slow cooking, in an earthenware jar — possibly one of the smaller jars that contained sesame oil from Tonkin — in an oven, with bits of bacon, onions, chillies, ginger and garden herbs. A simple sort of baked beans, but for all that much superior to the canned variety we now get. Much later, tomatoes were incorporated with the beans, and there are recipes that insist on butter and many spices that were only within the means of the rich.

Green beans were used when young and tender, and the best kind was always a butter bean, pale yellow in colour. It was steamed in wine and butter, with some herbs; or in a very little broth, and served with a covering of a sour sauce and a dusting of grated nutmeg. Cold, it was equally tasty with such a sauce. A green-bean *bredie* was a dish by itself, rich, savoury and filling. Sometimes little pieces of quince were added to it and, more rarely, a chunk or two of potato.

Green peas were treated in the same manner. Some kinds could be eaten, when cooked, with the pods, but commonly the beans were shelled, very gently steamed with butter and a little water with a snippet of onion, a leaf of marjoram and a teaspoonful of honey and served with a dusting of nutmeg. Mint was not supposed to be the best flavouring to blend with them and, indeed, mint does overpower the delicacy of their juvenile savour.

Indian peas, or groundnuts, were never eaten when fresh, but, when dried, were made into purées; sometimes they were first roasted, pounded in a mortar with chillies and breadcrumbs, salt and pepper, made into patties and fried in fat, but they were never popular, and their taste is not to everyone's liking.

Cabbage, Brussels sprouts and *red cabbage* were all much liked and there are many recipes for their preparation. Again, as these vegetables were old friends from the homelands, they were dealt with in accordance with European methods of serving and cooking. The only difference was that they were never overcooked, always sent to table with some butter and a grating of nutmeg on them, and steamed or stewed rather than plain boiled.

Cauliflower, spinach, celery, carrots, onions, leeks, shallots, parsnips and *turnips* could be cooked in much the same fashion and though, for them too, there are all sorts of recipes, the same qualification applied. Nearly all of them make good *bredie*, and all can be steamed or braised in accordance with the directions already given; flavouring is a matter of taste and discretion.

Gourd vegetables, of which the various *squashes, cucumbers* and *pumpkins* are the main representatives, were sometimes cooked a little differently, as the following recipes show:

Fried squashes. Peel them and slice thin; dust the slices with pepper, a little turmeric and salt; roll them in fine flour and fry them quickly in a shallow pan with plenty of fat; drain, pile on a dish, strew fine breadcrumbs over and serve them at once. It would be better to deep-fry them in a basket, as the Italians do, but the real *frittura* was almost unknown in South Africa.

Cucumbers with cream. Steam young cucumbers with a little white wine, herbs and salt; remove their seeds, and cut them up into square pieces; put in a shallow dish, with butter, pepper, salt, nutmeg and a cupful of thick cream; let simmer, shaking often. Serve with a dusting of dried parsley.

Boiled squash. Put the whole squash in a saucepan with a little water, salt and herbs. Steam till soft. Serve whole or cut into two parts, with melted butter.

This is the usual way of serving the small green, rounded squash known as *marakka*. If young enough its seeds are soft and entirely eatable, but older specimens must have the seeds scooped out before they are sent to table.

Pumpkin, cucumber or squash fritters. These are made with a purée of the cooked vegetable, spiced with cinnamon, mace, honey (or sugar nowadays), ginger and a little salt. A little rice flour or sifted meal is sometimes added to make a firmer dough, which is shaped into flat patties or cakes and fried in fat or butter, and served with a mixture of sugar and cinnamon, either as dessert or as an accompaniment of a *bobotie* or curry.

All gourd vegetables may be used for *bredies*, but as they contain much water, the stew pot should be left open to allow for evaporation and the cooking should be prolonged and very slow, great care being taken to prevent burning. Even at their best, such gourd *bredies* are not equal to those made from other vegetables, and their goodness depends much on what is added to them by way of spices and herbs.

Mielies, or *Indian corn*, came into the Settlement in the early part of the eighteenth century when the Company urged every householder to plant maize to augment the food supply for the slaves, as it was difficult to import sufficient quantities of rice.

Since then it has always been a favourite as a green vegetable on the farms, but it has never really come into its own in the towns. Even now hotel cooks do not seem to know how to serve it properly and usually spoil it in the cooking. Sugar corn is grown extensively for the market, but the best eating mielie is still the old-fashioned *bread mielie* which has a far larger grain and when eaten young is unsurpassed by any of the newer kinds. And let it be said that an old mielie, whose grain has already hardened, is quite unfit for the table; no manner of cooking it can make it worthwhile to eat, for it is tasteless, without flavour, and not easily digested. So choose young, fresh mielies, whose grain is tender, and whose 'beard' or *stigmas* are still transparently green, and treat them in accordance with one of the following recipes.

Boiled mielies. Divest the cobs of their outer leaves, but let the last, almost translucent layer abide; take away also the 'beard'; plunge them into boiling water, to which you have added some salt, and let them boil rapidly until the grains are soft. Take out and drain, and serve on a flat dish, handing round melted butter with them.

A few hints in connection with this: do not send them to table with butter on them; serve the butter separately; some people much prefer to butter them with unmelted butter; send them piping hot. The proper way to eat them is to butter them, grasp the ends of the cob with the hands protected by a napkin, and bite off the grain.

The guest who has a rocking denture is advised to cut the grain from the cob and eat it with a spoon or fork.

Baked mielies. Put the whole mielie, still covered with a layer of leaf, on the hot ash of a wood fire and rake over it more ash and some glowing embers. Turn it frequently; it generally takes from 10 to 20 minutes to bake properly; strip off the burnt leaves, and serve as with boiled mielies.

They can also be baked in the oven or grilled on a gridiron in this way.

Fried green mielies. Cut the grain from the young cobs, sprinkle with salt and pepper, and fry in fat till they are a golden brown; drain, heap on a dish, sprinkle with dried parsley, and serve.

Mielie bread (Indian corn pudding). Cut the grain from a dozen cooked cobs and pound it in a mortar; mix it with two beaten eggs, pepper, salt, a blade of mace, some grated nutmeg, a cup of milk and a cup of cream. Fill a greased mould with this mixture and steam for half an hour. Take out, cut into slices and serve with melted butter, or a sour sauce.

This is an excellent, delicious-tasting vegetable pudding which is usually served as an accompaniment to roast meat, particularly pork. It is not easy to make in perfection, but any care in its preparation is well repaid by the result.

A sweet dish is made from dried mielies, the recipe for which will be given later. From the cooked grain of fresh green mielies a number of made dishes can be prepared by mixing them with various other ingredients. A *mielie bredie* is not often met with, but is quite good. Another mixed dish is to stew the grain with braised onions and tomatoes; or mix it with eggs beaten up and fry the mixture to the consistency of buttered eggs.

Many other combinations will suggest themselves to the ingenious cook. One such is to steam the young mielies, entirely denuded of their covering leaves, in a little white wine, with herbs and spices; the result is something different from the ordinary 'boiled green mielies' and well worth trying.

Purslane (*porseleinblaar*) that grows profusely in every Cape garden in late winter and spring was, in the old days, and should be today, a favourite vegetable. Its little succulent leaves were gathered, washed and braised with ginger powder, mace, pepper and salt in fat; a tiny spicule of garlic was added, a wineglassful of wine was stirred in, and the result was an amazingly delicate, luscious and sapid purée, that was served with rice and potatoes.

Okra was introduced about the same time as tomatoes and the usual way to serve it was in the Creole fashion. The downy outer covering was scraped off, the pods were thrown into vinegar and water, dried, and then steamed or boiled in water till soft. Then they were drained and braised in a casserole with butter, chillies, a little sugar and salt to taste, and served on or with fried bread.

Sometimes tiny bits of pineapple were incorporated in the braise, which was glutinous rather than succulent.

Sweet potatoes. Three principal kinds were on the market, and all three are still obtainable. The best are the large-sized tubers that 'cut white'; they must be firm and old, woody tubers should never be used. They can be used just like potatoes; a favourite method is to bake them in their skins under the ashes or in the oven. In this form they are the chief food of the poor in country districts. A better way is to stew them.

> *Gestoofde patats* (stewed sweet potatoes). Peel and cut into slices four young, moderately sized tubers; put them in salted water, then take them out and dry them carefully. Place in an iron pot, with a large lump of sheep's tail fat or butter, a cupful of honey (or sugar), some sifted flour, a feathering of cinnamon, a blade of mace, and some salt; pour over a cup of boiling water; let it all simmer very slowly, shaking the pot but not stirring the contents which remain whole.

Stewed sweet potatoes should be translucent, golden with a slightly brownish tinge (topaz-tinted in fact) and exquisitely tender. They are served as a sweet vegetable with roast meat and roast chicken, and hardly ever as a dessert dish.

Rice. This cereal was indisputably the chief vegetable in the old Cape household, and is today still regarded as absolutely indispensable at every well-cooked dinner. The correct way of preparing it was the Indian way, which produced two kinds of boiled rice, one known as 'dry rice' (*droë rys*) and the other as 'wet rice' (*pap rys*). The rice was cleaned (not necessarily always washed, although some cooks rinsed it in several waters till the liquid remained clear; others held that this removed a good deal of goodness from the grains) and thrown into rapidly-boiling water. A little salt was added and the boiling was continued till the grains were soft; the rice was then strained on a colander, which was allowed to remain on top of the pot so that the steam from the water in which the rice had been boiled could rise up and percolate through it. In this way the rice grains swelled and lost enough of their outer moistness, while retaining all their inside sapidity, to become 'dry rice', where each grain was separate, distinct and entirely loose from the other.

If wet rice was desired, the grains were not strained off but were allowed to simmer slowly in the original water till they had absorbed almost all the liquid; the result was a pasty mass, in which each grain adhered to its fellows without, however, having lost its individuality and still retaining its shape.

Wet rice was preferred for some dishes; dry rice for others. It was regarded as distinctly bad taste to serve one kind with a dish that tradition prescribed should be accompanied by the other kind.

Rice was always served as a vegetable; a rice pudding was quite unknown, and the first recipe for it appears late and is obviously taken from a European cookery book — although it has been much modified so that, if its directions are followed, what comes out is not the ordinary insipid and gruel-like sweet of the nursery, but a glorified sweet pilaff of preserved peel, raisins, dates and nuts, cooked in plenty of butter and a rich custard cream.

Rice was also rarely made into sophisticated dishes, though it was much used for soups and was sometimes made into a *bredie*. The recipes for chicken, ham, mutton and fish pilaffs do not greatly differ from those that were familiar to Occidental cooks, except that they all prescribe a variety of spices and prolonged cooking; nearly every one can be paralleled by some particular Italian *risotto*. The most popular of these combined dishes is:

Yellow rice (*geel rys*). Take dry boiled rice; put it in a saucepan with butter, turmeric powder, a small piece of green ginger, a tablespoonful of moist brown sugar, a teaspoonful of salt and a little powdered chilli; add a cupful of stoned raisins; moisten with *bouillon*, and allow to simmer. One old recipe substitutes saffron for the turmeric powder. The rice should be 'wet' when dished up, with all the ingredients well mixed, and it should not be too sweet.

Two other combined rice recipes are:

Quince rice. Mix dry, boiled rice with grated green quinces and some pounded cheese, pepper, salt and a little powdered chilli; put in a greased pie dish; add a little onion juice mixed in a glass of sherry; steam, and serve with a meat sauce.

Rice with penguin eggs. Make a strong meat gravy; mix with a glass of sherry and beat into it a teaspoonful of sour fruit jelly (kei-apple jelly). Let it boil up and pour through a sieve. Put a layer of dry boiled rice in a pie dish, and place on it two hardboiled penguin eggs cut into quarters or slices; fill up with rice; pour over the sauce, bake for a few minutes in the oven, and serve.

vegetables

Tomatoes were a comparatively late introduction, but when the Malay cooks realised how useful they can be they did not hesitate to make *bredie* of them or to use them for mixed dishes. Their wateriness needs to be counteracted by prolonged slow steaming with the lid off the pot, to allow for evaporation. Most of the recipes for their preparation are, with the exception of the *bredie*, not original but copies from printed directives that have been adapted to local taste.

Thus *tamatie blatjang* (tomato chutney-sauce) is merely a variant of tomato purée to which various spices have been added with a fruit purée. A good tomato *bredie* made with fat mutton, spices, herbs and a glass of wine, should be neither watery nor greasy; it needs at least three hours of slow, steady simmering. But when well made it is one of the outstanding *bredies* and should be served with white 'dry' rice, boiled, buttered and nutmegged potatoes and a sweet chutney.

Chapter 10

Veldkos or Food from the Veld

Veldkos may be interpreted in two senses, either as 'food produced by or derived from the veld' or 'food to be eaten on the veld', veld being any uncultivated part of the countryside. In practice only the first interpretation is assigned to the word. In this chapter *veldkos* means edible uncultivated wild foodstuffs that are made eatable according to the old Cape recipes.

The earliest travellers relate how wonderfully prolific in 'herbs and plants' were the flat lands round Table Bay in winter and spring after the early rains. Jacquin, the famous gardener of Schönbrun, writing about a Cape sorrel, noted:

> '*Illam se invenisse anno 1653 in promontorio bonae spei ad pedem montis leonum, ubi magna copia colligebatur et ad naves deferebatur ut cum aliis herbis in olus coqueretur.*'

Before that date, however, ships sailing round the Cape had landed sailors to collect baskets of sorrel which, made into a stew, was regarded as a prophylactic against and a cure for scurvy.

Jan van Riebeeck found fine examples of wild asparagus, 'as good as anything in the homeland', growing on the slopes of Table Mountain. From his time onwards travellers have mentioned various wild plants that were used as foodstuffs by both Colonists and Africans.

Some of them are so rare, so local and little-known that they must be regarded as curiosities with which only a few cooks are acquainted. Others were, and to some extent still are, popular and comparatively easy to procure. The following kinds could all be had in season on the Cape Town market at the end of the past century,[1] when dishes made from them could be readily obtained at one or other of the hotels or boarding houses that specialised in Cape dishes. Today most of them would have to be procured through the intervention of some kindly farmer friend although, as a matter of fact, some of them are to be found within walking distance of Cape Town.

> *Wateruintjies*: The flowers and flower pods of the water hawthorn (*Aponogeton distachyos*) that blooms on waterpools from April to September.

> *Sanduintjies*: The corms of a blue-white Iris (*Moraea edulis*) in season in August to October.

---

1 The nineteenth century.

Geeluintjies: The corms of a yellow-flowered variety of the same species, reputed to be more delicate in flavour.

Bobbejaanuintjies: The bulbs of *Oxalis lupinifolia (Jacq)* or the corms of species of *Babiana* and *Cyanella*, season in winter and spring.

Sorrel: The leaves of the wild sorrel (*Oxalis pes-caprae*), in season from August to October.

Veldkool (wild cabbage): The flower buds of a species of anthericum,[1] often growing as high as five feet, and in season in April and May.

Jakkalskos (fox food): The fruit of a parasite, *Hydnora africana*, in season in the early summer.

Baroe and *kameroe*:[2] The large underground tubers of plants that grow in sandy and clay soil, usually *Cyphia* spp., in season in September to December.

Wild fennel and *wild anise*: The fleshy rootstocks of various plants belonging to the carrot family, in season in summer.[3]

Ghoo: The seeds of the wild almond tree (*Brabejum stellatifolium*).

In addition, there are many kinds of wild berries and fruits and at least one kind of *aloe* that are edible, and whose names figure in old recipes. As most of them are unobtainable on the market, nothing more need be said about them.

Water hawthorn (wateruintjies): This is undoubtedly the most popular of all the edible wild plants, and anyone who travels by road through the country will notice its beautiful white, strongly-scented flowers studding the surface of quiet wayside pools almost hiding the small, lancet-shaped leaves. It has a thick, fleshy bulb which is edible, but is rarely used, the flower buds being much preferred. Bundles of these can still be bought on the Cape Town Parade and sometimes in the streets from itinerant hawkers, four bunches making a *kooksel*, or sufficient for an average dish. The flowers must be fresh, partly opened, with the calyces bright green; if the buds are old and mahogany-coloured, they should be rejected. They will keep fairly well in a cool place for a couple of days. They are prepared as follows:

Stewed. Wash the buds and remove the stalks; put them in a stewpot with a lump of fat or butter, salt, pepper, a little chopped onion, a few thyme leaves and a bay leaf; let them simmer gently, then add a handful of chopped sorrel leaves, and allow to simmer for a little while longer; stir in a glass of sherry and serve.

---

1 *Trachyandra* spp., related to anthericums. See pp 226–230.
2 *Kameroe* was also called *kambro*, usually *Fockea* spp. See pp 309–310.
3 *Vinkelwortel* (fennel root) and *anyswortel* (aniseed root) are common names for *Chamarea* and *Annesorhiza* spp. respectively.

Some cooks always prefer to parboil the buds in a little salt water, throwing away the wine-coloured liquid, but this is not necessary.

Bredie. Braise good fat neck or rib of mutton, cut into suitable pieces, in a pot with some onion slices, a pinch of powdered ginger, a crushed chilli, a blade of mace and some salt and pepper. As soon as the meat is nicely browned, put in the buds, with a handful of sorrel leaves finely minced; let it all simmer for a couple of hours, adding a tablespoonful of wine from time to time, and stirring well. Finally stir in a tablespoonful of a good chutney sauce, and dish up with boiled rice.

With coriander. Proceed as before, omitting the spices; stir in a teaspoonful of crushed coriander seed; finish by stirring in a cupful of boiling cream.

With eggs. Make a purée of stewed buds, and mix it with cream, a pinch of tangerine peel pounded fine, and a teaspoonful of China (soya) sauce; fill small ramikin dishes with the purée, and place on each a newlaid egg; place in the oven till the egg is lightly set; powder with grated nutmeg and serve.

Soufflé. Make a purée of stewed buds and beat it till it is very fine. For each pound of the purée take four eggs; mix the yolks of these in the purée; beat the whites to a stiff froth, and fold in the mixture; bake in a quick oven and serve at once.

One recipe mixes chopped anchovies with the purée.

Baked. Mix a purée of stewed buds with boiled, mealy potatoes, well mashed with some butter and cream; form into cakes or balls and fry in butter or fat. Sprinkle with salt and pepper and serve.

With bananas. Peel and fry the bananas in boiling fat; put them round the sides of a deep pie dish, and fill the dish with a purée of the buds; pour over a couple of egg yolks beaten up in a cup of milk and bake in the oven.

With fish. This is simply any kind of steamed fish served on a bed of the purée and covered with either a sour or a fish sauce. It was usually garnished with peeled hanepoot grapes which had been preserved in brandy, and made an attractive, interesting dish.

As soup. The purée was stirred into a good chicken soup, to which a dash of cream was added; it was served with croutons of fried bread.

Tomatoes and potatoes were sometimes filled with the purée and either stewed or baked in the oven. The purée was also used as a filling for tartlets, as a basis for patties, and as a cold *sambal*. Instead of the usual admixture of sorrel leaves, which were intended to give a tinge of acidity to the dish, lemon juice or tamarind water was often used.

Wild cabbage was dealt with in much the same way, but as it has a less pronounced flavour, it was considered bad cookery to add chillies or too much pepper to it. It needed no preliminary parboiling, and was best prepared as a stew by itself, or as a *bredie* with meat and very little onion. Many epicures prefer it to *wateruintjies* and as a matter of fact its flavour is more delicate than that of any wild plant; while a creamed purée made from it far surpasses that made from spinach, broad beans or turnip tops. All that is required is to simmer it gently with wine, butter, mace and a little salt and pepper; mash it thoroughly when tender, and mix it with cream; then it is replaced on the stove, and allowed to heat quietly, without boiling, and served with dry white rice and boiled potatoes.

It is indeed so excellent that one wonders why no enterprising nurseryman has deemed it worth his while to cultivate the plant and introduce it to the general public as a garden vegetable. In season it grows abundantly on all the hill slopes in certain parts and can be gathered without difficulty, yet one never sees it exposed for sale on the streets and few, outside the country towns, know of its existence.

The bulb *uintjies* need different methods of preparation. In the first place, their collection in the field demands an exact knowledge of the different kinds of iris, for some species have bulbs that are not only not edible but poisonous, and there are some cases on record where children eating them have died. The native collectors, however, are fully aware of the distinctions between the different varieties, and their harvest may be trusted. Although there are several kinds, all the edible *uintjies* are cherry-sized and shaped bulbs, almond-white inside, and covered outside by a fibrous husk which is easily pulled off. They taste somewhat like chestnuts and, when boiled, have the same consistency, can be mashed easily, and blend perfectly with many flavourings. They may be baked under the ashes or in the oven, boiled like ordinary chestnuts, or made into a purée from which different dishes can be prepared.

Normally the bunch of bulbs, tied together by one of the rushlike leaves of the plant itself, is boiled in a little salt water, and served on a dish, each guest helping himself to a few of the bulbs, peeling off the husk, and eating the bulb with a little salt and pepper or melted butter. They are prepared more elaborately as follows:

Soup. The recipe for this has been given already, in the chapter on soups.

Creamed. The boiled bulbs are mashed to a fine purée which is passed through a sieve, mixed with grated nutmeg, salt, a little melted butter, and boiling cream.

Pudding. A creamed purée is made in accordance with the directions in the previous paragraph, and is mixed with honey (or sugar) and yolk of egg. The whites of the eggs are whipped to a stiff froth and incorporated in the mixture, which is steamed in a buttered mould. The pudding is served with a sweet sauce when it is used as a dessert dish, and with a sour sauce when it is dished up as an accompaniment to a roast. It is delightfully bland. As a sweet dish the addition of a few pounded bitter almonds improves it.

Wild sorrel, of which the stalks as well as the leaves are used, is added to *bredies* as a flavouring, souring agent. By itself it is rarely used, for its taste is far too sharp and acid, even when braised or stewed, to make a good purée. The old-fashioned sailors' *moes*, or pottage, was made by stewing wild sorrel with whatever garden herbs were available and a little salt and fat into a thick, pasty brew, to which a little rice flour was usually added. It was eaten with a spoon. It tastes very much like hotel spinach, but is decidedly more aromatic and much more acid.

A somewhat similar concoction of indigenous spinach-like plants is made by the Africans and eaten as a relish with their mieliemeal porridge. It is reputed to be exceedingly vitamin-ish, but that consolation will certainly not debar the good cook from damning it.

Jakkalskos is really the seed capsule of a parasitic plant, with curious, foul-smelling flowers, that grows on the roots of certain indigenous shrubs. In appearance it looks like a small, elongated coconut, with a rough dark-brown rind. Inside are found many tiny seeds embedded in a sweetish, aromatic, yellow pulp. It is usually partly covered with sand, and must be carefully looked for. Animals are fond of it and root up all they can find. It is therefore a rare thing, and also exceedingly local. The pulp is scooped out, beaten up with a glass of sherry and some grated nutmeg and a little honey, and is served as a cold custard.

Baroe and *kameroe* are underground tubers that sometimes attain the size of a football. They are baked under the ashes or in the oven, like sweet potatoes, and eaten with salt and pepper. Boiled, they are starchy, insipid and need a great deal of spicing and flavouring; even then the result is not worth the trouble. They are best made into a preserve, by boiling them in a thin syrup with peach kernels, ginger and a few featherings of cinnamon, when their crispness and faintly-bitter taste can be duly appreciated.

The turgid underground rootstocks of *wild fennel* and *wild anise* can be eaten raw for they are fairly sweet, with a pungent, aromatic flavour. By themselves they make an indifferent dish when boiled or stewed, for their flavour is far too intense and does not seem to be influenced by spicing. They make an excellent preserve which, like that made from *baroe*, is characterised by a delicious crispness, a tinge of acidity, and an agreeable aromatic flavour.

Ghoo is the fruit of the wild almond tree, and in appearance and size resembles a large almond. The husk, and to some extent the kernel also, contains a water-soluble cyanide salt that is decomposed by heat. The fresh ghoo 'bean' is therefore very poisonous; a couple of the raw kernels when eaten have been known to cause death. In practice the husks are removed and the kernels are placed in a sack which is put in running water for a week or more; at the end of the time they are fit for use.

They are roasted like coffee beans, in a pot with a little fat, and are then pounded into a powder, from which a drink like cocoa is made. This is known as *ghoo coffee*, and is an agreeable, refreshing and stimulating drink, especially when prepared with milk. Boiled in water, without previous roasting, the ghoo beans are reputed to be extraordinarily nourishing; it is alleged that when Grey's Pass was under construction, the road gangs lived mainly on ghoo beans and a wine ration and did better work than anywhere else. Such boiled ghoo beans are practically tasteless; to make them palatable, they are mixed with spices and salt, pounded and made into a purée, when their flavour is not unlike that of boiled peanuts.

Little need be said of the indigenous fruits and berries, some of which we will meet again when we deal with sweet dishes. The veld around Cape Town used to provide several species of edible berries that were in demand for sauces and garnishings, but today one must go much farther afield to get them. *Kei-apple*[1] *jelly*, made from the fruit of a plant that is used for hedges, is one of the most attractive-coloured jellies, with a bitter sour taste not unlike a Seville marmalade. *Kaffir plum*[2] *jam* and *stamvrug*[3] *jelly* are much more rarely met with, but are both excellent, each with its strong individual taste.

---

1 *Dovyalis caffra.*
2 *Harpephyllum caffrum.*
3 *Bequaertiodendron magalismontanum.*

Chapter 11

Egg Dishes

In Cape cookery egg dishes are prepared from the eggs of domestic fowls, ducks, peahens, turkeys, geese, ostriches and guinea fowl, and from those of the wild duck, bustard, plover, mollymawk and penguin. While in general the egg recipes are imitations and variants of older European ones, there are some that show interesting modifications.

Early visitors to the Cape — like De la Caille (who had the entrée to fashionable houses and could esteem the refinements of Cape cookery), Kolben (whose taste was of the pothouse variety), and Mentzel (who was much milder in his judgments about food, and who extolled the cleanliness and art of the Chinese eating houses that in his day were to be found in the neighbourhood of the docks) — wrote in praise of the egg cooking that they sampled. One of the earliest, a surgeon returning from India, tells us how in a 'free burgher's' cottage he was treated to 'a shapeless omelette, exquisitely made with crab'. We may take it that what the gentleman so much enjoyed was a 'fish with eggs', of which a recipe has already been given, made with pounded crayfish instead of fish.

I have been unable to trace, in print, the earliest mention of penguin eggs, but there is no doubt that they were used in Van Riebeeck's time. In my youth they were quite common and cheap on the Cape Town market; since they came under bureaucratic control they have become scarce, almost unobtainable, and very expensive.

As a delicacy 'Malagas eggs'[1] were regarded as superior; plovers' eggs, that could sometimes be bought, were not reckoned anything to be proud of; their flavour was said to be inferior to that of a Malagas egg. Wild duck eggs, bustard[2] eggs (*korhaan eiers*) and, very rarely, crane's or heron's eggs could on occasion also be bought at the market. One of my earliest recollections is that of being treated to half a pelican's egg, hard-boiled, by the late Mr Saul Solomon, the locally renowned liberal orator, at his house in Sea Point. As I remember, its flavour was harsher than that of a penguin's egg and its delicacy was not to be compared with that of a Malagas egg.

Turtle and tortoise eggs were also sometimes to be had; the former were always snapped up by the Government House steward, who was said to have a private method of preserving them, probably by packing them in coarse salt in an earthenware jar. Ostrich eggs — at first always from wild

---

1 Gannet eggs.
2 Undoubtedly *korhaan*, not bustard eggs are intended here.

birds, but in the middle of the past century[1] almost exclusively from the domesticated ostriches — were sold for a few pence each, but were regarded as coarse.

Fowls eggs, always easily obtainable, were sometimes as cheap as four pennies a dozen, and their cheapness no doubt encouraged the cooks to experiment in many ways to improve them for the table. There were already hundreds of recipes; no one has attempted to count how many different ways there are of dealing with eggs, but at a guess there must be more than half a thousand; and among so many directives it is inevitable that there should be a certain amount of overlapping.

Boiled eggs. My old preceptress, who emphasised her injunctions with good-natured taps of her wooden spoon on my head, insisted that penguin eggs should be boiled in sea water, steadily for 15 minutes. That produced a clear, transparent jelly surrounding an opalescent green yolk that crumbled readily to fine primrose-yellow flaky fragments, for nobody ever ate them soft-boiled.

Fowl eggs, for soft boiling, were put into cold water which was brought to the boil, when the eggs were taken out; if they were wanted hard-boiled, the ebullition was allowed to proceed for three or more minutes. If you wanted a crumbly yolk, that could be made almost into a powder, you boiled the egg for half an hour; then, according to the Ayah, you could preserve the eggs for several weeks by merely storing them in a jar of slightly salted water.

Among her favourite breakfast dishes were the following:

Orange eggs. Select a large, not too ripe, seedling orange (she invariably chose the Clanwilliam variety, which has a very thin skin and is grandly juicy), cut it in half, remove the pips, and scoop out a little of the pulp; sprinkle with salt, break into each half a newly-laid egg, dust with salt and pepper, and bake in the oven till the egg is nicely set.

She varied this by using avocado pears, large tomatoes, small squashes, baked potatoes, even small melons first sprinkled with grated nutmeg, salt and a few drops of rum.

More elaborately, she made:

Eggs on bacon. Chop up fat bacon; braise it with some chillies, a teaspoonful of chutney, minced onion and powdered ginger. Put it in a buttered shell (she used a small pearl mussel shell, which makes a good ramekin mould), break an egg on it, dust with salt and pepper, and bake till set.

Crayfish egg. Pound some of the soft, greenish-white flesh found adhering

---

1 The nineteenth century.

to the inner part of the carapace of a boiled crayfish with some salt, ginger powder, boiled egg yolk and some of the coral. Put in a small buttered pan; break an egg on it, and stand it in a vessel of boiling water till the egg is lightly set; dust with nutmeg and serve.

For a foundation she sometimes used finely-shredded fried snoek, pounded *bokkom* braised in a little butter with a few shreds of onion and a suspicion of garlic, or simply breadcrumbs soaked in a rich gravy and, to add piquancy, she sometimes mixed these combinations with a little curry sauce. Her generic name for these various very tasty dishes was *eiers met iets onder* (eggs with something underneath).

Similarly, she was fertile in her expedients to sophisticate her plain hard-boiled eggs. She halved and curried them, allowing them to simmer gently for a few minutes in a rich curry sauce, and serving them up with plain boiled dry rice. She took out the yolks, pounded them with spices, bits of fried fish, crayfish coral, or minced herbs, onion and lemon juice, replacing them neatly within the severed white and serving them with a sour sauce.

With ostrich eggs, an expert cook can have a positive holiday. The first thing to be done is to get at the contents of the shell. One makes a hole at the top end, and by gently shaking the shell the fluid white and yolk may be persuaded to run into a basin; it is almost impossible, by ordinary methods, to separate the white from the yellow. For that reason the most popular way of serving an ostrich egg — which by itself is the equal of more than a dozen hen's eggs — is to whip what comes down into the basin, and to cook it as:

Volstruiseierstruif (scrambled ostrich egg). Mix the whipped egg with a little minced onion, salt and pepper; melt a large lump of butter or fat in a pan; when it begins to brown, stir in the eggs, continue stirring till it is set; serve piled on a dish well dusted with salt and pepper.

This gives a rather watery, almost pasty result which it seems impossible to correct except by allowing the egg, before it is whipped, to stand in a cool place overnight and, before using it, to separate the top portion and scramble what remains. Even then, and even by using plenty of butter, it is not easy to get the rich flakiness of buttered eggs. The scrambled egg may be much improved by the addition of grated cheese. At a pinch one can make a heavy omelette with ostrich egg, but its taste and flavour are inferior to anything made from hen's eggs.

The best use for ostrich egg is as an egg substitute in baked cakes and puddings, where its coarse flavour is moderately well disguised. Old cooks used to boil the whole egg, for half an hour or more, till it was well set. It was then shelled, cut into slices, and used to decorate vegetable salads. In the early printed cookery books (not in any of my manuscripts) may be found a curious recipe for preparing an *imitation ostrich egg*, by covering an

egg dishes

orange-sized ball of pounded and cooked chicken meat, boiled egg yolk, spices and saffron, with a thick layer of a paste made with a white sauce and rice powder and steaming it in a round mould.

Penguin eggs are best served plainly hard-boiled in their shells. At table they are shelled, mashed up with a fork (that nearly always gets discoloured in the process), mixed with salt and pepper and a few drops of vinegar or lemon juice, and eaten with bread and butter. They may be made into scrambled or buttered eggs, served with a curry sauce, creamed, combined with anchovies or flaked fried fish, or covered with a cheese sauce. None of these can compare with the simple hard-boiled egg, which has always been considered a delicacy, although some people consider it overrated.

Gulls' and mollymawks'[1] *eggs* are by some connoisseurs more highly prized than penguin eggs. They should be simply boiled and eaten with a little salt, pepper and vinegar.

---

1 Mollymawk is an old word for a fulmar or petrel; Leipoldt probably means an albatross (Afrikaans = *malmok*), however.

Chapter 12

Game and Camp Cookery

When one considers the fact that the first settlers found South Africa teeming with game, it is surprising that the development of game cookery proceeded comparatively slowly. The manuscript recipes show no important modifications from the already known directives for the preparation of the flesh of wild animals that appeared in the printed cookbooks of the seventeenth century. The reason for this is probably the scarcity of game in the East with, as a consequence, the neglect of Malay cooks to deal with foodstuffs that were new to them. It may also be on account of the relative scarcity of game at the Settlement itself.

During the first 50 years game was undoubtedly plentiful in the environs of Cape Town, but it soon became so scarce that the prices in the open market were increased beyond the capacity of the pockets of most of the burghers. Mentzel, much later, records that the four huntsmen, who were the only people allowed to shoot game, could hardly get enough to satisfy the requirements of the Governor's household. While this is undoubtedly an exaggeration, and while a great deal of poaching must have occurred, it is clear that game was not a common foodstuff in poor or middle-class homes. It was prepared for the table in accordance with the recipes derived from Europe, and there are very few modifications of these that show a decided Oriental or local influence.

There has existed, however, from very early times what may be called an oral traditional repository of directions for cooking game that was preserved, augmented and improved by all those who were in a position where such game supplied their daily needs. These guardians were the hunters. First those who went out in small parties, camped on the veld for a few nights, and returned to the Settlement and, later on, those who adventured, with or without their families, far beyond the limits of civilisation. The methods that they used were rough and ready, but were influenced by age-old principles of gypsy cookery, probably imported by servants of the Company who had experience of improvised camp-cooking in the south of Europe where the Romany way of broiling under ashes and cooking in a covering of clay was still adhered to.

Much of it was forgotten in the Cape Colony, but it was remembered by those who went beyond the Vaal River and today it exists, in a modified form, in the Transvaal, where it is actively honoured by all those who have the leisure and inclination to indulge in that delightful avocation, camping in the Bushveld.

A glance through the old European cookery books shows at once that many of their recipes for game dishes are useless in South Africa simply because we have not got the necessary ingredients. We have no pheasants (ours are all partridges), no ortolans, ptarmigans, rabbits (except at Robben Island, whence one seldom gets an eatable one); and we disdain to use, except in our early, nursery years, sparrows and suchlike small fry. On the other hand, we have a number of excellent game animals and of others that, although they are not classed as game, are not only eatable but very good eating indeed, of whose existence the old Italian cooks had no knowledge. We have no chance of eating swans, but we have the flamingo, whose flesh is incomparably superior; our quails are in season extraordinarily fat and succulent; our snipe, ground partridges, and go-away birds vie with any ortolan or golden plover in Europe. We have a variety of wild buck, among which the eland, springbok, duiker and steenbok give us venison that is superior in quality to anything that Europe can produce.

So great is the variety of our wild animals that the cook in dealing with their flesh will find ample opportunity to exercise his ingenuity, to improvise where necessary, and to modify the old recipes in conformity to modern taste.

It is perhaps better to deal with each variety separately, but before doing so it is desirable to say a few words about the general methods used in South African camp cookery.

No camping outfit is considered complete without the stewpot, which is a round iron receptacle, with a well-fitting lid, standing on three spiked feet, which is known as the *drievoetpot* or tripod pot. Its capacity varies from a gallon to three or more, and it is usually swung, with the iron kettle, under the ox-wagon, though today it goes into the baggage compartment of the car. A frying pan and a gridiron are also required. The range and variety of equipment will, of course, depend on the size of the camping party and the particular whimsies of individual shots or cooks, but the four utensils mentioned are essential.

The iron pot is used for stewing, boiling and simmering; the pan for shallow frying, for pancakes, and for making special sauces; the gridiron for grilling; the kettle is solely for boiling water for coffee or tea.

Milk is almost never boiled in camp; indeed it is rarely used, except when it can be obtained locally, for condensed or dried milk serves equally well. Water sometimes has to be filtered before it can be used; green vegetables are scarce, but spices and dried herbs are brought with the groceries, and the camp cook generally has no need to stint himself; he can even get excellent flavourings by walking a few yards out of camp and picking the leaves of wild plants. Usually an oven is made by scooping a hole in an ant-hill, which is heated by burning wood inside; the loaves are placed in it as in an ordinary oven and the entrance is closed. Damper[1] is made in the usual way and either grilled on the gridiron or baked under the ashes.

---

1 Unleavened bread.

We may now proceed to consider the several varieties of wild animals that may require the cook's attention.

Pigeons. The large rock pigeon and the two kinds of green pigeon are the only ones generally used, though the ordinary turtle dove, the rameron and the speckled dove are also good eating. The green pigeon, especially in the summer when it has fed on wild figs, is tender, aromatic and fat; it needs no larding. In camp it is stewed, cooked with other game as a ragout, or grilled. The old recipes for pigeons include the following:

Pigeons with crayfish. Salt and pepper the carcase inside and out and stuff with pounded crayfish mixed with ginger, mace, marjoram, pepper and salt; if you like, you may add a little pounded chilli; stew gently in white wine, keeping the pot closely covered. Serve with wet rice.

Stuffed pigeons. Remove the backbone and breastbone; carefully remove as much meat from the bird as you can get out without breaking the skin; pound this in a mortar with a little marrow or suet, lemon peel, parsley, breadcrumbs and a little cream; add the yolk of an egg and a few shreds of anchovy. Fill the skin of the pigeon with this, and sew it up; place in a pot with some sliced onion, a little fat pork and a cupful of wine, and simmer gently, without allowing it to brown. Place on a dish, thicken the sauce with a glass of sherry and some arrowroot, pour over and serve with wet rice.

Pigeon stew (camp style). Cut the pigeons into quarters and put in the pot with any herbs or spices you may have, adding fat and chopped pork or game fat. Let it slowly simmer with the lid on, till tender; then add salt and pepper, a cupful of wine, or water if you have no wine, and let it simmer gently for several hours.

It is better when the pigeons are married, in the pot, to some other game, bird or mammal. At home the dish is finished by adding boiling cream, thickening the sauce, and stirring in breadcrumbs.

Quails: Deal with them as you would with pigeons. Or stuff them with any of the fillings mentioned in the chapter on meat; wrap them in fig or vine leaves, and stew them slowly in white wine. They are usually fat enough when in season to be cooked without larding or a wrapper of bacon.

Snipe and small game birds are treated in the same way, but the old Malay cooks eviscerated them only when they wished to stuff them; ordinarily they were not drawn, but enclosed in a mantle of fat pork and gently simmered with spices and herbs, and finished off with a dash of sherry. The small plovers are excellent when done in this manner.

Bustards: These range from the royal *gom pou* (*Otis kori*) that weighs as much as 60 pounds, to the various species of *korhaans* and *dikkops* averaging a few pounds in weight when drawn and cleaned. They are cooked exactly like a Muscovy duck — that is, stuffed with some kind of filling, covered with fat pork and pot-roasted or stewed. In camp they are camp-stewed by themselves or with other birds or game. They are excellent eating, and usually require no larding, but as they are protected game, one rarely has a chance to taste them.

Flamingo, too, is 'royal game', and cannot be shot. Formerly it was obtainable, though not easily, and I have eaten it on several occasions, and personally approved the two following recipes:

Flamingo supreme (flaminkbors). Remove the breast meat; cut it into neat strips; beat each with a wooden mallet; roll in pepper and salt; place in red wine and let them lie for a couple of hours. Take out, wipe dry, and place in a pot with diced pork fat, a blade of mace, a lemon leaf, a sprig of thyme, and a few peppercorns and cardamons; add a few spoonsful of wine, and let it stew gently with the lid on. Take out and place on your serving dish; thicken the gravy with flour, stir in a glass of brandy or sweet wine and a tablespoonful of lemon juice; pour over and serve.

Stuffed breast of flamingo. Carefully remove the flesh from both sides of the breastbone, and place it in red wine for a couple of hours; wipe dry and rub in pepper and salt and a little pounded chilli. Take a fairly coherent farce; mould it to fit the inside of the two breast pieces; wrap them round the farce and skewer with wooden pegs or bind with string. Put in a saucepan with a few cups of red wine, a bit of lemon peel or scented verbena, a few cloves and a handful of small onions. Let it simmer gently till tender; thicken the gravy with a white sauce and serve.

Flamingo flesh is equally good when simply shallow-fried in a little fat with pepper and salt. It is, of all bird flesh, perhaps the most tender, tasty and delicately flavoured, possibly because the bird feeds on an aquatic, plankton diet that imparts to its meat an extraordinarily savoury quality. An early Cape traveller maintained that soup made from it was claret-coloured, but this is a mistake; the flesh is dark, like that of a duck, but contains no pigment of any kind; when grilled, it is practically indistinguishable from beef as far as colour is concerned, but its tenderness is far superior and it seldom needs larding.

Herons and *cranes* are still sometimes sold by the butchers. They are prepared for the table like ducks, and are good eating, although they need larding and prolonged stewing, in *bouillon* or wine. The blue crane is considered the best; its flesh is dark, aromatic and delicate; its liver, broiled, is a delicious titbit, comparable to that of the Muscovy duck.

Wild duck, waterfowl. Of these there are several varieties, none of which is equal to the domestic species, and some of which have a pronounced oily, almost rank taste. Recipes for their preparation follow the oldest one in the cookery books, and no modification that is known to me is of practical importance.

Partridges. There are several kinds, ranging from the larger ones, equal in size to a domestic fowl, to the small *swempie* that weighs a few ounces, but is perhaps the best eating of all. From a gastronomic point of view their excellence varies considerably; sometimes one gets a partridge that is everything one can wish it to be; the next day one may have another of the same kind, prepared in exactly the same way, that is tasteless and insipid. The difference probably depends on the diet of the bird. One gets partridges that have a distinct aromatic flavour, sometimes very strong, reminiscent of mint or sage, and it is likely that these birds have fed on wild plants. At home all partridges need larding or at least swathing in bacon or fat pork, and can be prepared in accordance with the many recipes in the books.

The old manuscripts give the following directions for making:

Hunter's bredie. Take cleaned and drawn partridge, and a couple or more cleaned pigeons or any other wild fowl. Wipe them well, and rub inside and outside with pepper and salt. Put them in an iron pot, and lay on them strips of fat pork; add a few spoonfuls of fat, put the lid on, and let it stew slowly and gently; you may put some hot coals on the lid, and from time to time you must stir the contents, but you must not add water. Take care that it does not burn. Simmer it till the flesh falls off the bones, and serve in the pot.

That is the camp way. At home, one would add mace, coriander seeds, a shred of chilli and perhaps a few herb leaves. The result in both cases should be a whitish-grey, slightly pasty but exceedingly succulent stew. The method of making it is known as *rafeltjieskook* or 'stewing to shreds', and is excellent for partridges, hares and smaller buck.

Kwê-bird or *go-away-bird*[1] is a subtropical lourie of an ash-grey colour with a crest that it can raise or depress at will. In summer when it feeds on the highly aromatic Bushveld berries its flesh, which when stewed is as tender as marrow, is beautifully aromatic. As it is a comparatively small bird, half a dozen of its supremes or breast fillets are required to make a satisfactory dish. They are best simply stewed in fat, need neither larding nor spicing, and are just as good when they are grilled. Only private enterprise will obtain them.

Hare. The recipes for this animal's appearance on the dinner table are obviously cribbed from European textbooks; the main modification when stewing it is to do so without adding a drop of water as in the hunter's stew. This yields a fragrant, succulent and tasty dish, which is always served with wet rice and something sweet to accompany it. Another modification is that of the old-fashioned Dutch ragout known as *hasepeper*, in which the animal is cut up, stewed in wine, with herbs and spices, to which, when the stewing is nearly done, a cupful of its blood is added, beaten up with some vinegar or

1 The grey lourie.

tamarind juice. The gravy is allowed to simmer for a little while longer, and small dumplings of forcemeat or of the hare's liver are added; finally a little arrowroot is stirred in, and the ragout is served with wet rice.

In passing it may be mentioned that game was considered unfit for cooking if it was 'high'; it was allowed to hang for a few days, but in general cooks preferred to deal with it when it was moderately fresh, and some used it as soon as it was killed. To prevent tainting, it was salted and wind-dried. The old recipes give directions for 'removing any smell from game bought at the market'. This was not always successful, for Mentzel complains that some of the venison he tasted was not as fresh as it might have been. Nowadays moderately high game is not objected to, although something less odoriferous is usually preferred.

Wild buck. There are so many varieties that one can merely give a paragraph to some of the more easily obtainable ones. The manner of serving them is practically the same in all cases. In camp the meat, by itself or with the addition of wild birds or other meat, is put in the stewpot, with pepper, salt and plenty of fat, and allowed to simmer for many hours, practically for the whole day. The result is a perfect pot-roast, if the meat has been allowed to cook by itself, or a fragrant stew if it is a mixture. Sometimes potatoes or other vegetables are added a couple of hours before the meat is served. At home a grander ritual is followed.

Leg of game. Wash and dry it; lard it well with pork fat cut into narrow strips; rub in with salt, pepper, crushed coriander seed, brown sugar and a little chilli. Put the meat in vinegar to which you have added a cup of red wine; let it lie there for three days, turning it each day; if you like you may add to the marinade a couple of crushed bay or lemon leaves. On the fourth day take out, wipe and dry; dust with fine flour; put in a pan with plenty of fat, and let it roast; baste frequently with the butter and, when it begins to brown, baste with the marinade. When tender, take out, brush egg white over and place in the oven; boil the gravy and add to it a glass of sweet wine, pepper, salt and grated nutmeg, boil up, thicken with roux and serve with the roast.

With this one served wet rice, sweet potatoes and usually a salad. Some, however, served stewed fruit with it.

Fillets of game. Cut neat, regularly-shaped fillets from the neck or back portion of the buck (the best is from the muscles that lie along the spinal column), rub in salt, pepper and a little sifted flour; simmer in fat with a pinch of powdered ginger; make a good gravy sauce, and add to it lemon juice, chilli, a little sweet red wine and enough rice flour to thicken it. Dip the stewed fillets in lemon juice and powder them with pepper and salt; put them in a shallow dish; pour over the boiling gravy sauce and serve.

The largest of the antelopes in South Africa is the *eland*. Its flesh, especially the hump, is savoury and tender, and needs no larding. It is usually pot-roasted, but can be prepared in all the various ways that are used for beef.

The next largest antelopes are the *kudu* and the *hartebeest* whose flesh is far inferior to that of the eland although, when properly prepared, kudu steak and fillet, well larded, are tasty enough. Of the other antelopes, the larger *wildebeest* or *gnu* is the most common; its meat is tasteless and stringy, but its tongue, liver, brains and kidneys are considered delicacies. *Reedbuck* or *impala, springbok, blesbuck* and the smaller *steen, grys* and *ribbok* are much better; their meat is generally tender, faintly aromatic and, although they all need larding, their venison is excellent. It is largely used to make biltong, being slightly salted, cut into narrow strips and dried in the open air. The legs and shoulders of the smaller kinds are immersed in salt-saltpetre-spice marinade, and are then sun-dried as *wildsboutjies*, the meat becoming less dry than true game biltong, so that it can be cut into thin slices which are eaten like beef biltong. Today venison, usually springbok or blesbuck, can be obtained out of season from cold-storage depots, but is never so good as when obtained in camp.

Hippopotamus meat was formerly obtainable at the Cape Town market. At the earliest public market it was sold at two pence a pound. Today it is to be obtained only beyond the borders of our country, and there are few people who have tasted it. It has a peculiar flavour, intermediate between that of pork and beef, a slightly pasty consistency from its superfluity of fat between the muscle fibres, and a tough fascial layer over the soft parts that must be removed before it can be cooked. The breast and back muscles are reputed to be the best and choicest bits; they are pot-roasted with spices and herbs and are regarded as the greatest delicacies that the hunter can provide. Even when cooked in this way, the meat is apt to be greasy; it certainly needs the addition of wine or vinegar to improve it.

Giraffe meat is coarse and stringy, but parts of it are excellent, and the long, succulent tongue, properly cooked, is not only eatable but delectable. The expectant cook will be much disappointed to learn that the animal's well-developed bones are quite useless for marrow bones; with every care, all that results when such a bone is boiled or baked is a mess of yellow, unappetising oil that cannot be coaxed to a consistency that will enable it to adjust itself to a piece of toast.

Zebra flesh, on the other hand, I should without hesitation deem the tenderest, most savoury, and best flavoured of all game meat, especially when the animal is young. A zebra fillet, portioned into tournedos, is incomparably the finest meat that is obtainable in a Bushveld camp. It needs no preliminary marinading and is perhaps better without any sophistication. All that is necessary is to cut it into suitable pieces, pepper and salt it after, perhaps, rubbing it all over with the aromatic leaves of some veld shrub like *blinkblaar*,[1] and frying it in its own fat (which is of a deep chrome yellow colour) and serving it with its gravy thickened with a little flour and sherry.

Its succulent tenderness and its delicious flavour are a revelation to those who have never tried it, and it is astonishing that there still remains a prejudice against eating it. There is no reason whatever for this absurd distaste, for the animal is a clean grass feeder, is generally in prime condition when shot, and has no smell of any kind.

Among the earliest manuscript recipes for preparing wild animals for the table is one that gives directions for cooking:

> *Porcupine crackling.* Plunge the animal, as you would a sucking pig, into boiling water; scrape off the pens and the hairs; scrub the skin till it is perfectly smooth and white. Now skin the animal and discard the meat, which is not very nice to eat. Put the skin in a jar in salt water to which you have added a little vinegar, and let it lie in it overnight. Take it out the next day, dry it, rub it with a clove of garlic and put it in a saucepan with a little boiling water. Boil till it is tender enough to allow a fork to pierce it easily. Take it out and cut it up into pieces about the size of flattened apricots (about two inches square) which you may either grill or fry in a pan with a little fat. Put on the pieces some pepper and salt and send to table with plenty of rice, and lemons cut in halves.

This out-of-the-way dish would have delighted Elia, for its sapid crispness far exceeds that of ordinary pork crackling.

> *Roast leguan.* Take only the white flesh; cut it into thick strips, which you must powder with salt and chillies, and then put into a pan with some fat, a few coriander seeds, parsley leaves and a teaspoonful of chutney sauce. Put the lid on and simmer slowly till the meat is tender. Add a teaspoonful of China (soya) sauce and let it simmer for a few minutes more. Arrange the meat on a dish; thicken the sauce with a little roux, pour over and serve.

Leguans used to be obtainable on the Pretoria market, where there was a good demand for them from Chinese customers. Their meat is excellent when done in this way, without the slightest trace of any rankness or objectionable flavour, rather like chicken meat though of a more robust quality.

Elephant meat. This, too, the ordinary diner will not get a chance of sampling. On safari most of it is given to the camp followers. The foot, baked in an improvised oven or under the ashes, is regarded by many as a delicacy, but actually it has little to commend it, though a competent cook could no doubt make it into a palatable dish. The average man will probably much prefer sheep's trotters prepared in one of the conventional ways.

---

1 *Zizyphus mucronata.*

game and camp cookery

Python. Several kinds of snakes are eaten, not usually, however, by Europeans. The flesh of the python is tender, savoury and like that of a well-fed pig, but is generally so fat that it needs preliminary broiling, to separate from it some of its oily extravagance. It can then be roasted in a pot in the ordinary manner.

Selous, and other hunters, state that *lion meat* is as palatable as that of buck and on several occasions, in Bushveld camps, I have confirmed this opinion by preparing the meat in various ways. It is best fried as steaks, after marinading in wine and vinegar. When stewed it is apt to be insipid, though it is rarely stringy or tough. It makes excellent biltong of a delicate pinkish colour which, when grated, is hardly to be distinguished from buck biltong. The prejudice against using it is, however, so inveterate that the carcase of a lion or lioness, when the skin has been taken off, is either handed to the Natives, who regard particular parts of it as tit-bits, or boiled to extract the fat for soap-making.

There are several recipes for dealing with tortoises. These animals are still common in Bushmanland and the Bushveld, and some species yield several pounds of good meat, which must be extracted by chopping open the shell or, preferably, after boiling the animal rapidly until the shell falls to pieces.

Stewed tortoise. Take out the flesh carefully, taking care not to break the gall bladder. Separate it from the bones and gristly parts, and cut it up into neat pieces. Place them in the pot, with a little fat, a tablespoonful of sifted flour, salt, pepper and such herbs as are available, and allow to simmer gently, till tender. Thicken the gravy with breadcrumbs; add a wineglass of wine and serve.

At home, powdered ginger, a pinch of chilli, and a few tablespoonsful of a good stock are added, and the meat allowed to stew. Then a large tablespoonful of lemon juice is stirred in, and the stewing is continued for another 15 minutes. The meat is taken out, arranged on a dish, and the gravy, to which a cup of boiling cream has been added, is poured over it. It is generally eaten with wet rice and some sweet dish, either stewed fruit or sweet potatoes.

Tortoise in jelly. A rich jelly is made with seaweed boiled in a strong *bouillon*; a greased mould is coated with this, and sliced hard-boiled eggs are set in the coating when it is nearly stiff. Then follows a layer of braised tortoise meat, with pepper and salt, and preserved, pickled gherkins, sliced length-wise. The remainder of the jelly is poured over and the mould is put in a cool place till the contents are firm. It is then turned out on a layer of lettuce leaves, garnished with young radishes and carrots, and served with a sour sauce.

Tortoise in its shell. The meat is taken out carefully and cut into small pieces, which are braised in fat with a little onion, a clove of garlic, a crushed chilli and some salt. The shell is carefully cleaned, its inside rubbed with fat, and it is filled with the braised meat, mixed with bread crumbs steeped in milk, and a cup of orange juice. It is put in the oven and baked and served with rice and chutney.

Creamed tortoise. The meat is carefully cut up into comparatively small pieces, all the gristle being rejected. It is then simmered in white wine, with a little white pepper, powdered ginger and a blade of mace. When tender, salt is added, and a cup of boiling cream, which is allowed to thicken before the dish is served. Some cooks add a handful of white crumbs pressed out in milk.

Wild pig. The warthog and the bushpig are plentiful in certain parts of the Bushveld, and their meat is appreciated by both Europeans and Africans. It differs so much from pork in its flavour and texture that those who taste it for the first time will probably be unaware that they are eating pig's meat. All the recipes that apply to pork can be used for warthog and bushpig meat.

There remain some odd dishes, whose recipes cannot be found in old manuscripts but are enshrined in oral tradition. Every good cook knows about them for, as a master of the craft has expressed it, 'some of the tastiest concoctions cannot be served at an ordinary dinner, just as some of a juggler's best tricks cannot be shown before a large audience'. Here are a few for whose excellence I can vouch:

Baked ox head. An ox head, neatly trimmed so that it can stand upright on the neck part, is washed and scrubbed without removing any hair. Particular attention should be given, in this cleansing process, to the nostrils, ears and eyelids. The horns should not be removed. The whole head is placed in a large bread oven, and left there to bake for a day and a night. It is then allowed to get cold and replaced in the oven where it undergoes a further prolonged baking. When it is tender, it is taken out, put upright on a large salver and served just as it comes from the oven. The carver cuts through and reflects the skin from the forehead and cheeks, and serves to each guest some part of the underlying fat, a bit of the tongue, palate, or whatever is fancied.

One's first emotion, on seeing this immense and horrific roast — in which, if the head happens to be that of an Afrikaner ox, the horns appear to stretch the whole length of the dining table, while the baked eyes stare with an expression that is ludicrous as well as baleful, and the lips are drawn back to show the teeth in a sort of snarl that no living ox ever shows — is one of profound shock. Indeed, on the first occasion when I assisted, as General Botha's guest, at a party where this gruesome dish was the main and only item on the bill of fare, two of my fellow gourmets were so overcome that they had to leave the table.

Yet barbecued in this fashion, the fleshy parts of the head are exquisitely tender, as sapid as the meat of a young partridge, with a flavour that no beef can excel. As absolutely no condiments have been used in preparing the meat, each guest salts and peppers his portion at table according to his own taste. One is supposed to eat it with 'wet' rice, but any vegetable goes well with it and, personally, I have found it delicious when eaten with a plain salad.

It is, of course, a dish that cannot be ordinarily presented and there is no reason why it should not be made more attractive, if less imposing, by cutting off the horns, sewing up the eyelids and lips, and removing the hair before it is baked, but tradition insists that the way described is the only right way in which it should be cooked, served and eaten. And once one has tasted it, the memory of its surpassing succulence remains with one, just as the recollection of the bouquet, aroma and savour of an exquisite wine lingers through the years, stimulating the longing for a repetition of so perfect an experience in degustation.

From the sublime to the ridiculous one steps when, after tasting this delicious monstrosity, one is invited to eat:

Fried locusts. Nip off their wings, heads and legs, after you have plunged them into boiling water mercifully to kill them. What remains are the thorax and abdomen, which are the only parts that interest the epicure. You dust them with a mixture of pepper and salt (to which, for some absurd reason that I have never been able to understand, some people add a little powdered cinnamon) and shallow-fry them in fat till they are crisp and brown. They taste not unlike whitebait that, somehow, has been stuffed with buttered toast.

Less unconformable are some of the more common dishes that one tastes in camp. Made at home they would be finished off in the usual way skilled cooks perfect their concoctions — just that inimitable turn that converts the ordinary into the best, but made in the traditional fashion, with the means that are available, cooked by the slow, prolonged, cumulative application of heat, and eaten when one's appetite has been sharpened by a day's exercise in the open air, they are hard to surpass. The essence of their goodness lies in the slowness with which they have been cooked; any hurry in their preparation ends in something which it is hardly worthwhile to eat, except for the sordid purpose of satisfying hunger.

Camp soup. The large thigh bones of some of the bigger buck, containing marrow and having still on them some scraps of meat, are cut in half and placed in a large pot, which is filled with cold water. To them are added pieces of game, a generous portion of salt fat pork, a few handfuls of dried beans, peas and any vegetables that are to be had, such as carrots, potatoes and onions, and finally a handful of coarse salt. The lid is placed on the pot, which is then stood over the fire, where it is allowed to boil gently the whole day long. It is frequently stirred, and some pepper and whatever condiments — sometimes a few tablespoonsful of some bottled sauce — are available are added. In the evening the pot is placed where it can be heated by the camp fire. Its contents are now of the consistency of a well-made Italian *minestra*, but as a soup it is infinitely superior, though perhaps too rich, in a proud, even aggressive way, for in it float large lumps of marrow and over it half an inch of oil. Part of the supernatant oil is skimmed off; the rest is stirred into the potage when each member of the party dips into it with the ladle to fill his soup plate or pannikin and to select scraps of meat for individual consumption.

This soup, which is something more than a soup and not quite a stew, is so luscious and filling that when eaten with a piece of bread or damper, one needs little after it. Its ingredients have been so well blended that the liquid portion (sometimes so strong that if strained and set aside it jellies into a delicious *bouillon*) is a fragrant, well-flavoured rich thick soup, while the solid constituents are thoroughly impregnated with its savouriness. There is usually enough boiled marrow floating in the soup for each guest to get a fair share of it, and generally so much meat that the greater part of it returns to the camp kitchen to be consumed by the Native cook and his retinue.

Camp sausage. Meat left over from the biltong-making is passed through the mincing machine (in the old days it was pounded in a wooden mortar). Several varieties of game meat mixed make the best sausage-meat, to which must be added pork or game fat cut into dice, salt, plenty of pepper and such spices as can be obtained or have been brought for the purpose. The sausage-meat is kneaded with some vinegar and stuffed into the cleaned skins (entrails) which are then hung up for a few days. It may be dried again, to be eaten raw if desired, but more usually it is fried when still wet. The dried sausage will keep for months and, if soaked in a little salt water, can be used for frying or boiling.

Such game sausage is full-flavoured, and when it is to be fried it should be well-pricked; the bits of diced fat within it give it enough lubricant for grilling on the gridiron. It is excellent when simply fried in the pan, but is not so good when boiled.

Some campers still make the old-fashioned *blood sausage* with game blood mixed with breadcrumbs, minced meat, diced pork, salt and pepper. This, too, will keep, but is best used freshly made, when it is sliced and fried with fat in a pan.

Brain cakes. The brains of the buck are extracted, parboiled, mixed with a little minced onion, salt and pepper, and baked in a pan with a little fat. Or they are shaped into thicker cakes and rolled in flour and then fried.

Another way to do them is to dip them in a fairly thick batter, and fry them in fat.

Partridge in clay. Let the partridge be freshly killed and do not draw or pluck it. (Game birds are never allowed to hang till they are high, although they are generally plucked and drawn immediately they are brought to camp because they are sometimes not cooked for a couple of days; if the weather is cool, that does not taint them.) Cut off its legs just below the feathered part, and its head at the top of the neck. Coat the bird with a thick layer of clay that you have made into a dough, so that it is wholly covered. Place it on hot coals and shovel coals and ashes over it, replenishing them when they are no longer hot. When the clay has become hard and baked, rake out the bird and let the clay get cold. Then crack it with a stone, take out the partridge, and serve.

Most folk prefer to draw the bird before cooking it, but the undrawn bird is certainly more savoury. If the clay has been red hot, the feathers and part of the skin of the bird will stick to the fragments; the bird itself is cooked to a turn, and magnificently tender and savoury; all it needs is a little salt and pepper.

Other wild animals can be cooked in the same way, which is really an old Romany method of cooking. Apart from this we have no proper barbecueing ways of preparing food, though the old fashion, followed by Apicius, of baking foodstuffs under the hot ashes of a wood fire, is conveniently honoured in camp. As has already been mentioned, the ubiquitous ant-heap provides an admirable camp oven, in which practically anything can be baked, either in a pan or wrapped in fig or pawpaw leaves.

Whale flesh was, and still is, a common article of food and is a most nourishing meat. So, too, is the flesh of the *walrus* and the *seal*, both of which could still be obtained at the end of the past century[1] at the Cape Town fish market. All these are coarse-grained, generally with much fat between the muscle fibres, and with an oily taste that is, however, effectually eliminated by proper preliminary marinading, and adequate spicing when pot-roasted. A whale or walrus steak, grilled, is quite tender, tasty and eatable, but it is coarse compared with a good game or buck steak. Made into a stew, the way in which the old fishermen preferred it, with potatoes and cabbage, it is better. All three meats produce, when boiled, a very savoury and exceedingly nourishing broth, but it must be most carefully skimmed and flavoured, for its taste is not to everyone's liking.

1 The nineteenth century.

Chapter 13

Fruits and Sweet Dishes

The modern cook would find it difficult to make most of his sweet dishes if he were deprived of sugar and had to find an adequate substitute for it. Yet that was the difficulty that, 400 years ago, the old cooks successfully overcame. They had no sugar, but they used honey and the concentrated juice of sweet fruits, or the fruits themselves, to achieve results that we now would regard as unobtainable in the absence of sugar.

In our oldest recipes sugar is not mentioned; honey takes its place and is used in a manner that is no longer orthodox. For example, choice hams were preserved in honey; puddings and cakes, and even the first ices, were sweetened with it. The expressed sweet juice of the grape, the cherry and the plum was boiled, to make a concentrated syrup which was used when honey was not available.

The first Colonists at the Cape had access to imported sugar, but it was an exceedingly scarce and expensive article, whose use became general only in the eighteenth century. It was imported in the form of a coarse, almost black, unrefined sugar from China; later on it came in as a partly-refined, but still very moist, yellow; and still later as a white sugar, or as candy sugar which was a mass of well-defined crystals clustered round a bit of string. The early recipes give directions for powdering such candy sugar and also for 'clearing' unrefined sugar, when a transparent syrup was required for preserving fruit.

It is interesting to note that the quantities of sugar prescribed in those early days for the preparation of sweet dishes yield results that are much less sweet than what would be acceptable today, which may be either because the sugar then used, being unrefined, was more saccharine, or because (which is more probable) diners were content with a dish that was moderately sweet.

Another interesting point is that early Cape cooks used the contrasting flavour between salt and sweet; they served powdered salt with oranges, peaches, strawberries and melons; and every South African child who is well educated knows the improvement in the taste of a ripe quince when it is crushed on a rock with some seawater and eaten with some of the brine adhering to the pulp.

We owe a debt of gratitude to our founder, Jan van Riebeeck, who was at pains from the day he landed to establish an orchard at the Settlement, and who devoted much of his attention to introducing various fruits from the Fatherland. Within a few years it was possible to obtain many European fruits at the Cape and, later on, practically all visitors testified to the excellence of these. Lady Duff Gordon, who found little to praise in the

Cape cuisine, waxed eloquent over the fruit — melons, figs, apples, peaches and apricots — that she bought so largely and so cheaply. Nelson, in his evidence before a Select Committee of the House of Commons, spoke of the beautiful grapes that grew so abundantly at the outpost that he did not think was of much strategic importance. Today matters are somewhat different. Our apples are no longer what they used to be, and we can import better ones from Canada; our peaches and apricots have increased in size and diminished in flavour; our oranges are . . . but let us be thankful that we still have many kinds of most excellent fruit, chief among which stand our grapes.

In preparing fruit for the table, the old Malay cooks drew on their experience with tropical fruit. They hardly ever boiled fruit in water; they recognised that most fruits contain enough water to allow gentle steaming if one wanted to cook them, while for preserves it was necessary to impregnate them with the thin syrup by slow and prolonged maceration under an equally gentle heat. Fresh fruit was served without any accompaniment, but there was always a cruet on the table with powdered salt, pepper, ginger and cinnamon, from which the guest, if he so desired, could help himself.

Fresh melon, for instance, was usually eaten with a little salt and pepper, though some diners preferred ginger, and others salt and cinnamon. Fruit was dried in the sun, on a rough scaffolding; sometimes it was peeled, sometimes the rind was left on; the seed or stone was always taken out, and large fruit was cut into slices. Very ripe fruit was sometimes pounded and spread in layers on paper or cloth and allowed to dry in the sun, a little salt being strewn on it. This makes the once very popular but now hardly ever seen *plat perskie* (flat peach) in which the dried layer of mashed ripe peach is rolled up or folded into a square for use when travelling. It has a sour-sweet, slightly saltish taste, is a great thirst-quencher, and far more nourishing than any chewing-gum.

Some fruits were dipped into lye before being dried; this was generally the case with grapes. No sulphur was used in the old days, and no one was particularly impressed by dried fruit that had a pale yellow colour such as today appears to be the chief consideration. The peeled dry peaches that came from the farms in the South-Western Districts at the end of the past century[1] were unsurpassed in flavour, but their kind is no longer obtainable.

No Malay cook made *jam* in the modern way, by boiling the fruit till the individual shapes were merged into a stiff sweet purée; they insisted that even so sequacious and flaccid an ingredient as duneberries should retain as much of their original integrity as possible when boiled to make a jam. This, by the way, was always called a conserve.

Essentially their jam was fruit cooked gently in a thin syrup till the

---

1 The nineteenth century.

combination was so intimate that the syrup, as such, could no longer be distinguished and the whole had merged into a blend of fruit, fruit juice and sugar, varying in consistency but never so mushy that the fruit itself had disintegrated to an extent that destroyed its shape. They boiled it in a copper preserving pan that was kept scrupulously clean, and never scrupled to mix with it such flavourings as their experience had taught them would enhance the taste of the fruit that was its basic ingredient.

Great care was taken to skim the boiling liquid and to prevent burning, and considerable skill was necessary to detect when the risk of caramelisation was imminent (the stage of over-boiling as it was called), just as expert knowledge was needed to surpass the under-boiled stage when, if the process was regarded as completed and the jam bottled, it would inevitably crystallise.

A few jam recipes may be of interest.

Grape jam. Take any kind of grapes, not too ripe; pick the berries from the stalks, prick them with a needle, and place them for half an hour in salt water. Then put them in your pot, with a little cold water, just enough to cover them, and let them boil for a minute or two. Then add sugar, in amount half the weight of your grapes, a few featherings of cinnamon and a couple of inch-long pieces of ginger, and allow to simmer gently until the syrup has thickened round the grapes. Ladle out into jars, allow to get lukewarm, and pour over melted butter or fat. It will keep for very long.

Quince jam. Peel your quinces and cut them into neat slices. Put them, with the cores, in a little water and when they are soft, take out the cores. Now add your sugar, enough to equal the weight of the fruit, with your cinnamon, ginger and a blade of mace. Boil slowly, skimming frequently and taking care that it does not burn. If you wish you may add some *moskonfyt* to give it a colour (caramelised sugar does just as well).

Later recipes, obviously under European influence, say that the fruit should be 'minced'; they also give directions for making jams compounded of carrots, pumpkin, squash and suchlike soft things, that make a sweet purée. But the old cooks did not call these concoctions conserves, but spoke of them as a chutney or as a fruit purée, or thick fruit sauce which was occasionally served warm with meat dishes.

Chinese influence is equally obvious in the old methods for preserving fruit whole or in pieces, in thin syrups. This was also applied to some vegetables, just as in China they preserved bamboo shoots. The fruit or vegetable, if it was soft, was after peeling put for a varying length of time in brine or limewater, to harden its outside. It was then gently parboiled and after that allowed to simmer in the syrup, to which ginger, cinnamon, mace, tangerine peel or cloves were generally added. In a few instances brandy or rum was added. The result aimed at was to obtain a perfectly translucent preserve, replete with the original flavour of the fruit or vegetable but blended with other flavourings that enhanced its pristine virtue.

With fresh fruits, either whole or cut up, *fruit salads* were made, always with a little sugar and wine. Indeed, a fruit salad without wine was regarded as an exhibition of bad taste. The flavourings used were nutmeg, cinnamon, rose water, lemon juice, almonds, tangerine peel, preserved kumquats or citron, and occasionally rum or brandy. Vanilla came into favour in the middle of the nineteenth century, but the old cooks cordially detested it and against the old-fashioned flavourings, it cuts a very poor figure except in milk dishes where its peculiar, thick floral perfume seems to be kept in proper check. Even in these, however, nutmeg is less vulgar and more satisfying.

Some notes on the various fruits, with such special recipes as seem worthy of mention by reason of their local modifications, may now be given.

Apples. These were baked, stewed, puréed, made into jam, open tarts, pies, salads and soups, according to the printed recipes. The only modification that seems to owe something to local influence (apart, of course, from the usual Cape methods of combining the fruit with spices and flavourings) is:

> *Baked apple.* Choose large, not too ripe apples; wipe and core them; but you need not peel them as when baked your guests can easily remove the skins. Put the cores in water, with a stick of cinnamon, a blade of mace, some ginger and tangerine peel, and let them boil till the water becomes glutinous. Pour through a sieve and mix with honey. Dust your apples, inside the core, with sugar and a little fine salt, and put them in a pan to bake in the oven; when they are soft, fill them with the honey mixture and let them bake for half an hour longer, basting them well with what drips from them. Serve up on fried bread.

Some recipes direct that the apples should be filled with guava jelly; one advises a mixture of almonds and pine kernels pounded in a mortar with tangerine peel and rose water. The apples are much better if they are peeled before being baked. All manner of variations may be played on this recipe.

Apricots were dried, preserved in salt as *meebos*, or in thin syrup; made into jam, salads, purées, pies, tarts and, more rarely, into soups. The kernels were always used as an addition to jam and sometimes as a flavouring for sweet dishes; the dried fruit was in great demand for chutneys, and the half-ripe apricots for *atjars*. The following is the recipe for making:

> *Meebos.* Select your largest and very best apricots, which must be ripe enough to be soft but must still be firm. Do not peel them, but wipe them with a damp cloth to get rid of the bloom. Put them into thick brine and let them stay there for a day and a night. Then take them out; press out the stone from each one, and squeeze the pulp flat; strew some salt over and

put them in the sun. Cover them with a damp cloth at night, but uncover them the next day to let the sun get at them. Do not make them too dry. When they are ready — which will be in four days' time — put them on a layer of sugar in a jar; sprinkle more sugar over, and put another layer of fruit; continue till the jar is filled, with a thick layer of sugar on top. It will keep like this for many months.

Meebos made like this is a delicious sour-salt-sweet-meat; the commercial variety, made from mixed pulp, is a very poor substitute. Miss Duckitt, who gives a later recipe for it, states that 'it is a very nice sweetmeat and said to be a remedy for sea-sickness'. She had her own way of preparing it, which was to crystallise the dried meebos in a thin syrup.

Cape gooseberries. These were sometimes served raw, but more commonly used as an addition to fruit salads, fruit macédoines or fruit coupes. Cooked, they were made into jam, tarts, pies, purées and puddings, nearly always with the addition of cream and nutmeg. They were never dried, and seldom made into jelly for they contain very little fruit pectin.

Figs were dried, served fresh, made into salads, purées, jams, pies and tarts. Firm, well-grown but green figs were made into one of the finest preserves, which was prepared almost entirely in accordance with oriental methods.

Green fig preserve. Take the largest and firmest figs, scrape off the zest (thin outer covering) with a bit of glass and put the scraped fig immediately into salt water to which you may add a little lime water. Let them lie in it for two days; take out, wipe dry, and boil them very gently in a little cold water till they are soft. Take out and put them on a clean cloth, to drain. Make a thin syrup with sugar, water and a teaspoonful of rose water; put your figs in this when it is boiling and draw the pot aside and let them soak in it overnight. The next day boil them in it very slowly till they are quite translucent and have absorbed most, but not all, the juice. Bottle them at once and tie down with cloth dipped in brandy.

No spice or flavouring of any kind was used in this preserve, though later recipes make mention of mace, which is quite unnecessary. The fruit has a most delicious taste; it should be served with black coffee or a glass of sherry, both of which bring out its delicate, characteristic flavour. It should be firm, as translucent as a good fruit jelly, and as crisp as the best bits in a mixed Chinese chow-chow. When the syrup is allowed to crystallise round the fruit we get *crystallised green figs*, now also commercialised, but when home-made only slightly inferior to the preserve.

Cherries. These have always been scarce and — like the other smaller berry fruits, mulberries, loganberries, duneberries, strawberries, and the much less well-known rose apples or *djamboes* — were generally served fresh, in fruit salads, macédoines or coupes, with or without the addition of cream, wine, rum, spices and flavourings. Mulberries and raspberries were beaten

up with cream, lemon juice and a few drops of rum, while strawberries were soaked in wine, dusted with nutmeg or a little fine salt, but rarely served with cream. An excellent recipe is that for:

> *Mulberry pudding.* Pick up those that have dropped off the tree and select others that are ready to fall; they are the ripest, for which you will need the least sugar. Remove their stalks and place the berries in a saucepan with half their weight of sugar, a piece of cinnamon, a bit of lemon, a piece of tangerine peel and a little red wine. Let it come to the boil; press through a sieve and replace in the saucepan. Cut up a stale white loaf into slices an inch thick; cut off the crust, and place the slices in a mould which you have coated with butter. Pour over it your mulberry syrup, and put on it a layer of the mulberry purée. Put on it more breadcrumbs and go on in this manner till you have filled the mould, putting on top a layer of bread, which you have drenched in the syrup.
>
> Place on top a plate with a weight on it, and put the mould in a cool place overnight. Then take out the pudding and serve with a cold fruit sauce. You may also bake or steam it, but in that case it is better to butter the slices of crumb before you pour the purée over. Some people put bits of citron peel, pistachio nuts, almonds or preserved ginger between the layers, but these are not really necessary.

I agree. The pudding is excellent without any additional spicing, though a few drops of rum improve it.

Grapes and *currants.* These were used dried or fresh when in season, or cooked as jam; they were served by themselves or added to salads and coupes, or used as garnishes for fish and meat dishes. Hanepoot grapes were also preserved in brandy and sometimes in a thin syrup. Grape juice, partly fermented, was used as a yeast for bread and cake-making; a similar yeast was made from raisins. Elf was sometimes dished up with a garnishing of grape berries, peeled and steamed in white wine. Unripe grapes, stewed with honey or sugar and spices, made a good filling for tarts and open pies. Currants were made into jam, but more commonly used in cakes and puddings.

Plums and *prunes* were dried or served as stewed fruit, or baked in pies and tarts, or made into jam. The favourite flavouring was ginger or tangerine peel.

Watermelon. This was always served fresh, being sliced longitudinally at the table, so that the slices fell away from the central section, known as the 'crown', which was considered the best part. It was eaten by itself without flavouring and the flesh was never cooked. From the thick rind an excellent *watermelon konfyt* was made, by scraping off the green part with a bit of glass, steeping the rind in lime water, parboiling it, and then boiling it slowly in syrup, usually with some ginger, tangerine peel and a few cloves added. The result was an almost transparent green preserve, very crisp when well made, with a curious, nondescript flavour.

Melons, of which formerly the best was the large-sized, deeply ribbed *geel spanspek*, intensely fragrant, with pink flesh and extraordinarily sweet, were served fresh and eaten with salt, pepper or ginger. A preserve was made from the rind, usually much softer than that made from watermelon, dark brown in colour, and with no particular flavour. As an addition to fruit salads, melons were in great demand. The late variety, with a smooth white skin and green flesh, known as *winter spanspek*, was much smaller but deliciously flavoured, though by no means so fragrant.

Pawpaws. Common enough now, these were formerly scarce, imported and regarded more as vegetables than as fruits. Green pawpaws were made into soups and *bredies*. A little more ripe, they were stewed with honey or sugar, ginger and a bit of tangerine peel, making an excellent hot fruit dish. Nowadays pawpaw is usually served sliced and fresh with a lemon or a little sugar according to the taste of the eater. The old cooks treated it like pumpkin, and all the recipes for pumpkin cookery can be tried with pawpaw.

Avocado pear is best eaten by itself with whatever condiment is desired. As a salad it is too clogging by itself, and should be mixed, sparsely, with other ingredients. It contains a great deal of pectin, which gives it a bland, almost soapy consistency, and it needs for its due appreciation the contrast of a strong sour or salt flavour. With sugar it agrees badly, and it never appears to harmonise with wine.

Lychees. These formerly came, dried, from China and were known as Tonkin raisins. They were expensive and were served as dessert at fashionable houses. I have eaten them with fillets of sole and, prepared by an old cook who claimed to be descended from a Chinese convict, as a stuffing for quails wrapped and grilled in fig leaves. Today they are easily obtainable as they are widely grown in Natal and the Transvaal, and we ought to make greater use of them in our cookery. They are admirable when stewed in white wine, with a blade of mace and a little tangerine peel, make a good tart, and are excellent in pies.

Oranges. The old 'seedling orange', the best of which came from the Clanwilliam district where they have now been supplanted by the far less juicy navel orange, was the most popular. It was indeed the only kind referred to in the recipes. They were used fresh in salads or by themselves, preserved whole or in quarters in syrup, or made into marmalade. A favourite way of serving them was:

Baked oranges. Slice off the top of the orange and loosen the pulp, removing some of the seeds. Dust with salt and bake in the oven. Serve with a little powdered cinnamon and sugar.

Orange juice was much used for making orange jelly and cold orange pudding, in which the stiffening substance was the pectin derived from seaweed. As many fruit jellies were made with such seaweed jelly as a basis, the recipe for it may be given.

Orange jelly. Soak two handfuls of dried seaweed in cold water till the weed has swelled out and is soft; boil it in two cupsful of water with one cupful of wine; strain through a cloth. Whisk the white of four eggs to a stiff froth; beat their yolks with three ounces of sifted sugar, two cups of strained orange juice and a little grated orange rind, and incorporate in the seaweed liquor; finally whip in the beaten egg white and pour into a wetted mould. Let it stand overnight and, when turned out, serve with a garnish of orange segments and slices of preserved citron.

The seaweed liquor is practically a strong solution of pectin, which sets to a firm jelly when it gets cold. It has a curious taste — which is neither astringent nor woody, but between the two — and must be improved by some stronger and better-flavoured agent. It is merely a stiffening substance, but is cheap, easily made and acts as well as gelatine or isinglass. Although the latter was much used for jellies (as it was one of the chief means of fining wine), seaweed was preferred by many old cooks as it was said to solidify better and to be exempt from the enzyme action of some fruits like pineapple that interferes with the setting of animal gelatine.

Lemons, kumquats, pomelos and *tangerines.* All these are common, but, apart from their use as flavouring and sometimes as ingredients in salads, they are served only as fresh fruit, with the exception of the first two that are too tart to be eaten at table. Both cumquats and tangerines make an excellent preserve when boiled in syrup; neither needs any additional flavouring. Tangerine peel, dried, is extensively used as a flavouring for puddings, stewed fruits and suchlike things. It imparts a subtle, aromatic taste that combines excellently with anything that is sweet. The rind of the pomelo, or shaddock, like that of the large citron, makes a beautiful preserve with a flavour that is altogether its own. None of these citrus fruits is particularly useful for tarts or pies, although all are sometimes used for that purpose in combination with other fruits.

Guavas are such highly fragrant and strong-tasting fruit that it is always better to use them in combination, although stewed guavas, made with a little cinnamon and ginger, and served with a sweet custard or plenty of cream, need not be despised. They are excellent in a:

Guava salad. Peel and slice large, fully ripe guavas; those with pink flesh are to be preferred and you must remove as many of the pips as you can. Mix them with peeled and sliced oranges, a few tangerine wedges and peeled and sliced bananas; strew over powdered sugar and let them stand for a while in a cool place. Pour over a wineglass of sherry or white wine, give the salad a stir, dust with grated nutmeg, and serve.

As with all other fruit salads, there are many variations of this recipe; some folk add shelled nuts, diced pawpaws, peeled grapes, or even chopped citron and other preserved peels. One of the best additions is rose apple, broken and bruised. The salad is sufficient in itself, but is generally served with a cold custard or with whipped cream.

Loquats. These are eaten fresh or stewed, with or without spices. Tangerine peel goes well with them, and so does ginger. They make a good jam and a fairly well-flavoured preserve.

Pomegranates were formerly much more in favour than they are today. They were used to stuff meat, in the Oriental manner, and as garnishes. The modern cook has not much use for them and their preparation entails an amount of labour that can be devoted to better purpose.

Limes or *lemmetjies* make a glorious pickle and their juice, when mixed with rum, some nutmeg and sugar and broken ice, provides one of the finest drinks that one can wish for on a hot day. They are also preserved in syrup or salt.

Olives, although grown at the Cape, have never been extensively used. The old recipes are silent about them, although they are mentioned in one that gives directions for stuffing pigeons with a farce in which chopped olives are an ingredient. The wild olive has a tiny, acrid, and almost useless fruit.

Peaches. The ripe fruit is served by itself or stewed with a little white wine and sugar. The dried fruit is perhaps the favourite for a stewed fruit dish, and the following recipe may serve as a generic one:

Stewed dried peaches. Soak them in water and when they have swelled, take them out and dry them on a damp cloth; put them in a saucepan with half a cupful of sugar, a few featherings of cinnamon, a bit of dried tangerine peel, and a little grated lemon peel. Pour over a cup of sweet red wine, and put the saucepan where it can simmer gently. Shake it from time to time, but do not stir. When ready, serve up hot or cold, as you prefer.

To make it perfect one should add a few crushed peach and apricot kernels.

Nectarines are dealt with in exactly the same way as peaches. Both are sometimes served as fritters. They are peeled, halved, the stone taken out and each half dusted with sugar, ginger and cinnamon; they are then dipped in a sweet batter and fried in boiling fat. Orange slices, pineapple and other fruits that lend themselves to similar treatment may be fried in the same way.

Quinces are treated like apples. They make an excellent sambal, jelly and *bredie.*

Custard apple is always eaten by itself, but as an addition to a fruit salad it is excellent.

Bananas and *plantains*. These were known from the earliest times and there has always been a keen demand for them. They were served by themselves, baked, fried, stewed, made into puddings, jellies, salads or purées, but were never served plainly boiled as they sometimes are in the East. In their cooked form they are perhaps best when fried in fat, and fried bananas were regarded as indispensable when serving *sosaties* or a hot curry.

Mangoes were used only for chutneys and were rarely available on the market, which probably accounts for their relatively infrequent mention in the old recipes.

Jack fruit, which is now cultivated in Natal and the Transvaal, can scarcely be considered a fruit. It is a most delicate vegetable for its flesh, when steamed with a little butter, approaches in flavour and delicacy that of well-grown asparagus or *coeur de palmier*. Its large black seeds can be roasted like chestnuts, to which they approximate in taste.

The fruit of the *prickly pear*, when fully ripe and properly denuded of thorns, is sapid, aromatic and pleasant to the taste, but is rarely used in cookery.

That of the *Hottentot fig*, about which botanists are not yet agreed as to whether it can properly be called a fruit, is eaten by children. Lady Duff Gordon found it too sour for her taste. It makes, however, a good jam.

Rose apples or *djamboes* are very aromatic, and their usefulness as a flavouring agent is not yet appreciated; they are best as a preserve.

Grenadillas are best served beaten up with sugar, cream and wine, or as a water or cream ice.

There are many kinds of indigenous fruits, mainly berries, that are edible. So far they have not been popularised in cookery, although some of them have great possibilities.

There are no recipes among my old manuscripts for making water or cream ices. The reason for this is obvious, namely the want of ice or of refrigerating machinery in those far-off days. Ice cream was well known at the time when the Cape was first occupied, but it was prepared with the aid of stored ice which was not available at the Cape. It is equally obvious that the juices of all our Cape fruits can be used for making water and cream ices, as well as for making fruit drinks, for which recipes will be found in all printed cookery books.

As far as I have been able to ascertain, all our recipes for fruit drinks are copies of old European directives, with a few unimportant modifications, chiefly in the use of spices and additional flavourings. The 'harvest drink' mentioned by Miss Duckitt is a case in point; it is nothing but a variety of the age-old mulled wine that is described in the old cook books.

Chapter 14

Odds and Ends

The old recipes deal slightingly with milk. Its food value was to some extent dependent on its preparation and our forefathers, perhaps very properly, felt that if it was made into cheese it was of greater value to the community than when it was drunk as a liquid. Here are some of the ways in which they recommended that it should be prepared for the table.

Bread-and-milk. Take a piece of stale white bread and cut it into dice; pour over it a pint of boiling milk in which you have melted a teaspoonful of butter, and dissolved a tablespoonful of sugar or honey. Grate nutmeg over and serve.

Milk brawn. Into a cupful of seaweed liquid stir two cupsful of hot milk, which you have boiled up with a feathering of cinnamon, a cupful of sugar and a blade of mace. Pour into a wetted mould and, when set, turn out and serve with cream.

Sago milk. Boil a cupful of sago in three cupsful of milk with half a cupful of sugar or honey and a feathering of cinnamon or a piece of dried tangerine peel. Pour into a dish, grate nutmeg over, and serve. You may also bake it in the oven.

Fat milk. Boil three cupsful of new milk with an ounce of suet, half a cupful of honey or sugar, and a little grated fresh lemon peel. Pour through a sieve and serve with a dusting of grated nutmeg.

Toast and milk. Toast a slice of stale white bread; butter it and pour over it boiled milk that you have thickened with a little rice flour and to which you have added a lump of butter and a pinch of salt. Serve very hot.

Milk also enters into some of the old-fashioned drinks that were served on cold winter nights.

Milk and wine. Boil a cup of wine with half a cup of milk; when it boils stir in two wineglassesful of white wine; let it boil up; remove and set aside to cool; then pour off the whey that floats on top; mix with sugar and spices according to your taste. Serve hot or cold, as best pleases you.

Another foodstuff that was a favourite with the old cooks was flour in some form or other. Wheat flour was extensively used; barley, oats and rye and other cereals, including mielies, were at first not too popular. It was only in the nineteenth century that mielie meal became the staple food of the poorer class. It was prepared in much the same way as that in which the first settlers had made their flour *paps* or porridges of various cereals. Such *paps* are usually served with milk and sugar; sometimes a piece of butter is added to each plate. Oatmeal was rarely used, and then always with a good deal of salt added; it was sometimes baked in the oven and then made into a porridge and served with cream and honey. Kaffircorn porridge was a much later development. Mielie flour was never granulated, and it is worth noting that we have no local recipe for polenta or semolina.

> *Raisin mielies (gestampte mielies).* Take dried mielies and wet them slightly. Put them in a wooden mortar and pound them lightly, so that they break and their husk comes off. Put them in water to remove the husks which will float, and let them soak. Take them out when they have swelled a little and put them in a saucepan, with some salt, half a cupful of sugar, two cupsful of stalked and seeded raisins and a few featherings of cinnamon; add some water and let the mielies simmer slowly, stirring often. When they are soft and pasty, turn out and serve.

Although the mielies are broken, the fragments should retain their individuality in this dish and should be mixed intimately with the raisins, cohering to them by virtue of the gruel-like consistency that the mielies should have when properly cooked. This dish, which is not regarded as a dessert dish but one served with meats, may be made much richer and more like a pudding by adding cream, spices and a few drops of rum to it. From a nutritional point of view it is far more nourishing than any other mielie dish.

Bread was made with or without yeast. All visitors to the Cape who wrote before the nineteenth century and make mention of it declare that the brown and white bread that they tasted here was excellent. The wheat flour was crushed between stones; brown bread was baked with the wholewheat flour; for the white bread, the flour was sifted. The brown bread as made by Malay cooks was delightful when it was fresh and moist; when a few days old it was not so good. Their white bread came in various degrees of refinement, but never approached the thin, wooden consistency of white, steam-baked bread. It was nearly always slightly granular and, from a dietetic point of view, was quite as nourishing as their brown bread.

Bread was baked, usually, in an outside brick oven; only later was it prepared in an iron kitchen oven. A magnificent variety was baked in a pot, with hot coals on the lid and this was regarded, quite rightly, as the test of the artist's skill in baking bread. For yeast they used partly fermented must, crushed raisins, fermented dough, or dried hops and sometimes an indigenous plant that has similar properties.

> *Potato yeast (aartappelsuurdeeg).* Take a teacupful of dried hops and boil it in a quart of water with a pound of peeled and diced potatoes; let it cool

and add to it half a cupful of flour, three tablespoonsful of sugar mixed in a pint of water. Cover it closely and let it stand for a day and a night, when it will be ready for use.

Raisin yeast. Pound up two cups of raisins and put them in a wide-mouthed jar which you fill with water in which you have dissolved a little sugar. In a couple of days, when the raisins rise to the top, it will be fit for use.

Meal yeast (*soet suurdeeg*). Take a yeast pot (any earthenware jar with a closely-fitting lid) and fill it half-full with boiling water; put in, without stirring, two cups of unsifted wheat flour and a teaspoonful of sugar and cover it so that none of the moisture can escape. Let it stand in a warm place on the hearth overnight and add to it a cupful of hot water the next day, give it a stir, and let it remain till it begins to bubble and work, when you can use it.

Some recipes add salt to the brew but there seems to be no reason for this and the flour will ferment quite well — indeed better — without it.

Old yeast (*ou suurdeeg*) is simply a portion of the dough put aside in the yeast pot, which always contains spores of the yeast mould, mixed with lukewarm water and allowed to ferment. It is a convenient way of making yeast, but is stated to give a heavier loaf than the other yeast varieties.

The mixture of flour and water or some other liquid produced various kinds of dough and batter, and the directions for preparing these different kinds are usually precise. As a matter of fact, they differ in no way from those that were already in print in the early part of the seventeenth century, and they lay emphasis on precisely the same points that the best European cooks had insisted on in making dough — the necessity to keep it cool, to handle it as little as possible, and to allow it to settle.

A plain water dough was used for pies and simple tarts; an egg dough, much more complicated and resembling the French *feuilletage*, was invariably used for sweet tarts. The best cooks rolled it out 24 times, adding a little fresh butter each time, with the result that the subsequent baked layers were as thin as tissue paper and, when properly baked, as crisp yet as deliciously melting as a slither of crackling.

For the spongy dough, that required a good yeast, the recipe was almost exactly that given in the old printed books for what is now known as *baba* mixture. It produced a soft, pudding-like result that was invariably served with *moskonfyt* instead of the ordinary rhum syrup.

Another variety was transparent dough, made exclusively with butter and thrice-sifted flour, and so repeatedly rolled that my unmathematical mind boggles at the task of computing the number of final layers. Baking powder and bicarbonate of soda were never used; they are first mentioned

in recipes dating from the latter part of the eighteenth century and, although it must frankly be admitted that they have lightened the task of the cook, the doughs made without them suffered no less from their omission.

There were several 'secret' processes connected with the preparation of doughs and generally with cake-making that certain conservative cooks jealously guarded. These were never committed to paper but were preserved by oral tradition. Some of them were not worth all the fuss that was made about them, a few were of such a nature that no self-respecting cook would ever have employed them (as, for instance, one method of getting a fine patina on darioles and tartlets) while others were really of value. The manner of making 'filled pancakes', secret of my old preceptress with the wooden spoon, for example, was apparently unknown to other Cape Town cooks.

Filled pancakes (*gevulde pannekoek*). Make a pancake batter with thrice-sifted flour, a very little rice flour, the yolk, well-whipped, of two large eggs, and enough white wine to produce a thin batter that flows easily off your spoon. Whip it well and place it aside for a couple of hours before it is wanted. For your filling you want a couple of blanched sweet and one bitter almond, two pistachio nuts, and a tablespoonful of peeled pine kernels. Pound these in a mortar with a tablespoonful of butter, a few drops of rose water and a little powdered tangerine peel, and add to it a teaspoonful of honey, working the mixture till it is a stiff cream. Thin it slightly by adding more butter till it is of a consistency to spread easily. Put some butter or fat in your pan, add a little salt to your batter and pour into the pan enough of it to make a very thin pancake. As soon as it is browned on the underside, coat it quickly with your filling mixture, fold it, and put it on a hot dish; go on till you have enough pancakes. Pour over them a glass of rum and good brandy mixed, set it alight and serve at once.

Speaking from an experience that extends over 40 years, I can honestly say that I have never eaten more delicious pancakes than these, and that the European *crêpe suzette*, of later invention, is a bad second to them. My old Malay woman made them so crisp and knife-edge thin that it seemed impossible to fold them, yet she managed to do it with a dexterity that I envied and have never been able to imitate successfully.

There were, of course, many other recipes for pancakes with something or other inside them, and serving them with flaming rum and brandy was a common practice. The usual pancake batter was made with flour, egg yolk and milk, with a little sugar and salt added, and was served with powdered cinnamon, nutmeg and sugar mixed. It was never tossed, but always deftly turned, although it was usually made so thin that both sides were cooked without the necessity to turn it. The cinnamon and sugar was dusted on its upper surface, and it was rolled up and sent to table with a halved lemon for each guest — never a slice or a quarter.

Thicker pancakes were favoured by some cooks; in these the batter was mixed with various ingredients such as herbs and spices.

A salt omelette-like pancake was sometimes served with roast meat, for Yorkshire pudding was a much later introduction.

An old favourite, that has retained its popularity though it is now usually steam-baked and is even made from the horrible flour that cooks are not allowed to sift, is:

> *Raisin bread (rosyntjie brood)*. Make a dough with flour, salt, sugar, powdered cinnamon, grated nutmeg and a few cumin seeds. Add some raisin yeast and put aside in a cool place covered with a wet cloth; when it rises add stoned raisins and a cupful of good fat; knead well, shape into loaves and bake in the oven.

This, rather vague, original recipe does not give the amounts; few of the Malay cooks stipulated how much of each ingredient should be used and the reader was left in doubt on this point. It was presumed, apparently, that the intending maker of the dish knew for how many guests it would have to serve and could apportion the quantities as desired. Nowadays baking powder is used instead of yeast, and raisin bread becomes almost a Boston bread sort of cake, heavy and moist. In its original form it was, and should always be, delightfully crusty outside, and beautifully crumbly within. When fresh from the oven and still hot it is delicious eaten with butter.

Ash cake (as koek), which is really a kind of unleavened damper, was made as follows.

> *How to make good as koek*. It is better to sift your meal, for that makes the cake whiter, but if you cannot do so you may use unsifted meal. Mix it with enough salt to give it a good taste and stir it into milk or buttermilk till it is firm enough to knead. Add to it some tail fat and knead it well. It is not necessary to use yeast, but if you want it to rise like bread you may put some fermented must in with it, if you happen to make it in the time of wine-harvesting. Let it stand awhile before you use it. You must form it into cakes the size of your palm and about half an inch thick, and bake it on the gridiron. It is good eaten with fat or butter.

It is good eaten with anything, in fact, though perhaps best with butter and cheese, but it must be served very hot. It is the usual damper prepared in camp, where the flour is now commonly mixed with soda or baking powder. A coarse variety, known as *stormjaers* or *attackers*, is made by simply mixing meal with water and a little soda and baking the cakes in hot embers. It is filling, but leaves much to be desired from a culinary point of view.

Citron bread was made in much the same way as raisin bread, but is hardly known today. Preserved citron peel was cut into dice and was incorporated in a bread dough yeasted with fermenting must; usually ginger, tangerine peel and currants were added, and the result was really a not-too-sweet fruit cake. Gingerbread, which was another old favourite, was made in accordance with the old European recipes; the only modification seems to have been the use of tangerine peel.

Citron omelette. Chop up an ounce of preserved citron peel with a handful of stoned raisins and a little tangerine peel; mix it well with three beaten eggs; add a small glass of sweet white wine. Pour into a flat pan in which you have melted a little fat or butter, and let it set well; fold in two; scatter fine sugar over and serve.

Fried bread (*wentel teefies*). Cut slices of bread from a white loaf that is a week old or more, about a quarter of an inch thick and do not take away the crust. Soak them in buttermilk or, if you have no buttermilk, then in ordinary cold milk to which you have added a little white wine. Take out and drain. Then put each slice in some egg that you have beaten up well with a little salt; take out the bread and fry it on both sides in hot fat; strew cinnamon and sugar on each slice and serve.

Tarts were a feature in old Cape cookery. They were really open pies and were imitations of the old-fashioned Dutch *taart* (which itself was an imitation of the earlier, uncovered pies that probably came from the East) like the modern American 'pies'. Though there are many recipes for their preservation, some (indeed in the oldest printed cookery book extant) show interesting modifications.

Potato tart. Take mashed potatoes, two good cupsful, a cupful of sugar or half a cupful of honey, half a dozen fresh eggs, half a pound of blanched almonds, a few bitter almonds and a couple of peach kernels, peeled; a pinch of powdered tangerine peel and a little salt. Pound the nuts with the sugar, peel and salt. Whip the yolks and whites of the eggs separately, with a little rose water added to each. Mix the potatoes with the beaten yolk and pounded nuts and whip in the beaten whites. Line a dish with tart or pie dough, pour in the mixture and bake in the oven.

This mixture was sometimes put into a cloth and boiled as a pudding, or into a greased tin and baked in the oven.

Tarts were usually made with a very rich dough, repeatedly rolled and buttered, so that when baked it was exceedingly crisp and mellow. With this a deep soup plate was lined and the filling of the tart, which was its principal ingredient, was poured in. A decorated band of dough was placed on top as an edging and strips of dough were laid across the top in lattice fashion; these were brushed with yolk of egg and a little brandy before being baked to give the pastry a good golden colour; some cooks added a little saffron to the egg yolk.

The main thing in all tarts was the filling and for this there were many recipes. Probably the simplest was a fruit purée or jam, without any admixture. The best was undoubtedly the old-fashioned milk or custard filling, modified from the old Italian recipes in so many different ways that almost every cook had his, or her, own way of making it — and thoroughly despised anybody else's method. They were all very tasty, being well-baked custards intensively flavoured and sinfully rich.

A milk tart. Boil two pints of milk with a feathering of cinnamon, a bit of dried tangerine peel, a teaspoonful of honey and half a cupful of coconut milk, one bitter almond, shelled and blanched, and one peach kernel. Beat three egg yolks with a little candy sugar and stir them into the boiling milk; take off and pour through a sieve; add another egg beaten up with the whites of the three eggs and a small glass of sweet wine, and whisk well. Pour into the lined tart dish and bake fairly quickly in the oven.

Another milk tart. Take coconut milk, new milk and cream, of each an equal portion, and whip them well with a pinch of salt, the yolks of four eggs, a little grated nutmeg and a little powdered tangerine peel. When they are well beaten, add honey or sugar to sweeten; put the mixture on the fire and stir till it thickens, but do not let it boil. Then pour into your mould and bake. Sprinkle cinnamon and nutmeg on top.

A rich milk tart. You may make this by pounding in a mortar a handful of blanched sweet and one bitter almond with a few apricot or peach kernels, three tablespoonsful of sugar candy, a teaspoonful of rice flour, some flicks of mace and a bit of dried tangerine peel, which mixture you must wash with coconut milk through a sieve. With what comes through you must mix its own amount of cream skimmed from the morning's milk, and the yolk of as many eggs as will equal it in weight. When you have well mixed these you may add, also, the white and yolk of one egg beaten up with a glass of brandy or sweet wine. This you pour into the pie dish, which you have lined with paste rolled out 14 times at least, and you must bake it quickly in a hot oven. When done you may put on top of it some grated nutmeg and little crosses made of citron peel.

Coconut tart was made in the same way, its main ingredient being grated fresh coconut. *Nut tart* had a rich, juicy filling of pounded almonds, pistachios, pine kernels and walnuts, mingled with cream and egg yolk.

Pumpkin, squash and *vegetable marrow tart* were simply made with fillings of puréed vegetables. There was a special kind of gourd tart that needed a preliminary cooking, which was generally so good that it was served without waiting to put it in a tart.

Baked vegetable marrow. Pare and dice the marrow, which must not be too ripe. Put it in a pie dish with butter, sugar, cinnamon, nutmeg and a little tangerine peel. Bake it in the oven till it turns brown.

Although this was properly a filling for pies, it was used as a dish by itself; a little watery though it be, it tastes very good, and its liquidity may be much lessened by incorporating bits of toasted bread or dried breadcrumbs in it before it is baked. It is one of the easiest and nicest ways to prepare any of the gourd tribe of vegetables.

Closed pies were not usually sweet dishes, the word *pastei* being reserved, by usage though not by idiom, to pasties filled with some vegetable or animal material without sugar or honey. Piecrust dough differed in no way from rich tart dough; for the more moist kind of pies, a batter, that yielded a dumpling-like result, was sometimes used. The dumpling doughs were varied, and some recipes were, like those for milk tart, considered to be family heirlooms. Again, as a matter of fact, they differ in no way from old printed recipes.

Dumplings or *kluitjies*, considered as sweet dishes and not as meat, fish or vegetable farce boiled in soup or hashes, were made from a dough that was shaped into balls, pressed through a colander (in that way resembling the old-fashioned Hungarian *taronyha*) or rolled out and cut into strips, like Chinese noodles. They were then boiled, usually in milk, and served with sugar and cinnamon, or with a sweet sauce. The simplest dough was one made with water, egg yolk, butter, sugar and a little spice; a more elaborate one was where the dough was finally mixed with whisked egg white, this yielding a more friable, sponge-like dumpling. Where no sugar was added to the dough, it could be used for dumplings suitable to accompany meat, soup or vegetables. Typical recipes are:

> *Milk dumplings* (*melk kluitjies* or *melk frummeltjies*). Into a pint and a half of boiling milk stir two tablespoonsful of butter, a little salt and two cupsful of well-sifted flour, till you have a gruel-like paste; let it cool and beat into it three eggs; shape this dough into small balls and cook in boiling milk till they float. Take out, dust with sugar and cinnamon or nutmeg, and serve.

Into this dough may be incorporated currants, raisins, dates, or anything else you like; the dumplings also can be added to any meat dish. The dough may be rolled out and cut into thin strips, or pressed through a colander, and these strips and droppings boiled in milk, soup or wine and served as a dish by themselves — with a sweet sauce for dessert, or with a vegetable purée or gravy sauce, as a savoury dish.

> *Rice dumplings*. Mash wet boiled rice to a paste with eggs, rich flour and butter and a pinch of salt. Cook in boiling water, take out, drain and serve with a dusting of sugar and spice, or with a gravy sauce. Here, too, you may incorporate into the dumpling whatever dried or preserved fruit you fancy if you want a sweet dish, or add a herb flavouring if you wish to serve the dumplings with a meat dish or a soup.

A richer variety of dumpling was made with rice flour, cream, butter, egg yolk, honey and spices; a coarser one simply with flour, milk and salt.

The main point was that the product should be light, porous and neither granular nor flaky but something between both. As a dish for a cold winter's evening, dumplings boiled in milk and served with sugar and cinnamon were regarded as a generally acceptable finish to the dinner or supper. At the Cape they supplied, to a great extent, the need for farinaceous additions to a meal that in Italian cookery is met by the many varieties of *pasta*.

An interesting variation of such cookery is that in which Oriental influence is plainly apparent. Malay cooks, in their native country, were in the habit of making nut and farinaceous, and sometimes fruit, doughs, boiling or frying them in fat, and preserving them, sometimes for months, in honey or thick syrup made by evaporating fruit juices. Such delicacies, coloured with ochre, turmeric or saffron, heavily spiced and inordinately sweet, may still be bought in Indian bazaars. Occidental taste usually considers them too cloyingly nectarious specially when they are heavily perfumed.

In South Africa one kind, which is a trifle more in harmony with western ideas, has survived in:

Koeksisters. To three cups of sifted flour add one cup of moist brown sugar, a teaspoonful of ground cinnamon, half a teaspoonful of ground ginger, of cloves, of allspice and of tangerine peel, a little salt, four well-beaten eggs and enough melted fat to make it into a thick dough. Add some raisin yeast and knead it well in; cover with a wet cloth and let it stand until it has risen. Cut small finger-thin strips from it, roll them into figures of eight and boil them in boiling fat. Take out when they are puffed and brown and drain.

Then put them, while they are still hot, into thick syrup, flavoured with almonds, cinnamon or whatever you like. Take out after an hour and drain. They can be served as soon as they are cool, but can be kept for weeks and are better when they are a few days old.

The most delicious *koeksisters* are those made with rice flour and saturated in a syrup made by boiling nutmeg, while it still has its original covering of mace, with sugar. They are golden-coloured, translucent, and highly aromatic. They should be well drained in any case and should never be greasy. Today they are most commonly immersed in a syrup in which green figs, citron or tangerines have been preserved, and are never perfumed or coloured.

Eastern influence is also apparent in the recipe for:

Sweet cakes (soet koekies). Make a dough with four pounds of flour mixed with two pounds of moist brown sugar, a pound of creamed butter, half a pound of soft tail-fat, a little salt and a wineglassful of brandy. Pound four handfuls of blanched almonds, a few bitter almonds and a few peach kernels in a mortar with a quarter of an ounce of powdered cloves and the same quantity of powdered cinnamon; add four eggs, a little red ochre powder, and some raisin yeast, and knead this mixture into the dough. Let it stand for 24 hours. Then roll out thin and cut into shapes with a cup or knife; butter a large pan and set your cakes in it; put a piece of preserved ginger or citron on top of each cake; bake them in a quick oven for half an hour.

They were served with wine or coffee, and were very popular. Nowadays they are made without the almonds and with soda and are a poor imitation of the originals, which were a fine cross between a macaroon and an Oriental fruitcake. In one recipe the nut content is increased by the addition of pine kernels, which seems to be an improvement as it makes them more flaky; another modification is to add honey.

There were various sweetmeats, most of them emanating from the East. One of the earliest things I was taught to make was the age-old *tameletjie*, a kind of rock much in favour with all Cape children in the days when sweets were all homemade. It was prepared as follows:

Tameletjies. Take a cup of brown sugar, a lump of butter the size of a hen's egg, half a cupful of water and a pinch of salt; make a syrup that will 'crackle' when dropped into cold water. Have ready blanched, split almonds, some grated tangerine peel and a little cinnamon; fold pieces of paper into little square pannikins, smear them inside with fat, and put some almonds, cinnamon and peel inside each; pour the syrup on them and, when it is half set, put more almonds, peel and cinnamon in. When hard take off the paper.

We used various kinds of nuts, chiefly pine kernels, but sometimes the soft, fragrant embryos of leucodendron seeds for this sweet, and simply mixed all the ingredients in the syrup, which was then poured on to a buttered tin — the lid of a biscuit tin served admirably — and cut into pieces when set. It is really a highly spiced toffee, or better, a rock sweet, but more variegated than the ordinary almond rock. Some old Malay cooks made an interesting variation of it, in which 'butter nuts', the seeds of an indigenous melon, scraps of dates and a little moskonfyt were mingled with the almonds.

Another favoured sweetmeat was made with almond paste, rose water, citron preserve finely minced, powdered cinnamon and allspice and tangerine peel, sugar and honey, all beaten up with egg white. It could be baked as a sort of macaroon by itself, or enclosed in a coating of tart dough and either fried in fat or baked in the oven. Malay cooks were fond of flavouring these cakes with some perfume and, later on, vanilla was largely used for this purpose.

There seem to be no recipes for preserving flowers, although such delicacies were well known in Europe and in the East. My old Malay cook crystallised wild jasmine flowers – then common enough, but now rare – by slightly steaming them and then immersing them in a crystallising syrup made of sugar, green ginger and a pinch of salt. They looked rather draggled, but retained something of their fragrance and tasted, to children at least, very nice. Orange and lemon flowers were dealt with in the same way; gourd flowers were sometimes fried in fat and served with a dusting of powdered sugar and cinnamon.

Similarly the old manuscript recipes for *cheese dishes* seem to be mere copies of European originals. Cheese was made on some farms, but it was usually eaten fresh, with bread and butter, and was not even of much account as an addition to farinaceous and vegetable dishes. There are a few recipes for cheese puddings and cheese *vlae* or custards. Miss Duckitt gives several of these, but though they make savoury dishes they differ in no way from those already in print at the time. A little-known, but by no means locally original, way of treating cheese is the following:

> *Chilli cheese.* Pound three ounces of cheese in a mortar with a tablespoonful of powdered chillies, a tablespoonful of butter, a teaspoonful of powdered ginger and a pinch of salt. Whisk into it enough cream to make into a thin paste, to which add a well-beaten egg; put the mixture in a buttered pie dish and steam or bake it. Serve with a sweet chutney.

This is a fiery, cheerfully-biting, custardy dish, to which some cooks add a bit of saffron to give it a lemon colour. Its pungency is perhaps too forcible for most people's taste, but a sweet chutney, or a semi-sweet dish like stewed sweet potatoes, does a great deal to enhance its merits.

> *To use up old ship's cheese.* Collect all the stray scraps you can find; do not reject those that are mouldy. Pound them well in a mortar with powdered pepper, mace, ginger and cloves; add enough brandy in which you have steeped verbena and sweet thyme leaves to make it all into a thick paste; if you have a little sour cream, add it too; let the paste stand for a few days, when it will become mouldy; mix it well once more, adding more brandy, and fill a wide-mouthed jar with it. You may use it on bread or biscuits, for it will keep for a long time.

This is a very tasty and aromatic spiced cheese, which is improved by the addition of a little moist sugar, but certainly spoiled by adding mustard. It is, however, merely a variant of dozens of recipes for potted cheese, and has no claim to be South African, although it comes from an old Cape manuscript cookbook.

Nothing has been said about drinks, for the simple reason that those mentioned in the seventeenth and eighteenth century recipes at the Cape

odds and ends

are all familiar to European cooks. This may be surprising to many who maintain, for instance, that there are special South African ways of making coffee. That is a fallacy. 'Coffee was hardly known at the Cape in the seventeenth century; it certainly never came here with Van Riebeeck', as one writer observes, and it is improbable that our Founder ever served it at the Castle to his family or his guests. Its use was restricted in Holland till 1680 and only after that date do we find mention of it at the Cape. Coffeeimports from Java were of much later date.[1] Our methods of making coffee are not essentially different from those used in the early part of the eighteenth century in European coffee-houses.

There, too, they roasted the beans with a little fat, pounded them immediately before making coffee (grinding machines came in much later) and added salt, or a pinch of sweet herbs (later, by some foul mischance, changed to mustard) to the brew, which was always made with boiling water and, to settle the grounds, they sometimes used a hot poker or a burning brand, exactly as we still do in our camp cookery.

They also served sweet cakes and conserves with coffee, as that was merely a continuation of the custom of serving them with a glass of wine drunk in the forenoon or afternoon. There is thus nothing of particular interest in our coffee-making methods, and so far as I have been able to discover we have no other drinks that have any justification to claim a local origin.

---

1 Coffee plants were introduced in Java and were also sent to the Cape at the end of the seventeenth century. Coffee was actually produced on some Cape farms in the eighteenth and nineteenth centuries but, like indigo, its cultivation was not an economic success. (L)

Culinary Treasures

by

C Louis Leipoldt

Culinary Treasures

Written by C Louis Leipoldt under the pseudonym K A R Bonade
Translated from the original Afrikaans by Dr W L Liebenberg
Adapted for publication as *Culinary Treasures* by T S Emslie
Edited by T S Emslie and P L Murray

Contents

1

The Governor's Bean

It would be hard to find something more genuinely Afrikaans in a vegetable garden than the good old *goewerneursboontjie*,[1] or *hereboontjie*,[2] as it is also called. This is not something you are likely to find discussed in any overseas cookbook. Take for instance the *Larousse Gastronomique* — that comprehensive manual for the modern chef. There is no mention whatsoever of our admirable *goewerneursboontjie*, which is even overlooked in Afrikaans cookbooks, although here and there you might come across a casual reference to 'dry beans'.

Yet what could be finer than an old-fashioned *goewerneursboontjie* of the large variety? When green, they are magnificent; but it is a shame to pick them before they have reached maturity, and they taste much better when ripened in the sun. They are at their best when the pods have just opened, the two halves curling up to expose the treasure they have guarded with such care. And how splendid are the colours they display — subtle hues of red, black-brown, white and yellow. They lie there like fragments of the finest Amàndola marble. It is true that we now rarely see the *goewerneursboontjie* in all its old-fashioned glory, and it seems as if the species has become smaller, more wrinkled and less colourful. There are even some pale-yellow, dirty-white descendants to be found — inferior-tasting South American types that are far less pleasing aesthetically.

So try and obtain the good, old-fashioned variety if you can, preferably from a farm somewhere in the southwestern part of the Cape. Go for those that have grown in river soil and held their ground against the ravages of the southeaster. And please do not treat them like ordinary dry beans. These are aristocrats, entitled to their privileges, and they have their likes and dislikes. So keep them well dried and properly cleaned in an airtight jar, out of reach, where there is no chance of the jar being — as children might mutter in youthful, mock astonishment — mysteriously smashed by some inexplicable mishap. And do not for a moment think that this is too much to ask of an already overworked housewife. It is well worth the effort, for it preserves the flavour. As Ayah Mina — that wonderful old soul who taught me respect for the *goewerneursboontjie* — always used to say, 'The taste, *Kleinbaas*,[3] the taste is what makes it worth its weight in gold.'

I do not entirely agree. The *goewerneursboontjie* is not only the tastiest,

---

1 Lima bean, literally 'governor's bean'.
2 Gentleman's bean.
3 Literally, 'little master'.

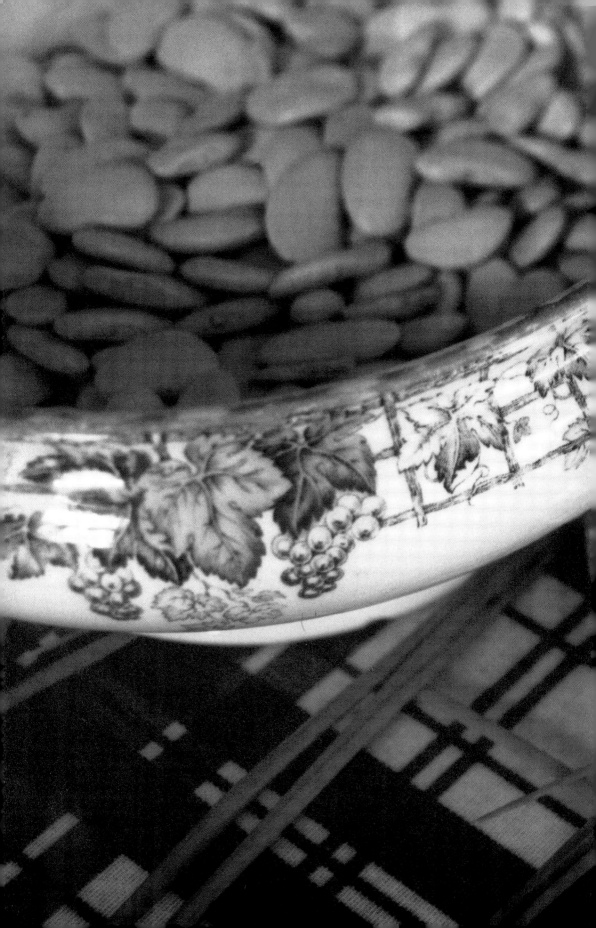

but possibly also the most nourishing of all our beans. Its nutritional value — those who speak of 'calorie value' are simply being foolish, for we do not choose our food according to how much 'firewood' it provides — is far more than that of meat or fish or fruit, and it contains just about everything one needs to live, including all the new-fangled vitamins so fashionable these days! Not *everything*, of course — you cannot survive on governor's beans alone.

And so? Since the cookbooks are unfortunately silent on how to prepare and cook them, allow me to offer a few recipes of my own. But be warned — long-suffering and patience are required when dealing with *goewerneursboontjies*.

To cook them, remove them from the airtight jar — a cupful is enough to start with. Examine them, and discard any that are not pristinely pure, perfect and pleasing to the eye. Wash them in cold water to get rid of any lingering grains, then place them in a clean saucepan and cover them with tap or fountain water. Let them soak awhile, but definitely not too long. Even when it comes to the lesser dry bean types, I am always horrified when I read the instruction in a cookbook to 'soak them overnight in cold water'. Phantoms of Carême and La Chapelle![1] That is no way to treat a governor's bean! Too long a soaking will stimulate growth, resuscitating its dormant lust for life and activating that most mysterious of chemical metabolisms that can ruin the taste in an instant. So soak them for an hour and a half at most, no longer.

Drain off the water and submerge them again, this time in lukewarm water with a pinch of salt. But in heaven's name, no bicarbonate of soda!

Nothing, alas, can preserve the magnificent colour of the beans. When cooked, they lose their colour and turn brown — light brown when cooked slowly and thoroughly, as they should be, or a darker brown when cooked too fast. Keep the lid on the saucepan, but give it an occasional shake, and add a bit of warm water from time to time so the beans remain submerged. When they are soft, take the saucepan from the fireplace, drain the water in a colander, and shake the beans dry.

For connoisseurs who prefer a simple, pure vegetable taste, they are now cooked and ready for the table. They are especially good when cold, for it is then that they have the genuine *goewerneursboontjie* taste — something between that of a chestnut and a dried medlar. You can serve them with a sour sauce, or as a salad with a simple mixture of vinegar and pepper, a touch of mustard and a dash of oil.

But what about something a bit more sophisticated, something more

---

1 A. Carême, author of a 5 volume work on French cooking (1835), perfected the art of *haute cuisine*. Vincent La Chapelle, author of *The Modern Cook* (1733), was Chef de Cuisine to the Prince of Orange and Naussau.

refined? Some of us are not content with sheer simplicity — we prefer the lily gilded, a whiff of perfume with the fragrant mignonette!

For the benefit of these connoisseurs, put the beans back in the saucepan with a pinch of pepper, ginger and mace. Add a cup of meat or chicken soup, and cook slowly with the lid on. In another saucepan braise a sliced onion (with a suspicion of garlic, if desired), and when it is light brown, mix in a few tablespoonsful of tomato sauce. Dilute with a few spoonsful of the soup in which the beans are cooking, then add the mixture to the beans, stirring carefully to keep them intact. Cook for a few minutes longer, and serve with a sprinkling of parsley.

Another method. Put the beans in the saucepan with a large tablespoonful of butter or soft, preferably chicken, fat. Add pepper, mace and herbs; and braise slowly, taking care not to break the beans. Serve with grated nutmeg or a sprinkling of parsley.

And what should one drink with it? It is a colourful dish, and aesthetics demand a wine of colour — so serve a red table wine, one that is not sweet.

10 April 1942

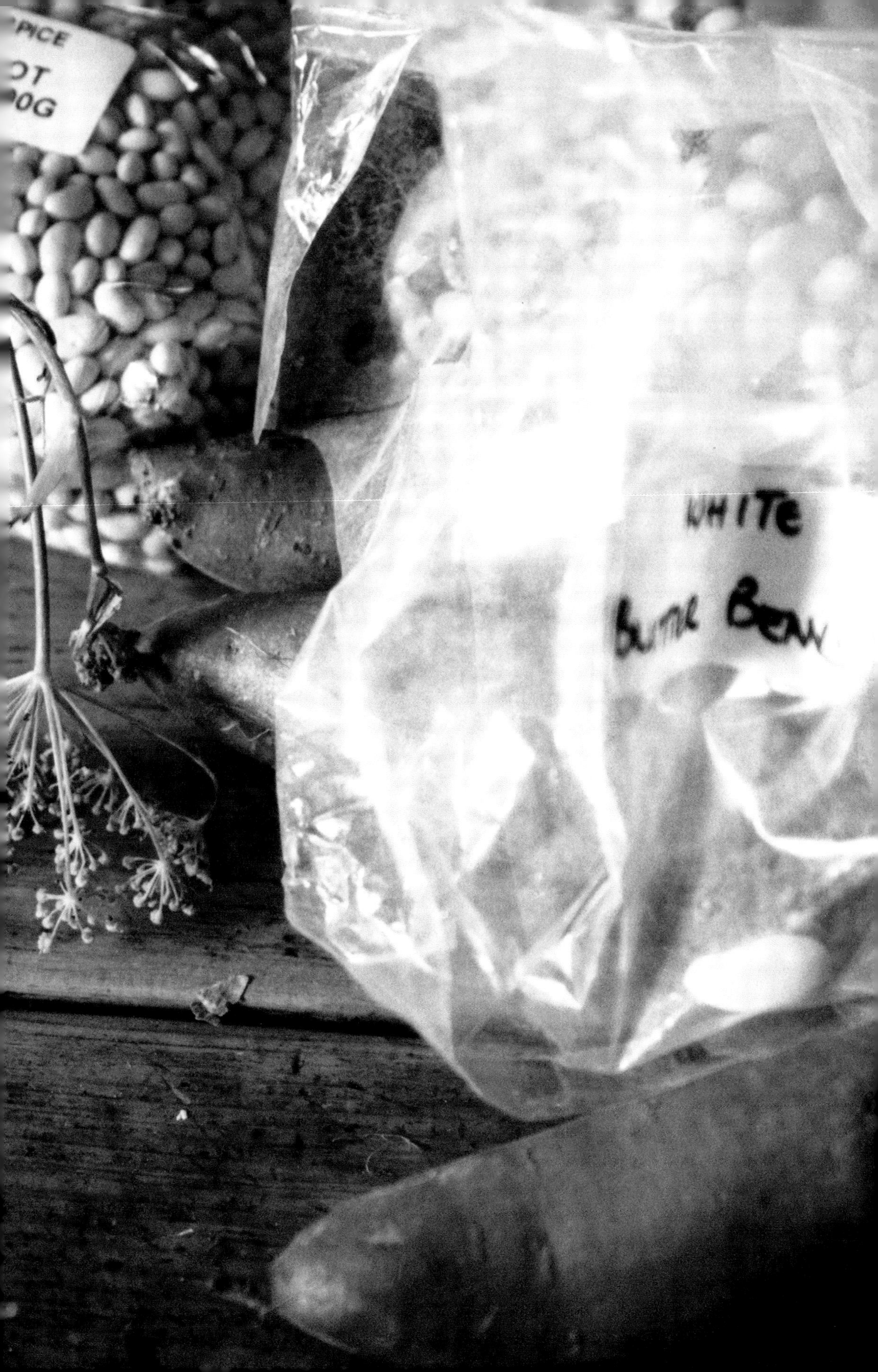
WHITE

Jakkalskos Soufflé

One of my friends from the Congo is a food connoisseur, a gourmet of the highest — or possibly the lowest — order. He is so fastidious a perfectionist that old Griet, who can just about make an excellent soup, and whom I have taught to sprinkle fennel leaves over a leg of lamb (when she remembers!), nearly choked when I announced: 'The gentleman who speaks with a hot potato in his mouth is coming for dinner tonight'.

My friend had asked me to serve him something truly indigenous. I replied that there was no such thing as an authentically Afrikaans dish, and that all we have are some traditional methods of preparing food.

'But give me a little while,' I told him. 'I'll let you know as soon as I have something good I can guarantee you've never tasted before!'

This was a promise I simply had to fulfil. What on earth could I offer him that was so Afrikaans he would be unable to find it anywhere in *Larousse*, that wonderfully exhaustive encyclopaedia of food?

Should I give him *wateruintjie*?[1] Alas, it was not the right time of year. Or *klipkous*?[2] But that could be had in Australia or Vera Cruz, that Cape Town-like city in the Gulf of Mexico. Or smoked ostrich egg in a parcel of puff pastry? That was a possibility, and he would definitely not find it under *Oeufs* in *Larousse*. But wait, there *was* something he would not find anywhere else on earth — *jakkalskos*.[3]

The know-all botanists call it the seed or 'fruit' of a parasitical plant, *Hydnora africana*, first described by Thunberg. That famous traveller mentions that the Hottentots ate it, but does not seem to have had the slightest idea that it could be cultivated. It is found in sandy soil, in the shade of a *melkbos*,[4] on whose roots it thrives as a parasite. The seed — if we are to believe *Oubaas* Marloth, who investigated this matter thoroughly and has a rather idealised colour picture of it in his expensive book — is carried down to the roots by ants. There it sprouts and, after a few weeks, the flower emerges from the sand. It is a somewhat strange flower with an unpleasant smell, but fortunately we do not have to worry about that — it is only the fruit we are interested in.

---

1 Water hawthorn, *Apogoneton distachyos*.
2 *Perlemoen*, or abalone.
3 Literally 'jackal food'.
4 A shrubby euphorbia, probably *Euphorbia mauritanica*, which Marloth describes as the main host (R. Marloth, *Flora of South Africa*, I, 178).

It is actually a kind of subterranean bulb, although — according to the botanists — it is not really a bulb at all, but a rounded fruit somewhat like a guava. It has a thin, mahogany-coloured skin, and juicy, custard-like flesh containing dozens of small seeds. Dr Marloth tells us that porcupines, baboons and jackals dig it up and feed on it. He could safely have added that, from time immemorial, two-legged connoisseurs have been doing much the same.

When I was young I often used to see the *jakkalskos* fruit at the old fish and vegetable market in Cape Town. In those days it was a celebrated and rare treat. The chef at the White House in Strand Street would sometimes serve it as a dessert. She would prepare it as follows.

Cut open the fruit with a silver or wooden spoon. ('Whatever you do, *Basie*, please don't use steel; somehow it makes a difference to the taste, and then *Basie* might just as well eat tapioca pudding.') Scrape out the soft inside and press it through a sieve to remove the small, hard, bitter seeds. Beat it up with a touch of cream, a glass of jerepigo (nowadays I would use a good sherry) and a pinch of fine sugar. Sprinkle with cinnamon, and serve with a biscuit in a cream glass.

Last year I managed to get hold of a few nice large specimens. One was already too old to use, but two were still fresh and juicy. I attempted, in the manner of Carême, a trial run, and invited my connoisseur friend over as the guinea-pig.

'This is a really strange kind of soufflé,' he said. He is a cautious man, and prides himself on not being easily led up the garden path when it comes to food. 'But I would never add cinnamon to medlars,' he added, in the tone of the master showing a youngster precisely how the ablative was correctly used by the Romans.

'This is, of course, not medlar soufflé,' I said. 'But tell me, how do you like it?'

'Interesting, but good,' he answered. 'With guavas I always add some maraschino. In this case it would definitely have been an improvement.'

'Wrong again,' I said. 'This is no guava, although you could possibly call it a younger brother — a subterranean younger brother at that!'

My dish was quite simple. The juicy inside of the *jakkalskos*, relieved of its burden of bitter pips, was beaten up with the white of three eggs, a little sugar, a tablespoonful of cream, and a glass of sherry. This was poured into a soufflé dish well greased with butter. As befits a soufflé, it was put into a glowing oven a few minutes before being served, with a grating of cinnamon on top, and taken to table as soon as it had risen nicely — the precise, exact, apostle-truth moment to serve a soufflé can only be learned by experience, often bitter experience. A soufflé, if it is truly a soufflé and not a bastardised flour pudding, should be served piping hot, soft as a cloud, and crispy-hard on the outside.

jakkalskos soufflé

The taste of *jakkalskos* soufflé is, well, impossible to describe, much as you cannot describe the taste of pineapple soufflé. Just try it yourself if you ever get hold of some *jakkalskos*. And have a glass of muscadel with it! Then you will truly be able to say: 'Now I've really eaten something indigenous to our own South Africa!'

8 May 1942

3

Sherry

It is customary — justifiably, in my view — to have something to drink before dinner. Our forefathers have done so from time immemorial. A *pimpeltjie* of wine before the meal was the expression in the old days, when that seaman's term still had currency. Today, nobody knows what a *pimpeltjie* is. But when I was young, the old ayahs in the cool shade of the vegetable market that used to be one of the sights of Cape Town used to employ that term for what we would now call a *pierinkievol*;[1] they also spoke of a *pimpeltjie* when referring to a 'small bunch' of something. But originally a *pimpeltjie* was a measure of wine, a small glass taken before the meal.

From a health point of view, there is something to be said for having a sip of wine before the main meal of the day. It is not just that alcohol stimulates the stomach to produce its digestive juices, but probably also the way in which the amino acids and oils in the wine enable you, twenty minutes later, to appreciate good food better.

The question, then, is not whether to drink, but what to drink. Definitely not those heavy mixtures of fortified wines, liqueurs, gins, Canadian grain-spirits, English beer-brandies, or even Russian vodkas, and absolutely not the one hundred and three variations of the American cocktail. They spoil your sense of taste and ruin your appetite. The only possible exception — but I would question even that — is the mixture consisting of one-third lime juice and two-thirds first-class Bols.

No, the very best drink before supper is a small glass of genuine sherry. It contains everything you need for the preparatory stimulation of the stomach lining, and too little alcohol to have a damaging effect on the appetite. Sherry — that is the best pre-prandial drink!

But what exactly is a sherry? I would be the last to defend, or even justify, the ridiculous fashion of giving the family names of established European wines to our Cape varieties. I shudder when I hear of a Cape hock or a South African burgundy. But with sherry it is different. Originally — in the distant past — it was a wine made exclusively in and around Xerez de la Frontera, in the south of Spain, by pressing red and white grapes with a wheelbarrowful of gypsum, and making from that a very light wine that could survive transportation, exposure to air and climatic change. It was then a very cheap wine, and not at all fashionable. The English soldiers in Wellington's army adopted it as their daily drink, and took a taste for it back to England (where it had, however, already been

---

1 Saucerful.

known since the time of Shakespeare), with the result that it became fashionable, especially in the western part of the country. English winelords then bought up vineyards in the south of Spain and spent a lot of money improving the wine.

Experts established that sherry was the only wine to undergo a double fermentation, but with the passage of time all sorts of superstitions arose about it. One of these was that it becomes much softer and better when sent on a journey around the world, heaven alone knows why. This legend of the overwhelmingly delicious quality of sherry that has circumnavigated the globe was undermined by one of the Walters. He bound a keg of sherry to one of his 'travelling' printing presses, letting it turn and shake about for eighteen months, and found that there was no noticeable difference between it and one that had been spared all the motion. Nevertheless, the fashion of sending shipments on a world trip gave us here in South Africa (or rather our forefathers, for we do not get it any more) the opportunity of drinking first-class sherries. The sherry of 1882 was especially famous — after the harvest of 1870 it was perhaps the best wine on the market — and the *raya* or second-class version thereof could cost up to £200 a barrel. For one or other reason a shipment was sold here, and some of it was still to be found at the old Poole's Hotel and, strangely enough, also at a well-known old boarding-house in Three Anchor Bay.

Today sherry is a 'made' wine, in the sense that it is not a pure harvest wine. It also differs in the way it is produced. When the grapes have been pressed and the first fermentation has taken place, the must is 'ignited' with a special germ, the so-called sherry *'flor'*, that induces a second fermentation. This causes just about all the alcohol to disappear from the wine, leaving it with more amino acids and oil-rich substances, and all this is due to a highly complicated chemical process about which the *cognoscenti* can tell us very little. It is, in fact, because this second fermentation is so complicated and mysterious that no one can tell in advance what the outcome will be. It may be an almost clear, quite bitter, very dry wine; it may be darker, richer, oilier; or it may be highly aromatic but very bitter. All three must first be blended and prepared for the market. This is done by adding wine-spirit or a sweet wine (when the *oleroso* or *amoroso* type is preferred), and especially by adding other sherries that have stood in barrels for years. The best sherries are blended by using the *solera* method. This simply involves, at the risk of undermining the mystique associated with making a good sherry, a shelf of sherry barrels arranged according to age. A good modern sherry is a blended wine in which the different older sherries are properly mixed. Assume, thus, that the sherry farmer started with a barrel of wine from 1920 and kept a supply of that and each subsequent year's produce up to 1940. The sherry of 1941 would then contain some of each year's wine, and it would thus obviously make no sense to speak of the sherry as a vintage wine. The sherry of a particular year could still dominate, though, in spite of careful blending by the *solera* expert.

Sherry is a wine that can stand exposed to the air without going flat. Indeed, it is better to uncork a bottle of sherry a few hours before drinking. It should be enjoyed without warming or cooling — normal room temperature is sufficient to allow the oily taste to come fully into its own. The unfalsified *fino* — almost colourless, aromatic, bone-dry, and bitter without any trace of brackishness — you will not find for sale. Only the KWV has it, for those who are able to coax it from them. The article for sale is the somewhat stronger, fortified, sweetened wine, of which every wine dealer has its own brand. I dare not name my own favourites here, and it is really not necessary to do so, for everyone should simply follow his own taste, or rely on a reputable wine merchant to make a recommendation.

The excellence of sherry is due to the quality of its various components, the most important of which are the oils, fatty acids and amino acids, and the least important of which is the alcohol content. It is a wine that should be sipped slowly and emphatically, preferably on its own. As a table wine I recommend it just before the meal, possibly with the soup (unless the taste of the soup is too floury — so not with a purée), and possibly even with a fish like *katonkel*[1] or *halfkoord*.[2] It really does not go with anything sugary, and it is far too proud of its own flavour to keep the inferior company of fruit and walnuts — its own nuttiness and its own fruity oils are sufficient, thank you very much! Therefore enjoy it as a *pimpeltjie* before the meal — preferably not the sweet variety — or as a drink on its own, for which the *oleroso*, darker, or semi-sweet varieties would be suitable, to be taken at about eleven in the morning, especially on a beautiful sunny day when the *vygies*[3] are blossoming and the sheaves of wheat are being brought in from the lands.

29 May 1942

---

1   Barracuda.
2   Yellowtail.
3   Figs, literally; a term used for all the plants in the Mesembryanthemum family.

sherry

4

Potatoes

It is indeed strange that we should classify potatoes as *groente*.[1] A potato contains neither vegetable juice nor chlorophyll. It is a subterranean food supply for a vegetable plant whose leaves, flowers, seeds and fruit we do not use at all. Other vegetable plants whose bulbous food supplies we also use — such as beetroot, various types of carrot, and turnips — have leaves that can be eaten. Beetroot leaves make an excellent stew, for instance, and carrot and turnip leaves can quite profitably be added to vegetable purées.

But with potatoes it is different. It is thought that the potato comes from South America, whence it migrated to North America about a thousand years ago. Scholars have argued about the identity of its original ancestor, but — in spite of considerable botanical research — the answer remains elusive. The general hypothesis is that the original plant had very small potatoes — about as large as the subterranean knolls of the species of *Kleinia* found in the *Springbokvlakte*[2] — and that by selective breeding it developed into today's larger potato. However that may be, it is safe to assume that the potato is one of the most important foodstuffs in the world today.

As such it must feature in any culinary reckoning, as indeed it has from days of yore. When La Chapelle wrote his authoritative *Le Cuisinier moderne en cinq volumes* in the early eighteenth century, the culinary art was already acquainted with no less than three hundred recipes for the preparation of a potato. In the somewhat ostentatious dedication to his book, 'A Son Altesse Serenissime Guillaume-Charles,[3] Henry Fris' — I challenge any matriculation student in this country to tell me who His Illustrious Highness was — La Chapelle commits himself to pure simplicity and pledges not to be a chef for the rich only. Nevertheless, some of his recipes are so extravagant that no modern housewife would follow them without adaptation. In one of his recipes for potatoes, for instance, he prescribes *inter alia* three litres of cream, half a litre of butter, and the beaten yolks of three dozen eggs. Ayah Toontjies would have had a fit at the mere thought of having to beat all those eggs!

Like his Italian counterparts, La Chapelle was well aware of the fact that potatoes are not as innocent as they seem. Like onions, potatoes are in fact

---

1 Vegetables, literally 'greens'.
2 Leipoldt is probably referring to *Kleinia stipuliformis*, which has knobbly stolons, from the area north of Pretoria.
3 This translation of Vincent La Chapelle's *The Modern Cook* (London, 1733) was dedicated to Prince William of Orange, whose Chef de Cuisine La Chappele was.

poisonous. Do not be alarmed at this chemical truth, for we consume many things that contain poison. Egg yolk, for instance, contains a particularly strong poison. And ghoo beans contain prussic acid, probably the strongest poison we know. Potatoes contain solanine — which, even in its weakest form, can cause painful stomach cramps. And indeed potatoes sometimes do cause precisely that.

In my youth the most prized cookbook in this country was *Aaltjie, of de Zuinige Keukenmeid.*[1] The first edition of this book mentions nothing about potatoes being poisonous, but subsequently an editor must have felt constrained to include a word of warning, for the third edition warns against potatoes that are 'not ripe' and that 'may be the cause of sudden discomfort'. The story is then told of a family that ate unripe potatoes and suffered such bad food poisoning that they were ill for days. Also mentioned is a case where potatoes occasioned death.

It is well known that poisonous solanine is found in the stalk and roots of the potato, especially in young potatoes that have not yet matured. As the potato matures its poison content becomes less, but solanine is produced once more when it starts sprouting. The answer is therefore not to use potatoes that are too young or that have sprouted, and — to be completely safe — to remove carefully the eyes of every potato. Boiling water dissolves the solanine, so when potatoes are well boiled even the young ones become harmless. But raw potatoes and young potatoes that are not properly baked or boiled can still, to this day, occasion 'sudden discomfort'. Be warned, then, and select full-grown, adult potatoes — those that, as it were, have matriculated or have the vote, but excluding those of marriageable age, for it seems — from the latest statistics, at least — that marriageable age is often accompanied by a poisonous precociousness.

There are numerous methods of preparing delicious potatoes, as is evidenced by the veritable 'commando' of recipes in *Larousse*[2] — which, by the way, is not at all comprehensive, for I know quite a few that are not included. Take, for instance, potatoes à la Ayah Toontjies.

'Take six medium potatoes of the mealy variety, *Basie*,[3] and cook until they are very soft. Remove any dust and sand, and scrape out the eyes. Put them in an iron pot, with a cup of water and a little salt, and let them boil with the lid on — until the skins burst, *my Basie*. Take them out and peel them with a pocket-knife, *my Basie*. Then place them in an earthenware pot, with a pinch of ginger, a sprig of plucked fennel and a large dollop of butter, and put it in the oven. Shake the pot occasionally, but let them absorb the butter thoroughly, *my Basie*, without getting burnt. Sprinkle with grated nutmeg and send off to table with a baked chicken.'

---

1 Literally, *Tiny Eel, or the Stingy Kitchen Maid.*
2 *Larousse gastronomique,* first published in Paris, 1938.
3 Literally, 'little master'.

In Vera Cruz I saw an old ayah do exactly the same, with only one difference — she sprinkled grated cinnamon instead of nutmeg and used a pinch of saffron instead of fennel. Both dishes are first-class, provided you use those mealy potatoes that are not so easy to find these days.

Ayah Toontjies's second recipe is also not to be found in *Larousse*.

'Boil the potatoes, as before, in their skins before peeling them. Boil six young turnips in the same way. Grease your earthenware pot well with fat or butter, and cover the bottom with a layer of diced potato. Sprinkle with grated cheese mixed with a little salt and pepper' — Ayah Toontjies was sometimes bold enough to add chillies, but this is a matter of taste, or perhaps more properly of inflicting pain! 'Cover with a layer of diced turnip; sprinkle once more with grated cheese; then another layer of potatoes. Cover with a *bobotie* custard (a cup of milk beaten with two egg yolks, a few spoons of cream, and a pinch of saffron or turmeric for colour) and place in the oven.' A delicious dish when properly cooked!

Not easy enough? Too extravagant? All right then, here is the simplest and perhaps — after you've tried all four hundred or more recipes — the very best way of preparing Parmentier's fashion-vegetable for the table.

'Take large, mealy potatoes. Clean well and cut out the eyes. Place in the oven, which needs to be quite warm (use a piece of paper to test the temperature). Let them bake until the skins start bursting open. Remove from the oven, and wrap each potato in a handsome little napkin. Serve with molten butter and a mixture of three parts of fine salt to one part of white pepper.'

Baked potatoes like these taste best outdoors on a cold winter's evening. But the potatoes really must be mealy, otherwise it is just a calcified ambrosia.

19 June 1942

5

Liqueurs

My old friend, Jaap Snoep,[1] is very particular about liqueurs. The other day he brought me an old bottle covered in cobwebs. 'It's a Van der Hum, sixty years old. My late *tannie*[2] kept it all this time, and it is really excellent.'

We opened the bottle. This was not easy — the cork was rotten and had to be extracted carefully, bit by bit. The liqueur was turbid, and though it still tasted somewhat like the old Cape liqueur, the resemblance was not great. To be frank, the old *tannie's* sixty-year-old liqueur was rather a disappointment.

That was to be expected. As in the case of brandy, no liqueur is improved by lying carefully corked up in a bottle for ages. The mysterious change that the wine-spirits and other ingredients of a good old brandy — from which a good liqueur should be made — undergo with time, is a chemical change that is largely due to the air to which they are exposed. In a well-corked, lacquered bottle, the only air that has contact with the liqueur is the small amount locked between the bottom of the cork and the surface of the liquid in the neck of the bottle. It can, therefore, when the bottle is kept upright, only influence a very small surface of the liqueur. Even when the bottle is kept on its side and the small amount of air may perhaps have a greater exposure to the liqueur, it is hardly enough to effect any change in its quality. It would, of course, be a completely different matter if the liqueur were stored in a barrel, but then there would not be a drop of it left after sixty years — it would have evaporated completely!

A good liqueur should, however, not lose its quality when stored with care. The deterioration of the old *tannie's* liqueur was simply due to the bad cork and, although I did not dare tell this to Jaap, the fact that it was not a first-class liqueur in the first place. I have, in my time, enjoyed a Noyau, or almond liqueur, that was more than two hundred years old, and it was still as pure and aromatic as if it were just a few years old.

Liqueurs are the alcoholic extracts of spices, with or without the addition of syrup. The alcohol content is — and should always be — quite high, otherwise there would be a danger of further fermentation, with inevitable deterioration in the taste. The main component of any good liqueur is therefore a first-class brandy; and the better the brandy, the better the liqueur will be. Do not think that you can ever make a fine liqueur from an inferior brandy.

---

1 Literally 'Stingy Jack'.
2 Aunt.

There are many liqueurs on the market, and it should be clear from the above definition that it would be impossible to limit the variety of spice extracts. The most important and popular types are world-famous. Among them are the yellow and green Chartreuse — perhaps the most famous, originally made by monks in Chartreux Abbey from honey, hyssop, cinnamon, saffron and herbs distilled with brandy and then mixed with a sugar-syrup; Curaçao, bitter-lemon liqueur, cherry liqueur, Danzig liqueur, Maraschino, Mastika and a variety of other liqueurs that contain relatively little sugar compared to the sweet Chartreuse; Van der Hum, and all the fruit-liqueurs. Liqueurs that are not sweet — for example, kümmel — are nearly all distilled liqueurs, with a high alcohol content, and are therefore hard tack. On the other hand, the *crèmes* of sweet liqueurs are mostly extremely sweet, with a high sugar content and less alcohol. Some, like *crème de cacao*, contain only enough alcohol to prevent fermentation, and are thus no more than a fortified sweet wine.

Our Afrikaans Van der Hum belongs to the *crèmes*. It is not our own invention, since a similar liqueur is made in the West Indies, and probably also in China. I have been unable to establish exactly how old it is. Nor have I been able to find any mention of it in print prior to 1850. This is a subject worthy of further inquiry, for this liqueur of ours is a product of which we can be truly proud; and I strongly recommend that research on the origins of Van der Hum be conducted as a labour of love by some student in search of a thesis topic. It is not mentioned in *Larousse*, but Baron Vaerst evidently knew it — a quotation from him is the oldest I have found. The earliest printed recipe I have been able to get hold of is that of Mrs Cloete in the first edition of *Hilda*[1] in 1891. I do, however, have a written recipe from the Schwabe family that was probably written in 1836, and is more or less the same as that of Mrs Cloete.

'Dissolve three pounds of black sugar-stick in six bottles of good Armagnac Brandy, and leave to stand for two days; mix a hundred Ceylon cloves with half a pound of ground thin cinnamon and the ground dried peels of five *naartjes*.[2] Add one ground nutmeg and a shred of mace. Pour the brandy over the mixture and stir well; leave to stand in a cool place in the cellar, covered with a wet napkin. Stir well daily. After two months, filter it two or three times through a cloth until it is nicely clear. Decant into bottles, cork well, and seal or cover the cork with beeswax.'

Variations of this recipe can be found in later cookbooks. Some suggest the addition of allspice or cardamon, others the use of a small piece of *bitterskil*;[3] one also mentions a few bitter almonds. I have tried them all, and still prefer the old Cloete-Schwabe recipe. It produces a first-class oily liqueur in which the taste of cloves mingles with that of *naartje*-peel. Our

culinary treasures

1   *Hilda's 'Where is it?' of Recipes* by Hildagonda Duckitt.
2   Tangerines.
3   Literally, 'bitter peel'.

218

best South African brandy is just as good — perhaps even better — than the French Armagnac or Cognac, and it is still possible to find some good brown or black sugar-stick, which is best dissolved by first grinding it.

Van der Hum is, of course, not our only liqueur. When I was very young I knew a Kukumakranka liqueur, made from sugar-stick, brandy, honey, cinnamon, orange peel and a few ground *kukumakranka*[1] seeds — a strange drink with a very odd flavour. There is also sugar-bush syrup liqueur, made from sugar-bush syrup,[2] brandy, *anyswortel*,[3] cloves and nutmeg — a shiny-yellow liquid with a fairly pungent taste. I still know *tannies* who make a loquat liqueur every year, as well as one who makes a very good liqueur from *kafferpruime*.[4]

10 July 1942

---

1 *Gethyllis* spp.
2 The nectar of *Protea repens*, the *suikerbos*.
3 Aniseed root *Annesorhiza* sp.
4 Literally, 'Kaffir plums', the fruit of *Harpephyllum caffrum*.

Our Cape Kitchen

In the good old days, when Cape Town still showed signs of being a real mother city, nurturing western civilisation, it was possible — in an old-fashioned way — to learn something of real Afrikaans cookery. A nation's culinary art cannot be judged by what is served in hotels and restaurants — to make an accurate appraisal, the connoisseur must have special friends with excellent cooks. The best traditional food is invariably found in private homes, not public eateries.

This is no less true of Cape Town than of anywhere else. Fifty years ago, the food in our hotels and fashionable cafés — such as that of Kamp — was mostly prepared and served in accordance with European standards. There were, of course, important exceptions, one being the famous White House in Strand Street — which had a good collection of game in its backyard. (I especially remember a young camel that, alas, did not survive very long.) The White House was well known for its excellent table. Even at eight o'clock in the morning, you could get sosaties with the customary fried bananas and no less than six different *sambals*.[1] Luncheon was something special, and from time to time the menu would contain delicacies such as turnip and tomato *bredie*, curried crayfish soup, saffron *bobotie* with almonds and raisins, and stewed *veldkool*.[2] Among the sweets was one that was prized by *plattelanders*[3] and Capetonians alike — thin, juicy, fragrant pancakes with a delicious topping made from eggs, cream and Van der Hum. Another hotel where the food was good and the cellar really impressive was the old Royal in Plein Street. Later, the Queens in Sea Point was also well known for its excellent table, but it did not specialise in genuine Afrikaans food.

Traditional Afrikaans dishes were found in private homes and in smaller boarding-houses. There you could enjoy first-class traditional fare, properly prepared over the moderated heat of a wood fire — we would not have considered scorching our food with a hot wire! The best known of the Afrikaans boarding-houses was probably that of old Miss Wahl in Queen Victoria Street, the popular home-from-home of many *platteland* Members of Parliament. The hostess was herself an excellent cook, who had the gift of being able to prepare simple yet exceptionally delicious dishes. Some of the house recipes — such as her crayfish salad, crayfish *frikkadel*,[4] bean soup and milk tart — were as traditional as you could get. One of the finest things available there was the coffee, served with plain cake and one or other fine preserve.

---

1 Condiments.
2 Literally, 'veld cabbage', *Trachyandra* sp.
3 Countryside dwellers.
4 Meatball.

34. WH I

The question remains whether we have a culinary art that can validly be described as genuinely and indigenously Afrikaans. In favour of this proposition is the fact that we do have certain food types — such as *klipkous*[1] and *wateruintjies*[2] — that are found only here, and we have at least one method of preparing food that is not to be found in *Larousse* — the preparation of porcupine skin. On the other hand, there is hardly any so-called 'Afrikaans dish' the preparation and contents of which were not known to our forefathers in Europe. *Bobotie*, for example, is described in an old cookbook published in 1609, years before the establishment of a European settlement at the Cape. Our *bredies* are nothing more than the meat and vegetable mixtures that were fashionable in the South of France, Spain and Italy during the Middle Ages. They would not, of course, have used mace, nutmeg, pepper and other spices — such additives were far too scarce then to have been used in the common kitchen. It was only after the Dutch East India Company started importing spices on a large scale — in one year over 100 000 tons from India — that the ordinary cook was able to get hold of them to add flavour to his dishes.

What we call traditional Afrikaans cooking can be compared to that found in the area south of the Ardour River in France. It is the part of France that was probably the longest under English influence. It is an area where the oxen are used — just like here — for working the fields and transporting goods, where beef is generally less tender and plump than in other districts, and where goat's meat, mutton and pork are preferred. There you will find the closest relative to our *boerewors* — sausage made of a mixture of goat's meat and pork, flavoured with spices and improved by the addition of sweet wine such as that from Jurançon. It contains the same little squares of pork fat that are so characteristic of good *boerewors*, enabling it to be properly *braaied*[3] over an open fire without depriving it of its juiciness. There you will also find the bean and fat soup so well known here, the grilled *pannas*[4] that are hardly known here any more but always used to be made when a pig was slaughtered, and also the stewed offal, with or without a turmeric or tomato sauce. There also you will encounter the habit of dishing up, in all its grisly splendour, an ox's head, complete with horns and skin, roasted in the oven — something completely unfashionable here but still found in the Transvaal. The last time I enjoyed it — and it was a real delicacy — I was in the company of General Botha, who expressly declared that the cheek of an ox-head roasted in this manner was the tastiest meat human teeth could ever chew.

Our contemporary schools for domestic science have thus far not managed to produce excellent cooks. Why, I really do not know — possibly

---

1 Ear-shell.
2 Water hawthorn, *Aponogeton distachyos*.
3 Grilled.
4 Scrapple. See p 245.

because our culinary art, like all our other arts, is still based on the English model. We are good imitators, but we seldom create anything original, of our own imagining — we are seldom roused by inspiration springing from an inner desire to create something of our own, willing to risk failure in the attempt. Our Afrikaans culinary art is about as feeble as our *volkspele*,[1] and these too are imitations of what we have inherited from Europe. Yet we have enough material to enable us to develop our own methods of preparing unique, characteristically Afrikaans food. We have seeds, leaves, herbs, roots and bark capable of imparting a very different flavour and taste compared with those embodied in conventional cookbook recipes. I do not know — and I really do not care — whether these innovations would actually be improvements. I plead only that we should try them. The art of cooking is, in essence, the art of making food tastier and more nourishing, and additives are both useful and necessary to this end. A dish without salt is not only tasteless, but also less nourishing than one that has been properly salted. Salt is a spice that needs to be used as carefully but also just as boldly as ginger, fennel, or cinnamon. I know a type of sage that improves the taste of a potato *bredie* twenty-fold when added to it, and a geranium leaf — a type that grows somewhere in the Eastern districts — that considerably enriches the flavour of a chop. If we were to take our cooking more seriously, we would utilise our indigenous treasures from veld and *kloof*. But without experimentation, there will be no progress.

7 August 1942

---

1   Folk dances.

Veldkool

Now is the season for *veldkool*.[1] Just after the winter rains, when the world is green and the veld is sown with sorrel, it is time to harvest this delicious veld food that city folk have hardly discovered yet. Once they find out how delicious *veldkool* is, it will quite possibly be cultivated in our gardens, as there is no reason why it cannot be 'tamed'. I have cultivated the smaller type in my own garden for years with hardly any effort, for it sows itself and provides enough each year for a few cookings. The larger, possibly more tasty, type is, however, less easy to cultivate. I tried sowing it, but without success. Then I tried transplanting it, similarly without success. But perhaps a more knowledgeable gardener, who knows more about such things, will be able to establish even the giant *veldkool*, that grows almost to the height of a man in the Karoo soil, in the vegetable garden.

Veldkool is, oddly enough, a type of lily. It belongs, so the botanists assure me, to the same family as our aloes and chincherinchees. The particular subcategory that *veldkool* belongs to is the genus *Anthericum*, most of the members of which are found in South Africa.[2] Most of them are edible, but some have a nauseatingly bitter taste, although I do not know of any that are significantly poisonous. The two varieties that are best known in the *platteland* are the little, small-leaved *veldkool* and the large, slime-leaved *veldkool*. Both are commonly called *Hotnotskool*, or wild cauliflower. In some districts the small-leaved variety is called *slaaikool*, and the broad-leaved one *steelkool* because it forms branches. The first is found in sandy soil, and its flower buds – the only part of the *veldkool* that is eaten – do not stand high above the ground. Sometimes it even becomes a creeper. The second variety is found in clay soil. It is particularly abundant in Karoo soil or in shale on the slopes of hillsides, although it is also found on plains where the soil comes mostly from sandstone. It has a much broader leaf than the smaller kind and is never a creeper, but has upstanding flower stems with four to twelve buds on each branch. Sometimes, when the veld is beautiful after the rains, it is easy to pick a whole batch for the pot in a few minutes. Only the flower buds should be picked – when the blossoms have opened they are no longer so juicy, and the fibre of the stems is tougher.

---

1 Leipoldt describes two species of *Trachyandra*, the low-growing *T. ciliata* ('*slaaikool*', salad cabbage) and the much-branching *T. muricata* ('*steelkool*', or stalk cabbage), which prefers clay, though he may also be thinking of the broad-leaved *T. falcata* which grows in sand. The 'giant *veldkool*' may be the (poisonous) *Drimia capensis*, which is superficially like a *Trachyandra*.

2 When the lily family was reorganised, the Trachyandras were taken away from the Anthericums and placed in the Asphodel family.

No research has been done into the vitamin content or any other nutrition provided by *veldkool*. But the experience of generations has been that it is an excellent vegetable, comparable to chicory, spinach and chervil, as far as its nutritional value is concerned. Like normal cabbage, it contains a reasonably large percentage of aluminium, which happens to be a slow-working poison that our bodies cannot use. But the fact that garden cabbage contains this metal has never stopped us from eating it, and there is no reason at all for avoiding *veldkool* simply because it contains a bit of aluminium.

I am not very impressed by the way vitamins are worshipped nowadays, but I would say that *veldkool* provides in abundance all the necessary vitamins that could be expected of it. Even if it contained none of these new idols, or lacked A to L, or whatever letter the known line-up of vitamins has reached, I would still put in a word for it.

For *veldkool* is truly one of the finest and most delicious vegetables to be found in sunny South Africa. Taste is, of course, not debatable. Jan prefers marrows to asparagus; Magriet has an aversion to scorzonera.[1] But I have never come across anyone who said no to a dish of deliciously prepared *veldkool*. And when I do meet someone like that, I shall know for sure that there is something wrong with him.

To prepare *veldkool* properly for the table, the freshly picked flower buds need to be soaked for a quarter of an hour in a bowl of salt water to get rid of sand and dust, and also any little bugs hiding in the petals. Then place them − the flower buds, not the bugs − in an iron or earthenware pot. Never use an aluminium saucepan, for that would spoil the taste. This is not a warning I need give the knowledgeable cook − she will know that it is a sin and a mockery of everything that is good to cook vegetables in aluminium equipment. But for the unschooled, this is a tip worth noting, especially nowadays when we are endlessly cajoled into acquiring such equipment for the kitchen. Cook the buds, very slowly, in a little bit of water; add, according to taste, some mutton, preferably from the rib side, with a morsel of fat. Take care with the fat, for *veldkool* must never be fatty; the fat, meat and *veldkool* should complement each other, and more or less melt together into a delicious mixture. Stew slowly over a moderately weak fire. Some cooks then press it through a strainer and add cream, butter and even egg yolks. My own view is that the only thing that really goes nicely with a well-braised *veldkool*, after it has been properly salted and peppered according to taste, is a bunch of yellow sorrel leaves, finely chopped and added when the *veldkool* is nicely soft. Garden sorrel can also be used, but its taste is a little too wild and spoils the fine flavour and peculiar plumpness of the *kool*. Many other recipes could, of course, be used to prepare *veldkool*. It could be served as a puree, as a tasty soup, as a soufflé baked in the oven,

---

1 A dandelion-like plant, with a black edible root.

as a pie, or as an open vegetable tart. I have also had it with a Mornay or cheese sauce, but prefer it in a simpler guise, without any additions that detract from its inherent delicacy. The one exception I would make to this is when it is served on occasion as the base of a sole prepared in the Florentine manner. The orthodox rule is to serve the sole on a layer of spinach. Try it on a bedding of nicely cooked *veldkool*, and see how wonderfully it enhances the taste.

One of the good things about *veldkool* is that it will never spoil the taste of even the most delicate wine. You can safely have a first-class Riesling, even — if you still have one in your cellar — a tasty Rhine or Mosel *Auslese* with it. I would not go as far as to say that *veldkool* would complement or improve the flavour of such a light wine — no vegetable, as far as I know, does that. But many vegetables do not go so well with good light wines, whereas *veldkool* definitely does.

28 August 1942

Grog and Bowl

Nowhere will you find greater ignorance of the meaning of words than in cookery. It is understandable. Every technical subject has its own language, its peculiar expressions, sometimes limited to a small coterie of connoisseurs — a kind of *argot* or kitchen language into which only the few have been initiated. One can therefore readily assume that some of the words currently in use originally had totally different meanings which have been lost and which learned scholars, in spite of all their sniffing around, have not been able to track down.

Such a word is 'grog'. Its etymology is that a British admiral, Vernon by name, had the habit, in 1709 or thereabouts, of always appearing on the officers' deck in a waistcoat of *gros grain*, a term that metamorphosed in the English language into *grogram* — or, as we would say, *skurwegoed*[1] — so that his sailors gave him the nickname of Grogram. It was this same naval chief who tried to protect his people from scurvy by giving them a daily portion of rum or sugar brandy, and according to linguists the name 'grog' for a mixture of brandy and other liquids grew out of this habit.

I find this explanation almost as farcical as that which tries to make us believe that the English 'sirloin' is derived from the story of King James I being so taken with it when he ate it for the first time that he bestowed a knighthood on the piece of meat. The truth is that linguists are as ignorant of the origin of the word 'grog' as they are unable to give an acceptable explanation for the etymology of the word *pons*.[2]

They are more authoritative when it comes to the word 'bowl', for its derivation makes sense — a drink that is mixed in a bowl, or in something that is round or bowl-shaped. We can readily agree with that, even though it tells us little about the type of drink that it is.

In practice — the cook's practice, that is — the two words 'grog' and 'bowl' are very different, because 'bowl' usually — though not always — implies a chilled or cold drink, whereas 'grog' mostly refers to a warm one. Grog and punch are more or less the same thing, with the simple difference that a punch is usually a much larger quantity of liquid whereas grog refers to a single drink. There are other differences as well, but I see no need to distract the reader with such technicalities.

In a nutshell, a 'grog' is something mixed in a glass, cup or small mug,

---

1 Coarse stuff.
2 Punch.

and meant for one or two people; 'punch' is the same kind of drink prepared for more than one person; and 'bowl' is a cold punch that usually consists of a mixture of white or red wine with fruit, herbs and flower petals, with or without sugar. There are exceptions to this rule — many of them. But if there were not an exception to every rule, our lives would be extremely dull and unpalatable.

Grog is typically a warm drink, suitable for cold winter evenings with the wind howling outside and rain dripping from the roof. It is under such circumstances that it is sought after, and its wonderful aroma fully appreciated. But there are also many kinds of grog and cold punch. All have as their main constituent alcohol, or wine-spirit, in the form of a good — though not necessarily first-class — brandy to which warm water (or tea, or any other kind of decoction or infusion of herbs or fruit, or whatever) is added, after which it is sugared to taste and flavoured with spice. It is in the skilful addition of herbs and spices that the real talent of a good grog-maker lies. Here, locally, we have an embarrassment of choice: *naartje* peel, aniseed leaf, *boegoe*,[1] *kukumakranka*,[2] and even sheep-bush[3] add flavour that you would not get if you were limited to East Indian spices like cinnamon, nutmeg, mace and tamarind. Then we also have lemon leaves, bay leaves and geranium leaves, all of which were used by the old people in warm grogs and punches.

Without the addition of wine-spirit or brandy, a grog is not really a grog but a *tisaan*, or warm tea (with or without sugar) — an infusion of herbs in boiled water. We still find this in the form of sage tea and elder tea — perhaps the only remainders of the many *tisaans* the Hugenots brought with them. With the addition of milk and cream, a grog becomes a cream or milk punch; when eggs are added, we have an *advokaat* or egg punch; and with a meat extract we have meat grog. These are, however, not proper grogs, but really just kinds of soup with a rather high nutritional value.

A bowl, on the other hand, is a cool drink, preferably chilled until nearly frozen, and it is best enjoyed on a warm summer's day. Its nutritional value is quite low, because the alcohol content is low, and the sugar content should also be low. The following recipe, from the old handwriting of Mrs Schwabe, will serve as an example.

'Take three flasks of light white wine, and pour into a bowl over two cups of white sugar, a teaspoon of chopped lime peel, a snippet of thyme, a ground peach pip, and a blade of mace. Leave overnight in a cold place. Mix, a few hours before serving, with the same amount of cold fountain water, strain through a cloth, and pour the infusion into a glass or earthenware bowl in which a handful of jasmine flowers, two dozen cleaned

1 *Agathosma* spp.
2 *Gethyllis* spp.
3 *Tripteris* spp.

strawberries and half-a-dozen mulberries have been mixed. Stir together well and allow to cool thoroughly. Serve with a punch spoon in large glasses; and add to each glass a pinch of ground cinnamon.'

Today I would add a few blocks of ice from the fridge, and omit the mulberries and perhaps also the peach pip — a piece of bay leaf would do better. The mace can also be omitted.

Every cook can try her own variations on these bowls. You could, for example, replace the strawberries with pieces of pealed pineapple for a pineapple bowl. For a peach bowl, use snippets of cooked, bottled peaches — canned peaches also make excellent bowls. All sorts of flowers can also be added, as long as they do not have too strong or sharp a smell — they mostly serve to give the drink colour and to make it attractive, but can also influence and greatly enhance its taste when used skilfully.

In English cooking the bowl is replaced by the 'wine-cups', of which the 'claret-cup' (light red wine with lemon peel, a piece of cucumber peel and some sugar, with soda water added), 'champagne-cup' (champagne with whatever additions are preferred), 'hock-cup' (Rhine or Mosel wine diluted with ice-water, cucumber peel, lemon peel and a few blossoms added according to taste) and 'fruit-cup' (any fruit juice diluted with soda water and whatever else). These bowls mostly contain soda water and therefore have to be prepared just before serving, otherwise they would lose the sparkling taste preferred by so many guests. The addition of a glass of brandy improves just about any 'cup' of this kind, except perhaps the champagne variety, which already has enough wine-spirit in it to make anyone who is not careful tipsy.

11 September 1942

grog and bowl

A Sucking Pig

'Paradox — an apparent contradiction.' This is how the dictionary defines something that the sensible cook would simply label a misnomer. A *speenvarkie*[1] is not really a pig that has been weaned — it is a pig that still suckles, that can in time be weaned — something that, if you were an expert cook, you would never consider doing. Such disregard for time would leave you with a *gespeende varkie*, a weaned pig, instead of a *speenvarkie*, a sucking pig.

The expert cook knows that there is an enormous difference between the two, both from a purely gastronomical point of view and from that of the butcher. The not-yet-weaned piglet is in a class of its own. It has something no older member of the pig family can ever have. Something . . . no, much more, since it is, as the oldest cookbook on the subject puts it, 'unique amongst the meats, a jewel without equal'. Such a crown jewel and kitchen pearl, indeed, that history tells of a time when only gentlemen of noble lineage had any lawful right to enjoy it. It is for precisely this reason that books on cookery and cooks are so full of tales, some pathetic, some silly, some simply banal, about the honour and respect accorded the sucking pig by our forefathers.

There was, for instance, the kindly earl who would deftly remove his hat whenever he met a group of sucking pigs. Brillat-Savarin, the food connoisseur, tied bows and tassels to his sucking pigs, just as the goodly king of Cockaigne did to his subjects, to show how highly he regarded the little creatures. And the learned monk of I-know-not-what abbey used a sucking pig to rescue himself from the hands of a heathen hero. Literature is well acquainted with the sucking pig. One of the very best pieces of English prose is the tale — sucked from the Prophet's fingers, but no matter — of how it came about that mankind prepared and savoured such a culinary jewel.

I stand back for no man when it comes to my genuine, unfeigned, passionate, total and sincere appreciation of the sucking pig, although I would not go so far as to acknowledge the little creature's excellent qualities in the way the famous Earl of Cuissy did. When I see it wandering around — the sucking pig, not the earl — I am not that interested. It is only when I see it slaughtered and ready for the kitchen that my enthusiasm begins and I wax lyrical as if it were Jacques Perk's rainbow.

And it is thus that I now approach it. First, as to its appearance, if it is a

---

1 Literally, a weaning pig.

real not-yet-weaned sucking pig, then it will not be too big, no more than a few weeks old. The sow's milk is still inside it and no other food has passed its lips. No sucking pig of ten to fourteen pounds for me, and not for you either if you want to eat a real sucking pig! A small one, about eighteen inches long from the tip of its nose to the curve of its tail, virginal, innocent, pure.

See to it that it has been properly scraped. No hair should remain, especially not on the head, nor around and in the ears. Wash it well inside and out, and dry thoroughly. The question whether to coat that beautiful white skin with breadcrumbs is something the expert cook would never ever even consider — the mere thought would be heresy! Drip, drip, drip — this alone will do to obtain that delicious, brittle crackling that should be the covering of the dish.

And what about the filling? Well, dear reader, let me plead with you and beg you not to gild the lily, not to sprinkle Eau de Cologne over our aromatic morning glory! Take care, therefore. Be extremely careful with the sage, rosemary, mace, and all the other spices. They are very useful when preparing the already weaned pig, but when it comes to the sucking pig they are superfluous. Its own little liver, fried in olive oil, then ground with bread crumbs and soaked in milk, pepper, salt and a few coriander seeds — there you have a filling worth more than even that suggested by Carême (who added cream and a pinch of saffron). Sow together well and coat the seam with lemon juice. Rub the skin well with a lemon and place the lemon (or if you wish a bay leaf) in its little mouth.

Place the little creature in a saucepan, deep enough to protect it from getting too much heat in any one place, add soft fat or butter, sprinkle with fine salt and a touch of pepper, and place the saucepan in an oven that should be quite warm — not quite as warm as that meant for Sadrag and his friends, but still warm enough to immediately, or at least within a few minutes, thicken the juices of the virginal skin. Turn the little creature regularly and keep pouring molten fat or butter over it. Do not be impatient — be thorough and make sure that not a millimetre of skin remains without dripping, and that the heat of the oven on the surface of the piglet is even. This is the only way to get the lovely golden-brown and ten times more delicious brittle crackling that should be as crisp and tender as a wafer. As soon as it is done, you can cover the saucepan with a lid and lower the heat. The little creature can be left to braise in the dripping, just long enough to cook its own meat properly. But again I advise caution. The precise moment for moving the little jewel to a cooler environment is something the expert cook will have learnt only through bitter experience.

Let us suppose that the moment has arrived. Take the piglet out of the saucepan and place it on a napkin in a shallow dish — this makes it easier to carve at table. Garnish by placing a small lemon in its mouth, a sprig of parsley around its tail, and keep it warm until it is taken to the table.

a sucking pig

What about the sauce? If it is a proper sucking pig, the dripping left in the pan will not make much of a sauce. It can, however, be used as the basis for a sauce. Mix a spoonful of buckwheat meal with a few spoonsful of good sherry or red wine and stir; add salt and pepper and, when more or less thick, half a cup of cream, sour or sweet according to taste. There you have your sauce, but as far as I am concerned, the Bonades always prefer to have the sucking pig without sauce, with good rice (cooked until a bit mushy), stewed sweet potato, guava jelly and mealy potatoes. More would be mere wantonness.

And to drink with it? On this the experts differ as widely as the public does on politics. My oldest cookbook, that of Scappi — he calls himself *Cuoco secreto di Papa Pio V* and his book was printed in Venice in 1579 — says 'definitely a tough red wine'. La Chapelle prefers a white wine that is 'not too sweet'. Between these two extremes every man can choose for himself. I have experimented on my own and can only say, with my hand on my waistcoat, that a white wine with 'body', with flavour and a slightly strong aftertaste, is just the thing for bringing out the full value of the little jewel. But it is a matter of taste. I know of many a connoisseur who has his sucking pig with 'communion wine', and I respect their taste. The Bonades are not fanatical dogmatists.

16 October 1942

10

Curried Meat

The old Ayah who gave me my first cooking lessons, in my early youth — and I must admit that, in all honesty, the old soul taught me more than *Maître* Escoffier, for whom I had the honour of washing dishes and filling a sucking lamb with chestnuts — always said: '*My Basie*, raisin rice and *pienangvleis*[1] — now that is something that *Basie* will never learn to make as it should be made. Only we Blacks can make it properly, not Dutchmen!'

In those days — I have said it was in my tender youth — I still had the cheek to suggest to the old soul that a woman could never really be a first-class cook. Father Abraham knew it. Remember the story of how he caught three men, there under the oaks at Mamre, when it was so hot. He told Sarah: 'Go and make the *roosterkoek*',[2] but he himself was busy in the kitchen with the tender veal, the curds and whey, and the sweet milk. That he could not, of course, leave to his wife, even though she was Sarah. Because Abraham, I imagine, was a sensible man, one who knew something about cooking. Veal with curds and whey — I bet the three men had a delicious meal.

Now that I am older I feel I must apologise to Ayah Hanna. I know that I cannot make curried meat as it should be made. The 'yellow raisin rice' — that is no miracle, although often enough one ends up with some kind of bungled Italian mushy rice. But curried meat — the real, genuine, unadulterated, traditional, unequalled thing — that requires far too much patience for my liking. I therefore appreciate it all the more when I happen to get some to eat. Even when made by a woman! I know a few who can prepare it excellently, even though not in Ayah Hanna's more or less ritual way.

I can still see the old soul in my imagination — she is long dead and buried, and the harvest festival at the time of her funeral was, as the family wrote to me (I was then too far away to contribute my own gardenia) the topic of conversation in the location for a whole month — there in the Bonade kitchen, busy preparing her curried meat. First, the meat itself. Good, fresh lamb or mutton — the ribcage, cut into neat, short pieces, carefully dried, with ground pepper, a bit of ginger powder, salt, and — do not forget — buckwheat meal rubbed into it. Buckwheat meal — where does one find it today? Who still grinds it? And yet, it is the very best flour for meat dishes.

---

1 Curried meat.
2 Grill-cake.

Then everything gets braised in soft fat with some very finely chopped onion. Before the onion can brown – it should just start getting the colour of an almost ripe loquat before you pull it aside – put the lid on the pot, and allow the meat to stew very slowly.

Take a copper mortar, dusted with buckwheat meal, and place in it a diced red chilli, a diced green chilli, two tablespoonsful of coriander seed, a snippet of green ginger, a pinch of coarse cinnamon (the thick kind, that is not really cinnamon but cassia, although it is always sold as cinnamon sticks and also taken for it by those who do not know better), a young orange leaf, a scraping of lemon peel, a clove of garlic, two large spoonsful of molten butter, a few cloves, six peppercorns, a piece of fennel stalk and, last but not least, a spoonful of turmeric. Now use the pestle, and pound and rub and grind what is in the mortar. Why? This is something I asked Ayah Hanna, and I must say that she did not answer me in the manner of the cheeky Temanite: 'Would a wise man with a windy knowledge give offence by filling his stomach with the east wind?' Politely and humbly, as it behoved a descendant of slaves to address the child of a Bonade, she said: 'My Basie, it is to get the soul out of it and into the meat'. And she added drily: 'If it is not fine, it might break the old master's teeth'.

Then make it into a cold, thick sauce. Dilute it now with something that requires equal patience – tamarind soaked in water, with the pips taken out, and then two cups of sour milk. I was told how to make that in an appropriately thorough manner, but never got the hang of it. I simply use any old curds and whey that have a bit of sourness, which would perhaps explain why my Dutchman's curried meat is never first-class.

Now stir it in and around the stewed meat, and let it braise – but definitely not cook. 'Bubble cooking' would spoil the sauce. And braising it too long makes it watery. Some people – but not the Bonades – mix a few spoonsful of tomato sauce with it. Others, who lack genuine turmeric, use curry powder, but the sauce is itself a homemade curry sauce and requires nothing else.

Nothing else? Well, not quite. Taste it. See if it has enough salt, and if not, add some. The salty taste should definitely not be overpowering, especially in the case of good meat.

There are those who make curried meat from cooked or roasted cold meat. There are also those who have mustard with milk tart! It is not for them that I am writing. May tinned food be their nourishment until the end of time!

There is no doubt that curried meat from the pot is well worth the effort. What to serve with it? The usual yellow rice with raisins, of course! But what else? *Sambals*, made of quinces, onions, cucumbers. Chutneys. Stewed prunes. It is a matter of taste. I prefer my curried meat, which I eat with a spoon, with rice, cooked dry, and a portion of *sambal* or chutney – nothing else. To each creature his own craving!

And to drink? No fragrant first-class wine, of course. That would be unfair, not only to the curried meat, but also to the wine. *Oom* Daantjie van den Heever, who really loved curried meat, used to tell me that communion wine was the best, but I shall merely say again that it is a matter of taste — every man should decide for himself.

Do not assume that *penang*[1] meat is just a common curry. It is an exalted, crowned, imperial curry. Even though it is named after a part of the globe that could hardly be regarded as paradise, it is what our heathen forefathers imagined the gods would eat. For there is reason enough to believe that the 'ambrosia'[2] the old poets spoke of was nothing other than some kind of ginger-chilli-turmeric curried meat.

6 November 1942

---

1 Curried.
2 Food of the Greek and Roman gods.

curried meat

11

Braaivleis

One of the most expensive cookery books you will find is a little one by a certain John Smith, printed in the year 1642, in which he describes the culinary art of the American Indians. It is a rarity that the Bonades are not wealthy enough to afford. The last one up for sale was bought for £900 and now forms part of an American library. But my grandfather, who was very keen on cookery, made use of the opportunity when he happened to get the book for perusal to excerpt a few pieces, among which was one on *braaivleis*.[1]

Most cooks in our country think of *braaivleis* as *gebraaide vleis*.[2] This is not entirely correct. Burnt meat is meat that has been exposed to a degree of heat that assails the outside of the meat so intensely that the juices in the outer layer of meat immediately coagulate and stiffen. When the heat is continued, the outer layer burns — a failure we often come across in hotels when we order chops and to our disappointment find that we are chewing pieces of burnt fibre.

Braaivleis, on the other hand, is meat prepared in such a way that the first shock of heat is just enough to bring about that coagulation of the meat juices in its outer crust, after which it is slowly and evenly *braaied*[3] — in other words, subjected to a more or less even heat that is high enough to cook the inside of the meat until tender without charcoaling the outer crust. *Braaing* the meat well is an art that requires the most diligent attention from the cook. It is so easy to ruin the meat when, for instance, the heat is too dry and too sharp. For that reason it is just about impossible to make good *braaivleis* with 'the wire', since an electric appliance cannot really *braai*. The American Indians knew well that *braaivleis* requires a moist heat. They enfolded the meat in leaves and roasted it in a hole in the ground. Even today this form of *braai* is used in America. On the large plantation farms in the southern states, in Virginia and South Carolina, a whole sheep or even a whole ox is roasted in this way. The hole is lined with flat stones and a large fire is stoked in it, and when it has burnt out, the meat is placed on the stones and covered with green leaves. On top of that another fire is made. A good cook can make a very tasty *braaivleis* with such a 'barbecue' — one that has all the characteristics of a piece of meat roasted in front of the fire or on a spit, and much juicier than spit- or pot-roast.

We prefer the pot *braaivleis* — meat that is roasted in an iron pot. Never

---

1 Barbecued meat.
2 Burnt meat.
3 Roasted.

use an aluminium pot! This is perhaps the easiest way, but I doubt whether it is the best, although the other way — *braaing* in front of the fire — can hardly be done in a modern kitchen. Our forefathers had their kitchens made for it. On a large, open fireplace, with the help of a wood or charcoal fire, you can *braai* a leg of mutton very nicely. All you need do, to make a success of it, is to turn the meat so that the heat roasts the surface evenly, and baste it well with fat or any juice that will prevent the charring of the fibres. When doing it in a flat pot, it is also necessary to baste the meat well, but then the meat (especially when covered with a lid) is exposed to less heat. This comes close to simply baking the meat, and the art of it is precisely to prevent that from happening, so that the meat will not bake but roast instead. When *braaing*, a chemical reaction takes place that affects the taste and tenderness of the meat. Too much heat will char the fibres, and even the smallest bit of charring will spoil the taste. On the other hand, too little heat will leave you with meat fibres that are cooked, that lack the *braai* taste completely and that are tough.

We usually tend to overdo *braaing*. That is to say, we tend to leave the meat over the heat too long with the result that, although there is no question of charring, it is too well done. White meat — chicken or veal that has been bled to death — is difficult to *braai* properly. For both of them the first shock of heat needs to be enormous, without charring the outside crust, but hot enough to form an even '*braai*-coating' on the outside, in which and under which the rest of the meat can then *braai* slowly and thoroughly. Both types require careful basting, preferably with their own fat or sauce. Beef, which in our country does not have much fat, needs to be basted even more, while mutton, which contains more fat, can be *braaied* easily in an iron pot. It is a matter of taste whether the cook will *braai* right through or stop *braaing* when three-quarters of the meat is done. Some prefer their *braaied* beef with the inside still raw — connoisseurs maintain that this is the only way of getting the best out of the beef. But that is certainly not the case with game, mutton or lamb. They have to be *braaied* through and through, without charring of course.

Grill or pan *braaing* are variations that are suitable for smaller portions of meat. They are, however, methods of *braaing* that, for various reasons, tend to make the meat quite tough, and the cook therefore needs to know how to counteract this tendency. One way of doing it is to marinate the meat beforehand by soaking it in vinegar, wine or a mixture of vinegar and oil for a few hours. Another is to separate the meat fibres from one another by pounding them with a stick or wooden mallet. Even a piece of hard old meat can be *braaied* in this way to produce a tender piece of *braaivleis*. A piece of beef, the 'cut' or 'steak', one and a half inches thick, can never be *braaied* tenderly on a grid or pan if not prepared in this way. The art lies in the cook scorching the piece of meat properly on both sides, without charring it, so that the inside can *braai* as much as you wish without acquiring the toughness of the outer crust.

braaivleis

Braaivleis goes with any vegetable — cooked, or raw as a simple salad. Many connoisseurs prefer something sweet with it and serve stewed prunes or peaches. Sharp sauces, such as horseradish, mustard or chutney, go well with *braaied* brown meat, but seldom with the white meats.

With regard to wines, the general consensus is that red wines go better with *braaivleis*, but naturally you would have to take into consideration what side dishes are served. No Bonade would think of insulting a good cabernet by swilling it down with a horseradish sauce, or with a cucumber salad doused in vinegar. A well-*braaied* beef 'cut' with potatoes and beans is a perfect accompaniment for the wholehearted appreciation of a dry red wine, and the connoisseur will enjoy the best imported red wines with it. A fruity white wine could also be served with *braaivleis* without affronting the taste of either.

27 November 1942

12

On *Pannas*

The other day an English friend asked me to translate the Afrikaans word *paljas*. When I tried to explain that it was just about impossible to express its meaning in English, he poked fun at my knowledge of language.

'Well,' I said, 'the Bonades are by no means language *indunas*.[1] But you should know that there are words in every language that are not easy to define, and are not even found in dictionaries.'

'Oh well,' was his reply, 'that's just another of your wild statements. I could give you the meaning of any English word instantly.'

'Okay,' I said, 'if you'd like to bet on it, give me the meaning of the word *scrapple*.'

'Oh dear . . . but there isn't such a word in English. Where does it come from?'

'There is, and it's a very good old English word. You'll find it in old as well as modern English cookbooks, although you might not find it in the Oxford Dictionary. Mr Fowler may think he knows it all, but he doesn't.'

'I don't believe that,' my friend said, quite upset, for he regards Fowler as the greatest authority on the English language.

'Look here,' I said, and I showed him Mr Grover's recipe. 'There it is in black and white: "Make scrapple on the same day that you butcher." Which we could translate into Afrikaans quite correctly as: "*Maak jou pannas op dieselfde dag waarop jy slag*".'[2]

This language-game with my English friend inspired me to try and find out whether we still make *pannas* today. To my astonishment I found that most women in our country are totally unfamiliar with the dish. The word is nowhere to be found in ordinary cookbooks. Mrs Dijkman makes no mention of it, and the encyclopaedic *Larousse* only lists *panache*, which it happens to define incorrectly. The correct meaning of *panache* you will find in La Chapelle's fourth book, although the recipe does not concur with that in old Westphalian cookbooks. Leipoldt's *Kos vir die Kenner* (which has no index, with the result that my patience was sorely tried by the time I found it on page 253) describes it, but says nothing about the name, and his recipe is also not exactly the same as that in the Bonade archive.

---

1 Authorities or experts (in context).
2 'Make your *pannas* on the same day that you slaughter.'

I consulted *Tannie* Lisbet on the matter.

She is one of the older generation that still says *harlie* and *hullie* instead of *hulle*, and is as stubborn as a scorpion when offered a cocktail. But her memory is still strong.

'Mother always told us,' she said, when I mentioned my problem, 'that it comes from Germany. It should actually be *pannhas* because it is made and baked in a pan. I cannot remember whether the recipe is to be found in *Aaltjie*.'

No, it is not in *Aaltjie*. That 'stingy kitchen maid' seems to have known as little about it as Mrs Dijkman and *Hilda* and *Larousse*. Nor is it to be found in the famous *Volmaakte Keukenmeid*,[1] published with permission in Amsterdam in 1755. I possess a rare signed edition, with the warning, in Dutch, that 'the publisher recognises as genuine only those copies that have been personally signed by the printer, Steven van Esveldt', even though it describes at length how to make *beulingen*,[2] for which *Tannie* prefers the French word *andoetjes*. Only in the cookery books published after 1800 do I find mention of *pan-asse*, *bloed-panes* and *Westphaliese Pannhas*. The English spelling varies as much — for example, 'Skrapil', 'Scruppel', 'Dutch skrappel' and Mr Grover's 'scrapple'.

Short and sweet, *pannas*[3] is a first-class dish, and the time has come to restore it to a place of honour, especially as it is so easy to prepare and tastes so good. Our recipe is taken from old Mrs Schwabe's personal *Notes*, and seems to be a translation of a much older recipe found in a German cookbook dated round about 1750. The Schwabes, who were well known in Worcester — the *oubaas* started doing woodwork there sixty years ago, and came from the city of Ulm — mostly practised the art of German cooking. Here is the recipe, without any claim to copyright.

'Braise pieces of liver, heart, brain, lung and other intestines of a pig in lard until well done. Grind well, and add a cup of blood, a few spoons of vinegar, salt, pepper, and coriander seeds. Cook in an iron pot any bones of the pig taken from the meat scraps with a bay leaf, a pinch of ginger, a few slices of onion, some rosemary, and a portion of grated lemon peel. After cooking it for one and a half hours, strain the soup through a cloth and place back in the saucepan. Add the ground heart, etc, and allow to boil slowly. After it has boiled up a few times, stir in enough wheat flour to make a stiff porridge. Stir well with a wooden spoon, to keep it from burning, and take care that no lumps are formed. Pour the porridge into a shallow tart pan and let it stand until nice and stiff. The layer of fat covering it will preserve it. To serve, cut in slices and roast in lard, with or without bacon.'

---

1 'Perfect Kitchen Maid'.
2 Sausage.
3 Scrapple.

I can assure you that, as old Mrs Schwabe would have said, it '*schmeckt sehr schoen*',[1] especially at eight o'clock with fried eggs and a piece of sour dough bread.

1 January 1943

---

1 Tastes very good.

13

Chicken's Eggs

There are hundreds of cookbooks devoted to eggs, and literally thousands of 'egg recipes'. In practice this super-abundant wealth of knowledge about the art of making eggs boils down to the fact that the egg is a foodstuff that not only lends itself to being prepared in all sorts of ways, but is also difficult to spoil — even when the cook is ignorant or careless.

In itself the egg is a microcosm — a small little world, as *Oom* Mias would have said — of an appropriate, well-balanced diet. Today one hears and reads much about malnourishment, about 'indispensable food ingredients' like vitamins and homeopathic particles of some or other metal, such as copper or silicon, without which, the experts tell us, it would be impossible to exist, not to mention the 'well-balanced diet'. Not long ago the know-it-all experts informed us that wheat, meat and coffee constituted a highly dangerous and unsuitable diet. *Oom* Mias, who has had a very amicable relationship with all three for seventy years and more, was underwhelmed when I informed him of this. His answer reminded me of the French grandfather who, when told that coffee is a slow-working poison, answered promptly: 'Very slow, I've been drinking it for eighty years.'

'*Ag* no man, Koos,' *Oom* Mias said, 'I can honestly say that meat and bread and coffee have never given me rheumatism.'

In a chicken's egg you will find meat as well as bread, and perhaps even — on this third point no Bonade can speak with authority, since our family does not dabble in any complicated chemical science — one or more of the ingredients of coffee. Which is to say that the egg contains all the necessary nourishment the human body could want. It contains fat, meat — the egg white, which is rich in protein — metal salts, carbohydrates, and complex acids of which science still knows very little.

It is also very handy, as it can be enjoyed without any further preparation, and is an easily digestible food every grain of which is used by the body. This is not something we can honestly say of all foods. Of every pound of meat we eat, our body probably uses only about a third — on the rest we waste energy that could be better used for something else.

The beaten raw egg — with or without something to make it more appetising — is a first-class food. It is often used in cooking, especially when making sauces. As soon as the egg is heated above a certain temperature, certain important changes take place. One is the coagulation of the egg white, which makes it hard and white. The whites of some eggs — penguin eggs, for instance, and plovers' eggs — coagulate without becoming cloudy or white. Their nutritional value is no less for this, as they contain the same protein as chicken eggs. Through heat the egg yolk — the yellow — also coagulates, although to a lesser extent — or rather in a less noticeable way, as the oil and fatty acids in the yolk influence and slow down the coagulation process. Every good housewife knows this and takes care, when stirring egg yolks into soup, not to let the soup boil lest it curdle.

How heat is applied to the egg is another point to be taken into account, as can be seen in the case of hard- and soft-boiled eggs. Complete coagulation of the egg white and yolk, as in a hard-boiled egg, requires no more from our digestive system than a partly coagulated egg — a soft-boiled egg, with the white not quite hard. Indeed, an egg that has been boiled for half an hour is more digestible than a soft-boiled egg. The yolk is even used for feeding babies that cannot tolerate milk or *meelbol*,[1] and is very good for use in dishes for the sick and convalescing. The thirty-or-more-year-old eggs that the Chinese are so fond of are always boiled for an hour and a half. Then they are shelled, cut into thin slices and served with a sour sauce. They taste a bit like turnips gone soft — what makes them delicious is the sauce they come with. I can also add that hard-boiled eggs can be kept for months, on condition that they do not come into contact with anything dirty, and all you need do to prepare them for serving is to boil them again for five or six minutes.

It is to be expected that among the hundreds of recipes, many ways of preparing eggs are to be found; and, curiously enough, some of those found in old cookbooks, and used by our forefathers here and in Europe, are now just about unknown by us. Take, for instance, poached eggs with a black, sour butter sauce, or with a wine sauce — referred to in culinary art as *a la Armenonville*. There are also countless 'coloured eggs' — yellow, green, red, and even rainbow. The prettiest are 'Cardinal eggs', in which ground crayfish eggs are mixed with beaten eggs, boiled in little pots, and decorated with more crayfish eggs to achieve a beautiful cardinal red colour. A more amusing than tasty egg dish is the so-called 'Dragon' or 'giant' egg that imitates the normal chicken egg on a grand scale. The preparation is somewhat tedious. The separated yolks of two dozen eggs are beaten and hard-boiled in a round mould, after which a layer of egg white is carefully hard-boiled in a separate mould. The large yolk is carefully placed upon it, then the mould is filled up with the rest of the egg white and the whole lot hard-boiled. If the cook manages to do it all without any cracks appearing, you will have a large egg that looks rather like a pretty white pudding. It is cut and served with a portion of béchamel or hollandaise sauce. As for the taste — I would not think it worth the effort since it is a lot of trouble for scant reward.

Every egg dish, if not herbed and spiced too much, will retain its egg taste, which goes well with any light wine. It is therefore not difficult to choose what to drink with an egg dish, and you can safely offer a semi-sweet white or red wine to your guests when it is served.

19 March 1943

---

1 Baked flour for infants.

14

Game I

To have game at its very best — to enjoy it as it should be enjoyed — you have to eat it at the campsite after a tiring but pleasant day in the veld, during which — if you like killing animals — you have taken part in bringing down a buck or — if you do not enjoy hunting — you have taken a walk with the hunters to enjoy nature. There, surrounded by convivial fellow-campers, you will encounter the old-fashioned 'hunter's pot' if the cook knows what is expected of him. This is game — preferably buck with partridge, pheasant or peacock — stewed without adding any water, and braised slowly for hours above a wood fire that is never sharp enough to eliminate the juiciness. When game is exposed to too much heat too rapidly, the result is 'frayed meat' — the way our old *tannies* were fond of serving hare — but that, too, makes an excellent dish.

Unfortunately we seldom get the opportunity of enjoying game under such conditions. We have to make do with a leg of game we get from friends who hunt or from the butcher. It is mostly blesbok or springbok, seldom smaller game such as grysbok, duiker or steenbok. As winged game belongs to a different category and requires a different treatment, I will for now restrict myself to buck.

The game we usually get is more often than not meat that has lost its stiffness and has already started decaying. This means that chemical changes have started taking place in the meat fibres that reduce the toughness of the muscles. The fatter the meat, the quicker is this process of decay. But game is usually not fat. On the contrary, you need to anoint it well, preferably with lard or hard suet. This needs to be done immediately, as soon as the leg of game is prepared. In our home we are also in the habit of marinading game. This not only makes it tender but also prevents the further decay that follows when the meat is simply hung. It is purely a matter of individual taste how far you allow the process of decay to proceed. We Bonades, for instance, do not like it when our game can be smelt outside the kitchen when it is roasted. Others like their game to announce itself from afar. One of the oldest cookbooks advises one to bury the leg of game and only use it when it starts showing signs of new 'life' — but so disgusting a preparation is surely not compatible with any civilised sense of taste.

The leg of game therefore needs to be larded. This is no child's play — it has to be done skilfully so that, when the leg is later cut, every slice will contain two or three pieces of fat. Use only good, hard lard — without skin of course — and preferably fat that has not been salted. Then comes the marinading. We Bonades use a marinade made up of three-quarters dry wine and one-quarter vinegar — some of our neighbours use vinegar only, others again only wine. *Tant* Hester always used to add a touch of saltpetre, but I do not consider this necessary. Before putting the leg in the marinade, it needs to be rubbed with salt, pepper, a pinch of powdered dry ginger, and a small piece — a very small piece — of garlic. Then place it in the lye, to which a bay or lemon leaf can be added. Let it soak for at least twenty-four hours. If it has been well larded, this will be sufficient. The lye then penetrates through the larding holes and the meat is thoroughly soaked. If you leave it to soak longer, it will get too soft; and too much acidity spoils the wild taste of the game.

Remove from the marinade, and dry well. Sprinkle with fine buckwheat meal — rub it in so that a thin layer is formed over the outside. Place in a pan or iron pot over a rapid fire with nothing but its own fat, and allow to brown on both sides. As soon as the outside has been browned, add a few tablespoons of fat to the pot or pan, with half a cup of red wine and salt and pepper to taste. Move the pot or pan to a cooler side of the stove, and allow the contents to braise slowly. Shake it often, keeping the lid well on, so that the sauce covers the meat. How long it should stew like this depends on the weight. Three hours would be enough for a normal leg of blesbok, but it is preferable to let it steam longer rather than shorter. Half-roasted game is never good to eat, and always tough. Test whether it is done by poking a piece of wire or a *sosatie*[1] stick into it every now and then. This is where your knowledge of cooking will show. A capable cook will know — by observing whether the poked stick is too dry or too moist — exactly when the game is done.

When it is ready, remove it, place it on a dish, and keep it warm in a cool oven until it is time for it to be served. Take the sauce and use it, according to taste, to make a simple 'own sauce' — a sauce consisting of nothing more than the juices of the meat, along with the fat and what remains of the wine — thickening it somewhat with fine flour or maizena and, of course, with the addition of further salt and spices to taste. Or make of it a more refined sauce, such as our forefathers liked. Beat up a few spoons of plum jam with a teaspoonful of good brandy, stir it into the sauce, and thicken it with fine flour. Or beat currant jelly into the sauce and add a cup of sour cream. All sorts of variations on this can be tried — it is, once again, simply a matter of individual taste. Some people prefer to have their game with nothing but its own juices; others prefer it with a portion of jelly, stewed prunes or sweet chutney. For game served in this way our Afrikaans taste demands a reasonably *pap*[2] cooked rice, stewed sweet potato and a simple salad. Dry cooked rice definitely will not do, but game goes well with vegetables such as cauliflower and carrots.

What to drink? There is only one kind of wine that really goes with

---

1   Kebab.
2   Soggy.

game and that is a dry red wine, preferably one of the more robust, honest kinds, like a cabernet or a shiraz. There are various excellent wines of this kind on the market, and most wine farmers make their own that are possibly even better than those you can buy over the counter. A touch of 'bitterness' in the wine, as a dash of pontac[1] would give, is recommended — it will strengthen the 'wild' taste of the game. This is especially good when the game is served with a cream sauce.

30 April 1943

---

1 A wine made at the Cape from the early days of settlement.

15

Game II

'That's not really true,' *Tant* Koba told me, when she heard I had written about the *braaing* of a leg of game, 'you can't really say that a *braaied* leg is the best kind of game.'

'Sorry, but that is not what I said, *Tante*. I made it perfectly clear at the outset that the best way of preparing game is to make "hunter's meat" of it.'

'That is not something I would know anything about,' said the old dame, whom no torture in the world would ever force to admit that men can cook better than women, and who therefore has but a vague notion of what we are capable of when out hunting in the veld with an iron pot and a hardwood fire. 'But the old recipe I got from the late Mrs Raats — that she got from her great-grandmother — wait, I'll see if I can get it for you . . .'

Now that recipe is not one that I would rate very highly. It goes as follows: 'Take three pounds of venison and cut it in pieces; some sausages; a pound of the minced meat of a hare with some fat . . .' *Tant* Koba declared it a *hutspot*.[1] I call it a mess!

Our own old Bonadian way of preparing a real 'frayed' dish — as was the custom at harvest festivals, or when participants in a funeral procession had to come from faraway farms and naturally had to be given something to eat — seems to me more appropriate for the palate of a true connoisseur. I must concede, in all honesty, that it is a difficult dish to prepare. It is about as difficult as making a first-class fish stew — called *bouillabaisse* by the French, which one used to be able to have at the White House in Strand Street — which requires many different kinds of fish. And for a genuine frayed game stew you need at least three kinds of game.

I can still remember when I was young — *ja-nee*,[2] as the Latin poet said, a day or a memory that is forever 'white-chalked'. On a remote farm somewhere, with large oaks and a magnificent poplar grove that for us children was a universe filled with countless possibilities, the *baas*[3] was fed up with the bush doves that were forever causing problems, swarms of them, as large as the grasshoppers spoken of in Exodus chapter ten. I doubt that I will ever see so many bush doves together again! *Outa* Augustus made a hiding-place on the lands from *kraalbossies*, leading from it a small furrow in which he sprinkled chaff and bran with the odd bit of rye. He then took up

---

1 Literally, 'hotchpotch'. A mixed stew.
2 Literally, 'yes-no'.
3 Master.

position in the shelter with a long *voorlaaier*,[1] and when hundreds of bush doves had descended on both sides of the furrow, head to head, to have a good feed, he let loose. We got more than two hundred bush doves from just that one shoot, and the next afternoon we had a frayed stew the like of which I have never tasted since. But I must admit, the conditions were different then. Where could you now, for love or money, get hold of three or four types of game in the Lowveld without going and hunting them yourself?

But let us say you do have the opportunity. Then proceed as follows – it will pay off, and your guests will mark the meal with white chalk for as long as they have memory and good taste.

Place a few pounds of the meat of any buck, preferably the soft strip off the back, in an iron pot; add a few doves, a Coqui francolin, a pheasant, and any other kind of game, winged or earthbound, that you can get hold of. If you can find some warthog, so much the better; if not, take a piece of lard, not too salty, cut it into little dice, and add it to the mixture. If you are using large game, with marrow in the bones, chop the bones open and there will be no reason to add any other fat. If you do not have game marrow, add a large lump of hard fat or butter.

Allow the mixture to steam slowly over the fire, and stir often so that it does not stick to the pot. No water is needed – the juice of the meat will be sufficient. Whether or not you add onions, spices, or even potatoes is a matter of personal preference. I do not consider it appropriate, but this is a matter of taste. The same goes for whether or not, later – when it is done and nicely 'frayed' – you should add wine, vinegar or cream. Wine gives it a darker complexion, and we Bonades like our frayed stew to be light. Vinegar does not really do for the taste what the old transport riders maintained it did – I think their stews were always made of half-dry meat and were therefore not very tasty. About the cream, especially if sour, opinions are divided. I admit that it gives a strange and, to my taste, very pleasant tang to the game, but it seems to me rather like the gilding of the lily that the old playwright warned against.

There is one addition I came across for the first time at a Dingaan's Day[2] festival in the Waterberg and that I can recommend passionately, with my hand on my heart, or rather, my stomach: dumplings of minced ham, small as little marbles, cooked in the stew. A real treat!

And to go with it? Whatever you like. A good slice of toast, fresh from the oven, coated with farm butter – try it, no matter how plebeian it may sound. Soggy rice, a baked potato or a sweet potato, stewed dry beans, salad, and any kind of vegetable. This is not important – just as no side dish

---

1   Muzzle-loader.
2   South African public holiday on 16 December, now known as the Day of Reconciliation.

really means much when you eat a good fish stew. Game stew, prepared in our old-fashioned 'frayed' manner, requires no more than a deep plate and the appetite of a connoisseur.

The first important matter, over which the cook should exercise great care, is that every piece of game added must be fresh — the smallest hint of decay will render it unsuitable for a proper stew. Secondly, the meat should be stewed slowly and patiently, without water, and should be properly shaken so as not to stick to the pot. Thirdly, the lid of the pot should be lifted as seldom as possible — the stew needs to cook in its own steam. The longer it stews, the better it will eventually be. The mistake made by those who do not know better is to let it heat up too quickly, with the result that the softer meats undergo that remarkable chemical process that gives the whole stew a burnt taste. This might add to the taste of a chop, but it is not appropriate for a stew.

Tant Koba agrees completely that it does not really matter what you drink with such a stew. If it is a first-class stew, you need not bother much about what to drink before you have taken a second or even a third helping. Thereafter, a glass of sweet wine will go down well. I would not recommend a first-class red wine. This would be fair neither to the stew nor to the wine. When two champions compete, it is difficult not to take sides.

14 May 1943

game

Wild Birds I

We have so many different kinds of winged game that many recipes are to be found under this heading in every cookbook. In one of my oldest cookbooks, written by hand in 1835, I found the following:

'*Partridge in Red Wine*. One medium-to-large partridge; one bottle of red wine; two large onions; one tablespoonful of buckwheat; one peeled lemon; salt; pepper; a lump of butter. Cut the partridge into nice, even pieces; add the onions; sprinkle with flour, salt and spices; steam slowly; add the wine. Put the lid on the saucepan and stew slowly; shake the saucepan well. When the partridge is nicely soft, remove and serve on a bed of cooked rice; sprinkle with parsley.'

This is a variation of one of the oldest recipes for winged game, but perhaps not the best. The cook who wishes to prepare fowl — especially wild fowl — properly must go to work in a precise and meticulous way.

First of all, with regard to the wild bird itself, the vast majority of them have dark flesh. In certain cases — pheasant, peacock and young partridges, for instance — a small part of the breast is more or less white, but even then not quite the white of a turkey or a farm chicken. The best kinds always have black or brown flesh. They are therefore not, from a purely aesthetic point of view, suitable for serving up cooked — they are, however, well suited for *braai* or stew meat. I have actually eaten 'green doves', plump after having fed on wild figs and marulas[1] for a few months — cooked and served with a white sauce *nogal*.[2] They tasted excellent, but the orthodox cook — trained in the school of Carême and La Chapelle, who maintain that the eye needs to be nourished as well as the mouth — would not have regarded it as a first-class dish. And I have to admit that this is not the best way to prepare 'green doves' — possibly one of the most delicious of all our wild birds.

Water birds like wild duck, African coot, heron, wild geese, etc, all have black flesh that is oily. They have a tough, somewhat thick skin that is quite difficult to completely rid of not only the large feathers but also the fluff. In most cases it is therefore preferable to skin the bird before placing it in the pot. An even better idea is to get rid of the oil, or lachrymal, gland carefully as soon as it has died. It is necessary to rid any bird of its intestines as soon as possible, and in so doing to take care that the gallbladder does not burst, as the tiniest drop of gall will spoil the taste of the meat. There is one exception to this rule, which is when you are dealing with tiny little birds —

---

1 The fruit of the marula tree, *Sclerocarya caffra*.
2 Moreover.

such as *mossies*[1] or *rooibekkies*[2] that are baked or *braaied* hard as crumbs and served on toast without removing their insides. Some connoisseurs are of the opinion that our quails should be prepared in the same way, but I prefer my quails properly gutted, even when served on toast.

How long do you have to hang wild birds before *braaing* them? This is a matter of taste. There is no inherent reason why the extra bit of flavour due to decay in the meat should be preferred above the natural 'wild' taste of the game itself. The high priests of the culinary art — I am thinking here of the venerated Brillat-Savarin — say categorically that a pheasant tastes best when prepared as soon as possible after being shot. This accords with what science teaches: that decay brings only one advantage, namely that it makes the meat fibres tender and thereby counters the stiffness that comes with death and causes the fibres to be tough. In many cases — for example, bustards and peacocks — the taste of decay definitely spoils the pleasant natural taste of the bird's meat. The tastiest meat of this kind is to be found in the breast of the flamingo, which is a delicacy unmatched among meats. It is, by the way, not true that a flamingo's meat, as the old Cape travellers used to say, is just as rosy as its feathers. It is black-brown meat with short fibres, exceptionally soft, and it requires little fat. The flamingo is, of course, no longer available as food — it has become 'royal game' like elephant or white rhinoceros. But it is still one of the most delicious birds you will find. I know of only one other that can compete, the breast of a juicy, fat, grey lourie that has been living on *moepels*[3] for a month.

Because a bird's meat is rather 'thin', it should always be well larded — something most cooks tend to forget. Placing a few strips of bacon across the breast of the bird is insufficient. It pays to insert thin pieces of bacon into the breast meat with the help of a large canvas needle, especially when *braaing* it on the grill or in the pan.

The filling is another thing the cook needs to consider carefully. The best filling is that in which one uses the liver and pluck[4] of the bird, finely ground, thoroughly mixed with spices and breadcrumbs, and soaked in milk. The spices need to be chosen with care. Some wild birds have a very delicate taste — for instance, Coqui francolin, speckled rock pigeon, and sand grouse, which should not be overwhelmed with sage, thyme or garlic. A good cook will know how to use even saffron and chillies in such a way that they add to the flavour of the game and do not drown it. But be warned about the fat. Whatever kind of fat you use — hard or soft fat, butter or oil — it has to be first-class and not the least bit rancid, as this will spoil the taste and may well make the meat tougher.

When preparing wild birds, especially wild water birds, we need to

---

1 Cape sparrows.
2 Waxbills.
3 Fruit of the red milkwood, *Mimusops* sp.
4 Heart, liver and lungs.

wild birds

make much more use of wine and vegetables. One of the oldest and best partridge recipes is that in which the game is braised with cabbage, and served on a layer of it. I have tried it with *veldkool*, with water hawthorn, and with the young pod leaves of some thorn trees in the bushveld. I have even tried it with the flower buds of an aloe, and it worked very well, but unfortunately that particular aloe is not easy to find. You can also stew birds with root vegetables — carrots, turnips and artichokes — as well as with fruit. A Cape dikkop[1] stewed with oranges and served with snippets of orange peel baked in oil will make your mouth water. In Natal I once had some bush partridge[2] served on a layer of stewed pawpaw. It was delicious.

The addition of wine, even just a few spoonfuls, when the bird is roasting or stewing in the pan, always improves it. It is also good to add a tiny bit of wine to the sauce, especially when thickened with flour. As for the birds themselves, the larger kinds taste better roasted than stewed. The smaller ones, on the other hand, usually taste better when stewed slowly.

Something the cook should remember is that an excellent soup can be made from the leftovers of any kind of wild bird the day after the guests have eaten it. The bones and skin, especially of water birds, will still contain enough to provide you with a strong soup that can be served either as a simple *consommé* — a clear soup made with egg white, of course — or as a thick soup with vegetables.

18 June 1943

1 The Spotted Dikkop.
2 Either the Crested or the Natal Francolin.

17

Wild Birds II

It would be difficult to say which of our wild birds has the best qualities from a culinary point of view. Years ago at the old Darling Street vegetable market, which some of us still remember well, wild birds used to be for sale. That was in fact the only place where you could find wild birds. I still remember how, as a child, I used to see cranes, dikkops, herons, flamingos (at that stage not yet 'royal game') and peacocks, as well as some not so 'genuinely noble' game such as red-winged starlings, cormorants and albatrosses. Today there is really only one place in Cape Town where wild birds can be bought, and that is at the fish market in Dock Street, but there you will only find sea birds — and they really do not taste good. The old Darling Street sellers used to tell me that, apart from the flamingo, which is without doubt the best, they rated the guinea fowl most highly. I would not regard it as the best, although I will admit that the taste of guinea fowl depends on the time it was shot and the farm it comes from. We still do not fully appreciate how much bird-meat is influenced by the food the bird eats. In America they understand this well. There a duck is rated up to three shillings per pound higher when it has been fed celery, and a Muscovy duck that has been fed turnips and cucumbers is even dearer. You also find the opposite. In the Rustenburg district I once shot a little swarm that was literally inedible — the taste was disgusting, indeed nauseating — and it turned out that the birds had fed on elderberries. I similarly found sand grouse (Namaqua sand grouse, although they are found throughout South Africa) that were inedible because of some or other food they had eaten.

It is simply a matter of taste which wild bird you prefer. Unfortunately we do not have much to choose from. Most of us have to make do with partridge, pheasant, bustard, guinea fowl or perhaps wild duck. Of these, one might take the guinea fowl and the wild duck as representing the two main groups — those with white meat and those with dark meat.

A guinea fowl, tame or wild, is usually quite plump, but not plump enough to be prepared without larding. Its skin, like that of the partridge, is not tough, and it therefore does not need to be skinned. But it is necessary to scald it to get rid of the fluff. The cook then needs to rub it well, inside and out, with butter or fat. Whether a tiny bit of spice — even garlic — should be added to the butter or fat is something every person must decide for himself. I always use a bit of crushed *naartje* peel mixed with grated nutmeg — it adds an extra touch of delicious flavour that is not strong enough to spoil the taste of the guinea fowl. Lard the breast, and as far as possible also the thighs, with very thin strips of bacon — without the rind, of course. Fill with a mixture of crushed liver, heart and lung, a few ground walnuts, a piece of lemon peel, breadcrumbs soaked in milk, and salt and pepper to taste. *Tant* Alida always used to add onions as well, but I believe this to be a mistake. An even bigger mistake is to follow the very English custom of stuffing it with sage. Remember, a guinea fowl, tame or wild, is a white-meat bird, delicate tasting and very tender. Therefore treat it with the greatest care. Baste it diligently in the oven, first with fat until nice and golden brown, then with its own sauce, to which you may add a few tablespoonsful of good jerepigo. When it is nicely done, add pepper and salt and serve as warm as possible with good potatoes, soggy rice and cauliflower. Stewed prunes are also a good accompaniment, as is any kind of red wine, or even a good bottle of white. It goes with everything.

Our wild duck is something completely different. It is, in the first place, a tough animal, with little 'short meat' and a hard, tough skin, which happens to be one of its best qualities. In the case of a moorhen or coot, I would recommend that you skin it — just as Apollyon did to Marsyas, but of course in a less cruel fashion. The one *oubaas* skinned the other alive, but that is not necessary when it comes to wild duck. Give the duck a good once-over, as it were, with a magnifying glass, to make sure that no little feathers remain; extract whatever you can find, and scald with a burning stick all the remaining fluff, especially round the neck and between the wings. Remove the oil glands; make sure that the crop is nice and clean; and cut off the neck as close to the body as you can. Carefully remove the innards and take care not to break the intestines and gallbladder. Wash and dry well, inside and out. Grease inside with butter, with or without a touch of spice. *Tant* Alida always used turmeric and I concur, although I cannot really say why — it is just the sort of habit you acquire with experience without really being able to give any reason for it. As regards the filling, this is something the cook needs to consider carefully. A duck filling needs to be tasty and should also add flavour without taking away any of the juiciness and definitely without making the meat watery. A firm '*braai* filling', as you would use for a hare or sucking pig, is therefore not desirable. Neither is a watery, porridge-like filling such as a pineapple-peach-guava mixture. It is true that the so-called 'Creole duck' gets a pineapple filling, but it is not right for our wild duck — it is usually a Muscovy or other, smaller kind of duck and has more 'short meat' than our yellow-billed or shelduck. The preferable filling is again one that uses the duck's own innards, assisted (since duck liver is a delicacy that should be eaten with the roasted duck) by what we can borrow from the innocent little farm chicken. Mix together well some minced bacon, chicken liver, a piece of duck liver, the duck heart, a piece of duck lung, a strip of red chilli, a cooked potato, a ground raw sour apple, a small onion, a piece of leek, a sprig of parsley, salt, coriander and pepper; dampen with red wine; stuff the duck with it; sow up and grease the seam well with butter. Smear the outside of the duck with fine breadcrumbs — preferably from bread made with buckwheat flour — and place in the saucepan above a thin layer of bacon. Put it in the oven and let it brown quickly; then pull it away and baste it well with fat and wine; allow it to roast very slowly. Some prefer the duck meat to be rare, still dripping blood when cut, whereas others like it 'well done like porridge'. Again it is a matter of taste, and I myself consider the right choice to lie somewhere in between. What the cook needs to bear in mind is that the skin needs to be completely edible. It is one of the most delicious parts of the bird, if well prepared. The duck's liver is cooked together with it and served up as an accompaniment, each guest receiving some. It is as delicious as Muscovy duck liver if properly cooked and not charred until it is hard and tough.

The best dish to serve with wild duck — and, for that matter, with any kind of roasted black-meat bird — is a good green salad, preferably made with vinegar and oil, not with mayonnaise. This is all you need — it goes best with the duck, and root or pod vegetables are too luxurious for a simple roast duck. With a salad like that you would of course drink a 'rough' wine — a first-class white wine with a delicate bouquet will not go with it. Therefore serve the guests a good farm wine — a sauvignon or a jerepigo, even a shiraz if it is not too tart. If you do not use salad, or if the salad is not made with vinegar, then a finer burgundy is what you want.

2 July 1943

wild birds

18

Our Brandy

There are few things about which there is more misunderstanding, prejudice and ignorance than our brandy — and yet it is really such a simple matter. I admit that brandy, viewed from a purely chemical perspective, is extremely complex — about as complex as bread or mieliemeal if you start unravelling them chemically. But no one really looks at what we eat or drink through the eyes of a biochemist. Life is far too short for such an exhaustive approach.

Our forefathers did not know brandy. They were only acquainted with alcohol in the form of fermented liquor such as the different types of beer, wine, fermented milk and other similar drinks in which the carbohydrates are converted to alcohol and carbon dioxide as a result of the work of bacteria. It was only when the Arabs, about twelve hundred years ago, accidentally discovered that you could distil something from these fermented drinks that is completely different in its effect on the human system that humankind came to know brandy. It was such a novelty, with such wonderful characteristics, that they named it 'life water', a name that brandy still has in French. The scientific name for wine spirits is nothing other than a translation — or rather an imitation — of the words 'spirit in itself', which expression was not meant to refer to anything learned but was simply considered an appropriate name for the end result of distilled wine.

Brandy is therefore the wine spirit that is derived from fermented wine when distilled. It is, however, not pure wine spirit, for we regard wine spirit — alcohol — as the particular chemical substance derived from any kind of fermented liquor when distilled. Thus from fermented rice you get arrack; from fermented grain vodka, gin and schnapps; from fermented peaches peach *blits*, and so forth. The basis of all is nothing other than wine spirit — ethyl alcohol. But brandy is something more and something much better than mere alcohol. It is wine spirit in which a whole range of chemical substances that are susceptible to conversion and change have been dissolved — which makes the whole better or worse, according to one's skill in making a good or bad brandy. No chemist knows exactly what brandy consists of, what the eventual conversion processes are going to achieve, or how the different combinations of amino and fatty acids are going to react with each other. Research on this topic is as difficult as that dealing with the making of wine, though in this case it is not so much a matter of the strange influences of bacteria that make studying the taste and quality of wines so very difficult.

For the layman it is not necessary to study the chemistry of brandy. I would also advise him not to try as it will only give him a headache. He should however know something about brandy as a drink, which is simple enough.

First, allow me to do away with a few misconceptions. Brandy is a poison — that is completely true. A poison is something that kills live cell fibres. Boiling water is therefore also a poison; so are vinegar, chillies and potato peels. We absorb these poisons into our bodies on a daily basis when we eat and when we drink coffee and tea. In some of our vegetables there are poisons that are much, much stronger than that in wine spirit. We can therefore readily admit that brandy is a poison. Anyone who dares to drink pure wine spirit will very quickly discover what a deadly poison it is!

The practical reality, of course, is that our body is a complex laboratory that daily extracts from what it consumes that which is suitable and useful for it, and converts and renders harmless everything that is poisonous. As long as we do not overwhelm it with a particular poison — like suddenly administering a lump of prussic acid it cannot possibly render harmless in an instant — it converts the poisons we eat on a daily basis into useful fuel and bricks for building tissue. Wine spirit is one of the poisons it is capable of converting very well indeed. It does this so easily that we can readily state that wine spirit is one of the best food fuels you can find. Thus the body can process, in much less time, a quantity of wine spirit having the same fuel value as an equivalent amount of meat, which therefore requires it to do less work. So while it is true that brandy is a poison, it is also a food and a fuel that is easy to process.

No brandy, however, consists of pure wine spirit. It contains many other substances and some of them — those we call amino acids — have a nutritional value that we have not been able to quantify. A lot of research will be required before we will know with any certainty why one food poison agrees with us better than another. We are still at the beginning of such investigations and the more we come to know about this, the more we will be forced to adjust our traditional views on food and nutrition.

One truth that research has proven beyond doubt is that the moderate use of a food that we find delicious is, in the long term, not damaging to the body, whereas the immoderate use of even the simplest food can impede the growth and development of our body tissues.

For us Bonades this is a great consolation. We are brandy drinkers — not heavy drinkers — and we have been taught from childhood to regard a good brandy as the best and most perfect product of the vine, and therefore as the crowning achievement of the wine farmer. When I was young old *Oom* Theofilus Schreiner once visited our district with Mrs Stuart, his niece. They recruited the whole confirmation class — with the exception of the brothers Bonade, who were too headstrong for that — and founded a 'Band of Hope'. They showed terrible pictures of what would happen to your stomach and intestines if you drank brandy. Our magistrate even protested against a picture of the liver of an official that . . . Need I say more? I know now that science has adjusted its view of the liver and the intestines considerably, and that the general opinion now is that a moderate user of brandy has just as much chance of living long and remaining healthy as someone who drinks no brandy at all. I remain mum about which of the two will enjoy his life more. This is a matter everyone should decide for himself.

Nor is it my wish to go on about abolition and the abuse of strong drink. I will restrict myself to brandy as a table drink. Now that I can console myself with the truth that brandy is no worse a poison than coffee or *mosbolletjies*,[1] I can deal with it as a delicacy.

One of the reasons we are still so against brandy – especially those who prefer to partake of alcohol in the form of imported whisky – is that there is still some prejudice against the so-called '*dop* brandy'.

There are two kinds of brandy to be found on the market. The one is pure wine brandy, distilled from distilling wine only, and the other is brandy distilled from distilling wine mixed with skins and sediment. The trade names for them are French. The French call the first *eau de vie du vin*, or 'water of life of the vine', and the second *eau de vie du marc*, or 'water of life of the skin'. The second has considerably more ingredients than the first, but that does not mean it is stronger. The 'strength' of a brandy is its wine spirit quality, and that depends on the way it is distilled – a technical subject I shall refrain from going into here. Connoisseurs regard a good '*dop* brandy' as more delicious and healthier than a good 'wine brandy', but it is simply a matter of taste if both are good. According to the law, we are now no longer able to buy '*dop* brandy' – at least not that which is made here. We are therefore concerned, when talking of South African brandies, solely with wine brandy.

I make bold to say that our best wine brandy can compete with the very best foreign types – even the famous cognacs from the Charente region in France – and do not have to stand back for them at all. The KWV has during the last twenty-five years done much to improve all our local brandies, and the best ones on the market are all blended with KWV brandy. Naturally each firm has its own 'type' of brandy, blended and made according to its own recipe. But in every type the main role is played by a good, ripe, completely natural wine brandy, that may not be less than five years old.

A lot of nonsense is spoken about 'old brandy'. Some – I trust not too many of my learned readers – still believe that there exists something like a Napoleon brandy, that is to say a brandy made before the year 1815. Now there are indeed brandies to be found that are that old, just as there are wines that are older still. But while some wines – not many – can remain in

culinary treasures

1   Must buns.

a bottle for fifty years or more and be improved by age, this is not the case with brandy. Once brandy is bottled and protected against the air, it remains unchanged. It neither improves nor does it deteriorate, assuming that it is well corked. There is perhaps one exception to this rule: a bad brandy becomes even worse with time in a bottle. Good brandy ripens in the vat, where the wood can breathe and the many ingredients can slowly but surely undergo chemical change. It is the vat that gives the brandy its colour, although it is normal in the trade to enhance the colour with additives allowed by law. It is not only the colour that is influenced by the wood of the vat but also the taste of the brandy and its nature as a liquid, and the longer the brandy remains in the vat, the better it becomes, although it is difficult to say at what point it could be regarded as overripe. It is not practical to keep brandy in the vat too long, for it evaporates, and a small vat of brandy will dry up after ten years. It is therefore clear that no brandy can stay in a vat for a hundred years. It is equally clear that brandy from 1815 that has been kept in a bottle will today be no better than it was then, and we have brandy today that is considerably better than that of earlier times.

The truth is that very old brandy is just about undrinkable, because it is so saturated with ethereal salt and volatile acids that it will burn your mouth and lips. A small quantity of such a very old brandy is used to blend a good younger one – it gives the younger liquid more body and a pleasant bouquet, aftertaste and oiliness. Such additives should however be used with the utmost care, for the 'blending' of brandy is a matter for the connoisseur and it is therefore done exclusively by experts attached to the large firms.

For the normal *afficionado* a good wine brandy of about ten to twelve years is just as good and tasty as a much more expensive one blended with an age-old liquid, be it imported or local. We now have many such good brandies on the market, and you can get them from any wine merchant. Try the different kinds. Pour a few drops of each in a dry wine glass – it is by no means necessary to use a large 'brandy glass' – and sample each first with your nose and tongue. (If you have false teeth with a metal plate, remove them before tasting; teeth with gold or metal fillings also do not help when it comes to judging brandy.) Warm the glass between your hands to cause the volatile acids to evaporate. Do not pay too much attention to the colour – unless it is too dark, the colour will in most cases have been enhanced by adding burnt sugar or something like that, which will not influence the taste very much. Too light a colour might make you suspect that the brandy has not matured for long enough in oaken vats, but your tongue and palate will be a better guide than your eye. Now taste the warmed liquid; 'feel' it on your tongue, and let it warm some more – so that the back of the palate can taste the flavour. Try to judge the extent to which the taste is even, oily and without 'bite' but still has a pleasant tingle. Then swallow and savour the aftertaste. Take a small sip of water and try another sample in the same way; and decide according to your own taste which brandy you prefer.

Now squirt a few drops of soda water in one of the glasses and try again. See which of the different samples passes the mixture test. A first-class type will immediately impart its good qualities to the mixture; its flavour will, as it were, be germinated by the carbon hydroxide; its tingling taste will be strengthened to a certain extent. On the other hand, you will, if you have a sensitive palate, immediately spot the lesser kind — that which still has some volatile acids that a good brandy should have given up to the wood of the vat. A subtle change in the aftertaste indicates the presence of the secondary wine spirit — a touch of bitterness might then even be noticed. Now compare your observations during the mixture test with those made when tasting the pure liquid, and make your choice.

The brandy you like most is the one that will best agree with you. Do not be impressed by labels or advertisements — make your choice according to your own taste. And then treat your choice with love and understanding. Enjoy it in moderation, preferably after a good lunch or supper, with or after coffee if you like it in its naked purity. Otherwise, again in moderation, with clean spring water, or, if you prefer, with soda water. And on a cold winter's evening, when the wind is howling outside and you are sure that your lambs are safely protected in the *kraal*, with warm water, a piece of cinnamon, a lump of sugar and a flake of lemon peel, as a warm drink.

10 September 1943

19

Water hawthorn

Now is the time for *wateruintjies*,[1] and my dear readers should understand clearly that one of the blessings that European civilisation brought to this country was to teach the 'uncivilised' how to make best use of their natural resources. My late *Tannie* Trifosa — there was no such name in our family, but *Oupa* called the twins Trifosa and Trifena because he happened to be reading the sixth chapter of Romans the day they were born (*Tannie* Trifena succumbed before the day she was to be baptised) — *Tannie* Trifosa used to tell me that the real water hawthorn harvest should be in spring. Her great-grandmother had told her that in the old days of the Dutch East India Company the people from the Hantam came to dig up the real hawthorn. But we no longer do that today — we only eat the upper part, the flowers. What she told me is true: Thunberg, who was apparently some sort of hawker around here,[2] tells us that people also did that in his time, and that the hawthorn was the bulb and not the flower. But when *we* tried to dig it up, we only found potter's clay and a dead water skunk!

We will therefore restrict ourselves to the hawthorn flowers and stalks — even from those, you can make a wonderful stew. It is a pity that they are so scarce nowadays. Previously it used to be possible to find a *klonkie*,[3] on the Parade or on any street corner, with half-a-dozen bunches of water hawthorn flowers for threepence each. Now you have to pay — can you believe it? — up to two shillings a bunch, and be thankful you managed to get it at all. The week before last I saw the *vlei* full of flowers — the smell was reminiscent of a funeral — but was there a *klonkie* to be found to wade in and pick them? Not a single one! I had to roll up my own trousers and, of course, the first thing I stood on was a jerepigo bottle. I am still limping, but we managed to return home with three or four bunches for the pot.

The Bonade recipe has fructified into half a dozen, and there will probably be further variations if the stuff becomes more widely used. It is really a shame that so much of our first-class veld food is so little known. We sell, just imagine, spinach — that has as little taste as a curried cucumber — for sixpence a bunch, and cauliflower for I know not how many shillings a head, and we treat with contempt water hawthorn, which is far more delicious and available everywhere for the picking. And in the veld there are many other delicious kinds of food that we neglect simply because we know nothing about them any more.

---

1 Water hawthorn, *Aponogeton distachyos*.
2 Carl Peter Thunberg (1743-1828), a famous Swedish botanist who stayed at the Cape from 1772-1775. He made three journeys to the interior, and collected 3 000 plants, of which 1 000 were new to botany.
3 Coloured boy.

When we start moaning and groaning on the subject of politics, or whatever else, there is no end to it ... but with all this fuss about the shortage of paper my space is limited – so I shall stifle my thoughts on the subject of the domestic training of the younger generation and return to the water hawthorn!

The secret of a good water hawthorn dish (as with every green vegetable dish) is the marriage of the green – in this case, the white – vegetable with fat. The basis of every stew should be a few pieces of fat mutton rib, well braised either in its own fat or with the aid of a bit of caul. *Tant* Tifrosa once showed me how she used ox-marrow for her stew, but that seems to me a bit extravagant, especially in a time of war when we cannot even get hold of enough good marrowbones for soup. I am also not convinced that marrow-fat improves the taste of a green stew. I think the particularly good taste that *Tant* Tifosa's stew had – and I grant that no one could make a better stew than she – was due to the sprig of rosemary she always added. We need to use herbs more. I recently searched in vain for a leaf of basil ... but wait, my space is limited!

Braise the meat well, and braise it properly – do not roast it! Slowly and carefully, for as the *Stingy Kitchen Maid* says: 'The stuff tends to burn very easily and therefore needs to be handled with care'. And once it has burnt you can forget about your stew. With vegetables it is different; when they have been 'lightly burnt', just take them from the fire immediately and place the top part in another pot – that way you can still save them.

In the meantime, wash the water hawthorn – taking only the flowers and flower petals and the youngest, softest stalks – in salt water; dry; and place on the fire in an iron pot with enough water to cover them. Allow them to boil. The water will extract the brown, bitter juice from the stalks, and as soon as it is reddish brown, the pot should be removed. Drain through a colander and throw out the red water – *Tannie* Trifosa always used it for her zinnias, and was genuinely convinced that it improved their colour. The things that superstitions can make people believe! Now add the water hawthorn to the braised meat, and add a lump of fat. Some say butter, but I cannot see why – fat and butter do not mix very well. Add, according to taste, a bay or lemon leaf, or a bit of whatever herb you choose. I have already mentioned that my old *tannie* was very keen on rosemary, and it is worth trying. Place the lid on and braise well for twenty minutes. Shake often, and take care not to let it burn.

Now take two or three handfuls of sorrel leaves – the yellow sorrel that grows in the vineyard is best.[1] If you use garden sorrel, cut the thick stalks away first and cut up the leaves well. Add boiling water, then dry well. When using the wild sorrel that is much softer, you do not have to carve up the

---

1 *Oxalis pes-caprae*, which is quite unrelated to culinary sorrel.

leaves first. Just bruise them well when getting rid of the water. Then add them to the stew and braise again. Stir well, so that the vegetables braise nicely in the fat and become oiled through and through. Take care that the heat of the fire does not become too strong, for then the stew will lose its green colour. To finish, the spice: add salt to taste, a piece of green ginger, a sliver of green chilli, and a thimbleful of fine white pepper. Dish up and serve with soggy rice.

I know that there are people who add cream. This is a matter of taste, but I prefer my water hawthorn stew without it. A puree of water hawthorn, like spinach without meat or fat — that is something you can add as much cream to as you wish. But the water hawthorn and meat stew should rely on its own flavour and richness, which it can do very well.

What to drink with it? One of our good white wines, well chilled and not too dry. A Riesling, if that is available, or else a Sauvignon. Both go well with the delicate taste of the water hawthorn that also pervades the meat.

24 September 1943

water hawthorn

20

Crayfish

According to what the old folk tell me, a taste for crayfish was not common in past times — at least not amongst white people. The Boer people never liked it much, and in my great-grandmother's recipe book, in which there are many recipes for fish dishes, crayfish gets no mention whatsoever. I regard it as one of the few bad traits of my otherwise well-nigh perfect family that there are, even today, Bonades who turn up their noses when crayfish is spoken of.

Sometimes, when quietly contemplating the nuances of human nature — in which pastime I sometimes indulge while attending to some or other delicacy on the fire — it occurs to me that one of the reasons why *Grootoom* Gieljam used to be regarded by the family as smelling a bit off was probably his love for this outstanding crustacean. I remember how he once took me to Kalk Bay, where he initiated me, from the rocks, in the art of catching small crayfish. They are no longer to be found around there, and even if they were you would not dare fish them out with a basket — one of the new laws, among the hundred thousand others in existence, is a prohibition on molesting small crayfish.

And yet, where will you ever find anything more delicious than these small, juicy, delicious little animals? When I speak of crayfish, I refer not to that red, hard-boiled 'factory' substance that is sometimes delivered or comes from cold storage at an exorbitant price, and that people in hotels, in clubs and — yes, believe me — in private homes use to make 'crayfish salad'. I refer to the small crayfish that really are worth eating, or the larger ones, preferably female, that are almost as good.

Try and find one of them. Get hold of it while still alive, struggling, and able to pinch your fingers with relish; one that is still — well not quite black, but that strange green-blue, blackish body colour with various hues of gold, depending on how the light catches it. And please do not throw it into boiling water. If you are extremely sensitive and a member of the Society for the Protection of Animals, you may kill the little ones first by slipping a knife into their heads. Miss Duckitt advised that for crabs, but while admitting that there was a measure of cruelty in immersing crayfish in boiling water, she readily agreed that it was the most common method. Her own cook, she tells us, always cut through the neck of the crayfish with a knife, and those who consider this a more merciful method could do likewise.

I place my crayfish, small or large, in a pot with a cup of sea water, a few strips of seaweed, a few slices of lemon, two or three Pittosporum leaves, a quartered onion with a piece of onion leaf, and a sliver of mace. Then I put on the lid and place the pot on the fire. Within ten minutes my crayfish is done. When eaten very hot with a sour sauce, it tastes delicious, like soft-cooked beetroot, like something you cannot imagine if you have only tasted the type of crayfish that is bought wholesale and cooked *en masse*. But it tastes even better if you let it soak for a few hours in the soup in which it was boiled until it is cold through and through.

You can make a number of delicious dishes from crayfish cooked in this way. I shall touch on only a few. One of them is made according to an old recipe of Mrs Schwabe from Worcester. In her day they used to get the crayfish from Kleinmond or Gordon's Bay, and then it was still fashionable to sell only the very best 'maiden crayfish'. Her recipe is similar to that found in the recipe book of Miss Elizabeth Raper, written in 1756, which appeared in print for the first time in 1924 when the Nonesuch Press reprinted it in a deluxe edition, of which there is probably a copy in our State Library. The two recipes differ slightly, and that of Mrs Schwabe is to my mind more acceptable.

Crayfish in its shell. Take all the flesh out of the shell, tail and legs, especially the fatty meat just beneath the shell; crush it fine in a mortar along with an equal weight of ox-marrow or caul (the marrow is better!) and stir in some salt, pepper, breadcrumbs, two egg yolks, a cup of whipped cream, a pinch of chilli, and a tablespoonful of lemon juice. Fill the empty shells with it and place them in the oven until baked.

It is delicious, but today I would replace the breadcrumbs with rusk-crumbs because our government bread is completely unsuitable for any culinary work of art. I would also put a few lumps of butter on top when I take the shells out of the oven. I have also, on occasion, added a pinch of saffron to the mixture, which gives a beautiful colour to the dish. For variation you could add any garden herb, and I always find that a piece of *naartje* peel goes well with any crayfish dish.

A second recipe is one I inherited by word of mouth from *Grootoom* Gieljam. He always used to prepare his little crayfish on the beach after boiling them in seawater.

Egg Crayfish. Take out the flesh and cut it into small shreds, the smaller the better; braise with a bit of onion, chutney, thyme, pepper and a crushed chilli in butter or fat until it just starts getting nice and brown; add a few beaten eggs and stir briskly until it is all quite thick.

We always used to enjoy this simple dish on the Kalk Bay rocks, and not a morsel would remain for the *klonkies* who were watching eagerly. In my kitchen I always used to adjust it — I would hardly say improve it — in various ways. I would add a glass of brandy, which makes the eggs a trifle watery but improves the taste. Or a few oysters, two or three anchovies, and a few spoonfuls of ground almond. You could also play different tunes with spices, but beware of garlic.

A third recipe comes from one of the oldest handwritten manuscripts known to me, and I rather think that this is the way the Chinese cooks served it in the olden days when they had little 'eating houses' on the spot where our Broadcasting Corporation office stands today.[1] They were then the most knowledgeable cooks in the country, and we are indebted to them for many of our Afrikaans cooking methods.

Pineapple Crayfish. Crush the meat, especially that of the claws, and mix with cream, ginger, mace, a teaspoonful of honey, a pinch of ground red chilli, a tablespoon of Chinese (soy) sauce, and a pinch of salt. Cut out the inside of a pineapple so that the peel forms a hollow container. Cut part of the inside of the fruit into small strips, add the crayfish mixture and stir together. Fill the pineapple with it, place in a pot with a little water, put the lid on tight, and allow to steam for twenty minutes. Take the mixture out of the peel, cover with a sour sauce, and serve.

This is perhaps a bit complicated, but the dish is well worth the trouble. When made in the right way it looks a bit like crumpled mielie bread but, as for the taste, that is ... well, quite unique. The pineapple flavour is particularly good. I sometimes replace the soy sauce with a glass of good brandy.

22 October 1943

1 That was in 1943. Today the African Life Centre is to be found there.

21

The Genuine *Uintjie*

Writing elsewhere on the subject of *wateruintjies*,[1] I made the point that it is not really correct to regard them as *uintjies*,[2] and that the name really only applies to the bulb and not the foliage and flowers that we now use for our water hawthorn stews. An *uintjie* — really nothing but a tiny onion — is, as far as I know, always a bulb, and also always that strange kind of bulb that is surrounded by tissue and can be shelled. Such genuine *uintjies* have been known for ages. The old travellers who traversed the Cape a hundred years ago,[3] from Thunberg on, mention it. They say that the indigenous people used such bulbs for food, and they say it without any hint of surprise. This is itself unsurprising — after all, our forebears in the old European motherlands also ate *uintjies*. In the famous *Herbaal* of *Baas* Gerhardt,[4] the merits of different kinds of *uintjies* were expounded on — some were suitable for inner or outer use as medicine, others again for peasant food. Without exception, they are all foreign to us here in South Africa. Our own kinds of *uintjie* were, of course, unknown to *Baas* Gerhardt.

After asking around a bit, I discovered that there is a difference of opinion among our own *uintjie* connoisseurs as to the genuine article. The name *uintjie* is generally given to an iris or *vlablom*,[5] so well known as a food that the learned botanists gave it the name *Moraea edulis*, or edible *vlablom*. There are many kinds of *Moraea* in our country, and some of the bulbs are poisonous, like those of the related family *Homeria* that we call the tulip. Then again there are edible tulips, although I would not advise anyone to make a tulip stew without a thorough knowledge of them. In his list of Afrikaans flower names, Dr Muir gives the name *uintjie* to our *wateruintjie* and *Moraea edulis* only. Dr Fourcade, who has a thorough knowledge of the flora in the Humansdorp to Knysna area, also knows of only the two types of *uintjie*. In the southwestern districts (real *uintjie* country!) other kinds of *uintjie* are to be found. *Bobbejaanuintjies* are the bulbs of a *Babiana* type, which grows between the stones of the Olifants River and the Kamies Mountains and is rather difficult to dig up, although baboons manage it quite easily. *Hotnotsuintjies* are the bulbs of a type of sorrel, *Oxalis lupinifolia*: the beautiful picture of this type of flower in the quarterly magazine of the Pretoria herbarium was a painting of *uintjies* sent from Springbok to an

---

1 Water hawthorn. See p 269.
2 An edible bulb, literally 'a tiny onion'.
3 The mid-nineteenth century. Leipoldt is being a little vague here. Thunberg was in the Cape from 1772-1775.
4 Gerard's *Herball* (1597).
5 Literally, 'custard flower'.

uintjie eater there, and of which a few bulbs just happened to land in the garden by mistake. Another delicious kind is the bulb of *Cyanella capensis*, *bokuintjies* or *klei-uintjies*. Then there are also the little bulbs of the different *Moraea* types: in the Sandveld, for example, there is the large yellow *uintjie*, the purple *uintjie* and the *witblom-uintjie*, as well as the *slymblom-uintjie* and the *kaneel-uintjie*. They are all part of the *Moraea* family, and once you have seen the flower you will not easily confuse it with the simpler tulip flower.

We may quite possibly have many other edible bulbs. According to *Baas* Gerhardt, the bulbs of our chincherinchees are edible, and also those of *ferweeltjies*.[1] In comparison with the real, genuine *uintjies*, *Moraea edulis*, they are, however, all quite inferior.

When I was young there used to be an abundance of *uintjies*. An *outa* who was a shepherd used to bring bunches of them to the village. For a few *oulap*,[2] you could buy a bunch of anything from fifty to a hundred little bulbs that must have taken three to four hours to dig up as the *uintjie* embeds itself deep in the ground and, moreover, it is usually in the hard Karoo clay that it finds its shelter. In sandy soil it is, of course, easier to dig it out, but connoisseurs will tell you that clay *uintjies* taste much better than sand *uintjies*.

A bunch like that provides plenty of food. Cut off the stalks and cook the bulbs with just enough water, preferably lukewarm, to cover them, and do not cook for too long. Fifteen to twenty minutes will suffice. Take them out, allow them to cool, and you can then eat them with relish as they are easily shelled. They taste like young potatoes or chestnuts; some kinds are less sweet than others, and the *Bobbejaanuintjie*, usually the largest, is mealier and therefore perhaps more suitable for further preparation. But cold cooked *uintjies*, eaten just like that, are already a delicacy.

You could, however, also experiment a bit. Crush them fine in a mortar with a touch of nutmeg, mix with cream and a beaten egg, and place in the oven — which should be just as warm as that in which you would roast a guinea-fowl. If all goes well you will have a delicious soufflé on your hands.

Alternatively, stir the crushed *uintjies* with a touch of sugar, a pinch of ginger and two or three eggs; and cook slowly in a earthenware pot. You will then have a delicious pudding that can be served with *moskonfyt*[3] as syrup, or with a wine sauce. If you would like a first-class soup, add a few cups of milk to a scraping of lemon peel, salt, a pinch of white pepper, and ground *uintjies*. Bring it to the boil once only and pour into the soup tureen, in which you have already whipped up an egg with a teaspoonful of cream and a little brandy. You could wish for nothing better. If you would like a thicker

---

1 Sparaxis.
2 Pennies.
3 Grape syrup.

soup, add more ground *uintjies*; if you would like it thinner, more milk. My old *tannie* always used to sprinkle chopped parsley over it, but I do not fancy that, although it does make the white soup look pretty. *Uintjies* 'blend' well with all kinds of spice, because their own taste is not too strong. But still you have to be careful, as it is easy to spoil the *uintjie* taste by an excessive use of herbs or the use of herbs that are too strong.

The *tannie* whom I have already mentioned had vegetarian leanings in her latter days, and was thereby a very bad example to the family. We Bonades have always been liberal people: we eat everything that is tasty and cannot be bothered about what Dr Hay, or whoever, has to say. Anyway, my old *tannie* sometimes used *uintjie* purée to make 'artificial chops', just as some people now make them from lentils and beans. I consider it heretical to do such a thing, but each to his own taste. What this does show, however, is that with the *uintjie* as a foundation you can get up to all sorts of dietetical tricks.

If only we could get our *uintjies* onto the market! What would a Carême not have been able to do with them? My own experiments are curtailed year in and year out for lack of sufficient material. But I have been fortunate enough to succeed in making a delicious *uintjie* ice cream. And next year I shall try to use *uintjies* instead of chestnuts for that crown jewel of the culinary art, a Francatelli pudding!

29 October 1943

the genuine *uintjie*

22

Biltong

When the long-awaited Great Afrikaans Dictionary appears, we will probably obtain certainty about the derivation of the real meaning of the word 'biltong'. I am familiar with what the lexicographers say about it, but their explanations do not entirely satisfy me. I would encourage them to do a bit more research to try and find out whether there was not some bastardisation long, long ago.

The Bonades' own library, which is reasonably well stocked, contains nothing at all helpful concerning the derivation of the word. My old *tannie*, relying on her recollection of what her great-grandmother told her, was convinced that it meant nothing other than what it should mean. 'It goes without saying, Karel,' she would always say, 'that it looks like a tongue and is cut from that part of the ox that it would not be decent for me to mention.'[1] She was a prudish old dame, who never managed to convince me. For I have never seen biltong that looks like a tongue, and biltong made from the buttock is not what I would call first-class. It is fillet that makes the best biltong, although I must admit that the large muscle often recommended for biltong (for example by Mrs Dijkman, and in our earliest cookbook, printed in Natal)[2] does make quite good biltong.

In Switzerland I came across genuine biltong. There they call it *bindenfleisch*, and it is under this name that it is known by *Larousse*. In Mexico I found biltong under the name of *carne secca*, which means 'dried meat'. Later, in South America, I came across it under the name of *tasajo*. It is found everywhere in the world for, after all, it is nothing more than dried meat.

For such dried meat there are as many recipes as there are for onion soup, some simple, like that of Dumas[3] (who always carves his onions with a razor), and some highly complicated, like that of Scappi,[4] who adds garlic, *duiwelsdrek*,[5] thyme, and who knows what other herbs and spices.

But just as in the case of onion soup, the taste of the biltong depends upon the quality of its main ingredient, the meat. It does not matter whether it is game or the meat of a tame animal, whether you make your biltong from a sable or from an ox — if your meat is not first-class, your

---

1 The Dutch word *bil* refers to a buttock.
2 See p 26.
3 Alexandre Dumas (the Elder), author of *Grand dictionnaire de cuisine* (1873).
4 Bartolomeo Scappi, author of *Cuoco Secreto di Papa Pio Quinto* (1570).
5 Asafoetida.

biltong will be no good. This is seen all too clearly in the awful dried-out ostrich biltong we sometimes have to make do with here in the south, and that tourists take to be the genuine version of our South African delicacy. I do not believe in trying to eliminate all evils in our society, or even in trying to curb them, with strict laws, but deep down I consider that nothing is as objectionable as when my fellow citizens palm off such 'biltong' to ignorant foreigners. I know that in trade, as in the law, the principle holds: 'let the buyer beware'. But we have some fine assets — our wine, our brandies, our penguin eggs, our biltong — and it is in our own interests to make sure that these products have a good name.

Therefore, quality meat is the first prerequisite. A tip for the hunter: do not be satisfied with just cutting away what you cannot use at table, then drying it out on a string next to your tent. Choose some of the best meat. Preferably a muscle without sinew: the thick muscle-meat found alongside the spine, known as the *haasvleis*.[1] Cut off all the fat — there is enough fat in the tissue — and game biltong should never have outside fat. Rub it well with a mixture of salt, coriander seed, pepper, nutmeg, a touch of saltpetre and some vinegar to moisten it. Hang it up to be wind-dried. Rub it once again, and hang it up again until properly dry. Then you will have a first-class biltong that will be easy to grate, shave or cut into thin slices, that will keep for years and never lose its flavour if you keep it away from moist air. I know that this is not the usual way of doing it. The typical hunter leaves it to his workers to make the biltong. They cut what they get, muscle and sinew and whatever else comes with it, do not always salt it evenly, never use spices, and the biltong is seldom cut with skill. I grant that even biltong made in this way can taste good, but in comparison with that which is made with more care . . . well, there really is no comparison.

Beef biltong is something completely different. It should not be grated, for well-made beef biltong is too moist to be scraped or grated. The proper way is to cut it into thin slices, which are then eaten with butter on nice fresh brown bread. Making this kind of biltong requires patience and knowledge. It also requires a good, preferably young, fat ox, with muscle tissue that is not yet tough. The biltong maker should choose his meat as soon as the ox is slaughtered. My oldest Cape recipe, that of Mrs Schwabe, says: 'Take the round muscle that leads to the bottom part of the leg, and choose one that is about as thick as your forearm'. I do not know exactly what she is referring to. There are different round (ie buttock) muscles and I myself would, as I have said, prefer the thick round muscles found next to the spine above the walking muscles of the fore or hind legs. But whatever you choose, prepare it well. Cut it so that it is even and longish, but not more than at most eight pounds in weight — a weight of three or four pounds is probably best. Lighter pieces will dry out too quickly. Remove

---

1 Fillet.

carefully every piece of sinew you can see. It is not necessary to remove all the outside fat as well; a certain amount of fat round part of the biltong is actually recommended.

Once a piece is cut and dried a little, beat it a bit with a piece of wood — that will bruise the outside tissue somewhat so that the pickle can penetrate better. Rub with a mixture of salt, pepper, saltpetre, coriander seed, nutmeg, mace, and a pinch of ground ginger. My old recipes say 'with saltpetre, salt, brown sugar and anise'. The brown sugar I will go along with — the anise never!

Is the pickle necessary? Opinions differ. The best beef biltong I have ever had was pickled biltong. The *tannie* who made it — and she was a master of the art — let it lie for days in the mixture already described, which she moistened with brandy and vinegar. Every day she rubbed the biltong well; every third day she squeezed it a bit and then put it back into the pickle. Then she dried it well, covered it with cheesecloth and hung it in the chimney, where it stayed for nearly three months. Now that was real biltong! It was hard as a stone on the outside, and inside it was as soft and tender as lamb. A slice of it was like a cut ruby, red and transparent, and so beautiful and even that you could look at it with delight even while your mouth was watering to taste it.

Let me add this. Of all the meats, biltong is possibly the easiest to digest, and the best food. I do not know why. But it is a fact that thin slices of beef biltong (and the same holds for grated game biltong) almost melt away in your stomach. They are digested without using much energy. This makes biltong, if it is first-class, one of the best foods for sick people. But then a bad, and especially a dirty, fly-bespeckled biltong is an inferior food, and much more so if a quarter of it consists of indigestible sinew.

26 November 1943

23

Delicious Snail Dishes

In *Oom* Danie's vineyard there are many snails. 'They don't really do any harm, *Neef*,' *Oom* Danie said to me, 'but if the workers don't get rid of them, they may multiply.'

'*Ag nee*,' said *Oom* Danie a bit later, when I told him that his own forefathers had imported the snails from European vineyards, 'that is too terrible for words.'

'No, really *Oom*. They made only one mistake. They wanted to have the large, Italian snail here, but it perished on board ship and only the vineyard snail survived the journey.'

'And what on earth did they want to do with them?' *Oom* Danie wanted to know. 'Was it to get rid of some or other louse? But vines don't have lice!'

'No, no, it was to eat them, *Oom*.'

And to *Oom* Danie's dismay, I took a few dozen of his vineyard snails to the kitchen and made a snail dish. It took quite a bit of persuasion to get the old fellow to try them, but after the children and even *Tant* Hessie had declared it to be '*lekker*',[1] he did. Now *Tant* Hessie makes a snail dish every now and then.

For the vineyard snail is a real delicacy! Well prepared, it is one of the most delicious foods there is.

It is also called the garden snail, and its scientific name is *Helix aspersa*. Here in South Africa we have over six hundred of its nephews and nieces, and some of them I consider to be much more delicious. There are, for instance, the beautiful large veld snails of the Bushveld — the striped one, *Achatina zebra*, yields nearly one and a half ounces of meat. The largest is *Achatina immaculata*, which sometimes weighs more than a pound, but that is unfortunately only found in the dense parts along the coast of St Lucia Bay. Then there is *Metachatina kraussi* from Pondoland, and also the tasty white-yellow veld snail from the Richtersveld, with the long scientific name of *Trigonephrus porphyrostoma*. Then there are literally hundreds of smaller snails, of which the tiniest (and from a culinary point of view worthless), *Opeas sublineare*, was discovered by the late Dr Purcell in Namaqualand. It is a longish snail barely as large as a thin *naartje* pip. All these smaller kinds are possibly edible, but not worth the effort to clean.

Snails usually eat vegetables — there are a few carnivorous types, but

---

1 Delicious.

they need not be considered. Some are regarded as inedible because they cause sickness in the eater. This is due to the fact that they feed on poisonous plants such as black nightshade and hellebore, and also, in the case of the vineyard snail, because they sometimes, without any harm to themselves, feed on young leaves sprayed with some or other poison. It is well known that snails can tolerate chemical poisons that are deadly to other animals.

With a bit of care, however, it is easy enough to collect snails that are completely harmless. The snail is one of the oldest of foods. Our forefathers ate them raw — it was only later that cooks discovered how to prepare them in a refined manner for the table. The vineyard snail was always the most popular, but the Roman snail, which is larger, was the more famous. Today snails are still a popular food in Europe, where they are fattened artificially by snail farmers who prepare them for the market and see that they are given only the finest vine leaves and salad or cabbage to feed on. Nice juicy snails, fattened for the market, are quite expensive. Their price before the war was about two shillings a dozen, which was good value. It is perhaps too much to hope for that snails will become popular here in South Africa, but they are still a nutritious, useful food; and where there are vineyards or vegetable gardens we will always be able to gather enough of them for a good snail dish almost all year round. But take care that the snails have not fed on certain plants they love, such as the agapanthus or bush marigolds found in the garden. It is best to take snails from vine-leaves, for then you can be sure they are healthy and harmless.

Say you have collected a dozen beautiful medium-to-large snails. How should you prepare them?

There are many options, but one recipe that can serve as a model for all the others is the following. It is none other than the recipe preferred by the famous Carême.

'Wash the snails well in salt water; then put them in lukewarm water — never use boiling water, as this congeals the jelly-like substance in them. Take them one by one in your hand and remove the snail with a bent piece of wire from its shell, placing it in a saucepan with some cold water. Boil the shells well in water with a bit of soda, until they are cooked clean. Then remove them from the water, brush them inside and out with a small brush, and place them on a piece of paper to dry.

'Now take the saucepan with the snails and cover them with a glassful of white wine and a few spoonsful of strong meat *bouillon* or meat soup; add a sliced onion, a blade of mace, a teaspoonful of chopped parsley, a scraping of garlic, and salt and pepper to taste. Stew slowly over a not-too-rapid fire — it usually takes not more than twenty minutes for the snails to become nice and soft. Now remove them and replace each one in its shell. Thicken the sauce in the saucepan with some fine flour or maizena and an egg yolk, and pour some in each snail shell, so that the shell is nicely filled to the top.

Finally, close the door of each snail house with a layer of butter. Place the shells in the oven to warm well, and serve covered with what remains of the sauce. Your guest takes a little wooden lance, picks every snail out of its shell, and eats it with relish. Six snails are usually more than enough for each guest as they are quite rich.'

There are several other methods — *comtesse Riguidi*, *à l'arlésienne*, *à la bourguignonne* (supposed to be the favourite of our Huguenot forefathers), *à la chablaisienne*; *à la poulette*; *à la Brimont*, and so forth, that — if you feel like it — you could look up in *Larousse*. But the recipe given above is one of the best — it brings out the genuine, unspoiled taste of the little animal, and I speak from experience when I say that it really is delicious.

Have it preferably without any accompaniment — it is worth it. But if you really wish to have something with it, eat it with some toast and butter that can be soaked in the sauce. What to drink with it is a matter each must resolve according to his own taste. I prefer a not-too-strong red wine — therefore not a Burgundy, but rather a claret. Some connoisseurs declare that you can only have a swig of Bols with snails; others again prefer a sweet white wine. It is all a matter of taste.

7 January 1944

24

The Pawpaw

When I was young, we never used the word 'pawpaw'. We always used to call it a *'bobotie* fruit', or simply a *'bobotie'*, that grew here and there on the old farms, but was rarely found on the Cape market and therefore regarded as a bit of a scarcity. Today everyone calls it *papaya* or 'pawpaw', and the *bobotie* that we get to eat is mostly not the real thing.

We regard the pawpaw as a fruit and usually eat it raw. But it is as good — or even better — as a vegetable. No one really knows where it comes from. The botanists claim that *Carica papaya* (as it has been scientifically baptised, and the American *papaya* that we are not familiar with is not even its cousin) originally hails from South America, whence it was carried across the Pacific Ocean to a multitude of islands found in that great sea, so that it has become naturalised in each and every tropical or semi-tropical country. The tree grows wild in the tropical jungle, but seldom bears the beautiful large fruit that we find on our cultivated trees. In its wild state the pawpaw is not much to write home about. It is edible, but that is about all. *Oubaas* Lindley,[1] who knows his jungles well, wrote somewhere: 'All tropical fruit are edible, but there are few that are really worth eating'. He probably had the wild pawpaw in mind when he made this pessimistic remark.

The tame pawpaw is found — on the market and in the fruit shops — when it is already ripened until soft. It is then full of fruit sugar, and you can serve it on its own as a sweet dish. Even in this state, it is not to be missed as a *hors d'oeuvre* or dessert, with or without lemon and sugar. When ripe and soft, you cannot do much more with it. It is then only suitable as an ingredient for a fruit salad, although a good cook will on occasion, for instance when he has a wild duck or coot, whip it up with mace, breadcrumbs, an egg yolk and a pinch of nutmeg as a first-class filling. When less ripe, you can stew it. Cut it into neat squares, after peeling, and place the pieces in a saucepan with a cup of brown sugar, a glass of brandy, a piece of *naartje* peel, and a shard of stick cinnamon. Stew slowly but well. Serve with whipped cream. My old *tannie* always used to add a glass of Van der Hum, but that does not really make much difference if there is already some cinnamon and *naartje* peel in the syrup. The less ripe, the better this recipe will be. I prefer to make my stewed pawpaw with hard, not-at-all-ripe fruit. Then it comes out beautifully white when stewed carefully and well — stewing it too quickly makes it go brown. Both taste good, but I prefer the nice white one.

You can also make a pudding of it. Grind the flesh of the fruit to a

---

1 John Lindley (1799-1865), a famous botanist and horticulturalist.

pulp, and mix with sugar, spice (choose according to your own taste, but possibly ginger, cinnamon and a pinch of allspice is best — nutmeg will not do, nor will cloves or *naartje* peel), the yolks of a few eggs, and a few spoons of finely sifted flour. Some people also add finely chopped grapefruit peel, a few raisins, and ground almonds. You can stuff this pudding with just about anything, Carême said, but as overloading does not ennoble the end result, I would advise you not to be too extravagant with the flavours. Place in a mould or in a cloth sprinkled with flour, and steam slowly. Serve with a sweet-sour butter sauce. Or even better, if you want to be very Afrikaans, make a sweet sauce from *skilpadbessies*[1] or, if you can get them (this is alas no longer so easy), from wild apricot berries,[2] and pour it over the pudding. The beautiful red colour goes well with the creamy yellow pudding, and enhances the taste.

You can also make pawpaw ice cream. Beat together, this time with cream, sugar syrup, grated lemon peel, egg yolk, and a few drops of orange oil. Place in the fridge and, as soon as it starts stiffening, beat again and add a squeeze of lemon juice. Freeze well, and serve with sweet cookies or rusks. You can decorate your ice cream — which is by no means to ennoble it — by pouring over it an iced thick sweet sauce, made from strawberries or raspberries. That is what the American cooks call a 'sundae', although they indulge in it every day of the week.

Preserved and crystallised pawpaw is something I have seldom come across, although there is no reason to be scornful of it. The fruit needs to be quite green, and the preparation is as for *spanspek*[3] preserve. I have also come across pawpaw jam, but this was made from dried pawpaw, which is unknown here, although it is sold in America.

I esteem the pawpaw more highly as a vegetable than a fruit. But then it needs to be barely full-grown and the pips still need to be quite white. Steamed in water and served with a sour butter sauce, it is a fine dish. You can also make a first-class soup and a tasty purée with it. For the soup, take a medium-to-large green fruit, peel and remove the pips. Cut into pieces. Chop up a large onion and fry along with the pawpaw in butter, without spoiling the colour. Add some chopped parsley. Pour onto it four cups of water (or meat soup, if you prefer), move the saucepan to where there is less heat, and let it cook for an hour and a half. Strain through a colander, forcing the vegetable through it. Then place it back in the saucepan, with a blade of mace, and salt and pepper to taste. Allow it to boil, rub a tablespoon of maizena into a cup of sweet milk, and add the mixture to the soup. Stir well, and allow it to cook for a few minutes. Serve with toast. This soup can be made richer by adding half a cup of cream and a lump of butter.

---

1 Literally 'tortoiseberries'; the fruit of *Nylandtia spinosa*.
2 Probably the fruit of *Dovyalis caffra*, the Kei apple.
3 Musk-melon.

A tasty way of serving pawpaw is that of my old *tannie*. She diced her peeled green pawpaw and steamed it softly for twenty minutes, adding salt. Then she took a deep earthenware dish, greased it with butter or fat, and decked it out with a layer of cooked pawpaw, a layer of peeled tomatoes and chopped onions on top of that, then another layer of pawpaw, and so on until the dish was full. Over that she poured a cup of meat-roast sauce, and put the dish in the oven to bake. I can tell you, it was a feast! But as far as I remember, her masterpiece was the filled pawpaw. She cut it in two, took out the pips, and boiled it for ten minutes in salt water. Then she took it out, let it drip, and filled it with a *frikkadel*[1] filling made of minced ham, mushroom sauce, and egg yolk to bind it. She put a sail yarn around it, baked it in the oven, and served it with a white or sour sauce. Delicious!

My memory of this last dish is not quite as pleasant as my recollection of its taste, for it was while eating it that I — then still wet behind the ears — decided to make known to the world my knowledge of nature. I enquired whether the *bobotie* tree in my *oom's* garden was male or female, which *tannie* found 'unedifying' — with the result that my *oom* and I were soon visiting the garden where there was a quince-hedge.[2] Whenever I eat filled pawpaw today I can still smell the *borrie* quinces.

21 January 1944

1   Meatball.
2   Canes for administering corporal punishment to errant boys, *kweperlatte*, were selected from the quince hedge.

25

Mielies

Of all our imported vegetables the mielie[1] has probably become naturalised the best. We are very much a mielie-eating nation. Whether or not this is an advantage we can defer until later. I do not, for the moment, wish to expound on the nutritional value of mielie meal — that I will leave to the Food Council, which can inform us according to latest scientific hypotheses. I wish merely to say something about the mielie as a vegetable for the table.

This happens to be what it is really well suited to. What can be more delicious, soft and appetising than young corn on the cob, properly done, creamy-white or golden-yellow, each 'pip' as round and fat as if it were chiselled on the cob? What genuinely Afrikaans dish do we have that can compete with a Transvaal *tannie's* mielie bread? Anyone who has eaten either, or both, will savour the experience deep in his memory.

But when dealing with mielies, as with any other kind of vegetable, one should not go about it as though neither art nor taste is required to make a delicious dish of it. Choose the mielies carefully, bearing in mind what a healthy, well-cultivated mielie should look like when commandeered for use. I emphasise that one should pick 'healthy' mielies. So many of those we are offered today — and that at two hundred per cent more than we used to pay for them — are not as healthy as they should be. The mielie is the seed of a grass, of which the 'beard' represents the *stamens*. Pollination takes place with the help of the wind, and the quality of the mielie pip depends upon whether the pollination has taken place properly or only partly. Furthermore, the appearance and juiciness of the mielie pips are influenced by the nutrition the mielie plant has extracted from the earth and the air — both before it 'flowered', and after pollination. Just like people, all vegetables require certain minerals for their health — phosphates, calcium, iron, and probably many other elements as well. They only need a little, but when even that is lacking they cannot develop into healthy vegetables, and the bulbs or seeds that we use are then not completely first-class. The first thing you will notice is a lack of firmness — the mielie pip, for instance, will no longer have the beautiful, round, shiny appearance it should have. This is the result of too little moisture. The second is a change in colour — the pip will no longer be an even white or yellow but will have a greyish appearance and the leaves will be wilted, with yellow or brown freckles. The older the mielie, the worse it gets, but you may also find noticeable signs of undernourishment and unhealthiness in young mielies.

---

1 Maize.

Avoid such mielies. Choose only young ones with proper pips arranged in even rows. You will of course not find them in completely straight rows – nothing in the mielie world is completely straight: those rows that look straight are really growing in a spiral. At least, this is what my friends who know something of botany tell me – and who am I to broadcast 'clever remarks' on the subject?

Should one cook the mielie with or without the inside leaves? The Americans always cook it with the inside leaves, which are removed along with the beard when the mielie is done. Our way, which I happen to prefer, is to peel off the leaves, to rid the mielie of every strand of beard, to immerse it in boiling water for a few minutes, and then to cook it slowly with some salt in the water. Maria then sees to it that it does not cook for too long. It is difficult to know exactly when to stop. Cooking for too long will remove the juiciness from the pips – they are then no longer nice and round, but develop sides, and the one no longer huddles shoulder-to-shoulder with the other as it should, but leans over a bit, as if shy to maintain its place in the row. I admit wholeheartedly that I have not yet mastered the art – as every Ayah appears to have done – of cooking mielies perfectly. Therefore I appreciate them all the more when I come across them on the farm in the mielie season, especially when they are still the old-fashioned 'bread mielies'. They compare to the smaller sweetcorn that has become fashionable as the old-fashioned *spanspek*[1] compares to the modern small ones you first have to keep in your fridge before you can enjoy them properly.

Leave the mielies to dry in a colander as soon as they are done, without letting them cool down, and serve – not with just anything, of course. A good green mielie can stand on its own legs – or pips. If there is butter on the table, those who want to spread it on their mielie may do so. But please do not serve molten butter in a little saucepan with your mielies! And please, not the affected 'mielie sauce' I have come across on occasion, of butter, nutmeg and egg yolk. This is an insult and an affront! The taste of a well-cooked green mielie is too delicate and too fine to be blended with any other taste or flavour. And for precisely that reason one should also not have any wine with one's mielie. Wait until you have dealt with it properly before you reach for your glass. And of course, it must be eaten 'off the cob'. To cut away the pips and devour them with a spoon or fork – well, that is about as abominable as serving it with nutmeg and a sour sauce.

Mielies also make an excellent purée that can be used as the foundation of a delicious soup. One of the best recipes is the American corn soup with mussels; another is mielie and green bean soup. The vegetarian can also bake all sorts of mielie cakes if he wishes. This is, however, not the best way of using mielies. The cooked green mielie on its own is the best way to have it.

---

1 Musk-melon.

The one exception is our delicious Afrikaans mielie bread. Made from young mielies, it is one of the best dishes I know — even when made from mielies that are past their best, it is a work of art that deserves to be more widely known. I find it nowhere in the recipe books of other countries — even the all-knowing *Larousse*, who has plenty to say about the most insignificant of things, is silent about it. But in South America, home of the mielie, it is well known and popular enough, although it is seldom found in restaurants. Our own Afrikaans recipes differ in some respects from each other. In the older ones, eggs are seldom used. The boiled green mielies are cut from the cob, ground, beaten up with milk, cream, a touch of sugar, a pinch of salt, nutmeg — some recipes say mace — and salt to taste, then placed in a mould and steamed. The addition of eggs makes the 'bread' richer and binds it somewhat more, but this is not really necessary and the old people prefer it without eggs. When it has been properly steamed, the 'bread' is cut into slices and served as a vegetable dish with meat. It can also be served with a sweet sauce as a desert. Either way, it is a tasty delicacy and can be regarded as one of our genuine Afrikaans dishes, one that tastes as good warm as it does cold.

17 March 1944

mielies

26

Cooking with Grapes

'No, what are you talking about? You can't cook grapes!'

The young woman had learnt domestic science in a modern school — I believe she even did it for matric, something that further lowered my already declining respect for examinations, as the woman cannot even cook a potato properly. She can go on about vitamins and nutrition until the cows come home, but she is ignorant of the art of cooking!

Imagine saying that one cannot cook grapes!

Going back to my childhood, I can see old Ayah Hanna, the cook at the old White House in Strand Street, standing at the kitchen table. I can hear, coming from the yard, where *Oubaas* Haylett kept some kind of zoo, the clacking of pheasants and the cooing of tufted pigeons, as from the kitchen you could see the cages and admire the game. It is February again — but not like today — for Strand Street was not then a place where the life of a pedestrian was in danger, and the horse-tram that went by was a decent, controlled mode of transport unlike the hazardous commotion one experiences nowadays. On the table was a basketful of Canaan grapes, enormous bunches such as are seldom seen today. The Ayah was busy peeling the grapes and carefully removing the pips.

'It's for the fish, *Basie*,' she explained, and when I later had some fish it became as clear to me as daylight that you could indeed in certain instances cook grapes with great success.

The Ayah's recipe for grapes with fish is well known to cooks. What Carême has to say about it is that the grapes should not be too sweet, although he uses muscadel grapes that I find far too sweet. As we no longer get the Canaan type of grape, I would recommend one of the newer Algerian kinds, or perhaps a Waltham Cross or Raisin Blanc, but any table or wine grape can actually be used. They have to be peeled carefully and the pips removed, then you steam them without water — they are juicy enough for that. They can then be used in a variety of dishes.

One of them is sole. Fillets of sole, with mussels stewed in white wine, a blade of mace, a pinch of salt and a touch of anchovy, served on a layer of grapes (cooked as described above), is a beautiful dish that is still too little known. The same can be achieved with steamed hake or shad. The strange aftertaste given to the fish is something one has to get used to, but it is well worth the effort.

Peeled grapes, even peeled black grapes, are — with a few exceptions — never coloured, but always white or light green, transparent and nicely soft.

The colour of a grape — which is actually a highly complex sugary combination, a glucoside — is due to the skin only; and only when the grape is very old or bruised will some of the colour permeate the flesh of the grape itself. When you cook black grapes, the flesh will also acquire something of the colour — as for instance with Isabella or Katalba grapes, that are otherwise very nicely green when cooked. The pips contain tannin, which leaves a bitter taste when cooked with the fruit. One should therefore get rid of both pips and skins.

It is rather strange that here in our winelands, where we regard grapes as the most important fruit for a quarter of the year, the product of the vine is so seldom used in the kitchen. Take vine leaves. You never find them in the home, except perhaps to decorate a bunch of grapes. Yet there are many ways in which they can be used. From young leaves you can make soup, a sort of *julienne* with a delicate taste. You can wrap *frikkadels*[1] in vine leaves, then roast or braise them. Quails in vine leaves is a well-known dish in Europe, and is well worth trying here. The young stalks of the vine can be steamed and served as a kind of spinach or asparagus; in Germany they are eaten like that, as are the young stalks of hop plants. Older leaves can be used as a wrapping for chops stewed in butter.

We do not use grapes for sweets either, although it is one of the best fruits to serve stewed or steamed, with or without the addition of sugar and spices, either hot or cold. In America grapes are often used in a dessert of sugared fruit. Here we seldom find a dessert like that containing grapes. Perhaps this is due to the fact that the preparation is a lot of trouble and requires some patience. The skins have to be taken off and the pips removed, which is a bother and takes time. But without a little trouble you will not get far when it comes to the art of cooking.

There are some so-called table grapes, especially those destined for the export market, that cannot really be eaten in any way other than cooked or as an addition to another dish, as far as I can see. One of them is the beautiful Flaming Tokai — that is oh-so-grandly coloured and perfect in appearance, but tastes a bit like chaff. Try cooking with it, adding a bit of nutmeg, when you do a nice fat leg of lamb. Or in a fruit salad consisting of orange, pineapple and pawpaw. For that it should be steamed first, for as it stands it is not a particularly nice grape. When my friends give me a basketful as a gift, I shell the grapes and cook them (without first taking out the pips) with sugar, cinnamon and white wine, and make of it a *macédoine*[2] with the help of some seaweed. Better kinds of grape do not require this cumbersome treatment. Hanepoot, for instance, can be added to a fruit salad just like that, or steamed and served with fish or meat.

I once treated the domestic science *niggie* to dove breast — called

---

1 Meatballs.
2 Fruit in jelly.

'supremes' by well-read cooks — with a little mound of steamed hanepoot grapes, served on a piece of toast dipped into a meat sauce with a dash of brandy in it. She later asked me whether it was something out of a tin. And this is what we call a matriculated girl! Why on earth do we waste so much money on what we call 'education'?

31 March 1944

27

Vegetable Dishes

In the end, after all is said and done, we get our nourishment from the ground. The scientifically enlightened person will rightly object: 'Excuse me, Mr Bonade, but that is wrong. We get it from the sun.' But that matters not, for sunbeams — or at any rate the life energy radiated by the sun — are gathered by the plants, and anyone who eats them uses this energy. The cattle eat grass and crops, and meat-eating people eat cattle and get energy that way. But we can just as easily go direct to the source of energy, eating the vegetables themselves.

I am not proposing that we should all become vegetarians. There is no reason at all for giving up meat completely, although as a nation we tend to eat more meat than we really need for our nourishment and health. But we can mix meat and vegetables, and so enjoy the best of both.

Green, uncooked vegetables are only used in salads — and far too sparingly. It is not clear whether such uncooked vegetables really transfer all their energy to the body. The human body is not really equipped, like that of a sheep or a hamster, to extract the last bit of nutrition from a lettuce leaf. But we manage to get enough for our daily requirements, which makes it worthwhile eating vegetables raw.

To get more out of them, they should be cooked, but in such a way that the nutritional value is improved not lessened. My niece, who underwent a course in domestic science at university, tells me that cooking vegetables often destroys their 'vitamin value'.

'Don't cry, darling,' I told her, 'but vitamin value is not something the good cook bothers about. He knows only too well that it is a minor consideration and that the main thing is to serve the vegetables in a way that makes them tasty and digestible.' She prefers not to believe me and quotes learned experts and newspaper advertisements telling us that there is more treasure to be found in guavas than in gold mines. This kind of 'learning' makes me despair of the future of our nation.

Do not, therefore, make too much of vitamins when you are dealing with vegetables. A carrot, a turnip, an onion, a cabbage or cauliflower, spinach, mielies, maracas, sweet potatoes, runner beans or cucumbers — whatever vegetable you can get hold of — is something that is improved and ennobled by proper cooking, and can just as easily be spoiled by careless treatment in the kitchen. Preserve the flavour of the vegetables, where possible preserve the juicy crispness that makes them 'snap beneath your teeth', and preserve especially the valuable minerals. Do not therefore 'boil it up in cold water'. That is a good way of making vegetable soup, but it is not how to cook vegetables properly. Cook them in water that is already boiling if you must, but rather steam them in their own juices, with the lid tightly on. Very juicy vegetables, like cucumbers and brinjals, are done in a few minutes; others, that may look as juicy but are not – like pumpkin and marrows, which have more fibre – take longer.

And please do not add any bicarbonate of soda. Bicarbonate of soda has a specific purpose in cooking, to curb sourness, but never to preserve the colour, be it green or yellow, of cooked vegetables. Use it, therefore, when you need a purée of tomatoes or a tomato soup, and then with great care and skill. But do not simply add it when cooking beans, peas, cabbage, or any other green vegetable. There is one exception, steamed purslane – a vegetable used all too rarely by us, although it is found in every garden and farm yard – with sorrel: this requires a pinch of bicarbonate of soda.

Spice, salt, pepper – well, that is a matter of taste. I find that we tend to overdo the salt. Most vegetables need little salt and, especially when they have a delicate flavour, just as little spice. My old teacher in the culinary art always used to add herbs, and there is a lot to be said for it if the flavour of the herbs does not drown but enhances that of the vegetable. I do not like cooking young peas with mint because the mint overwhelms the shy, delicate taste of the peas; a leaf of rosemary, on the other hand, brings out their taste as does a dash of sugar. In the case of a vegetable with a strong flavour like asparagus, herbs or spices are neither necessary nor advisable, although I have had this vegetable stewed with ginger and nutmeg. Sheer barbarity, as one would expect from my niece with her theoretical training! It was her concoction, and that after she treated us to 'cocktails'!

Of all our vegetables, cabbage is perhaps treated with the least respect. And yet it is one of the best, and also one of the most delicious when prepared properly. There are literally hundreds of different kinds, and every year a new one is cultivated that can in one way or another claim to have advantages not possessed by its predecessors. But in the end the one kind does not differ all that much from the other. They all have strange, juicy leaves, rich in mineral salts and vegetable acids, and a pleasant taste.

The best way of cooking a cabbage is that described in our old recipes. Steam the cabbage, after washing it thoroughly in cold water. (Some recipes say: 'let it lie in cold water for a few hours', but that does not improve the taste.) As soon as the cabbage is soft, which usually takes fifteen to twenty minutes – depending upon whether you have to do with a very young head or one already going grey. Put it, as my oldest recipe says, 'in a colander and pour cold water over it. Shake dry, place in a saucepan with butter, nutmeg and pepper, and allow to steam slowly'. In this way you preserve the green of the leaves, if that is what you want. The greenest cabbage is *boerekool*,[1] with its frummeled leaves – it does not, however, have a very fine taste.

---

1   Kale.

Brussels sprouts, a refined type of cabbage, requires careful — one might almost say loving — treatment. When cooked just a little too much their fibres lose their juicy crispness.

Another vegetable we do not treat well is the turnip. The taste and flavour of a turnip are regarded as being less than aristocratic, and only rarely will you find a dish of well-cooked turnips. Yet there are few root vegetables that taste better than young turnips, steamed quickly and then '*gefruit*,'[1] as the old Dutch cookbooks say, in butter. You have to use young turnips, as an old turnip root that has become spongy should never appear on a civilised table.

And what a delicious treasure we neglect by using cucumbers only for salads! Here and there I find them with a filling of mince meat that is suitable neither for them nor for the guest who is worthy of something better. A young steamed cucumber is a fine dish, but it needs to be prepared skilfully lest it become too soggy. One has to go to work with the same care one would use on all the different kinds of marrow. The old Cape way of dicing them and roasting them in the oven with cinnamon and sugar is a variation we should not forget. But the best, apart from simply steaming with or without butter and nutmeg, is the Italian way: very young marrows that are still milky are cut in thin slices and cooked in boiling oil.

28 April 1944

---

1 Fried until brown.

Baking under the Ash

The old way of preparing food by baking or roasting it under the ash is not, as many assume, a genuine Afrikaans custom. It is found in the cooking of every nation. Those who nose around to discover everything about the habits of our forefathers maintain — albeit with some reservations — that a certain ritual meaning used to be attached to the custom of cooking food 'under the ash'. It originated, they say, from the secret gatherings of the druids, who used to roast human flesh at clandestine meetings in the lanes of the priests — all of oak trees. If this were true, the custom of 'roasting under the ash' would have come to us from England. In fact it came direct from France, where in the district of Perigord it is still today regarded as one of the noblest ways of preparing food. Historically we have inherited many customs from the border area that previously used to be English and where, during the time of the English occupation of the south of France, English customs became deeply entrenched.

But the historical aspect is not our primary concern. What we are interested in is the method by which it is done.

Baking or roasting under the ash used to be easy on a traditional open fireplace. Today it is very difficult. So please do not try to 'roast under the ash' with electricity. Moreover, I take it that my reader is serious enough about the culinary art to regard it as something great and beautiful, and would therefore hardly wish thereby to dry out his food.

As there are no longer open fireplaces, we will have to make do with the dry heat of the oven. Roasting under the ash is something we can do while on an outing in the veld — food prepared in this way is also at its best in such an environment. What is more delicious than a lamb chop *braaied* on a grill under rhinoceros bush[1] smoke? Or what is juicier and tastier than a pheasant roasted beneath the warm ash? Not to mention a meat dish roasted in an anthill oven. Many of my readers may never have had the opportunity of trying out something like that but, if they do get the chance, let me beg them to roast a sheep's head, a large Muscovy duck, a turkey or a little lamb in it. One of my not-to-be-forgotten memories is of the first time — it was on the occasion of a Dingaan's Day[2] feast — I tasted an ox-head that was roasted whole, with its horns and skin intact, in an anthill oven. The meat of the cheeks and the palate — well, I can only make a gesture like that of the Coloured elder when he spoke of the juice of the vine in his sermon!

---

1 *Renosterbos, Elytropappus rhinocerotis.*
2 A South African public holiday on 16 December, now known as the Day of Reconciliation.

With our current problems in the kitchen we do not have to completely deny 'baking under the ash' its rightful place. In a good Swedish oven, even the much more expensive new models one finds nowadays, you can 'bake' very well. I find potatoes baked in an oven like that just as tasty as those baked under the ash, and that goes for sweet potatoes too. The connoisseur will perhaps claim that it depends on the kind of ash you use. I will grant this when it comes to *taaibos*[1] ash. It may have a real, though very slight, influence on the taste of a sweet potato. But that could also just be the imagination. When you roast or bake beneath the ash, you do not get the direct blending of food flavour with smoke flavour that you would get, for instance, when you *braai* a piece of meat on the grill over a wood fire. By roasting in an anthill oven, you can of course influence the food made in it. I know of an old *tannie* who, after the oven was nice and warm, cast a handful of the leaves of a certain bush into it — the bush had a strong herblike smell, and the meat roasted in that anthill oven was particularly delicious. I never managed to find out what bush it was as the *tannie* was very secretive about it.

Another way is to 'pot' cook. Put the food in an earthenware or iron pot after first stewing or cooking it a little, and while the fire is burning beneath it, place hot coals on the lid. In this way you will get heat from above and below. It is an imitation of 'baking under the ash', but too tedious and bothersome, and the heat cannot be controlled. The schooled cook uses a 'salamander' to give his food — such as soufflés — a brown colour on top. This too is not the genuine way of roasting under the ash.

We should 'roast under the ash' much more than we do. Take potatoes, for instance. I maintain — and I can support this with all sorts of wonderful scientific arguments — that potatoes are never worth more than two *oulap*[2] a pound; at a higher price they simply are not worth eating as they have very little nutritional value — about as much as milk. If you peel and cook them, they are worth even less. You should therefore always cook them in their skins. Potatoes that are cooked unpeeled are, however, not to everyone's taste and require further treatment before being served. But when they are roasted under the ash, you get everything that is in them. The same goes for sweet potatoes. Remember also that this way of cooking clearly shows whether the potatoes are first-class or not. A second-rate potato will not bake evenly and will never be mealy, while the least bit of *vrotpootjie*[3] will also immediately be apparent.

We can use this method of cooking food for a number of other vegetables too, and of course also for any kind of fish or meat. The larger fish do not even have to be wrapped in paper or dough; just as in the case of the ox-head, its skin can be used to temper the heat. Perhaps the best

---

1 *Rhus*. The leaves of some species are resinous.
2 Pennies.
3 Blackleg.

galjoen I have ever tasted was one – an enormous one – that had just been caught and was baked on the beach under seaweed ash. Time and again I tried to make as delicious a galjoen in my own kitchen, without success. Possibly because it is only under such conditions that one is fortunate enough to achieve the same taste, flavour and juiciness.

To cover the meat or fish first with clay is a way of cooking I have very seldom seen amongst our people, but it is worth remembering. Another wonderful memory is how I once had *jakkalskos* that was *braaied*; the fruit – it is really the seed tube of an underground parasite – was first folded up in pumpkin leaves, then placed under the ash until the outside peel was charred. Concerning chestnuts and *barsmielies*,[1] I need say nothing – this is more or less child's play in comparison with the serious preparation of food under the influence of dry heat from above, below and around. This is what 'roasting or baking under the ash' means, and it is one of the very best ways of cooking food.

28 July 1944

---

1 Bursting mielies.

29

Greens

Greens are, briefly (remembering that, as Multatuli declared, all definitions are problematic, and this one is therefore also disputable), the green leaves of garden vegetables, or sometimes the as yet undeveloped fruit or seed that contains the green plant colour, called chlorophyll by the learned people. It is therefore largely leaf-fibre consisting of cellulose, in which all sorts of chemical substances are to be found. These chemical substances are what give greens their nutritional value.

It goes without saying that chemical substances, no matter what their nature, can be transformed by heat or by interacting with other chemical substances. This happens daily when we boil, braise or in some or other way prepare our vegetables for eating. In most cases the change that the vegetable undergoes is not so drastic that its nutritional value is greatly reduced, but it is enough for the cooked green to differ from the raw version. The tubes within the tissue of the leaves hold vegetable juice that contains amino acids and mineral solutions, and the most important changes brought about by cooking the vegetable take place in these juices. Some of them are coagulated or stiffened by the heat; others are transformed into more complex substances; yet others are destroyed, either by the heat itself or by being dissolved in the water in which we cook the vegetables. The last of these is something the good cook will deliberately try to achieve when dealing with a vegetable containing bad-tasting or even poisonous ingredients. Sorrel, for instance, which is loaded with the poisonous sorrel acid, loses most of it when boiled because the poison dissolves in the boiling water and is thereby removed. Similarly the first boiling of water hawthorn rids that delicious vegetable of the aftertaste left by the chemical substance that gives the boiling water its reddish colour. And in the same way young potatoes boiled in water lose the dangerously poisonous solanine they contain.

Most greens can be enjoyed without such preparation, and it is possibly a good thing to eat some raw vegetables every day. They have a crispness that is pleasant and tasty. Who does not enjoy a beautiful head of garden lettuce, with or without a salad dressing of oil and vinegar? It is a pity that we only find lettuce good enough for being served uncooked — there are many other grasses and vegetables that could be served up in the same way. Purslane, for instance, which you find shooting up as a weed in every garden after the winter rains, is excellent as a green (even though it is not all that green) eaten raw, and it is even better when stewed with butter and cream. Cabbage that is not too old is another good green; and some pulses, such as young beans and peas, can be served up raw as a table salad.

The nutritional value of raw greens was appreciated by our forefathers long before the discovery of vitamins. When the Dutch East India Company's homeward bound fleet dropped anchor in Table Bay, one of the first duties of the captains was to send their sailors to go and pick basketsful of 'mountain sorrel', which was then known to be a first-class prophylactic against the dreaded scurvy. We now know that nearly all vegetable juices, without exception, contain amino acids and vitamins, and that it is healthy to include raw vegetables and fruit in our diet.

But please do not go on about it! Keep a clear head. The human being is not a grass-eating animal. He cannot digest grass as easily as sheep or cattle do. They have stomachs specially designed for that – they can heat the grass in a way that would give you or me a high fever. We do not have the requisite internal laboratory; and although we eat raw vegetables daily, for the sake of our health, for the taste and for variation in our diet, it is highly questionable whether we would remain healthy if we lived only on raw vegetables. I know that there are people who say that they do just that, but I have never come across any that are shining examples of health. I therefore prefer to eat my vegetables properly prepared and cooked.

This can be done in more than one way. You can boil the vegetables (as is most commonly done) in water, but this is not the best way and it always seems a bit extravagant to me. Each vegetable contains enough water to be cooked in its own moisture. All you need do is apply the heat in such a way that it will not burn, and will preserve its taste, where possible its colour, and its nutritional value. As far as colour is concerned, there are many superstitions amongst cooks. In one of my oldest cookbooks, I find the following: 'to preserve the colour of green peas, use a teaspoonful of Bicarbonate of Soda'; and elsewhere: 'the beautiful green of Brussels sprouts is preserved if you boil them with a bit of alum'. I reject both – alum no less than bicarb. We need them as little as we need boiling water to cook our vegetables in. Cook vegetables in their own juices, braise them with the help of a little butter or fat, and if you want to be lavish add a spoonful of whatever you wish – wine, vinegar, brandy or fruit juice – but do not add it for the purpose of *boiling* the vegetables.

Reserve boiling for vegetables you wish to drain first. In this case, put the vegetable in lukewarm water with a pinch of salt, boil quickly, and drain in a colander; then prepare further – for example, as a stew in the case of water hawthorn. But as a rule, cook your vegetable in its own vegetable juice, with the lid on tight, and just long enough to make the fibres soft and juicy. Only then should you get going with the salt and spice. Prepared in this way, the most common vegetable is a delicacy. I know of no more delicious vegetable than a cabbage, cut in four, steamed and then stewed with a bit of butter, nutmeg, salt and pepper. When well prepared it preserves its green-white colour, and as for its crispness – the quality prized so highly by Chinese cooks – it is just one step behind the raw cabbage we use as a salad. There is no need at all for Bicarbonate of Soda, or whatever.

As long as it is braised slowly and consistently, and the vegetable is not exposed to the air but kept braising in the warm steam of its own environment, its colour will not change much. And it will taste a thousand times better than cabbage boiled in water.

15 September 1944

greens

30

Herbs in the Kitchen

I recently enjoyed lunch on a Boer farm. It was a normal, simple Boer lunch. This was the menu: bean soup, roast leg of mutton, soft-boiled rice, boiled potatoes, stewed green beans and beetroot salad, followed by stewed dried peaches with custard and coffee.

Quite as ordinary a lunch as I have enjoyed probably hundreds of times on other Boer farms. But this one was memorable because the *tannie* who prepared it was a real culinary artist. Seldom have I enjoyed food that was cooked and prepared as well as that afternoon. The soup had bacon in it, was salted just right, and also had a bit of leek leaf added to it. The beetroot salad, although without oil, had some finely chopped parsley in it. The potatoes, nice and mealy, had been given just the right kiss of butter and nutmeg. The beans came with a delicious egg sauce. The stewed dried peaches were prepared in the traditional way, with a piece of cinnamon, a scraping of *naartje* peel and a glass of sweet wine. Even the rice was first-class, with just enough salt not to spoil it. What really made an impression was the roast leg of mutton. It had a particularly pleasant aftertaste and was so juicy that, had I not seen the bone, I really would have thought it a very young little lamb. But it was the leg of a full-grown sheep, and not too fat either.

'*Nee, Meneer* Bonade,' the *tannie* said to me later, 'it is not a matter of hanging it. I don't like hanging my meat for too long, especially not mutton. It was roasted in the roasting pot after being rubbed with coriander and sage. My late mother always used a bit of fine flour, and I also like adding some herbs where possible.'

Later on she showed me her herb garden. Under an old apple tree in the vegetable garden, exactly where it belonged, next to the broad beans, the cucumbers and the marrows. There were about a dozen and a half herbs: parsley, tame sorrel and grey fennel, even rosemary and thyme, not to mention a bunch of *swartstorm*[1] that appeared to be a bit starved, I could not help noticing.

'*Ja*,' said the *tannie*, 'it needs sea air and sand, and I'm not sure it's worth the effort – it isn't much good for cooking.'

I agree fully. *Swartstorm* can be good for headaches – my doctor friends question this, but I know of a *niggie* who swears by it and prefers it to aspirin – but its value to the cook is minimal.

---

1 *Cadaba aphylla*, a usually leafless shrub from arid areas.

I take off my hat to that *tannie*. She realises the value of herbs in the kitchen. Today's cook does not know much about herbs. When he does use them, it is likely to be dried herbs like pepper, saffron, turmeric or coriander. A hundred times not half as good as freshly picked herbs from the garden! Just try! See what a bit of sage does for a coot, rubbed into it after you have first skinned it; or what effect rosemary can have on a chop. I do not even have to mention a lemon leaf in brawn or sosaties, or the value of a bay leaf as a surrogate for it. One of my friends tells me that the leaf of the Cape Pittosporum[1] — not the Australian kind, which has a sharper smell — is excellent in a *bobotie*. I have not tried it, but I can imagine that it would have an interesting effect on the taste. Here I am merely pleading for the common or garden kitchen herbs that can be planted and cultivated in every vegetable garden. It is a pleasant hobby to keep a herb garden. There are those who collect postage stamps and manage to find great pleasure in it. For the housewife I would recommend collecting herbs — live herbs — and seeing how many different kinds she can find. It is surprising to hear how many different kinds there actually are. Most girls do not even know half a dozen — even when they have negotiated the matric exam.

How the addition of herbs transforms our food, or at least its taste, has not been ascertained. It is possible that in some cases the herb oils have a chemical reaction with the outer tissues of meat, perhaps also of vegetables, but that is not something we know much about yet. Another explanation is that the soluble ingredients of the herbs blend with the juices of the food and thereby change the taste. We know far too little to be dogmatic about that either. As a practical cook and lover of good food, I only know that the use of herbs makes a considerable contribution to making food tastier, more delicious, and perhaps even more nutritious.

This does not mean, however, that we should make too much use of herbs. Moderation in everything is a rule that holds for the modest cook as well. Some garden herbs are used for just about everything. Parsley is an excellent example; mint another. These are unfortunately the only two that most cooks have any intimate knowledge of, and they therefore have to suffice for all purposes. I recommend giving them a desperately needed holiday from the kitchen, and in their absence some rosemary, fennel and a few nephews and nieces could be invited to assist us.

Herbs are not spices. Do not therefore confuse the taste of cinnamon, a spice, with that of coriander, which is actually a herb, although we use its seed more than its leaf. The good cook combines, where necessary, herbs and spices. Without both you will not be able to create a good curry, or for that matter a *bobotie*. When the food is sweet, spices are normally used — exactly why I cannot tell. And a meat dish sometimes benefits from a concoction of mixed herbs and spices. Ginger with pork, allspice with quails,

---

1 *Pittosporum viridiflorum.*

and similar combinations are well known. In the culinary art of our forefathers it was a common thing to add spices to meat; today it is the exception rather than the rule.

To return to the herb garden: take good care of it. Nearly all herbs are fond of shade, with only a few exceptions — among them tame sorrel, which needs a lot of sun. Therefore protect the others against sunburn. It is good to water them well — that brings out the quality of the herb. We will probably get to know more about herbs in time, because it is quite likely that South Africa will produce some important new herbs that will sell well — especially for use in the manufacture of perfumes. Then our kitchen herbs will perhaps regain the respect that is their due.

22 September 1944

31

Kambro and Baroe

At the end of the previous century,[1] when Cape Town still had its beautiful vegetable market, that tourist attraction and bargain-shop for every housekeeper — a pleasure we no longer have in spite of our more civilised lifestyle and increased municipal rates, there was still a chance of buying some *kambro*[2] and *baroe*[3] in the capital city. Today this is no longer possible and one has to travel sixty or eighty miles to get hold of these delicacies. First-class *kambro* is to be found growing on the Worcester common. It is also abundant in the Karoo veld near Citrusdal, but I know of no other place where it can be found — at least of a sufficient quality to be used by the cook. In our Cape Peninsula you will find nephews and nieces that have tiny, insignificant little bulbs. But the real, genuine *kambro* is found in Karoo soil, clay, where it grows best.

It is a frail, delicate creeper with tiny, yellow-grey flowers and milk in its stalks. For that reason livestock do not feed on it, although they do chew off the leaves in times of drought. The plant contains the food in its bulb, which can range in size from a little cucumber to a medium-sized watermelon. One of the largest I have come across was displayed on the *stoep* of the old White House in Strand Street where it was admired by Cecil Rhodes, *Oubaas* Merriman and Jan Hendrik Hofmeyr when they were there for lunch one afternoon. It was nearly three foot long and about eighteen inches in diameter. Last year a friend sent me one that was nearly as big, but it was spongy and not worth cooking.

As in the case of the sweet potato, it is the subterranean bulb that is regarded as a delicacy by the connoisseur. It is in fact nothing more than a fusion of plant fibres containing water, or rather a solution of all sorts of ingredients, that gives the *kambro* bulb its odd flavour. My old friend Dr Marloth analysed it and told me that the nutritional value consisted largely of a certain plant sugar, called inulin, the same as is found in artichokes and in the *veldpatats*[4] that grow on the *Springbokvlakte*. In the tissue itself there is, however, as with sweet potatoes and potatoes, a lot of starch, and I would say that the bulb is therefore just as nutritious as those two cultivated garden bulb vegetables. However, it also contains an ingredient that has a somewhat bitter taste, which is why some people are prejudiced against the *kambro*. With the right treatment, however, the cook can remove this bitter taste and get the best out of the bulb.

---

1 The nineteenth century.
2 *Fockea* spp. The plant Leipoldt describes was probably *Fockea edulis*, although the 'nieces and nephews' may have been *Cyphia incisa*, which was also called 'kambro'.
3 *Cyphea* spp., probably *Cyphea volubilis*.
4 Veld sweet potatoes, the rootstock of *Commicarpus pentandrus*.

Kambro can be prepared just like sweet potatoes. Peel it, and slice or dice it. Then put it in some salt water for an hour or so — this will draw off some of the bitter taste. Then cook it in its own steam and water. Pour off the first water. When it is soft, add sugar, cinnamon, *naartje* peel or whatever you prefer if you would like a sweet *kambro* dish. I have also had *kambro* stew, made with bacon, sorrel and mutton-chop. It tasted a bit too watery-mealy, and I do not consider the bulb to be suitable for a vegetable dish either. It is as a jam that it comes into its own. *Kambro* jam is a rarity today, but when the old *tannies* still made it, it was often seen at the agricultural shows and church bazaars, and it was always first-class and well worth eating. Some recipes say that the slices should lie in limewater — as is the custom with green figs when making jam — but that is not necessary. The most important thing is that it should be cooked soft rapidly and evenly at first, so that there are no raw pieces among the slices. Then dry them and place in a boiling sugar syrup (old *tannies* always used to add a large tablespoonful of *bossiestroop*,[1] and I must say that it gives the jam a really nice taste) that should not be too thick, because the slices need to be completely soaked in it. Cook until the slices are nicely transparent, and bottle immediately while still warm. If the syrup is too thick, the jam will crystallise quickly and this will spoil the taste. When it is properly thin it can be preserved for years in a bottle without the slightest change. As for the flavour, most recipes say that ginger, cinnamon and almonds are also used, but my own choice is for a bit of wild fennel bulb, boiled with the *kambro*, a bay leaf, and a shaving of grated lemon peel.

Baroe is something completely different and it is, I am afraid to say, no longer available. The authorities on plants call it by a wonderful name. The bulbs are also not as large as those of the *kambro* — sometimes as small as allspice or peppercorns, and it does not really have a pleasant taste. It is found almost wherever there is clay, but the largest and best bulbs are, once again, found in Karoo soil. The little flowers are pink, and the stems contain no milk. To prepare it you do exactly as you would for onions, but in fact I think onions are more worth the effort than *baroe*. There is another kind of veld food of the same name that comes from the northwestern districts, especially from Namaqualand. Of that I have no experience, and it is also not something that can be cooked or baked.

There are probably other bulbous plants in the Suurveld and the Karoo that will reward experimentation. In the Transvaal we also have a subterranean bulb with as delicate a taste as an artichoke, and just as much plant sugar. In Namaqualand we have subterranean *fungi* that are highly regarded by connoisseurs, but this kind of veld food warrants another discussion.

13 October 1944

---

1 Sugarbush syrup, the nectar of *Protea repens*.

32

Milk Food

One of my readers wrote to ask whether I was not 'a bit mistaken' when I said the other day that 'the nutritional value of potatoes is very little — about as much as that of milk'. He asks: 'Is milk then not the food containing vitamins A, C, B and D, just about all the minerals, 3 per cent protein, 4 per cent sugar, 3 per cent fat, and just about everything the body needs? To compare that with potatoes, which consist of not much more than starch, is, as far as I can see, not quite right.'

I speak only as a cook, not as an expert on the health value of foods. From the point of view of the cook, vitamins do not mean a thing — they are not something the cook is concerned with, nor do they matter to the guest for whom he is preparing the food. As far as I know, most of the so-called vitamins are transformed when exposed to heat; therefore, again from the perspective of the cook, they are only of use when the food is eaten raw or half-raw.

But nutritional value is something every cook should know and understand something about, and there is no difference of opinion at all about the poor nutritional value of potatoes and milk: a hundred grams of milk has a nutritional value of exactly 65 calories; a hundred grams of potato has exactly 76 calories. There is therefore little difference. In 100 grams of potato there is 78 per cent water, 1,8 per cent protein, 17,2 per cent carbohydrate, 1,1 per cent ether extracts (fats), 13 milligrams of iron salts, 0,51 milligrams of phosphorous salts, and other similar mineral salts. In 100 grams of milk there is 87 per cent water, 3,3 per cent protein, 4,6 per cent carbohydrate, 3,2 per cent fat, 120 milligrams of lime salts, 0,1 milligrams of iron salts, and 0,95 milligrams of phosphorous salts. There is therefore very little difference between the two, except that the phosphorus in milk is found in a fat compound and milk therefore contains a larger quantity of fatty acids. That is all.

Milk is something without which no cook can survive, as it is one of the best emulsions we have. But it is also one of the most expensive foods we can use, a food that moreover, especially in the cities, is extremely difficult to keep pure because such an emulsion is a first-class breeding ground for all kinds of airborne germs. On the farm, direct from the cow, uncooked milk is something anyone can drink and enjoy quite safely; in the trade even pasteurised milk is not always completely pure and free of germs. The only way of making it pure and safe is to boil it first, and in the process — at least so the district surgeon, who of course knows much more about the subject than I do, tells us — its vitamins are damaged.

I repeat that as a cook I am not too concerned with vitamin values. *Neef* Kerneels, who recently had a job working with tanks somewhere in the far north, tells me that they were given many vitamins, but that he benefited much more from chewing a piece of old-fashioned dried peach roll. If only we could get more of that today! It must be about ten years since I last saw peach roll in a Cape Town shop. The sweets that *Neef* Kerneels gave me are a poor substitute.

But let us return to the subject of milk. In the kitchen it has three main uses. One is to thicken and give body to soup, sauce and such-like. You can just as well use oil beaten up in warm water, but milk is always at hand and well suited to the purpose. The second use is for mixing with flour and using it to bind. And the third is to use it as a food in itself. I am now dealing only with the third use of milk.

What we call *melkkos*[1] is usually some or other farinaceous food (like *frummeltjies*, dumplings or macaroni) boiled in milk and then served in it, sometimes after it has been thickened with butter or cream or something else. Who does not recall cold winter's evenings as a child when Mother served a soup tureen full of delicious, soft white-flour dumplings swimming in thickened milk, with cinnamon, mace and perhaps a bit of allspice? Today's government flour is not suitable for such dumplings, but we can still make them with fine buckwheat flour or even sifted cornflour. The serious concern for the cook, when preparing such a dish, is to get the dumplings light. Recipes differ on this, but old *Tant* Alie always reckoned that it was definitely necessary for the cook to have an ice-cold hand and for the milk to be boiling hot as every dumpling was drowned in it. The art of making good dumplings has all but disappeared, but it is worth resuscitating – the milk dumpling is one of the best foods we have and, when well made, one of the easiest to digest.

A second milk food is custard. By this I do not mean those milk puddings that are stiffened with the help of additives of starch or something similar. They are sold in little packets and, although I admit that they save time and can taste good enough when nothing better is available, I cannot – with the very best of intentions – even think of beginning to compare them with a homemade milk-custard in which you can taste the egg and cream. Such custard – whether steamed, cooked or baked – has its own characteristic softness that is unique and incomparable. No other food can give you this soft yet firm substance. You can try starch, gelatine, roux – everything that is used to bind – without ever succeeding in getting as delicious a combination as milk mixed with eggs. The only thing you have to be careful of is that it must be well-mixed and the heat must be as even as possible so that it does not curdle. Curdled custard is a monstrosity one might expect from an electric oven!

---

1 Milk-food.

And do be careful with spices and flavours. Milk does not tolerate excessive use of them. It requires only the slightest, microscopical whiff and vapour, and one can spoil it with too much cinnamon, too much *naartje* peel and — especially — too much ginger. The almond and vanilla flavourings that are so often used usually overwhelm the delicate taste of the milk and eggs. A bitter almond and a sweet almond, peeled and boiled in milk, is really all you need. We Bonades have never had much time for vanilla — it is, despite all that can be said for it, a grossly overestimated flavour.

Another way of enjoying milk is as ice cream. You can make ice cream without milk, but that would never be first-rate. Milk, eggs and cream, beaten up as for milk custard, is the basis of every good ice cream.

I prefer to use milk powder to cook with. It is completely safe, pure and clean, and in the long run much cheaper than the milk you have to buy from a dairy for more than its economic value. There are different kinds on the market, and they are now all made in South Africa, so you can rest assured that you are supporting the industry of the fatherland. Just be careful and follow the instructions meticulously when making milk from milk powder. It is not difficult, but requires a degree of time, patience and effort — all of which are fully repaid.

27 October 1944

33

Seafood I

For those who have any imagination, it is always a source of wonder how much there is for which to thank the sea. The sea that many of us have never seen and know only from hearsay! The sea that is sometimes depicted as a cruel monster that devours all and gives nothing in return! And yet the sea without which we would not be able to exist, that is companion to and — to an extent — lord of our steadfast world!

What on earth — the reader with a logical mind might ask — does the sea have to do with our kitchen or our cellar?

Just think back. Our earliest forefathers, who went without clothes and knew nothing of the art of cookery as we understand it today, obtained all their food from the sea. Shellfish and seafood of all kinds were what they lived on. You only have to dig in the dunes along our coast and you will find shell middens — the remains of our forefathers' dinners, discarded after their contents had been eaten by the guests.

Today there is still much food to be found in the sea. Men of learning, who think so far into the future that they can see our steadfast world not being able to produce enough food to feed its increasing population, already anticipate that we will have to get most of our food from the sea. What they have in mind is, first, the sea's wealth of plankton, that enormous supply of small plant-animals on which the huge whales thrive. It is exceptionally difficult to prepare a meal from plankton. We have tried, but up to now the results have been unpalatable, even though the nutritional value is high. I am sure that in time we will manage to fashion plankton in a form the cook will find useful and cheap, but it has not happened yet.

There are, however, many other types of seafood that we know well and should make better use of than we do at present. Some are already popular; others less well known and still regarded with a measure of suspicion. Which is not fair, for the accomplished cook is able to turn them into tasty dishes that deserve respect, especially in these times of controlled food.

Take, for instance, a common seafood like periwinkles. Every child knows them after playing on the beach once or twice. They are crustaceans with about as much nutritional value as chicken's eggs. You can eat them raw, with or without a sour sauce. You can stew them, with or without spices, onions or whatever you prefer, into a tasty ragout. The more aristocratic members of their family — mussels, oysters, *perlemoen*[1] and about

---

1 Mother-of-pearl.

twenty other kinds — are perhaps not so abundant, but with a little effort and patience one can get hold of them as well. I remember how as a child I used to see more than a dozen kinds in the old vegetable and fish market in Cape Town. In those days seafood was something the old people really liked. On Fridays you could enjoy it to your heart's content at the White House in Strand Street, and in Kalk Bay there was a place where the cook used to prepare it excellently.

Some people regard seafood with distaste. It is too mushy for them. But the accomplished cook knows just how to neutralise this mushiness so that it loses its unattractiveness. An oyster eaten raw with lemon and pepper cannot but be mushy but, baked in a crust of dough that has been rolled out ten times, it is a completely different matter. Similarly when it is turned into a delicious oyster soup, with cream and milk and a bit of grated cheese over it. However, the connoisseur prefers eating his oysters raw. Only in this way, he declares, can he fully appreciate their delicate taste. That does not, however, prevent the cook from making all kinds of mixed dishes from oysters, and there are hundreds of oyster recipes that are well worth trying.

The same goes for mussels. We have different kinds of mussels, of which the large blue ones and the nearly square white ones are the most popular. Today they cost more than they did a few years ago, when it was still possible to get them for a hundred a shilling at the fish market. But even at the higher price they are an economical food because their nutritional value is high and they can be prepared in a variety of ways to make an exceptionally tasty dish. There is also no fear of them being detrimental to your health if well boiled, taken from a part of the sea that is not polluted with sewage, and fresh — that is to say still alive, with their shells closed tight. Put them in some fresh water, and wash off all sand and slime. Then place them in boiling sea or salt water, and boil well for five to ten minutes. This will kill the shellfish, and open the shell. All the sand and dirt inside the shell will then enter the water. Now take the mussels and keep them warm. Pour the water in which they have been boiled through a cloth to purify it of sand and other dirt. This water can then be used as the basis of the sauce in which they are served, which can be prepared according to a variety of recipes. Most require onions, a slice of garlic, parsley and pepper, with or without a glass of brandy or wine. Pour the sauce over the mussels and serve them in their shells. There will be no sign of any mushiness — mussels prepared in this way are soft, tasty and nutritious.

Our old Cape cooks also used to take the cooked mussels from the shells, mince them with a sausage machine, and prepare the minced mussels in various ways. First as a powerful and tasty mussel soup, with milk, cream, some grated cheese and nutmeg. Then as mussel *frikkadels*,[1] with parsley, some vinegar and wine, a lot of pepper (some cooks add turmeric, or even

---

1 Meatballs.

seafood

317

curry powder), and fried in boiling fat. Or baked in a dough tartlet which the French cooks call *vol-au-vent*. Another way is to make mussel *bobotie*. Follow the usual recipe for meat *bobotie*, mix the mussel meat with a bit of ginger, a lot of pepper, a bay leaf, parsley, vinegar and a spoonful of finely chopped pickles of the old type. Add half a dozen seeded raisins and a few blanched almonds, cover with egg-custard, and bake in the oven. It becomes, in a word, delicious.

15 December 1944

34

Seafood II

Under seafood we should also include seaweed. This is something we tend to use far too little. 'It's a shame,' the old *tannie* said to me, 'that people no longer know how to eat seaweed creepers!' This is the kind that grows on sea-bamboo. Its colour is brilliant red in the deep-sea water, but when washed up and bleached by the sun it is a dirty grey or yellow. There are many other kinds that are edible, but for the moment I shall concentrate on the creeper.

Collect some — it is easy enough, especially after the southeaster has been blowing, because then it washes up on the beach *en masse* — and take it home. Store it in a tightly closed tin. When using it, take a few handfuls, soak it in cold water, wash it well, then place it in a saucepan with enough water to cover it completely. Boil slowly until it starts swelling and becoming soft, then take the saucepan away from the fire and let it draw slowly, stirring well every now and then. Strain it through a cloth after a few hours, and what you get is the decoction of the seaweed that serves as a basis for a jelly or custard. For a simple jelly, mix the decoction with sugar, spices, lemon juice, and a glass of sweet wine. Pour into moulds — preferably small moulds — and place in a cool spot or in the fridge. Pour it out as soon as it is nicely stiff, and serve with cream or a sauce. It should not, however, stand for long when taken out of the mould, as it can easily become runny.

The decoction can also serve as a base for a fish soup, made from the bones and heads of any type of fish, and thickened to taste with minced fish or crayfish. The famous Chinese soup made from birds' nests is nothing other than such a seaweed soup. It is made with the decoction served boiling hot, well peppered, and flavoured with all sorts of additives. The ingredient of the seaweed that gives it its gelatinous quality, a pectin called *agar-agar*, is quite similar to the fruit pectin we use for making fruit jelly. We used to be under the impression that the pectin, just like gelatine, does not have much nutritional value, but now we know better. In some countries seaweed is used as a peasant food, and there are many different kinds that are suitable. It is braised, with or without spices and butter or fat, then served as a stew. It is sometimes mixed with vegetables, but the connoisseur prefers it without any intrusive accompaniment and finds the taste good enough on its own.

Let us return to our very best seafood. This is the *perlemoen* (abalone) or *klipkous*, known to scientists as a kind of *Haliotis* or pearl mussel. Stewed *klipkous* is a South African dish that has achieved well-deserved fame among connoisseurs. It is a dish we can regard as genuinely indigenous, for we

prepare it according to recipes that differ significantly from the way in which *Haliotis* types are prepared in other parts of the world — for example in Australia, where it is also a popular food, now even available in tinned form.

To get hold of *klipkous* is about as difficult as finding first-class beef. It used to be sold for next to nothing on the fish market in Cape Town. For a few *oulap*,[1] you could get three or four large *perlemoen*. Now you have to order them days in advance, and then wait for the tide and the weather to play along with the fisherman's comfort in getting them from the rocks where they live.

But say you have managed to get hold of a few large *klipkous*. Put them in cold water and let them lie there for a good half-hour. Then brush thoroughly the bottom, the sucker, with a strong brush — rub hard and remove as much of the green slime as possible. If that cannot be done with the brush, use a blunt knife and scrape it well. Now take the animal from its shell. Cut away the beard, remove the innards and throw them away. What remains is the hard, white body of the animal. Place that on a block and pound it with a piece of wood until the gristly edge is flat and soft. Pound it evenly and carefully, taking care not to break it, but make sure that every part of the gristly outer wall is soft. Then dry it well with a moist cloth, and cut it into two or three equal pieces. Place them in a saucepan with a cupful of tail- or kidney-fat, and add a blade of mace, nutmeg or ginger, as you please. Place on the fire, which should not be too hot, and close the lid tightly. Shake now and then while stewing for ten to fifteen minutes, no longer. Remove the lid and test the *klipkous* to see if it is nicely soft. It should be soft enough for a normal table fork to penetrate easily under its own weight without having to exert any pressure. If it is not yet soft enough, close again and allow it to steam in the fat a few minutes longer. How long is something only the experienced cook will be able to judge. If heat is applied too long, the danger is that the meat will be too tough — and when it comes to *klipkous* this is a horrifying thought and would be completely unforgivable.

When it is nicely soft, take the saucepan from the fire and remove the pieces of meat. Place them in a dish, sprinkle a little salt, pepper and nutmeg over them, and keep them warm. Now make a sauce with the fat — or butter, if you prefer. For that you will need a small quantity of fine flour, a glass of good brandy, and a cup of sour milk or curds and whey. First make a fat or butter sauce with the flour, stirring it constantly so that lumps do not form, then add some fine salt and a pinch of pepper. Remove the mace or ginger, and stir in the curds and whey. Finally, add the brandy. Serve separately in a sauce dish. The *klipkous*, which should be nicely white and soft as marrow, can be served either in its own dish or on a slice of toast covered with some of the sauce. It is one of the most delicious seafoods I know.

---

1 Pennies.

The most important thing is to cook the *klipkous* without a drop of water or a grain of salt. Either would make it tough, while the butter or fat will make it nicely soft. It is hardly necessary to add that the *klipkous* should be fresh — the slightest bit of aftertaste will spoil it.

What to serve with it? This depends on your own preference. The Bonades have the habit, probably inherited from the time when our farm was still a beach farm and the old *tannies* could serve *klipkous* every day, to have it with dry rice or mealy potatoes only. I have also had it with yellow rice and raisins, and that was not bad. Another old *tannie* served it with cooked cauliflower, as white as the *klipkous* itself. But if you ask me, it does not really matter what you eat it with. *Klipkous* is a dish that needs nothing but itself. It stands on its own merit, and there is no need to add anything.

What to drink with it is completely a different matter. *Perlemoen* has its own unique taste, and quite a strong taste at that. It cannot easily be smothered by anything else, and it is so very soft that in itself it will not overwhelm any good wine. The choice of wine is therefore wide open. Some connoisseurs prefer a light, somewhat sweet wine, like the different kinds of what we now call Sauternes. Others prefer red wines, jerepigos or pontacs, if they are not too sweet. I myself tend to prefer a dry white wine with *klipkous*, but in the end it is a matter of individual taste. Just one bit of advice. When you have finished the *klipkous*, take a *pimpeltjie*[1] of good brandy. Now that '*het smaakt*',[2] as our forefathers used to say.

12 January 1945

1 Tot.
2 Tastes good, literally 'has taste'.

35

Seafood III

Of all the favourite *strandkos*[1] of my youth, *perdevoetjies*[2] were perhaps one of the most popular. They used to be made at least once a week at all the old beach and holiday places that were then fashionable. *Perdevoetjies* were easy to obtain: you could take them, large or small, without much trouble, with a blunt knife or a piece of barbed wire, from every rock that was accessible at low tide. The *outas* and Ayahs used to sell them for thruppence a half-bucket, and for an extra penny they would clean them for the cook.

Nowadays it is not so easy to get hold of edible *perdevoetjies* — I mean those found in the sea. The other kind, found on rocks alongside rivers, cannot be regarded as edible — they are succulents, not animals. The sea *perdevoetjie* is a shellfish with quite a thick sucker, and it is this sucker that one eats. The animal is taken out of its shell, the innards are scraped out, and the sucker is then pounded with a piece of wood until soft. The procedure for preparing it is more or less the same as for *klipkous* (*perlemoen*), the only difference being that all sorts of spices are added to stewed *perdevoetjies* and they are sometimes served with vegetables — such as purslane, which makes a first-class accompaniment. The old Ayahs maintained that a cutting of wild fennel root[3] was indispensable when making the real thing. I must admit that it does give stewed *perdevoetjie* a unique flavour that improves it, but where would you find wild fennel root today? Certainly not in a city or *dorp*. You would have to find it and dig it out yourself and, believe me, getting it out of the ground is no child's play.

A *perdevoetjie* stew needs to be cooked long and slow — perhaps two or three hours on a mild fire — but not *too* long. In this respect also it differs from *klipkous*. And again, add no water or salt before the *perdevoetjies* are soft. Well cooked, they are wonderfully soft and about as good as thick offal stewed in milk. Poorly done, they are inedible — tough as leather and delectable as a stone. Take special care not to have sick *perdevoetjies* in the saucepan — these are the old animals that have gone yellow, have shrunk inside the shell, and are easily removed. Their suckers are always rather soft and they 'kook rafeltjies',[4] as the old *tannies* used to say — a sure sign that they are not completely healthy. And do not take any shells from rocks in the immediate vicinity of an urban sewage system: they will not really be

---

1 Beach food.
2 Possibly the 'Horse's hoof' slipper limpet, *Hipponix conicus*.
3 *Chamarea* sp.
4 Literally, 'cook fronds'.

polluted — and in the heat that the *perdevoetjies* are exposed to during the process of cooking, no germ will have much chance of survival — but they easily acquire an unfortunate flavour that may just spoil the dish.

Of course we also count fish and other marine animals as seafood, but I have written about fish elsewhere and, although there is much to add, I need not do so now. The kind of seafood we have been hearing about so much recently — whale meat — will also have to wait for a later discussion. Having said something about shellfish, I will restrict myself to two particular kinds of seafood, the value of which has not been adequately recognised simply because there is a strong prejudice against them. I refer to octopus and squid.

Both are traditional foods in other countries. In Lourenço Marques,[1] for instance, both are eagerly snapped up when they arrive at the fish market, and here at the Cape too there are people who like both. When properly prepared an octopus is one of the most delicious dishes that can be served. The cook has to know, however, what parts of the animal to select if he does not want tough pieces in the octopus stew. The octopus should not be too large, and only the tentacles should be used. Skin it and cut off the suckers with a pair of scissors. Then pound well with a piece of wood, so that the meat is bruised but not broken. Discard the thin end of the tentacle — it consists mainly of sinews that are tough when cooked. Now stew slowly — once again without water — in fat or butter, and add what you wish, according to taste. Some old Ayahs added potatoes and made quite a thick, dry stew, almost like braised snoek and potato stew, which is also the usual way in which Chinese octopus is prepared. But others prefer a juicier stew, which actually amounts to a kind of thick soup. It is served with toast sprinkled with some grated cheese, and is not to be missed. Another way of preparing it is to stew the octopus with similar pieces of fish in a curry sauce.

The squid, which seems to be more popular than the octopus, is a cousin. It is known as *tjokka* at the fish markets and is a favourite food of the Coloured people, who know from experience how good it tastes when properly prepared. It is, however, by no means an easy task to prepare it properly. Mrs Aagot Stromsoe provides a few recipes for preparing it in her first-class little book on fish and fish dishes, *Do You Know How to Cook Fish?* and I do not have anything to add except to say that the cook who has not tried to make squid stew is advised first to have a chat with one of the old Ayahs at the fish market and to ask how you tell whether a squid is fresh or not. Because a dead squid rapidly deteriorates in taste and texture, and the 'ink' contained in the squirting-pouch is the first thing to undergo a change.[2] This ink is regarded by the expert cook as an indispensable ingredient of the sauce with which the squid is served. It has an odd taste,

---

1 Since renamed Maputo.
2 In Afrikaans the squid is known as an *inkvis*.

which can be tempered by adding coriander and a glass of brandy. First fry some sliced onion in butter or fat, then stew the pieces of squid in it until nicely soft. Stir in the 'ink' with some cream and flour, to make a thick sauce, and stew slowly, with the lid on the saucepan, until everything is soaked through and through. Different spices can be added. The best is a little ground ginger, mace and rosemary, but all sorts of other spices can be used according to taste. Serve with mushy rice.

As a table drink to go with it beer is perhaps the best, but any good table wine would be agreeable. Currying squid is not really recommended, for the curry overwhelms the unique, delicate flavour, rendering it almost unrecognisable.

9 February 1945

seafood

36

Green Peas

Pulses are perhaps the oldest food known to humankind.

My old aunt, who is glancing over my shoulder as I write, just shakes her head.

'As far as I know,' she says, in that dreadful, oh-so-sweet manner she adopts when she wants to demolish me, 'our dear Lord said that for food He gave us the plants that have seeds and all the trees that bear fruit. Is that not what is said in Genesis 1 verse 29?'

'Absolutely right, *Tannie*,' I answer, not at all put out, 'but *Tannie* is forgetting that pulses also have seeds, and the scientific know-alls maintain that pulses like lentils and peas, not grasses like wheat and rye, were our very first food.'

'They have a lot to say,' *Tannie* snaps at me. 'Today they talk of vitamins that the Holy Scripture doesn't even mention. All just talk.'

'I agree completely when it comes to the vitamins, *Tannie*. But please . . . I have to have this piece ready before this evening . . .'

By the way, *Tannie* is one of the few cooks of my acquaintance who knows how to do things with peas. I have her to thank for being able to distinguish between peas and peas, for having learned the difference between peas that honour their name and peas that could just as well have been acorns.

Cooking peas – peas suitable for the table – are young peas, not those usually passed off as cooking peas that you have to pay a fortune for in these days of controlled vegetables. Real cooking peas are young, soft, virgin green, juicy and plump. You usually only get them if you have a row of peas in your own garden. Do not wait until the pods are thick and fat – the less they look like a water-loving creature's thigh the better they are for the pot. Watch your peas closely, therefore, and as soon as the pods show signs of bulging, pick them and shell them. Then you will get the young peas the connoisseur prefers; and, believe me, there is no vegetable that comes near them.

To prepare such young peas requires expertise and what *Tannie* calls *'n slag*.[1] When it comes to expertise, I agree. Concerning *'n slag* – well, one could argue endlessly about that without coming to any worthwhile conclusion. I know of an old Ayah who, according to the general testimony

---

1 A knack.

of the families she cooked for, had a remarkable 'knack' of colouring tartlets a beautiful golden yellow. When she told me her secret, however ... well, since that day I have always been a bit nervous when presented with a golden yellow tartlet.

To return to the young peas, for heaven's sake do not wash them. It is possible that a worm might hide in the pod, in which case just show him that he does not belong there. That is all that is really necessary. Place the peas in a saucepan, with just enough water — or preferably a bit of meat soup — to quench their thirst when it starts getting hot. Close the lid and let them cook in their own steam without adding anything whatsoever. To add mint, lemon peel, nutmeg, or whatever is an affront to them and an insult to your own taste. And do not cook them for too long. Very young peas — I am dealing only with them — do not require more than a quarter of an hour in the saucepan. As soon as they are soft and mushy, take them from the fire, sprinkle with a pinch of sugar and salt, and add a lump of butter — the best available, of course. Shake the saucepan, without taking off the lid, until the peas are well oiled by the butter. Serve immediately. My, now that is really an excellent dish to serve a guest!

When peas are older, swollen with more body, the cook can still prepare them in this way. Indeed it is the usual way of cooking peas. But the connoisseur will not like it. The fully-grown pea does not have the soft juiciness of the baby pea, and this is why it is smothered with mint that overwhelms the taste of the pea. No, use the full-grown pea for making soup or purée. An excellent soup can be made of it — the so-called *Potage St Germain*. Its basis is a good *consommé*, preferably made of chicken bones and veal. Cook the peas in the manner mentioned above and mash them. Then cook them for a half an hour in the soup, strain through a colander, and heat until the soup is even and velvety. Add spice, salt and pepper, and bring to the boil again. When it starts bubbling, add a cup of cream or two cups of milk and serve immediately with toast.

Some cookbooks suggest that one should colour this soup by adding spinach juice to give it a nice green appearance, but I disagree — just as I oppose the idea of insulting peas or indeed any green vegetable by cooking them with bicarbonate of soda. Green pea soup does not have to be leaf-green. The more cream or milk you add, the less green it will be — but it will not taste any less good.

My old aunt interrupts me again. 'Just imagine, who would make pea soup without onions? You don't seem to have the faintest idea of what is appropriate. Why don't you tell the people ...'

Well, there are cooks who start by frying sliced onion, sliced leek, a slice of sour apple and a snippet of mace in butter, adding it to the pea purée and then boiling it all up together as a soup. This is purely a matter of taste, and I am liberal and tolerant enough not to regard this as heretical. But I myself prefer my *Potage St Germain* without onion, celery or mace. A

green peas

333

combined vegetable soup is something I regard very highly — but this is something different from a green pea soup.

Speaking of heretics, heresy is — according to the dictionaries — the wilful rejection of a generally accepted doctrine of faith. There are no such doctrines in the art of cooking, for otherwise there would be no culinary art. Cooking is learned through experimentation and experience, and sometimes by accident. If *Oom* Karools — who was in France during the last war[1] and there acquired the habit of sprinkling cheese over his soup — always wishes to eat his pea soup with cheese over it, I shall not feel obliged to drag him to the pyre in a chequered *sanbenito*. The fellow has his own life to lead and his own taste, and that is that! But the taste of green peas has a character of its own, and I regard it as worthless and unnecessary to try and improve it by adding and supplementing all sorts of things. It is a different matter when you are dealing with dried peas, but that is a separate topic.

16 March 1945

---

1 World War I.

37

Dried peas

Dried peas, like other dried pulses, need to be prepared in a completely different manner. Dried pulses are the seeds of ripe pulses in which the food for the seedling — called the germ proteid by men of learning — has developed so far that it contains a number of ingredients that the young pea does not have. Unfortunately we have not advanced far enough to know exactly how the change takes place inside the pea, or inside any other pulse such as lentils or beans. For the cook, however, it is enough to know that such changes have taken place, and he does not need a chemist to point this out to him. Experience and common sense reveal that dried peas contain much less juice and liquid than green peas, and that they need to be soaked before use; also that they are much harder, much more wooden than when they were in the pod. The knowledgeable cook will also have learned, using his sense of taste, that dried peas have a completely different taste and flavour from green peas.

Do not think, therefore, that you will be able to make green pea soup from dried peas. I know only too well that this is done. The holy saint — well, I cannot for the moment recall his name, and it is too much bother to leave my typewriter in order to go and look it up in *Larousse* — once made cabbage stew using partridge. This was on a day of fasting, and there was reason enough for the transformation. But I am bold enough to imagine that the partridge remained a partridge, and my colleagues in the culinary art fully agree — today we still have partridge cabbage stew, and it is a first-class dish. I am only trying to say that you cannot make a green pea soup from dried peas, even if you call it — coloured as it might be with spinach juice or one or other green colouring from the chemist — *Potage St Germain*. It would simply be bad pea soup, for if you want to make soup from dried peas they need to be prepared completely differently.

Not that I wish to compare the two. No good cook would do that, for he would know that every food has its own characteristics and that it is unfair to compare one dish with another. Such comparison would in the end amount to nothing more than a matter of taste. Thus while I have waxed lyrical about the real *Potage St Germain*, I would not hesitate to join in the refrain if someone else were to sing the praises of dried-pea soup.

It is, indeed, one of the soups on which the poetic imagination can be given free rein, as is the case with onion soup or the much more aristocratic *bortsch* of our Russian friends. But to merit such praise, a dried-pea soup needs to be prepared, served and eaten properly.

First the dried peas themselves. They can be green or yellow. That, again, is purely a matter of taste, but most cooks prefer the yellow kind, whole or split. Look them over well. Pick out the bits of dirt from among them. Then put them in cold water and wash them thoroughly to remove any dust that may still cling to them, also to select those that have been eaten by weevils and are spongy — to be fed to the chickens. Wash them under the tap, and when they are clean and shiny put them in a saucepan with enough water to cover them completely. Leave them to soak for a few hours.

In addition, take a piece of salted bacon, a piece of leftover ham still containing the bone, a piece of celery stalk, sliced onions and leeks (here I am in complete agreement with my old *tannie*), a bunch of herbs (I use bay leaf, sage, thyme and rosemary, but there are of course many other combinations), white pepper and a small teaspoonful of brown sugar. No salt, as there is enough in the bacon and ham leftovers to pickle the soup. If necessary the cook can add a bit of fine salt just before the soup is served.

Brown the sliced onions and leek in a saucepan, and add a few cups of good chicken or meat soup. Allow it to boil and bubble. Add the other ingredients, along with the soaked peas, and pull them aside so that they can cook slowly — very slowly. Scoop off the foam, but keep the lid on so that the soup will not evaporate. Cook slowly but well — this is the art of obtaining a good, well-cooked dried-pea soup. When the peas are mushy, pour the soup through a colander, take away the bone, and after the peas have been mashed fine — a purée made of it, to use the fancy term — put the rest back in the saucepan and boil well once again. Some cooks now add a new piece of bacon or dice an earlier piece, which is braised until soft before adding it. But the soup will already be strong and tasty enough without it. Stir well to ensure that the soup is even and velvety, as in the case of green pea soup. Nothing more is required. Serve it with diced bread baked in fat.

'*Ja-nee*,' says my old *tannie*, 'the Bonades like a *klitsel*. Say something about the *klitsel*.'[1]

This is true. The Bonades, spoiled by habits formed in times when the cook still held sway in the kitchen and could make decisions without supervision, always tried to gild the lily and perfume the violet. I add this purely out of interest because I feel as a connoisseur that it is unnecessary, even inartistic, to further enrich dried-pea soup that is properly cooked with good bacon and ham bones. But those who insist on having their soup so strong and tasty that they do not require anything else to eat thereafter might like a *klitsel*.

The cook pours — into the warmed soup tureen in which the pea soup will be served — a cup of cream and the yolks of a few eggs, which are then

---

1 Mixture beaten together.

beaten up, with or without adding a glass of brandy. The boiling-hot pea soup is then poured onto it and served immediately after being stirred. My own opinion on the matter, although I know only too well that *ou-Tannie* will regard me as a heretic, is that this is completely unnecessary. Well-prepared pea soup can stand, unassisted, on its own merits.

With a purée of dried peas — as also with one of green peas — the cook can get up to all sorts of tricks for his vegetarian guests. The vegetarian 'meat dishes' all have such a purée as a basis with or without the addition of ground beans, peanuts or nuts. In a vegetarian restaurant in Cologne I once had a baked 'duck' that was made completely from dried peas. The purée is then usually shaped into neat triangular pieces, a chicken bone is stuck into the one side, a paper collar is folded around it, and the piece is then fried and served as *cotelette à la Maintenon* — in imitation of the well-known lamb chops that derive their name from the lady friend of Louis XIV. That gentleman was not particularly refined when it came to table manners as he had the habit of eating chops with his fingers and then wiping them on the table cloth. Hence the paper collar that was originally attached to keep the royal fingers clean.

16 February 1945

dried peas

38

Tameletjies

The bell ringer who used to come and tug at the bell-rope on the market three times a day was an old half-caste. Everyone called him *Stomparmpie*.[1] His right arm had been blasted off years before when he let the fuse on a dynamite shell burn too quickly when they were busy breaking stones out of a quarry. This incident dates from my youngest childhood, and I cannot remember whether he got *voldoening*[2] for the accident as the law would stipulate nowadays. But what I do remember well is how the old fellow taught us children to make *tameletjies*.[3]

In those days sugar was quite expensive. It had to be imported from the East and West Indian islands and came in grass bags, so that when we spoke about a sugar bag, it was always a grass bag—and one beautiful and neatly woven—that we meant. When a new batch of sugar arrived, the shopkeeper used to send out samples in paper envelopes, each with about one and a half ounces of sugar and the price marked on it. The samples came to us children and were most welcome. Usually — especially when it was that moist, dark-brown Demarara sugar — we tucked in immediately. But there were times when we had enough self-control to keep it for making sweets — which were also useful and attractive to the young ones. How wonderful it is to beat up molten sugar until it forms white *kapok*,[4] a *kapok* that you could knead and twist into little sugar men, oxen, wagonwheels or whatever your childish imagination inspired you to. The artistic cooks call it '*fondant*' — we always used to call it *witkleisuiker*.[5]

Coffee samples also used to arrive in the same way. It might be news to my reader to hear that South Africa used to import coffee — tons of it every year. Now do not look at me as though I am plucking it from my imagination and presenting it on a tray decorated with poplar leaves. I am speaking the gospel truth, but to give an explanation would be beyond my ability. It had something to do with a foreign law, a trade agreement, and a clever way of making money by picking up each other's acorns. But it is a fact. What is more to the point concerning the coffee is that it came in envelopes as raw beans. And there was no pleasure in chewing raw coffee beans. We therefore had to roast them first. Some kinds — especially Java, paper-bag number three — would then taste quite good, especially when chewed with pine nuts.

---

1 Little stump-arm.
2 Satisfaction.
3 Sugar candy.
4 Snow.
5 White clay sugar.

Old *Stomparmpie* taught us how to make *tameletjies* the old-fashioned way. It is a kind of sweet that you do not find anymore. But, strangely enough, I came across the old recipe in one of my mediaeval cookbooks. The cooks of the Middle Ages — about 1400 to 1550 — had a tough time with sweetness. Sugar was a scarce commodity for them and they could not afford be too extravagant with it. Honey and fruit juices had to be made use of to add to the sugar supply, and egg white had to be incorporated to make the sugar look more than it really was. Nuts were also added, which is how we came to have marzipan — one of the greatest aids in the mediaeval kitchen.

The *tameletjie* is therefore one of the oldest sweets known to us and most definitely comes from China, where sugar was well known from the earliest times. The traditional way of preparing it was exactly as old *Stomparmpie* taught us.

First make sure that you have a mould. We used to use the lid of a shoebox. It was handy and could be used over and over again. It was greased with butter or fat on the inside to make sure that the *tameletjie* did not stick to the paper. The sugar would be melted in a little pan, usually seized from the kitchen without parental permission. It would then be prepared over a little fire in the garden made with appropriate care and some token of solemn ceremony under the large medlar tree. Next to the fire there would be three flat stones on which the little pan could be placed with safety, no matter how furiously the flames would leap up around it. Old *Stomparmpie* would determine the exact moment for taking the pan from the fire by poking a pointed stick into the molten sugar and rubbing a drop of it carefully between his fingers. It is, however, better to let the drop of molten sugar plunge into a cup of water; then you will not risk blistering your fingers. But the former was his way of doing it, and whenever I make *tameletjies* I still do it without thinking, even though I know only too well that it is against the rules. The aim is to judge whether the sugar has reached '*tameletjie* point', which is slightly higher than '*fondant* point' and a bit below 'caramel or burning point'. For a good *tameletjie* there should, however, be a touch of caramel or burnt sugar in the end result, and it is therefore a task for the connoisseur to determine when it is just right.

In the meantime we would crack open the pine nuts, take out the nuts, get rid of their shells, and split each nut in half. Sometimes also a few almonds if they could be found. But the almonds had to be blanched first, which was easy enough if you first put them in warm water, but took much longer if you had to use your teeth or fingers. Our tutor always used to have a pinch of ground stick-cinnamon at hand — I now suspect that it might in fact have been cassia and not real stick-cinnamon, for that was then very expensive — and if we could get *Ouma* to give us a few 'green almonds' (pistachios) out of her pantry (which we sometimes managed to do, even though they were then more or less priceless), we added them as well.

When the molten sugar was exactly right, *Stomparmpie* would hold the pan over the shoebox lid and drip a thin layer into it. 'Quick now with the nuts,' he would urge, and we would sprinkle some of our preparation on the layer of sugar, over which we then sprinkled some stick-cinnamon (or cassia). Then we waited, with the pan over the fire again, to keep the sugar in check. Then another layer of sugar, this time to the top, and on top of that the rest of the nuts. In a few minutes the *tameletjie* would be hard as a stone. It could now be taken out of the shoebox lid — a beautifully transparent sweet, the colour of topaz, with the pine nuts in it like white streaks in a piece of Amandola marble. And it tasted as good as only a *tameletjie* could.

Today we have sweets that are made by the ton. Machines mould them and cut them up. All sorts of chemical products colour and flavour them. It is mass production, a boring repetition of the same taste and the same appearance. Very seldom do we find our traditional sweets, unadulterated *tameletjies*, true to the old recipe. And yet they are so easy to make. Every cook can beat up his own *fondant* sugar, and make a number of elegant sweets for the meal or thereafter. It really requires no special knack — it is one of the cook's easiest conjuring tricks. And the combinations that are possible! Mix some butter with the *tameletjie* sugar and you will get a more brittle product; add a spoonful of cream and you have a juicy *tameletjie*; add a few drops of fruit juice, Van der Hum, or whatever, and immediately you have something else, although not necessarily something better.

To my mind the traditional pine nut *tameletjie* is still one of the finest sweets our country has produced. It is just a pity they are now so hard to find.

25 May 1945

39

Sausage

There is perhaps no single dish so well known and so widespread throughout the world as the sausage. It happens to be one of the oldest dishes in the history of the art of cooking. In the first printed cookbook known to us, that of Scappi,[1] the cook of a famous Pope, you will find various recipes for making sausage. Scappi was Italian, and it is actually Italy that we have to thank for our culinary art. Today so much is made of French cooking, but in the end French cooking is nothing more than a refined form of the Italian art, and here and there it even misses something of the taste and juiciness that is so characteristic of Italian cooking.

But to return to the sausage! In today's Italy, despite all the changes it has been through, the art of sausage-making is still well known, and there are literally hundreds of kinds, from the frail, fine *solticchi* to the enormously large *mortadella*. The sausages also differ greatly as to their ingredients and taste. None that would qualify as a good sausage is made exclusively from one kind of meat. A proper sausage is a mixture of meat, spices and sometimes other ingredients, but it is also a mixture of different kinds of meat. Minced meat of one kind, even when stuffed into an intestine, is by no means a sausage — that is what you would call *sosys*,[2] which again is none other than the old Latin *salsisia*. This *salsisia*, which is described by Petronius, is minced meat rolled out, salted — hence the name, derived from *sal*[3] — and then fried on a warm plate. Today we call it *frikkadel*.[4] Only when two kinds of meat are minced and mixed together, properly spiced, and then stuffed into an intestine do you have our contemporary sausage. Who came upon the idea first, heaven alone knows!

An old Chinese cookbook, from a thousand years before Scappi, tells of minced food fried in wrappings that consisted mostly of vegetables, groundnuts or fruit. The Latin writers talk of *sosys*-es that must definitely have been real sausage. One recipe for it says: 'Take the breast meat of quails, the fat meat of a young lamb, the leg of a hare, lean pork, grind it, and mix with honey, salt, garlic, aniseed, coriander and a handful of bran. Stuff the mixture into little bags and roast them under warm ash.' What the little bags may be is left to the reader's imagination. Carême thinks that they were vine leaves sown together; another expert is of the opinion that they must actually have been cleaned intestines. I have tried the recipe twice, and the result is excellent — if one is not too liberal with the honey, that is.

---

1 Bartolomeo Scappi, author of *Cuoco Secreto di Papa Pio Quinto* (1570).
2 Not a real sausage, an Afrikaans word parodying the sound of the English word.
3 Salt.
4 Meatball.

Cooking food in little bags is probably one of the oldest methods experimented with in the art of cooking. It is easy to understand why. Our forefathers did not have metal pans and saucepans in abundance. It is indeed odd to read today that an important Roman household did not have a frying pan — it only came into use much later, at more or less the same time as the fork. Earthenware pots were too expensive for the poorer people, and they therefore had to make do with leaves and the innards of the animals they slaughtered. One of the traditional dishes still highly regarded today by genuine Scots is *haggis*, a pudding of minced meat cooked in a sheep's stomach — or, to put it more precisely, wrapped in the cleaned stomach of a slaughtered sheep.

Every country, and just about every district, in Europe has its unique kind of sausage. Some are world famous. The tiny pork sausages of Vienna, which we now import in tins from Argentina (not nearly as nice as those in Austria) have become truly cosmopolitan. The same holds for different kinds of salami, which should really be made with horsemeat. The salami we buy in shops has a bit of sugar added to imitate the taste of horsemeat, which is slightly sweet. There are all sorts of recipes for preparing sausage, and of such a variety that you could write a voluminous book about it all.

For us, however, there is but one kind of sausage that stands out from the rest. This is our traditional *boerewors*,[1] which is alas seldom found in its genuine, noble, unmatched, inimitable form. What passes under that name is usually a mill-ground meat of the toughest kind, mixed with far too many breadcrumbs, and some coriander, salt and pepper. I am in complete agreement with my old aunt who was given some the other day at a *braaivleis* and pushed it aside in disgust, saying: '*Dis mos nie wors nie, dis sommer gemors!*' ('This is not *boerewors*; it is just rubbish!') You see, she herself is a first-class sausage-maker. When I have sausage at her place, I refrain from food altogether the day before, in the knowledge that I will be indulging in the priceless dish she will serve me, along with homemade white bread (in her house you will never find government bread, only the genuine white farm-bread, crumbly, soft and easily digestible) or a portion of mushy rice.

'You know, my child,' she says, '*boerewors* must be made with mincemeat, very, very finely minced, except for the bacon. The bacon should be diced and added to the mince. Then, my child, when it is *braaied* on the plate, the fat will melt out and keep the sausage nice and moist. Yes, my child, it should be moist but crispy, so crispy that the outside cracks as you eat it.'

Exactly! And that goes not only for the finely minced meat. My old aunt always adds a bit of pork and mutton, although the basis of her *boerewors* is beef. And no leftover meat either! No — only selected thick, soft, round sirloin, and first-class pork. The meat is finely minced, then well ground,

_____

1 Literally, 'farmer's sausage'.

sometimes even pounded with a mortar. The pork is diced and frayed, then mixed with the rest of the meat. The mixture then gets its *opskiksels*:[1] a glass of wine, a glass of vinegar, a tablespoonful of brandy, and salt to taste. (Always a bit more than is really necessary, in my opinion, since too much salt influences the taste of the herbs, but on this point *Tannie* simply will not listen to me. When I quote from my cookbooks, she simply says: 'My child, I keep to the commandment of Moses, who says: "You should not go with the majority in things that are wrong".' What can one say?) And then coriander (clean, new seed, without the slightest trace of weevils), pepper, a pinch of ground ginger, a leaf of sage rubbed to pieces, bruised rosemary, and — be careful with this one — a suspicion of garlic. Everything is well stirred, so that it all clings together — something that is not easy, and requires a strong arm. Then it is stuffed into the well-cleaned intestines, with the help of *Tannie's* old fashioned little copper sausage-stuffer, and hung up in a cool room until it is used.

This kind of sausage is a pleasure to eat. It is the apotheosis of sausage when it is *braaied* on a grill over a rhinoceros bush fire in the open air. Or even in an iron pan on a common Swedish stove, or an Aga if you are a millionaire. I can also recommend it strongly when wind-dried while hunting. No biltong tastes better, and I know of very few dried sausages abroad that can compete with it.

But the stuff that now passes for *boerewors*! Ichabod — three times Ichabod![2]

1 June 1945

---

1 Trimmings.
2 The glory has departed. Biblical, the name given by Phinehas's wife to her son to mourn the loss of the ark.

40

Sosaties

There is perhaps no other single dish that can be regarded as more genuinely Afrikaans than *sosaties*.[1] Yet it is by no means unique to South Africa, and it is known in many different countries around the world. In Russia, for instance, you will find pieces of veal, pork, onions or preserved cucumber skewered together on a stick and roasted on the grill. The pieces of meat are first soaked in sour milk, then rolled in salt and pepper, rubbed with a clove of garlic, and roasted. The taste is of course not like that of *sosaties*, but the method of preparing it is more or less the same. In the south of France, in that beautiful Ardour valley — from where we get some of our dishes — you will find another kind of *sosatie*. The meat is first ground, then mixed with bacon and stuffed into a little gut. These sausages are then pickled, after which they are strung up on wooden pegs and roasted under the ash or on a grill.

Tant Alie says: 'Those are by no means *sosaties* — they are just some of that French rubbish you get in their restaurants.' She knows all about it because when she was still young enough to be courted by her male contemporaries, she paid a visit to Paris. According to her it was then a very strange place, certainly not what it is today or was in my time! I never had the misfortune of eating any rubbish there, although I must agree that I never came across any genuine *sosaties*.

'No,' says *Tant* Alie, 'to tell the truth, child, you don't get *sosaties* like our late *Ouma* Liesbet used to make any more. Now *those* were real *sosaties*!'

She explained to me at length exactly what kind of *sosaties* they were. And since I must say that *Ouma* Liesbet — I never knew her, as when I was born she had already exchanged her earthly existence for a heavenly equivalent, and all that remained was the memory of her unrivalled cooking, especially when it came to making *pannas*,[2] brawn and Spanish-reed chops, about which I may have something to say at a later stage — that *Ouma* Liesbet used to be exceptionally orthodox in following the rules when making her *sosaties*, I can do no better than tell the reader how she went about it.

First, the meat. The basis, the foundation, the cornerstone of a decent *sosatie* is pork. And not just any old pork. Today we tend to cut *sosaties* from whatever piece of meat we get hold of, and we are only too pleased to get some. But on the farm it used to be different. When a pig was slaughtered —

---

1 Kebabs.
2 Scrapple.

which happened regularly every month, because *Oupa* Hermaans was very fond of it – they carefully cut the *hasievleis*[1] from the vertebrae just below the ribs – long, soft strips, with quite a lot of fat between the fibres, but not enough to make it rancid. The strips were then cut into even pieces, dried well, and placed in an earthenware bowl on a layer of orange leaves. Then a moist cloth was draped over it, and the bowl was placed in a cool spot, where the large mulberry tree cast its shade upon the windowsill. Then pieces of mutton, about a third of the amount of pork, and preferably from the leg of the lamb, but sometimes also the fillet, were cut up and a few pieces of good, thick, soft bacon added to it. This too was dried and then mixed with the pieces of pork in the bowl.

Then onions were cut into thin, even slices – medium, fresh, strong onions that had not first been dunked in boiling water to lose part of their manliness to the water, but onions that were strong and juicy. A layer of onion slices was strewn in another bowl, and on top of it was placed a layer of meat pieces, with a raisin here and there – freed of its pips, a dried apricot or a cut-up *platperske*[2] and, like little red jewels amongst it all, some small chillies. Then a layer of brown sugar, mixed with some curry powder, salt, pepper, and good coriander seed that the weevils had not got hold of. Then another layer of sliced onion, this time with a small piece of onion leaf (*Ouma*, as far as I know, never used garlic for her *sosaties*) and a few of the orange leaves on which the meat had previously been laid. Then another layer of meat, sprinkled once again with the curry powder, brown sugar and so forth. All of this was then covered with a last layer of sliced onion. Now it was ready for the sauce or curry pickle.

For this *Ouma* used a cup of red wine, two cups of good wine-vinegar – she would never have dreamed of using white or malt vinegar, and I would not recommend it either, for that would merely amount to diluted acetic acid with no trace of a wine flavour – a cup of water, a teaspoonful of salt, a few peppercorns, and a tablespoonful of good curry powder. She put it all together in a saucepan on the fire and warmed it up slowly, stirring it to give the curry powder the opportunity of learning to swim in it evenly. The moment it began to bubble she took it off the heat and poured it over the sosaties, always enough to cover the meat properly. The sosaties were then placed back in the cool spot where they remained until morning. Perhaps they would be stirred with a wooden spoon during the night, but it was better just to leave them alone until the following morning. Then it was stirred, and *Ouma* would always add a cup of sour milk or cream. I consider this worth doing, but on this point many people disagree – being of the opinion that *sosaties* do not need any milk. In any event, the meat and the onions had to be stirred and mixed well, then left until the meat had absorbed enough of the flavour of the other ingredients. How long is a

---

1 Fillet.
2 Dried peach.

problem that every cook has to solve for himself. Personally, I would go for less than twenty-four hours; otherwise the meat becomes pickled and loses its childlike innocence.

Then the sticks had to be cut, preferably from green bamboo, although I admit that nowadays this might be virtually impossible to find. And take care, for if you are not used to doing it you risk inflicting some terrible wounds on your fingers. See to it that each of them has a sharp point, then string the pieces of meat onto the sticks, with a piece of bacon between every two or three pieces of meat. The *sosaties* are now ready for *braaing*, which should be done on a hot grill or over glowing coals – I prefer the coals. Some *braai* it in a pan in the oven, but that is not advisable.

While the *sosaties* are *braaing*, pour the sauce through a colander. The strained fluid is then heated in a saucepan; and what remains in the colander is put in a pan with a bit of fat, baked until soft, then stirred into the warm sauce once more. Boil the sauce until it starts thickening and serve it with the *sosaties*, but in a separate gravy boat. Do not of course forget about the rice or, if you prefer, the mealy boiled potatoes. And with this meal one drinks a good red farm wine – not the best, since the *sosaties* have too sharp a taste to complement a truly first-class wine.

13 June 1945

sosaties

41

Brinjals

In my youth we used to talk of *eiervrugte*,[1] a literal translation of the English 'egg-plant'. My Dutch friends use the French word '*aubergine*'. In Afrikaans we say *brinjal*. But whatever you call it, it is a beautiful vegetable. Hardly a 'fruit', even in the sense in which an avocado is a fruit, or a tomato. Because, although there are those who eat brinjals raw – just as there are those who chew cabbage, turnips and onions, it is not really a vegetable I would recommend for a salad. No matter how pretty it may look, you first have to tame the brinjal with heat before you are able to really enjoy it.

But then, properly prepared for human consumption, it is also one of the most delicious vegetables that the garden or veld has to offer. One knowledgeable cook maintains that it is in fact the most delicious, and devotes a whole chapter to its virtues. Well, taste is not really something you can argue about. It simply varies too much. No one person will have exactly the same preference for a 'taste' as another. It is, of course, completely true that there will be a measure of concurrence about which foods are tasty and which are not, or which are sour, salty or sweet. The scientific know-alls tell us that these are the only three distinctions a sensible person can make, but the knowledgeable cook knows better. He understands only too well that there are all sorts of additional subtle tastes, mixtures of those three, blended so fine that you would never tell them apart – unless you have refined and 'educated' your sense of taste.

So please do not try to make a salad out of brinjals. When raw you could make better use of them as trimmings on the table. I recently met an old *oom* who planted some persimmons. 'I don't eat the stuff,' he told me, 'but the wife says they look beautiful amongst the other fruit.' He knew what he was talking about.

Select your brinjals with care. Discard those that are wrinkled, wilted or a bit dried out. Also those that are too large or too old: they will be spongy and tasteless, even with the best treatment a cook can give them. Take young ones that are firm, juicy, and display their youthfulness. There are different types. The best are probably those that are really white or cream-coloured, but you seldom find them on the market. If you do not grow them yourself, they will be very difficult to get hold of. The second best is the medium-to-long kind, purplish-blue, with hues of reddish-brown here and there. Then come the medium-sized round ones with a brown colouring. Last come the large brown or purplish-red round ones, sometimes as large as a football.

Peel the brinjal neatly. The cookbooks say you should do it with a sharp knife, which is possible but rather difficult. You can also put it in boiling

---

1 Egg fruit.

water and then pull off the skin, something that is not quite as easily done as it is with, for instance, a tomato. And if you wish, you could also cook it with its peel. But whatever you do, the peel will always be hard. I would therefore make a case for using the sharp knife.

Now cut the brinjal into slices and lay them on a dry cloth. Sprinkle with a bit of fine salt and allow them to lie in peace for half an hour. By that time they will be sweating and coated with moisture. Dry them well, and they will then be ready for cooking.

But how? Frying? Well, then you would need boiling fat or oil to dunk them in – preferably in a wire basket – and let them fry until nice and crisp. This is how the Italian cooks many of his juicy vegetables – marrows, brinjals, cucumbers or pumpkins. The result is a thin, crisp slice, just like a potato chip, that is fried until it is cracklingly crisp. Sprinkle with fine salt and serve on a napkin. You could also fry the slices in butter or fat in a pan. They will be a little less crisp, but have more flavour. Sprinkle finely snipped parsley and a puff of white pepper over it.

These are both simple methods, but neither really brings out the very subtle taste of the brinjal. That you will only get when you stew them slowly, with or without butter. Put the slices in a pot or deep pan – an earthenware saucepan is perhaps best – with salt to taste, a pinch of fine ginger, a shred of mace, as much pepper as you like, and a large lump of butter. Then stew slowly over a temperate fire until nicely soft. Some people stir it; some add a tablespoonful of thick cream. Again this is a matter of taste. Brinjals stewed in this way are delicious enough without anything added. A refined way of serving them is to make little tartlets from the best cake dough, fill them with stewed brinjal, then bake them in the oven until nicely brown. But these days you do not find good flour for making tartlets, and a tartlet made of government flour is a monstrosity as far as I am concerned.

I have, however, had brinjal tart – the open kind that the Americans are so fond of. The brinjal is cooked, mashed and mixed with sugar, a glass of wine, cinnamon and a pinch of salt, then used as a tart filling. One can also dice the brinjal, then bake it in the oven with butter, cinnamon and sugar, as is the old-fashioned way with marrows.

There is also stuffed brinjal, where the poor thing is filled with mincemeat – or, if you are a vegetarian, with a surrogate made from ground walnuts, carrots and some breadcrumbs – then baked in fat. But none of these is as good as stewed brinjals.

What about the pips? Well, if the brinjals are young and virginal, you really do not have to worry about the pips, and an old brinjal with hard pips is hardly suitable for the table. Middle-aged ones with pips that are still reasonably soft can be fried or stewed, pips and all. If you are fussy you can cut away the pips, but in the process you will also lose something of the flavour that gives the brinjal its characteristic taste.

3 August 1945

42

Cold Soup

It is purely a matter of habit that makes us always eat our soup warm, and preferably boiling hot. There are many delicious cold soups that can come in handy when you need to put a meal together quickly. Cold *consommé* is well known. It is simply meat soup, preferably made from mutton, beef and pork, that has been kept in the fridge for a while until it has formed a jelly. If it is a weak soup, like you often find in hotels, it will not have the ability to gel. All you will get then is an ice-cold, sometimes utterly tasteless, watery kind of food, with possibly even a bit of hard fat swimming around on top.

This is the ultimate in ignorant cooking. A cold soup should have no fat at all, whether swimming or not. The fat should be carefully scooped off. An oil soup, as I will describe in a moment, is something different. There the fattiness is so interwoven with the other ingredients that it becomes an integral part of the soup.

There is a first-class cold *bortsch*, or beetroot soup. It is simply boiled chicken soup with beetroot cut up and added. They are cooked together until the chicken soup has acquired a beetroot flavour, put on one side and, when cold, strained through a cloth, and the expressed juice of a few young beetroot then added. This makes the soup wonderfully red. Spice and salt and place in the fridge, but do not allow it to gel. That will only happen if the chicken soup is strong and hearty — as it should be. As soon as it shows signs of wanting to gel, remove it from the fridge and beat it a little with an eggbeater. It should be fluid when served, with just a touch of crispness.

Sweet cold soup is always a fruit soup, and can be made in different ways. A good orange soup is made by taking a few spoonsful of maizena, a few spoonsful of sugar, a blade of mace, cinnamon and a cup of water, putting them all together on the fire and stirring until the mixture becomes thick. Move the pot away from the heat, remove the cinnamon and mace, add four cups of orange juice and a pinch of grated orange peel, and boil it up once more. Remove from the heat and add — carefully while stirring slowly, lest it curdle — the yolks of three eggs. Remove from the heat once more and beat repeatedly; and when too thick, dilute with water. Put it in the fridge and serve with almond rusks when nice and cold. This soup is easy enough to make, but whenever I have not made it myself it has always been a complete flop. It requires a special knack for beating in the eggs.

During my travels overseas I came across an interesting soup. They call it a *gazpacho* — but it is actually a mix. I really like it, especially on the farm in winter, when there is the opportunity to add all sorts of veld food. But I must admit that it is an acquired taste. Still, those who are willing to try something new can make it, as follows.

Take a handful of any kind of herbs available — the greater the variety the better. You could for example use the following: thyme, mint, rosemary, beetroot leaves, lettuce leaves, mustard leaves, sorrel leaves, the inside leaves of a cabbage — in short, any kind that can be used for a salad, including young onions or leeks, young carrots, and a mealy potato. Cut up or grate it all very fine, and mix. Stir in, drop by drop, a mixture of two spoonsful of good salad oil and a tablespoonful of wine-vinegar (never use the white shop vinegar — it is pure acetic acid, probably made from wood) in which you have first dissolved a teaspoonful of fine salt. Stir it all thoroughly — the more it is stirred, the better. Then pour over it four cups of water and stir well once more. Place it in the fridge and serve with pieces of toast, or — my preference — cheesecake. A bit more oil can sometimes be added to give the soup body. But the big secret is to crush all the herbs, all the elements in it, to such an extent that they will impart their flavour and an enjoyable juiciness to the soup. If one of the ingredients tends to dominate too much, this is because the stirring and the mixing have not been done thoroughly enough. It should be a properly 'blended' mixture in which all the flavours can be tasted without any of them being a dictator.

There are those who first cook this mixture, then strain it through a cloth, and only then place it in the fridge. But then it amounts to nothing more than a meatless vegetable soup, of which there is an infinite variety. The novelty lies precisely in the fact that it is not cooked. It is, in other words, a more or less watery salad. In America it is always made with the addition of cream cheese, sometimes also with shelled nuts, like Brazil nuts or almonds, but this is a somewhat refined touch that really does not belong here. A cold nut soup is something else for which there are many recipes. It is made more or less like the abovementioned orange soup — the basis is always a custard of maizena or rice flour, whichever you wish, and the nuts, eggs and spices are also added according to taste. Sometimes raisins or fruit preserves are also mixed in. The variations are as incalculable as those of ice cream.

9 November 1945

cold soup

43

Christmas Drinks

'Merry Christmas' implies cheerfulness, happiness and a mood of homely, convivial cosiness. I admit that this may be possible when food is not plentiful and there is no chance of any liquor, but I realise equally that it is more easily achieved when the festivities are celebrated around a table well laden and when the host has seen to it that a suitable quantity of drink is provided.

We Bonades are not teetotallers. We are moderate people, farming folk with a tradition of viniculture, based on the *dictum* of old King Solomon that 'he is a fool who allows wine to dumbfound him'. And we honour that tradition just as much on Christmas day as we do on any other day of the year. We know that wine can make you cheerful, happy, cosy and convivial. The scripture says so, and we agree.

As a young upstart I used to help *Oupa* Jan fill four or five bottles of sweet wine on Christmas morning. We unfortunately no longer get that type of natural, unadulterated farm wine. I remember vividly its colour — not quite red, and also not quite gold, the colour of a fire opal with the shine of a *naartje* peel. In my mind's eye I can still see a few drops on the little tap, me carefully transferring them with my forefinger to my tongue, and I can still hear *Oupa* saying: 'That is not done — you will get your glass at table this afternoon.' These days, unfortunately, I no longer get such a glass of wine. According to law our wine farmers have to blend their sweet wine with spirits when it contains more than so much sugar, or whatever. Heaven knows why, but this is what the law stipulates, and as long the law dictates, I see no way in which we will ever again, even at Christmas, be able to enjoy a first-class sweet wine — as fine as that decanted by my *oupa*.

And yet, sweet wine is just about indispensable at the Christmas meal. Therefore we have to make do with what we can get, and even with the added sixteen per cent of spirits there are still nice, palatable sweet wines to be found. They are mostly red or reddish-yellow fortified wines, of the class we call 'Port', although they really are not port wines at all. They are blended wines, sweet and heavy, with a fairly high spirit content and rarely an exceptionally good bouquet, although they sometimes have a passably good taste. As heavy wine they should be used in moderation, preferably after the meal when coffee is served. It is not advisable to drink them before.

No wine farmer — if he is a good wine farmer — will allow his Christmas guests to spoil their palates and their appetites before the Christmas meal with the now fashionable mixtures called 'cocktails'. A glass of good sherry — either completely without sweetness, with the genuine, bitter, 'nutty' taste that the 'flor' gives it, or for those who are more partial to something with a grain of sweetness, the darker, sweeter type — is, however, something that can always be recommended as an appetiser before the meal. It can even accompany the soup, especially a hearty meat soup. Even when there is already some sherry in the soup — and my old *tannie* never served a meat soup for Christmas without adding a few tablespoons of good sherry before the soup tureen was taken to the table — a glass of sherry will go with it admirably.

Since we usually have our Christmas meal in the afternoon and Christmas day tends to be rather hot, the table wine should be light, chilled and delicious. There are quite a few good white wines to choose from. Those cultivated from the Riesling grape are regarded as being the best, simply because they are at present made and blended with care. They are the lightest wines on the market and can safely be enjoyed with most of the dishes served at the Christmas table. It is sometimes argued that they are too sour, but that complaint is completely unfounded as our white wines contain less acidity than most of the imported ones. They should be served as cold as possible. Half an hour in the fridge is the best way of chilling them, and when there is no fridge at hand they can be opened, wrapped in a wet cloth and placed in front of an open window to catch the draft for half an hour before being brought to table.

A red wine should not be chilled, but can also be opened half an hour before the meal. There is perhaps less to choose from among the red wines. There are the lighter types with more or less the same alcohol content as the white wines, then there are the heavier Cabernet types, with a darker colour, a much better bouquet and a stronger flavour. Some of those now being sold are first-class wines that do not have to stand back for imported table wines, and they are all healthy, unadulterated wines that no one need be afraid of. One of the greatest benefactors of mankind, the famous Pasteur, expressly declared: 'Table wine is the best, the safest and the healthiest drink one can drink'. The Bonades underwrite this pronouncement, on the authority of generations of experience.

But what about sparkling wine? It is fashionable in certain circles to present sparkling wine as something special. This fashion is simply a form of snobbishness, for sparkling wine is never a natural wine and the wine connoisseur will never prefer it to the real thing. While champagne is an imported sparkling wine, and the imitations that we get here cannot by any means be compared to it, we have amongst our own natural wines many that are far superior to the imported sparkling ones. In time we will probably find a sparkling wine of our own that will be able to compete with the Italian sparkling wines — which are, of course, not champagnes — but as yet we have none. We do have wines, white and red, that sparkle and that the wine merchants sell for more than our good wines. We can mix our red and white wines with sparkling water if we wish — that makes a very useful drink for those who like it, and on a warm summer's day such a mixture is

refreshing and delicious. But this is not the best way to drink wine at table. It is equally inappropriate to add a block of ice to your wine glass.

For the afterdinner party, in the afternoon or in the evening, and for the younger generation who have not yet come to understand the seriousness of drinking wine, we can make all sorts of drinks in which light wine plays a large role. The most popular mixtures are those consisting of a light wine, fruit juice, spice and something that lends a distinctive taste or attraction to the mixture, such as flowers, ripe fruit or herbs. Such mixtures can be sweetened by adding sugar, syrup or *moskonfyt*.[1] For a heavier mixture some brandy or a glass of liqueur could be added, but then it needs to be drunk with care, for a mixture like that can be extremely seductive. My old *tannie* left handwritten recipes for several such mixtures — they were served to us young people on birthdays and festive occasions. The two that follow are copied from them.

Mulberry drink. 'Take two cups of fresh mulberries, cleaned, and grind in the mortar with two tablespoons of brown sugar; pour over it a bottle of red wine. Stir well and place in front of the window (or preferably in the fridge). For use, put in a can and stir in a pinch of nutmeg, ginger and mace; add six bottles of soda water and serve in glasses with a mulberry in each.'

I would use more sugar, but this is a matter of taste. It is a good, enjoyable drink that is as pleasing to the taste as it is to the eye.

The other recipe is not really for children, and is more or less a kind of punch that most people will find far too sweet.

Apricot drink. 'Peel and de-pip three dozen medium-size apricots; crack open half a dozen of the pips and take the white part, bruise it, and add it to the peeled apricots; add a cup of good brandy; mix with two cups of white sugar and beat together well; let it stand for a few hours and then add two bottles of white wine, a cup of ginger syrup, a glass of Van der Hum and two glasses of sweet wine. Beat well and let it stand until it settles. Decant without disturbing the precipitate at the bottom and mix with two bottles of soda water. Serve with a piece of ice in each glass. This tastes even better when made with dried apricots.'

There are many such fruit-wine mixtures, but it is questionable whether in the end they taste any better than a good glass of wine by itself. But as the host and hostess have to cater for everyone on Christmas day, it is advisable for them to be well acquainted with the art of making such mixtures. When you have among your guests some who are so opposed to wine that they refuse to try it even on Christmas day, the wine can be left out of the mixture, and a clean fruit 'bowl' concocted.[2]

23 November 1945

---

1   Grape syrup.
2   See Chapter 8 on Grog and Bowl.

44

Oysters

Brother Jan's eldest finished matric with a first-class pass, and is now enrolled as a first-year medical student. Would I please keep an eye on him, wrote Brother Jan, and see to it that everything was all right?

My memory of the little chap — it had been about ten years since I last saw him — was of a bolt-upright, skinny as a fishbone, short-pants, barefoot youngster with mischievous little eyes, a turned-up nose pointing skywards to such an extent that it always seemed to be smelling something unpleasant, and front teeth that a yappy little dog would be proud of. Now I am confronted with a fellow stretching an inch and a half further into the air than I would be able to myself if my rheumatism would allow me to straighten up — a fellow with smoothly plastered hair, the foreshadowing of a moustache on his upper lip, the even more suggestive blue-black along the jaw, and the inkling of that cheeky, half-embarrassed attitude his generation is afflicted with when confronted by older people for the first time. The turned-up nose was just as turned-up, and the teeth just as white as before, but the young man was now grown-up and no longer gave the impression of a hungry, moulting chicken. The yellow tie swaying in the wind — convincing evidence of his rank as a first-year student — and the grey blazer had nothing in common with the short-pants of ten years before.

It did not take us long to leave behind the protocol-like relationship between uncle and nephew, as *Kleinjan* at his best is quite adaptable. Within an hour I had got to know everything about the family, the farm and his school adventures. It was apparent that *Neef* already felt at home in his new environment, especially after the initiation ceremony that — it pains me to say — is still the habit at institutions we recklessly still call 'universities'. It was just as apparent that he would not let himself be intimidated by anything that *Omie*, or whoever, said, taught or advised.

When it was time for lunch I took him to a place where I sometimes enjoy the midday meal. There the waiter came straight towards us with the news that they had oysters in stock. I ordered two dozen without thinking. *Kleinjan*, his couldn't-care-less, 'you won't impress me' attitude notwithstanding, was in awe of the scene at the club, and his lively banter quietened down somewhat. When the oysters came, he stared at them like a Kalahari Bushman seeing a motorbike for the first time.

'Now what on earth is this, *Omie*?' he asked, and I imagined that I saw his turned-up nose flipping a centimetre higher.

'Oysters, man, the very best! We're fortunate to get them today. They're usually flown to Johannesburg, and it's seldom we get the opportunity of eating them here.'

'Eat, *Omie*? . . . *Si* . . .' His politeness made him bite off the word in his mouth[1] just as I swallowed my first oyster, appropriately baptised with a drop of lemon juice.

'Of course. Look, you take them like this,' and I showed him how. Unfortunately, just as I was busy baptising it, his oyster went into a spasmodic convulsion.

'But what the . . . *Omie*, this thing is still alive . . .'

'I should think so. You'd never eat *dead* oysters — that would be far too dangerous. Come now, don't be so childish. If you want to be a doctor, you'll have to get used to trying everything, and I give you my word that you'll enjoy this. There, now swallow it down . . .'

'Please . . . no . . . *Omie* . . . *Omie* must excuse me. It looks . . . it looks just like *dermskraapsels*.'[2]

'Well then, have your *dermskraapsels*, or have you never eaten sausage? If you don't want your oysters, give them to me. I'll eat them for you, and you can order yourself some soup. But I must say, *Kleinjan*, I thought that Brother Jan's son would be able to show he's a man, even when it comes to oysters.'

Kleinjan did not order soup. He took a swig of his beer and followed me with his eyes — no longer mischievous but really afraid, as if he had come across a cannibalistic *omie* — as I devoured one oyster after the other. Only at the end, after I had encouraged him several times to order something for himself, did he ask me in a whisper, '*Omie*, is that really nice?'

I regard it as a civilising task to teach someone to eat oysters, and though I am by nature — like all of us Bonades — impatient, especially with people who are full of themselves (that is to say, who do not agree with me), I did my best to bring my nephew around in a most avuncular way to try just one oyster. And then just one more! There were, however, only half a dozen left, and we could not order any more, oysters being so rare these days. My reward was *Kleinjan's* well-considered opinion: 'Yes, I must admit, *Omie*, they really are not bad.'

Yes, *nefies* and *niggies*,[3] oysters really are not bad. That is, if you eat them properly — without all sorts of additions that end up spoiling the pure, undefiled, immaculately innocent, genuine oyster taste with other tastes and flavours that are a real sin to the oyster connoisseur. Serve it in its shell. Open it yourself if you have the slightest fear the waiter will let the point of his knife slip into the animal's tender flesh. Make sure that you at least get it served with its muscle still functioning so that it can shrink. And do not

---

1 *Kleinjan* was about to say '*sies*', which expresses disgust.
2 Scrapings of gut.
3 Nephews and nieces.

come and speak of cruelty or barbaric treatment of a defenceless little animal. Such ultra-ultra-humanitarian excuses do not hold for a cook. Will he who gives in to them ever dare eat duck liver pâté or tortoise soup or crayfish salad or stewed eel? I would ask whoever holds forth along such lines to honestly guarantee that the mielie feels no pain when you strip off its leaves or the watermelon when you cut it open. Was it not the portly *Oubaas* Chesterton who put his vegetarian friend in his place by asking: 'And why should only the salt and the mustard suffer?'

Therefore see to it that your oysters are still alive and eat them either (and preferably) in their virginal innocence without adding anything, or with a drop of lemon juice to soften slightly the saltiness still clinging to them. Do not fry them — that is to do them an injustice. Make no soup from them — that is to adulterate something delicious and pure into something complex and artificial. Eat them with a piece of bread and butter. If you have the opportunity, try them with a bit of caviar in a sandwich. But never with red pepper or onions or anything else that could spoil the fine taste of the oyster. You should therefore also be careful about what you drink with them. You do not actually have to drink anything, since they contain enough water themselves. But if you must, then choose between a good beer, preferably a dark type, and a white wine that is not too sugarless and that should, of course, not be sparkling. For us older Bonades — since as you see, the younger generation still has much to learn — champagne with oysters is from the devil and not mentioned in front of Christian children — *inter Christianos non nominanda sunt*, as the Old Father says. And never think that, if you bear these tips in mind, you will ever be in danger when eating oysters. They are the most innocent and delicious animals ever to come out of the sea.

21 December 1945

oysters

45

Our Daily Bread

Now that the war is over, we might be getting bread again. What we have been getting instead is . . . well, the Bonades are not in the habit of using bad language — they rather suffer in silence. For does Solomon not say: 'A fool lets his anger rail, but the wise one calms it down'?

I do, though, still manage to eat good bread from time to time. When my petrol ration justifies it, I drive to the farm. *Tannie* still has the pure, genuine farm flour that is ground in the old mule mill — a contraption that is now as rare as a young woman who is satisfied with the nails that our dear Lord gave her. And she — I mean *Tannie*, of course, not our oh-so-stylish young woman — still sifts it from time to time to produce a first-class fine flour. I am not sure whether it is unlawful or punishable, but if I were in her shoes I would do exactly the same. Because I simply refuse to eat bread made from war flour. That is . . . but what did Solomon say?

And what is there more delicious, tasty, healthy and attractive than a loaf of freshly baked farm bread? With farm butter or soft fat on it — I prefer the beautiful, yellow-brown soft fat remaining in the saucepan after a plump chicken has been turned into a blessed food offering. It has a taste that is unique, and with a sliver of biltong on top — what more on this earth could the most refined gourmet want? Bread made of sifted flour is always nice and white — its colour differs from that made of unsifted flour. *Tannie's* is usually grey-yellow and grainy, with a crust — ah, that crust!! It commands more than one exclamation mark. For the crust is surely one of the most important parts of a good loaf of bread — like the crisp skin of a roasted sucking pig — at least it should be. Alas, in the city bread we have been getting it is like . . . but let me not forget the old king's admonition.

Tannie has her own, secret way of baking bread, and I will not give it away here. But I once tried baking my own bread. The oven was nice and hot, there were no unwelcome visitors in the kitchen, and there was a bowl full of sifted flour. For one with some talent and an inclination towards preparing food, the temptation was very great indeed. I nearly succumbed, but fortunately my sense of honesty prevailed over my spirit of inquiry. And I received my just reward for that restraint in the face of the devil of temptation when *Tannie* later asked me if I would not show her how 'a learned chap' makes bread. I fear the invitation was meant somewhat sarcastically, as she knew only too well that I had no 'knack' with baking cake or kneading dough, but challenges are there to be taken up by a knight, and so I tried. The result was first-class, and *Tannie* graciously complimented me, although I know she preferred her own way of doing it to mine. She maintains that farm bread requires no milk, and she prefers old leaven to the bought yeast that I use. Well, each according to his taste.

I take ten cups of sifted flour — not sifted from the rubbish you get today, but from pure farm flour — three cups of milk, four tablespoonsful of sugar, two tablespoonsful of sifted salt, a lump of butter, and a cup of warm water. The milk is boiled up with the sugar, salt and butter and, when lukewarm, I stir into it a packet of that shop yeast that *Tannie* dislikes. Then comes the lukewarm water, and some beating mixes it all together nicely. I slowly add the sifted flour and stir until I have a good dough. This dough is then kneaded — I admit that this is something I do not do half as well as *Tannie* or even Ayah Rosa, but it is an indispensable requirement — why, I really do not know. One of these days, as soon as I have my own sifted flour, I shall try and see what happens when you bake without kneading. But my recipe says: 'Knead . . . knead until it is properly soft and plump'. Then it is covered with a damp cloth until it has 'risen' properly. This normally takes six to seven hours, and it is therefore best to make the dough in the evening and to let it rise overnight. As soon as it has risen nice and high, the breads should be shaped, either long or round, as you please, and greased with some butter or fat. They should then be left to stand until they are twice as large as when they left your fingers, then baked in a hot oven. My first batch was not like *Tannie's* white bread, but in my opinion it was first-class. The Ayah said it would have been better 'if *Baas* had added a mealy potato'.

I will try that one of these days.

But when will that be? How much longer will the aftermath of war last, and when will we have flour to bake with again?

11 January 1946

46

Tongue

There are different types of tongue, like the malicious tongue or the false tongue, but that is not my concern now, although I would like to say that the Bonades have had to endure much bother and discomfort from that kind of tongue. However that may be, the tongues I would like to deal with are the kind you can touch with your own tongue without being hurt by them.

There are also different tongues of this kind for, as *Neef* Frans tells me, every animal in existence has a tongue. *Neef* Frans did a dissertation on lizard tongues for his doctorate at one of our universities and, listening to him, it must be the most wonderful, strange and scientifically interesting tongue in the world. But I have never heard of cooking gecko, or of rock lizard tongue as a dish for the table. A crocodile tongue is so tough and disgusting to look at that when I once had the opportunity of trying to practice some culinary art on it, it all became too much and I abandoned the effort.

To come to my topic: the tongues we normally bring to the kitchen are those of oxen and sheep, of which only the former is really worthy of the culinary art. Smaller tongues — those of sheep, pigs and even smaller animals — are usually cut up and used for brawn or a ragout. (It is, by the way, high time that we found a good Afrikaans word for ragout: in its original French it means something that is tasted again, for a second or subsequent time, *ragouter*. In French cooking it is a meat stew made from already roasted or cooked meat with vegetables and spice: therefore a kind of warmed-up second-hand stew. Even we Bonades do not have a family word for it. My grandmother on my mother's side used to just say *ragoe*, with the *g* pronounced very softly. The Dutch members of our linguistic family do not have a suitable name for it either. But once I set off on a side trail, I never manage to outspan — so let me leave etymological puzzles on one side.)

It is only when you go along on a hunting expedition that you discover how delicious other varieties of animal tongue are. The tongue is, for instance, the only part of a wildebeest that is to my mind suitable for the connoisseur's table. The same holds for the tongue of a zebra and — although my hunting friends will not agree — the tongue of every kind of grass-eating game, as opposed to that of game like kudu or impala that eat leaves and branches. A camel's tongue looks quite delicious, but it is too tough, has a thick skin, and does not taste at all good. I may have been unlucky with the only camel tongue I ever had the opportunity of eating, but I remember being as disappointed with the camel bone marrow, which was a really awful oil. My experience in this area is admittedly limited, and I will not place myself in the pulpit on the subject. We Bonades only stick to a belief in the face of being burned at the stake when we definitely know more about the matter than those who dare to contradict us. And since my readers will more than likely not have had much to do with the tongue of game, I need say no more about it.

I will therefore restrict myself to ox tongue, which – when all is said and done – is still the only kind of tongue the cook can shed a tear about when it is not properly prepared for the table. We use it fresh, when it is at its best, but it is also good salted and pickled, and when dried and smoked it has an exotic appeal that I find quite fascinating. All the cookbooks describe at length and quite exhaustively how to prepare it in those different guises, and it would take up many pages to repeat it all here. One or two things that every cook should know about cooking ox tongue may, however, be appropriate and even educational at this stage, simply because one usually finds, if the tongue dishes served in hotels are anything to go by, that this knowledge is rarely acquired.

As regards fresh tongue, the first and most important point is that when cooked, roasted or stewed, it must be genuinely *fresh*. The least cause for concern should be taken as proof of guilt – a fresh tongue that is the slightest bit 'gamey' will not do. Even when you try and overcome the problem with vinegar, spice or other ways of making it smell or taste different, in the end the result will be a complete failure. And a fresh tongue spoils very quickly, especially when the air is warm and humid. Therefore put it in the fridge, or in a cool place, as soon as it comes from the butcher, and use it as soon as possible. Cook by dunking it in boiling water, then letting it cook slowly for an hour where the fire is not too hot, with a bit of lemon juice or vinegar, and some salt, in the water. Some also add herbs, a carrot and an onion, but this is not necessary. A cooked tongue is something very tasty in itself, so flavoursome and soft that it could almost be served without further preparation. However, most cooks prefer to peel off the skin and refine its outer appearance by removing any superfluous pieces of meat and some of the cartilage and sinews in it. When tongue is served cold, it is put in the fridge with a weight on top of it in some of the water in which it was cooked, which then forms a jelly around it. Before it is put in the pot, it should be properly prepared: all the fat should be cut away, the bones inside should be taken out, and it should be rolled up and fastened with a little peg to keep it together. It should not be cooked for too long or it will become mushy; but it must be cooked sufficiently or it will be tough.

Cooked tongue serves as a basis for many first-class tongue dishes, to which French cooks have given wonderful names. You can slice it up, dice it, cut it into round pieces, or just do as you please; and it can then be fried or stewed. The dish is given its particular name according to the kind of sauce used. The best of the many tongue dishes are perhaps those in which quite

tongue

367

thick slices of cooked tongue are stewed in a sweet wine with herbs, almonds and raisins. The sauce is thickened with some fine flour and a beaten egg yolk. A small spoon of lemon juice is added, and the dish is served as hot as possible.

A salted tongue is first soaked in fresh water for a few hours, preferably all night long, then slowly cooked in unsalted water that is replaced at least once. It should be cooked quickly the first time, then again 'lukewarm'. The result is a tongue that is baby-soft, and that asks for nothing more than mustard and a good soft-boiled potato — with nutmeg and butter of course, and a glass or two of red farm wine. Many different dishes can be made with salted tongue, but most of them seem to involve unnecessary trouble. For cooked, salted tongue is a dish in itself — a delicious dish that, if well prepared, will honour any cook.

Dried tongue is a completely different matter — so different that my views on this subject must wait for another occasion.

22 February 1946

47

Camp Food I

If there is one kind of cooking we farm people understand, it is the art of preparing good food where we camp or outspan. It is actually an art that we Bonades should know well but, to tell you the genuine, gospel truth, our family has somewhat lost the touch. In the old days, as my grandfather often told me, it was the custom to spend New Year's Day somewhere in the veld. They would take the large tent-wagon with a team of oxen, and *Ouma* and the girls would collect provisions for days before the great outing. They would take three of the farmworkers with them — *Outa* Doors, April, who was in charge of the oxen and had to look after them, carry wood, do odd jobs, clean fish, and on occasion go and look for bait for *Oupa* in the rock crevices, and Toontjies, who had to assist *Ouma* in making food for the men. I have a vague memory of one of these outings, but I was far too young to remember much. With the arrival of the motor car, the tent wagon made way for the lorry and — I do not really know why — we became more civilised, urban, refined — spoilt I would say — and we seldom undertook anything more challenging or old-fashioned than half a day's picnic somewhere on the farm.

But old-fashioned camp life, as I later rediscovered it in the Transvaal at a Dingaan's Day[1] festival in the Lowveld, was a revelation of what Boer women can achieve. I speak not of the kind of food we took along with us — brawn, sausage, bacon, *koeksisters*, buttermilk cake, *sosaties*, pickles, pickled fish, and dried fruit. Those we still take along today when we Bonades go for a picnic in the motor car, along with all sorts of tinned food that are not to be frowned upon. What I am talking about is the food prepared at the campsite, more or less fresh from the veld.

There are, for instance, the meat dishes. The game or birds that the men shot would hang for a day or two. The exception was partridge and dikkop, that were immediately cleaned and put into an iron pot along with bacon, salt, herbs and a bit of farm wine to stew, with the fire below it and coals on top, until it was time to eat. Prepared in this way, even an African coot is a delicacy.

Hare was always served in the farm style. This, I believe, is a variation on one of the very oldest recipes, but it definitely differs from the 'jugged hare' and stewed hare recipes you find in the cookbooks. We always used to cook the hare in shreds, or rather braise it, with onions, herbs and a glass of wine, and done in this way it was as tender and tasty as you could wish it to

---

1 South African public holiday on 16 December, now known as the Day of Reconciliation.

be. The game was always roasted in the iron pot, in more or less the same way as the fowl. In the Transvaal I saw *tannies* bake in an anthill oven, but this did not appeal to me and they also tended not to lard the meat properly. Our game is almost always too lean to eat without lard, and the more thoroughly it is larded the better.

Tame meat, whether mutton or pork, is, when it comes to camping, always at its best in the form of chops. To *braai* them properly, you need a hot fire, made of leadwood[1] or thorn-tree[2] wood in the Transvaal, and in the southern parts any wood that makes good coals. Here in the Cape Province we are privileged to be able to place a layer of rhinoceros bush over the coals, which imparts to the chops a peculiar, fragrant taste, but this is a refinement lacking at most campsites – instead you can rub the meat with herbs according to taste. But choose your chops well and see to it that they are soft and tender. First give them a tap with a clean stone or a piece of wood – not too hard, for you do not want to break the fibres – you should only bruise them a little to get rid of the stiffness. Salt them – a pinch of fine ginger in the salt goes down well, and some people are very fond of coriander or aniseed. Dry them well: a wet chop will never *braai* as well as it should. Then place them on the grill – if you have not brought one along, you could make do with one improvised from *Oom's* wire fence, but it is generally preferable to take your own along. First grease the grill with a bit of fat, and make sure that it is nice and hot before laying the meat on it. Three or four chops can withstand the fire ordeal together, but look after them well and see to it that you turn them over as soon as they are well browned on the one side. When done, serve immediately with or without a lump of butter. If you have such civilised implements as knives and forks with you, a lump of butter is recommended, but a chop should actually be eaten just like King Louis XIV enjoyed his – with the fingers. His Majesty did that at table, however, and not when out camping. His favourite, *Tannie* De Maintenon, found it so unbearably rude the way he always used to dirty his jacket – the one with the golden fleece on it, no less – with dripping fat that she ordered the cook always to serve the king's chops with a piece of paper lace around the bone. That is how we came to have *Cotelette à la Maintenon* – mutton chops with frumpled pieces of paper around the pieces of bone. The way they are usually served in hotels, there is – if the truth be told – not much difference between the meat and the paper when it comes to taste and juiciness.

Therefore see to it that your camp chops will not suffer such reproach. They should have good flavour, and be soft and tasty. It is no small matter to achieve all this with a grill, which is why some people prefer to *braai* them in a pan. I have nothing against that – a chop fried in a pan can be delicious – but it can also be the opposite. It all depends on the way it is

1 *Combretum imberbe*.
2 *Acacia* sp.

braaied. A proper chop should retain all its juiciness, so the fire should be glowing hot to scorch the surface of the meat, which should then be roasted right through. The result is a piece of juicy meat that almost melts in your mouth.

What to eat with it? As far as I am concerned, I can imagine nothing nicer than a piece of white farm bread, well plastered with farm butter, its inside just as soft as the meat should be with a beautiful golden brown crust into which your teeth — be they false or natural — can bite with relish. Vegetables and other additions? I know that camp hospitality ensures that they are always close at hand, but I really think them superfluous. A good slice of bread and a chop — they go together like husband and wife, and to separate them from each other is an offence and a sin.

29 March 1946

camp food

48

Camp Food II

On our veld picnics we never used to make soup. In the hunter's camp, however, soup is one of the most popular dishes enjoyed by the light of the campfire. Nowhere have I tasted a better camp soup than in the Lowveld at a bushveld camp where the hunters knew what they were doing.

Camp soup is much more than just a normal soup. Carême, one of the greatest experts in the history of cooking, maintains — and I think he is absolutely correct — that soup should only be used as an appetiser. Therefore it should, according to him, consist of a thin, preferably clear solution of cooked vegetable or meat juices. Meat extract has a stimulating effect on the mucous membrane of the stomach, just like a glass of good sherry. It therefore improves the appetite and the digestion, even though it has no great nutritional value in its own right. You could give it nutritional value by mixing it with flour, milk, wine or anything else that provides nutrition, but a solution of meat or vegetable extract is not really what you would call food. And when food is added to it, as in thick soups, it becomes a dish that should not be served merely as an appetising prelude to the meal, but as a part of the meal itself, and it is then used as much for its food value as for its taste.

This view of soup is not shared by Chinese cooks, who sometimes serve a nutritious soup between or after other dishes, but not beforehand. They would, however, agree with me that hunter's camp soup is the most appropriate evening meal for the open veld.

Such a soup is cooked slowly all day long. Early in the morning a large iron pot is filled with water. In it is put whatever vegetables are available — usually potatoes, onions, dry beans, lentils or peas — and whatever remains of the hunters' booty in the form of bones with a fair amount of meat still on them. Salt and pepper are added at an early stage — other spices are not usually at hand, although someone who is familiar with the bush can add a lot of flavour to soup by adding some of the leaves and herbs usually found in the immediate vicinity of the campsite. There you will usually also find some root vegetables that can be used. The soup is cooked slowly and stirred from time to time with a spoon or a piece of clean thorn-tree wood. A civilised cook will try and scoop off the foam, and especially the fat that may be floating on top, but in my experience this is never done, and it is precisely for this reason that the result is so remarkably hearty and tasty when you have it the same evening. It is a thick, doughy soup that is served along with the marrowbones and the meat, and it is a meal in itself. After such a bowl of soup you need hardly touch the *braaivleis* that invariably follows — it is so nourishing that nothing more is required but the usual *aposteltjie*[1] with coffee, and then your pipe.

Another camp dish that is unfortunately no longer fashionable is *askoek*.[2] This is the old-fashioned name for any kind of *roosterkoek*,[3] which has been called by many names. There is a collection of recipes written by an old *tannie* in 1815, the year Napoleon was defeated at Waterloo. The reason I mention Napoleon is that he, according to one of his contemporaries, was very fond of *askoek*, which he always used to gobble up with goat or chicken fat in such a greedy fashion that it would leave him suffering from stomach-ache. Well-prepared *askoek* will never give you stomach-ache when chewed properly. The old *tannie* agrees with me on this point. She starts by telling us that the flour does not really need to be sifted flour, but that it should be 'new' flour, 'stone-ground fresh', from which I gather that she means common *boer*-meal that has not yet been spoilt by weevils. Such flour is then mixed with salt and bicarbonate of soda and slowly stirred into a mixture of water and milk until you get quite a stiff dough, which can be left under a damp cloth until it is time to bake the *askoek*. Pieces of dough are then plucked from the lump and flattened into cakes 'about a hand's breadth wide and as thick as a thumb'. They are laid on a layer of warm ash with a coal or two still showing here and there, covered with more warm ash and left like that until both sides, top and bottom, are nice and hard. Then they are taken out, as much of the ash as possible wiped away, and served immediately. The camp guest cuts open each cake with his pocket knife — with his *herneuter*, as the old people used to call it — and spreads butter on the inside, if he has some; otherwise it can be had with sauce.

These days we use a grill for *askoek*, with the result that the little cakes are not evenly baked, but it does not really matter. The important thing is that the outside of the cake should be brittle while the inside remains soft, dry and delicate. Some recipes say that the dough should be made with milk — this makes the inside a bit moist, but perhaps tastier. It is, however, not at all necessary to add fat or egg yolk, as then the *askoek* would no longer be an *askoek* but an ash bun, something too refined for the campsite ambience, where simplicity is the paramount virtue.

There is perhaps no better dessert to round off a campfire meal than a pancake. The pancake dough is easy enough to make: a bit of fine flour, a pinch of salt, a few eggs beaten up, and enough milk — you can use tinned milk if no fresh milk is available — to make a thin dough, thin enough to drip easily from the spoon. The pan should preferably be small, no more than nine inches wide, and the fire warm enough. Put enough fat in the pan to grease its surface when molten and allow it to heat up well, until it starts smoking. Then place a tablespoonful of the thin dough in it and shake the

---

1 A round, hollow tea cake with a 'lid'.
2 Literally, 'ash-scone'.
3 Griddle cake.

camp food

pan so that the dough covers the whole of the bottom evenly. If the fire is hot, the pancake will be ready in barely a minute, and if the layer of dough is thin enough — as it should be — it will not even be necessary to turn it over. This the artful pancake-maker does easily enough, either with a knife or by giving the pan a deft flick, but that requires skill and experience, and if you are not good at it the pancake will more than likely end up in the fire. Therefore make your pancake thin, as thin as possible, and be content with having it baked nice and golden-yellow from below. Sprinkle with sugar, put on a plate next to the fire, and cover with a warm plate. Continue the work — and it should be done quickly, with haste, so that you can have a dozen pancakes piled up within a quarter of an hour. Then you can ask someone to hand them round while you continue making more. A bit of nutmeg and cinnamon mixed with the sugar is always delicious, and if syrup or honey is available it will go well with this simple camp pancake. You could even leave out the eggs, but then it is advisable to add a pinch of bicarbonate of soda to the dough, and it is possible that the pancake may then be a bit tough.

5 April 1946

49

Our White Wines I

A few correspondents have asked me to say something about our white wines. They would like to know which is the best brand to buy, why it is the best, and in what respect it differs from others that are available.

It is not for me to recommend particular brands, for by doing so I would open myself to the criticism of being partial and, which would be much worse for us Bonades, the accusation that I rate my own taste higher than that of my readers. Fortunately I do not suffer from this form of snobbishness. And I always remember, when writing these pieces about food and drink, what a great Frenchman said about another Frenchman who is still regarded as a more famous chap than the one who gossiped about him.

The criticising Frenchman — his name was Baudelaire and there are those, some of the Bonades amongst them, who regard him as an excellent poet who also had good taste when it came to food and drink — was bold enough to say that Brillat-Savarin, who is admired by all Frenchmen as the high priest of the table, was nothing but a puffed-up, ignorant, uncouth, uneducated, inexperienced braggard who denounced himself in his own words as someone who knows nothing at all about the holy science of the art of cooking and eating. All the stupid Brillat-Savarin had to say about wine in his widely read and world-famous book on the art of eating was a single sentence: 'Concerning wine, it is an invention of Noah and is made from the juice of the grape'.

Imagine! A thick tome dedicated to the art of cooking by someone who pretended to be a connoisseur and professor of the art of eating, a man who spent his whole life in a wine country — and such a banal summary.

I could easily go along with Baudelaire's scoffing at such an expert, but I like to be fair and therefore I did some research of my own. My literary investigations revealed that the famous Brillat-Savarin, well acquainted as he was with the kitchen, knew nothing whatsoever about the cellar, and that on one awful day he treated his guests to some not so clear white wine. Now French white wine is never really first-class, and if it is not a sparkling wine there is normally not much to be said for it. But still, neither Brillat-Savarin nor his guests had the right to conclude from this one unfortunate incident that French white wine cannot sometimes be good.

The same goes for our white wines. At present they are not yet as good as our red wines. We have red wines that can compete with the best European red wines. We have blended Cabernets with a flavour next to which even a *Nuits St George* cannot hold its own, with a sparkle and a colour that compares well with that of the best brands. Our white wines, however, are not as good as they ought to be, or could easily be if only our winemakers would take more care and our infernal legislation would allow them to be treated in the modern way.

Our white wines are inferior when it comes to flavour and what the French call *velouté*, which means velvety plumpness, something that, as it were, allows the tongue to perceive the taste of a watery solution. This is their greatest deficiency, but there are also others, for instance their too-high alcohol content.

The lack of flavour is to a certain extent due to the fact that our white wines are less acidic than the European ones. Yes, I realise that this statement is contrary to the accepted view. Just the other day I treated one of my friends to a choice Riesling, as soft and palatable as you could wish for, but after the first sip my guest said: 'Oh no, this always gives me acidity in my stomach — I would rather have a whisky and soda'. I did not tell him what old Dr Hahn said about imported whisky in his evidence before the select committee of Parliament — he would simply not have believed it. And when he told me that the only white wine he could drink without getting heartburn was *Liebfraumilch*, I realised that it would be quite impossible to instruct him in the most elementary oenology. For I agree completely with Multatuli who said: '*Er is moed nodig tot het voeren van den strijd tegen misverstand*'.[1]

The more acid a wine contains, the easier it is to preserve the flavour that comes originally from the leaves of the vine. In the trade it is no longer a secret that leaf extracts are sometimes, with the greatest care of course, added to European wines for the export market. I also see no ethical reason why not, on condition that we know that such doctored wines are, like champagne, no longer natural. To improve the flavour of our white wines I would not, however, recommend this method. We should rather carefully select the grapes to be used for making our best white wines. Not that we should wait to get *edelvrot*[2] grapes, although I look forward to the day when one of our farmers will make us a real *auslese* white wine, but a bit more attention could be given to the selection of the grapes and especially to the fermentation of the must in the vats. One of the most flavoursome white wines I have tasted here was a mixture of sémillon and sauvignon, quite a sweet wine, that was not for sale in the shops because it had too low an alcohol content. There is no reason at all why our white wines cannot be given more flavour with proper treatment and without making use of extracts.

The velvetiness of our white wines depends upon the quality of that strange gelatinous substance that science calls 'pectin'. Unfortunately we have to ward off this pectin instead of encouraging it to remain in our white

---

1 'You need courage to take up the struggle against misunderstanding.'
2 Noble rot.

wine. Why? Simply because it makes our white wines murky by entering into a marriage with the iron sometimes found in the must and giving birth to an odd pair of twins. One of these composite substances is soluble in wine, the other is not and makes the wine murky. And the funniest thing about it is that the one can easily be converted into the other by being exposed to light. A bottle of murky white wine can be made clear again by placing it in the sun; and it becomes murky again when placed in the fridge. The French call it *casse* — not really a sickness but a quality of white wine that is not good for the trade. If the law were to allow us to prepare white wine according to modern methods, for instance by adding prussic acid, we would probably never have to complain about *casse*. It would allow more pectin in our white wine and thereby give us a plumper wine that tastes more like jelly.

It is also possible to make a natural white wine without adding alcohol. On our wine shows we get such wines — I can remember tasting a first-class natural wine on the last show — flavoursome, soft, lovely, not sweet, and yet with a certain pectin quality that made it somewhat oily. A few weeks ago I tasted it again, in the form of a white wine sold over the counter with a certain amount of alcohol added, and — well, what would you expect? According to the law you cannot sell wine containing more than 20 grams of sugar per litre if it is not strengthened to more than 16,6 per cent with alcohol. According to law we are not allowed to sell a natural sweet wine over the counter, and the law will not allow us to get rid of *casse* by preparing our young wine properly.

24 May 1946

50

Our White Wines II

In the previous piece I quoted a saying of Multatuli about misunderstanding, not with any intention of implying that it is not necessary to fight misunderstanding but simply to indicate that I had no appetite for getting involved in an argument with a headstrong fellow after a fine midday meal. Our wine farmers should, in their own interests as much as that of the public, stand together and bravely go on the offensive against misunderstanding about wine. The Bonades will support them boldly in every attempt to educate the public and inform them about wine, white as well as red.

One correspondent asks: 'What kind, what brand of white wine should I buy?' This is a fair question that should be answered by the wine industry. In California the wine farmers and the wine merchants have joined hands to inform the public. They put an amount of money aside for systematic propaganda. What they mean by that is practical guidance like, for example, the distribution to every library of wine lists in which the brands are indicated, with information about their alcohol content and acidity level. Something like that is what we need here.

I know of only one restaurant in the country that presents its guests with a more or less complete list of indigenous wines. Even this list is not complete: a few names are missing, and the information provided is not always accurate and is open to misinterpretation. But I notice that it mentions fourteen different brands of white wine, and they are all, at least within the limitations mentioned in my previous piece, good, proper, drinkable wines. Not one of them dates from before 1938 — they are therefore all relatively young wines, just as — to tell the truth — nearly all the brands you will find on the shelf are, although not necessarily unripe, still in their youth. It would not be appropriate for me to mention any particular brand here, for reasons that my readers will understand, but I betray no secret when I refer to the white wine of 1931, produced by the *Nuy* farms, and still available over the counter a few years ago. This was one of the best and most flavourfully blended white wines you could then buy. Today there are first-class brands from the districts of Tulbagh, Paarl, Stellenbosch, Somerset West and the Cape that will be as good in a few years' time.

My advice to my correspondents is: order a case of each of the different brands. Store them in a cool place in the pantry or cellar, and give them a chance to rest well before trying them out. Wine is a living thing — it gets tired quite easily. Try a glass that has been shaken about on a motorcar journey and compare it with the same wine that has rested properly in the fridge for a few hours. This is one of the reasons our wines seldom make a first-class impression in the dining cars of the railways. At sea it is a different matter — there the wine is given proper rest, and the motion it is exposed to is less protracted and unsettling than it is during a journey on a gravel road.

Therefore allow your wine to rest. Then try two or three brands, one after the other, and do so under proper conditions. White wine loses much of its peculiar flavour when it does not meet the tongue chilled — only a fortified sweet white wine tastes acceptable at room temperature. The knowledgeable reader may immediately say: 'Yes, but what about sherry?' I beg your pardon! I fully agree that sherry is an exception to the rule, but then it is also an exception to many of the things that hold true for most wines, simply because sherry is a different kind of wine that cannot really be compared to other wines. But when it comes to white wine, drink it chilled — not quite iced, but well chilled. Twirl it around in the glass and smell the bouquet. The most important test of any kind of wine is the nose test. You can immediately tell not only whether the wine has flavour, but also whether it has an improper smell. Then, while the mouth is still half-open, taste it — not only in your mouth but also at the back of your throat, where the taste and fragrance more or less melt together, and the real *aroma* becomes noticeable. Then the swallowing — the more or less tangible feeling when mouth, palate, tongue and throat come together to deliver judgment on what is passing over them.

It is only by establishing the brand that best appeals to your own taste that you can decide to buy that which will be best for you. It may not be exactly what your friends and acquaintances prefer, and it is therefore advisable to acquire half a dozen different brands for the cellar. No one has been able to establish with any certainty how much time white wines require to reach full maturity. My own experience is that they can remain in the cellar for four to six years without deteriorating, and I have tasted some of *Oubaas* Philip Rabie's white wine that was twelve years old and could still be called delicious. But it will require much research before we will be able to speak about it with any certainty. The white wines now available over the counter are still very young and could do with another two or three years in the cellar before being drunk.

I started off saying that our wine industry could do much to clear up misconceptions about wine. Many people still have not the faintest clue. For instance, they think a red wine is made from red grapes and a white wine from white grapes, that sparkling wine is a champagne, that imported wines all contain less acid than indigenous wines, and that the label on an imported bottle of wine is as reliable as a dividend cheque from a gold-mining company. On the contrary, the sparkle of a wine has nothing to do with its foam — a foaming wine is a wine that still contains carbon dioxide from the second fermentation, it is not a natural wine; and champagne, which is a foaming and very seldom a sparkling wine, is one of the most meddled-with wines in the trade. Our indigenous wines have less acid than any imported ones. The well-known brands of imported wines are no proof that the wine in the bottle really is what it purports to be, and the most popular brands are all blended wines. *Liebfraumilch*, for example, and *Beaune* are trade names that do not mean as much as that of even a second-rate wine. A red wine is made by letting the skins of the grapes ferment along with the must — the colour comes from the skins, and there are only a few varieties of grape that have rosy juice (*Katalba*, for example, and *Pontac*). These are all minor details that we Bonades have known since our youth. But the city youth do not know these things and grow up under the impression that wine (how few of them ever get the opportunity of drinking natural wine!) is a solution of alcohol, made from grapes and discovered, to the curse of humanity, by Noah.

Heaven knows, we do not want our children to grow up to become 'overblown, ignorant, uncivilised, uneducated, inexperienced braggards', do we?

I recently had quite an odd white wine, in some respects very individual. It had a unique flavour, something between that of sorrel and rosemary. It was nicely sparkling, with a 'wettish' taste, an equally lovely aftertaste, very acidic, and with a low alcohol content — I would say about eleven per cent. The colour had a light green shine to it, and I was precocious enough to think that it was made from a Furmint grape. But it was not. It was wine made of wild grapes from the Knysna forest, where the grapes are as black and large as *gros colman*, as sour as vinegar, and possessed of a pip that burns your tongue like a chilli!

7 June 1946

51

Freshwater Fish

In a farmhouse on one bank of the Groot River, I once enjoyed some very fine fish. It was a thick piece, boneless and soft, grilled over the coals, with a pleasant flavour and a somewhat sour aftertaste. When I asked what it was the *tannie* said: 'It is the fillet of the *moddermorgel, Meneer*. We cut it out, pickle it in vinegar, then bake it.'

The barbel of the Groot River — which is what we are talking about — is also found in many other rivers, and is one of our largest and most delicious freshwater fish. It can weigh up to sixty pounds, has a flat stump of a head with long outgrowths around its mouth, and a greyish-brown colour. It is not a pretty fish, and also not one that anglers are fond of, as it fights and will not easily allow itself to be hauled in. It is only its weight that makes catching it with hook and line difficult. And once you have caught it, you find yourself not really knowing what to do with it. It is so revoltingly ugly and its skin is so slimy that you have to be quite resolute to regard it as food.

And yet, when prepared as described above, it does not taste bad at all. I have dealt with it in different ways and over time I have come to the conclusion that it can be regarded it as a delicious fish if one knows how to go about cooking it.

All the deep-water river and freshwater fish suffer from the apprehension that they might have a muddy taste that will be unpleasant, even disgusting, to the connoisseur. One of our best freshwater fish is the carp, which is far too seldom used as its meat is first-class if cooked properly. It is not enough just to clean it, then cook it in the pot or pan or *braai* it on the grill. That way you will get the full benefit of its mud and stand little chance of enjoying the genuinely fine taste of the meat itself. The old *tannie's* method can be used for the large carp. You can cut fish chops — strips — out of the thick meat, marinade it first in a mixture of wine and vinegar with herbs, then *braai* it in the pan or on the grill. If the fish is too small for so generous a treatment, you could also, after cutting off the fins and skinning it (as the skin is not worth preserving), marinade the whole fish and then bake it, covered in breadcrumbs, in a pan. From such pieces you can then make first-class fish preserve, with the necessary addition of fried onions and a curry sauce. Therefore do not pass over the barbel or the carp.

Our best and perhaps tastiest freshwater fish is the yellowfish, well known throughout the land. As a sporting fish it is one of our best, since a yellowfish of two pounds or more can put up quite a fight and give the angler enough work landing it with a thin line. We usually *braai* it whole in the pan, but that is not the best way of doing it as it is very bony and it is a bother having to get rid of the bones during the meal. Divided into pieces, a *braaied* yellowfish can be pickled and, after a few days, if you have used good vinegar, the bones will be soft. But no one really wants to eat bones with their fish. For my part, therefore, I prefer to cut up a yellowfish at the outset so that I have properly formed pieces to work with, and as few bones as possible. I then salt and pepper them, and if they are not fatty enough, lard each piece with a strip of bacon, and cook them in white wine with a blade of mace or some herbs. Or I bake the pieces in a pan. One must be careful not to cook or *braai* them for too long, as the taste of yellowfish is very fine and the meat requires just a few minutes on the fire. The knowledgeable cook will be able to adjust this recipe in countless ways. He might braise the pieces with special sauces — tomato sauce, mushroom sauce, curry sauce, etc — and in this way prepare a very fine fish dish that will not have to stand back for sea fish at all.

In some rivers you get a small fish, barely the size of a largish tadpole, slender and grey-white. It has no proper name and, as far as I know, is not normally eaten. But it is actually a very fine little fish. I have at times got hold of dozens of them in a pillow case used as a net, and prepared them tastefully in the way European cooks prepare sardines.

It is done as follows. Dry the little fish properly so that not a drop of water remains. You do not even have to clean them or scrape off any scales. Take quite a large pot and place in it enough oil or hard fat to half-fill it. Allow the fat to heat until a blue smoke starts rising from the pot. This means that the oil or fat has reached a temperature far above that usually required to cook meat or fish. Place the dried fish in a wire basket and place the basket in the boiling fat. Keep it there until every little fish is nicely brown. Take out, sprinkle with salt and ground dry parsley, and serve promptly. You can eat them skin and all, like chestnuts. It may not be a 'large' dish, but it is definitely a welcome change and well worth trying. In Europe such small fish are counted among the tastiest dishes and, when available, they fetch high prices as connoisseurs regard the 'whitebait' of the Thames — which is nothing other than our little river fish — as one of the tastiest dishes there is. The orthodox accompaniment to such crisply fried little fish is small pieces of rye bread generously spread with butter.

Our freshwater fish are quite plentiful and we make far too little use of them. There are many kinds and, as far as I know, they are all edible, although some kinds, such as the Transvaal tigerfish that anglers are so fond of, have hardly any edible meat and are so bony that they are impossible to prepare for the table. All the recipes for sea fish can also be used for fresh-water fish, and the cook will have enough opportunity of showing off his art and skill preparing river fish in different ways. I would make a special plea for cooking it in wine and adding certain herbs that add to the taste, such as rosemary, mace and fennel leaf; also, where necessary, for a proper larding of the fish when it is not fat.

27 December 1946

52

Red Wine

The sad history of *Grootoom* Gieljam is something our family prefers not to mention. When I was young it was the custom to send children out of the room when the conversation came round to *Grootoom*, which of course naturally made us young ones all the more curious. It was only in my matric year that I gathered he was *kinds*[1] by the time he died. My maternal *ouma* filled me in.

'We knew he wasn't all there, my child,' she told me. 'It started with his aversion to red wine. One of the abolition missionaries came along, and Gieljam chopped down his vineyard. Can you believe it?'

The Bonades have always been fond of wine, and they are not afraid or ashamed to say so because they adhere to Scripture which, of course, states clearly: 'God makes the grass grow for the animals and plants to serve mankind, to bring forth wheat for bread from the earth, and grapes for wine to gladden the hearts of men'. And they know that as well as old Mr Pasteur, who said when the doctors inducted him as an honorary member of their Academy (he being a teacher in physical science and never legally having had the right to cut out anyone's appendix) that wine is not only the best and healthiest of drinks, but also one of the best assistants to the expert cook. In our home there was therefore always wine on the table, and in the kitchen or pantry — always *red* wine. I am not saying that white wine is not just as good for cooking, but red wine is the experienced cook's aid and refuge *par excellence*.

Its redness is due to ingredients that scientists have not been able to agree upon. What we do know for sure, however, is that it is a strange colouring that undergoes a remarkable change when exposed to air — as old Mr Pasteur would have said 'by oxidisation' — and that also makes a big difference to the taste and flavour. It is precisely this change in the wine that is of so much value in the art of cooking, since it can be used to improve the taste and aroma of some dishes, especially those consisting mostly of animal proteins. Just about every kind of meat, wild or tame, is improved by red wine; tough meat soaked in it and then cooked is more tender than meat merely cooked in water. A beefsteak that has been lying in red wine for a few hours gains considerably in taste and juiciness. And this has nothing to do with the wine spirit — the alcohol — of the wine. Wine spirit causes the meat juices to coagulate and is therefore not at all suitable for softening the meat. Therefore use red wine with quite a low alcohol content — preferably

---

1 Senile, literally 'child-like'.

farm wine that has not been fortified. Naturally, on the stove or in the oven the alcohol quickly evaporates and what remain are the ingredients that make wine so eminently suitable for kitchen and table use — the amino and fatty acids, and the colouring that so easily changes into something new and keeps the scientists baffled.

It was, according to my maternal *ouma*, one of the proofs of *Grootoom* Gieljam's being a few sandwiches short of a picnic that he objected to the use of wine in stewed mutton. 'And that is the recipe we still use today, my child,' the old lady told me. 'How on earth could we prepare it without red wine? A change of taste? But of course, my child, that is exactly what we use it for. It makes a big difference, my child, whether you first braise the meat in red wine or make do without it.'

How many farm cooks know that today? We use all sorts of bottled sauces, about which most of us cannot say with any certainty what the ingredients are, and we neglect farm wine. This is because our people just do not know any better. I am not saying that the prophet's conclusions are correct. We are not quite finished. But they are writing quite a lot in the newspapers about malnutrition that, it is said, is quite common, not only amongst the blacks in the Transkei, but also on our Boer farms.

As a cook I am bound to say, with my hand on my heart — I really do not know what this means for in truth it is an expression which, taken at its word, is not accurate, and why the assurance of an anatomical impossibility should contribute anything to the reliability of what I may say is beyond me — to say, therefore, that red wine is just about indispensable if you want to prepare good food for the table. Everyone knows that you can make do without it, just as you can manage in the kitchen without vinegar and butter and herbs and mustard and oil and nutmeg and cloves and pepper, and all those things that contribute so much to making food enjoyable and tasty instead of just edible. As with herbs and spices, red wine is one of nature's gifts that is of great assistance to the cook, enabling him to serve food in a manner that maintains nutritional value and stimulates appreciation and relish.

Therefore try it with any recipe or dish where before you used only water. Make it an ingredient of coloured soups, of meat, vegetable and fruit soups. Stew meat in it; add some to curries and stews. Try it in all sorts of ways. The art of cooking remains in many ways an unknown domain in this country, an expanse in which you may with advantage dare to explore and try out a thing or two yourself. I have done so many a time, and with felicitous results in most cases. There have been failures, of course, but these I do not regret.

I once stewed ghoo beans in red wine, and what came out of the pot was about as sad as the history of *Grootoom* Gieljam.

17 January 1947

red wine

53

Zebra Meat

'Not even the *volk*[1] eat zebra meat,' my Bushveld host assured me. 'They use only the fat for making soap.'

This sounded a bit strange to me, for we Bonades have always been endowed with a sense of realism. The *volk* will eat any kind of meat, and in addition many a thing you would hardly honour with that name. Just think of what happened when the last wildebeest was slaughtered.

I had eaten zebra meat before, years ago when trekking somewhere along the Magalakwyn River. And according to my memory it was definitely quite tasty, a tender meat, as old *Oom* Danie told me in my young days. *Oom* Danie was a transport-rider and later made a small fortune delivering acacia for firewood to the people living in the then still embryonic Kimberley. He was one of those who contributed to the deforestation of the plains in that area, but one should grant that our people then knew very little about the topic of soil erosion — that we hear so much about today.

To cut a long story short, *Oom* Danie explained that there was no meat on earth that could hold its own against zebra meat. A young zebra, in his opinion, provided meat without equal. Years later I ate some donkey meat in the form of chops that I took for first-class lamb chops. My host assured me, however, that it was the meat of a young donkey, a very young, innocent animal that had never consumed anything but milk. It really tasted good. And why on earth should it not? Horses, donkeys and zebras are not only the most beautiful four-footed animals in existence; they are also, in respect of their eating and living habits, the cleanest. Take for instance the zebra. It only eats grass. It does not nibble, like many an antelope, at bushes with leaves that sometimes have a turpentine-like resinous oil that imparts an awful taste to the meat. It drinks a lot of water — an unbelievable amount: you have to see it drink at a dam to appreciate how much it really consumes. It is always nice and plump — what happens to underfed zebra heaven alone knows, since the animals you find in the veld are always admirably fat, as if taken care of by a stable boy. And talk about clean — you would go a long way to find a wild animal that is cleaner.

Oom Danie did not tell me anything about how to prepare zebra meat for the table. As far as I remember, he cut a piece of meat, salted and peppered it, and *braaied* it over the coals. Nor have I found anything about it in the cookbooks. There are, however, many recipes that provide information on how to cook and prepare horsemeat — ragout of horsemeat,

---

1 Workers.

horse chops, horsemeat sausage, horsemeat salami, horse mince, grilled horsemeat, spiced, stewed, smoked horsemeat, horse ham, horse mousse, and dozens more. But when it comes to zebras and camels, the cookbooks have nothing to say. The enterprising cook has to draw on his experience and find his own way.

My first problem was to find a little zebra. You have no idea how difficult that was, but we Bonades are persevering people. I eventually convinced my host that, in this time of scarcity of soap, it was undoubtedly his duty to make zebra fat available to his workers for soap-making. He agreed to shoot an old stallion, and although I tried to explain that something like that would be quite tough, and perhaps even completely inedible, I could not get him to change his mind on that score. I naturally did everything I could to put my case as convincingly as possible. There was, for instance, the argument that a zebra, if shot when still very young, would be spared all the trouble that lay ahead — just imagine the cruel prospect of being caught and eaten by a lion, not to mention a Cape wild dog! But it was all in vain. It was an old stallion or nothing, and with that I had to be content.

The stallion was one of the largest zebras I have seen — quite old, too, since its teeth were already worn away. But it was plump, smooth and beautiful to look at. The slaughtering is not worth dwelling on. My part was the inside fillet — a large, smooth piece of meat, or rather two pieces. I tried it the very same evening. Perhaps this was not quite fair to the zebra meat. A few days in a marinade would possibly have improved it, but I wanted to use the one piece for biltong, and I wanted to see what kind of meat it would turn out to be if *braaied* immediately.

I cut my piece of inside fillet into proper 'tournedos', or round pieces, each about two inches thick and a hand wide. They were then pounded with the handle of the knife, cut nice and even, and rubbed with a mixture of salt, pepper, young *blinkblaar*[1] twigs, and some wild wormwood[2] I found growing along the river bank. Then they were *braaied* in an open pan with a spoonful of butter. After being nicely browned on both sides, I poured a glass of sweet wine over them and braised them in it for a while. The result was a dozen tournedos that, as regards their appearance and aroma, no Carême would have been ashamed of. A little sifted flour and another glass of wine made a tasty sauce of what remained in the pan, to which the *blinkblaar* gave a tang. On each round chop was placed a soft, fried piece of tomato, and the sauce was poured over it all. My zebra dish was ready!

During the cooking I did what every good cook does and tasted the stuff in the pan. It was beautifully soft, with a very good taste — so tender that a fork easily sank into it. The tenderest wether chop could not compare.

---

1 *Zizyphus mucronata.*
2 *Wilde-als, Artemisia afra.*

zebra meat

The camp guests reacted according to their nature and their sense of taste. One of the *tannies* pulled up her nose, left the bouma, and in her disgust drew comparisons that were not altogether appropriate. Another camp mate carefully took a small piece on his fork, but never got as far as tasting it. We were pleased about that later on as only one piece had been provided for each guest, and we ended up with two more to divide amongst the rest of us. Those who were brave enough to taste it all agreed that it was first-class meat. Of course comparisons were made — with eland, mutton and pork — but those were all plucked out of the air. Zebra meat is *sui generis* — unique in its taste, tenderness and flavour. And the biltong, which was dried out fourteen days later, was just as delicious.

In future I will give preference, above all other Bushveld game, to zebra meat. And I will definitely, when I have the opportunity again, get hold of more than just the inside fillet.

24 January 1947

54

Brawn

Paging through an ancient recipe book — it is more than three hundred years old and unfortunately has nothing to do with our family, so I cannot really brag about it — I happened to read, with reference to brawn: 'This dish is not suitable for a high table; the commoners enjoy it, though'.

The cook, dead and buried for three hundred years and more, produced a recipe I cannot honestly recommend for a dish as beautiful as brawn. It reads: 'Cook a lamb's head, a pig's head, and five or six chicken feet ...' Peas and flour are added, and — can you believe it? — snippets of garlic and 'leftovers of salted herring ...' Now that is really a nightmare of a brawn!

Where today do you find the real, genuine brawn that *Ouma* used to make in the old days? Nowhere, I fear. It is perhaps for that reason that we find crude imitations, sometimes as hard as Cape salmon cooked to death, sometimes as tough and tasteless as vegetables cooked in the English manner. But the real thing is something completely different that melts away in your mouth and leaves you with the feeling the Israelites must have had when they tasted manna for the first time.

When a pig was slaughtered, it used to be the wedding feast of true brawn. Head, trotters and selected pieces of meat were cooked up slowly and patiently, together with orange leaves, sage, a bay leaf, allspice, nutmeg, ginger, and sometimes even a tiny piece of saffron, in enough water to cover everything — but not drown it. When the meat was tender and fell from the bones, it was dished out of the pot and spread out on a clean tablecloth, and we children used to help pick out every little bone and piece of sinew. Then back in the pot. There was always a bit of a commotion between *Ouma* and our cook at this stage. The cook would want to 'clean up' the 'soup' that was in the pot — which was done by beating it up with a few ground egg shells, then straining it through a cloth. In this way you get a clear brawn in which the pieces of meat lie buried as if they are caught up in an iceberg. *Ouma* was however against this, and I think she was right. A good brawn should not be clear. If you want a clear brawn, you may as well make it like the cookbooks of today tell you: by dissolving a few spoonfuls of gelatine in water, putting snippets of meat in it and letting it gel. That is no brawn; it is an imitation meat jelly that would never make you think of manna eaten in the desert.

Therefore back to the soup, without 'cleaning it up'. Cook it slowly once more with the addition of half a cup of mixed wine and vinegar, and some lemon. The lemon is not strictly necessary, but my late *ouma* always maintained that it added just the touch that made it perfect. Some connoisseurs prefer a squeezed lemon cooked up with the soup and meat — it is a matter of taste.

When everything is cooked up nice and evenly, the pot is taken from the fireplace and its contents worked on once more. The larger pieces of meat are reduced in size; the swimming orange leaves and sage are removed — only the bay leaf may remain, and if necessary a few new orange leaves can be introduced. Salt and pepper are now added, the whole is warmed up again, the foam taken off the top, and it is then ready for pouring into moulds. These were the old-fashioned rippled copper moulds, each one large enough to hold one and a half or two pounds of brawn. The brawn was dense enough to suspend the contents evenly during the process of stiffening. While stiffening, the fattiness floats up to form a thin layer on top that protects the brawn against penetration by bothersome and unwanted germs. *Ouma's* brawn could be kept for weeks without any fear of spoiling. But the best time to eat it was two or three days after it had set.

Now that was real brawn! Soft, tasty, flavoursome, with a pleasant mixture of different tangs, a velvety smoothness like that of old wine, yet a firmness that would have pleased a Chinaman, although there was nothing crisp in it, nothing that would crunch under your teeth. That is what *Ouma's* brawn was like!

I challenge anyone to come and tell me that it was unsuitable for a high table, or ever would be. It was the glorification of the best to be found in a pig's head and trotters, the jellied fifth essence of excellence — an unsurpassable work of art. And with that, Amen!

31 January 1947

55

Atjar

Dreams of the Far East . . . the smell of melatti and the different noises of the *desa*-bazaar . . . palm trees and 'kabous' . . . volcanos and impenetrable jungles . . . man-eaters and pirates . . . headshrinkers and opium smokers.

With a bit of imagination you see and feel all of this when you hear the word *atjar*.[1]

And I can imagine that what the word really refers to has contributed more to the pleasure and satisfaction of humankind than many a thing the wonderful East has provided, created and preserved.

We do not find it any more today. And, my goodness, do not come and tell me that it is still made; that in every Afrikaans cookbook and in some English ones you will find recipes for it and its preparation; that it is still to be found here and there; that it is not yet as dead as the dodo of Mauritius. This is all nonsense. The traditional atjar, as we Bonades used to know it — at a time when confirmation still lasted a year and a half, when it was still the custom for a civilised person to present you with his snuff-box, when girls did not yet make themselves ridiculous by making their fingers look like they have been caught in the pantry door, and when you could still sometimes find something worth reading in a newspaper — that kind of atjar has disappeared completely. It has melted away like snow on the Cederberg mountains in August.

There are those who are able to speak without emotion about the dying off and disappearance of old habits, old friends, old fashions and old things, and who would not shed a tear about the loss of something our forefathers loved and cherished. They are, as the Latin poet said bluntly, 'unfeeling stones that do not notice the slow erosion of wind and rain'. It is they who today satisfy themselves with So and So's Pickled This and That, Tom Dick and Harry's Sauce, Potdamn's Pickle, *Ouma's* little Wake-me-up, and heaven knows what else is scraped out of bottles and tins and served up with our best dishes.

We Bonades are different. We like the old stuff. We are loyal to what our forefathers cherished. And one of the *tannies* still makes the genuine, traditional atjar.

---

1 Pickle.

This very summer month is the right time for it. When I happen to be in the vicinity, I am sent to the garden to gather the necessary *ingrediënte* (*Tannie* would never say *bestandele*[1]).

'Please don't bring old mielies,' she would warn, 'and the marrows must be no larger than a ha'penny.'

And what did not go into *Tannie's* atjar! Small gherkins, you could just about say with their mother's milk still on their little teeth — which is completely silly, of course, as someone with teeth would not be drinking mother's milk any more — small mielies, an inch and a half long, young cucumbers, as soft and juicy as they come, green beans and yellow beans, small walnuts, the insides of hard, crisp, white heads of cabbage, pieces of pure white cauliflower, green and red chillies, almonds, raisins, apricots, peaches, far from fully grown *naartjes*, small lemons, celery, carrots, little turnips, little radishes — just about everything that a garden and fruit orchard could provide. And still *Tannie* would sigh that in her great-grandmother's time still more would be used. 'Especially,' she would say with a sad smile, 'the preserved bamboo and the young nuts they got from India.'

I know for sure that this was completely correct. We still have the bills from Batavia and Colombo in which mention is made of '*bamboesen voor 'n atjahr en vogelnesten uit Tonkin*'.[2]

But we did manage to contribute this and that to help *Tannie* make an excellent and tasty atjar. Stem ginger, wild aniseed root (she gets that from a girlfriend from the Hantam) and grapefruit peel. Also, of course, turmeric, a tiny bit of saffron, onions, garlic, coriander, peppercorns, and all kinds of nuts.

This was boiled up in the usual salt water until everything was nicely soft. *Tannie* always added a handful of seaweed. Then it was poured out onto a tablecloth and sorted — what was bruised and less than first-class was discarded. The 'pickle' was boiled in wine vinegar, with salt, a glass of brandy and a tablespoon of turmeric. ('Yes, I know, my child, that many people use ——'s curry powder, but it is really not necessary and I find that it makes the atjar murky, my child.') The boiled *ingrediënte* were placed in a large, wide-mouthed flask, the boiling pickle was poured over them, and there they stayed for a day or two. Then they were boiled up again, slowly and carefully, with *Tannie* tasting now and then, and here and there, and where necessary a tablespoonful of honey was stirred in, or sometimes brown sugar — but atjar must be full of flavour, sharp, tangy, and therefore not too sweet. ('Yes, my child, there are those who make it into a pure jam, but my late mother always used to say it should bite, you know, my child,

---

1 Ingredients.
2 'Bamboo for an atjar and birds' nests from Tonkin.'

bite — especially with a roast.') Then it was put back into the flask, the pickle was poured over it, and the bottle was carefully sealed.

'After three months,' said *Tannie*, 'it is ready. But it is better to wait a year, my child, especially if the walnuts and almonds are on the old side. Then they will be nicely saturated.'

I think there is nothing finer with either a roast or a bobotie than one of the small green mielies out of *ou-Tannie's* atjar.

21 March 1947

Three Hundred Years of Cape Wine

by

C Louis Leipoldt

'*Si le vin disparaissait de la production humaine, je crois qu'il se ferait dans la santé et dans l'intellect de la planète un vide, une absence, une défectuosité beaucoup plus affreuse que rous les excès et les dèviations dont on rend le vin responsible.*'

—Baudelaire

Contents

Introduction

Born and bred in a wine-growing district, initiated, from my earliest youth through a novitiate that stretched through many years, in the practical knowledge of wine-making, and pricked by a permanent and pervasive curiosity to learn what could be learned about wine, it is only natural that my interest has concentrated upon the wine made in my own country, South Africa, and that such time and energy as I have been able to devote, in the leisure leased from other avocations, to the study of so attractive a matter, has been spent in gathering information about the wine industry in this country. It may be that the précis of what I have gleaned is of instructive interest to others who, like myself, are lovers of good wine, and who may wish to know something about the vicissitudes through which the wine industry in South Africa has passed during the past three hundred years. Such a summary of the facts cannot possibly be complete, and this book does not pretend to give a full history of the wine industry in South Africa. All that it purports to give is an account of how that industry started, what difficulties it had to surmount, and what opposition and enmity it had to fight against before it achieved its present stable position.

It appeared to me that a bare outline of the story of our wine industry might be usefully enlarged by an account of wines in general, of the grapes from which they are made, and of the popular fallacies that have clustered around them. The book, therefore, consists of two parts, the first dealing with the history of the wine industry, and the second with South African wines as they are today. The concluding chapter, on the future of the wine industry in this country, is necessarily polemical, and contains merely the stray thoughts of a wine-lover who is seriously concerned about the development of the industry in South Africa.

My indebtedness to those who have helped me to compile the narrative is so great that it would be futile, and perhaps invidious, to attempt to acquit myself of it by apportioning my gratitude in individual thanks. In the text I have mentioned where such help has been given; in the bibliography,[1] the available sources of such information as has been used have been indicated. There remains, however, a host of friends who have freely placed at my disposal private papers and memoranda from which I have culled generously, and to them my thanks are profound.

C Louis Leipoldt
Cape Town
August 1946

---

1 No bibliography was ever prepared. Leipoldt died in April 1947, and this work was first published in 1952.

Chapter 1

The First Vintage

The Dutch East India Company, that most profitable combination of unblushing piracy and commercialised Protestantism, wanted a halfway house on the long, dreary, and dangerous voyage from the Texel to Tandjong Priok. Mr Secretary Van Dam had long urged that some such repair station should be established, farther south than St Helena, and more midway than Ceylon. The Lords Seventeen, who never passed a resolution without previous prayerful and shrewd practical consideration, asked for a memorandum. The best site for such a small settlement as they had in mind — a store, a shop, a simple landing wharf and shed for repairs, with perhaps a hospital, and, in the future, some tilled plots where green corn and vegetables, so necessary for the health of the crews, could be cheaply grown — was one of the two bays at the southern end of the African continent, the Cape of Good Hope. Little was then known about the place, though much was imagined. Its high mountain bastions shut out all sight of the country beyond, where, if the Portuguese were to be believed, lay the lands of man-eating savages and the fabled town of Vigiti Magna. But since the intrepid Cornelis Houtman had sailed round it, on his way to India, many other ships, principally those belonging to the Company, had cast anchor in its waters, and their captains had sounded their depths and reported the best and safest parts of the roadsteads. Sometimes a vessel had been wrecked on the sands of Table Bay and castaways had lived for weeks, even for months, on the shore, until rescued by the home- or out-going fleets. From such chance residents the slight knowledge of the country that Mr Secretary could communicate had been obtained, and even for that he had to go to outside sources. There was, for instance, Sir Thomas Herbert, who in 1638 had published a book in which he described what he had seen at the Cape during a stay that appears to have given him an opportunity not only to climb Table Mountain, but to glean something about the natives and the soil. Sir Herbert, who came when early spring was flushing the hills with green, wrote enthusiastically:

> 'The Earth abounds with roots, herbs, and grass aromatique, redolent and beneficial; such as I took notice of I may dare to name; Agrimony, Mynt, Calaminte, Betony, Plantain, Ribwort, Spinage, Sorell, Scabious, Holy Thistle (of which beware), Coliquintida, all the year long, Nature roabing the fruitfull Earth with her choicest Tapistry, Flora seeming to dress her selfe with artlesse Garlands, Alcenoe and Tempe serving as Emblems to this Elysium.'

What was more to the point, returning sailors reported that there was most excellent grass, and sorrel to be had by the basketful to save scurvied men from death, while from the native could be bartered sheep and cattle, though these were rarely spied from shipboard. Indeed, instructions had been given to all the Company's ships that touched at the Cape not to omit to take in water and a supply of sorrel that in spring and early summer grew luxuriantly on the foreshore.

From two seamen, who had personal experience of a short stay at the Cape, Mr Van Dam obtained particulars that he elaborated into a memorandum. We may take it for granted that he spurred his directors on to pay some attention to the matter, and he was so far successful that his estimate of cost and the general scheme that he had submitted were provisionally approved by them. But they wished for further comments on the memorandum, and a young surgeon in the Company's service, who had once been an assistant factor but had blotted his copybook and been disgraced as a result, although he still had a good friend in high quarters, was ordered to study the document. His criticism, and the knowledge that he displayed in suggesting improvements of the scheme, impressed the Lords Seventeen, and when it was finally decided to adopt the secretary's proposals, Johan Van Riebeeck was deputed to lead the expedition and establish the repair station.

He arrived here in the first week of April 1652, and immediately set to work. A fort was built, a site selected for a garden, and a portion of land prepared for sowing. Among the commander's company were two men who probably had specialised knowledge of agriculture. One was the head gardener, Hendrik Boom, who brought with him his wife and family; the other was Jacob Cloete van de Kempen, destined to become the ancestor of the family whose name is indelibly associated with the wine industry at the Cape. Neither of them knew anything about viticulture. Indeed it is quite possible that their ignorance may have been responsible for the failure of the first vine cuttings that were planted in the settlement, but on this point there is very little to be gathered from the only records of the time, the commander's logbook or *dag-register*, and the copies of letters sent home.

We may pause for a moment to discuss whether or not there was any intention, at the time when the settlement was planned, that wine should ever be made there. Certainly there is no mention of such a design in the formal instructions issued, before he left Holland, to the commander. There is, however, ample documentary evidence in the Company's archives to prove that the directors interested themselves greatly in the provision of wine for their outgoing ships, and that the problem of supply was one that caused them a great deal of worry. Wine, especially natural, unfortified wine, was then rightly regarded as an admirable drink, especially to correct the insipid and often almost undrinkable water that remained in the casks after a three months' voyage. Ships' captains carried with them, as a standby in all cases of illness on board, Conrad Knuthman's *Medulla Destillatoria et Medica*, whose initial chapter describes *Des Weins gute Tugenden*, and mentions the usefulness of natural wine in the treatment of scurvy and as an adjunct to food, while in a later chapter it deals, as faithfully as any fanatical prohibitionist pamphlet can state the case, with the abuse of wine.

All sailors knew and appreciated the value of wine of a long voyage. The Company ordered that no ship should embark on the journey to the East without carrying an amount of wine sufficient to give the crew at least a weekly ration. Unfortunately the wine shipped at Amsterdam was usually of such poor quality that it sickened or turned to vinegar before it reached the equator. Better-class wines could be procured at Lisbon or at Bayonne, but for obvious reasons they could not be called for by the Company's ships, and, because of their expense when imported overland, could be supplied only in small quantities for the use of the captains. Commander Van Riebeeck knew these facts, and, as he was a medical man of some experience, he probably realised that if he could make wine at his halfway settlement, it would greatly help to maintain the health of the crews of all vessels touching at the Cape. He had hardly been a month in charge of the infant Colony when we find him writing home, asking the directors to send him young trees, berry-shoots and vine cuttings; the latter, he says, are likely to flourish on the mountain slopes as excellently as they do in Spain or France. There is no evidence that he brought any cuttings or slips with him. He may have done so, for it is quite likely that his enthusiasm for gardening had prompted him to bring some with him, but they may have perished on the voyage out, or failed to root. What is more likely is that he brought with him grape seeds. These were then used by nurserymen to propagate vines from Turkey and Persia, but their germination was a matter of chance, and if they were sown broadcast and ploughed under — as tradition reports that they were — it is not to be wondered at that they failed to grow.

The first cuttings that were sent from Holland arrived at the Cape at the end of 1654, nearly eighteen months after the commander had urged that they should be sent out. They were probably short, three-inch-long slips of young vines from the Rhineland, buried in wet soil and sewn up in sail cloth which was supposed to be kept wet on the voyage, for that was then the common way of sending them. Nothing more is heard about them, so we may conclude that they were rotten when they arrived, or, if any survived the voyage, that they were mishandled in the planting. A year later, in February 1655, another consignment was sent. There is no record of what varieties were included in this parcel, but at that time the Company's agents were in touch with a grower who had available cuttings from France, Germany, Spain and Bohemia. Our best oenologists are of opinion that this first parcel, from which derived nearly all the later stocks in the Company's vineyard, consisted of Muscat, Green Grape, Muscadel and French Grape, but we have no reliable record and their classification can therefore be conjecture merely. This parcel arrived at the Cape on the 22nd of July 1655, having taken nearly five months to reach its destination, which, if we take into consideration that the cuttings must have been imbedded for at least a couple of months before they were sent out, could scarcely have favoured

the first vintage

407

their budding. But apparently more precautions had been taken in their despatch, and certainly greater care was given to them, for most of them grew, and a year after their arrival the commander writes home to say that they were flourishing. In that year several more parcels of cuttings were forwarded, and these, too, succeeded. The gardeners were not viticulturists, and the commander himself had had no experience of starting a vine-nursery, but among his men was a German, whose name has not been handed down to posterity, who had practical knowledge of such things. He showed Boom how to nurse the cuttings, first in wet earth to encourage the formation of rootlets, and afterwards to layer the divided cutting so as to strengthen and elongate it. When the plants became sturdier, local cuttings were made, and these answered well. In 1657 Commissioner Van Goens noted in his report to the directors that the vines were sprouting and showed promise of reaching maturity.

The first vineyard plot was somewhere in the Company's garden and was necessarily an experimental nursery. Here grew the vines from which, on the second day of February 1659, wine was first made at the Cape. The occasion is thus immortalised in the logbook:

'February 2, 1659. Today — God be praised — wine pressed for the first time from the Cape grapes, and from the virgin must, fresh from the coop, a sample taken ... pressed from the three young vines that have been growing here for two years ... yielding 12 mengles must (15 litres) from French or Muscadel Grapes, the Hanepoot Spanish not yet ripe.'

On this interesting passage our first historian, Theal, comments:

'From the vintage of this season (1659) a small quantity of wine was made for the first time in South Africa. The fruit used was Muscadel and other round white grapes, and the manufacturer was the commander himself, who was the only person in the settlement with any knowledge of the manner in which the work should be performed. The event is recorded on the 2nd of February and it is stated that the Spanish grapes were not then ripe, though the vines were thriving. There is no mention now to be found of vine stocks from Spain, but this observation appears to verify the common opinion that the Hanepoot was brought from that country. This is not the only importation of plants of which the record has been lost, for the introduction of European flowers is not mentioned in any of the documents of that date still existing, though the rose and the tulip are incidentally spoken of as blooming at this time in South African gardens.'

That Van Riebeeck himself pressed and fermented the must is merely conjecture, for there is no proof whatever that he had any personal practical experience of winemaking. It is quite as likely that someone else, who had travelled in the wine-growing countries — such as, for example, the Scottish artisans or the assistant surgeon who had been to Italy and France — knew far more about the business than he did. As there was no press the juice must have been expressed by hand, while the fermentation must have proceeded in one of the casks in which wine had been imported. Nothing is stated about the quality of the wine, a somewhat remarkable omission when we remember how dithyrambic the commander could be about other things.

The success of the first vintage, even though the yield was so miserably small, encouraged the enthusiastic Van Riebeeck to contemplate a larger vineyard. He had induced Commissioner Van Goens to grant him a plot of land on what was later to be known as Green Point Common, then a well-watered, bush-grown expanse of level country, backed by a lake that abounded with waterfowl. Here he planted an experimental vineyard and cultivated a garden, but he soon found that the site was not well chosen, for the lake overflowed in winter and part of the soil was brack. Commissioner Cuneus, an even more complacent superior than Van Goens, was good enough, in direct contravention of the Company's standing rules, to allow the Commander to exchange the Green Point freehold for a 101 morgen plot on the south-eastern bank of the Liesbeek River, near its source. Here the land was rich, varied and well-watered, with ample shelter against the southeaster wind that in summer tore the vegetables in the Company's garden to shreds and must have ruined the experimental vinery had it not been protected by a wall of bush.

The first vineyard that in South Africa had any pretension to be so called was planted here, and for some time its presence gave a name to the place, which was known as 'The Wine Mountain' (Wynberg). Later on the name Wynberg was transferred to the higher ground on the south and east part of the valley behind the mountain and the commander's farm received the name of *Bosheuvel* or 'Hillwood'. It may be of interest to the reader to summarise the history of our first wine farm, which today can no longer boast of having the smallest connection with the industry.

When Van Riebeeck left South Africa on his way to Java, where he was later to become Governor of Malacca and Secretary to the Council, his holding, to which under the Company's regulations he was never properly entitled, reverted to the common land of the settlement. Only by grace could he be compensated for the work and expense he had lavished on it, but as his industry — even though misapplied, as Mr Secretary Van Dam most likely would have expressed it — was patent, such grace was vouchsafed to him. The Council of Policy resolved:

'18 July 1661. As at Mr Van Riebeeck's farm at the *Bosheuvel*, oranges, lemons and many kinds of Dutch fruits flourish, as does also the vine, it is resolved to take this place for the Company, and to plant a large orchard and vineyard there. The expenses to which the commander has been subject, and all farming implements now there, are to be valued by the next commissioner who arrives at the Cape. There are now growing at the place 1 162 young orange and lemon trees, ten banana plants, two olive trees, three walnut trees, five apple trees, two pear trees, 19 plum trees, and 41 other sorts, besides some thousands of vines. As the Company has a small orchard at the Rondebosch, a nursery is to be formed there.'

This resolution was sent to the Lords Seventeen, but they would have none of it. They had no faith in vineyards and orchards; let the settlement grow corn and supply cattle; that was all they asked for. And for heaven's sake keep down the expenses! Mr Secretary Van Dam — or his no less cantankerous successor — had moodily worked out a statement that the *per capita* cost of the settlement at the Cape of Good Hope was much in excess of what the original estimate, dating back ten years ago, had been. With such growing expenses, and no possibility of quick piratic gains from the capture of richly laden Portuguese ships, the Company despaired of paying six hundred per cent on its capital. *Bosheuvel* must be sold by public auction to the highest bidder, and the purchase price credited to the 'income account'.

Jacob Cornelis Rosendaal, of Amsterdam, a free burgher, who seems to have originally been a farmhand before he enlisted in the service, bought it for the equivalent of £100 and sold it to one Tobias Marquard, who was the first to register its title. When Marquard died in 1690 Cornelis Linnes bought it from the estate for £437. Mr Linnes was a favourite of fortune. He had entered the Company's service as a clerk and slowly climbed the ladder until in 1685 he was promoted to be chief salesman, and in 1691 to be *Landdrost* of Stellenbosch. The fact that he paid what was then a high price for a farm showed that he, too, had disobeyed the regulations and done a little private trading. When he was ordered to Stellenbosch he sold *Bosheuvel* to Guillaume Heems, of Bruges, who came out as a colonist, and had, it seems, considerable private means. Heems lived on the farm and much improved it, and after his death in 1726 it was apparently — there seems to be some doubt here — bought by his son, Martin Heems, on behalf of his young grandson, Guillaume Heems. Jacob van Reenen bought it, many years later, for £267, and sold it to Jacob Neethling in 1758 for £400, who in his turn sold it to Jan Roep for exactly the same sum. Jan Roep was a most enterprising and hard-working German colonist, who had emigrated from Hanau in 1755 and had established himself in the settlement. He greatly improved the farm and sold it in 1783 to Peter Henker for the sum of £2 267. It passed from Henker in 1804 to Justus Keer, who sold it in 1805 to Honoratus Maynier, of Leipzig, a Stellenbosch burgher with ambitions, an acquisitive disposition and a literary education, a rare thing in those days. The new owner added 77 morgen 100 square roods to the place at a yearly quitrent of one pound eleven shillings and sixpence, beautified the buildings, planted many oak trees and changed *Bosheuvel* into *Protea*. After his death in 1836 the farm was sold by auction and bought by Andreas Brink, who in 1842 sold it to Honoratus Maynier, a grandson of the former owner. Finally it passed into the possession of the trustees of the Colonial Bishopric Fund, which paid £3 100 for it and rechristened it Bishopscourt. Little of the original farm can today be identified. Even the site of the first vineyard is not to be fixed with any certainty, nor that of the relatively large orchard of more than a thousand orange and lemon trees. But none of us who have any feeling for the past or today appreciates Cape wine can wander within its limits without kindly thoughts of the enthusiastic ship's surgeon who here gave the first practical proof that the Cape can be a great wine-growing country.

Had Van Riebeeck realised that, had he guessed that in this pleasant, sylvan environment, busy with his vineyard and his garden, he would have been spared the sorrow and disappointment that awaited him in Java, he might have retired as a free burgher and, like Simon van der Stel, made a great wine.

During his tenure of office at the Cape, the settlement gradually learned to grow its own wine. From 1652 to 1660 it imported all its liquor, and some of it was very bad. From Europe it bought gin and beer and French, German and Spanish wines, and French, Spanish and Portuguese brandies. The commander's table was well supplied with good wine, imported at the Company's expense; the men drank ration wine that was an indifferent Medoc brand, usually thin, often sour. Their beer and spirits ration pleased them more, but led to trouble on occasions. The first serious case of disobedience resulted from a too-generous ration of brandy to a soldier who insisted on disturbing the commander's sleep with a kettledrum. The first really scandalous behaviour was that of the layreader and schoolmaster who had to be repatriated because he got continually drunk on gin. But, on the whole, the community was a sober, temperate set of folk, and there was no clamant demand for restriction.

In 1657 the first free burghers were settled on the land in two parties. Harman's Company obtained plots in the Groeneveld, the country lying 'between False and Table Bays', where they were supposed to confine their bucolic activities to corn growing. Stevens's Company, more fortunate, held lands around Rondebosch, in the area known as the *Hollandsche Tuin*. Nine persons in all, and each one of them a worthy servant of the Company, but none even a third-rate farmer. They were all offered vine cuttings. They grew these for grapes; none, as yet, had the slightest desire to emulate the commander and establish a vineyard. There was no money in it, they argued. One could grow rich much more quickly by illicit cattle trading or by selling farm produce to the ships, if only the Company would permit such a thing.

These were the first farmers, but two years before the Company had so far relaxed its stringent regulations as to allow its servants at the Cape to have small gardens and keep a few cows and pigs. Hendrik Boom, the gardener, was the first to take advantage of this permission. His energetic wife, Annetjie de Boerinne (Annie the Farmer), obtained the first monopoly to sell milk and dairy produce to the ships. Later came other monopolies. In 1657 no one was allowed to buy liquor from the incoming ships; the vintner's licences came much later, and this primary attempt at prohibition met with little success.

From 1661 the settlement began to take more interest in winegrowing. Rosendaal, who had bought *Bosheuvel*, made wine and so did Cloete. They had a ready local sale for their produce, which appears to have been a pure, natural, rather earthy-tasting red wine, a trifle too sweet to be called dry. Wouter Schouten, visiting the Cape in 1658, mentions the vegetables, the fruits and the farmers, but says nothing about wine, for the excellent reason that none was yet made. On his return from the East, in 1665, he describes some of the vineyards he saw, and gives an account of his reception by a free burgher, whose house had no window panes and who lived a simple life without any amenities, but had home-made wine. Surgeon Frikius, somewhat later, found the farmers very hospitable. Many had 'small vineyards, from which they make their own wine'. He describes a meal he had at one farmhouse, where the good wife gave him 'a most excellent salad, cabbage, well-tasting mutton, fish, an omelette and good bread, with butter and a trifle of cheese; for this I had to pay one schelling'. The wine he tasted was 'very drinkable', but he had to pay extra for it, 'half a riksdollar for one measure'. Elias Hesse, the forester, found the wine from the Cape that he drank at Batavia 'not very sweet'; the women 'sugared it before they drank it'. On his arrival at the Cape he drank the local wine, which he found 'very good'. Lastly we have the testimony of Christopher Schweitzer, the accountant, who lodged for some weeks with a free burgher living on 'the slopes of the Devil's Peak'. He found the wine thin but good, and states that the grapes were 'most excellent', but that his host had to get up in the middle of the night 'to scare the wild beasts away from his vineyard'. The learned Osorius, Bishop of Silva, is quoted by another traveller as an authority for the assertion that the wine he tasted in the East was too sweet, but there is no proof that this refers to wine from the Cape, and as the bishop travelled before 1661 it is hardly likely that he ever tasted Cape wine. The French Jesuits who were entertained by Van Riebeeck were regaled on choice Rhine wines, perhaps also on Spanish wine. It is regrettable but true that we have no record that tells us anything about what our first vintage was like, nor what was the quality and quantity of its successors for the first five years after the founder's departure. From that date, however, far more information is available that needs a separate chapter.

Chapter 2

The Growing Industry

Commander Van Riebeeck was succeeded by Commander Zacharias Wagenaar, an ill man, disgruntled and cantankerous. He had no love for the free burghers, whom he described as lazy, avaricious and impudent. They had managed to obtain a few privileges, although these were little in comparison with the many restrictions that the regulations fixed upon them. In 1665 the Council of Policy passed the following resolution:

> 'Of all the free inhabitants, those who keep canteens have the easiest lives and are the most prosperous. Farmers, fishermen and mechanics are constantly requesting to be allowed to set up canteens here and there. There are now four canteen keepers, who have hitherto paid nothing for their privileges. In future they are to pay as in India. Jacob van Rosendaal is to hold his licence for six months only, as in future this privilege will be given by turns to poor people who have families to provide for.'

Already both the free burghers and the private gardeners had seen the advantage of winegrowing, though they scarcely imagined that it would lead to a brisk export trade. The commander viewed this new tendency with some concern. The growing slave population needed rice, which had to be imported at some expense. Maize had recently been introduced, and the authorities tried to encourage its production. But the most pressing need was grain, barley, corn and oats, and the harvest never came up to expectations. That was not surprising, for labour was scarce and draught animals almost unobtainable. Only in 1666 could the free burghers, now numbering 16 families, buy horses from the Company's stud; these were sold by auction and proved a great boon.

A year after the new commander's induction the settlement was much perturbed by the appearance of a 'crescentic comet', whose luminescence in the eastern sky, after sunset, was held to be a precursor of divine wrath with the community that had so often transgressed the honourable Company's regulations. One Ernestus Back, a jovial fellow, had been entrusted with the spiritual comfort of the free inhabitants; he taught their children with the help of a chapbook, and lent a hand with the fermentation of their wines. But much must, that is a highly inebriating liquor, made him run amok on occasions, which caused scandal and led to undignified complications, especially when it happened on the Lord's Day. So on the 1st of January 1665 appeared a proclamation, a model of pious hypocrisy, that was to be the first specimen of that sorry legislation that still afflicts us whereby Sunday is designed to be twenty-four hours of enforced idleness with its concomitant result of moral, intellectual and cultural stagnation. To back it up, Mr Ernestus Back was bundled off to Batavia in disgrace, and with his and the comet's disappearance from the scene, the settlement calmed down and the free burghers made more wine.

They got their cuttings from Rosendaal's vineyard at *Bosheuvel* as well as from the Company's farm at Rondebosch, where some thousands of vines were now growing. The grapes from the latter vineyard were foot-pressed, for as yet there does not appear to have been a proper winepress in the Colony, and the wine was used exclusively for the ships. It was this wine that was sent to Java, where it arrived sometimes in excellent condition and sometimes in an undrinkable state. It was there noted that 'the Cape wine is not to be wholly depended on, being at times muddy and distasteful, though in general it stands the voyage better than wine brought from Surat or from the homeland'. Obviously its manufacturers knew very little about blending or fortifying, and as little about how to stop the fermentation in wines of high sugar content — those made from the Muscadel and Spanish grapes — which, in the opinion of those who had drunk them when they were fresh, could be compared with the rich wines of Anjou. There was a demand for such sweet wines. James the First had set the fashion by preferring 'Frontignac, Muscadello and Canary' to the tart French wines of the day — then generally known as 'wine of the Pontacq' — and high officials in the Company agreed with his choice. But such wines demanded great care in the pressing, fermenting, blending and, above all, in the maturing, together with the most scrupulous cleanliness. New casks were unobtainable at the Cape; the wine had to be sent to the East in old ships' casks, often dirty and sour. In the circumstances it is not amazing that so much of it reached its destination in a thoroughly bad condition; the wonder is rather that some of it improved on the voyage and pleased the taste of the Indian officials.

Some of it was sent to Mauritius, which in 1664 had been reoccupied as a settlement affiliated to the Cape, and found much favour there. Later on this export assumed fair dimensions, though for many years the main market for Cape wine was to be the Company's eastern possessions.

There is no information to be gleaned from the records as to individual vineyards, but from later accounts it seems clear that the two chief ones, both of which served also as nurseries, were *Bosheuvel* and *Rustenburg* where the Company's wine was made. Cuttings were properly layered and some new varieties were undoubtedly obtained from seeds that had been brought direct from India. We may assume that there were small vineyards attached to the plots of all the freeholders, and there was probably not much to choose between those who farmed far behind the mountain and those whose holdings lay closer to the settlement. As the farming population increased, more attention was paid to wine growing and less, perhaps, to wheat, mainly because of the scarcity of labour. There was as yet no over-production of grapes or wine. In the season grapes could easily be disposed of, and the wine that was made found ready purchasers in the canteens. In 1665 the first open market was started, where farm produce, including game — eland, rhinoceros meat, penguin eggs and hippopotamus fat — could be bought very cheaply. Spirits and foreign wines could only be bought at the canteens, whose owners, again, were only allowed to buy from the Company's central store. In no case was anyone allowed to buy liquor from incoming ships. The first licence to purchase wine and spirits from officers of ships calling at the Cape was granted, by special resolution, to Wouter Cornelis Mostert in 1668; it was limited to a term of three years at an annual fee of 100 guilders. Two years later Rosendaal was granted the privilege of selling wine of his own making, and in the same year the Council minuted:

'As most of the free men lead idle lives about the canteens, it is resolved to permit only the following persons to sell strong liquor: Wouter Cornelis Mostert, who is one of the oldest residents; Hendrik van Surwaarden; Tielman Hendriks; Joachim Marquard; Jan Israels; Joris Jansen; Steven Jansen; Elbert Diemer; Jacob Rosendaal (who is showing great diligence in extending his vineyard, and is therefore privileged to sell wine of his own making to the free people and to people of the ships) and Mathys Coeman. In reply to the question: What is to be done with the grapes which flourish here in such abundance and which are cultivated not only by the Company but by individual farmers, the Council resolves: Wine has already been sent to Batavia, but whether it will pay the Company to purchase from individuals remains to be seen. Ships are abundantly supplied with grapes in the season. Individual farmers may be allowed to send surplus wine to Batavia for sale, upon payment of three riksdaalers freight per half aum and such duties as may be imposed.'

Theal comments:

'This was practically throwing the Eastern markets open to the Cape wine farmers to make the most they could in. But so far from being viewed as a privilege or a concession by the colonists of those days, it was held by them to be equivalent to a prohibition of wine making. They wanted their market on the spot, for they were too poor to wait for a twelvemonth for the price of their produce. Neither were they a people inclined to run any risk, and therefore their idea of a good market was a market where the price of everything was fixed, where a man could reckon to a stiver what his wine would bring before it left his farm. The freedom of selling in India was thus no inducement to them to increase their vineyards.'

This is altogether too sweeping a statement, and does not take into account the practical difficulties under which the budding winegrowers laboured. If the Company had had such bad luck with the shipments of its own wine, it could hardly be possible for the farmers, who had still greater stumbling blocks to climb over, to ship their produce without such a loss as they could ill afford to contemplate. The obvious thing was for the Company to buy their surplus at a fair price and use it for such purposes as it was suitable for. Probably some of the wines were superior to those made at Rustenburg, and a proper blend, such as the farmers could not themselves undertake, might have produced an article that would have found a ready sale overseas.

That was the opinion of the Council in India, which in 1676 sent out a certain Hannes Koekenberg, who was reputed to have had considerable experience in Alsace in the blending of wines. A proper wine press was also imported, and the newly arrived expert was stationed at Rustenburg. The petition of the winegrowers to be allowed to sell their wine to whoever wanted to buy it, but that a proper tax should be levied upon it, was referred to the directors. In 1677 the lease of the garden and vineyard at Rustenburg was renewed to the old tenant at 3 000 Cape guilders a year, but the tenant was permitted to pay the whole rent in wine at 20 riksdaalers the half-aum, and to sell the wine by wholesale or retail at a fixed rate. He was also granted an exclusive privilege to deal in spirits, and to make brandy, for which purpose the Company would provide him with a still upon payment. The Company also undertook to provide suitable casks for the winegrowers, and commissioned the cooper, Adriansen, to make a sufficiency of 'leggers, aums and half-aums.' Whether these concessions had anything to do with the newly arrived expert or were merely granted upon instructions from the Council of India, there is no doubt that they gave encouragement to the winegrowers. In 1678 part of the surplus vintage was distilled; the resultant brandy was not of good quality, but that was to be expected for its makers had as little knowledge of the technique of distilling as the first settlers had of winemaking. A year later the privilege of selling wines and spirits within the limits of Table Valley was put up for sale by public auction, and in the same year the Company, on instructions from the Council of India, decided to buy wine at 80 riksdaalers a leaguer from individual winegrowers, such wine to be shipped experimentally to Ceylon and Mauritius. The next year the wine expert left. He had apparently farmed a vineyard in partnership with a certain Hans Troost, who was allowed to take over his share of the common vineyard and indebtedness.

The settlement was now expanding. On the Peninsula itself there were 87 farmers, with 55 women, 117 children, 30 European assistants or paid servants, and 191 slaves. Their living they made out of the soil and out of trading, and there can be no doubt that trading, legitimate and unlawful, was much more profitable to them than farming. Their canteens were retail shops, for which they bought the liquor at the Company's magazine, according to a fixed tariff that allowed them a fair profit. Some of them, like Cloete, Botma, Bezuidenhout and Rosendaal, who before they entered the Company's service had had some experience of farming, had flourished, farming 'forwards' as their vernacular has it, while most of the others, who lacked both their knowledge and their application, had failed. The new colonists who entered the settlement were, in general, men of a different class: they were free emigrants from Europe or old servants of the Company who had a sense of responsibility. From these newcomers much more was to be expected than from the first settlers. They probably had no illusions about what awaited them on arrival at their new home, for the Company's officials in Amsterdam made it perfectly clear to all colonists that their future depended entirely upon whatever decisions the local commander might make. They swore allegiance to the Company and promised to obey its numerous and often tyrannical rules and regulations, and if, on arrival or after a few months' experience, they found that these prohibitions made profitable farming almost impossible, they had no one to blame but themselves, for they had been properly forewarned. It was deplorable, from their point of view, that the commanders had shown so little of the fatherly interest in the free burghers that Commander Van Riebeeck had displayed, for each of his successors had been a cold and indifferent official of the Company, none with the slightest intention to share in their interests or even to encourage their hopes.

Now they were to get a new commander who, while he was no less bureaucratic and official-minded than his immediate predecessors, was, like the founder, a man of some culture, with a great fondness for agriculture and with ample means to indulge his taste.

He was Simon van der Stel, the son of Adriaan van der Stel, of Amsterdam, who had been commander of the Mauritius Settlement where his son had been born. The new commander had been educated in Holland, where his family had much influence, which made his promotion in the Company's service unusually rapid, for when he assumed command at the Cape he was barely forty years old. He left his wife, for some reason that has not been disclosed, with her family at Amsterdam when he came out, but brought with him his four sons, one of whom was to succeed him in his commandership when he retired.

Van der Stel was a small, dark, dapper, dignified official, a gentleman whose courtesy and charm, tactfulness and friendliness in private were only surpassed by his stiffness and protocol affinities in public. He was as busily energetic as an emmet in his official capacity, and as cheerfully indolent as a grasshopper when at home. His inherent faults were a tedious prolixity in despatch writing (which the Company, very likely, deemed a virtue) and an opinionative fussiness that probably earned him the hearty dislike of his subordinates. His compensatory good qualities were his love of the beautiful, a naturally kindly disposition and, on occasion, a shrewd common sense tempered by an all-too-complacent reliance upon the goodness of Providence. He loved good wine, good food, good furniture and good company. If he stood too often upon his dignity and had more than his fair share of family pride, and if, too, he was altogether too fond of the money that makes it possible for a man to enjoy good things, let us charitably overlook the matter in grateful remembrance of the fact that he gave South Africa its first great wine.

He assumed office with much pomp and ceremony on 12 October 1679, and lost no time in visiting all parts of his little dominion. Among the servants of the Company who came out with him was one Jean Marieau, who had knowledge, from personal experience in the south of France, of winemaking and wine-blending, and it is probable that to this expert must be ascribed the credit of having later on prepared for the commander's table a wine that excelled all wines hitherto produced in the settlement. We know little about him; his name appears once or twice, but beyond that the records are silent. It is permissible, however, to fancy that his help and skill enabled the commander to improve both his vineyard and his wine.

Van der Stel went beyond the limits of the settlement and found the well-wooded valley beyond the Kromme River to his liking. He called it Stellenbosch and settled some of the small farmers from beyond Wynberg there, fixing at the same time a site for a Company's outpost at the foot of the Hottentots Holland Mountains. He did not like the way in which the farmers neglected wheat-growing to devote their energies to winemaking, which had now become quite profitable as the Company bought most of the vintage that they could not dispose of by retail sale. He therefore resolved:

> 'On account of the vine flourishing here so well, many persons are inclined to neglect other farming and to plant large vineyards. It is therefore resolved that henceforth every person who shall plant a morgen of vines shall be bound to cultivate six morgen with other crops, and so in proportion, that the object of the Company may not be defeated.'

Later on, when wine farmers were 'selling their wine at a price far in excess of that fixed by the Council,' a *plakaat* was issued forbidding wine farmers to sell wine to anyone without the written permission of the authorities and penalties for infringement were fixed.

Still later, when he had had ample proof of the slovenly manner in which the grapes were gathered, pressed, fermented and stored, he induced the Council to pass the following resolution:

> '26 June 1686. Taking into consideration that by the untimely cutting and pressing of the grapes the Cape wines are sour, biting and unpleasant to the taste, and that experience has shown that these wines can be notably improved if the grapes are allowed to ripen, it is resolved that the inhabitants shall in future not be at liberty to press any wine before the vineyards have been visited by a committee and pronounced by the commander to be of the requisite maturity. A penalty of 60 riksdaalers is to be enforced for infringing this regulation.'

At this time the Company's vineyard at Rustenburg had 100 000 bearing vines, while the farmers between them owned a total of some 303 000 vines. The settlement now consisted of 254 men, 88 wives and widows, 231 children, 39 paid assistants and 310 slaves. The commander busied himself with the Company's farm and garden, but he much wanted a farm where he could experiment with winemaking, for like the founder he was keenly interested in agriculture. Time and again the Company had insisted that its officials should not engage in private trading or farming, but Van der Stel had sufficient influence to get the directors to waive this rule in his favour. There was a large tract of land next to the last farm from which the free burghers had removed to occupy a new farm at Stellenbosch, and this was derelict. It was granted to the commander in 1685, 891 morgen, 380 roods and 28 square feet in extent. He took possession of it in the same year and named it *Constantia*. There is no truth in the story that he called it that in honour of his wife. He never saw her again after he bade her goodbye on leaving Holland, and although the name might have had an ironical implication it is much more likely that it was chosen for some other reason. Whatever that reason may have been, the name was to become famous among wine lovers.

Chapter 3

The First Constantia

Simon van der Stel lost no time in improving the large farm that he had obtained. He planted many trees, mostly oaks, for windbreaks, for decoration and for wood. He built roomy quarters for his many slaves and a commodious dwelling house for himself and his family. He laid out a choice garden and a larger vineyard than at that time had been established elsewhere in the settlement and stocked it with nearly 100 000 vines. Most of these were rooted cuttings that he had obtained from the Company's nursery gardens at Cape Town and at *Rustenburg*, but he probably bought others from Rosendaal at *Bosheuvel* and odd lots from the free farmers when they pruned their vines. He also raised vines from seed that came to him from the East and from the Canaries. His main plantations were of Muscadel, Green Grape, French White Grape and that beautiful vine, Pontac, whose leaves turn to an early autumn tint when all its neighbours in the vineyard are yet green, and whose grapes are among the few that yield a naturally red juice. It is quite likely that he also planted Shiraz, Aramon, Pinot and Cabernet, though we have no definite proof of this.

From this vineyard, in due course, he gathered his harvest of grapes, which at first must have been comparatively small. In the planting, pruning, manuring and general cultivation of his stocks, he had the expert help of the Company's gardeners, one of whom, Oldenland, was a well-read and travelled man who had some knowledge of botany. The owner's own knowledge of viticulture was good enough to prevent him from making some of the mistakes that he had observed among the other vine growers in the Colony. He took care to give his vines space and air, and some of them at least he trained on low palings. His vineyard was kept scrupulously weeded and he tended it according to the rigid rules laid down in the *Gardener's Manual* that gave precise directions when the vines were to be tilled, manured and watered. There was ample labour, for he not only had his own property in man but he could make use of the Company's slaves, although strictly speaking he was supposed to indent for those and to debit himself in the Company's books with their working time. In practice, however, this supposition was generally overlooked and the higher officials made use of 'Company's labour' for their own purposes when it suited them, knowing that the most they would be exposed to would be a mere reprimand from the Lords Seventeen. In Van der Stel's case, moreover, it may be assumed that he had discussed the matter with the Secretary before he left Europe, and that he had been assured that he could use such labour where and when the immediate interests of the Company were not affected. An assurance of this kind had been given more than once to commanders and governors in Java, who had been allowed to use the Company's slaves, and sometimes even the Company's sailors, to beautify their tenements and cultivate their gardens. It is also probable that similar permission was granted him to make use of the Company's cooperage, press and implements. He reported most of his doings to the Council in India, and at no time did the authorities ever hint that he was going beyond the limits that they had set for their higher officials. On the contrary, although they sometimes sharply differed from him in opinion as to what was best for their interests in other matters, in this they appear to have been gratified by his pioneering zeal. They raised his salary and as a final mark of their approbation they gave him the rank of Governor in 1691 and appointed him an honorary member of the Council in India.

His energy was remarkable. He travelled to the unknown parts beyond the limits of the settlement. He devoted much care and attention to the Company's garden, that under his fostering supervision became the foremost botanical garden south of the equator until the far larger and more favourably situated rival at *Buitenzorg*, under the able management of Teysman, surpassed it. But he found time enough to attend to his new estate, although he lived in town and spent much of his leisure in entertaining visitors at the new guesthouse that he had built on the spot where now the Houses of Parliament stand. He superintended the cutting and pressing of his grapes, introducing the methods of wine-making that he had seen in the south of France or in Germany, and the results amply repaid his unwearied energy and attention. His grapes were cut when they were fully ripe, thus assuring in the must a high sugar and a low acid content; they were carefully brushed to free them from earth and dirt and were pressed after removal of all stalks. This careful handling was in strong contrast to the haphazard manner in which other winegrowers dealt with their grape crops. It is not surprising, therefore, that the 'Governor's wine' rapidly won a reputation for itself — a reputation that in due time would travel far beyond the limits of the settlement and win for it the first mark of international fame that South Africa obtained.

There can be no manner of doubt that Van der Stel made several and different kinds of wine. From the Green Grapes and White French, and from the Hanepoot and Pontac, he probably made a thin, dry wine of low alcoholic strength that could be sold to the ships, given to the slaves — who by that time had become accustomed to their daily ration of a locally made refreshing liquor that was far cheaper and less intoxicating than the arrack that they had previously been allowed on occasion — or exported. It was this wine that when sent to Batavia was found to be 'no better than some previous samples we have had from Cabo.' From the Pinot and Hermitage he probably made a good beverage wine of higher quality that he reserved for his own use. But those were the days in which the favourite wines were of the type now known as 'liqueur wine' and in Holland, as also in England, those who could afford it drank the syrupy, bland and beautifully aromatic

Frontignac or Lunel of which James the First was so fond. This type was considered to be the finest and best, and it was this type, therefore, that Van der Stel set himself to produce.

He succeeded beyond his expectations, for 'Constantia', the sweet red and white wine that he made on his private estate, was for nearly 200 years regarded as one of the most outstanding wines of the world. It is assumed, by competent oenologists like the late Drs Hahn and Perold, that it was originally made from White and Red Muscadel grapes, blended, very skilfully, with a small quantity of Frontignac. This white variety, probably a pure White Muscadel and Green Grape wine, was oily and smooth, with a strong Muscat *bouquet*, but lacked the suavity and grace of the red. The latter, that in time became a rich topaz colour, was a magnificent liqueur wine; bland aromatic, less pungently scented, a harmoniously soft wine, full of individuality and character. It must have been known and appreciated some years before we find the first mention of its name. Murray's large dictionary suggests that the name was first used in 1797 in Holcroft's edition of *Stolberg's Travels*, but long before that Constantia wine had already obtained a worldwide reputation. In the archives at Batavia it is mentioned as early as 1692 in a note that reads: 'The Constantia wine of the Honourable Governor of the Cape of Good Hope . . . in the small cask . . . and the three larger casks containing the Company's wine'. A little later we find a note stating that 'the Constantia wine is of a far higher quality than any yet sent out, but it is manifestly procurable in small quantity only'. After 1720 there are frequent references to Constantia wine, but by that time the vineyard was in other hands and it could no longer be regarded as Van der Stel's wine.

Its original maker resigned his gubernatorial responsibilities in February 1699, and retired to his farm where he lived a dignified, easy life. He was succeeded by his son, the notorious Willem Adriaan, who distinguished himself more by his trouble than by his winemaking. Simon, who kept himself out of the quarrels and disputes in which his sons foundered, died in 1712, respected and to some extent beloved by those who had known him. There is some doubt about the conditions under which he died, for apparently his death did not take place at his farm, but in the house of one of his friends. Before his retirement he had extended his domains to include practically all the land lying beyond *Constantia*, and was not only a large winegrower but farmed wheat and cattle on an equally large scale. At his death his estates were sold by auction, and the original farm *Constantia* was cut up into two separate farms, while the rest of his estate was also subdivided.

Before that date we have singularly little information about *Constantia*. What we have derives from travellers and visitors whose accounts show that they never were privileged to inspect the Governor's vineyards and cellars, and who therefore gathered their data from casual intercourse with the residents. Valentyn does not appear to have had first-hand knowledge of Constantia wine. Chaplain the Reverend J Ovington, in his voyage to Suratt in 1696, wrote as follows:

'Their very Wines, in which they will suddenly increase to a great Plenty and Variety, are now able to supply their Ships and to furnish the Indies with some quantity, where they sell it by the Bottle at a Roupie. It is coloured like Rhenish and therein they pass it under that spacious Name in India, but the Taste of it is much harder and less palatable; its Operations are more searching, and the strength of it is more intoxicating and offensive to the Brain ... The Impositions which are laid upon Wine and other Liquors that are sold by Retail seem almost incredible, especially when the small number of People that are presumed to drink them is considered. For in the Town of the Cape are not reckoned above 500 Inhabitants, besides those that are brought in Ships and come out of the Country; and yet the annual impost upon Europe Beer and Wine is four thousand one hundred; and Brandy, Arak and Distill'd Waters pay twenty Thousand Gilders Yearly to the Governor of the place for a Licence to sell them. All which taxes summed together make up above twenty-eight Thousand Gilders Yearly, which, according to our Accounts, raise between two and three thousand Pounds, for the liberty of selling Liquors by Retail. This exorbitant Fine upon the Tavern and Tipling Houses makes them exact extravagant Rates from the Guests that drink the Liquor, who are indeed the people that pay it. For he that resolves to drink Brandy must pay at the rate of ten Shillings a Bottle for it, and the Cape Wine, which in Cask is sold for less than six Pence a Quart, is in the Tavern half a Crown, and such proportionately are the excessive Prices of the rest. A tame submission is the only Remedy for these Impositions, from which there is no Appeal or Relief, which is apt to imbitter the Lives of the People, nor can any be very happy who are subject to the Tyranny of a Government that is under no Restraint. The Arbitrary Proceedings of the Dutch Commissaries in India have been much resented, and have likewise raised loud Complaints against them by the injur'd Factors, but have met with very little redress ... The present Governor, Min Heer Simon Vanderstel, who lives with his Council, is a very kind and knowing Person, is maintained in Grandeur and lives Honourably. His publick Table wants no Plenty, either of European or African Wines or Asian Liquors; and whatever the Land or Water or Air affords in that place is served up in his bountiful Entertainments. To Complete the Magnificence of which sumptuous Fare, all the Dishes and Plates upon the Board are made of massy Silver, and before the departure of their Fleets, the Dutch Commanders are all invited to a publick Repast, where they drink and revel, bouze and break Glasses, what they please; for these Frolicks are the very life of a Skipper, and the Governor, by indulging these wild, licentious Humours, ingratiates with them more than by anything else he could devise.'

Chaplain Daniel Beckman, who visited the Cape a few years later, has merely a short note on its wines:

'They have lately improved their Vineyards, so they have plenty of White and Red Muscadello Wine, and another pleasant, though small, White Wine. The Muscadello is sold for from 20 to 24 pounds the leaguer, which contains 160 gallons, and the others at 10 to 12 pounds.'

Captain William Dampier, who probably assisted at one of those wild orgies at Government House of which the chaplain wrote, praised the table grapes which he thought the best fruit at the Cape:

'The country is of late so well stocked with Vineyards that they made abundance of Wine of which they have enough and to spare, and do sell great quantities to Ships that touch here. This Wine is like a French High Country White wine, but of a pale yellowish colour; it is sweet, very pleasant and strong ... Notwithstanding the great plenty of Wine, the extraordinary high Taxes which the Company lays on Liquor makes it very dear, and you can buy none but at the Tavern, except it be by stealth. There are but three Houses in the Town that sell strong Liquor, one of which is this Wine House or Tavern; there they sell only Wine; another sells Beer and Muur; and the third sells Brandy and Tobacco, all extraordinary dear. A Flask of Wine which holds three Quarts will cost 18 Stivers, for so much I paid for it, but it was privately at an unlicensed House, and the Person that sold it would have been ruined had it been known.'

I have already said that we have very little authentic information about the original *Constantia*. We know that the house in which the retired Governor lived was completed in 1692 and that it was later on broken down and rebuilt, probably by Thibault assisted by Anreith, nearly a hundred years later. It was this gabled, newer house that perished in the fire on 19 December 1925, was afterwards rebuilt, and is now one of our historical monuments. But the *Constantia* Manor House that the visitor admires today is certainly not similar to the house that Van der Stel lived in. That building was drawn by Van der Heydt in 1714, shortly after the original proprietor's death, when *Constantia* farm had already been cut up into *Constantia*, *Little Constantia* and *Bergvliet*. *Constantia* itself had a chequered history. Its various owners did not treat it with the respect that it deserved as the first great farm in South Africa, and in 1759 it was bought for a beggarly 3 000 guineas by one Jacob van der Spuy, who seventeen years later sold it, at a small profit, to Jean Serrurier. Neither of these seems to have improved its vineyards, nor enhanced the reputation of its wines, but in 1778 the place passed into the hands of Hendrik Cloete, who was destined to make it one of the show farms of the Peninsula. Its buildings were then in ruin; its vineyards were weed-grown and rank, and much of it was being used for grazing. In a later chapter the revolutionary improvements that Cloete made will be described and the history of the famous *Constantia* wine continued.

Perhaps it is this want of accurate knowledge that has crystallised round *Constantia* so much that is legendary and untrue, so much that is fantastic and absurd. The authority of Bernardin de Saint Pierre, who visited the Cape in 1771, started the story that the farm had been named after 'Madame Constantia, daughter of a Governor of the Cape'. Saint Pierre was a bright, imaginative young man, whose local descriptions are veneered with a specious plausibility, but whose testimony is generally inaccurate and worthless. Unpublished references to *Constantia*, dating back to the time when Simon was still alive, are rare, although they do occur in private letters among family records that I have been privileged to read. In the early years of the nineteenth century they abound, for Constantia wine was then attracting much attention and its excellences were extolled in military and literary circles.

It is highly improbable that the inchoate vineyard of Van der Stel yielded its best before 1698, a vintage year that was said to have been very good, or that his true 'Constantia wine' was exported much before 1702. In that year it was certainly known, under its own name, both in Amsterdam and at Batavia. It was sent out in small casks that were emptied on arrival and returned to the farm. Export in bottle was begun much later, and there is no evidence that any particular kind of bottle, different from that in which European wine was imported into the settlement, was used at that time. The wine that was exported was undoubtedly of a very high quality, so individual and characteristic that connoisseurs at once recognised that it was altogether different from the liqueur wines of the South of France, the Canaries, Italy or the Levant. That fact should never be forgotten by winegrowers in South Africa. Our wines, if they are to hold their own in competition with other wines on the world's markets, should have their own individual characteristics and excellence; they should not be passable imitations of wines already on the market from other wine-growing countries, but local wines of outstandingly high quality, possessing merits of their own that entitle them to the respect of all unprejudiced wine lovers. Simon van der Stel, the first who in this country realised that truth and tried to shape his wine policy in accordance with it, succeeded in producing one wine, at least, whose fame, even if it has outlived the wine itself, should serve as an inspiration to all winegrowers in this country.

There is no man living today who has drunk Van der Stel's original Constantia, and to tell the truth we possess no reliable information regarding its composition. The nearest to the facts that we can attain is the record of the Constantias exported after the Cape passed into the possession of the British, when Lord Macartney, in 1798, bought a cask of it from Mr Cloete of *Groot Constantia* at the rate of £52 10s for the leaguer. It was wine of this quality that was later on exported under the name of 'Constantia wine', but most of the wine labelled as 'Constantia' and sold under that name, even by reputable wine merchants in Europe, was most certainly not produced at *Constantia* and was merely an imitation of the famous 'Governor's wine'. What reached Europe before 1840 was consigned to private persons and very little of it could have been available for the trade. The Constantia that was analysed, somewhere in the early twenties of the past century, by Dr Prout as a wine with a specific gravity of 1.0810, with an alcoholic content of 13.42 volume per cent, equivalent to approximately 23.4 degrees proof spirit, must have been quite a different wine from the later Constantias that were exported after 1840, with a much higher alcoholic content. The late Dr Perold, who has tasted some of the 'old Constantia wine' still to be found in some famous Continental cellars, was always of opinion that it was by no means the same as the wine that had been analysed by Prout. His own experiments, conducted over many years, inclined him to the belief that a wine could be made from overripe Steen grapes that closely resembled the original Constantia, both as regards its low alcoholic strength and its characteristic aroma and savour. His experiments in this connection were unfortunately interrupted by his premature death.

In the circumstances all that we can truthfully aver is that the original Constantia was a magnificent, pre-oidium, liqueur wine, unique in its low alcoholic strength for such a full-bodied wine, exceedingly aromatic with a rich, sparkling colour and with a delicious flavour. Its low acidity probably prevented it from having much of a bouquet; no description at least makes mention of that feature. It improved with age, as all such full-bodied wines do, but lost something of its colour, becoming lighter but throwing no crust. It is much to be regretted that no adequate description or analysis of it has been handed down to us, and that for all our knowledge of it we have to depend on what was known about the Constantia exported long after the Governor's death. There is, however, no reason why its counterpart should not again be produced in South Africa when winegrowers realise the importance of making a distinguished liqueur wine that in time can establish for itself the same reputation that our first Governor's wine had.

Note to Chapter 3

Simon van der Stel's father was a cooper by trade, who afterwards rose to high rank in the Company's service and was murdered in Ceylon.

In the portentous instructions to Van der Stel, dictated by Commissioner Van Rheede in 1686, a small part is devoted to the wine industry. The Commissioner was of opinion that there was 'every reason to anticipate that we can get more, and better, wine'. 'At present,' he comments, 'only about twelve morgen are planted with vines', which evidently refers to the Company's vineyards, from which he estimates that after four years 144 leaguers would be obtained yearly. But it is evident that the Commissioner thought the wine industry was merely a side issue; the main point was that the settlement should grow sufficient grain, wheat, barley, maize and rice, to make it self-supporting and rid the Company of the expense of importing foodstuffs for its now rapidly increasing population.

Chapter 4

Development in the Eighteenth Century

After Willem Adriaan van der Stel became Governor, the hitherto fairly placid routine of the settlement at the Cape changed in a manner that has provided students of its history with interesting material for discussion. No good purpose would be served by joining in the debate about the rights and wrongs of the matter. The case of Willem Adriaan is no longer a matter of conjecture. Theal, in the first place, and Professor Fouché, in his appendix to the *Diary of Adam Tas*, have so utterly demolished the arguments in favour of the view that he was a good-natured, much-maligned man that few will today give him even the benefit of the doubt. He was an oppressive, tyrannical rascal, bilking the Company, bullying the free burghers on their pelting farms and trying, until the directors dismissed him, to establish the first great vested interest at the Cape. His father had furnished him with a tedious prosy memorandum, wherein had been pointed out that wheat growing was being neglected by the free inhabitants who were now all trying to become winegrowers. They had not made much of a success of the business, for with a few exceptions the wines produced were of poor quality, and there was already some over-production for which no market could be found. The new immigrants, the French refugees, had, contrary to what is generally believed, done very little to improve the industry. Among them, so far as can be gathered from the records, there were barely three who had any practical experience of winegrowing, and one alone who could be said to know anything about winemaking. This amateur expert was Isaac Tallifer or Taillefer, of Thierry, who came from Middelburg in 1688 with his wife and children in the Company's ship *Oosterlanda*, and who, after a few years' tilling of his glebe, made excellent wine, reputed to be the second best in the Colony.

The new Governor had his own farm, comprising many hundred morgen, near the foot of the Stellenbosch mountains, which he called *Vergelegen*. No expense, either on his or the Company's part, was spared to make it a most imposing undertaking. The vineyard boasted almost as many vines as the rest of the Colony possessed; though there are differences in the estimates made when the value of the estate had to be assessed, we may take it that there were approximately 250 000 bearing vines. Yet the wine that was made here does not seem to have been of a high quality, although probably many more kinds were produced, for we hear of Stein, Hermitage and Madeira wine, exported by the Governor 'from his own demesne' to Batavia. The evidence shows that the Governor attempted to obtain a monopoly in at least the export wine trade, and among the complaints that were made, and fully proved to the satisfaction of the Lords Seventeen, was the accusation that he was trying to establish a ring, buying through nominees and cornering the retail trade. He paid no attention to the good advice contained not only in his father's memorandum but also in the long and carefully detailed report compiled by Cornelis Joan Simonsz, who had strongly urged that the free burghers should not be ground down by unnecessary and vexatious restrictions, that the Company's officials should not be allowed to compete with them in trade or farming, and that minor officials should be permitted to have freehold plots for their own domestic use.

In the circumstances the agitation on the part of the colonists against the Governor's harsh and grasping administration was hardly surprising. The Company took a commonsense view of the matter, recalled the Governor and made some trifling concessions. The fine estate at *Vergelegen* was cut up, the manor house broken down, and thereafter no high official of the Company, still drawing a salary, engaged in private farming on a large scale.

From this time, too, we have far more accurate details about viticulture at the Cape. The settlement had been growing steadily in population and importance. It was visited by many strangers, some of whom remained for several months as temporary residents and left us an account of the conditions they found there. The documentary evidence in the archives at Cape Town, Batavia and The Hague now also supply us with much further information from which it is possible to sketch the development of the wine industry in the eighteenth century. For the most detailed accounts of that development we are indebted first to Otto Mentzel, who dealt with the earlier part of the century, and secondly to Captain Robert Percival, whose description applies to its last years and the early period of British occupation.

Otto Mentzel arrived at the Cape as an *Adelborst* or midshipman in the Company's service in 1732 at the age of twenty-three, and served first as a tally-clerk and later as a tutor in Captain Alleman's family. He was a well-educated young man and had ample leisure and opportunity during his ten years' sojourn here to become well acquainted with local conditions and customs. After his return to Europe in 1741 he obtained some other employment, and in 1781 published a biography of his protector, Robert Alleman, that gives much interesting information about contemporary events. Six years later appeared his *Beschreibung des Vorgebirges der Guten Hoffnung* in which he incorporated much of what had already been printed by others, but also his own comments and criticism together with much original matter that he had himself accumulated. An excellent translation of his book has been published by the Van Riebeeck Society, with an instructive introduction and explanatory footnotes by Professor Mandelbrote of the University of Cape Town.

The tenth chapter of that book is devoted to viticulture at the Cape, but throughout the work there are many interesting references to wine farming. He mentions that the free farmers treat their labourers to a wine ration; describes the Company's gardens at Rondebosch and Newlands; and gives much information, most of it accurate, about the wine districts. The wine made in the Tygerberg area he found:

> 'The worst of all the wines ... only palatable if mixed with other mellower wines. It does improve with age, but becomes very harsh and heady so that when it is old and settled it is also gross and strong, causing a heavy hangover. Two kinds of it are stocked: old dry wine and new sweet wine; the old wine mostly from Tygerberg, and the sweet from grapes grown around the Salt River. ... Most of the ordinary Cape wines have the drawback that they make those who become drunk on it bilious, for which reason the drinkers are all too soon incited to quarrel and fight. In the respectable wine houses the proprietors generally take pains to get wine from grapes grown in Hottentots Holland, around Stellenbosch, Salt River, Roode Zand, Zwart Land, Drakenstein and Fransche Hoek.'

His account of Constantia contains nothing new, except a criticism of a second-hand statement with reference to 'a certain Kluthe (*sic*) now the owner of one of the *Constantia* vineyards.'

> 'The said Kluthe prides himself on corresponding with several European potentates because of his trade in wine with them, but this may be just the common African method of boasting. ... I would not dispute that when ships touch there they may order some wine from him, and on their return take it to their rulers, but that would always have to be done with the consent of the Company or of the Governor. ... A third of all the wine that is made at *Constantia* has to be delivered to the Company at a fixed price, and as the Company makes an almost incredible profit it may well be that it also buys the remainder at the yearly market value, makes a gift of a portion to European Courts and sells the remainder at great profit at public sales. The little that is sold by the owners per bottle to friends returning from India is of no consequence, for the inhabitants of the Cape do not think much of it because it is too racy for their taste. The cost is also too great for them, as they have to pay two guilders for a flask containing little more than two champagne bottles. ... The wine sold in various parts of Europe under the name of Constantia wine or Vin du Cap is no other than the wine from Hottentots Holland, which bears the closest resemblance to the Constantia type. It may also at times be mixed with Madeira or De Palma wine, but that it should besides have been boiled, brewed or adulterated and treated in other ways is absolutely incredible, for its own body cannot be imitated as it shows an immediate effect on the faces of the drinkers and warms their blood in a noticeable but pleasant way. If the wine lacks this quality it disavows its fatherland and is no true African wine, least of all from *Constantia* and not even from Hottentots Holland.'

He instances the slanderous statements that have been made about the adulteration of Constantia wine, and regrets that many writers whose names he mentions have published information about conditions at the Cape that is not true, a regret that will probably be shared by many of us who know that the tendency to draw wrong conclusions from incomplete data is not confined to eighteenth-century writers on South Africa. The one author he had most in mind was the then celebrated Kolben, whose account of Cape wine and wine making is, however, of little interest. He does not mention Lequat, who in 1707 found Cape wine quite drinkable, and though he names Forster who accompanied Captain Cook and visited the Cape twice, he appears to tar him with the same brush that he uses for De la Caille, Taehard and Merklein. Forster, however, writing in 1777, has an interesting note on Cape wine which reads:

'The wines at the Cape are of the greatest variety possible. The best, which is made at Van der Spuy's plantation at *Constantia*, is spoken of in Europe more by report than from real knowledge. Thirty leaguers at the most are raised of this kind, and each leaguer sells for about £50 on the spot. The vines from which it is made were originally brought from Shiraz in Persia. Several other sorts grow in the neighbourhood of that plantation, which produce a sweet wine that generally passes for genuine Constantia in Europe. French plants of burgundy, Muscadel and Frontignac have likewise been tried, and have succeeded remarkably well, sometimes producing wines superior to those of the original soil. An excellent dry wine which has a slight agreeable tartness is generally drunk in the principal families and is made of Madeira vines transplanted to the Cape. Several low sorts, not entirely disagreeable, are raised in great plenty and sold at a very cheap rate, so that the sailors of the East India ships commonly indulge themselves very plentifully in them whenever they come here.'

Mentzel's own account of the wine industry obviously relates to conditions as he found them in 1732-41, and although he doubtless profited from what he had learned from published sources, it is clear that he depended mainly on his own observation. He starts by telling us how vineyards are laid out, and gives some interesting details about the difficulties winegrowers had to contend with. Vines could not be trained on stakes, for the southeasters were too strong. The small 'sucker' insects were a plague; they appeared before the buds burst and destroyed the bearing shoots; hand picking was the only way to deal with this pest. Then there were birds and dogs. The former could be kept away by scaring and — so the farmers averred — by cutting down trees in the vicinity of the vineyards; indeed, one of the excuses advanced for the lack of tree planting which Simon van der Stel had made compulsory was that trees encouraged the birds. The dogs, however, were a greater nuisance; they not only ate the grapes before these were quite ripe, but they wantonly tore bunches to pieces, apparently for the mere love of snapping at them. Slave boys were stationed in the vineyards to keep them away, and most vineyards were surrounded by a moat and a hedge or stone wall to keep them out. Mentzel describes the Hanepoot grape, which was his favourite eating grape, and the method of making it into raisins. With regard to the Muscadel he tells us:

'The red muscatel, of which delicious red wine is made at *Constantia*, is undoubtedly also the most pleasant to eat, but only a very good friend can get any of the grapes. The white is not pressed separately at *Constantia*, but together with other kinds. In other vineyards, however, white muscatel wine is made of this type alone, without being mixed with others, and makes a very pleasant, delicious and invigorating drink for those who have not made wine drinking a mere habit. Whether I have myself drunk genuine Muscat wine of Frontignan or Lunell I cannot say, but instead of the muscatel wines which are openly sold in Germany under this name I prefer the Cape wines. Besides the fine and really delicate Muscat flavour, it has this virtue that it does not make one as sleepy and intoxicated as those which are sold in the present-day (German) wine shops under the name of "Sack-muscat," from which those who have been intoxicated by it are dreadfully sick the next day.'

He agrees with the Abbé de la Caille that 'the inhabitants of the Cape do not yet know how to treat their wines properly', and goes on to describe winemaking as then carried out.

'When the grapes have been trodden and crushed with bare feet, they are left in this state in a vessel for four or five days without further treatment, so that the whole mixture may ferment for a while with the husks ... Then it is pressed out either with a press, or better still with a squeezer. He who possesses neither press nor squeezer has everything pressed out by hand, but obtains less wine and can use what remains in the husks for brandy only ... Two Muscat nuts are taken (according to whether the barrel is small or big), stuck on a slightly bent iron wire, set alight and hung over the bunghole of the barrel, the peg having been loosened in the bunghole to allow the Muscat nut a little air in which to burn. As soon as the nuts have burned out the wine is poured in and the barrel bunged tightly. Red wine, or rather the barrel in which it is contained, may not be muted, as this would remove the red colour of the wine. For this reason, too, the pure unadulterated red wines are the healthiest, and invalids are allowed by doctors to drink them. After a few days when the lees has drained off somewhat, the red wine is drawn into another barrel in which also two Muscat nuts have been burnt; this is repeated several times until the wine has become quite clear. Then another Muscat nut is burned over the wine and the barrel is tightly corked, and the wine left undisturbed for several weeks, after which it is sold or put into smaller casks for home use. At the Cape little red wine is drunk and I doubt if one leaguer of it is sold for every hundred leaguers of white wine. A boiled wine is made ... very sweet and delicious to drink. As it does not ferment properly it remains thick and retains all the crude stuff; it is therefore unhealthy.'

He then describes conditions in the vineyards during the wine season which, for the white wine, started 'at the end of February or the beginning of March.' From his account it is clear that while some wine farmers were careless and slovenly, others had already adopted the better methods that had been introduced by Van der Stel, Taillefer and the brothers De Villiers, who had been sent out as 'vignerons' by the Company early in the eighteenth century. There was no general use of a wine press; some of the farmers pressed by hand; most, however, trod the grapes in big vats, allowing the must to be contaminated and dirtied, not only from the earth adhering to the bunches but from oddments that got into the vats. One of these outside contaminants, much feared at the time, was a small spider that was said to give the wine poisonous properties, a superstition that probably originated from the death of a grape gatherer who happened to be bitten by the venomous *Lathrodectus* or Button spider that lurks in grain lands and vineyards. This superstition was evidently not unknown to Mentzel, for in his biography of his patron, Alleman, he tells (quite unbelievably and wholly from hearsay) how Governor Van Assenburg and two of his aides had been almost immediately killed by drinking at *Constantia* a bottle of wine that had been poisoned by a spider. As a matter of fact, although it was suspected at the time that Van Assenberg's death might have been the result of slow poisoning, it occurred several months after he took to his bed and his illness does not seem to have had the slightest connection with *Constantia*.

Mentzel asserts that barrels were very scarce and expensive; those sent to Batavia did not come back (this was certainly not true; the small casks in which Van der Stel's wine arrived at Batavia were all sent back, and there is ample testimony that the Indian authorities tried their best to meet the wants of the Cape wine farmers). The farmers used mainly the teak wood arrack casks, but white wine turned a nasty reddish-brown colour in them. There is reason to believe, however, that most of the imported arrack came in earthenware jars, and that the *djati*-wood casks which Mentzel refers to were specially made for wine farmers. He narrates in detail the various steps taken to ferment the white wine musts and to sulphur the casks and has an interesting note on 'flat wine'. This was partly fermented wine, drawn off within twenty-four hours after fermentation had started, and then strongly sulphured. 'But as not everyone can successfully make such a flat wine,' he continues naïvely, 'I am inclined to believe that there is yet another trick to it, which I did not try to find out as it would have been of no use to me. Such wine cannot be drunk on account of its sickening sweetness. It is, however, bought at a much higher price for sweetening the sour wines.' He goes on to say:

> 'Not all Cape wines are suitable for maturing. What is not good wine by nature and quality (or, as I think, has not been properly prepared) is not improved by long seasoning, but only becomes sharp and prickly, as

they say here. Really good, well-prepared and well-cellared Cape wines improve with age; only the vessels in which to store them are lacking. All the same I have seen on the farms of prosperous wine farmers vats so large that they held eight ordinary leaguers, that is forty-eight Berlin pails, which were kept merely for seasoning the wine. A farmer called Van der Liet, who lived about ten to twelve hours from the Town, had a very large one made of Batavian teak which held still more.'

The muted, drawn off and settled wine, he tells us, was allowed to remain undisturbed for a few weeks and then fined with isinglass; if it cannot be clarified by the isinglass, 'well-washed fine sand, or well-scraped chalk and the ash of vine branches are put into it'. It is highly improbable that this was the method generally used for fining wines, for blood was the most common and the cheapest fining material and was already extensively used by all farmers. Eggs were used by Van der Stel, who also imported much isinglass, but both these methods were expensive and for the cheaper local wines blood was certainly the most popular fining material, although Mentzel does not even mention it.

He concludes:

'Every sensible man will surely presume that for good winemaking something more is necessary than what has been described. However, this is how it is done, and if one speaks about it and wonders if the wine does not need further treatment the answer always is: "I should like to know what else could be done with it?" Truly, friend, did you not know better you would tackle the matter differently. Many colonists do indeed know the secret of making good wine and make wines that stand the test and grow mellower with age, but they are not such fools as to give away their secret and make good wines more common. . . . In the less warm mountainous regions the grapes are seldom ripened properly, but the farmers make as much profit as though their wine is equal to that made in the Tygerberg. For they make vinegar of it which they can sell at a like price in the Town, where an unbelievable quantity is consumed.'

On the whole Mentzel's opinion can be accepted as he knew something about wine and winemaking, and was a much better judge of the conditions under which wine was made than either Kolben or De la Caille. His account, as I have already said, applies to the first half of the eighteenth century, although it was published nearly thirty-six years after he had left the country. It contains, however, much less information than we have a right to expect from so inquisitive and well informed a chronicler. Little, for instance, is said about the sweet wines, nor is any light thrown upon the manner in which the first sweet white wines were made. The free farmers stated in their *Contra Deductio* that the credit of first preparing such wines must be ascribed to one of them, Paul Selyn, who is mentioned in Tas's *Diary*; they use the words 'who made the first sweet wine at Cabo'. There is no evidence to support this claim and it is much more likely that Van der Stel, or one of his experts, made the first sweet wine. Before that time musts were allowed to ferment fully, with the result that a thin, dry wine was produced; apparently the only way to interrupt the fermentation was to boil the must, and the use of alcohol to 'fortify' the wine and prevent further fermentation was, if not quite unknown at the Cape, at least not general. All that may be said to have changed after 1702 when Van der Stel's superior sweet wines were being made.

From 1689 the Company had bought wine from the free farmers at £5 a leaguer for use on its ships. The sailors' wine ration was prescribed by the Company's rules and its strict enforcement, now that wine was available at the Cape, prevented much scurvy and sickness on board. Cape wine was used, even in India, as a wine ration for slaves, and its usefulness for that purpose was never questioned. Undoubtedly our 'tot-system' of today dates from that time, when it was recognised that a ration of good wine is one of the healthiest and most valuable food adjuncts that can be given to a labourer.

In 1715 the first excise was levied, at a rate of 4s 2d on every leaguer of wine pressed. There had been absolutely no wine tax on the farmers before then and this small imposition was not resented by them. But from this time onwards we meet with proclamations, legislation, regulations, restrictions and prohibitions that became increasingly vexatious, absurd and calculated to make South Africa a spirit-drinking country where drunkenness is far more frequent than in any other wine-producing country where such restrictions do not exist and where every citizen, irrespective of colour, can obtain pure natural wine whenever he wants to drink it. The incalculable harm that such restrictive legislation has done to the community, and more especially the non-European part of it, will be discussed later.

In fairness to the Company, that with all its Calvinistic hypocrisy was not so foolish as to imagine that a community could be made sober by legislation, it must be said that the first taxes on wine were imposed purely for revenue purposes, just as the licensing system had been introduced to help in financing the settlement. In 1719 the Company agreed to pay £6 a leaguer for wine for the fleet, and £8 a leaguer for old wine to be used in the hospital, an encouraging sign that it was alive to the importance of improving the quality of the wines. From Amsterdam the directors wrote asking that samples of Cape wine should be sent over in larger casks as the consignment that had arrived in small half-aums turned out sour. In 1772 the consignment sent to Middelburg was declared to be quite poor in quality, and another lot, sent out later in bottles, was also condemned. There is some reason to suspect that private meddling, to use a mild word, was responsible for these failures. It was in the interests of the wine farmers to have a local market, and they probably did not like to see the Company buy up their wines at a set price and resell them in Europe at a profit when they were not permitted to do the same. Only in 1789 did the directors give their consent to colonists to export wine to Holland and then only on the condition that it was sent by their own return fleet and at a freight charge that exceeded £2 a leaguer. Exportation to Batavia and to Ceylon averaged several hundred leaguers per year, and the majority of wines sent to the East were reported to be excellent, of good keeping quality, and well liked by the recipients. This export reached its peak in 1751-54, but after that year dropped alarmingly, simply because the restrictions on the sale of wine had become increasingly severe. In 1754 a duty of 32s per leaguer on wine supplied to foreign ships was proposed, but on behalf of the winegrowers the Governor objected so strongly that the directors did not press the matter. Similarly when they suggested that the wine farmers should distil their surplus wine there was no ready response, and in the end they contented themselves by levying a tax of £1 a leaguer on all wine sold to strangers.

The reports from Batavia on Cape wine were always much more favourable than those from Europe, but the Lords Seventeen commended Constantia. They wrote:

'This wine is of such a quality that it can be classed as a distinctly superior wine, which already has a reputation in Europe. It should be husbanded for the Company's use, provided such can be done at no unnecessary expense.'

At that time *Great Constantia*, where Jan Colyn held sway, produced 10 to 12 leaguers of the red wine for which he received about £17 a leaguer, and from 20 to 24 leaguers of the white variety which sold locally at £10 a leaguer. The Company probably resold at Amsterdam at something like £100 a leaguer.

An interesting record in the archives contains the copies of affidavits submitted in the request to the directors, signed by the winegrowers J van Renen, Tielleman Roos, Berend Jacob Artoys and Nicolas Gideon Heyns in 1779. The petition sets forth the grievances under which the wine farmers 'groaned', asked for the abolition of the office of *Kellermeester* (cellarer) and his assistants, that free trade in wine be permitted, that more cooperage should be given, especially in the form of wood and staves so that farmers could make their own casks; that coopers should be encouraged to start their own open shops (*werkwinkels*), and that more encouragement should be given to farmers to produce their own *maag* wine. In the accounts of prices affixed to the request are stated the prices at which some wines were retailed to ships. One Danish oxshead of Cape Madeira fetched 28 riksdollars, one half-leaguer of the same wine sold for $22\frac{1}{2}$ riksdollars, while one half-aum of red wine fetched 33 riksdollars. The winegrowers alleged that the cellarer was constantly interfering by threats and cajolements to get wine into his own hands, and it is plain to see that Mr Pieter Hackert was no favourite. One D Wieser, who made an affidavit to support his fellow winegrowers, was particularly clamant. He states that he had a farm near Rondebosch and that he took great care in preparing his wine. 'Our wine,' he avers, 'nearly equals that of *Constantia*, and strangers have paid us 25 Spanish dollars for a half-aum. Our vineyard has 100 000 vines, which give us from 40 to 50 leaguers, while the Paarl-Frenchhoek vineyards give 100 leaguers per 100 000 vines. They irrigate their vineyards, which give much must but bad wine. We mature our grapes till they are almost raisins and our wine is consequently of a good quality and not to be sold at the miserable price the cellarer offers.' Other deponents stated that they had been forced to sell their vintage at 27 riksdollars per leaguer; indeed one, J A Myburgh, had been compelled to sell his at the absurd price of 19 riksdollars the leaguer. So much graft and dishonesty on the part of the cellarer was proved that the case for the deponents was thought worthy of consideration, but events interfered and prevented the directors from taking further steps in the matter, which remained in abeyance until the settlement had changed hands.

The Company's restrictions on the sale of wine were merely survivals of regulations that in the seventeenth century were by no means rare. In other winegrowing countries the wine farmers had matter for complaint. When in 1618 the old law forbidding French wine merchants from buying wine within a radius of forty miles from their wine houses was reaffirmed, the *Syndic des Vignerons de Ruei, Suresne, Nanterre, Coulobe, Argenteuil et autres vignobles du plat pais* formally complained to the king, who was good enough to revoke the obnoxious edict. But the Cape wine merchants had no court of appeal except to the Lords Seventeen and their petitions had to be forwarded by the local Governor, who always accompanied them with explanations and criticism. As up to the end of the eighteenth century the directors of the Company did not think that their Colony at the Cape had much prospect as a winegrowing country – certainly not one that could compete with France or Spain – they paid little attention to the wine industry and neglected what could, with proper care and organisation, have become one of the Company's best assets.

In 1746 an attempt was made by both parties to end a state of affairs that was proving vexatious to both. Theal writes:

'For a long time the wine farmers had been making complaints of there being no sale for the produce of their vineyards, then from 2 000 to 4 000 leaguers a year, and to relieve them the directors have resolved, if no other remedy could be devised, to substitute wine for spirits to a large extent in their ships and Indian establishments, provided a moderately good article could be obtained. The Burgher Councillors, on behalf of the farmers, addressed the Governor, General Van Imhoff, on this question. The Governor replied by offering them free trade in Java upon payment of 16s 8d freight and £2 10s a leaguer duty. The burghers replied that such a privilege would be of no use to them. The Governor then proposed that the tax on wine should be increased from 4s 2d to 12s 6d a leaguer, that upon payment of this a fee of 4s 2d to the Fiscal and a fee of £1 0s 10d to the licensed dealer, the burghers should be at liberty to sell without let or hindrance to all visitors, Dutch or foreign, at the best prices they could obtain, and that the Company should purchase at £5 5s 10d a leaguer sufficient for its own needs, which would have been an average of four leaguers for each ship leaving the port in addition to a quantity to be sent to the Netherlands and Batavia for ships coming to the Cape and for the use of the work-people in India. With this proposal the Burgher Councillors on behalf of the farmers expressed themselves satisfied.'

In his chapter on the revenues of the Colony, Mentzel has this to say about the revenue derived from viticulture:

'The tithe has not been imposed upon wine products because it would have been regarded as too crushing a burden in view of the existence of licences for the sale of wine. The Company imposes an excise rate of 20 stivers per leaguer on wine pressed. The licencees retail about 2 000 leaguers. Unlicensed persons who sell wine in quantities of not less than half a leaguer purchase 3 000 leaguers and the Company buys 185 leaguers, while 1 800 leaguers are privately consumed. . . . The licences bring in 70 000 gulden yearly.'

Only after the middle of the century did the wine trade become organised at the Cape, and herein it was behind Batavia, where the importers were much more careful about both the goods they sold and the goods they bought. Even the Company, that had so great an interest in wines, kept fewer skilled artisans at the Cape than they did in Java. In the return of persons in the Company's service for 1778 we find 'One master cooper,' 'ten journeymen coopers,' and 'one tapster' or *Wynverlaater*, a word that is applicable also to one who blends wine although it was usually given to the man who transferred wine from one cask to another. At Batavia there were three such tapsters besides several butlers, while at the Cape there was only one butler and one butler's mate. It may not be without interest to note what the Company paid for imported wines sent to Batavia, as these prices may be compared with the beggarly £6 for ordinary Cape wine and £20 for Constantia wine that it paid to winegrowers at the Cape. The prices in pounds per leaguer were: White Naples: 16-23; Red Beno Carlo: 28-36; Oporto: 25; White Frontignan: 47; Lunel: 52; Medoc: 28; Toulouse: 28; Bergerac et St Fort: 15; Margaux: 22.

There were constant complaints about the last four, that stood the journey across the equator very badly. The Italian wines were always better than the French, with the exception of the Lunel and Frontignan, that were regarded as choice wines in the same category with Constantia. Oporto wine was never popular, either at the Cape or Batavia, and was never regarded as an aristocrat among wines but simply as a manufactured wine. The quality of the Constantia sent to Amsterdam also varied considerably after 1740. In 1780 we have a report signed by Willemz, Hoen and Schouten, wine brokers, which reads:

'The quality of the Constantia both white and red is so miserably poor that it would be prejudicial to the Company's interests to sell any at auction. We are returning you a few bottles to taste for yourselves, together with the confidential report of the tasters. We found the white Constantia marked I W C worst, not to be compared with the white Frontignan or Bezier of Celte, which sell at 36-50 gulden per hogshead.'

At about the same time we find an official at Batavia writing home to state that:

'The white Constantia from the Cape is a far superior wine to anything else sent out. The red is now darker and with less bouquet than former consignments, but it is still a great wine.'

It is possible that the 'much darker' consignment was the mixture of Muscadel and Pontac that later on was substituted for the original Muscadel-Frontignac blend, but there is no documentary evidence of any kind to show what different musts were used for the various vintages. About this time we hear of *witte Pontak wyn*, and of 'very sweet Pontak that has a Muscat odour,' which seem to have been attempts to make imitations of the original Constantia type. Cape Madeira, Cape Pontac and Cape Muscadel were by this time well-known wines on the Batavian and European markets. All three were full-bodied, aromatic sweet wines, much esteemed, but not really comparable to Constantia under which name all three were sometimes sold. The 'Madeira wine from the Cape that had the glow of a fire opal and the flavour of something divine' that Platen tasted on his travels in Belgium was probably a Cape Madeira. The taste of this wine was popular in south Holland and, whereas the real Madeira was an expensive and uncommon wine, the Cape article, which some wine lovers held to be superior, was sold at auction at a much cheaper rate. From the Cape also came — but only to Batavia, never to Holland — a 'white wine made from Green Grape, very pleasant and dry,' and, curiously enough, a '*Boene* (Beaune) dry red wine from the Drakenstein.'

Captain Cornelis de Jong, who visited Cape Town first in 1792, found much to admire in the wine that he tasted there. At *Bergvliet*, where he ate tortoise eggs and wondered at the wild flowers, he sampled 'a very pleasant white wine'. At *Constantia* he drank the liqueur wines and found life very pleasant, and incidentally complains that Le Vaillant had abused its hospitality. Most travellers in these early years agreed with the verdict, given many years later by Schrumpf, that the community was on the whole sober, and that excessive drinking, chiefly of spirits and malt liquors, was confined to the town taverns and indulged in largely by the visiting sailors and soldiers. The Malays were cited as exemplars of sobriety, a reputation that they have retained to this day.

In general, however, it may safely be said that at the time when the settlement at the Cape of Good Hope passed from the Company into British possession, it was not yet regarded as a great winegrowing country. It had achieved one outstanding wine, Constantia, but the quantity of that particular kind was so small that, like Tokay essence, it could never be anything but supremely dear and, in Europe, beyond the reach of any except the Company's directors and their friends or those they specially wished to favour. The demand for good wine was amply met, so far as Europe and, to a limited extent, America were concerned, by the winegrowers of France, Germany, Italy and Spain and Portugal. The overland route supplied India with Italian and Levant wines. For the Cape the only market was on the spot, or, under conditions that appealed only to the richer farmers, in Java. For the local market there was far too large a quantity produced every year to enable prices to be profitable, but the industry was still developing and it needed only some direct encouragement to make it develop along the right lines.

Chapter 5

Cape Wine in the Early Nineteenth Century

On 16 September 1795, the settlement of the Dutch East India Company at the Cape of Good Hope surrendered to the English force in command of General Clarke and Admiral Elphinstone. That force had landed on the western shore of False Bay, marched across the estate that had once belonged to Governor Simon van der Stel, fought a few skirmishes on the way, and occupied Cape Town with very little loss. In that brief campaign that lasted barely three days only one man on the settlement side had distinguished himself. That was Daniel du Plessis, of the Swellendam Volunteers, whose stand had so impressed General Clarke that when the surrender had been arranged and the terms signed at *Rustenburg*, the Commander-in-Chief requested the honour of Mr du Plessis's company to dinner. After all, the invaders had come as friends to occupy, on behalf of the Prince of Orange, allied with them in their opposition to French Jacobinism, that in those days smelt as rank as modern Nazism, a Dutch possession to save it from being swallowed up by the enemy. Misunderstanding and divided counsels had interfered with the peaceful occupation, for protective purposes, that had been planned. Colonel Gordon and the Dutch Governor had been at cross-purposes about the matter. Contradictory instructions had been given and a good deal of confusion had resulted. But the Colonel had wanted to save bloodshed and had understood what kind of action was contemplated by the invading force, so there had really been no great delay or difficulty in settling the terms of capitulation. The old customs were to be recognised; no new taxes were to be imposed; the settlement was to be held on trust for the Prince of Orange. Three weeks later Colonel Gordon realised that the Prince's part in the arrangement was merely decorative. His reaction to this discovery, that to a man of his imagination and talents should not have been surprising, resulted in a fit of melancholy in which he committed suicide. The Governor was despatched to Holland, where he wrote memoranda to explain his part in the affair, and the occupying force took over the administration of the country. On the night of the surrender some of the soldiers and sailors, under the influence of the good wine of the country, had a hilarious time, and one small party of them visited the *Constantia* cellars and did some damage to the property, about which the owner bitterly complained, as his letter, now in the archives, shows. But the settlement, as a whole, was but slightly disturbed by the change in government, which lasted for nearly eight years. By the treaty of Amiens the Cape was returned to Holland and was formally handed over by General Dundas to General Janssens and Commissioner De Mist on 20 February 1803. Three years later, on 18 January 1806, it was again surrendered by General Janssens to another invading force under General Baird, and practically the same procedure was followed as eleven years before. This time there was no pretence at protection; the fight was between enemies. The defeated General Janssens was sent to Europe, exchanged and made a Marshal of France by Napoleon, who intimated to him, quite courteously, that so magnificent an officer never surrendered twice. Alas, misfortune dogged him, for at Meester Cornelis, in far-away Java, he found himself in practically the same impossible situation as on Blaauwbergstrand, and surrendered to Gillespie.

By the London Convention of 1814 the settlement was finally ceded to Great Britain, together with Demerara, Essequibo and Berbice, in consideration of the full payment of all the Swedish claims against the Netherlands and the payment of an additional three million pounds sterling.

The close of the eighteenth and the opening of the nineteenth centuries thus mark the beginning of British rule at the Cape, an *interregnum* of a few years, too transitory for any revolutionary administrative changes, and the final establishment of the new regime which outlasted the new century. For our purpose, so far as the wine industry was concerned, we may take the period from 1795 to the end of the nineteenth century as a whole, neglecting the interlude that had, after all, no viticultural significance.

For the study of this long period we have much more informative data than were available for the preceding years. The documentary evidence obtainable from the records during the first occupation is ample and interesting, but enshrined in a mass of irrelevant material that makes the task of extracting it wearisome and tedious. There is, however, much printed material in the narratives of visitors and residents, whose accounts are generally more accurate than those of their predecessors. There are also letters and private documents that may be consulted and that offer valuable additional information.

During the administration of Major-General James Craig no important change was made in the relations between the winegrowers and the government. This was in accordance with the terms of the capitulation that prescribed that no new taxes should be levied. On 15 October 1795 regulations were issued for the wine houses. These laid down that the vintners were to have the exclusive privilege of selling Cape wines and brandy by retail to be drunk in the tavern and all wines of a smaller quantity than a half anker, and that they could buy their wines when and where they pleased. All vintners were to sell 'a pure and good wine only,' and the Fiscal was given power to inspect supplies. No tavern was allowed to remain open after nine o' clock in the evening or during the hours for divine service on Sundays; no gaming was permitted in taverns and vintners were not permitted to take pledges for wines consumed or bought, conceal deserters, or supply drink 'incautiously' to guardsmen.

These regulations were necessary because control of the taverns had been lax during the former administration. Mrs Kindersley, a visitor from

India, who visited *Constantia* and found its wine 'very rich', remarked upon the number of wine houses. 'The finest fruit' [at the Cape], she wrote, 'is the grape. . . . The vintage is in autumn, which is about March and April, when a considerable quantity of wine is made; the white they call Cape Madeira; the best red is a sort of Tent.' Lord Nelson, in the evidence before the select committee, doubted the strategic value of the Cape, but admitted that it was a good victualling station, an immense tavern, as he called it, from which the fleet could easily be supplied with wine. It would seem that at first the authorities in England overlooked the possibilities of the wine industry in their newly acquired territory. Only when traders, under licence from the East India Company, established themselves in Cape Town, was it realised that Cape wine was something out of which a reasonable, and sometimes a large, profit could be made. Under the administration of Earl Macartney and in the first term of Major-General James Dundas, no great improvement or change is to be chronicled. Winegrowers found a steady market after the great fire that in 1798 destroyed the military stores, but the records give little information about the production of wine and for a more or less accurate account of the state of affairs we have to rely upon the summary given by John Barrow, who wrote:

'Wine and brandy may be considered, with wheat and barley, as the staple commodities of the Cape of Good Hope. Grapes grow with the greatest luxuriance in every part of this extensive Colony; but the cultivation of the vine is little understood, or, to speak more properly, is not attended with that diligence which in other countries is bestowed on it. Hence the wines are susceptible of great improvement and the quantity of being increased indefinitely.

Ten or twelve distinct kinds of wines are manufactured at the Cape and each of those has a different flavour and quality at the different farms on which they are produced. From difference of soil, from situation and management, scarcely any two vineyards of the same kind of grape give the same wine. By throwing under the press the ripe and unripe grapes, together with the stalk, most of the wines have either a thinness or a slight acidity, or, for want of a proper degree of fermentation and from being pressed when overripe, acquire a sickly saccharine taste. An instance of the former is perceptible in that called Steen, which resembles the Rhenish wines, and of the latter, in that which is known by the name of Constantia. It is generally supposed that this wine is the produce of two farms only of that name; whereas the same grape, the Muscadel, grows at every farm; and at some of them in Drakenstein the wine pressed from it is equally good, if not superior to, the Constantia, though sold at one-sixth of the price; of such importance is a name.

This wine sells at the Cape for 70 to 80 rix dollars the half-aum, a cask which ought to contain 20 gallons, but the avaricious propensity of the proprietors, increasing with the demand for their wines, has led them to fabricate false casks, few of them that come to England being found to measure more than 17 or 18 gallons; many not above 16. And if they find out that the wine applied for is to be sent abroad they are sure to adulterate it with some thin wine. For, according to their own returns, the quantity exported and consumed in Cape Town, as in the case of Madeira wine, greatly exceeds the quantity manufactured.

By a settlement made between the Dutch Commissaries General, in the year 1793, and the owners of the two farms of *Great* and *Little Constantia*, the latter were bound to furnish, for the use of Government, 30 aums each, every year, at the rate of 50 rix dollars the aum; which was regularly taken, after being tasted and sealed up in the presence of persons appointed for that purpose, by the English Government, to the no little annoyance of the Great Lord of Constantia, who is the son and successor to the man of whom Mr Le Vaillant has drawn a very entertaining portrait. The wine was paid for out of the Colonial Treasury and the whole of it, under Lord Macartney's government, sent home to the Secretary of State for the disposal of His Majesty.

The quantity of Constantia wine exposed in four successive years was: 1799, 157 half-aums, value 11 752 rd; 1800, 188 half-aums, value 14 070 rd; 1801, 173 half-aums, value 13 007 rd; 1802, 210 half-aums, value 15 745 rd. The best-bodied wine that is made at the Cape is the Madeira, considerable quantities of which were usually sent to Holland and to the Dutch settlements in India. The Americans, also, have taken small quantities of late years in exchange for slaves, a trade that seems susceptible of very considerable augmentation. The English merchants at the Cape have made up cargoes of the different sorts of wines, both to the East and the West Indies, and they have been tried in the northern nations of Europe. But they universally complain that the wines seldom agree with the samples and they frequently turn sour; so little regard for reputations have the Koopmen of the Cape. Confined to this spot from their birth, they have had little opportunity of improvement from education and none from travel and are consequently ignorant of the nature of foreign trade. If their wines are once on board ship they conclude there is an end of the transaction, and, if previously sold, whether they arrive in good or bad condition is no concern of theirs.

The country boor, having no surplus stock of casks, is under the necessity of selling to the merchant in the town his new wine; and here it is mixed and adulterated in a variety of ways. The pipe is called a legger and contains eight half-aums or 160 gallons, and each legger pays to Government a duty on entering the town of three rix dollars. The price paid to the farmer is generally from 20 to 30 rix dollars the legger, which, after adulteration, is sold from 40 to 60 rix dollars, and frequently at the rate of 80 to 100 rix dollars.'

Barrow states that in the four years 1799 to 1802, 21 649 leaguers of wine and 1 665 leaguers of brandy passed the barrier into Cape Town. Of this 800 leaguers of wine and 100 of brandy were exported, not including the Constantia; the rest was consumed in town. He estimated the export value of wine and brandy at about £10 000 a year. In his general criticism he suggests that the wine trade might be improved by ensuring a proper number of casks for maturing the wines, which could always find a ready market locally. The squadron alone consumed over a million pints of wine a year, and Cape brandy was considered better for the sailors than the imported rum. He also advised that vines should be trained on espaliers and that the government should import vine growers from Madeira who could give practical demonstrations of dealing with the Sercial and other wines used for making Cape Madeira. Finally he echoed Van Riebeeck's sighingly expressed hope: 'O for some Chinese to teach our free inhabitants how to cultivate their ground and to get the best out of it!' He also gave an account of a model winegrower's statement of expenses and incomings, which was later on copied — without acknowledgment — by other writers, notably by Carmichael and Percival.

The former of these commentators was a captain in the 72nd regiment stationed at the Cape, who had ample opportunity to form an opinion from personal observation. He found the Cape wines 'generally with an earthy taste', and lamented that so little was being done to improve them. Quite rightly he put his finger squarely upon one of the factors that had made the winegrowers apathetic. 'Among the terrible reactions produced by the slave trade,' he wrote, 'none is perhaps more merited or more evident than the dissoluteness of morals and ferocity of disposition which it creates among the people who are concerned in it.' This judgment was delivered at a time when it was seriously proposed to barter Cape wine for American slaves. The Captain's observations on the mischievous activities of 'the newly established Temperance Societies imported from America' appear to be the first mention of these detestable fanatics whose unbridled fervour has occasioned so much harm to South Africa by its implicit denial of the dietetic usefulness of natural wines.

Captain Robert Percival, writing about the same time (1804), gives such an interesting account from personal experience that his chapter deserves to be quoted in full.

'About Wineberg, Round-a-Bosch, Witte Boem and the other spots in the neighbourhood of Cape Town are several fields, planted with vines, well fenced in and bounded by hedges of low oak trees, myrtle, quince and others of the shrub kind, to keep off deer and cattle and to shelter them from the violence of the winds. These fields are also laid into lesser divisions with hedges, the better to secure the tender shoots from the violence of the blast. The vines are planted and brought up in these enclosed spaces in regular rows or ridges, like drills of potatoes or beans in Europe. They are not suffered to spread out their branches or to grow up, except one or two particular species which produce the grapes used at table or dried for raisins; these are permitted to grow and spread in the same way as our hot house vines, and are usually planted against the walls of their houses; the shoots form pretty arbours and shades before the windows or over the porches of their doors, spreading very much and bearing abundantly.

'In the vineyards the plants are regularly pruned and never suffered to grow more than three feet high; they are supported by twigs crossing each other and interwoven to keep the shoots from dropping or falling to the ground with the weight of the fruit. These vines have the appearance of low currant bushes, being seldom suffered to grow higher. About Constantia and Wineberg, to the south of Cape Town and eastwards at the Villages of Fransche Hoek, Drakenstein, the Great and Little Parl, and further on towards Stellenbosch, Swellendam and the adjoining country, are a number of vine plantations, and no production is here so abundant or so profitable to the planter. It is computed that an acre of vines may contain about 5 000 stocks or shoots, which may produce, on a moderate calculation, 700 gallons of wine.

'The wines made at the Cape are of various qualities and are called Constantia, Muscadel, Moselle, Cape Madeira, Vin de Grave and Rhenish; the latter is so called from some resemblance in taste to the European wine bearing the same name. They are all very much inferior to those of Europe; rather from the mode of manufacturing the grape into wine and from not paying proper attention to the culture and nurture of the plant than from any natural defect in the quality of the grape; for it is a well-known fact that the grapes in general at the Cape are inferior to none of any part of the world, and some kinds are even much richer than those which, in Europe, produce far superior wines. The Dutch have never arrived at any perfection in the art of making wine or the rearing of vine shoots. As this subject appeared to me of very considerable importance, I bestowed some pains in collecting information with regard to it, and the observations which I was enabled to make may be found not altogether uninteresting.

'The defects in the Cape wine proceed from the avarice of the planter on the one hand and his extreme indolence on the other. His contracted disposition prevents him from ever foregoing a little present emolument for much greater acquisitions in prospect. Antipathy to laborious exertions and a sordid desire of saving combine to prevent the planters from allowing the grapes to be raised to any height from the ground by standards, as this would require more work and care in the management of them and a greater expense of wood for supporting the shoots; though at the same time it is allowed that it would materially improve the quality of the grape besides adding considerably to the produce. It is indeed natural to suppose that the fruit, by growing so near the ground, imbibes many corrupting particles; nor can it be doubted that it is from the soil in which it grows that the grape derives that particular flavour peculiar to the wine made at the Cape of Good Hope. The Dutch planter also, not content with the fruit itself, often mixes both leaves and stalks in the wine press to increase the quantity by the addition of their juice. The grapes are too often pulled before ripe from the fear of losing any by birds, insects or other causes; nor is the wine allowed a sufficient time to purify itself by a proper fermentation and to acquire a ripe and agreeable flavour, but is immediately from the press put into butts which are well caulked up with lime. A quantity of sulphur which at the same time is thrown into it is all the further means employed for its purification. I have often perceived a sediment in Cape wine, which when analysed was found to be impregnated with sugar of lead and sulphurous particles. The Dutch allege that the dearness and scarcity of wood, with the violent winds that often prevail, will not allow them to suffer the grapes to grow higher, and that the juice from the leaves and stalks gives a greater zest to the wine. These arguments upon examination were considered by our countrymen as extremely futile and not justified by experience. Since the English arrived in the settlement, some farmers have at their suggestion considerably improved the quality of their wines and have paid more attention to the planting and squeezing the grapes. Our countrymen indeed have it not in their power to become adepts in the making of wine, as that is not a species of produce granted to their climate; but good sense and activity soon find remedies for defects in new situations; and the English at the Cape found themselves under the necessity of attending seriously to this article from the exorbitant prices which the merchants charged for European wines. At one time the different regimental messes were forced to come to a resolution not to drink any but Cape wine; and this had a temporary effect in lowering the price of port, which had been raised to a degree altogether extravagant. The Cape wine has one good effect upon the body that it keeps it moderately open; and a bottle or two serves to a European as a purgative draught. A constant and free use of it, however, irritates the bowels, probably proceeding from the sulphur and other substances used in fining it; and perhaps still more from the quality of the wine itself which has naturally a great degree of acidity.

'A few Englishmen undertook to make wine here, and for some time succeeded very well, but not having the advantage of a large establishment of slaves, and of being themselves proprietors of the ground, they were at length compelled to abandon their undertaking by the jealousy of the Dutch, who discouraged these adventures by every means in their power and employed every art to prevent Englishmen from interfering in this article of trade. The grapes are in general not inferior to those of Lisbon or France, and are reckoned in many instances, as I have observed, to be of a richer and more luscious quality. It is therefore a matter of serious regret to the possessors of the

Cape that this valuable article has not been attended to, as the revenue of the Colony would be benefited in a degree not to be calculated by an extensive cultivation of vineyards and a great trade would by this means be established here to all parts of the world. The resources arising from such a trade would at once tend to stimulate the industry of the inhabitants and afford the means of general improvement. The Dutch hitherto have appeared to be altogether blind to their true interests; the farmers go on in their old and rude way, equally inattentive to private advantage and the public good. Though the quantity of wine made at the Cape is very considerable, yet it is little esteemed from its poorness and insipidity, and comparatively no advantage is derived from its sale to the settlement. In India no Englishman would buy it; nor would the captain of an East Indiaman think it worth room in his ship. Were the possession of the Cape of Good Hope to remain permanent with Great Britain, in some little time, by attention to this valuable article, great and solid advantages might be secured to this country. The British would no longer be compelled to accede to those extravagant demands and extortions of the planters in the island of Madeira and other foreign countries from whence we are at present under the necessity of purchasing; and less inconvenience would arise when at war with France and Spain, from our having excellent wines made in a British Colony.

'The sweet, luscious and excellent wine called Constantia, so highly esteemed in Europe, is made in only one particular spot at the Cape of Good Hope. The village where this wine is made is called Constantia, whence it derives its name. The village of Constantia is delightfully situated near the foot of a range of pleasant green hills about halfway between Musenberg and Wineberg. It is distant about eight or nine miles from Cape Town, with which it is connected by a pleasant and romantic road, having several very handsome houses and gardens belonging to the Dutch on either side of the way. Every stranger who arrives at the Cape, if his time and other circumstances will allow of it, makes a point of visiting the village of Constantia, and those famous wine plantations; for these, with the Table Mountain, are looked upon as the great and first objects of curiosity at the Cape. There are only two houses on the estate, but the offices, farmyards and stores, where the wine is made and kept, are so very extensive that Constantia obtains the name of a village and appears so to the eye. Round the vineyards, dwelling houses and offices are pleasant groves of the silver tree, besides oak, elms and other smaller plants which completely shelter it in every direction and hide it from the view till you wind round the hill and come quite close to it. There are two distinct and separate plantations of vines here, each of a different colour and quality, though both are called Constantia wines. The first farm, called *Great Constantia*, produces the red wine of that name; and at *Lesser Constantia*, in its vicinity, the white is made. The farm, which alone produces this richly flavoured wine, belongs to a Dutchman, *Mynheer* Pluter (*sic*) and has been long in his family.

'The grape from which this wine is extracted is a species of the Muscadel, extremely rich, sweet and luscious. Its qualities proceed in some measure from the situation and soil, which are particularly favourable; but the exquisite flavour is chiefly to be attributed to the great care taken in the rearing, dressing and encouragement of the vines, in preserving the grapes wholly clean from sand and free from the ravages of the insects which usually attack them when full ripe. With the cleanliness and healthy state of the grape when put into the press, another cause contributes much to the goodness of the wine, thus not suffering the leaves, stalks or unripe fruit to be mixed in the press, as is done by the other Dutch farmers. If the same attention was paid to the vines in other parts of the Colony and the same precautions used in compressing the fruit, Cape wine would no longer labour under its present disrepute. The grapes of *Constantia* are indeed larger and have a richer and more fleshy pulp than those of any other farm, and consequently give more juice in proportion. There must, however, be many parts of the soil equally adapted to the rearing of grapes as this of *Constantia*, although from negligence overlooked; for those spots that require least trouble in the turning up or dressing are universally preferred by the farmers here in laying out their plantations.

'The quantity of wine made on the farms of *Constantia* on an average is about 75 leaguers a year, each leaguer containing upwards of 150 gallons of our measure. It is a sweet, heavy and luscious wine, not fit to be drunk in any quantity, but chiefly suited to a dessert, as a couple of glasses are quite as much as one would desire to drink at a time. It is even here excessively dear and difficult to be procured, and must be often bespoke a considerable time. The captains of vessels touching here, who have wished to procure a quantity of it, have been frequently obliged to contract for it a year or two before the wine was made.

'Under the Dutch government the farmer divided the produce into three parts; one third he was obliged to furnish, at a certain price, to the Dutch East India Company, who sent it to the government in Holland. Another proportion was furnished to certain of the inhabitants of Cape Town, chiefly the people in high office and power, at the same rate; and the remaining quantity he was at liberty to dispose of at what price he could to the passengers and captains of ships of all nations. The price to strangers varied according to circumstances; when there was any deficiency in the produce of his farm, the price was always raised in proportion. The Dutch inhabitants of Cape Town, at whose houses and tables the passengers are accommodated, rarely ever produce a drop of this wine, except upon very extraordinary occasions. The Dutch, indeed, are sufficiently careful never to open a bottle of this valuable liquor at their tables, unless they perceive it may serve their own purposes. A rich Englishman who has made his fortune in India, and from whom they expect a handsome present of tea, sugar-candy or muslin, is honoured now and then with a bottle of Constantia at the dessert; but a British officer who is not supposed to be flush of money or valuable articles, except where he is a favourite with the lady of the house, may go without it all the time he remains here.

'When a bottle of Constantia is to be bought at Cape Town, which is but seldom the case, and even then it requires some management to secure it, it is never sold under a couple of dollars. But it generally happens that strangers, although they procure this prize, are still as far as ever from tasting real Constantia, as there is another kind of sweet, rich wine which the Dutch frequently pass off for it.

'One may fortunately, by dint of persuasion, get at the village of Constantia, from *Mynheer* Pluter, a small cask containing about twenty gallons for ten or twelve pounds sterling; a stranger can seldom procure a larger quantity at the same time; indeed he must always be particularly recommended to take any quantity he can obtain, and also to prevent having the other heavy, sweet wine imposed on him for Constantia. Mr Pluter has a great number of visitors to his farm who are equally attracted by the beauty of the place and the desire of seeing the vine plantation, with the manner of making the wine. He is in every respect a complete Dutchman. For though used to such a variety of the first company and gentlemen of high civil and military situations, who always pay liberally and whom it is strongly his interest to encourage to his farm by civility and a suavity of manners, he is generally morose, uncouth and churlish in his manners; and it is rare to see him in good humour, though he gains a great profit by entertaining his occasional guests with his nectar. Money is the idol of the Dutch; yet they receive it without thanking those who bring it, or encouraging them to come again by civility and attention; and when they have once received their extravagant demand, they laugh at the folly of our countrymen for their indifference in parting with that money which is their own idol.

'I was so unfortunate as not to find this gentleman in a good humour during the two or three visits I made to his farm, and could scarcely get a bottle of wine, or leave to look at his wine vaults and presses, not having brought any particular recommendation from his friends at the Cape, which from pride he regularly extracts. I relied, however, on what I knew of a Dutchman's partiality for English customers, but on my requesting leave to see the place, he himself came out and informed me that the gentleman was not at home. The other officers who were along with me, however, and who understood his disposition better, and the requisite management, got some of the slaves, for a present, to get us wine, and shew us the plantations and manner of manufacturing the grapes into wine; nor did we take the smallest notice of the owner's surliness, and boorish manners, when we afterwards met him, but went on to satisfy our curiosity, and obtain the wine and information we wanted. If company arrives before he is dressed and has got over his usual quantity of pipes of tobacco, he denies himself, and does not wish to admit them, unless he is pretty sure of getting hard dollars. Those perfectly acquainted with this take care to let the slaves see the cash, on which he sends any quantity into an arbour in the garden, and when the bill is called he charges two Spanish dollars a bottle, equal to 11s 6d British. Some allowance must certainly be made for *Mynheer* Pluter's moroseness, as it is impossible for him at all times to attend to the reception of his visitors, some of whom by their teizing and forward loquacity, might render themselves extremely troublesome, and disagreeable to his grave and solemn habits. His slaves are exceedingly attentive and communicative when allowed to wait on and conduct strangers, finding it highly to their advantage as they always get something for themselves.

'Mr Pluter's wine vaults are very extensive and neatly laid out, and everything is in much better order than at other wine farms I have seen. In the vaults and wine cellars of the merchants of Cape Town, the wine is kept in very large butts or vessels somewhat shaped like the hogshead, but the rotundity is vastly greater in proportion. Those vessels are made of mahogany, or a wood very much resembling it, very thick, highly polished, and kept clean as our dining tables; they are bound round with great brass hoops, and the edges are also secured by the same metal, so that no accident or time can damage them. Each of those butts or reservoirs, which they call leagers, though an inapplicable term, as a leager is a measure of 150 gallons, will contain from six to seven hundred gallons. The bung-holes are covered with plates of brass hasped down and locked, the cocks are also strong and large with locks and keys to them, so that the slaves are prevented from embezzling any of the wine, as they are never opened but in presence of one of the proprietors. Some of these leagers are elegantly carved and ornamented with various figures.

'The next wine in estimation to the Constantia is a kind of Muscadelo or, as they call it here, Cape Madeira. The colour of this wine is a deep violet, and the appearance thick and muddy. Cape Madeira is a heavy, sweetish wine, with a stronger body than the generality of what is made here; for the various kinds of white wines at the Cape are thin, light and acid. A person may drink five or six bottles without being intoxicated; and it is this wine which is generally used at the tables of the colonists. Except the red Constantia, no wine made at the Cape is ever so high coloured as port or claret.

'I scarcely ever drank any palatable wine at the tables of the Dutch, as they produce mostly unripe wine for domestic consumption; while they dispose of that which is become ripened, for this wine becomes wonderfully improved by age, to the captains of trading vessels. This is an invariable custom which they scarcely ever deviate from; as the wine is reckoned in with the board and lodging at the Dutch houses, and no extra price paid for it, they generally give their guests a new, insipid, and very indifferent sort, such as may be had in the wine houses for two or three pence a bottle. There are two or three kinds of sweet wine made, but too heavy to drink after meals. The Steen wine has a sparkling quality and tartish taste, something like Vin de Grave, but much inferior in flavour. The Hanepod made from a large white grape is very rich, but scarce and dear, and only used by the ladies at their parties in the same manner as the Constantia. The grapes from which this wine is made are chiefly dried and preserved for raisins to eat at dessert . . . Cape Madeira and the other wines of first quality are sold at from twenty to thirty pounds a leager of 150 gallons; formerly it was much cheaper; and the common or poorer sort generally drunk at table, on the first arrival of the English, might be had for fourpence or sixpence a gallon, but was afterwards raised to a shilling. A leager of the poorer species brings about eight to nine pounds British currency.'

The 'brandy-wine' he found 'awful stuff, with a strong resemblance to Irish whisky, only harsher and more fiery'.

Notes on the Cape of Good Hope in the year 1820, London, 1821, has a chapter on Cape wines:

'The multiplicity of bad wines sent from the Cape has sunk the whole in the estimation of our countrymen, and it is now a drug on the market. Why the grapes of the Cape should not yield good wine is a question often asked, and for the most part unsatisfactorily answered. The reason may partly be sought in the process. The grapes, ripe and unripe, sound and unsound, with stalks and filth of all kinds, are pressed together and no wonder that bad wine is the consequence. This is the general process among the Boors, but not all the pains and attention that have been devoted to the business by one or two individuals of Cape Town have produced anything that can compare with the wines of Madeira and France. There is still a harshness and acidity peculiar to the Cape wines, and heartburn has been observed to be a common consequence of drinking freely of them. . . . Some have thought that the clayey soil, in which the vines take root, other that suffering the fruits to grow so near the earth, are among the causes of the characteristic flavour of the wine. . . . No doubt, soil and climate have great influence in modifying the growth and flavour of fruits. The grape of Constantia loses its properties at a distance of half a mile from one particular farm, and the wines of France are known to make a totally different wine when transported into other countries of Europe. But it is notorious that the best vineyards of this Colony are upon the strong clays; and if the soil of the Cape really imparted any peculiar qualities, it would surely be discoverable in the fruit, so that it still remains a puzzle why good fruit should not make good wine.'

The writer remarks on the general sobriety of the wine-drinking communities.

An Account of the Colony of the Cape of Good Hope, with a view to the information of emigrants, published in London in 1819, gives little that is not in Barrow and La Caille, and is obviously a compilation:

'The vine growers or wine boors, as they are called at the Cape, are the most opulent cultivators of the soil in this Colony. Their lands are chiefly freehold, exempt from almost all taxes, and capable of any sort of cultivation. The general size of their farms is about 120 acres, English, and the culture of the grape, with an elegant garden, generally occupies the whole. Descended from the old French families who first introduced the vine into the Colony, they retain much of the suavity and communicativeness of their ancestors; and in this respect, as well as in the general comfort of their establishments, impress the stranger with a feeling of their respectability and decided superiority to their neighbours. But the French language is never heard amongst them and a French book of any kind is rarely seen. The produce of their vineyards is brought to market from September to the period of the new vintage in February or March, but principally in the last four months of the year. Here it is subject to a rate of three rix dollars per legger of wine or brandy on passing the barrier, but no duty is laid upon it in the vineyard or when sold in the country. The only taxes to which the grower is subject are a small capitation rate toward repairing the highways leading into Cape Town, and what is called the lion and tiger money, a district rate originally levied to defray the expenses of exterminating these animals, but now devoted to the general exigencies of each division. Fourteen or sixteen oxen are required to convey two leggers of wine, of the weight of from two tons to two tons and a half, over the deep sands of the isthmus. These are sometimes kept, during the greater part of the year, at loan farms belonging to the proprietors on the east of the mountains or they are hired for the occasion or put to graze.'

This writer estimates that the immigrant will need a capital of 25,160 RD if he wants to be a wine farmer, and gives the following budget:

Outgoings

Cost of estate	15 000
15 slaves at 300 rd each	4 500
80 wine leggers at 12 rd	960
Implements for pressing, distilling	500
Three teams of oxen	500
Two wagons	800

Horse, wagon and team		900
Household furniture and utensils		2 000
	Total	25 160

Upkeep is estimated at

Interest at 6 per cent		1 509
Clothing for slaves, 15 rd per year		225
Corn for bread, 36 muids at 3 rd		108
Tea, coffee, sugar		150
Clothing for family and contingencies		350
Duty at barrier on 120 leggers		360
Wear and tear, parochial assignments		120
	Total	2 822

Returns

100 leggers marketed at 30		3 000
20 brandy at 50		1 000
Wine and brandy sold to country Boors, with the fruit and poultry brought to the Cape Town market are more than sufficient to balance every other contingent and extraordinary expense		
	Total return	4 000

Total profit 1 178 rd or approximately £294.

On an equally optimistic estimate he returns the yearly profit for the grain farmer at £143, and his opinion favours the wine farmer.

George Thompson in his *Travels in Southern Africa* (2 vols, 1827) found the country fairly sober; there was little drunkenness. He comments on wine:

'With regard to wines the colonial interests of the Cape cultivator have been sacrificed to those of the foreign winegrower in a way which would not have been tolerated in a contest between the colonial spirits of the West Indies and the foreign spirits of France or Holland. At the period when universal war made it doubtful how long we might be able to procure from our enemies or our allies a cheering glass to alleviate our troubles, it seemed good to His Majesty's government to open at least one resource for our drooping spirits by giving every possible encouragement to the growth of wine "to make glad our hearts" within our own territories. By a government proclamation issued 19th December 1811, the cultivators and merchants of the Colony were directed to the subject of the wine trade, as a consideration, of all others, of the highest importance to its opulence and character and such proclamation, after authoritatively demanding from the settlement a serious and lively attention to their interests, promised "the most constant support and patronage on the part of government" and that no means of assistance should be left unattempted to improve the cultivation and every encouragement given to honest industry and adventure to establish the success of the Cape commerce "in this her great and native superiority." This proclamation was followed by the appointment of a Wine Taster and Examiner of Casks – by the repeated publication of the best advice and information as to the best method of culture and the management of the wine – by the offer of *premiums* to those who planted most largely and those who produced the best wines – by a promise that the old channels of this trade should be reopened and new ones found, and by a variety of regulations, all evincing most strongly the lively interest which government took in promoting this trade and which were fully ratified by the Act of July 1813, admitting Cape wines to entry at one third the duty on Portugal wines (Memorial to the Treasury, 1824). The effect of these measures fully answered the expectations formed of them; the Colony rapidly advanced in wealth from the ready sale of its surplus produce, and additional property has since been embarked in this trade to the extent of at least half a million sterling; while in England, the wine drinker of moderate means, driven from the use of the higher class of foreign wines, as well as by their increased and increasing prime cost, as by a high rate of taxation, found in the equally wholesome, though perhaps less palatable, produce of our Colony a medium between the entire desertion of his accustomed habits and a resort to the less gentlemanlike system of grog drinking. That the extension of the colonial system to this new species of wine should give umbrage to those "whose craft was in danger" from its introduction will excite little surprise; and consequently Cape wine has ever been marked out as an object of execration by the "Foreign Wine Trade" – its quality traduced, and the dangers of frauds upon the revenue pointed out to government with a dexterity which, coming from a quarter so practically conversant in the tricks of the trade, could not but be perfectly convincing. The consequence of this organised hostility was that when the duties on foreign wines was lowered nearly one half and the Cape duties left at their old rate, the interviews between the Cape merchants and those with whom the power of relief rested very much resembled the parley between Yorick and the mendicant Friar. "But the best reason of all was that I was predetermined not to give him a single sous." The palpable cruelty of prematurely withdrawing a protection which at once depreciated the value of each person's property, who had been *tempted* to invest it in this now proscribed article, to the extent of at least one-third, drew forth from the Colonial Department, highly to the credit of their humanity, very strong remonstrances upon the subject. But it had become a Treasury question; and *there* its significance amid the press of the more important matters affecting the enormous revenue of Great Britain could not procure for it the same favourable attention; and the decision, which was attended with such fatal consequences, was lightly justified, both in and out of Parliament, by sarcastic remarks upon the wretched trash under consideration, or upon the iniquities of adulteration, to such an extent that the rank fiery Sherry, the acid north side Madeira, the meagre Teneriffe of former days, were no longer to be found at the taverns neat as imported. Whether before the introduction of Cape wine any method existed of at once defrauding the revenue, and adding to their own profits by the mixture of ingredients more pernicious than the juice of the colonial grape, is best known to the trade, but they have been sadly libelled from the days of the "limed-sack" of Falstaff to the modern times of sloe-juiced port, if the introduction of Cape wine has been the first thing that has led them into temptation. As to the intrinsic bad quality of Cape wine, as furnishing a reason for driving it out of consumption altogether, I must contend that it is as yet premature to form a judgment. The only well-founded complaint that I have ever heard of it is a certain earthy flavour, disagreeable to the English palate, in a great part of the wines (for some are entirely free from it) and in regard to the causes of this there is such a diversity of opinions, of which a long course of practical experiments can alone determine the correctness, that the space of about a dozen years (during which short term only has any attempt been made to discover a remedy) seems scarcely sufficient to enable us to come to a fair conclusion. That the praiseworthy efforts now being made by his Excellency the Governor, the Commissioners of Enquiry, and other leading persons of the Colony, to promote the improvement both of its wines and spirits, by the establishment of a committee consisting as well of gentlemen of the highest chemical attainments as of those who have long been extensively engaged in the practical details of the trade, will in a reasonable time be productive of favourable results, I have no doubt. In the meantime the Cape of Good Hope has at least a good claim to a full and adequate protection to her staple produce as any other of our more influential colonies, whose liquid or solid productions are forced upon the home market by protecting dues. The loss of property has already been too considerable, and still further depreciation must take place in 1830, when an additional duty of *twenty-five per cent* is to be levied, unless the Lords of H M Treasury can be induced to reconsider the question.'

He shows that the wheat farmer is now better off than the wine farmer and consequently more people are growing wheat, for which the country is not really suited.

John Splinter Stavorinus (*Voyages to the East Indies*, 1798) states that Van der Stel very carefully tested the soil at Constantia to find out the amount of saline matter in it before he planted the vines. He describes how, on his little excursion to Stellenbosch, he everywhere obtained 'a good glass of wine', mentioning Albertyn's farm at Klapmuts and the Melcks' farm on the Berg River.

'I have observed that we never drank any wine of one and the same flavour, at two different places; every soil that produces wine, gives a different taste to it. The vines, which are planted by themselves, like currant bushes, are set in rows, three feet from each other, and when they are pruned are not more than two, or two-and-a-half, feet above the ground. They are planted in rows, and not close to each other, in order to afford room for the labourers to go between them, to weed the ground, without damaging the vines. A thousand of them, it is calculated, will produce a leager of wine, and sometimes more. Albertyn van de Klapmuts had a vineyard close to his house, with fifty thousand vine plants, which yielded him annually seventy leagers of wine. The pressing of the grapes is performed in a more simple manner here than in Europe. The slaves gather them, and put them into a vessel, the bottom and sides of which are bored full of holes; this is set in the inside of a larger one, upon a crosspiece of wood laid at the bottom of the latter; this outside vessel has a spigot and faucet, through which the juice, as fast as it is pressed out, runs into a tub placed beneath. The grapes being heaped up, in the inner vessel, to the brim, three or four slaves, after having washed their feet in a tub of water standing at the side, get upon the fruit, and holding themselves fast by a rope fixed to the ceiling, trample upon it, and squeeze out the juice as long as they are able. In the meantime the must that runs out is put into large high vessels to ferment. If the aperture be obstructed by grapes, or stalks, so that the juice cannot easily run out, they push them away with a stick, to the end of which a few brushes are fixed. The trodden grapes, before they are further pressed, are put upon a coarse strainer, made of rattans, on which they are rubbed with the hand, till the husks go through it, the stalks remaining behind, which are thrown away as they are supposed to make the wine austere and bitter. The husks are then put into the fermenting vessel, which the next morning is in full fermentation; during this process the thick parts subside, and the must grows clear, when it is barrelled off, being first filtered through a wicker basket. The grounds remaining in the fermenting vessel are afterwards put into a square vessel pierced full of holes, and placed in a larger one with a spigot and a faucet at the side; at the top there is a screw of wood or metal, by means of which the last drop of juice is pressed out from the husks. From the dregs and husks that remain over from the last pressing, brandy is distilled. No yeast is used for accelerating the fermentation.'

He describes his visit to Melck's farm, where he found one hundred and fifty leaguers of wine properly stored.

'Melck could neither read nor write . . . He was a native of Prussia, and had arrived at the Cape many years ago, in a very low station. Understanding the burning of lime, the making of bricks, and something of agriculture, he had entered, as head servant, into the service of the former proprietor of this farm, but which, at that time, had not by far the same extent as at present. When his master died, he married the widow (which does not unfrequently happen in this country), and extending his enterprises from day to day, he at length obtained from the Company the exclusive farm for the sale of wine and spirituous liquors, by which he cleared one hundred thousand guilders (about £9 000 sterling) in one year, chiefly by the arrival of the French fleet at the Cape. This enabled him to undertake still more important objects, so that he once bought up all the wine produced in the country, which amounted to some thousands of leagers. Though this did not conduce to the benefit of the public, yet it sufficiently shows the spirit of enterprise which animated the man.

'The vineyards of Constantia consist of two farms, called *Great* and *Little Constantia*. Their annual produce is of red wine about fifty pipes, and of white about ninety; yet the vintage here, as in other places, is different in different years. These two farms were for a long time the only spots which could produce this delicate wine; but lately some other farms in this district, and in a few other places, have been able to bring their wines to the same degree of excellence. But as the Company reserved to themselves the exclusive sale of Constantia wine, which frequently was considered as contraband, and was not to be bought or transported to Europe under that name by individuals, they hit upon the expedient of giving their wine, which in point of goodness does not yield to Constantia, the name of *maag* or stomach wine.'

(He[1] was at the Cape in 1774.)

cape wine in the early nineteenth century

---

1 John Splinter Stavorinus.

Chapter 6

Cape Wine in the Early Nineteenth Century
(Continued)

Lord Macartney's successor, Sir George Younge, was an enthusiastic gourmand, a lover and critic of good wine, elderly, inclined to be irascible and peppery, pompous as is the nature of such characters, and not at all clever. Very naturally, therefore, he made mistakes, and his administration was so unsatisfactory — 'fuddled,' indeed, as one of his superiors complained — that he served barely a couple of years. But in that time he learned to appreciate Cape wine, and never lost his taste for it. He did his little best to improve viticulture within the limits over which he ruled. He visited the wine farmers and was popular with them, sampling their produce and commenting frankly as he sipped. Duoro Port, Malmsey, Madeira and Lunel were then still the favourite club wines; the Rhenish and lighter French types had not yet achieved fashionable popularity, while the great Italian and Hungarian wines were hardly known in England. The Cape produced its incomparable *Constantia*, its interesting Pontac that when sweetened was better than most of the exported Portuguese wines, and its manufactured sherry and Madeira that varied considerably in quality. They were produced in surplus quantity, but there was still no free trade for the winegrowers, and Sir George quickly saw the advantage of obtaining an English market for them. Several difficulties, however, had to be overcome. Wine merchants in England knew very little about them, for only a few years before the Governor's arrival had the Cape vintners exported them to England and the West Indies. Now these export types were blended wines, a little good wine being mixed with a great quantity of inferior stuff, that, heavily fortified, was sent out, usually in cask, to be further sophisticated on arrival in England. The result was that, as a member of the House of Commons expressed it, 'Wine from the Cape was regarded as a drink only suitable for tipplers and bargemen'.

Sir George, who knew better, urged that Cape wine should not be penalised by a heavy duty and by long delays at the docks. He strongly advised that it was in the interests of the Colony that a revenue from the export of wine should be raised, and as the first champion of 'colonial preference' his advocacy was crowned with surprising success. On 9 June 1800, the House of Commons decided that 'all spirits imported from the Cape of Good Hope should be subject to the same duties and drawbacks as those imported from the West India colonies, and that all wines from the Cape should be subject to the same duties and drawbacks as those imported from Portugal'. The Treasury informed Sir George that the charges would work out approximately as follows: 'Cape wine, per tun of 252 gallons, carried in English bottoms: Customs £16 16s; Duty £20; Convoy duty £1 6s 6d; total charges £38 2s 6d. Total charges for Cape wine per tun, carried in foreign bottoms: £40 18s 6d.' These were very satisfactory rates so far as the Cape vintners were concerned, for they yielded a handsome profit on exported wine.

In a letter to the Secretary of State, dated 22 October 1800, Sir George wrote in some detail about canteen conditions at the Cape. The wine was so heavily adulterated that some of his soldiers had died through drinking it; the canteens made enormous profits; one held by a Mr Kemble, a recent arrival, realised £1 000 a year out of cheap wine. The government had found it necessary to appoint inspectors, in accordance with the old regulations that had never been scrupulously carried out, to ensure that good wine only was sold. Two months before he had issued a proclamation appointing Mr Richard Blake 'Wine Taster' and Mr Arend de Waal 'Assistant Wine Taster', with full powers of entry, and with authority to stop all casks coming into Cape Town at the barriers to take samples and to reject impure wine. A tax on brandy was also under consideration.

These innovations were resented, not so much by the winegrowers, perhaps, as by the trade, which by that time had become firmly established at Cape Town. The wine farmers, indeed, seem to have liked Sir George personally, and appreciated his interest in their doings. He founded the first Agricultural Society in South Africa, under the title of 'The Society for the Encouragement of Agriculture, Arts, and Sciences', of which he was president, with Mr Barrow as secretary. 'Beyond talking,' remarks Theal, 'this society did nothing,' but that is not quite fair, for it did stimulate interest among the more progressive wine farmers, and led to the first tentative efforts to hold a show of agricultural products in the Governor's garden. What was of more importance was the establishment of a department of agriculture and an experimental farm at Klapmuts under the supervision of Mr William Duckitt, an expert from England, who was paid a salary of £40 a month. This farm, like most experimental farms in South Africa, spent much money without a proportionate return, but it stirred interest in new methods of tilling the soil, Mr Duckitt being of an ingenious mind and a great admirer of his improved plough that was designed to revolutionise the industry and supersede the old machinery for preparing the ground. Whatever may be said about his administrative deficiencies, Sir George's interest in matters agricultural certainly deserves better appraisement than that which our historians have given him.

Their doubts about the wisdom of much of what he did in other directions appear to have been shared by the authorities at home, who summarily recalled him, and appointed a commission to investigate the charges that had been made against him. One of these was that he had infringed the eighth clause of the Articles of Capitulation, that stated that no new taxes should be levied, by levying a tax on spirits. The Commission found this charge unproved, as nothing had been done that could in any way be regarded as an innovation. The objections against the stoppage of wine at the barrier were no longer valid as wine was now freely admitted. The unpopularity of Mr Blake, the Wine Taster, was natural, but the official did his work without prejudice and there was no reason to abolish his office. For several years, however, this official was a source of much outspoken criticism.

General Dundas, who succeeded Sir George, was far more concerned with the military aspect of affairs than with the agricultural development of the Colony. He was far-sighted, and realised how helpful the possession of the Cape would be to whoever held India. The Cape station was now increasingly popular with the squadron as well as with the military, and the original settlement of Van Riebeeck had expanded to a size undreamed of by Mr Secretary Van Dam. The Officers' Mess was at Wynberg and at the Castle; the navy had made Simonstown into almost a rival of Cape Town, and at both places the lodging houses and taverns catered amazingly well for visitors. In the memorandum of Egbertus Berg, that used to be (and perhaps still is) in the Berlin Library, these matters are noted, and some slight, but appreciative, reference is made to Cape wines.

> 'They are most splendid wines, but are unfortunately sold too young, too adulterated, and too rank, which has given them a bad reputation. Constantia is an exception, but this is a rare wine, and strangers are usually cheated with Muscadel. Cooperage is provided in insufficient quantities. . . .'

At that time, 1801, brandy was already being distilled from the surplus vintage as a matter of business. The raw spirit was not very good, and the final product, after three years in cask and suitable blending, was stated to be 'something like Spanish spirits, but harsher'. A long time was to pass before Cape brandy was given the attention and care that it merited.

Another visitor who relished Cape wine was Brevet Colonel Arthur Wellesley, of the 33rd Regiment, afterwards to be far better known to fame as the Duke of Wellington. Although he had quarters at the Officers' Mess at Wynberg, he preferred to spend most of his spare time in two private rooms in a house belonging to a Mrs Berg at Mowbray, where he assiduously studied military science to make up for the time lost when he had been a rollicking major. He rarely accepted invitations, but made an exception in favour of his friend Walker, a member of the largest merchant firm in Cape Town. Mr Walker, who report said was related to a well-known laird in Scotland, was a bachelor, rich, hospitable, and generally esteemed both for his honesty and his business acumen, and his weekly dinners were held to be the best to which anybody at the Cape could be invited. That was mainly because Mr Walker was served by a very loyal butler, Hendrik Heger, known to the officers as 'Cheap John', a slave and descendant of slave parents, whom his master had emancipated and made major domo at the Newlands house. The butler was a connoisseur of Cape wines, and his wife was a talented cook, whose curries, kabobs, sausages served with fried bananas, and other delectable compositions were the talk of the town. To this hospitable bachelor establishment Colonel Wellesley came fairly regularly, and, as Heger many years later told a curious reporter, found the Pontac and the Madeira from Mr Cloete's farm to his liking, and said so. The dinners were sometimes Bacchanalian, but 'the Colonel never took over-much wine, and always rode home by himself' while some of the other guests had to be given temporary sleeping quarters before they could travel back to Cape Town. Very little has been discovered about Wellington's stay at the Cape, and we are grateful for 'Cheap John's' reminiscences, that are buried in the files of an old local newspaper. About the Duke's host we know a trifle more. Mr Walker's firm failed disastrously, after a series of unfortunate speculations in Rio de la Plata, and soon after the bankruptcy his partner died. The house at Newlands had to be sold, the servants dismissed, and everyone expected that Walker would retire to Scotland where he had rich relatives and influential friends. But he stayed on at the Cape. His former slave and butler, who had prospered and saved, had a cottage at Wynberg, and shared it with his former master for thirty years. Mr Walker survived him, but still refused to leave South Africa, preferring to go to the New Somerset Hospital, where Dr Bailey cared for him, and where he died a few years after his faithful and devoted emancipated slave.

The documents in the Cape Archives give some information about the official Wine Taster reappointed by the proclamation of December 1811. The letter book of this official covering the period from July 1816 to April 1826, when the office was abolished, contains much interesting material. In one letter the writer complains that a great deal of inferior wine is clandestinely exported as 'sea stores', especially to St Helena, and that some farmers had bought imported French wine to mix with their own wines for exportation. He instances cases of attempted bribery and evasion of the law. The letter book gives full details of the Wine Establishment, and is annexed to the day-book that lists the quantities and value of wine registered every month for export, with the names of the vintners, destination of the consignments, and much varied information. The official ledger book is also preserved; this gives all particulars about the wines brought to the barriers. The reports of the Wine Taster are bound up with the ordinary 'Letters Received' and contain little that is of general interest. In the Orphan Chamber reports (Vol 93, Colonial Office) are to be found several other interesting documents in connection with the Wine Establishment. There is a letter from W Caldwell, the first Wine Taster under the new régime, with draft instructions, hints about viticulture, and observations on the then existing methods of making wine; another listing the various sorts of Cape wines (Pale Madeira; High-coloured Madeira; Yellow Madeira; Old straw-coloured Madeira; Very old Madeira; Pale deep Madeira; Old Muscadel; Straw-coloured Muscadel; Very old deep-coloured Muscadel; Very old Steen; Pontac, etc). The various functionaries appear to have carried out their duties conscientiously, and to have had rather a thankless job. Bourke's letter to Bathurst, explaining why he had abolished the office of Wine Taster, is not in the archives, although the reply to it, dated 3 October 1826, has been preserved as No 820. In the Report of the Commissioners of Inquiry it is stated: 'The recent abolition of the wine taster's fees has superseded the necessity of any particular remarks from us. The amount collected by this office upon wines exported during the year 1825 was Rds 15 575 or £1 168 2s 6d, and we are not aware of any corresponding advantage that was gained throughout the whole period of its existence. It was an old office that was revised in the year 1812, and some of the worst wine that has been produced in the Colony was suffered to pass the Wine Taster's office, to which much of the unfavourable opinion that has been obtained of the wines of the Colony may be attributed.' The Rev Mr Leibbrandt, in his memorandum to the Select Committee on the Export of Cape Wine in 1888 (to which I am indebted for much of the information in this note) is of opinion that 'the temptation to pass and approve every cask submitted to the Taster's office was irresistible in the face of the financial condition of affairs at the time'.

The records of the Council also contain matters pertinent to the consideration of the state of the industry when the Wine Establishment was abolished. Eighty wine farmers submitted a memorial in December 1825 in which they pointed out that while they could very well bear the tax on wine when there was a definite market, the fall in prices and the failure of the vintage that year had reduced their incomes by one half, and that 'their chances of livelihood are accordingly seriously imperilled unless relieved by the kind of intercession of the Governor in Council'. The memorialists were informed that while no definite answer could be given, the subject was under consideration, and His Majesty's Government had already been approached on the matter. At further meetings of the Council it was minuted that Earl Bathurst had replied that no reduction could be made in the duties on Cape wines, but that abolition of the Wine Taster's fees might be considered if it could be effected without exposing the colonial revenue to a great loss. On 3 July 1826, the draft ordinance abolishing the office of Wine Taster was formally approved by the Council.

General Dundas was still unhappy about the trade's criticisms against Sir George's 'restrictions'. In a letter to the Right Honourable Henry Dundas on 23 July 1801, he wrote:

'The public have by no means relished the Wine Tasting Establishment which is attended by many grievous inconveniences to the proprietor of the wine sent up to Cape Town on account of the casks being opened at the barriers affording the means as well as the temptation for slaves and others to break open and drink the wine. The Establishment through experience having been attended with no sort of use, it is my intention to defer taking any steps until after the new vintage.'

On 27 August, he issued a proclamation that abolished this vexatious restriction, but the Wine Taster and his assistant were allowed to continue their work, which earned the cordial approval of the regimental doctors who had raised objections to the quality of wine sold to the garrison.

When the *interregnum*[1] came, the new administration found so much else that demanded immediate attention that it had no time to study viticultural problems. Commissioner de Mist seems to have appreciated the importance of the industry, and General Janssens, who was his own quartermaster-general and took an active and laudable interest in the welfare of the troops under his charge, saw to it that the canteens were regularly inspected. The harvests were, on the whole, good, and much wine was made, though it is to be feared that most of it was not of excellent quality, for an increasingly large quantity was being used for distillation. The number of wine farmers increased, for there was now a ready local market and a fair expectation that export would be profitable. The English firms that had settled at Cape Town during the First Occupation[2] remained, and those that dealt in wine exported wine not only to Europe but to India and to America as well.

When the administration again changed, the new Governors became increasingly interested in the industry. It was even suggested that wine farming might be extended far beyond the existing wine districts. Colonel Cuyler, in a letter to the Colonial Secretary, advised that 'farmers from Stellenbosch should be encouraged to settle in the Zuurveld to produce corn and wine'. The importance of the export trade was fully realised. Thus, the Earl of Caledon, writing on 21 March 1810 to the Earl of Liverpool, remarks:

'I beg to attract Your Lordship's attention to the encouragement of the ordinary Cape wines and brandy. The Constantia has been hitherto the sole wine usually exported to England, but it is even here an extremely expensive wine, being in price about 100 rd or £20 for 19 gallons. But, My Lord, I send you eight kinds of the common wines and some Cape brandy with their prices, and if it be the pleasure of His Majesty to encourage the growth of wine in this Colony for the supply of the Navy or for Home Consumption, and to reduce the duty to that upon the home-made wines and spirits, I have little doubt of this Colony becoming in a few years competent to supply any demand that may arise.'

On 14 March 1807, General Grey had issued a proclamation reaffirming the right of the administration, under the contract made by the Dutch East India Company in April 1793 with the proprietors of the farms *Great* and *Little Constantia*, to demand from each farm 30 aums of wine; that is, 15 aums of red wine and 15 aums of white wine, at the rate of 150 guilders or 50 rix dollars the aum. This proclamation authorised a committee consisting

---

1 1803-1806.
2 1795-1803.

of John Murray, His Majesty's Commissary General, two members of the Court of Justice, and Mr W S van Ryneveld, to select and set aside 30 aums from the vintage of 1806.

Sir John Cradock's proclamation of 19 December 1811 stated that 'this Colony can produce as excellent wines of various sorts as perhaps any country in the world' — the first direct and official enunciation of a great truth that is even now not generally recognised. Sir John, himself no mean judge of the quality of a good wine, demanded from winegrowers 'a serious and lively interest, as wines are losing their reputation', and promised that adequate premiums and rewards would be given and that an Institute of Wine Tasters would in due course be established to give help and advice to farmers.

Action, however, lagged upon intention, and nothing practical seems to have been done, until in 1814 the government widely distributed a 'general advertisement' that gave the wine farmers the benefit of expert opinion on what could be done to improve matters.

> 'The present moment is most favourable to the introduction of Cape wines into general use, but this is not to be accomplished with effect without the total abandonment of the present system conducted as it is under a false principle and full of error throughout.'

This was certainly a frank and perhaps not wholly fair condemnation of the methods then in use, but it was in part justified by the deterioration in the product of the vineyards. The advice given was that vines, now far too closely planted, should be more widely spaced, and trained on espaliers of bamboo or reed, not more than four feet high, to prevent damage by the southeaster wind; that all vineyards should be scrupulously weeded; that existing vine plots should be drastically thinned; and that great attention should be paid to removing shoots and leaves so as to give the grapes sufficient air and sunlight. Further, the greatest care should be taken in gathering the harvest, and in pressing the grapes and eliminating all rotten and immature berries. 'The grapes should be pressed out by men's feet.' All casks should be washed out with brandy and the greatest cleanliness observed. Farmers were to be allowed to send their wine into town after the first fermentation, and the wine merchants were to take it over at that stage. The wine merchant, the advertisement went on, had then to further improve the wine by keeping it in his possession for at least sixteen months, separating it at the end of that time into four different qualities and blending his final wines accordingly. After 1 January 1813, all wines had to be shipped in pipes of 100 gallons each, half-pipes and quarter casks. The Government would grant:

- a gold medal, value 300 rix dollars, to the farmer who led the greatest number of vines, not fewer than 2 000, by 1 September next;

- a gold medal, value 200 rix dollars, to the farmer who planted the greatest number of new vines, not fewer than 2 000, properly spaced, of that species only from which is produced Cape Madeira, by 1 September next;

- a gold medal, value 150 rix dollars, to the farmer who produced the best Cape Madeira;

- a gold medal, value 100 rix dollars, to the farmer who sent in not less than five leggers of Cape Madeira of the most approved quality and uniform flavour;

- a gold medal, value 100 rix dollars, to the farmer or merchant who submitted the best sample of wine considered to come nearest in flavour to real Madeira;

- a gold medal, value 300 rix dollars, to the wine merchant who produced the best certificate of the superior quality of wine shipped by him, not less than fifty leggers, from any foreign market within the space of fifteen months after shipment.

A committee, consisting of Messrs H Alexander, W S van Ryneveld, J A Truter, C Bird and F W Forster, was appointed to report on the matter of wine licences and to advise if these could be changed to a uniform tax. It finally reported against any change, Mr Truter and Colonel Forster expanding at great length upon the pros and cons of the difficult problem of adjusting matters to satisfy all concerned. On 10 January 1812, the Government issued regulations for the Wine Taster's office. From these it appears that the official had to seal all casks for export and to keep samples of all wines tasted; he must not taste wine before 8 am nor after 3 pm; must not trade in wine in any way; must keep books; must report on any bad wine, and when he refuses a certificate of export must inform the Governor, who may, if necessary, 'publish the names of parties attempting so serious an injury to the interests of the settlement.'

Up to this time the wine farmers had been singularly fortunate in escaping serious disease in their vineyards. The common pests had been mainly entomological; birds and dogs, about which earlier observers had complained, no longer did much damage, while sun-scorching, millerandage, and leaf blight could be kept under control. Now, however, a more dangerous condition was noted, apparently by Mr M van Breda, who in his diary in 1819 (quoted by Dr Pappe) reported a rust disease that affected the Hanepoot grapes more than the Stein variety. This was probably the first observation on a serious disease, oidium, that forty years later was to cause considerable destruction in the vineyards.

During Lord Charles Somerset's administration the industry developed more or less satisfactorily. The Deputy Judge Advocate, who was also the Deputy Quartermaster-General and Aide-de-Camp to the Governor, and a gentleman of 'elegant taste', was appointed Wine Taster, with Mr W M

Ludley as Inspector of Casks and Mr G Paton as bookkeeper to the Wine Establishment. The wine merchant's annual licence was reduced to 50 rix dollars, but the licence for foreign wines and beers was fixed at 200 rix dollars. It is interesting to note that licences were required for many other purposes, for instance to erect a tent near the wharf, to remain in the Colony, to leave the Colony, to cut timber, and to go on a visit to the Caledon hot baths. Instructions to the wardmasters and captains of watchmen and to the watchmen themselves emphasise the importance of preventing abuse of spirituous liquor. In 1829 the wine farmers and merchants made the first conjoint effort to better their wares; they established a Joint Stock Company at Stellenbosch to improve the quality and price of wine. The shares were limited to 100, each of 1 000 rix dollars, which could be paid by the shareholder in cash or in 15 leaguers of new and 10 leaguers of matured wine. The prospectus stated that 'Mr Poleman has in his possession samples which show, without any possibility of doubt, that wine can be made in this Colony capable of competing with the best samples of sherry or Madeira'. The Company exported two cargoes of 'superior wine' in 1831, but after that we hear very little about its activities.

At this time the following statistics were published:

Cape districts: vines in bearing, 2 601 650; wine made, 1 461 leaguers. Stellenbosch: not stated; wine made, 12 500 leaguers. Worcester, Tulbagh and Clanwilliam: not stated, 6 500 acres planted with vines; yield not stated. Swellendam: not stated; 100 acres planted with vines; not stated.

From other sources we learn that Worcester district produced 789 leaguers of wine, and 153 leaguers of brandy in 1829, while the district of Clanwilliam produced 48 leaguers of wine and 23 leaguers of brandy. A local publication stated: 'There are now five varieties of wine made at *Constantia* from a vineyard of 120 000 vines; 30-40 leaguers at each farm, red and white, Frontignan and Steen.'

Sir John Cradock appointed a committee in 1814 to consider if it was worthwhile to modify the licensing fees. The committee, after taking evidence from both the merchants and the winegrowers, suggested the following taxation in *lieu* of the existing licensing fees:

Ten rix dollars on each leaguer of wine; 20 rd on each leaguer of brandy, brought into Cape Town or Simonstown, subject to a drawback on exportation.

Five rix dollars and 10 rd on each leaguer sold in the country, and three and six rix dollars respectively on wine and brandy used by the grower for domestic purposes.

Wholesale merchants' licences to be increased from 50 to 200 rd.

All retailers to take out a quarterly licence at 30 rd.

A duty of 2 rd on each half-aum of wine and of 6 rd on each half-aum of brandy bought for retail from merchants or growers.

From this time onwards a number of ordinances appeared modifying the existing taxation on wines, sometimes in a bewildering manner; the principle enactments were those of 9 December 1829, 26 June 1832, 27 June 1832, 7 August 1832, 20 December 1832, 4 June 1834, 10 December 1834, 5 October 1846, and 30 March 1846, the last having reference to conditions under which liquor could be sold beyond the limits of the Colony.

Contemporary publications contain much that is interesting to students of Cape wine, but it is impossible to extract all the relevant references. The following must suffice.

In 1830 a local firm advertised for wine that had not been produced from 'clay subsoil' and advised that greater care should be taken in cleaning grapes before pressing. A writer in the *Bengal Hurkaru* declared that Cape wine was generally so earthy in taste that it was unpalatable. In a letter in the *Cape Literary Gazette* of 2 January 1832, obviously written by a vintner who was an expert, the writer complains that wines from the country are usually inferior and seldom up to sample and specification. The 'wine committee's recommendations,' he complains, 'have not been followed, for prejudice and private interests were too strong . . . Instead of imitating other wines, we should produce a wine with a character of its own . . . Inferior wine should be used solely for distillation.' These criticisms are supported by the artist Milbert, who drank Constantia but found it 'heady'. He visited a Stellenbosch wine farm and gives a good description of what he found there. The Stellenbosch growers were more progressive, apparently, than those in the Cape district. At a dinner held on 7 February 1824, Mr John Collison, the wine merchant, who had already done much to stimulate the production of good wine, presented a silver cup to Mr C J Briers for his 'Cape Madeira,' and another for 'Cape Hock' to Mr J M Helsdingen, both Stellenbosch farmers. In his speech he commented favourably on the good quality of wines that came from this district, but earnestly urged his hearers to concentrate on quality rather than quantity. His action and example were in striking contrast to the 'discouragement by wine merchants of our local wines' of which '*Bystander*' complained in the *Cape Literary Gazette* in 1832, a complaint that had already been voiced by Adam Slokker's letter in Afrikaans to the *Zuid-Afrikaan* in 1830, who stated that wine could be had at Swellendam for sixpence a bottle (*Wyn in Swellendam is seks pens vir een bottle.*) By proclamation (3 January 1812) wine merchants had been forbidden to export wine in bad casks; the casks had to be approved by the wine taster and to be marked and reserved for export use; no one could use them for any other purpose, under a penalty of 100 rd; wine farmers were repeatedly warned not to ask too much for their new wine. They were now also vexed by further restrictions, and complained that the Wine Tasting Establishment served no longer any useful purpose. Wine merchants were well able to judge the excellence of wines offered, and there was no need to salary three government officials with 5 200 rd a year (the Wine Taster drew 3 000; the Gauger and Tester of Casks 1 500, and the Bookkeeper 700 rd) to test wine that came into the cellars of Cape Town and Simonstown. In the circumstances, it was decided to abolish the Wine Tasting Establishment, a decision that was generally approved.

The industry was now in a bad way, through over-producing without a corresponding active market, but perhaps more through the determined efforts that were made in England to depreciate the quality of Cape wines exported. There is no doubt that good wines sent out from South Africa were deliberately adulterated on arrival in England, with the result that, apart from the high-class Constantia, available only to the friends of the administration, no really drinkable Cape wine could be bought in that country. On the Continent matters were not so bad, but comparatively little was sent to Holland and Germany, and none to France. The reports on consignments that reached Germany were favourable, but freight and excise made export to that country highly unprofitable. The Indian market offered a solution, and for a time Cape merchants toyed with the idea of sending most of their blended wines to Calcutta. A letter dated 1825 from John Trotter, a Calcutta wine merchant, states:

'On arrival of your wines in India, three great objections were entertained. These were: the peculiar earthy flavour of some samples; excessive fieriness; and, in all, want of age and aroma. I am persuaded that if the earthy and saccharine flavour could be eradicated, there would be considerable market in India for Cape wines. ... They were first sent to Bengal in 1812; that consignment was very good.'

Trotter recommended better blending, and pays high tribute to the excellence of samples from Collison & Co, whose brandy particularly impressed him.

By an Ordinance in Council on 3 July 1826, the office of Wine Taster was abolished, and exporters of wine were relieved from the duties formerly levied by this official. The following year the tax levied for gauging casks was repealed, and in 1828 the licensing taxes were in part repealed in favour of direct levies on production; farmers were allowed to sell *bona fide* product of their lands outside a twenty mile limit of a town or ten miles from any licensed house or store, on payment of a yearly licence fee of a little over three rix dollars. Notwithstanding these concessions, the conditions under which the winegrowers farmed their vineyards were not conducive to the production of high-class wines. Even in 1815, the Colonial Agent in London had crabbed their wares. In a letter to the Cape, he wrote: 'Cape wine is so inferior that its importation is hardly worthy of financial consideration'. 'It is hardly any use,' wrote an English vintner to a Cape Town merchant in 1819, 'to send me your Madeira; there is no sale for it, as it is damnable poor stuff.' Yet this 'damnable poor stuff' was drunk by the Governor and by the officers of the mess and considered excellent. One cannot but believe that the campaign against Cape wine in England was organised, deliberate and calculated to decrease the export from the Cape in favour of an increased import from France whose wines were now coming rapidly into favour, and Portugal, whose port was now being expensively advertised, with almost as much ingenuity and recklessness as vitamins are today.

All this tended to depress the wine industry at the Cape, and the imposition of further excise duties nearly killed it. Somerset, writing to Bathurst (who liked Cape wine, especially the Madeira) remarks:

> 'The wine farmers can at present scarcely find any market for their produce, and from the measures which have lately been adopted in England to facilitate the introduction of French and other foreign wines, it is not likely that their prospects will brighten.'

While a Mr P van der Byl writes to Captain Hare on 6 October 1825 to complain bitterly about the woes of the wine farmers: 'Profit from it has so much decreased that we now consider horse breeding much more lucrative, and we are deeply grateful to His Excellency for what he has done in this matter' (horse breeding). In the same year Martin Mulders, a descendant of one of the oldest wine farmers in the Colony, petitioned for protection of Cape brandy, 'which is now the only hope for the winegrower who cannot make a profit out of wine'. The Government Commissioners reported that as in the division of Stellenbosch the growing of wheat had been a secondary object to the production of wine, the situation was serious enough to demand immediate attention.

Chapter 7

Weathering the Storm

Sir James Emerson Tennent, in his *Inquiry into the Operation of the Wine Duties on Consumption and Revenue*, published in 1855, affirmed his conviction that 'should any Chancellor of the Exchequer come to the determination . . . to take wine out of the category of articles from which, as *luxuries*, it has been hitherto customary to raise a revenue and transfer it to the class of *necessaries*, with an almost nominal duty, it is but justice to the trade that they should be early apprised of such an intention, in order that the continental growers of wine may be prepared for any increased demand in this country, and that the trade at home may be enabled to take the necessary precautions for its own reorganisation under such a revolution in the economy'. In his preface, Sir James sighingly admits that the wine trade in Great Britain is 'a craft which in some of the branches seems to justify the ancient title of a mystery.' His now almost forgotten treatise contains much that is of interest to Cape winegrowers, and is particularly instructive where it deals with the evidence given to the House of Commons Committee of 1852, of which he was a member, on the subject of adulteration. Quoting Dr Gorman's testimony, he writes:

> 'No natural sherry comes to this country; no wine house will send it; the article you get is a mixed article; if they gave you the natural produce of Xeres it would not suit you; in all probability you would say it was an inferior wine; our taste is artificial because we are not a wine-drinking people. If your tastes were directed to natural wines, Spain alone could supply this country with hundreds of thousands of butts of beautiful choice wines, which are not known in this market . . . because you would not drink them.'

> Another witness, a Mr Lancaster, a wine merchant, told the committee:

> 'The most iron prejudice rules over wine, and a new wine coming into the market will not even be tasted. A man would be almost mad to introduce a new wine here; he would have to go and look for every separate customer from door to door.'

The consensus among those who appeared before the committee was that the prevailing taste was wholly for fortified wines. The statistics quoted amply support this view. From 1786 to 1794, port wine accounted for 75,67 per cent, Spanish for 16,67 per cent, Madeira, Sicilian and Canary for 4,02 per cent, and the lighter French and Rhenish for barely 3,64 per cent of the total consumption in Great Britain; Cape wine was not drunk at all. In 1825 Cape wine had partly established itself in favour; it represented 8,37 per cent of consumption, as against 1,834 per cent for Rhenish and 6,56 per cent for French wines. In the following year it reached the zenith of its popularity, and stood third on the list, Port heading the consumption with 46,77 per cent, Sherry coming second with 26,78 per cent, and Cape wine 10,41 per cent. After this year its consumption steadily declined until in 1851 it was but slightly in excess of three per cent, while Sherry had increased to over forty per cent and French wines, expecially the heavier types, to over seven per cent. Dealing more especially with Cape wines, Sir James states:

'From the Cape our importations have been decreasing year by year since 1825. Up to that period a fictitious demand for this cheap colonial wine was created by the excessive duties on foreign growths, which paid 13s 8d and 9s $1\frac{1}{4}$d a gallon, whilst Cape wine was admitted at 3s and 2s 5d. Under this artificial stimulus the consumption rose to 670 000 gallons in 1825, but after the reduction of the duties on foreign wines in that year, and subsequently in 1831, it declined to—

465 773 in 1840;
246 132 in 1850;
182 322 in 1853.

'The history of the trade in Cape wines is an illustration of the fact that, in the absence of those qualities which consort with the tastes of this country, *mere cheapness* cannot force a wine into favour or maintain it in uniform demand. The existence of a discriminatory duty on Cape wine at the present moment, in the face of a declining demand, serves no other purpose than to keep up the supply of an ingredient for adulteration (it is used in the manufacture of what are called "British wines" of some of which it forms the basis), and its decreasing importation shows how little it is sought after, even for this base use.'

Sir James's solicitude for the mysterious trade interests might reasonably have been charitable enough to embrace the Cape winegrowers, who, after their golden years, saw themselves suddenly, and through no fault of theirs, deprived of that measure of protection and encouragement on which they had founded their industry. Sir George Younge and Lord Charles Somerset had both realised the importance of that industry, and had done all in their power to foster and develop it by bringing about a greater measure of co-operation between the wine merchants on the one and the wine farmers on the other hand. The vintners, too, had done their best to safeguard common interests, and there is no proof that the adulteration of Cape wines, apart from the addition of extraneous spirit to suit the English palate, was their doing. On the contrary, the reputable Cape Town exporting firms blended their wines with great care, purchased the best that could be had in the country, and sent out consignments that were identical with the samples. While the Wine Establishment lasted, the Cape government, to a large extent, guaranteed the quality of the wine exports. The sophistication of Cape wine began after its arrival in England, and there are abundant proofs that vintages of a particular year that were found excellent by continental tasters were described as 'pretty awful' by wine judges in England, a difference that can only be accounted for by wilful adulteration. One of the pioneering Cape wine merchants, Mr John Collison, was indefatigable in urging wine farmers to produce quality wines. The government had appointed a wine committee in 1826, 'to inquire into every circumstance relative to the culture of the Vine, the manufacture of the Wine, together with its treatment up to the moment of exportation, and the age at which it is to be exported; with a view to ascertaining the cause of its not being of a better quality and flavour . . . and to suggest such measures to be adopted as may conduce to a general improvement in the wines of the Colony'. This committee did excellent work. Answers to a questionary issued by it to all wine farmers provide interesting and instructive information about the methods then in general use, and show that the most progressive growers were careful and conscientious. The committee's wine expert, Mr Daniel Dixon, gave lectures, replete with hints that a hundred years later earned the cordial approval of the late Dr Perold, who wrote in 1936:

> 'What Dixon said about fermentation in small casks is as true today as it was then, and an insufficient fortification of fermenting must may still very easily result in a sick, sweetish wine being obtained. Further, he was quite right in laying stress on the value of press must obtained from grapes that have been harvested fully ripe, since the pectic and other matters that give the wine its best quality are in the layers of cells immediately inside the husk of a fully ripe grape and too little of this gets into the must when the grapes are merely crushed. If the grapes are well trodden by the human foot, more of these valuable materials get into the must than when they are crushed in a grape mill.'

The state of the industry at the time when the wine committee was started was already precarious, although few except the winegrowers, the vintners and the government realised how heavily the repeal of the protective duties would damage it. The agriculturist Teenstra, who visited the Cape in these years, found the industry flourishing; he describes his visits to the *Constantia* farms, where he tasted the different kinds of wine and was most hospitably entertained by the widow Colyn, and concludes that the Colony can produce much wine of a desirable quality. Sir George Keith, many years before, on his visit to South America, had touched at the Cape and, although he does not seem to have noted anything about the different kinds of wine, agreed with the Admiralty that the Colony was an excellent base for the supply of wine to the squadron. The statistics of production and export give perhaps the best indication of the success that had attended the combined efforts of all interested to effect some improvement in the industry:

Year	Leaguers produced	Leaguers registered for export	Leaguers exported
1812	11 979	2 152	—
1813	6 724	2 824	—
1814	8 697	2 341	—
1815	14 365	3 647	—
1816	15 398	4 111	4 418
1817	10 713	9 076	9 105
1818	12 382	5 580	6 399
1819	13 343	4 621	4 805
1820	15 210	4 712	4 338
1821	16 254	4 221	5 005
1822	15 348	7 600	7 253
1823	21 147	7 939	7 013
1824	16 183	7 966	8 013
1825	No return	—	5 814
1826	No return	—	6 026

During that time French wine was liberally imported into the Colony, to the amount of 42 000, 46 000, 47 000, 20 000, 28 000, 45 000 and 25 000 rix dollars in the years 1820 to 1826. Foreign brandy to the amount of 1 414 749 rix dollars was imported during the same period.

The chief exporting wine merchants at the Cape were then Collison, Sheppard, Venning, Hertzog, Bergh, Couvin, Sandenberg, Herman, Watson and Thomson, but many others exported in retail quantities, and some private speculators bought up 'registered for export' wine and consigned it to wine merchants in England or America, Calcutta or Canton. One such enterprising gentleman afterwards made an unusual pother about his failure to obtain a sufficient profit from his adventure, and wanted the British government to indemnify him. This was the energetic Mr Strombon, who had resided at the Cape for many years before General Baird's forces landed on the shores of False Bay, and claimed to have given considerable 'moral and intellectual support' to the invading party. He was treated with marked consideration by the newcomers, and embarked upon various speculative undertakings on the strength of his standing with the authorities. One venture was the consignment of 22 000 gallons of Cape wine to England at a loss of £3 000. A second consignment of the same quantity to 'Mozambique in the *Good Hope*' resulted in a loss of £4 000. He claimed £48 000 from the government, but his hopes of redemption foundered on the rocks of Lord Bathurst's cold indifference, and the 'Strimbon case' which at one time caused a mild susuration in the lobbies of the House of Commons is today of interest only to the antiquary.

The Cape vintner could export his wine to England under far more favourable conditions than when the Colony was still under Batavian rule. His wine paid an import duty of 2s 6d per gallon in England; import duty in Mauritius was 6 per cent *ad valorem*; into Rio, 15 per cent *ad valorem*; into van Diemens Land also 15 per cent *ad valorem*; and into New South Wales —

which had not yet started to grow its own vines — 5 per cent on the invoice price. In addition there was a rapidly growing local market. The Navy alone took between 18 000 and 20 000 quarts yearly, while the garrison bought all its 'common wine' by contract from local dealers.

Another profitable branch of the trade was private custom. Every householder bought wine, for that beverage was then considered indispensable in a civilised household, and as much wine was used in the kitchen as on the table and in the sitting room. The various 'day-books' of Cape Town merchants give interesting details about this private custom. One, in the South African Public Library collection of manuscripts, gives the prices and amounts of wines bought, sold locally, and exported. The best-class wines were bought from Myburgh (hock type), van Schoor (sweet white, Muscadel), Dickson (Steen), Cloete (Cape Madeira; Pontac; old wine; Frontignac), and among the clients were all the local officers, from the Governor downwards, the Governor of New South Wales, Sir John Herschel, George Rex of Knysna, reputed a bastard of the royal family, Sir William Burnett, a high-class London physician, and wine lovers in China, Bombay, Madras, Montreal, Washington and Leipzig. This merchant exported large quantities to Rutherford Bros at Washington, and to many other English and continental firms, but it is curious to find that he rarely sold any imported wine, and it is evident, from local diaries of the time, that in private houses little French or German wine was drunk, although both were served at regimental mess dinners. Some wine lovers, however, did import high-class wines from the continent, and the late Dr Hahn used to relate how he had been acquainted with an old gentleman who still held, as a splendid trophy, a bottle of the famous 'Comet Steinberger of 1811' that had been imported in 1826, and was 'at the time we tasted it perfectly undrinkable, of course'. Most local clients bought regularly to the value of 30 to 50 rix dollars a month, and the prices varied from 60 rd for sweet muscadel to 10 rd for new wine per half-aum. The wine merchant paid less and less for his wines as the supply became larger. In a letter to Bathurst on 24 October 1826, Major-General Bourke wrote:

> 'The price of wine is not more than £2 5s a leaguer of 152 gallons, which hardly pays the cost of carriage to the market, but growers will have to sell as they have neither casks nor store room nor capital to enable them to hold out for a better market.'

The cost of carriage, indeed, was of great importance to all winegrowers outside the peninsula. By the proclamation of 1815 they were not allowed to bring wine into Cape Town or Simonstown except at certain seasons of the year, and this proclamation was only repealed by Sir George Lowry Cole in 1832. The road from Stellenbosch and Paarl across the Cape Flats was not then a hard road, and the heavy wagons had to struggle through stretches of wind-blown sand, making the journey a long, tedious and trying pilgrimage that when the southeaster blew was particularly disagreeable.

We get some interesting information about the wine industry, curiously enough, in the report of an appeal to the Privy Council that in those days excited Cape Town and for a while raised passionate discussion in England. A Cape Town wine merchant named Anderson had refused to liberate one of his slaves who claimed that under an old Dutch *plakaat* she was entitled to manumission for reasons that appear to be self-evident to common sense but were apparently most obnoxious to the lawyers. Her plea was rejected by the Cape Courts and, with the Governor's consent, she was allowed to appeal, through her curator, to the Privy Council, where Mr Sergeant Lushington and Mr Brougham appeared for the respondent, Anderson. The appellant won her case, and in the documents affixed to the full shorthand report (by the late Mr Gurney) appears a letter from Anderson's London agent, a Mr Strachan, that contains a paragraph on Cape wine:

'I have purchased (for you) 15 puncheons of Cognac at 2/9d per gallon. Good Cape wines have been for some time scarce and in demand. I heard of one parcel of fine quality being sold at £34 in Bond; I therefore hope yours will be choice, and the nearer the quality of Sherry the better. There is some little demand for Pontac, but I have never been able to get rid of the Pipe per *Cornwallis*, and the quality has been objected to. I do not consider that it is any disadvantage to Cape wines arriving here in winter; they do not taste so well on the Quay when chilled with cold, but soon recover in the vault, and all the Cape wines improve very much by keeping, as I have experienced in the last parcel by the *William* ... Messres ... do a good deal of business, but I should think at considerable expense in travelling about the country to take orders for single pipes; besides, they do not sell from the London Docks, but bring the wines to their own cellars and make them up. In point of fact they do not stand very high there, and buy brandies (payable in Capes) on very disadvantageous terms. The Excise here do not permit samples of spirits to be shipped; however, the broker for the *Robert* managed to get samples for the 15 puncheons on board.'

From this it seems clear that the trade in England deprecated the 'making up' of Cape wine as much as did the vintners at Cape Town. The latter, however, were powerless in the matter, and they and the winegrowers had to submit, indignantly but helplessly, to the virulent condemnation of Cape wines by members of the House of Commons when the question of duties on wine came under discussion. Some of the remarks made by possibly well-intentioned but utterly ignorant members of Parliament were particularly galling to those who, like Lord Bathurst, knew the facts, and it is to his Lordship's credit that he consistently opposed the proposal to remove the protection from colonial wines. None acquainted with conditions at the Cape could have credited the statement that 'the winegrowers there are waxing rich by the sale of the worst trash that it is possible to imagine', or 'the Cape vintner pays nothing towards the revenue and is richly rewarded for his idleness and corruption'. One excitable critic complained that Cape wine was 'poisonous' and had caused the death of 'many of our brave soldiers and sailors exiled to that part', which was probably an exaggeration of the incidents reported early in the century when there had been no government control of the taverns. The obvious reply, however, would have been to point out that more than one brave sailor and soldier had died in English ports after a debauch of gin and adulterated wine.

A more unkind assertion was that the winegrowers did nothing for the country. They, at least, could then and can now claim that they were the first to devote a portion of their profits to some cultural object. In March 1818, Lord Charles Somerset had imposed the one rix dollar tax upon every cask of wine and spirits entering Cape Town as a special fee for testing and gauging the wine, but he had immediately given the assurance, in reply to a question from the winegrowers themselves, that the proceeds of this tax would be devoted to the establishment and maintenance of a public library. A public committee was formed, and the library was opened two years later. In 1823 the Treasury decided that the method of financing the institution was unsound; the wine tax proceeds were then paid into the funds, and an annual grant of £300 was given to the library committee. When in 1827 the wine tax was finally repealed, the library committee received a commutation allowance of £921, and decided to appeal to the public for further support. The South African Public Library, one of the best institutions of its kind in the southern hemisphere, may thus be said to have been founded in the first instance by the exertions of the winegrowers. It is a sad reflection that it contains, even today, fewer books on wine than many a parochial library in Great Britain.

In March 1825 the Cape Government was advised of the changes that the Treasury proposed to make in the current excise. These were changes that had been discussed long before they came before Parliament, and Lord Bathurst had opposed them, while Somerset had written strongly to point out how adversely they would affect the Colony. It seemed as if the authorities in England were as unconcerned about the fate of the winegrowers as, a century before, the old Company had been, and that all that was required of the Colonists was that they should contribute all they possibly could to the revenue. There appeared to be still some doubt, among the Treasury officials, about the success of the substitution of the sale of licences and the imposition of extra duties in place of the system of farming the retail of liquors. The 'Pagter' or monopoly holder had become insolvent in 1822, when the payment to revenue was 133 333 rd. Under the new system, from 1823 onwards, there were 45 licencees permitted to retail Cape wine and brandy and foreign brandies at 1 500 rd; 66 licences to export liquor at 250 rd and 21 licences to import liquor at 250 rd. Even the committee of the Commons was satisfied that the change was not so bad as might have been expected.

The other alteration, however, that in the wine duties, was reckoned a disaster by both the government and the wine farmers at the Cape. In March 1825 the difference between the duties on Cape and other wines entering England would no longer be in favour of the Cape. French wines would be charged 6s a gallon if conveyed in British ships; Cape wines if conveyed in British ships would be taxed 2s a gallon and 2/3d if carried in foreign bottoms; all other wines would be taxed 4s if shipped in British ships and 4s 4d if carried in foreign vessels. In 1831 this was again modified; henceforth the duty on Cape wine was fixed at 2s 9d per gallon; all other wines would pay 5s 6d a gallon. The protective premium over French and Canary wines that the Cape had, for more than 12 years, possessed was changed effectively to the benefit of the competing wines that had a shorter sea passage and consequently a far lower freight in their favour.

The Colonists thought it very unfair and unjust that such changes should be made without hearing their side of the case. Constitutionalists have not failed to find, in the proceedings of the meeting held on 16 July 1831 at Cape Town, the first indication of that sturdy democratic sensibility that has made the Cape Colony, along with Canada, the first champion of the real as opposed to the theoretical freedom of a community. It was a meeting thoroughly representative of the wine industry, and also of the general commercial and professional class in the Colony, but it is interesting to note that here, as in the case of the establishment of a public library, the wine industry took the lead and gave guidance to the rest of the community. The meeting was called, by advertisement, primarily 'To take into consideration the state of the wine trade', but it developed into a general review of the constitutional rights of the Colonists, and ended with a petition to the King for a legislative assembly composed of representatives freely chosen by the inhabitants. Comic relief was supplied by the facetiousness of a certain Mr A M Buckson, who acted as a voluntary Bottom and vigorously defended the case for mulcting Cape wines. Mr Michael Breda, one of the most respected farmers in the Colony, was unanimously voted to the chair, and wisely confined his remarks to introducing the speakers. The first of these was a wine merchant, Mr Ebden, whose integrity, experience, progressiveness and skill none could question. He asked the meeting to endorse the first resolution which amounted to a statement of the case, and was worded as follows:

'That as a matter of National Policy for the interests of British Commerce, and for the purpose of raising a large revenue within this Colony, Government held out the most solemn assurances of protection and support to all who should invest their capital in the Vineyards, or employ it in the preparation of the Wines of this Colony for the supply of the British market; and it was on the faith of these assurances that the immense Capital now fixed in that Trade was withdrawn from other occupation and diverted to it.'

He pointed out that the state of the Colony was not so prosperous as it had been. A violent storm had caused damage; harvests were poor. The decision of Lord Althorpe, the Chancellor of the Exchequer, to lower the protective duties at this time on one of the chief products of the Colony came as a great blow. By the equalisation of duties Cape wines would be made to pay almost 200 per cent, while the duty on foreign wines would be under 100 per cent. As a wine merchant he knew that what was said about Cape wine was often wholly untrue. Such wine was adulterated in England, but pure natural wine was exported. He cited his own consignment of Cape Madeira, that the Excise officers seized on arrival in England, averring that it was not Cape at all but real Madeira wine.

Mr Advocate Cloete, in seconding the resolution, reminded the meeting that in 1811, when England could get no wine from the Continent, the Cape was naturally and rightly regarded as a source of supply of this valuable commodity. The Governor had in that year by proclamation urged the people to increase the supply of wine, and the government had done all in its power to encourage wine farmers. The British Parliament had in 1833 agreed, in the proper spirit of co-operation, to grant a preferential tariff for Cape wines. Much relief had been given to wine farmers by lowering the import duties on material that they needed for the industry. Premiums had been paid for good wine; prizes and medals had been given. Indeed, every inducement had been held out to Colonists to become wine farmers, and to others to sink their capital in the industry. As a result more than a thousand wine farms had come into existence; more than 30 million vines had been planted and were bearing grapes, while the industry gave work to 30 000 people and represented an invested capital of 21 million rix dollars. Under the old tariff Cape wine had a protection amounting to £28 per pipe and the annual return of wine production rose from 7 335 leaguers to nearly 20 000 leaguers in five years. In 1824 the labour employed by the wine industry was one-third of the entire labour in the Colony. Now all that would be changed, and the wine from the Cape would have to compete, heavily burdened, against French and Canary wines. It was untrue to say that Cape wine was bad, adulterated, over-acid, or poisonous trash; we exported some of the best kinds of wine, and were not responsible for what happened to it when it reached England.

The meeting passed the first resolution, and then agreed upon the following three extra resolutions:

‘That if a change of circumstances renders it convenient and wise for Great Britain to introduce changes into her policy with regard to Foreign Trade and Commerce, justice requires that some provision should be made for the protection of the capital thus sunk, it being impossible to withdraw it in any shape from its present employment without enormous loss to the Community, and the unmerited suffering of individuals engaged in the Trade, and the total ruin of the Wine Growers.

That the Wines of this Colony cannot yet compete on equal terms with those of Europe in the British Market; but the proposed equalisation of duties on all wines would place us in fact immeasurably below the Foreigner, in what was held out as our proper and natural market; and that an *ad valorem* duty, or a duty equal to one-third of that levied on Foreign Wines, would sufficiently protect this branch of our trade, and redeem the pledges made to those now engaged in it by the British Government.

That Memorials, founded on the Resolutions now passed, be drawn up and signed by the Meeting and transmitted to the House of Commons.'

In speaking to these resolutions Mr Collison, one of the best-known Cape Town wine merchants, pointed out that Cape spirits paid the same duty as French spirit while spirit from other colonies paid only half that duty. The assertion that Cape wine was uniformly bad was entirely false and absurd. It needed maturing and improvement, no doubt, but what was exported was generally of fair quality and did not in the least merit the strictures that had been passed upon it in the House of Commons, while some consignments were of excellent quality. In the memorial for the information of the House of Commons — to which that dignified body did not pay the slightest attention — statistics and details about the wine industry were given, the gist of which has been imparted to the reader in the foregoing pages. The petition, resolution and memorial had no practical effect; the duties remained as they had been intended to remain, and the contemptuous remarks about Cape wine made in the British Parliament (and often repeated in published writings since) remained uncontradicted, with a nuance of credibility over them which took generations to dispel and is even today not totally removed.

To those who are interested in the adulteration of Cape wine, then generally prevalent, may be commended Charles Tovey's *Wine and Wine Countries*, the introduction to which is devoted to a description of the manner in which 'South African wine' was produced in England. In justice to the author, who was a wine connoisseur and very well able to tell good from bad wine, it may be stated that he was good enough to class real Cape wine as being 'not amongst the very worst of wines.' 'Things are better than they were 20 or 30 years ago,' he writes (in 1862), 'and the wine is much improved. A parcel may occasionally be met with that will bear comparison with Sicilian Marsala, to which we believe it at all times to be superior as regards vinous merit ... We concur in the opinion of those who think that in no wine-growing country is there scope for greater progress than at the Cape. Care and science properly bestowed, upon her vinous products, would compensate for any outlay or expense. If instead of quantity, quality became the consideration, the evil would be remedied. The overdose of wretchedly-made spirit with which the wine is drugged, prior to its shipment for England, entirely destroys whatever good character it might have originally possessed. We have met with persons — residents at the Cape — who informed us that excellent wine was to be drunk there from their own vineyards; they likewise stated that the red wine, when of a proper age, is good, sound and very palatable; both the red and white wine being drunk by the inhabitants in preference to any other. Our informants assured us that the wine was quite different from that usually sent to England; as indeed it needed to be. It would be a source of gratification, as well as of benefit, to the mother country, to have it in her power to encourage the growth of her settlements; and it is a stigma and a reproach to perpetuate a character for producing bad wine, when the fault is shown to be remediable; especially in a country so favoured, and where nature is free from any share in the blame.'

With this opinion the wine merchants and the more progressive winegrowers at the Cape agreed. When it became obvious, as it did after a short while, that the Exchequer did not intend to 'give relief to the wine industry in this country by a just and judicious readjustment of the wine duties', they set themselves sturdily to cut their losses and to devote their attention to the other markets at their disposal. The best of these was the local market, at that time not yet restricted and hampered by absurd legislation. For the 'fine wines' there was still a payable offset abroad, without resorting to questionable practices. Long before Sparrmann had pointed out that some Cape wines had strong individual characteristics that could stand transportation overseas. In the German edition of his book he refers to one which he calls the 'Magellanischen Schluckchen' that tasted 'like a Spanish tint,' and another that resembled 'a Rhenish hock.' He held a high opinion of the veritable Constantia, and in his French edition writes:

> 'Les amateurs accautumés à se payer de vains noms, boivent souvent avec délices un vin de Constance imaginaire, qui n' a rien de commun avec le veritable que le nom.'

The Cape Town vintners took this fact into consideration. They blended their wines with some skill, and produced varieties that, without masquerading under well known names of types with which they had no real affinity, possessed a dignity that appealed to continental and Indian customers, and even won praise from the wine merchants of New York. 'Your light wines,' writes one of these Americans, shortly after 1834, 'have arrived safely, and we are much pleased with them, as they appear to be less acid and at the same time more pleasant than the French wines we have been getting.'

This, apparently, was a dry red wine, sent through the firm of Borrowdale and grown somewhere on the peninsula. Possibly it was the 'light red table wine' of which Sir John Herschel ordered a regular monthly half-aum while he sojourned at the Cape.

From now on we obtain more information about the industry from the daily press than from government reports, and the main sources are the newspapers and private documents, together with district reports from the various resident commissioners that are filed in the Archives. Full returns of production are not available; such statistics as there are, up to 1860, are incomplete. Valuable information is obtainable from the published reports of agricultural shows, that from now onwards became annual features and in the course of time were to be regarded as of national importance.

The leading wine farms were still the three *Constantia* estates, though other farms in the Peninsula, and a few in the districts of Stellenbosch, Paarl and Worcester were becoming known as producers of fine wines. The following press notices of the *Constantia* farms date between the years 1830 and 1834:

'*Sebastian Hoof Constantia*, formerly the Country Residence of the English Governor of the Cape, and exchanged in 1806 by Sir D Baird for *Newlands*, is 400 acres in extent, the greater part of which is suited to the production of the luscious Constantia wine. About 40 acres were planted by the late Mr Sebastiaan Valentyn van Reenen in 1817, all in one year, with the different sorts of grapes which now produce on an average 60 Pipes of red wine, white Frontignac, Steen and Pontac Constantia. The vineyard is enclosed with a double hedge of oak and quince; it is considered the largest in the Colony and lies upon a sloping hill with an eastern aspect. Its distance from *Great Constantia* on the lower part is about 50 yards. Its ground has been worked in one year with the Miner plough by the skilful English farmer, the late Mr Wm Duckitt.'

An advertisement:

'TO STRANGERS
Intending to visit the Original
Old Constantia
known by the name of
Great Constantia.

In consequence of several Constantias having latterly sprung up, it has been thought useful by the Undersigned to publish the following

Travelling Directions

for the information of Strangers, by which disappointment may be prevented.

Passing the Toll Gate at the Military Lines, the Road between Cape Town and Simons Town is kept to a little beyond the seventh milestone, when it branches off through the Village of Wynberg, down the Wynberg Hill, until in view of the Estate Alphen (of Mr D Cloete). Here turn off to the left over the Bridge, keeping the Main Road to Hout Bay for about two miles till you reach the Constantia Cottage. Here right in front, will be seen in large letters, arching an entrance, the word 'CONSTANTIA'. This is *not* Great Constantia, but on the left a small board will be seen directing the Traveller to the proper road, which followed half a mile farther, will bring him to the real Constantia named

GREAT CONSTANTIA

known for upwards of 170 years, and the Property of the Undersigned.

It being the chief object of the Proprietor to maintain unimpaired the just celebrity of the genuine Constantia, he never sacrifices the quality of his wines to produce a large quantity, and he can now confidently offer to the Public his unrivalled Stock of Genuine Constantia Wines consisting of Pontac; Frontignac; White, Red; which may be had either in bottle or cask.

NB – For the convenience of Masters of vessels, Passengers and others, a quantity of the genuine article is constantly left on hand in Cape Town at Mr Gaums, 14 Castle Street, and at Simons Town at Mr Martin's, where also orders may be left.

J P Cloete'

A later advertisement states that Mr Cloete has appointed Mr Jan Albertus at his store, 2 Castle Street, as his only agent. Mr William Hollett, of the Freemasons Tavern, 32 Hout Street, advertises that he has taken out a retail licence and has for sale: 'Champagne, 50 rd per doz; Superior Port and Claret, London Particular Madeira, and Prime Sherry at 26 rd per doz; and a variety of Foreign Wines at equally reasonable prices. The best Cognac can be had at 6 rd per gallon, or 1½ rd per bottle; second quality Genuine Hollands and Superior Jamaica Rum 4½ rd per gallon or one rd per bottle; Mauritius and Cape spirit at half that price; Old Cape Madeira at 6 rd per doz; younger Cape wines at 3 rd per doz.' The General Store or Big Butt at 39 Dorp Street (then a much more fashionable locality than it is now) advertised 'Old Wine two skellings per bottle; young wine four dubbeltjies; Cape brandy two skellings per bottle'. Another advertisement reads:

'For sale at No 1 Newmarket Place, about 120 Leaguers of Old Wine, brandied and prepared for the London Market. Samples can be had after the 15th January 1824. The Purchase Money may remain on Interest for five years upon giving good Security. The Store and Stuckvats to hire for one or two years if required . . . H Ball'

Travellers, too, occasionally report on the wines. Joubert, writing in 1847, remarks:

'*Le petit vignoble de Constance produit l'un des meilleurs vins connus; c'est un vin liquoreux sans exces, doux, fin, spiritueux et d'un bouquet extrémement suave; on lui attribue de merveilleuses qualities hygieniques; mais il ne se recueille qu' en petite quantité; on se le dispute au Cap même, et il est tres rare de l'obtenir en Europe par voie commerciale; on ne peut avoir confiance que dans quelques flaçons apportés par les amis des propriétaires et reçus comme présènt.'*

The anonymous 'Indian Officer', who visited the Cape in 1843, went much farther afield than merely the environs of Cape Town, where he stayed for some time. He reports most favourably on the old Cape Town boarding houses, where wine was always served with the midday meal. Mrs Gunn in Burg Street charged seven shillings and sixpence a day; Mrs Usher in Wynberg and Mrs Savins in Roeland Street, sixpence a day more, while Mrs Van Schoor, who had a house in the fashionable Strand Street, priced her board and lodging, much patronized by officers and officials, at nine shillings a day. The unknown officer went to Paarl and beyond and noted—

'... the fine farm of Mr Hugo, the Field Coronet of the District, who is well reported of far and near, and who will readily open his house for the reception of visitors and strangers. The wine made on this farm is the best of its kind in the Colony. It is one of those originally planted by the French Protestant Refugees, who were located by the government of the day in this favourable position for the culture of the vine, and from one of whom Mr Hugo is descended.'

This was apparently the ancestral farm of the Hugos at Paarl, where the South African artist, Hugo Naude, spent many of his boyhood years, and where good wine is made today.

From what the contemporary records tell us, it is clear that the vintners and the winegrowers resigned themselves to the task of making the best of a bad situation. Their exports to England declined steadily. Some of the winegrowers turned their attention to farming and horse-breeding, but the more progressive and further-sighted maintained their faith in the industry in that anxious time that saw the close of the middle of the last century.[1]

weathering the storm

---

1 The nineteenth century.

Note to Chapter 7

Interesting information about the adulteration of Cape wine during this period may be obtained from contemporary issues of *The Lancet*, a scientific journal that from the first had vigorously championed the use of natural wine as a healthy beverage, and as forcibly and consistently condemned the taste for fortified, highly alcoholised wines. In 1867 it published the following analytical table, compiled by Dr A Dupré, showing how a Cape wine, at 18s a dozen bottles, compared with other wines on the London market.

	In 1 000 parts of						
	1	2	3	4	5	6	7
Ranenthaler 1864 18s	74,4	6,74	1,18	0,175	0,256	0,431	0,581
Ranenthaler 1862 54s	88,3	4,45	1,78	0,2392	0,218	0,4572	0,4596
Hattenheimer 1862 40s	99,7	5,25	0,67	0,253	0,201	0,454	0,521
Steinberg Cabinet 1858 120s	97,4	4,113	1,305	0,2944	0,236	0,528	0,499
Light Claret 1865 15s	90,5	3,38	2,22	0,17	0,144	0,314	0,5056
Cape Wine 18s	241,0	2,244	1,47	0,3348	0,2922	0,627	0,8276
Port 1864	185,6	3,075	0,84	0,1288	0,3018	0,4306	0,6202

1 = Alcohol
2 = Fixed Acids
3 = Volatile Acids
4 = Alcohol converted into Volatile Ethers
5 = Alcohol converted into Fixed Ethers
6 = Total Alcohol in Ethers
7 = Ditto, calculated

Previously it had published an elaborate analysis of many other wines of all kinds, including some much more lightly fortified Cape wines, and had commented favourably on the general excellence of the latter and deplored the tendency to add 'extraneous spirits' to beverage wines.

Chapter 8

The Day-Book of Jacob Cloete

There are few remaining private records of winegrowers of these early days. The Myburgh and Cloete manuscripts in the Archives contain relatively little that is of general interest. I have read other documents that contribute much more to our knowledge, and among these is one of the most interesting journals kept by a winegrower in the early part of the last century.[1]

By courtesy of the Misses Cloete of Plumstead, I have been allowed to browse through the day-book of their grandfather, Jacob Cloete, the owner of the farm *Groot Constantia* in the first half of the last century, and one of the makers of the three famous wines that have won for themselves an international fame.

The book is a big, soft calf-covered ledger, with many pages of unruled, thick, linen-woven paper, half of them closely covered with writing in various scripts, some obviously made by thick-nibbed goose quills, others by the pinpoint pens of a later date, in inks that have faded to dull dirty brown. It is a complete record of the income and expenses of a typical wine farmer of the first half of the period, who starts by summarising what his assets and liabilities are, and gives full details of his various activities. Its interest is enhanced by a number of contemporary letters and odd notes that have been preserved between its pages, by the information it supplies about dealings in wine at Cape Town during the period 1824-60, and, last but by no means least, by the certified copy of the agreement between the owners of Constantia wine and the Honourable East India Company, dated 2 April 1793, by which the proprietors of the farm pledged themselves, in perpetuity, to supply the Company with 15 aums of red and 15 aums of white wine every year.

Mr Cloete started his day-book in 1824 when he assumed possession of the farm. He begins by recording his assets, starting with 'a list of such goods as have been obtained by me from my mother, the Widow Hendrik Cloete, Senior, by purchase at auction or out of hand' with the prices paid for such goods. Among these he enumerates the following—

The farms *Groot Constantia* and *Steenbrassems River*, as well as the right to the *Strand Fontein*	240 000 gulden
307 half aums Constantia wine	142 608 gulden
Cooperage, tools and apparatus	15 351 gulden

---

1 The nineteenth century.

In the last item are included two presses (300 g), one copper still with accessories (300 g), 80 leaguer casks (3 200 g), two large *trapbalies* (100 g), and two stikvats (250 g). On the next page he details what he paid for the eighteen slaves bought at the auction on 9 October 1824, a total of 92 250 gulden; he also bought furniture and 'extras' to the amount of 10 154 gulden. For his slaves he paid fairly high prices, probably because they were trained on the farm and well acquainted with the work on the vineyards and in the cellars. For Klaas van de Kaap, later on 'mandoer' or head slave, he paid 3 050 rix dollars; for Patrys and Jonathan, both Cape born, he paid 2 700 each; for Tobias, from Mozambique, 2 300; for 'Mathys van Mozambique, together with his wife, Serronie, and his boy Isaac, both Cape born', 4 500; for Esau, Nero and Frans, all three 'sturdy Cape slaves', 5 950; for Hoop, of Mozambique, 1 850; for September, *'van Goegies, met syn brouw Mariserra van Mozambig en een jongetjie, Ontong, van de Kaap'*, 4 900; and for the four other slaves, from Malabar and Ternate, 2 800 rix dollars. His total expenditure on assuming possession of his farm was thus well over 500 000 gulden, against which he reckoned various sums owed to him amounting altogether to some 60 000 gulden. Every year he notes his income and expenditure, down to the smallest detail, and this part of his day-book is of considerable interest to all students of domestic history. It is, however, of lesser importance to students of the wine industry at the Cape, but I may be pardoned, perhaps, for including two paragraphs that are worth quoting.

'1 August 1824. The aforementioned Green came to reside with me as tutor to my children at a wage of 25 rix dollars per month, and continued until 1 May 1825 . . . rd 225. Books for my children . . .43 rd 5 st.'

(*'Aug 1. Is gezegde Green by my koomen inwoonen als informator myner kinderen teegens RD 25 per maand en gecontinueerd tot den 1 May 1825 . . . Aan Boeken etz, voor de kindere . . .'*)

'Juvenile emigrants: William Henry Priestly was apprenticed to me on the 8th day of May, 1834, for the term of five years (*vide* indenture). John Derham was apprenticed to me on the same date for the term of eight years (*vide* indenture). Paid to Mr Ewan Christian for the apprenticeship of the said Priestly £8, and to the same for the apprenticeship of the said Derham £12.'

In a letter which has been preserved, Mr Cloete's son-in-law, William Hiddingh, writes—

'Dear Papa. I have just fested (*sic*) your apprentices from board the *Munster Lass*; there is only *one* for you, and you will see him yourself before opening this letter I dare say. His passage money I paid to Thomson and Watson, four pounds ten shillings, and had to go on board for him myself; *ergo* boat's hire and some little trifling expenses yet to pay for his sustenance three or four days on board ship. He seems a very good boy, but small for his age . . .'

Of greater interest is the careful record of 'persons to whom wine has been sent'. Mr Cloete kept this wine register from January 1824 to December 1859, and it is undoubtedly one of the most complete and accurate wine sales books of the last century kept by any wine farmer at the Cape. In comparison with it the Bergh register, now in the manuscript collection of the South African Public Library, and the Elsenburg (Myburgh) papers deposited at the Archives, are much less informative. It is possible that some other registers exist, and if so, those in possession of them should make them available for study, and should deposit them in some safe place, like the Library or the Archives, to be carefully preserved. We know so little about the wine industry in the last century, especially in the first half of it, that such scraps of information as may be obtained from old family papers are to be gratefully welcomed. In these early years of the last century there were wine farmers, like the Worcester Hugos, the Paarl Bosmans, and the Clanwilliam Moutons, whose wines, to judge from what those who sampled them wrote about them, rivalled the Constantia wines. Wine farmers – or at least some of them – then took a pride in their sweet wines, and there were no silly statutory restrictions to prevent them making as good a wine as Mr Cloete's Constantia red with an equally low alcoholic content. Those who remember the *Nagmaal* wine of Brakfontein, and that lovely Muscadel prepared by 'Koos Mosterdpotjie' will readily agree that our preposterous wine legislation has not fostered but rather retarded the evolution of our superior sweet wines.

Mr Cloete rules his pages into four columns, the first for his Constantia red, the second for his white Constantia, the third for his Frontignac and the fourth for his Pontac. All the sales were recorded in half-aums, and the prices, up to 1843, are given in rix dollars; after that date the prices were given in pounds, shillings and pence. Where other wines, or brandy, were concerned, a marginal note was made, and where the wine was delivered in bottles (usually brought by the purchaser to be filled on the farm), a corresponding entry was made. Here and there a special note shows that further precautions were taken. For example, wine for a sovereign potentate, the King of Prussia, had to be specially bottled and cased; wine sent to van Diemens Land needed extra careful packing. There are several letters that show how pernickerty some of the customers were. One wrote: 'I cannot understand how it is that your wine is so altogether different from the Constantia I tasted in London; it seems to me that the voyage disturbs its quality'. Mr Cloete should have referred this gentleman to the evidence given before the House of Commons wine enquiry committee, where a wine merchant stated that the rankest trash was sold in London as 'pure Cape wine', and that the adulteration practised in regard to Cape wine was 'worse than any other in the trade'. Usually, however, clients left it to his discretion, both as to the selection and the packing of the wines, and there are numerous appreciative letters, from all parts of the world, testifying to the excellence of his four 'perfect wines'. This is no place to describe them, or to discuss the differences that may have existed between them and the real

Van der Stel Constantia. Indeed, it is now quite impossible to have any certainty about such differences. The Constantia that Mr Cloete sent abroad can be judged on its merits; there are several bottles of the 1854 vintage still in existence, and the Misses Cloete have two of an even older date. The Van der Stel Constantia has vanished like the famous 'Comet Steinberger' of 1811, which, if any exists, would no longer be drinkable. We can only conjecture about its quality, and for such assumptions as we make we have to rely entirely upon contemporary evidence.

The wines with which Mr Cloete's day-book deals were all analysed, exhibited, and tasted, and there is ample testimony about their excellence. The red Constantia had an alcoholic strength of 13,42 vol per cent; the white of 14,50 vol per cent; the Frontignac and Pontac had a slightly higher strength. The price charged for the first, in cask, was 200 rix dollars per half-aum; for the white it was the same; the Frontignac was 250 rix dollars per half-aum; and the Pontac 100 rix dollars. The Steen wine was sometimes sold by the pipe, and most of Mr Cloete's customers referred to it as 'hock', though he himself never mentions that name. He had common sense sufficient to appreciate the fact that Cape wine gains nothing whatsoever by masquerading under a Continental name, and infinitely much if it makes a distinctive name for itself, as his own Constantia had done, by inherent excellence and individual merit.

He had special labels designed and printed in Germany, for the Constantia that was sold on the Continent. In forwarding samples of these labels (shield-shaped; for the *Rother Constantia Wein*, a mauvy pink; for the *Constantia Pontac Wein*, a dark orange; for the *Constantia Frontignac Wein*, yellow; and for the *Weisser Constantia Wein*, white), his agent wrote cheerfully that he need not worry about the adulterations in England: 'Here your wine has an established reputation, and needs no bush'. For the wines he sold in bottles from the cellars, as for the bottles sold in Cape Town and Simonstown by his agents, Albertus & Gaum, he used a plain blue label with 'White-Red Constantia made by J Cloete, *Groot Constantia*'. The bottled Constantias sent to the Exhibitions of 1851 and 1854 bore similar labels; afterwards, there appeared at the bottom of the label a small note to the effect that: 'This wine has been crowned at the . . . Exhibition'. No special bottle was ever made, nor is there any evidence that one was ever used, at the Cape, for Constantia wine. The high-necked 'Constantia wine' bottle, with the impressed seal, that has been associated with Constantia wine, was, I believe, made for the Wembley Exhibition by Messrs Burgoyne. Among the letters in the day-book is one from the European agent, written in the early 'fifties, stating that he did not want to send 'the bottles you ordered, as I consider it absurd to pay so much for them as is asked'.

A glance through the day-book, and a perusal of the letters that have been found in it, will dispel some of the mistaken impressions about Constantia and its owner in the first part of the last century that may have been gathered from the accounts of stray visitors like Captain Percival,

Captain Paterson, Le Vaillant and others. It is obvious that so famous a farm was an attraction to every stranger who had the means to visit it or the money to buy its produce, and that its proprietor would have lacked both common business sense and commercial acumen if he had gratuitously insulted stray travellers or treated them with studied discourtesy. That this was by no means the case is definitely shown by the day-book with its letters, which records every sale made on the farm, even in cases where the buyer's name has been forgotten and the purchase was comparatively trivial. Apparently a supply of wine in bottles was kept on the farm for visitors who wished to buy one or two bottles (which was then permissible, however great a felony it is considered, today, to be), although for the most part such retail purchase was discouraged, by referring the would-be buyers to the Cape Town and Simonstown agents.

Mr Cloete's clients were in all parts of the world, and many well-known names are to be found in his day-book. In Cape Town he supplied Government House, the Admiralty at Simonstown, and the various regimental messes. His agents supplied local hotels with a dozen bottles at a time, but one of his constant customers was Mr Russell, of the Masonic Hotel, then the favourite resort of foreigners who visited Cape Town. Another good customer was Dr Samuel Baily, who bought largely for his hospital, and whose monthly orders sometimes exceeded 2 500 rix dollars. The Navy bought sometimes to the extent of 1 000 rix dollars; the French Government at Bourbon fairly regularly for 1 500 rix dollars. Among the individual clients whose orders exceeded 1 000 rix dollars at a time may be mentioned Sir Thomas Bradford, Baron Van der Capellen, Sir Richard Plasket, Lord William Bentinck, Lord Cecil, Sir Edward Barry, Earl Dalhousie, Viscount De Gissignies, Viscount Comberbere, Mr Nathan Dunn, 'on account of Chinese merchants'; Government of St Helena; Sir John Wilson; Mons D'Epinay, 'on account of the King of the French;' Archdeacon of Madras; Comte De Richemont; Sir Robert Grant, Governor of Bombay; Earl Clare; Hon F Cavendish; King of Prussia; Mons Belting d'Lancastel, Directeur General del' Interieur de l'Ile de Bourbon; Sir Willoughby Gordon; Baron von Hugel; Sir John Franklin; Lord Elphinston; Count Van Limburg Stirum; Governor of Ceylon; Sir William Nicolay; Governor of New South Wales; French Commercial Mission to China; Marquis of Tweeddale, and many others.

When a French ship arrived at Cape Town or Simonstown, Mr Cloete had many orders; indeed, one of the largest received in a single day was from a party of French officers who each purchased a half-aum of all four kinds of wine. Another remarkable sale was to a Dutch midshipman of the Frigate *Prins Hendrik der Nederlanden*, who probably followed his captain's example, for Captain Jonkheer H A van Karnebeek bought half-aums of all four wines. In 1851, it is interesting to note that 'Jonkheer G R G van Swinderen of Friesland, on account of Messrs Hoogendonck Tulleken, ordered to be forwarded to Messrs Heukelom of Amsterdam and Vollehoven two half-aums of red wine; forwarded in the ship *Padang*, Capt Van der Lint.' Although there is no mention of the visit in the day-book, the French poet Baudelaire was a guest at *Constantia* when he arrived at Cape Town in 1841; he was so much impressed by the wine he drank there that he wrote the much-discussed *Constanz* poem that has puzzled his critics for half a century.

His local customers were practically all Cape Town and Simonstown residents who could afford to pay for quarter-aums or ankers at the high prices at which he sold his wines. Among the best were the naval and military officers, who bought for their mess and wardroom. The 7th Dragoons were particularly fond of his Pontac; the navy preferred the red Constantia; Sir John Herschel and Sir Henry Pottinger – who both continued buying (through Mr Secretary Montague) long after they had left South Africa – preferred the white Constantia, which I remember the late Dr Daniel Hahn once called 'the finest wine ever produced on the Cape Peninsula', an opinion not shared by a former French consul at the Cape who, in 1872, wrote to Sir Henry Barkly that the Constantia Pontac was the best wine at the Cape. This, however, referred to the Van Reenen Pontac, and not to the Cloete wine.

Where local clients wanted wine by the bottle, they applied to the agents. Mr Cloete's advertisement, that appeared regularly in all the Cape Town papers, gave full directions to strangers how to find the farm, and ended by intimating 'for the convenience of Masters of Vessels, passengers and others, a quantity of the genuine article is constantly kept on hand in Cape Town at Mr Gaum's, 14 Castle Street, and at Simonstown at Mr Martin's, where also orders may be left'. Where clients wanted a shipment in bottle, they either brought their own bottles – as the ship's pursers invariably did – or were charged for the bottles and casings. The shipments overseas were made regularly every month, and always to order, delivery being through the agents, Maclaren, Watson & Co, and Borrodiale. Similarly the wines sent to India, America and the Continent were consigned to agents on receipt of orders. Here and there an experimental shipment was made. For example, there is an almost pathetic entry which reads, 'Mr R Matthew of New South Wales, 8 h-a red and 8 h-a white on my account; 6 h-a Constantia and 10 h-a ordinary wine; shipped', against which there is, in pencil, the remark *als verloren opgegeven* (given up as lost). An interesting entry is 'Mr R Grisold, wine to the value of 450 rix dollars, in exchange for two mules'. This client must have been the Mr Grisold, well known to Clanwilliam wine farmers, who endowed the English congregation of that town, was a generous benefactor to the local library, and for many years the owner of the well-known *Warmbad* farm near Citrusdal. He was one of the yeomen farmers who came out in the brig, *Fanny*, and refused to knuckle under to Mr Parker when the latter tried to settle some of his emigrants in the Olifantsrivier Valley, and as a lover of good wine he must have appreciated Mr Cloete's products. Such exchange of wine on a system of barter appears to have been fairly common. Among the papers in the day-book is a list of groceries, to be imported from the East, by the captain of the sailing ship *Admiraal de Ruyter,* in payment for Constantia wine received. The list includes 100 lb tamarinds, 2 bottles trassie (a fish condiment now quite unknown here, but at one time regarded as quite indispensable for the preparation of certain dishes), six dozen birds' nests, two jars minced pineapple, two pots nutmeg preserve, two pots red fish, two canisters tea sugar, and two jars preserved bamboo. Where he made visitors or friends a present of his wine — and such entries are frequent in the day-book — he left the cash received column blank. Among the letters in the book are acknowledgments of such gifts, warm in their appreciation of the generosity of the donor and the excellence of the wine. There are also similarly appreciative letters from customers, mostly from French officers. One, in placing another large order, writes: 'Please select your best wine; my friends are Councillors of the King, and have tasted Constantia at court, and I should like to give them your best'.

For the years 1855 to 1859 his farm sales averaged £2 200 a year, exclusive, apparently, of local sales through his agents. From 1824 to 1848 the wine trade at the Cape was suffering from the severe reaction consequent upon the repeal of the protective duties, and Cape wine was at a discount in England. Constantia retained its reputation, but its high price and comparative rarity made its sale far less profitable than in later years. The following Account of Sales from Mr Cloete's London agents is a fair summary of the conditions of the English market at the time.

'Account Sales of 12¼ Casks Wine shipped by Messrs Hovill & Russell per *Gladiator*:

> Sold 12¼ Casks Wine, No 11/22, J P Cloete; containing 348 galls, £25 per pipe of 92 galls £94 11s 4d.

Charges:

> Insurance, nil; Orphans dues 5s 6d; Customs entry 3s 6d; Freight and primage, £4 2s 1d; Pierage 1s; Stamp for Bill of Exchange 4s 6d; Postage 2s 6d; Broker's Commission 15s; Landing and housing rate £1 14s; Rent 23 weeks, £2 6d; Hovill & Sons Commission 2½ per cent £2 7s.

> Balance carried to credit £80 3s 3d.

Above we hand your Account Sales of 12¼ Casks Sweet Wine at the highest prices we could obtain. We have on our own responsibility omitted your order for bottles, until the freights get to a more reasonable rate, believing you would be grieved if we paid 40s to 50s per ton for goods of so small a value . . .'

And this at a time when he could easily get £12 per half-aum for his Frontignac, without the bother of shipping charges and agents' commission.

In the circumstances it is not to be wondered at that he found his trade with the Continent, where his wine was much appreciated and where he had little to fear from imitation Constantias, more profitable than export to England on commission. So far as can be judged from the day-book, after 1843 he seems to have confined himself more and more to private clients and to have sent less and less of his wines for sale on commission to England.

His day-book is a document of historical value that is of permanent interest to all those to whom the study of the development and progress of the wine industry in this country appeals, and I trust that it will find an abiding home either in the South African Public Library or in the Cape Town Archives.

Chapter 9

The Industry in the Middle of the Nineteenth Century

From the records available in 1850, the state of the wine industry at the Cape is reflected in the following returns of wine and brandy production in what were then its chief magisterial districts:

	Cape Division	Malmesbury	Stellenbosch	Paarl
Wine (pipes)	260	853	11 640	12 000
Brandy (pipes)	–	15	43	621
	Caledon	Worcester	Clanwilliam	Swellendam
Wine (pipes)	322	1 012	85	1 120
Brandy (pipes)	57	500	248	28
	George	Beaufort	Albany	Uitenhage and Port Elizabeth
Wine (pipes)	350	280	43	12
Brandy (pipes)	680	500	8	90
	Fort Beaufort	Somerset	Cradock	Graaff-Reinet
Wine (pipes)	38	754	2½	No return
Brandy (pipes)	14	20	290	No return
	Colesberg	Victoria	Albert	TOTAL
Wine (pipes)	No return	9	No return	28 870
Brandy (pipes)	No return	0	No return	3 114

These statistics are interesting. They show, for instance, that some wine farmers, more especially in the outlying districts, where frontier trading was brisk, turned most of their wine into spirits. The returns for the Cape division were incomplete, for obviously much more wine was produced in that area which, with Paarl, Stellenbosch and Worcester, headed the list of vine-growing districts. No figures are available for the number of vines planted or in bearing, but various estimates were made, ranging from 80 to 90 million. The districts of Clanwilliam and Swellendam had many vineyards, and even as far east as the border districts viticulture was found to be profitable. The encouragement given by the government, and by the various local agricultural societies, headed by the influential and progressive Cape of Good Hope Agricultural Society, that organized shows and assisted with advice and sometimes with practical help, was having its effect, and the Cape Town wine merchants reported satisfactory improvement in several directions. The information, distributed in pamphlets, by experts like Messrs H Jarvis and C Juritz and Dr Gird, about modern methods of fermenting, racking and fining wines, was sound, although at that time much of the knowledge about these matters was theoretical and practical rather than scientific. Pasteur's epoch-making experiments had still to be undertaken, and very little that was accurate was known about the chemistry of wines.

Cyrus Redding, in his *History and Description of Modern Wines* published in 1851, devotes a few pages to South African wines. He wrote:

'The vineyards of the Cape of Good Hope are some of them in the vicinity of Cape Town itself, where the beauty of the climate and equality of the temperature are particularly favourable to vine cultivation. The proper choice of a site for a vineyard was seldom taken into consideration by the Dutch, who first planted vines, under the governorship of Von Riebeck (*sic*), in 1650 (*sic*). At least, so the Dutch say, but on the revocation of the Edict of Nantes, the Dutch settled a colony of emigrant French, at Franschehoek, a secluded valley, and the residents at the Cape give them the merit of the introduction. Their descendants are still the principal vine growers. There are many places where the soil is exceedingly favourable, but these are neglected for situations which have been chosen from local convenience, the caprice, or mistaken policy of the planters. The fertility of the land near the first settlements was very great, and on that account the less applicable to vine culture, yet vineyards were planted in such places very early after the Dutch began to bring in the land (*sic*). It is not far from Cape Town, or about halfway between the Cape and Saldana Bay (*sic*), so well known to seamen, that the Constantia, both red and white, celebrated among the first class of sweet wines, is grown. Of the two, the preference is given to the red, though both are luscious, and the white is remarkably full in the mouth. Both are what the French call *vins de liqueur,* and are drunk as such. The vineyard is very small, and is divided into two parts, belonging to different proprietors, called the Higher and Lower Constantia, separated only by a hedge, and having an eastern exposure. It was named from the farm on which it stands, and the farm from the wife of the Dutch governor, Van der Stel, who formed [?] it. The wine of both vineyards is nearly alike in quality, though the Cape connoisseurs pretend that there is a considerable difference. Formerly, when the Cape belonged to the Dutch, their East India Company always took off a third part at a fixed price. Three score years ago, the wine sold for between two and three shillings per bottle on the spot. It lies about eight miles to the west of the town, and the produce both of the red and white does not exceed eighty to ninety pipes annually, though some have calculated it at twelve thousand gallons. The soil of the *Constantia* vineyard is a sandy gravel, lying upon a gentle slope. The vines are of the Spanish muscadine species, and cultivated without props; when pruned, only a small number of buds is left for bearing. The wine is pressed after the grape is freed of the stones and every extraneous substance. The casks are deposited in a cellar, where the air has a free circulation, upon a level with the ground. The price of Constantia varies from a hundred to a hundred and forty dollars the half-aum of nineteen gallons. The other wines run from twelve dollars as high as seventy-six.

'Stellenbosch, so called from the Dutch governor Stel, and the bushes which covered it, is a second wine district, north of False Bay, by the Stellenbosch river. Stel seized upon large portions of territory for himself with more than Dutch cupidity, and drew a great profit from the vineyards and cornfields in that part of the colony. He constructed a reservoir in the mountain to water his farms and vineyards, which he conveyed in a channel by his wine cellars to a mill where he ground his corn. The valleys are described as being very fertile in corn and vineyards. Drakenstein, another settlement to the northeast of Stellenbosch, was settled by French refugees in 1675. In Simon's Valley, one Von Blesius planted vineyards, and, as well as Stel, seems to have turned the country into a source of private profit, until an ordinance from Holland, in 1707, forbade the civil officers of the colonies to traffic for their own advantage in wine, corn, or cattle. It appears that wherever land was proper for the growth of corn, vineyards were introduced, and to this conduct the bad quality of most of the Cape wines may be ascribed. There was no care discovered in the choice of the site or soil. The beauty of the vineyards at the Cape seems to argue against their existing site and mode of culture. Two vineyards in 1722, near Cape Town, were described as the most beautiful in the world, one fourteen hundred paces long by two hundred and thirty-five, with a rivulet through the midst. The Dutch placed high duties upon the wine sold at the Cape to strangers touching there during the infancy of the Colony. Dampier speaks of the strength and sweetness of the wine in his time; but he probably alluded to the Constantia. In no wine country is there room for greater improvement, nor is there any in which care and science, properly directed, would earlier exhibit their effects. No method recommended by European science or experience prevails. The improver would have to encounter very considerable obstacles. That it would be highly beneficial to Great Britain as well as the Colony, there is no doubt. Things are undoubtedly better now than they were twenty years ago, but amendment is very slow. The obstinacy of the Dutch character is proverbial. Old habits can with difficulty be overcome in a long series of years. The boors are a very ignorant, dogged race of people, and not at all of speculative habits, but content to do, in the same mode, what their fathers did before them, and no more, contented with "the wisdom of their ancestors".

'Except a soil consisting of volcanic remains, there are traces of every other species of land congenial to vine culture. There can be no doubt that were vineyards planted on the sites better adapted to their growth, and the grapes selected with due care, a vast deal of good wine might be sent from the Cape into Great Britain. The quantity of produce is now the only object kept in view by the farmer. The vines are not always propped for the common wines. It is observed already that they never are propped for the Constantia wine, but left too frequently to grow like currant bushes in England, and even to rest upon the ground. From this custom, perhaps, arises one cause of the earthy taste of the wine. The customary mode of doing everything as it has been done before, together with an inveterate adherence to precedent, renders it very difficult to effect the least amelioration. The Dutch farmer presses his grapes under any circumstances that will ensure quantity of product. Carelessness in training and dressing the vines also equally contributes to perpetuate the bad nature and bad character of the wine in a country where nature is free from any share of the blame.

'The wine grown at the Cape is both red and white, and the larger part is dry. They have, besides the red Constantia, a red wine called Rota, and various wines grown at Stellenbosch, Drakenstein (*sic*) and Perle (*sic*). The real Cape Madeira is a boiled and mixed wine, and used to be sent to Holland, India and America. The farmers sell their new wine to merchants at Cape Town for thirty-six dollars the leaguer of fifty gallons, which the latter retail at an advanced price, adding execrable native brandy. They also ship it off to the quickest market, rarely having capital to retain it in their own hands until it is properly matured by age. The greater part of the wine produced goes by the general name of Stein wine, some of which, when carefully prepared, and after due keeping, is really excellent when about seven years old. The absurdity of government interference exists at the Cape; tasters, inspectors, and what not, get a living upon the wine owners, mere tools of the government, for which the people are taxed. The wine is not permitted by these agents to leave the grower's hands under six months or longer at their caprice. A duty, equal in some cases to one half the price of the wine, is laid upon that which enters Cape Town for consumption. The entire product of the vineyards of the Cape is calculated at fourteen thousand leaguers, of which the Colony consumes six thousand; two are sent to St Helena, and the rest exported, a large part to this country. From the Parliamentary papers in 1817, the total quantity was then estimated at about twenty-one thousand pipes and upwards. The importation was as follows, in tuns, from 1816 to 1820:

1816	1 631 2 21
1817	4 218 0 29
1818	8 648 0 15
1819	1 648 8 19
1820	1 925 0 60
	13 071 3 18 (*sic*)

Of which were exported again   1 928 1 17

Total consumed in Great Britain in 5 years 11 148 2 1 (*sic*)

'A large proportion of Cape wine is used in England to deteriorate the growth of other countries, by making what are called cheap wines. In the six years ending with 1849, the quantity decreased from 349 257 imperial gallons in 1844 to 241 845 in 1849, as returned to 5 January 1850. It is singular that British example has been unable to make an impression upon Dutch doggedness in the way of improvement, and that efforts, if made, have been directed as ignorantly as that of the older Dutch, with an utter disregard to later precedent. Yet tolerable wine is to be drunk at the Cape itself, from its own vineyards. Red Cape drunk at a proper age in the country is a sound, good wine. Who would believe this, from the specimens tasted in England?

'The merchants at the Cape are more careful of their cellars and appurtenances than of the wine they export from them. In these they deposit the produce of their purchases from the farmer in large tuns, made of a hard dark wood, holding six or seven hundred gallons each. The bungs are kept locked down by brass plates well scoured, and only opened in presence of the owner.

'The grapes were first brought to the Cape from the banks of the Rhine. The muscadine grape, as before stated, is found there, as well as other European species. The fruit is rich, full and fine, and has none of the earthy taste found in the wine. It is therefore very probable that this taste is further aided by the stalks and stems, for the grapes are neither picked nor sorted, ripe from unripe, except for the Constantia, and what earth may cling to them all go into the vat together, the whole management being generally entrusted to emancipated slaves. The casks, too, are ill prepared for the wine. The vintage labour takes place in February and March. The process of fermentation is ill conducted; even the operations preceding the vintage are rude, and managed as coarsely as cider making in Devonshire. The grossest manure is applied to the vines. It is therefore not wonderful that Cape wines have become depreciated in public opinion. This is the more to be lamented, because the mother country possesses no colony where a more congenial soil exists, or where better wines might be grown. The reduced duties, and extent of the home population, would secure a consumption for a superior wine, which would render the Cape in return pecuniary advantages that could not fail to be felt by the Colonists. It is wonderful that English speculation, securing a few French cultivators, has not made new attempts to raise the character of these wines, of which even the worst find a market. The return would not be slow, the capital secure, and a little patience recover the market for any distinct, well-characterised wine which might be grown. There is, however, another obstacle to be overcome in the ill-managed fiscal regulations of some of our colonies, and the arbitrary enactments of military governors ignorant of everything but regimental duty, whose will is too often the sole law by which everything in them is regulated. Until this system is abolished, and the colonies become self governed in all things of which they have true comprehension, little emendation is to be expected.'

The Colony was now self-governing. Under the Letters Patent that granted it a constitution, the first election for the Legislative Council took place in January 1854, and the successful candidates were proclaimed on 16 March. The first election for the House of Assembly took place in April and the successful candidates were proclaimed on 22 June 1854.

In its first session the new Parliament considered the report of a Select Committee of the Wine and Spirits Ordinance No 9 of 1851, that had laid down the rates for wine and spirit licences, and postponed its further consideration until the next session. The newly elected representatives of the people were men who were well acquainted with conditions in the Colony, and not likely to be rushed into panic legislation. They contented themselves with a general discussion of the subject. Already the ranks of the total abolitionists were closing in in an attempt to foist, under the guise of 'temperance restrictions' (an unfortunate choice of words characteristic of the muddled thinking of these fanatics), a number of vexatious controls upon the winegrowers and vintners. Their activities, however, demand a chapter to themselves, even at the risk of interrupting the chronological sequence of the account. On the other hand, the farmers were now not only more enlightened but also more active in promoting their own interests. The Cape of Good Hope Agricultural Society, formed in 1831, was now an important and popular organisation that held annual shows and did its best to foster the development of the farming industry. In its annual report for 1862 it wrote:

> 'Your Committee are happy in being able to report that Oidium Tuckeri, which devastated the vineyards last season, has been greatly checked by the more general use of flowers of sulphur, the remedy first suggested by Mr McGibbon, Superintendent of the Botanic Gardens and afterwards by the European Vine Disease Commission. ... Your Committee, from personal observation and the information collected, hope that the disease is fast becoming less malignant. They advise, however, that the application of this remedy shall be as zealously persisted in next season as it was in the last.'

In subsequent annual reports the Society urged the establishment of an experimental agricultural farm. It was so much shocked by the falling off in the wine exports that it saw little hope for lucrative wine farming, and thought it highly desirable that the wine farmers should turn their attention to other cultures such as silk, chicory, flax and tobacco. In private letters of this period one finds unmistakable proof of the despondency that resulted from the curtailment of the export trade in wine.

'I have no reason to suppose,' writes one wine farmer, 'that my crop will be worse than last year. As a matter of fact, we have got the new rust well in hand and, although it is a nuisance having to sulphur the vines, we are gratified by the results. But what is the use of making wine when there is, or will be, no sale for it? It is all very well to say that I must turn it into brandy and send it to Kimberley, but we have been wine farmers for generations, and there is quite enough spirit in the country as it is.'

The 1866 annual report of the Cape of Good Hope Agricultural Society reflects this gloomy opinion about the prospects of the wine industry. It reported that 'wine farming has received a heavy blow from which it may be difficult to recover', and suggested that as a precautionary measure winegrowers should experiment with linseed, cochineal and new kinds of tobacco. A year later it reported that no suitable natural wine was obtainable to send to the Paris Exhibition, and that it was useless to include wine exhibits in the next annual show. Wines were, however, seen on local shows, and the reports in the contemporary press contain the names of prizewinners in Worcester, Tulbagh, Paarl and Stellenbosch. At the Cape Town show, held in the grounds of Government House in 1883, the first sign of a reanimation in the industry was to be seen when, in the class of 'Wine' (the produce of this Colony and exhibited by the Grower; Vintage 1882), prizes were awarded in the following classes:

Best 3 Leaguers Greengrape (not sweet).
Best 3 Leaguers Steen.
Best 3 Leaguers Hanepoot (not sweet).
Best 3 Leaguers Dry Pontac.
Best 3 Leaguers Sweet White Muscadel.
Best 3 Leaguers Sweet Frontignac.
Best 3 Leaguers Sweet Pontac.

Each sample to consist of not fewer than three quart bottles.

A special prize was awarded to 'the best three leaguers of wine, the produce of this Colony, vintage to be stated by the Exhibitor; silver medal and open to all competitiors, any age.'

Good wine was still in demand, and when Prince Alfred visited Stellenbosch the reception committee, headed by Dr Mannerschmidt, who was himself a connoisseur of wine, tried its best to secure the best local wines for the formal luncheon under the oak trees. Old Constantia was served, and a wonderfully 'soft' wine that came from the Tulbagh district. We are not told if His Royal Highness, and the midshipman who accompanied him on the visit, were impressed by the wine, but 'the Prince's entourage found the wine delightful, and expressed a desire to buy of it, if obtainable'. As a change from the strongly fortified Ports and Sherries of the wardroom, the natural wines served at that luncheon must surely have been appreciated by the visitors.

Many references to Cape wines can be cited from the reports of local shows. At Swellendam in 1864 the judges stated:

'The wines gave no satisfaction to the judges. It is impossible to get any flavour or bouquet out of wines that have been boiled for half an hour in the sun. The wines ought to have been tasted the day previously and

in a cool place. Sample XX of Mr J C Beyers, resembling a Burgundy, was considered very fine. Messrs Marillac Bros, who have undertaken to produce wines and spirits of the same body and flavour as Continental wines from Cape wines, sent samples for competition. The imitations produced were 'Golden Sherry', made according to the receipt of a Cadiz merchant; 'Hunt's Port', made according to the receipt of an Oporto wine grower; 'Hennessy's French Brandy', made from the spirits of wine of Messrs Barry and Nephew, which was so highly commended by the judges of the Cape Town Exhibition, Messrs Anderson, Walker and Leibbrandt, in 1862. The following prizes were awarded: Silver Cup: for 16 Imperial gallons or ½ aum white wine − J Z Herman; red wine ditto − J J Barry; Dr Pontac made in district − J L Beyers.'

Among winegrowers whose names figure prominently in the prize lists may be mentioned P J Haupt (Stellenbosch; Green grape), J Louw (Paarl, Pontac), Keyter (Worcester; Hanepoot), Roos (Stellenbosch), and, of course, Jacob Cloete and S van Reenen.

A 'General Committee' to promote the interests of the Colony at the great 'Universal Exhibition' of 1855 was formed, with His Excellency the Governor at its head. Among the many sub-committees into which it was split was the 'Wines and Spirits Sub-Committee,' consisting of Messrs E Chiappini, G Prince, and D G de Jongh and M C Vos, senior, all winegrowers and vintners. The sub-committee circularised the wine farmers and the vintners, and printed an 'informatory note' on the wine industry, which is not as informatory as one wishes it might have been. We learn from it that the 'current prices of Cape wines, locally,' are as follows: White, ordinary, £8 10s to £9 per pipe; superior, £9 to £12 per pipe. Pontac, sweet, £24 to £26 per pipe; dry, £12 to £13 per pipe. Steen, £11 to £13 per pipe. Frontignac, £7 10s per half-aum. Muscadel, white and red, £7 10s per half-aum. Constantia red, £12 per half-aum; white, £18 per half-aum. Constantia Pontac, £12 per half-aum. The general interest in the forth-coming Great Exhibition stimulated discussion, and in the contemporary press there are frequent, and sometimes instructive, references to Cape wines. A fairly representative selection of Cape wine was despatched to London, where the greater part of the consignment arrived safely, though some samples were unworthy of being exhibited. Among those that attracted the judging committee's attention were some samples sent out by the firm of Prince, Collison & Co of Strand Street, whose bottled wines were already well known 'in Rio, Canton, Melbourne and Calcutta.' Dealing with the sweet wines (A13; cases 26-31) the committee reported:

'These wines, on which, in Europe, adulteration and mixing are often practised with a view of selling them at a reduced price to the consumer, are remarkable for a kind of *gout de terroir* (*sui generis*) without analogy with any other. They have that peculiarity, when they are pure, that they leave the palate perfectly dry after degustation, although they contain a large proportion of saccharine matter. They are dessert wines, much esteemed for their delicacy and aroma. Proprietors Messrs N Colyn, J P Cloete and S van Reenen of Constantia . . .

We feel a lively regret that in a Colony which is so essentially a wine-growing country as this is, there has not been brought forward a single specimen worthy of the attention of the Committee of the seven or eight different sorts of dry wines which might become very desirable if care were taken in their manufacture. We are firmly of opinion that this product may attain, in consequence of the superior quality of the grapes, a degree of perfection much greater than it possesses at present. Moreover, the wines of ordinary consumption at the Cape, containing already in themselves from 18 to 20 per cent of alcohol at 33 degrees, to which is still added on exportation from 10 to 12 per cent, it results that this article of produce is considered only as raw material reserved for the wants of the distiller in case of a bad vintage in Europe, a matter worthy in this respect alone of fixing the attention of the (wine) merchant.'

Which, however badly expressed it may be, was a caution certainly deserving the attention not only of the wine merchants but of the wine farmers as well.

An interesting private memorandum, dated 1854, states that 'among those who are familiar with the Cape wines, it is now considered that the red wine, known as "Sweet Paarl" and manufactured by Bosman on his farm is nearly equal to the best Constantia, and is much cheaper'. Unfortunately there is no further record of Mr Bosman's wine, about which we know as little as we do about the 'most excellent wine of a Mr Keyter whose farm lies between Darling Bridge and Worcester', and who, later on, obtained the first prize for his wine at the agricultural show held at Worcester in 1860. This latter wine was eulogistically described by Mr F W Reitz, the father of the late President Reitz, as 'of a very superior quality, and of an excellent taste which is said to be due to the soil in which the grapes grow'.

William Hawes, in his description of the Cape Colony printed in 1859, wrote:

'Wine production could be much increased. Oudtshoorn has only now been thrown open for vines . . . It is a great mistake to sell Cape white and red wines as "Cape Sherry" or "Cape Port". Good Cape wine will always have a peculiar flavour, as Madeira or Marsala or Sherry has, and it is only producing an unfair and injurious comparison to call it by any other name than that to which it is legitimately entitled. The goodness and cheapness of Cape wine now on the market will secure it a ready sale, and from experience we can say that the public at present have no knowledge of the quality of the best wines. Time is all that is required to improve the average quality and therefore the price that it will realise to the grower.'

Here again the advice given is thoroughly sound, and our wine-growers, who are still obsessed with the fancy that they should be ashamed to call their wines by some local name but proud of letting them masquerade under names that by no stretch of the imagination can fairly be applied to them should take particular heed of the caution enshrined in the second paragraph.

About this time the Annual Register, avid to give snippets of information to its readers, printed a note on Cape wines:

'The wines of the Cape are of three sorts — good, bad, and indifferent. That excellent wines are made here is most certain and they are seldom known to produce that acidity or at least stomach complaints as in the case of wines manufactured elsewhere. Much error prevails as regards the real purity of good Cape wine. Such wine has never been known to disagree with a rightly constituted and healthy constitution. It has been the fashion to decry Cape wine, but we think it is a fashion, like all others of mere worldly notion, that is fast passing away.'

Wilhelm von Meyer in his *Reisen in Sued Afrika* (Hamburg 1843) had already discussed the salubrity of Cape wines, and from the Continent there came frequent testimony to the excellence of some of the samples exported, an encouragement that was to become more frequent after the Franco-Prussian War when German merchants patronised the Cape vintners.

One of the best testimonials to the excellence of Cape wine came from a connoisseur. Monsieur L'Héritte had been French Consul at Cape Town for many years. A frequent customer of Jacob Cloete, he had also made himself acquainted with other sorts of wine than that made at *Constantia*, and had on occasion acted as a judge at agricultural shows where wines had been exhibited. He departed, much regretted, to take up his duties at Elsinore in Denmark, and a few years later wrote to Sir Henry Barkly a letter that is worth quoting almost in full:

'Why are your Cape wines so despised that certain London taverns, as it were, have the following inscription on their ensign-boards "Here at least no Cape wine is drunk"? Simply because the exporters, in order to increase their profits, export only the most ordinary sorts, which are represented as the best, and chiefly because the wine is exported and brought to the market being too young and without having achieved its fermentation, and the result is that in consequence of the very strong dose of alcohol that must be added to it, like in all southern wine-producing countries, it is at the same time too strong and too much sugared. When leaving the Cape in March, 1869, I took with me three sorts of wine in bottle (unhappily not more and in very small quantity). One was Pontac, prize wine of S van Reenen at *Constantia*; the second was Cape Sherry 1st Quality of Mr E K Green of Cape Town, and the third Dry Old Pontac of the same Mr Green. Well, these three wine sorts have become altogether perfect, and the best connoisseurs among my friends like them very much, not because they come from a distant country, but because the wines are really excellent. The Pontac Prize wine has become so dry that it is almost a little bitter, but of a bitter dryness which connoisseurs like best. It is really a unique wine, and if this wine as it becomes in course of time, were more generally known, it would create *furore*.'

It is to this wine that Mr F W Reitz alludes in the article that he wrote for the *Cape Monthly Magazine* Vol IX 1861, describing his visit to *High Constantia*, then owned by Mr S van Reenen. He drank and much appreciated the 'Prize Pontac', and preferred it to the old Frontignac that was considered by the proprieter to be the best wine made on the estate. Oidium, he remarks, had already damaged the vines, but was kept in check by sulphuring the 100 000 bearing vines on the farm. The article is illustrated by one of the first photographs taken of the old farmhouse, and contains interesting information about the conditions under which the wines were made.

One of the most interesting books on viticulture is that written in 1860 by A Haraszthy, Commissioner of the State of California (*Grape Culture, Wines and Wine Making*, New York, 1862), who visited all the European wine-growing countries, and gave a racy, readable account of his travels with many instructive details about the various wines that he tasted on the way. His note on Cape Wines reads as follows:

'The Cape of Good Hope produces three sorts of wine which are commonly designated Cape Wines. The most celebrated is the Constancia, so called from a mountain of the same name two leagues from the promontory. It may be classed among the first quality wines, second only to the Tokay. This is sweet, spirituous, very agreeable in taste and exquisitely spicy. The white one is a little less sweet than the red one. In former years only some 900 hectolitres, or about 22 950 gallons, have been produced, which was sold at the place of its growth for 80 or 120 cents the bottle, while the common one is sold for one cent. The grapes are left on the vines till they become shrivelled. After the Constancia follows, in quality, the Muscat, which is grown on the False and Table Bay. In Europe it sells under the name of Constancia, notwithstanding its inferior merit. The best kinds of this wine are those of Beker and Hendrik. The third sort of Cape wine is the Stone wine; though dry, it has a good taste. It is raised in the districts of Gerlen (sic) Drachenstein, and Stellenbosch. The red wines are there known under the name of Rota; they are somewhat like the Spanish wine of this name. They are dark, of good body and spirit, and a pleasant odour. Recently the quality of the Cape wine has been impaired, because the wine growers look more for quantity than quality. In 1806 only 6 909 pipes were exported; while in 1817 there were 17 000 pipes, and in 1822, 23 000; and since then a constantly increasing amount has been sent abroad.'

This writer quotes M de Szemere on the subject of the then altogether too prevalent adulteration of foreign wines for the English and American markets:

'All is false in the wines; the color, the strength, the flavor, the age — even the name under which they are sold. There are wines which do not contain a drop of grape juice. Even science is impotent to distinguish the true from the false, so complete is the imitation. You may every day see advertised in the French newspapers the *Sève de Médoc* of which a small flacon, costing three francs, is declared sufficient to give flavor to 600 litres ... Fraudulent adulteration is practised at Paris and Cette on the most colossal scale. Certainly one half of the Parisian population drink, under the name of wine, a mixture in which there is not one drop of grape juice ... In a very recent trial, the chemist, after reporting every ingredient of which the wine was composed, observed that if one of them were in less quantity he would have been unable to distinguish it from the natural wine. The prosecuted wine merchant, who was present, listened attentively to the chemist's report, and at last asked him which ingredient it was. The chemist very imprudently told him, and the accused immediately answered: "I am very much obliged, sir, and I don't regret now my 40 hogshead of wine which will be destroyed because now I am certain of my business". ... If France in 1857 consumed more than she can produce in some years, is it unreasonable to doubt whether she would always be able to export natural and unadulterated wines? In any case, can one believe that in such circumstances old French wines could be found anywhere but in private cellars? ... It is a fact universally known, that to all wines exported to England is added more or less brandy (and in most cases not Cognac, but what is quite another thing, corn, fig, sugar brandy); thus the Rhine wines receive an addition of 2-5, the French 4-7, and the Spanish and Port wines 8-15 per cent of alcohol.'

Fashion in wines changes, like everything else that is subject to popular taste. A hundred years ago the best wines, according to Leuch (*Weikunde*, Nuremberg, 1847) were the following:

Red wines, first class: Romanee Conti, Chambertin, Richebourg, Vougeot, La Tashe, St Georges, Corton, Lafitte, Latour, Chateau Margeaux, Haut Brion, Hermitage.

White wines, first class: Sillery, Montrachet, St Bris, Carbonnieux, Sauternes, Barsac, Beaumes and the Preignac, Hermitage and Chateau Grillet.

Liqueur wines, first class: Tokay, Lacrimae Christi, Constantia, Syracuse Muscat, Rivesalter, Commandery from Cyprus.

Dry wines, first class: Johannisberger, Rudesheimer, Deidesheimer, Badenweiler.

Among the second-class wines, much inferior to the first, 'Muscat and Rota from the Cape' were listed among the liqueur wines, and 'the dry Xeres' among the 'dry wines' in which class, too, Port wine was listed as an inferior second-class type. Among connoisseurs a foaming wine was regarded as in every way distinctly third class, an opinion which today would be considered unfair by some wine lovers, although most of us would probably agree with Sir George Yonge that a still Champagne, properly matured, is aesthetically and gastrosophically far superior to a Grande Mousseux, no matter what vintage.

In 1861, under the provisions of the Treaty of Commerce with France, the House of Commons passed the new wine duties, that reduced the existing import duties on wine to 3/- per gallon with a further reduction from 4 April 1862 to 1/- per gallon on all wines with less than 26 degrees of proof spirit, 2/6 per gallon on all wines containing more than 26 but less than 42 degrees proof, and 3d in addition for every degree of strength beyond 42 degrees of proof spirit. On all wines shipped in bottle and containing less than 42 degrees of proof spirit an additional duty of 2/6 per gallon was to be paid.

This change in the English wine duties acted as detrimentally upon the export of Cape wines as the former removal of the preferential protection tariff had done. The Colonial Parliament, still young enough to take itself very seriously, appointed a Select Committee to report on the effect that the new tariff would have upon the wine industry, with the usual power to call for evidence and submit recommendations. The report of the Select Committee is one of the most interesting and instructive documents in the history of the wine industry at the Cape.

The 'Wine Trade Select Committee of 1860' reported that:

'The Imperial Government having decided upon placing the wines of all countries upon an equal footing in so far as regards duty chargeable theron upon importation into the United Kingdom, the Committee are of opinion that it would be useless to endeavour to obtain any protective measure in respect to the wines of this Colony ... The Committee, whilst they consider that the alteration in the rate of duty above referred to will, in the beginning, have a depressing effect upon the wine trade here, are of opinion that good Cape wine will continue to command remunerative prices in the English and other markets, and if the wine growers and others engaged in the trade only exercise proper care and attention in the manufacture and preparation of their wines, and refrain from shipping wines of an inferior quality, the Committee, bearing in mind the greatly increased consumption of the article in the Colony, see no reason to fear that the wine trade of this Colony will sustain any permanent injury from the withdrawal of the protective clause hitherto in force in regard to wines the produce of the Cape of Good Hope.'

This highly optimistic opinion seems scarcely to be warranted by the testimony of the witnesses heard, and was certainly not justified on the facts. In 1817, when the export of Cape wine to England reached its peak, the Cape supplied one-seventh of the wine imported into the United Kingdom. From 1856 to 1860, Spain and Portugal together supplied three-fourths of a total importation of nearly nine million gallons per year, while France and South Africa supplied approximately 700 000 gallons per year. After 1860 France exported a yearly average of over two million gallons to England, while the Cape export dropped from 126 951 gallons in 1861 to 29 457 gallons in 1864, while the exports from Spain and Portugal showed appreciable increases, the importation of 'sherry' from Spain reaching in 1864 nearly eight million gallons, out of a total of 15 500 000 gallons imported. Of this grand total only 1 800 000 gallons were under 26 degrees proof, the more fortified wines still accounting for four-fifths of the whole consumption of wine in the United Kingdom.

Giving evidence before the Committee, the Hon. H C Jarvis, one of the largest shippers in Cape Town, said he always had to fortify his wines above 26 degrees for the English market, although he considered that they could easily travel below that strength. The English trade wanted spirituous wines, and in the trade spirit, generally corn spirit, was always generously added. He used only grape spirit, although corn spirit was cheaper. The natural wines he bought were low in alcoholic strength. His advice was that winegrowers should seek a local market, and distil more brandy from their surplus wine, for brandy was 'at the present moment at an enormously high price, beyond any reasonable rates'. The quality of export wine could be much improved. Mr J B Ebden, who had been shipping wine from 1810 to 1850, said that the English trade preferred strongly fortified wines, and the stronger our export wines were the more likely were they to command a profitable price in that market. Mr D C de Jongh told of his own experience in shipping natural wine. In 1856 he had exported 40 pipes to England, one half pure natural wine, mixed with fine old wine and six per cent of spirit. The young fortified wine had sold for £2 more per pipe than the far finer old, less spirituous wine. Mr J J de Villiers, who had shipped to the Continental vintners, said the 'generality of our natural wines contained about 26 degrees', with which his customers were satisfied. He had shipped a young fortified wine and a fine old matured wine with no spirit added, and the report from his agents in London was that the young wine had been preferred to the old which was said to be too weak.

Eight years later another Select Committee was appointed, this time to report on 'the practicability of relieving the existing distress among wine farmers'. After taking evidence (not transcribed) this Committee reported:

'There undoubtedly exists at present very great and to some extent unprecedented distress amongst the wine growers of this Colony and those connected with them, which has arisen mainly from circumstances beyond the control of the sufferers. To relieve their distress by legislative action entails many and great difficulties . . . Your Committee are of opinion that an Association with a large command of capital having for its main objects the manufacture of Cape wine on improved systems and the storing of it for a sufficient time to mature previous to its disposal in foreign markets, would help materially to remove the strong prejudice now unfortunately existing there against it, and enable it to obtain a position to which it might and ought to aspire.'

The Committee therefore recommended the House of Assembly 'to express its readiness to give favourable consideration to applications from companies properly established and managed for that purpose'. Such applications, unfortunately, were not forthcoming. The wine industry appeared to have reached the nadir of its prosperity and to be slowly sinking into a decrepitude from which it could never be regenerated.

This report achieved nothing, and five years later, as the position had become worse, parliament appointed another Select Committee to report on the state of the wine trade. Mr Jarvis now testified that the Cape had practically lost its market in England. The only wine that could be profitably exported was 'Geropega', which he considered an inferior Port type and which was extensively used in manufacturing wines in England. The French wine trade was also interested in Geropega, which was bought to blend with the lighter French wines so that these could still be introduced in the London market at a lower duty. Hamburg Sherry, he stated, had altogether driven out Cape wine from the English market, and that notwithstanding the fact that wines of a Sherry type were produced at the Cape that were equal to any Spanish Sherry imported into England. 'I have myself tasted a wine from Worcester,' he told the Committee, 'that is equal to any Sherry imported into the United Kingdom.' He had personally interviewed Mr Adderley and Mr Gladstone, and represented to them most strongly how the South African wine growers were affected by the new duties, but had found them implacable. Questioned about the quality of the wines produced here, he said that he thought better wines were made in 1817 on certain farms, and that the best wine now to be had came not from old wine-producing districts but from beyond the mountains, from the districts of Worcester and Robertson. The soil in the Breede River valley he considered ideal for wine production. Mr A B de Villiers thought that better brandy was now being distilled than ever before, and some of it was equal to the best French brandy. He was of opinion that there was considerable room for improvement in the making of wine; for instance, the customs introduced by the Huguenot settlers had not tended to benefit the industry; grapes should not be cut for pressing after they had been heated in the sun. There was no reason to suppose that Cape wines could not travel unless they were heavily fortified; formerly, when the voyage to Europe had lasted several months, there was something to be said in favour of fortifying the wine, but with the quicker transit by steamship there was little to fear. Other witnesses confirmed these opinions, and the Committee had authoritative statistics about the wine industry to rely upon. It therefore reported:

'That His Excellency the Governor be requested by respectful address to bring to the notice of the Imperial Government the following statement of facts relative to the Wine Trade of this Colony:

(a) That induced thereto by the assurance of at all times finding a ready and profitable market for their wines in England held out to them by a former representative of Her Majesty in this Colony, thousands of the inhabitants of some of the Western Divisions have devoted all their means and time to the cultivation of the vine, and are at present unable to avail themselves of any other means of subsistence.

(b) That in consequence of the warm latitudes our wines have to pass on the voyage to England, our wines cannot arrive there in a sound condition unless fortified and shipped at a strength varying from 26 to 30 degrees including alcoholic strength.

(c) That by the terms of the Imp. Act 25 Vict. Cap 22, our wines are in consequence of circumstances above stated subject to the higher rate of duty, viz 2/6 per gallon, and therefore labour under a very serious disadvantage in the English market where they have to compete with Continental wines of the same value, which, being produced so near England, require no such fortification and are liable to only one shilling per gallon duty.

(d) That owing to the above circumstances, the effect of the Act mentioned has been to reduce the quantity and value of the wine exported from this Colony to the United Kingdom from 1 002 449 gallons valued at £153 379 in 1859 to 30 679 gallons valued at £5 213 in 1864.

(e) That this enormous decrease in the value of an article upon which so many thousands of the inhabitants of the Western Districts are entirely dependent as their only means of subsistence, has caused a very serious distress amongst them, which is daily increasing and seems likely to end in their entire ruin unless some means be devised to alleviate it.

(f) That with a view to such alleviation, and in consideration of the facts stated, H.M. Government are requested by this House to alter the existing tariff of custom dues on wine so as to allow all wines not exceeding 33 degrees of alcoholic strength to be imported at a rate of duty not exceeding one shilling per gallon.'

The Committee also recommended that the Colony of Natal be asked to lower its import duty on wines and brandy, and that the licensing fees should be modified. Already parliament had attempted to legislate in regard to the wine trade, and to consolidate the old ordinances with regard to licensing and the sale of wines and spirits. Already the old conception, that wine was a necessity, was slowly but steadily losing ground to the new suggestion that it was merely an article of luxury that could legitimately be taxed. Prohibition fanatics had so far not been very vociferous in public or in parliament, but the 'Good Templar' sect was growing in numbers and importance, and its influence was increasing. This aspect of the matter will be considered in a later chapter.

To the requests and remonstrances of the Cape Colony, the Imperial Government replied, politely but firmly, that it could not repeal the wine duties. The reasons for this decision need not be discussed. The fact occasioned widespread dissatisfaction among the wine farmers. Many sold their farms and trekked; many others dug out their vines and started other crops.

Chapter 10

Struggling Against Adversity

Thrown upon their own resources, compelled to relinquish their foreign market, and conscious of the growing prejudice against their industry, the wine farmers and merchants looked forward to an unhappy period of depression and loss. Fortunately for them, the development of the country beyond the borders of the Colony, the discovery of diamonds[1] and, later on, the exploitation of the gold resources of the Transvaal,[2] gave them a market nearer at hand, of which they made full use. It was true this market clamoured for spirits rather than for wine, but the consumption of wine in the Colony itself was increasing in an encouraging manner, and much less beer was imported than in previous years. Mr J X Merriman, always a good friend of the wine industry, and Mr J H Hofmeyr, another staunch champion, both stated in parliament that they were glad to see that a taste for good wine was being developed in the public that had hitherto been far more partial to spirit drinking. The advertisements in the contemporary newspapers reflect this growing popularity of table wines. The Paarl Spiritus Maatschappy advertised that its Cape Town branch 'has always on hand a choice stock of old Cape wine, of Madeira, Sherry, Hock, Aromatic Hock and of Pontak, equal and in many respects preferable to the Port wine generally imported into this Colony'. Another local firm stated that it had on hand 'choice Cape wines that will bear comparison with any imported article'. Agricultural shows, held at various centres in the Colony, played some part in advertising the produce both of the wine farmers and of the vintners, and increasing custom came from the Eastern Border districts, from the Free State, and especially from the diamond diggings, although the trade in brandy far exceeded that in natural and blended wines.

Very little wine was now exported to England. The samples sent to the various exhibitions overseas had not attracted much attention, but had brought some orders, chiefly, however, for the sweet and fortified wines. These were very favourably reported upon at London and Vienna, where several prize medals were awarded to Cape merchants.

Of the Cape wines sent to the Vienna Exhibition of 1873, where all the wine-producing districts of the world were represented, Henry Vizetelly, one of the judges, reported as follows (*The Wines of the World*, 1875):

---

1   1867.
2   Gold was discovered in 1886.

'The Cape of Good Hope sent samples of well-nigh all its wines to Vienna, including its Ports and Burgundies, its pale and brown Sherries, its sweet and dry Madeiras, its Pontac, its Steen, its so-called Frontignac and, above all, its celebrated Constantia. Unfortunately the majority of them were so charged with alcohol as to shock Continental palates already sorely tried by the highly spirituous samples exported by Portugal and Spain. Russell & Co of Cape Town sent ten different kinds of wine, but only in a single instance of a dry Pontac did they secure the classification of No 1, which obtained for them a medal of merit. Collison (sic) & Co's samples were very much better, more especially the sweet varieties, although one specimen of so-called Sherry was found to possess sufficient merit to be classed in the first rank. This wine, although by no means of the Jerez type, was evidently the produce of some sweet Spanish grape, and with the exception perhaps of a small amount of added spirit was to all appearance a perfectly natural wine of exceedingly rich flavour. Three other of Collison's samples were classed 1, of which the best was their red Constantia, very bright in colour, a little too sweet to the taste, not particularly spirituous, and with a full amount of that refreshing sub-acidity which alone renders these luscious *vins de liqueur* tolerable. Next came the syrupy wine termed Constantia Sweet Pontac, intensely deep in colour and of the consistency of molasses, and then a Constantia Frontignac, a white wine of fine flavour but too sweet and spirituous for its higher qualities to be readily discernable. For these samples Messrs Collison & Co secured a medal for progress, medals of merit being given to Messrs J P Cloete and Cloete Brothers for other samples of Constantia and Frontignac. There were only four exhibitors of Cape wines, and the whole of them secured medals, invariably, however, for *vins de liqueur*, excepting in the single instance of the Cape Sherry exposed by Messrs Collison & Co.'

One of the best testimonials to the excellence of Cape wine came unsolicited to a winegrower in the Worcester district. Mr Koos Hugo, who had his vineyard on a peculiarly favoured spot where the vines needed no irrigation whatever, made a luscious, amber-coloured wine that won renown throughout the Colony. There was very little of it, and few of his friends were privileged to get it; but among connoisseurs, such as Baron Von Babo and Dr Hahn, it was always reckoned one of the best wines ever made at the Cape, in some respects superior even to the original Constantia, with which it had, however, no close affinity. It was a clean, sparkling, delicious, fine, magnificently harmonious, not too saccharine wine, grandly individual, so that although some saw or tasted in it a fancied similarity to a superb Sauternes, and others again likened it to a liqueur Furmint wine, its characteristics were definitely its own, and comparison was altogether pointless. By chance a bottle of this wine reached Germany, and was so favourably reported upon that the German consul at Cape Town was instructed to obtain a half-aum of it for the King of Prussia, who had recently been made Emperor in the historic Hall of Mirrors at Versailles.

Unfortunately Mr Hugo had none to spare; his wine was in great demand as a *Nagmaal* or communion wine, and the supply had been bespoke for several vintages to come. Some years later, however, the first South African Plenipotentiary ever sent abroad to negotiate with a foreign government, himself a son of the district and known to Mr Hugo from boyhood days, begged a dozen bottles to take with him to Berlin. There he handed them over as a gift to Prince Bismarck, who, not to be outdone in generosity, responded by presenting the envoy with three bottles of the 1846 vintage Steinberger, of which the whole 123 gallons had been bought at the Eberach sale in September, 1858, by the King of Hanover for 6 000 florins or £120. One of these bottles was opened by Dr Hahn at the Captain's table in the saloon of the Union *S S Athenian* on her arrival at Cape Town, and I, a very small boy at the time, was permitted to swallow a sip. My recollection of that famous wine is that it was not to be compared with *Oom* Koos Hugo's product, with which I was quite familiar, nor with that of *Oom* Abram Mouton, of the historic farm *Brakfontein*, who made a *Nagmaal* wine almost, but not quite, equal to the Worcester wine. It is interesting to add that Mr Hugo was afterwards informed, through the proper channels, that his wine was preferred by the Emperor Frederick in his last illness when he was allowed to take it a teaspoonful at a time. Sir Morell Mackenzie, who attended him, stated that his royal patient 'liked a fragrant Cape wine that had been difficult to procure'.

Many years later, I asked Dr Horell who, as Sir Morell's assistant, had attended the Emperor throughout his illness, about this wine and was told: 'It was exclusively reserved for the Emperor's use, and there was very little of it. H.M. wetted his lips with it very frequently, but could hardly swallow, but for some reason he preferred the Cape wine to the other fine wines.' Dr Horell added naïvely: 'I tried to get a similar wine in London, but all the Cape wine here is practically undrinkable'.

Many years later, another wine farmer, who also made a fine, pure natural wine, was visited by the Governor, who, when presented by the host with a half-aum of it, was so impressed by its virtues that he placed an order for a yearly supply. Like Bismarck, he, too, sent a present in return, a case of bottled wine. The wine farmer presented most of the bottles to the local parson, alleging that the wine was too fierce for his taste. The parson opened one bottle, and did not like it either, so the odd half dozen bottles were put in the pantry where they remained until 1901, when an officer, visiting the parsonage during the Anglo-Boer War, discovered them to be . . . Chateau Yquem 1865.

The wine farmers had now to contend with an enemy far more dangerous than tariffs or 'temperance' fanatics. This was a disease of the vines that demands a few paragraphs to itself.

The grape vine, like every living thing, suffers from disease. The fermented juice of its fruit, wine, which may also be said to be in the category of things that have life, has, too, its illnesses which lead to decay and death. The diseases of wine are the concern of the vintners; the sicknesses of the vine are matters of grave interest to winegrowers, and two of them have in the past fifty years very seriously endangered the existence of the wine industry.

The first of these grave diseases is *Oidium*,[1] a parasitic fungus disease of the vine, endemic in North America. It reached Europe in 1845, and was investigated by Berkeley, who discovered that it was caused by a sprouting fungus to which he gave the name *Oidium tuckeri*, in honour of the gentleman who had first drawn attention to its occurrence on grapes growing in a hothouse at Margate. It is now known to scientists as *Uncinula necator* (Schwein) and has been responsible for much damage to vineyards throughout the world. At the Cape it was first reported by Dr Pappe, who found it on Lachrima Christi grapes in Mr P Myburgh's vineyard in 1859, and mentions the fact that as early as 1819 Mr M van Breda had described a somewhat similar rust that affected Hanepoot vines more than it did Steen grapes. Mr McGibbon, the Curator of the Cape Town Botanical Garden, was appointed in 1860 by the government to investigate the disease, and in his report he states that he met with it first in Mr John Proctor's vineyard at Paarl; he found it also in vineyards in other districts, but was of the opinion that its ravages could be stayed provided the affected vineyards were immediately treated by sulphuring the vines, which had been found to be a fairly effective remedy against the parasite. Since then our knowledge of the disease has enabled winegrowers to deal with this pest in such a way that it can now be said to be under control. Some varieties of vines – such as Muscat, Steen and Pontac – are much more susceptible to oidium than other kinds. The fungus attacks the surface of the whole plant and causes permanent damage to the stem, the leaves and the fruit; it rapidly multiplies and spreads through the vineyard very quickly when the conditions are favourable. Where the air is dry and warm, oidium does less damage than in places where warmth and moisture, with little movement of the air, are found. The remedy against the oidium is vigorous and intelligent sulphuring, which is particularly necessary where the vineyards are irrigated. The dry sulphur, when it comes into contact with the fungus and with the surface of the vine, forms sulphuretted hydrogen, a gas that is intensely poisonous to the parasite.

The second serious vineyard pest is an insect known to science as the *Peritymbia vitifolii* (Fitch),[2] though winegrowers prefer to call it by its older and more popular name of Phylloxera. It is this pernicious and yet biologically intensely interesting little animal that has caused a revolution in

---

1   Powdery mildew of grapevines.
2   Now *Daktulosphaira vitifoliae*.

the wine industry, and that at one time threatened to destroy every vineyard in the eastern hemisphere. To its ravages we owe the destruction of millions of vines, and the total disappearance of old wine types made from grapes grown on vines that have now been killed by it.

This horrible little insect, as hideous as a girl in trousers, has a sex life whose surprising aberrations make, by comparison, the wildest imaginings of modern pornographic novelists appear like anaemic virtuosities. It has three mature phases, the sexually fully developed form, the pathogenic precocity that lays eggs without being impregnated, and the curious root parasite that evolves from the leaf galls and actively propagates the species. Those interested in its amazing life cycle will find a full, though somewhat restrained, account of its biological history in M Cornu's *Etudes sur le Phylloxera vastatrix* published in the early eighties of the last century,[1] when it had already caused more than £40 000 000 damage in France, reduced the price of vineland from £250 per acre to a mere £10 per acre, and put several million people out of employment. Briefly, its activities, mainly underground upon the root system of the vine, sap the life of the plant and kill it within a few weeks. It is thus an example of that absurd kind of parasite, similar to the plasmodium that causes malaria, that in due course destroys its host and does so without, apparently, any compensating advantages that we know of. Much more investigation is required before we are able to say, with any suspicion of truth, that we have penetrated behind the secret of the *Phylloxera vastatrix* or its analogous mysteries in the world around us. We do know that it may be killed by suitable poisons, but we have no great hopes of applying these remedies without destroying the vines. Fortunately we have found out that there are certain American rootstocks that appear to be completely immune from the attacks of the insect, and the salvation of the wine industry lies in the utilisation of such immune stocks, upon which a variety of wine grapes can be grafted and propagated. Before this discovery was made, however, three-fourths of the European vineyards had succumbed to the pest, and time and patience and much expense were needed to develop new plantations.

The disease made its appearance in French vineyards in 1863, but was first tracked down by Asa Fitch in America in 1854. Six years later it manifested itself in hot-houses at Hammersmith and thence spread rapidly to the Continent, and east and south. At the Cape it was anxiously looked for. Indeed, from an article in the *Cape Monthly Magazine* of 1872, it appears that in 1866 a winegrower reported that a strange affection had blighted a portion of his vineyard. The description stated that there were parched patches among the vines that were at first attributed to a want of manure, but a liberal application of what was thought to be wanting caused no improvement, so the help of an expert was called in. Dr Becker investigated the matter, but no report was made and no further action was taken.

1 The nineteenth century.

Apparently the 'blight' was thought to be the effect of oidium, just as some years previously oidium had been taken to be 'ordinary rust'. In opening Parliament on April 27 1860, the Lt Governor-General had spoken comforting words:

'Upon the appearance of the mildew in the vineyards, I appointed a Commission to investigate the nature and prevalence of the disease, and I sought for information, through Her Majesty's government, regarding its history and treatment in Europe. The latter has been promised. Although I have not yet received the report of the Commission, it is satisfactory to know that the chief injury to the crop has been owing to a well-known disease of periodical visitation, the rust, and not to the dreaded mildew, whose ravages have been comparatively limited. Its appearance, however, affords a warning which I trust will not be neglected, and will lead to increased attention in the cultivation of the vines, to a careful observation of the first appearances of disease in them, and to the adoption of precautions against its extension. The recently declared policy of the mother country with regard to the import duties upon wines calls for corresponding efforts on the part of our growers to improve the quality of their produce. If these be made, I believe we shall shortly have nothing to fear from a competition upon equal terms with the wines of other countries.'

Brave words indeed at a time when, in Europe, wine farmers were tearing their hair out by handfuls in despair of saving their ancestral vineyards. For it was known that there was no effective remedy against the new pest and the experiments on immunity had not yet borne fruit. A somewhat similar situation had contemporaneously arisen in the east, where the quinine planations in Java were threatened with extermination by the dreaded canker disease of the nursery plants, a threat finally averted by Teysmann who discovered resistant stocks upon which quinine could be grafted. When in 1886 the presence of *Phylloxera* was incontrovertibly demonstrated in vineyards at Helderberg and Constantia, the knowledge obtained by experiments on resistant rootstocks was available, and could be applied with comparatively little loss of time or of stock.

Already in 1880, thanks to the foresight of the wine experts, the Cape government had passed the 'Vineyards Protection Act', implementing the summary proclamation of January 26, 1880, issued under Act 9 of 1876, that gave it authority to inspect vineyards and destroy affected vines and take all steps necessary to stay the extension of the disease.

These steps, in brief, were the gradual replacement of non-resisting grape varieties by others grafted on *Phylloxera*-immune American stocks such as Aramon, Jacquez, Rupestris de Lot, and Riparia. The most commonly used today is Jacquez. Thanks to these precautions *Phylloxera*, which, like the poor, is always with us, has ceased to be an alarming pest. It can be kept within the bounds, and need not scare any intending viticulturist. On the whole it has not done so much damage to South African vineyards as it might have done, thanks to the precautionary measures that were taken to check its spread. In the outlying districts — in Clanwilliam, for instance — it ruined many vineyards, but in the chief wine districts its ravages were not half as serious as in France. Today practically all vineyards are of vines grafted on pest-resistant stocks, which although their rootlets are not absolutely immune from attack, are yet sufficiently guarded, by some means that we do not yet fully comprehend, to protect the plants from damage. Much more investigation is needed before we are able to say in what way the must of particular grape varieties is influenced by such resistant stocks. It is popularly presumed that pre-phylloxera wines were immensely superior to wines made from grapes now grown on root-resistant stocks, but this, like so many other popular presumptions about wine and wine-growing, is a mistake.

Before the policy of replanting was enforced, reliance was placed mainly on quarantine, destruction of infested vines, and the use of chemical remedies that are now proved to be useless and to do more harm than good. A Phylloxera Commission was appointed by the government; its members were Mr Roland Trimen, Professor Macowan, the Government Botanist, and Monsieur Peringuey, a distinguished French wine merchant who was also an enthusiastic entomologist. The last was deputed to visit all vineyards, and put in force the destruction of the infested stocks, for which some compensation was paid. Much dissatisfaction was caused by this policy, and later on, in 1889, a Select Committee was appointed to investigate the whole matter. The Committee reported that while the enforcement of regulations undoubtedly had caused dissatisfaction, it could not recommend any relaxation of the vigilance that had so far prevented the wholesale extension of the pest.

'Considering that the produce of our Colonial wine farms is estimated at nearly half a million pounds sterling per year, and that the disease has as yet extended over only portions of the Cape and Stellenbosch divisions, but that there it has proved itself as destructive as in any European vineyards … the Committee hold that the efforts of the Government, rather than being relaxed, should be redoubled in vigour in combating the spread of the evil.'

The recommendations were: more stringent quarantine; prohibition of the use of vine leaves or twigs in packing; more compensation for the destruction of infested vineyards; prohibition of importation of grapes, vines, tubers or plants from abroad, and finally replanting of the vineyards on Rupestris and Riparia stocks.

The government was alive to the necessity for action. It appointed a Government Viticulturist, bought the Constantia estate to establish thereon an experimental farm, and stirred its almost moribund department of agriculture into emmet-like bureaucratic briskness. The decision to bring an expert out from Europe to advise the industry was made in the teeth of some opposition, but was generally approved of when it became known that a real expert had been selected and that he would be given, within such limits as are demanded by departmental prestige, a free hand to improve the wine industry.

Chapter 11

The Industry Gets Expert Advice

In the early eighties of the last century,[1] winegrowers at the Cape had the benefit of their own experience in wine making, of the advice and help of wine merchants who were mainly blenders and had themselves no practical experience of modern methods of making wine, and of such assistance as they could obtain from the Department of Agriculture which at that time had no great prestige and not a single expert on viticulture. It was generally admitted that Cape wines could be greatly improved, but there was apparently none capable of demonstrating how such improvement could be practically effected. Dr Daniel Hahn, the lecturer on chemistry at the South African College, and Professor A Fischer, the lecturer on agricultural chemistry and experimental physics at the Victoria College, Stellenbosch, were both wine lovers, expert analytical chemists, and greatly interested in matters oenological, but they were not viticulturists, and their knowledge was to a large extent theoretical. Nevertheless the government had called upon both to report on the wine industry, and both had given evidence before Select Committees, strongly urging the establishment of an experimental wine farm, under the direction of an expert viticulturist, and the introduction of improved methods in wine and brandy making. Dr Hahn, in an exhaustive report published in 1881, which contains a good description of the various wine districts, with instructive comments upon the soil and climate, had expressed strong views about the advantageous position in which the Colony, regarded purely as a wine-producing country, was placed.

> 'Of the first four conditions for the success of viticulture — soil, climate, capital and knowledge,' he wrote, 'the Colony possesses two, soil and climate of the best possible quality, and this country must become, when capital and knowledge are brought to bear upon the two former, one of the greatest wine-producing countries in the world.'

In Parliament, representatives of the wine-growing districts had repeatedly urged the government to 'take steps to improve the conditions of the wine industry,' although they had failed to suggest what such steps should be. That great wine lover, John X Merriman, on assuming ministerial responsibility, decided that the time had come to implement the recommendations that had been made so often by former Select Committees, and to initiate a programme of scientific development. Discussing the matter with his friend, Dr Hahn, he asked for concrete proposals, whereupon Hahn drew up a private memorandum in which it was

---

1   The nineteenth century.

suggested that a qualified expert should be obtained from France or Germany, not only to report upon the state of the wine industry in the Colony but to give demonstrations and practical advice to winegrowers. Hahn did not consider himself fitted to recommend anyone for this post, as he 'had lost touch with the younger qualified men in Europe,' but advised that the government should consult Professor Planchon, Director of the *Jardin des Plantes* at Montpellier, Dr E Rotondi, Prof A Blankenhorn, Director of the Oenological Institute at Karlsruhe, and Freiherr A von Babo, all recognised as among the foremost European oenologists and ampelographists. Mr Merriman accordingly instructed Mr Charles Currey, the Commissioner of Crown Lands and Public Works, to ask Sir Charles Mills, the Colony's Agent General in London, 'to be good enough to institute inquiries with a view to ascertain whether a class of experts exists from which a person could be selected to examine and report upon the best means of improving the wine industry of the Colony', on the understanding that 'the man selected must be of such a calibre that his opinion would be received without hesitation as that of a master' (letter dated 24th October, 1883). Mills replied on November, 1883, stating that he had consulted with the Agent General for the Australian Colonies, and had learned that in Victoria and in New South Wales the government had decided to leave such matters entirely to private enterprise, and that only in South Australia the government had stepped in to help the wine farmers. New South Wales had indeed asked that an expert should be sent out, but the Agent General had 'after personal inquiry on the Continent and mature consideration, prevailed upon his government to abandon the proposal'. In the circumstances Mills suggested that the best thing the Cape government could do was to grant free passages to carefully selected, intelligent and skilled vine dressers from Germany and Italy, who could be placed among the wine farmers and, as wine farmers themselves, teach their neighbours how to make good wine.

Mr Merriman did not take this reply patiently. The Agent General was informed that what the government wanted was not a number of selected immigrants, but a scientific expert of indisputable standing, and was instructed to apply at once to the celebrities named by Dr Hahn, asking them '*de vouloir bien avoir l'obligeance de lui recommender les noms d'un ou plusieurs candidats possédant le [sic] connaissances practique et scientifique necessaires pour entreprendre le travail indique par le M le Doc Hahn*'. (Letter 19 December 1883.) This was done, and Mills wrote back in February 1884, forwarding letters from these experts, some containing interesting and practical suggestions. In a later despatch, the Agent General submitted an application from M Foex-Mortimer, a professor of agriculture and agricultural engineer, who offered his services for five years, at an annual salary of £1 000, and another application from a protégé of Blankenhorn. Neither candidate, in Dr Hahn's opinion, was of the outstanding ability that was required and no provision was made in the estimates for a viticultural expert, but after further correspondence the government decided upon the appointment of Baron Carl von Babo, who was recognised as an acknowledged expert on viticulture.

His first report, presented to the government after the 1885 vintage, gives such an admirable picture of the wine industry at the time, and contains so much that is still of lively interest to winegrowers after the lapse of nearly half a century, that no apology is necessary for extensively excerpting from it.

After a general review of viticulture in the Colony, and suggestions for improving the vineyards, with special reference to siting, he discusses the different varieties of grapes.

'It is most fortunate that the different kinds of grapes grown in the Colony produce a very excellent wine. This is of great value, because the introduction of new kinds would endanger the whole viticulture of the Colony by carrying the Phylloxera to South Africa. The law prohibiting the introduction of vines, etc, has removed all danger, and it was made just in time to keep this plague from South Africa. The Phylloxera *was not in the Colony* when the law came into force, because its presence in the Colony would have shown itself by this time. The most rigorous enforcement of this law is the surest protection of the Cape Viticulture. But in order to be prepared for any emergency it is necessary for this Colony to follow the example of France, Germany and Austria. The Cape vines must be grafted on American vines as basis ... They are obtained by importing the seeds of the best kinds of American vines ... Vines of different kinds can be produced. But only a proper method of mashing, pressing and of manipulation of the wine in the store will show what sort of wine each variety of grape will produce.'[1]

He found the most popular varieties to be Green Grape, a vigorous grower which 'will certainly produce a good wine for export.' Hanepoot he thought should be kept for making raisins 'until a better manipulation of wine has been generally adopted,' but he rightly recommended it as an export grape. Stein produced 'a most delicate wine'; the Muscadels were excellent for sweet wines. Of the dark grapes, Pontac was the most valuable, and its must gave a very excellent dark wine 'which equals the Bordeaux and will always find a market in Europe.'

After dealing with climatic conditions and vineyard pests, with particular reference to oidium, he discusses the wine crop, and comments on the difficulty of estimating the yield from the number of vines.

---

1   Many new varieties of grapes had been imported: among the best of these was undoubt-edly the Hermitage grape. McGibbon had a small experimental winery in the Botanical Gardens in 1856 where he grew 33 different kinds of grape vines, listed as variants of *Vitis vinifera*; among them were Verdelho, white Nice, Water Hanepoot, Syrian, but no Riesling or Hermitage. (L)

'As soon as the Cape wines are properly prepared and manipulated, they will be the best material for mixing and improving light and inferior European wines. These two facts, *viz* that the yield of the vineyards is greater at the Cape than anywhere else in the world, and that Cape wine, when well prepared, is a superior article, secure the future of the Viticulture at the Cape, although it may be several thousands of miles from the principal markets of the world. If the juice of the Cape grape is properly treated and prepared for the European taste, it will always find a market in Europe.

In the sun of South Africa the grapes ripen to perfection, and South African grapes are an excellent material of which to make wine, which will find ready customers. But in consequence of great negligence and bad or insufficient manipulation, a wine is produced which does not deserve the name of "wine." This is borne out by the ill success of the numerous attempts made with a view to exporting Cape wine to Europe in large quantities. The fact that small samples of better wine arrived in a sound condition in Europe does not disprove the fact that the bulk of the Cape wine would not stand the journey to Europe. I have frequently heard the opinion expressed that no wine made at the Cape could stand the voyage to Europe. This is entirely erroneous and false; all wine merchants in Europe know perfectly well in what condition a wine must be, in order to stand a sea voyage, during which it is exposed to very high and very low temperatures . . .

It is unjustifiable to give Cape wine a name to which it has no claim. Why are certain Cape wines called Sherry, from a locality in Spain? Are they, perhaps, afraid to appear in public without a mask? Who is to be imposed upon? The consumers at the Cape know all about the origin of this sort of Sherry and there are no foreign consumers. Besides, the new label does not improve those wines of which the flavour would penetrate through the most beautiful label with a famous name. It is entirely useless and misleading to adopt foreign names for Cape wines; such names as Constantia, Paarl, Breede River, and Montagu on the labels of bottles containing properly prepared and manipulated Cape wine will read as well as Sherry or Madeira. A really good article does not require a high-sounding name; it will recommend itself by its properties. Also the name Hock is false and unjustifiable; it means Rhine wine; but the character of the wine which goes under this name is just the opposite of the wine which is called Hock at the Cape. Good Cape wine under its true name will soon become known and famous . . .'

Here, again, is sound advice that our winegrowers and merchants should follow. Mr Jacob Cloete once replied to an agent's letter asking him to 'send some Hock, or as near it as you have,' honestly and succinctly: 'I make no Hock. I am sending you a good dry white wine.' But from time to time there is a resuscitation of the silly argument that foreign geographical names, that by custom and time have become associated with wines made in particular localities, have no patent rights and that they may be glued on wine bottles that contain wine that never came from such places.

'Some very old wines are met with here and there, and they are very good, but in quantity too insignificant for export. It was the old wines which in former times established the reputation of the Cape wines. Something very superior was then meant by the words 'Cape wine' and it is to be hoped that this old reputation will be re-established, to the benefit of the active, ambitious and unprejudiced wine farmers and wine merchants at the Cape.

'It is the manipulation of the wine that is to be blamed for the quality of the Cape wine. The cutting of the grapes, the separating of the ripe from the unripe grapes, the collecting of the grapes before pressing, is [sic] all done, with a few exceptions, in a careless manner. But the climax of the untidy proceedings is reached in the tramping of the grapes ... A number of half-naked coloured men, in a state of active perspiration, are tramping the grapes in the first tub; thus the feet break the grapes, and by the elasticity of the sole, the seeds, etc, remain unbroken. Only the juice runs off and, if this were passed through a sieve, only the pure grape juice would be obtained. But during the tramping some other substances are added to the juice. From the floor of the wine stores, which are saturated with acetous germs, the trampers carry on their feet a large amount of detrimental substance into the juice, and also the sweat of the men goes into the juice; although the latter does not perceptibly increase the quantity, it certainly imparts a most objectionable bouquet to the wine.'

He advises the use of European grape mills, which do not crush seeds or stalks, and the use, for fermentation purposes, of closed casks.

'Juice, husks and stalks are thrown together in the fermenting tubs, and the astringent harsh tannin is thus extracted from the husks and stalks, imparting to the wine that unpleasant scratching taste. The fermenting tubs are open, and the juice can absorb from the air any quantity of those germs which are, later on, a standing danger to the quality of the wine. All the bouquet compounds can freely escape during fermentation from the open vessels. These bouquet compounds, which are so characteristic of the Cape grape, would also be in the wine, if the making of the wine were better ... The fermentation of the juice of dark grapes should only be carried on in closed tubs; the fermentation of the juice of white grapes must be done in casks provided with fermentation bungs.'

The report abounds with practical hints, and well repays perusal, even at this time when elementary science has been widely popularised, by every winegrower. There is a section on the export of grapes that anticipated much of the development that has since taken place in this branch of viticulture, and a long paragraph on raisins. The concluding chapter is devoted to 'Proposals and recommendations with regard to the improvement of the wine industry.' In it he remarks—

'The first experiments made with a view to the introduction of the vine into South Africa have been successful. The conditions required for the growth and development of the same are very favourable. In the course of time this branch of agriculture spread all over the Western Province. Even under the most primitive and simple treatment, the vine yielded the most beautiful crops. Although the wine which was produced here was made contrary to the best principles, it always found a ready market in the Colony. The better wines could even be exported to Europe. In the course of time, viticulture became the most important branch of agriculture. The consumption of the wine did not, however, keep pace with the extension of the viticulture and the increased production of wine. As a large proportion of the wine produced was inferior, much wine remained unsold; and it did not always pay to manufacture the wine into brandy, because the price of brandy was often very low. The surplus wine, which cannot be sold, ought to be exported; but with this we have arrived at a point which presents very great difficulties. There are rich and populated countries which could easily absorb all our surplus production of wine, but the attempts made to introduce our wines to these markets have not been successful ... Those who tried these experiments did not set to work correctly ...

'In order to give a correct idea as to the share which the Cape has at present in the wine trade of Great Britain, I quote the following figures, taken from the *Wein-Merkur* of February 1885. The imports were in 1884: Dark wines, 8 817 166 gallons; Light wines, 6 321 479 gallons; total, 15 138 645 gallons. Of this, the Cape Colony only exported 64 584 gallons (about 500 leaguers). In 1883, it exported only 49 872 gallons ... The wine farmers are at present in a most critical condition. Some years ago they worked with a very great profit, because the prices of wines were high. Gradually the prices went down and many were half ruined. This state of depression did not come on suddenly; its consequences could have been avoided. But the necessity of assisting and supporting the wine farmer was not recognised in time, and the present state of viticulture, wine export and wine trade is the consequence of the indifference shown with regard to this all-important branch of agriculture.'

He proceeds to give his recommendations that, in brief, are that an experimental wine farm should be established, that ocular demonstrations should be given to wine farmers and wine merchants, for 'neither the farmer nor exporter knows how wine fit for export is to be made, and it is necessary to teach both.' Model farms should be started in the various wine-growing districts, and the government should take the lead in investigating the many problems in connection with the wine industry. The Baron was a thoroughly scientific-minded man, and he fully realised how much there was that he did not know about wine. The bacteriology of wine was, as yet, in its infancy, but he knew enough to understand that many of the mysteries in connection with the ageing of wine, the deterioration of good wine under certain conditions, and the variability of wine from the same bin could only be solved after prolonged and painstaking investigation with the combined assistance of the chemist, the bacteriologist, the botanist and the plant pathologist. His report, although written in a hard and crabbed style, is a readable and instructive document that deserves a better fate than to be buried in the 'Annexures to the Votes and Proceedings of the House of Assembly' for the year 1886.

In the same volume as the Baron's report is to be found a memorandum on the general state of agriculture in the Colony by Professor A Fischer of the Victoria College at Stellenbosch. The professor is in general agreement with Baron von Babo on the imperative necessity of establishing an experimental agricultural station, but deals more particularly with the wheat and grain industry. Incidentally, his report, although an official document, contains an amazing tirade against the Jews who are stigmatised as among the worst enemies of the farmers, in a long paragraph that might have been penned by the late Dr Goebbels himself, for it displays just the right mixture of truth and falsehood to make an appeal to the passion and prejudice of anti-Semitism. There is some evidence that this violent diatribe, occurring as it did in an official parliamentary document, was resented in certain quarters, and that Dr Hahn, whose courage and sense of fair play was never questioned, vehemently protested against its inclusion. The records, however, do not show that any official action was taken in the matter which was allowed to drop.

Baron von Babo remained on as Government Viticulturist until his contract expired. His salary was so low that he did not see his way clear to renew the contract, and preferred to engage himself in private enterprise. Meanwhile he had been given charge of the newly purchased estate at Constantia, which he found in a neglected condition, but with the help of convict labour the farm was greatly improved, and the wines that were made by the Baron, according to his own process, were regarded as sound. The government engaged a student, recommended by the firm of Deinhart & Co of Coblentz, who had gained practical experience at the German viticultural farm at Geisenheim as Government Viticulturist, and brought him out in 1888. He was Mr Clemens Mayer, and his work at Constantia could hardly be said to have been thoroughly satisfactory. In 1889, less than a year after he had assumed office, a Select Committee was appointed to inquire into the working, management and condition of the Government wine farm at Constantia. The Committee heard evidence, the gist of it to the effect that some of the wine made on the farm had turned sour and contained far too high an amount of acetic acid, that the lectures given and the curriculum generally were not such as to encourage even the few students – fewer than half a dozen – who had entered, and that the management was not satisfactory. In its report it recommended that the services of a competent overseer should be secured to take charge of the farming operations, that more supervision should be exercised over the students, and that greater discrimination should be shown in granting diplomas. It thought that the results so far obtained in regard to wine making were unsatisfactory, even while recognising the fact that wine making in this Colony is still in an experimental stage, and suggested that, while the manufacture of light wines should not be discontinued, more attention should be paid to the manufacture of sweet wines. The expert witnesses concurred in the opinion that excellent wine could be made, and had indeed been made, but also in finding that there was a deplorable lack of uniformity in the quality of the wines submitted. The Committee concluded that the evidence did not warrant the recommendation that the farm should be disposed of; it should be placed in charge of a thoroughly competent and experienced manager, preferably one with some knowledge of local conditions. The mistake that had been made was one that is not unknown in government departments, namely to replace a known expert, whose services had been requisitioned by private enterprise, by someone at the same low salary whose experience and abilities are not those of an expert. The Constantia farm had showed, under Von Babo, what could be done under expert direction, and much later on equally valuable work was done at the viticultural stations at Paarl and Stellenbosch.

There was now a general feeling among the wine farmers, given expression to in letters to the press and at public meetings, that some measure of co-operation might be usefully tried. The difficulty was to suggest in what way such co-operation could be organised. The excise on brandy and on distilling wine had been modified, revoked and again imposed and modified, and the price of spirits had fluctuated with an irregularity that was appalling. The solitary distiller from grain petitioned Parliament for relief, because he had been ruined. But the winegrowers fared no better for, although there was a keen demand for brandy, there was also much illicit distilling that produced liquor devoid of any vestige of grape spirit, and the price of natural wine oscillated between £2 and £3 per leaguer.

The Select Committee appointed by the House of Assembly on 29 May 1888 to report on the means for establishing some regulation or supervision of the export of Cape wines was presided over by Mr J X Merriman, and reported that, in the face of the evidence, 'Your Committee do not feel themselves at liberty to recommend any compulsory regulation of the wine export on the lines attempted in former years.' The evidence before consisted in the replies to questions put to the leading wine merchants, and in a memorandum on the duties of the Wine Taster, complied by the Keeper of the Archives, and another memorandum furnished by Mr H J Jarvis, who excused himself on the ground of his great age and his state of health, from tendering evidence in person. Mr Jarvis stated that he had himself had experience of what happened when under the Wine Establishment an attempt had been made to exercise some control over the quality of wine exported. He wrote:

> 'If the object of the Committee is to revive the Wine Taster's department, I fear it will have no beneficial effect towards the improvement of the quality of our wines for exportation; the remedy was tried and failed; improvements are now being attempted. It is to the grower we must look in the first instance, that he takes more interest and pains with the vineyard, selection of the grape, cellar, and the making of the wine ... If the wine merchant receives a good sound article from the grower it is very easy for him to manipulate it, and to make it a good sound exportable article, and as the duty of 1/- is the standard for a good and sound wine I have no fear of its not *regaining* its lost credit in the British market. What is required there is a uniform, sound quality, an article which the consumer can depend on receiving from his correspondent; such wines are produced from the Green and Pontac grape ... I had a long experience of what was required for the London market, and its greatest requisite was a wine of sound and *uniform* quality; to attain that, I would advise all exporters to give their wines the benefit of exposure to the summer sun before shipment; it has a wonderful effect in mellowing and improving the wine ... It was the act of Mr Gladstone's treaty with France which ruined the trade (in 1860) and from which the Colony is still suffering, but which can again be revived by careful means. Whilst in England in 1870 and 1871, I did all in my power to induce the several authorities to give the trade some relief. It was admitted *by all* that the Cape wine trade had been hardly dealt with.'

Among the witnesses examined by the Committee, Baron von Babo, formerly the Government Wine Expert, was of opinion that 'all the light, bright wines with bouquet can be produced here.' If the export of wine could be controlled in such a way as to exclude wines that were not perfectly good, it would be of great advantage, as opinion abroad in regard to Cape wine would soon change. Green grape wine could be bought for as low a price as £2 10s. A taste for light wine would have to be cultivated; the prevalent taste was for sweeter, stronger wines. Mr C F Sedgwick, in answer to the question, 'Do you think our wines, when properly prepared, compare favourably with those of other Colonies?' said, 'Yes, they surpass them. I am speaking of our wines as compared with Australian wines. Our wines are also superior to the inferior class of European wines, such as Mediterranean wines; at least, that is my opinion and, I may say, that of the best judges in London.' Mr F Green concurred; Mr P Marais stated that what 'had got Cape wine a bad name in England is that they have been accustomed to take all the bad stuff from every part of the world and pass it off for Cape wine.'

All the witnesses agreed that government control would do very little to improve matters and would present great practical difficulties. Professor A Fischer, the Secretary for Agriculture, was of the opinion that the quality of the wines produced had improved, and that a good, wholesome class of wine was being exported; his department was already testing wines on voluntary submission by winegrowers. All the witnesses agreed that young wine likely to 'turn' should not be exported. Mr J H van Ryn, who in five years had shipped about 3 000 hogsheads to England, said that there was an increasing demand for lighter wines; in three years he had exported 30 000 gallons, mostly to the Continent where there was no difference of duty between the light and heavier wines. He thought the consumption of wine locally had fallen off. The witnesses did not think that much would be gained by offering a bounty to winegrowers; wine farming was a business proposition, and the yield should depend upon the quality. This sound advice was followed by the Committee, which did not recommend a bounty, but advised that the duty on staves and fustage might be modified.

In the eighties another attempt, this time better organised, was made to secure co-operation between winegrowers and the exporters. The late Mr J H Hofmeyr, generally known to his contemporaries as 'Onze Jan,' took a leading part in the movement, and presided at the meeting in Cape Town, held on 18 January 1888, at which it was decided to establish the *Cape Town Wine and Export Syndicate*. Winegrowers from all parts of the Colony attended the meeting, which had been well advertised, and promises of support came from others who were unable to be present. Mr Rhodes, for example, telegraphed from Kimberley that he was willing to take five shares; Barnato, too late for allocation, applied for a number of shares, and among the other subscribers were some of the best-known farmers and merchants. It was unanimously decided to offer the appointment of General Manager of the Syndicate to Baron von Babo, the Government Wine Expert, at a salary of £300 plus a bonus of five shillings on every leaguer of wine exported. Amidst a chorus of local commendation and in the expectation of quick and enduring success, the venture was launched. How unsubstantial were its hopes and how total was its failure can be seen from the first report, presented by the directors in August 1889 when the first and last annual meeting of the Syndicate took place. The Directors explained that the Syndicate had been formed 'for the purpose of finding an export for the surplus production of Cape Wine.' Its subscribed capital was £5 800 in £100 shares, the amount paid up being £5 050. Operations started in February 1888, when premises were hired at a monthly rental of £40. The running expenses totalled £100 per month. Wines were bought direct from the winegrowers, and were blended into the following Syndicate specialities: *Tafelberg*, a light red wine, 'similar to claret'; *Green Kenya* and *Stein Kenya*, light white wines 'similar to Rhine wine'; *Hanepoot Red,* and a *White Hermitage*. All were guaranteed to be pure natural wine, to be shipped in casks of 63 imperial gallons. Samples, generally in lots of six bottles of each variety, were shipped to Hoffman and Hefter (Leipzig), K S Scholtz

(Lubeck), Peycke and Rascher (Hamburg), A P Sjoberg (Malmo), W Dull (Amsterdam), A Stein & Co, Army and Navy Stores, and Civil Service Supply Association (all of London), Mayer and Co (Bordeaux), M Berliner (New York) and Currie Fraser and Co (Mauritius). The reports on these samples, went on the directors, were favourable, but the value placed on the wines as an article of commerce was very disappointing. It had been hoped that France, where the phylloxera had devastated many vineyards, would have welcomed these wines, but the Bordeaux agents had been very discouraging, and export in that direction would scarcely be profitable. The discovery of gold in the Transvaal, and the sudden increase in the European population there, had also justified the belief that an export trade could be built up in the north, but here too the results had been 'most disappointing.' An export trade in light wines, the directors concluded, was quite unprofitable; winegrowers must look for local markets, and could only make a success of a co-operative syndicate if it was a strong company with a capital of at least £30 000. If such a company could be formed it could take over the remaining assets of the Syndicate — chiefly the stock of wine in the cellars — but if there was no prospect of forming such a company, the directors advised immediate liquidation. The shareholders agreed, and were lucky enough to get back a substantial portion of the money they had invested. The failure of the undertaking, so auspiciously started and, so far as we can judge, so excellent managed, was a great discouragement to subsequent attempts at co-operation, nor did it serve, apparently, to drive home the lesson to the wine farmers that their best market was in South Africa itself. Curiously enough the wines bottled by the Syndicate were not sold locally. All of them were superior to most of the wines obtainable at the time in Cape Town hotels and bars; one, *Tafelberg*, was a table wine of excellent quality, and exactly the type that appeals to those who wish to drink a light beverage wine. The curious reader will find some documentary notes on the activities of the Syndicate in the letters preserved with the Syndicate's Minute Book in the S A MSS collection[1] in the South African Public Library. Among these is a report, unfortunately unsigned, from the London agent, on the samples received. It gives the following analysis:

	Green Kenya	*Stein*	*Tafelberg*
Density of wine	990.30	990.28	992.68
Density of distillate	981.21	981.00	982.12
Spirit as proof strength	25.6	26.6	25.0
Acid as tartaric	54%	61%	25%
Residue per cent	2.29	2.28	2.52
Ash	Clear	Clear	Clear
Condition	No deposit	No deposit	No deposit

'Neither of the two white wines was quite free from the characteristic odour and taste associated with Cape wines. This

---

1   The South African Manuscript Collection.

objectionable flavour was, however, greatly modified and the improvement leads one to hope that at no distant date these (white) wines will be of a true hock type ... Cape wine is prejudiced by its old reputation, and its value in the London market is depreciated ... Its intrinsic value is certainly higher than its commercial value.'

Chapter 12

Later Development

The end of the last century[1] saw the wine industry at the Cape more or less stabilised as a growing agricultural asset with limited possibilities of expansion. Legislative interference that will be discussed in more detail later on was hampering its growth and development, but could be considered as a passing phase likely to be modified, or even to disappear, when the economic problems of the Colony were understood and the antagonistic, or at least negative, attitude of a part of the public to the winegrowers gave way to a recognition of the national importance of their product. Co-operation and scientific improvement of the methods of making wine, in the light of the great discoveries that had been made about the fermentation and maturing of wines, were still lacking. There was, however, encouraging proof that individual wine farmers fully realised the significance of these new methods and were experimenting in the right direction.

They were greatly helped by the information, experience and criticism given and gained at the annual agricultural shows, which now paid more and more attention to wine exhibits, although the rewards to which successful competitors could aspire were not as yet even moderately encouraging. At the Western Province Agricultural Show, held at Rosebank in March 1894, the prizes offered in the wine section ranged from £3 to £5, distributed among six classes: Hermitage, dry Pontac, Sherry, Hock, dry Muscadel, and four varieties of sweet wines. Among the prizewinners were Bam & Co, Collison, Paarl Wine and Brandy Co, Paarl Berg Wine and Spirits Co, Philip Faure, Kufner & Malzer, and Barry & Co; the report on the exhibits was very favourable, and a few wines were singled out for special praise. Cape Town wine merchants could now, in their advertisements, refer to the awards that had been made to them. Henry C Collison Ltd, whose stores were in Sir Lowry Road, specialised in F C Brandy, old Montague Dop, and referred proudly to the prize medals gained at the International Exhibitions at Paris, Amsterdam and Bordeaux, and to the fact that they were 'sold agents for the Cape Government Farm Wines, manufactured at Groot Constantia by the Government Expert, R Dubois, namely Hermitage, Sauvignon Blanc and Constantia Berg.' J Sedgwick & Co of Strand Street, established in 1859, with a depot in St George's Street, advertised forty different kinds of wine, and had gained first prizes at successive Cape Town shows for Hermitage, Stein, Greengrape and Hanepoot wines. A 'Wine Merchants' Guide' in a contemporary handbook gave interesting particulars about the various firms in Cape Town, while Dr

---

1 The nineteenth century.

Hahn's official account of the wine industry was printed and reprinted in the several editions of Noble's authoritative Directory.

The outbreak of the Anglo-Boer War[1] did not at first impede the development of the wine industry. Indeed, it rather stimulated the production of wine, for the local market for that product suddenly became far brisker than it had ever been, and large quantities of young wine were disposed of at remunerative prices to supply the demand at the various camps and canteens all over the country. Only in the second year of the war were some of the wine-producing districts directly affected, but the damage done to the vineyards was limited and made no difference to the production in the four main wine-producing areas. When the war was over, the great surplus of imported wines held in stock at the military canteens was sold by auction, often at ridiculously low prices, and for a few years afterwards some well-known European wines could be obtained at local hotels where no one would have dreamed of ever buying them. As late as 1915 I met with some of them in a small Transvaal hostelry, and was told that they were the remnants of several cases sold by the Army Supply Store in 1902.

When the war was over, the temporary boom in demand abruptly ceased and the over-production in the following three years once more became a problem that seemed incapable of solution. The export to the Transvaal was increasing, but although the war had made thousands of visitors acquainted with Cape wines, the demand from abroad was still small. More and more it became clear to the wine producers that in order to put the industry on a profitable footing, co-operation and attention to the production of a superior quality of wine were necessary. The Cape Government had done its moderate best for the industry by offering free expert advice, establishing another experimental farm and publishing informative articles in the *Agricultural Journal*, while the Agricultural Society had developed its wine section at the annual shows into something that was really stimulative and encouraging. In the war years the shows had necessarily to be curtailed. At that of 1901, for instance, the six classes of wines exhibited differed in no respect from those shown in former years. At the 1906 show the prize list showed certain changes. Entries were called for in nine different classes: Port type, Burgundy type, Claret type, Sherry type, Sauterne type, Hock type, Sweet wine, red and white Muscadel and Hanepoot and Pontac. Among the prizewinners are the High Constantia Estate, the Western Wine and Brandy Company, and the Castle Wine Company. Subsequent shows were planned on the same lines, with the addition of an exhibit of table and wine grapes, as the export of the latter, thanks mainly to the pioneering efforts of Mr Charles Chiappini, the Trades Commissioner in London, was becoming a profitable venture. It was only after Union, however, that the Agricultural Society decided to hold an annual 'special wine show,' to give winegrowers facilities to advertise their

---

1 October 1899.

product. The first of these wine shows, that are today a popular feature and have done much to encourage the winegrower, was held at Cape Town on 17 October 1912. The annual report for the following year stated—

'For many years a show for producers only had been held under the auspices of the Western Province Board of Horticulture, but as that body had become defunct, having been merged into the newly formed Agricultural Association of the Province of the Cape of Good Hope, the Agricultural Society took over the management of the show. These shows have contributed in no small degree to the vast improvement which has taken place in recent years in the manufacture of Cape wines, and it would be a pity to let them drop. There is little revenue to be derived from a fixture of this nature, and a good deal of expenditure is incurred, but the government was good enough to assist with a monetary grant so that the Society did not suffer any financial loss. At the same time, it was decided to provide classes for matured wines at this Show instead of at the Annual Show in February. The wine merchants heartily co-operated and, in addition to entering samples for competition, put up tastefully decorated stands where samples of their wares could be obtained.'

This 'special wine show' was held at Libermans Building in Burg Street, but it was unfortunately so badly attended — probably because it had not been adequately advertised — that the trade was discouraged and pressed for a return to the old custom of including a wine section in the annual Western Province Agricultural Show held in February. In later years the wine show was better patronised, and was held at some centre in the wine-producing districts. Today it is usually held at Paarl, which is a convenient centre, and is always well attended and well worth a visit by the wine-lover who wishes to satisfy himself that quality wines can be produced here. The great development that has taken place during the last two decades is well illustrated by the prize lists of the 1912 and the 1946 shows. The latter lists no fewer than fifty-five different classes, divided into the following groups: Dry White (sixteen classes), Novice class; Dry Red (fifteen classes), Novice class; Sweet White (five classes), Sweet Red (six classes), Novice class; Zone group (five classes). Among the prizes offered are the following—

Ten leaguers of blended Sherry (finished article) ready for market and conforming to trade description of Dry Sherry not less than two years old (Perpetual Silver Floating Trophy, value 20 guineas, presented by E W Sedgwick).

Twenty leaguers Dry White Wine with a maximum strength not exceeding 21 proof spirit. The wine to be analysed by the KWV Analyst before judging, and a certificate covering the results to be handed to the Secretary. Messrs Bertrams, High Constantia (Pty) Ltd, to have the option to buy Prize Wine at an agreed price (Perpetual Silver Floating Trophy, value £25, presented by G N Maskell, Esq).

Twenty leaguers Light Dry White Wine, unfortified, suitable for export, 1945 vintage (Stellenrust Silver Cup, value 15 guineas, presented by the Hon R Stuttaford. To be won three years in succession or four times in all before becoming the property of the Exhibitor).

Twenty leaguers pure Riesling (Monis Regina Cup, presented by Monis Wineries Ltd, to be won three times in succession or four times in all before becoming the property of the Exhibitor).

One hundred leaguers Dry White Wine, suitable for export, unfortified (The C W H Kohler Silver Floating Trophy, value £25, presented by the Co-operative Wine Growers' Association of South Africa, Paarl. The Cup to be held by the winner for the year following the award when it must be returned to the Society).

Seven leaguers Claret type, light bodied, blended or otherwise (Silver Cup, value 15 guineas, presented by J Rubbi, Esq. To be won three years in succession or four times in all before becoming the property of the Exhibitor).

Ten leaguers of a blended Dry Red Wine, full bodied, unfortified, with a maximum of 24 degrees proof spirit (Silver Floating Trophy, value £25, presented by Mr Hugh Bairnsfather in memory of his son, Mr Peter Bairnsfather Cloete, with a replica to the winner each year).

Twenty leaguers Red Export Wine, of full Burgundy character, as near as possible to French Burgundy (Silver vase presented by Cuthbert Burgoyne, Esq, of London, in memory of his father P B Burgoyne, Esq).

Twenty leaguers Light or Full Bodied Dry Red Wine, matured in wood, suitable for export and unfortified (Silver Cup, value ten guineas, presented by the Quality Wine Growers' Society; to be presented in alternate years for 'Light or Full Bodied Dry Red Wine' and 'Light Bodied Dry Red Wine').

One hundred leaguers Dry Red Table Wine, suitable for export, full-bodied, unfortified (C W H Kohler Silver Floating Trophy, value £25, presented by the Co-operative Wine Growers' Association of South Africa, Paarl).

One hundred leaguers Dry Red Wine, suitable for export, light-bodied, unfortified (Silver Floating Trophy, value £26 5s, presented by J A Meyer, Esq, Editor of *Wine and Spirit Review*).

Perpetual Silver Cup presented by the Vine Products Company of London for 'Medium Sweet Red' not exceeding five degrees Baume or nine degrees Balling Apparent suitable for export overseas.

Silver Cup, presented by J McDonald, Esq, to the exhibitor gaining the largest number of points on the Show, excluding Prizes gained in competing for other Cups and in Novice Classes.

Silver Cup, presented by P B Burgoyne, Esq, to the exhibitor gaining the largest number of points for Dry White Wines, excluding Prizes gained in competing for other Cups and in Novice Classes.

Silver Cup, presented by Messrs Stephen Smith Ltd of Bow, London, to the exhibitor gaining the largest number of points for Dry Red Wines, excluding Prizes gained in competing for other Cups and in Novice Classes.

Silver Cup, presented by the late W H Lategan, Esq, to the exhibitor gaining the largest number of points on the Show, excluding Novice Classes.

Perpetual Silver Cup, presented by the *Wine and Spirit Review*, for the exhibitor gaining the most points in the classes for Sweet White Wines, excluding Prizes gained in competing for other Cups and in Novice Classes.

The Frank Myburgh Perpetual Floating Trophy, presented by some of his admirers as a permanent record of his services to the wine industry, for the best and most outstanding exhibit of Dry White Wine (Hock type).

Silver Floating Trophy, value £25, presented by Stellenbosch Farmers' Winery for the best and most outstanding sample of Dry Red Wine on the Show.

The Cups to be held by the winners for the year following the award, when they must be returned to the Society.

Basis of point awards — Three points for a first prize, two points for a second, and one for a third.

These awards show how far the wine industry has advanced during the past twenty years. The advance has been made in spite of great difficulties, many disappointments, much hostility even from quarters in which it had a right to expect support and friendly encouragement, and the still effective opposition that comes from prejudice that is rooted in profound ignorance. For a wine-producing country, South Africa is amazingly unenlightened about wines, their dietetic and nutritive value, their importance in the cultural life of a people, and their economic significance. Formerly, when a knowledge of good wine and an appreciation of its virtues were reckoned marks of well-breeding and of a cultured mind, the public was less prejudiced and better informed than it is today, and propaganda and publicity are needed in the interests of the winegrowers if this ignorance is to be dissipated.

After the Anglo-Boer War the Cape government decided to engage the services of another Expert Viticulturist. The Groot Constantia Wine Farm, which had been bought in 1885 for £5 312 and in repairs and re-equipment with fustage had cost altogether some £13 000, had been managed by a practical farmer with more or less satisfactory results so far as its wines were concerned. Between 1885 and 1903 the total cost in overhead expenses had been over £34 000. The profit and loss account for the farm from 1885 to 1894 showed that there had been a total profit of approximately £7 000, and the accountant's report stated that: 'It is estimated that the farm, if put up for auction, would realise £25 000 and the fustage £3 000.' The manager, Mr De Waal, while on a trip to Australia, met Mr Raymond Dubois, Principal of the Viticultural College at Ruthenglen in Victoria, and suggested that he should be invited to serve as Government Viticulturist. The Department of Agriculture accordingly invited Mr Dubois, who, it is interesting to note, had already in 1901 applied for the post of lecturer in viticulture to the Elsenburg Agricultural School of the Victoria College at Stellenbosch, but had been turned down, to accept the post at a salary of £500 and travelling expenses. The Victorian government protested against this attempt to filch from it one of its experts, and some acrimonious correspondence ensued before Mr Dubois obtained permission formally to apply for the post. On his arrival he found that he did not have a free hand and complained that difficulties were put in his way. A Select Committee was appointed that, after hearing evidence, reported strongly in favour of Mr Dubois's claims, recommended that Groot Constantia should be retained as a viticultural farm, that help should be given to the Victoria College to establish a chair of viticulture, that railway facilities should be granted to students and farmers who might wish to visit the experimental wine farms, and that more American stocks should be provided. The Committee affirmed its faith in the eminent suitability of the Colony for the cultivation of the grape and declared that by judicious expenditure and scientific advice and assistance, wine can be produced in this country suitable both for home consumption and for export. Another Select Committee, a year later, was even more emphatic. The experts, it heard in evidence, agreed that excellent wine was being made, but that much remained to be done before the general quality of Cape wines was worthy of the industry. Mr Dubois, a recognised expert who had reported to the French government on Algerian wines and to the government of Victoria on Australian wines, said that few wine farmers took care to let their wines mature; they left it entirely to the wine merchants, and no farm wine was ever allowed to mature; a full-bodied, heavy Burgundy type of wine could easily be made, and Mr Burgoyne, the largest buyer in England, bought Australian wine of this type at an average of 2s 6d a gallon and could not get enough to supply the demand. Mr Rene Santhagens, a wine expert of great experience, who afterwards became one of the foremost wine manufacturers in the Union and made quality wines of a superior class, said that in 1898 he had made wine at one of Mr Rhodes's farms that was excellent in quality. He did not consider that the best wine was being made at Constantia and declared emphatically: 'There is not one cellar in the whole Colony fit to guarantee good wine.' He considered the Cape the best wine-producing country as it had all the natural conditions required for the making of good wine, and thought that winegrowers should concentrate on satisfying the local demand that was rapidly growing, and that there was no need to look to foreign markets. All the witnesses agreed that co-operative wine farming would be an ideal solution of most of the existing difficulties, and the Committee recommended that steps should be taken to bring this about. In 1905 the government started a scheme under which co-operative wineries were enabled to get Treasury grants, and several such societies were founded, struggled on for some years, and then gave up the ghost. A few survived and are still active, but several years were to elapse before real co-operation was achieved.

In that direction some progress has, fortunately, been achieved by the co-operation that, in the teeth of much opposition, has been organised amoung viticulturists and the vintners. Perhaps the greatest and most important factor in the development of the industry has been the establishment of the Co-operative Wine Growers' Association of South Africa, popularly known by the initials of its Afrikaans title, the KWV (*Koöperatiewe Wynbouers Vereniging*).

This Association, that today exercises a wise and prudent control and may yet develop into a national supervisor and regulator of the wine trade, is the result of private initiative inspired by the will and desire to promote the interests of the consumer as well as those of the producer. The years following the Anglo-Boer War had been a period of great hardship and much distress to the winegrowers. For revenue purposes a fairly heavy excise had been levied. The Phylloxera, notwithstanding the efforts that had been made to check its spread, had ruined many vineyards, whose owners did not have the necessary capital to rehabilitate themselves by replanting vines grafted on immune stocks. The price of wine had dropped alarmingly; some growers were unable to get more than 30s per leaguer, a price that made winegrowing impossible. There was no hope that a government, so strongly influenced by the prohibitionist faction, would ever consider the grant of special bounties to the winegrowers, and to do them justice the latter had never clamoured for such state-aid, thereby showing a most praiseworthy self-reliance that has, unfortunately, never been imitated by other agriculturists. The wheat farmers, for instance, whose product costs the taxpayer far more than he would have to pay if he imported his wheat from abroad, has depended wholly upon increasingly large subsidies that in practice amount virtually to a tax upon food. An increase in the revenue by an excise had for many years been contemplated, although the first attempt to impose such a tax had not been particularly lucrative. Ultimately, however, it was imposed, meeting with strong opposition from the wine farmers and from the trade. In 1909 a large public meeting at Cape Town asked the government to take immediate steps to alleviate the distress among winegrowers, and a deputation called upon the Prime Minister, Mr Merriman, who, while sympathetic, being himself a winegrower, did not see his way clear to repeal the excise or to hold out any hope of implementing the various recommendations that had been made by the Select Committees in the past. Union was in the offing, and the wine farmers were told that agitation and a loss in the revenue returns might jeopardise the negotiations that were afoot to bring the four self-governing South African colonies into a co-operative Union that would be able, in time, to deal with the liquor problem as a whole. With this bitter consolation the winegrowers had to be content. They formed a small private association, The Wine Farmers' and Wine Merchants' Association, that did good work, but could not achieve the wholehearted co-operation so urgently desired, and after a few years the Association was dissolved. The first Great War, coming shortly after the declaration of Union, and before there had been time to deal properly with the many problems of the liquor trade, hampered the efforts of those who were earnest in trying to promote co-operation between the wine farmers and the vintners. In 1916 another attempt was made, and at a well-attended meeting of winegrowers called by the Paarl Farmers' Association and held at Paarl on 13 December 1916, it was decided to form a 'Co-operative Viticultural Union of South Africa,' a title that was afterwards changed to the more appropriate 'Co-operative Wine Growers' Association of South Africa.'

The principal mover in the matter was Mr C W H Kohler, the first President of the Association, who wrote the original constitution, and has shown himself an enthusiastic champion of co-operation. He was a successful winegrower, whose wines have gained first prizes at successive wine shows and was intimately acquainted with the wine industry to the development of which he gave the best years of his life.

Briefly put, the constitution of the newly-formed Viticultural Union stated that the Union was formed with the object of regulating the price of wine and brandy produced by members and to promote the sale of their products. Membership was confined to *bona fide* producers of wine and brandy, who pledged themselves never to sell their products below a price that had been fixed by the directors, and to submit themselves to such rules and regulations as the directors, with a view to safeguarding the interests of all concerned, might make. The regulations would only come into effect when agreed to by four-fifths of the winegrowers in the Western Province, but as soon as the Union was established they would remain in force unless two-thirds of the members were in favour of changing them. The draft constitution was unanimously accepted, with the proviso that the Union should not prohibit the planting of more vineyards. Financed by voluntary contributions from the winegrowers, the Union was established, and held its first meeting at Paarl on 2 November 1917. A year later it was floated as a company under the old Companies Act of 1892, under the title of the Co-operative Wine Growers' Association of South Africa Limited, with a nominal capital of £100 000 in ten-shilling shares. When the Company was registered the price of wine rose from £2 10s to £4 per leaguer. At first the vintners opposed the Association, but in time they saw that their own interests were best served by effective co-operation, and they joined the Association and financed it liberally. They agreed to buy their stocks through the Association and entered into contracts which fixed a minimum of £5 for distilling wine and £7 for natural wine. In 1918 the Association had 1 807 members, and was already in a flourishing position.

That success was maintained. Circumstances conspired to help its development and hasten its advance. There was an unprecedented demand for wine and brandy after the war, and the price of wine rose rapidly. The Association had to deal with any surplus that there might be. It agreed with the wine merchants to fix the price of wine for distillation at £9 per leaguer, and that of natural wine at £11, and that any surplus which could not be sold, distilled or stored would be destroyed. The wine merchants formed a special company, the South African Wine and Spirit Corporation Ltd, which dealt with the Association on their behalf. After 1921 various difficulties arose. Some of the members objected to certain of the regulations, and appealed to the courts, whose decision was against the Association. Much hard work had to be done, especially when the 'boom' years had passed. The curious reader may read about these vicissitudes and the manner in which they were met, in Mr Kohler's autobiography that has recently been published (*Kohler van die KWV*, 1945).

The later history of the Association can be summarised in a few paragraphs. In 1922 it was registered under the Co-operative Associations Act. It was a voluntary, mutual co-operative society, and had no power to compel any winegrower to join, nor had it any direct means to control production or prevent over-production. It could act only by means of its regulations, subscribed to by its members who had voluntarily undertaken to abide by them. In the circumstances it was hardly to be expected that all winegrowers would submit to have a voluntary co-operative association prescribing for them what contracts they could undertake, and when some members found that they could sell their wine at a slightly higher rate than that fixed by their Association, they did not scruple to do so. After due consideration, the Association approached the government to ask for more extended powers. The matter was carefully studied, and in 1924 a Bill 'to provide for the control and management of the wine and spirit industry and for matters incidental thereto' was introduced as a government measure, and was passed and placed on the statute book as Act No 5 of 1924. This Act, as amended by Acts 17 of 1928, 23 of 1940 and 23 of 1946, is now the charter of the KWV, and gives it the power to exercise that control which it could not adequately do as a purely voluntary association.

The Act provides that wine for distilling purposes may only be acquired through the KWV, which may fix the price; the Association is given absolute power in this respect, for the Act says clearly: 'No person shall sell, acquire or utilise wine of the vintage of 1924 or any subsequent year . . . by any means whatsoever for the purpose of distilling or converting it into spirits by any means whatsoever except through or with the consent of the KWV.' The Association 'shall' withhold such consent from a winegrower who is not a member; it shall supply wine for distillation in the ordinary course of trade; all winegrowers shall render to the KWV returns of all wines and spirits in their possession. The Act applies only to the Cape Province but may be extended to the other Provinces if five per cent of the winegrowers are members of a similar co-operative body when similar powers of control as are now exercised by the KWV may be granted to it. The Governor-General is empowered to make regulations under the Act. The Association is not to discriminate against wine or against the buyers or growers of wine that is sold for consumption as wine (which is defined as wine or must of any description, and includes grapes, grape juice, grape syrup, raisins and lees of wine) and cannot impose restrictions of any kind on the freedom to buy or sell wine. Clause 6 of the Act defines what is potable spirit.

The control vested in the Association has been judiciously used, and the result has been that the industry has flourished since 1924. At Paarl, the headquarters of the KWV, much good work has been done in oenological research, in the blending, manufacture, and maturation of wines, in investigating the bacterial diseases of wines, and in the making of perfumes and extracts. These services, initiated by recognised experts, are of incalculable service to the wine industry, and are an excellent example of what can be accomplished by skilful co-operation and intelligent organisation. The industry owes a great deal to the KWV and to these experts, and will in the future owe still more when the Association has extended its activities into spheres which lie close to the ground that it has already so ably exploited. The Society has recently, in cordial co-operation with the trade, undertaken the supervision of all wine exported, with the result that Cape wine when it leaves its native shores is furnished with an authoritative certificate of purity and worth. This is purely a voluntary development, and it is highly desirable that a similar co-operative body should guarantee the excellence of all wine sold in the country.

A Wine Commission was appointed in 1935 to enquire into the conditions of the industry, and as a result of its labours the Wine and Spirits Control Amendment Act of 1940 (Act No 23 of 1940) was passed. This gives the KWV additional powers of control and supervision mainly directed to prevent over-production. The Association is now by law empowered to fix the price of good quality wine in relation to that of distilling wine; to supply members with limited quantities of matured wine and brandy in exchange for distilling wine, and to limit the production of alcohol by assigning to each winegrower a quota of the quantity of wine or spirit which such winegrower may produce during any year.

In 1926 the KWV started exporting, and it is today the biggest exporter of wine and spirit in the Union. Export wine must, in accordance with government regulations, be certified by government officials to the effect that it is true to type, sound, and in every way conforms to the export regulations. By Government Notice No 895 of 1935 the use of certain French names in respect of wine, brandies and champagnes produced and sold within the Union is prohibited. This prohibition has caused much heartburning, but there can be no doubt that it is a sound check upon any attempt to exploit public ignorance and prejudice.

Unfortunately there appears to be no means of preventing the adulteration of Cape wines in foreign markets. How greatly such adulteration has in the past damaged the reputation and sale of Cape wine has been explained in previous chapters. It would be highly disadvantageous to the industry if similar methods were in future allowed to impair the quality and affect the sale of Cape wine overseas.

Chapter 13

Restrictions and Prohibitions

Before the Cape Colony obtained the benefit of self-government, its liquor legislation was a matter regulated solely by the interests of outsiders, who did indeed pay attention to local conditions and customs where these could be harmonised with the demands of the Imperial government, but on several occasions flatly declined to modify their policy to suit the wishes of Cape winegrowers and wine merchants.

Such legislation, during the first 200 years of the settlement, could scarcely be called restrictive or hampering. It was designed solely to regulate the retail trade in spirits and wine, and in some measure to protect the public against imposition of various kinds. Later on it was broadened, to exact from the growing wine industry some return for the security and help it received from a stable government and the protection accorded by authority. Even then it never contemplated that the winegrowers should be directly taxed, and it was only after the Company had realised that by farming out the tavern licences the revenue from the settlement could be much increased, that the licensing fees came to be regarded as valuable income that could not be relinquished in any circumstances. In the previous chapters reference has been made to the various ordinances that fixed and modified these licensing fees, and there is no need here to linger over them.

When the settlement finally passed into other hands, further changes in the liquor legislation were inevitable. These changes were necessitated by the varying local conditions, and were generally of no great importance. They affected merely the conditions under which the licensees were empowered to retail, export, and purchase wine and spirits, and their general tendency was to broaden rather than to restrict the rights and privileges of the wine merchants and viticulturists. Ordinance 30 of 1826, amended by Ordinance 54 and repealed by Ordinance 93, consolidated the various regulations then in force. Ordinance 67 of 1829, and Ordinance 80 of the same year, dealt with the same subject, and were both repealed by Ordinance 93 of 1832, which remained in force until it, too, was repealed by Ordinance 29 of 1846, and Ordinances 94, 95, 96 of 1832 and 2 and 9 of 1834, all introduced some slight change, but none departed from the general principle that the sale of wine was in the interests of the community and that the growth and manufacture of wine were to be encouraged and promoted. In 1851 Ordinance 9 repealed all previous liquor legislation and laid down a new set of rules and regulations that were modifications, in no way revolutionary, of all the old ones, and again there was no vestige of any desire to inflict unnecessary restrictions upon the trade or the industry.

This liberal and enlightened policy was possible and practicable when the public at the Cape, in strong contrast to the public in England, still looked upon wine as a *necessity* rather than as a *luxury*. The Cape was a wine-producing country, the oldest in the Empire, and its community had from the days of Van Riebeeck learned that wine was of food value and that light wine, while it gladdened the heart of men, was never a communal danger. There is ample evidence to support this statement. Wine was drunk in every family; it was given to the Coloured servants as a matter of course; to children at school and to children at home; as a ration to the soldiers, and even to sick convicts. It was extensively used in the home; all the old Cape cooks thought it indispensable for the making of their dishes. There is a full record of an interesting murder trial in the early part of the last century[1] that gives, in the evidence of witnesses for the Crown, some curious and instructive facts about the supply of wine to slaves, from which it appears that the masters were of opinion that those labourers who received a triple ration of wine daily fared better and did more work than those who, for various reasons — the strict Moslem slaves refused a wine ration — got no wine. When the first boarding school for boys was started, resident pupils received a glass of wine with their midday meal. Old pupils of the Diocesan College state that this custom prevailed in that institution, and declare that the wine ration kept them in excellent health, and that no parent ever objected to the custom. In every middle-class family, in town as well as on the farms, wine appeared regularly on the table at the midday meal, and all children belonging to such families learned to drink wine.

Such drunkenness as existed was generally caused by drinking spirits or adulterated wine, highly fortified, and was found chiefly in the neighbourhood of canteens. In Cape Town it was not very prevalent, and all the accounts we have from travellers and residents confirm Mrs Kindersley's opinion that 'on the whole, considering it is a shipping port and a garrison town, the settlement is commendably sober.' Major Fawcett, much later, was of another opinion, and lamented the fact that the 'canteens have brought the Hottentot to ruin and debasement,' but he was a violently prejudiced gentleman, fanatically prohibitionist himself, and his testimony must be cautiously received. That there was much insobriety among the straggling natives, who wandered from town to town, did a little work here and there, and spent their earnings forthwith at the nearest canteen, was undoubtedly true. The German missionaries permitted no canteen to be established on their properties, and where they worked in a town area, as at Worcester, they persuaded their congregations to agree to drastic punishment for drunkenness, though they themselves took wine and had no objection to wine drinking, in moderation, by their Coloured flocks.

It was, however, the missionary agitation, supported by what a contemporary called 'the pestilential disturbance of those busybodies that

---

1 The nineteenth century — Eds.

come from America and call themselves templars,' that initiated the campaign against wine as a necessity. That movement received strong support from the propaganda of the egregious Dr Philip, of the London Missionary Society, whose exaggerations and libels upon the community at the Cape are now a matter of history. Good Templar lodges were established at Cape Town and elsewhere, and much acrimonious discussion ensued in the press and on platforms. The Cape community took an amused interest in the discussion, and even as late as 1866 it was not regarded as serious or as imperilling the wine industry. Mr De Lima printed some extravaganzas in favour of the campaign, and Mr W Brittain, of St George's Street, published Mrs Harriet Beecher Stowe's *The Pledge Taken* and *The Wife's Gift*; neither had any great popularity and they are both today rare items of Africana. 'Temperance' tracts for some of the mission schools also fall into this category; they were broadsheets printed by tender, and some of them are now exceedingly scarce, the only copies being in the Berlin, and possibly the Elberfeld libraries. In the beginning of the century Werninck, reporting to his society (*Brieven der Zendelingen*, 1817) states that in the Klein Drakenstein area there is little drunkenness among the farm labourers, though everyone of them drinks wine. Knobel (*Family Papers*, 1856) reported that in the Bedford and Uitenhage districts drunkenness is rarely seen among the Natives, except such as come from missionary stations where they have been forcibly prevented from drinking wine; 'when the restraint is taken away, they drink freely, and not being used to it, they drink much more than they can carry.'

An impetus to the 'Temperance' agitation was given by the support lent to it by the Scottish ministers of the Dutch Reformed Church in the first half of the century. The Dutch Reformed Church parsons had always taken a commonsense liberal view, and had time after time reaffirmed their opinion that there was no harm in wine making and wine drinking, while they had always vigorously protested against abuse of wine and forcibly condemned drunkenness as a vice. They drank wine themselves, and were good customers of the winegrowers, as the books of the wine merchants conclusively show. They held no narrow, prejudiced views, and when Dr Philip indulged in outrageous statements, they promptly gave him the lie, and testified to the sobriety of the wine-growing community. The newcomers, totally unacquainted with the local conditions, and much impressed by the drunkenness among the Natives, soldiers and seamen, that they saw in Cape Town, joined in the new movement for 'temperance reform,' and their influence, especially beyond the borders of the Colony where they visited and ministered to the emigrant farmers, was undoubtedly directed towards effecting restrictions in the liquor trade.

Such restrictions had already been applied in the areas under missionary control, but the results had not been good. While independent testimony (such as *Kretzchmar* in *Suedafrikanische Skizzen*, 1858) affirmed that there was little drunkenness among Natives and Coloured labourers who

received wine rations at their farms, reports from magistrates and justices of the peace throughout the Colony stated that it was rampant among vagrant Natives and those who came from mission stations. For all that, the 'Temperance Party' clamoured for prohibition for the Natives, attacked the wine ration system on the Western Cape farms, and demanded more stringent legislation. The time was not yet ripe, however, for the public to acquiesce in such restrictive measures. The Cape now had self-government, and in the debates in Parliament the liquor question was more than once referred to. The 'Temperance Party' had as yet no champion in either the Legislative Council or the Assembly, and the matter was therefore discussed in a sober, commonsense manner. In the debate on the Lands of Missionary Institutes in 1854, several speakers paid tribute to the general sobriety of Natives and Coloureds, while in the contemporary press the extravagances of the 'reformers' were held up to ridicule and the public was warned that their intention was to get some measure of prohibition. A Select Committee reported on the petition of certain residents in border areas where grants had been made to Coloured and Native landholders on conditions that prohibited the establishment of licensed premises on the land, a clause that had been practically dictated by missionary influence. Witnesses before the Committee stated that in their opinion the establishment of canteens under controls would tend to decrease drunkenness which was now becoming more common because of the smuggling of spirits. The Kat River Settlement, completely under missionary influence, was referred to in particular as one of the places where such drunkenness was known. The Committee reported in favour of the petitioners. Another Select Committee later on dealt with the question whether or not such restrictive clauses in grants in freehold to Native landowners should be allowed, and again heard evidence, which more or less confirmed what had been said by previous witnesses.

In the Orange Free State, one of the first acts of the new government had been to pass an Ordinance (No 10 of 1856) of 47 clauses, dealing, on more or less the same lines as the Cape laws, with the sale and purchase of liquor. Clause 25 of this Ordinance introduced for the first time in South African legislation a definite colour bar in wine drinking, as it prohibited the sale to or consumption by Non-Europeans of wine, forbidding even the gift of a glass of wine to a Non-European and making drunkenness a crime (*misdaad*). This Ordinance was amended in 1880 and again in 1883, but the relevant clause was left unaltered.

The Cape Legislature was not to be stampeded, as yet, into passing similar restrictive legislation. It amended the 1851 Ordinance by Act No 10 of 1860, which laid down further rates for licences. This was repealed by the Retail Wines and Spirits Act of 1864, which was designed to consolidate the regulations, but which was itself repealed by the Retail Wine and Spirits Act of 1868. Further legislation was passed in 1875, 1876 and 1879, but long before that, in 1865, the Incorporation of Kaffraria Act had fixed, so far as the new Native Territories were concerned, drastic restrictions on the granting of liquor licences in that part of the Colony. In 1884 an Excise Act was passed, amended in the following year, and repealed in the next. In Act 28, 1883, a clause was inserted forbidding the granting of a liquor licence in any Native location or area defined by the Governor within which no liquor licence may be granted or liquor supplied to any aboriginal native. The Liquor Licensing Act Amendment Act of 1885, though more liberal in some respects (it retained the Sunday privilege clause against which the prohibitionists had violently protested), contained the same clause, and in the Penal Code for the Transkeian Territories of 1886, the colour bar in drinking was trebly underlined. The Police Offences Act of 1882 made 'drunkenness in any street, road, lane or public place, in or near any shop, store, hotel or canteen' an offence under the Act. Act 15 of 1892 adds a little to the restrictions already imposed, but gives one concession to the winegrower — it empowers him to destroy dogs trespassing in his vineyard! Act 25 of 1891 and the several Acts passed to protect the industry against phylloxera have been referred to already and need not detain us.

The Wine, Brandy and Spirits Act of 1906 is interesting because it attempts to define wine as 'the product solely of the alcoholic fermentation of the juice or must of the grape.' Dry wine is defined as wine produced by the complete fermentation of the sugar contained in the juice or must of the fresh grapes from which it is made; sweet wine, as wine containing sugar derived from the juice or must of the grapes from which it is made and not from raisins; sparkling wine, as wine surcharged with carbonic acid gas and to which cane sugar and pure wine spirit may or may not have been added. This was an improvement on the Liquor Law Amendment Act of 1898, and was an attempt to deal with certain problems on scientific lines.

When Union came, the overwhelming influence of the northern Provinces, that in all legislation affecting the Natives and Non-European element invariably called the tune to which the Cape dutifully danced, led to amending legislation that restricted still further and that has now brought about compulsory prohibition for practically three-fourths of the population of the country. The trend of such legislation is more and more restrictive, and the repeal of certain Cape laws, such as the Pure Natural Wines Facilities Act of 1907, the Light Wines Licences Act of 1908 and the Sale of Pure Natural Wines Amendment Act of 1909 are gloomy forebodings of the reactionary tendency that has been at work since Union. The strength of the prohibitionists is the result of active and energetic propaganda that is allowed to go unchecked and uncontradicted. It derives much of its force and appeal from the skilful use that it makes of the feeling against the Native and the Coloured, masking its innate illiberalism and intolerance under the guise of a charitable concern for the interests of the Non-European. It should be the task of the winegrowers and wine merchants to expose this blatant hypocrisy, and to demonstrate to the public the inherent fallacies of the premises that wine is not only a luxury but a deadly and insidious poison that it is the duty of the state to suppress.

The trade and industry are at present governed by the consolidated Liquor Act of 1928 (No 30) as amended by the Liquor Act Amendment Act of 1934. This is a comprehensive measure of 176 clauses, repealing practically all liquor legislation in all the four Provinces that existed before it was passed. Under this Act off-consumption licences for the sale of liquor are classed as: wholesale, foreign liquor, brewer's, bottle, and wine farmers' licences, while on-consumption licences for the sale of liquor are classed as: restaurant, hotel, bar, wine and malt, club, theatre or sports grounds, temporary, and late hours occasional licences. A board is set up in each district of the Union for the consideration of all applications for the grant, renewal, transfer or removal of licences, such board to consist of the magistrate and four other members to be appointed by the Governor-General, two of whom shall be members of an urban local authority. A member of the board may not be: holder of or applicant for any licence; a brewer or distiller; a person engaged in making wine or spirits for sale; spouse, partner, agent or employee of such three; any officer or agent of any partnership or association of persons or society interested in the sale or the prevention of the sale of intoxicating liquors, or anyone who during the preceding three years has held office in any association or society having as its main object the suppression or the promotion of the liquor trade, any person employed directly or indirectly, as an agent for making any application for a licence; any person who carries on business or is interested in the premises in respect of which a licence is asked for; any unrehabilitated insolvent; the chairman or member of committee of any club that is applying for a licence; any person who has had a sentence of imprisonment without the option of a fine imposed upon him within the Union or elsewhere and has not been freely pardoned. Three members shall form a quorum. The board has power to summon witnesses and take evidence on oath; review and appeal in regard to its decision are provided for by allowing appeal to the Supreme Court. Applications for licences must be minutely detailed, and particulars of such applications must be published; objections to them must be lodged not later than seven days before the annual meeting of the board; the police must make a full report on the application, but such report may be seen by the applicant and by the objectors. Under clause 40, prohibitionists are practically invited to address the board 'generally on the question of the desirability of reducing or increasing the number of licences, hours, or times, withdrawing, with-holding, granting or enlarging other powers.' Clause 53 states:

'No licence under this Act shall be granted for the sale of liquor (*a*) in or within half a mile of the boundary of any native location or native village established under the provisions of any law; (*b*) in or within three miles of the boundary of any area set apart under the provisions of the Native Land Act . . .'

Clause 60 retains the local option prohibition areas that existed before the passing of the Act. The board may not grant an on-consumption licence or bottle store licence in an urban area in the Cape Province if a memorial signed by the majority of the voters in that area disapproves of such a grant. The number of licences that may be granted in urban areas is limited by the number of parliamentary voters; the licensee must have special qualifications; the premises must be approved by the board and certain types of business may not be carried on there. The board may fix the days and hours of sale under any licence, and the maximum and minimum quantities to be sold under the several licences are laid down. Liquor may not be supplied or delivered to any person under the age of 18 years; provision is made for the prohibition of supply to confirmed inebriates.

Clause 94 states: 'Save as is otherwise specially provided by this Act, no person shall supply or deliver any liquor to any Native, and no Native shall obtain, or be in possession of, any liquor.' In the Transvaal and Orange Free State: 'No person shall sell or supply or deliver any liquor to any Asiatic or Coloured person, and no Asiatic or Coloured person shall obtain or be in possession of liquor.' In Natal, no Asiatic may be in possession of liquor off licensed premises, and may only be supplied or obtain liquor for consumption on premises. Provision is made for exemptions in some cases.

In the Cape Province, farmers may give their Native, Coloured or Asiatic labourers, over the age of 21 years, one and one half pints of unfortified wine or Kaffir beer, provided that such wine shall be consumed during intervals of not less than two hours and in not less than three equal portions. In the Orange Free State, an employer may give his male employee of 18 years or above one single drink of intoxicating liquor per day in quantity not exceeding one quarter of a pint in the case of spirituous liquor and not exceeding one pint in the case of liquor of any other kind to be consumed when received and in the presence of such employer. Non-Europeans may, under certain conditions, obtain letters of exemption from these restrictions. Women and any person under the age of 18 years are not allowed to be employed on licensed premises. Special chapters are devoted to Kaffir beer and native liquors, to methylated spirits, intoxicating medicines, powers of police, etc, and a long list of offences is added.

With this Act must be read the Transkeian Territories Liquor Law of 1933, which summarily enacts that liquor may not be supplied to 'prohibited persons.' A prohibited person is declared to be 'any person other than a European,' but two other classes are mentioned, and an exception is made in favour of the Non-European who, not being an Asiatic or a Native, is in possession of immovable property of a certain value. This Act is much more restrictive than the consolidating Act: it practically proclaims the Native Territories to be prohibited areas.

A more scientific, although in some respects very bad Act, is the Wines, Spirits and Vinegar Act of 1913. This states that no wine shall be sold that has added to it, before, during or after the making thereof any substance other than those mentioned in the Act. These mentioned substances are yeast, isinglass, gelatine, eggs, albumen, Spanish clay, kaolin or tannin, common salt, pure caramel, sulphate of lime, metabisulphite of potassium or sodium or sulphurous oxide, tartaric acid, natural products of the grape vine, and brandy, wine brandy, grape brandy or wine spirit. No wine containing 20 grammes or more of sugar per litre shall be sold unless it contains not less than 16.6 per cent of alcohol by volume, but this shall not apply to sparkling wine and to any wine produced from grapes grown on land owned or lawfully occupied by the seller and sold by him to any person who lawfully carries on the business of selling wine. No person shall manufacture or sell under the name of champagne or as a wine of champagne type, sparkling wine in which the excess of carbonic acid gas arises from direct admixture of the same. Sparkling wine is defined as wine surcharged with carbonic acid gas and to which cane sugar and wine spirit may or may not have been added. Further chapters deal with brandy and provide most excellent safeguards for its distillation and purity.

The legislation that gives a certain amount of control over wine production to the KWV has already been dealt with.

An interesting side issue of liquor legislation is the survival of old servitudes on land granted for occupation on condition that no licensed premises would be established on the farm. In course of time such land has been proclaimed as townships, cut up into erven, and developed into flourishing urban communities that, by virtue of the original servitude, must remain perpetually 'dry.' Such townships can have no bar licences in any circumstances, no matter what may be the wish of the majority of the residents; they are condemned to an enforced prohibition that can be removed only by an Act of Parliament, and any attempt to obtain such redress would be vigorously opposed by the prohibitionists. The reasons for imposing the original restrictions are in most cases obvious; in one glaring instance, the condition was inserted in the lease because the farm was on the direct road between Simonstown and Cape Town, and the authorities objected to the establishment of a wayside canteen that would attract soldiers and sailors from the respective naval station and garrison. There is today no valid reason for enforcing the restriction, but it is perpetuated in the title deeds of the farm which is now a flourishing residential and commercial township. Another interesting point is that there are some unrepealed exemptions that may provide lawyers with several moot questions when their importance in enforcing prohibition upon the Non-European population is recognised.

Chapter 14

Wine

In the foregoing chapters a brief and necessarily incomplete account has been given of the origin and development of the wine industry at the Cape from the first vintage in 1659 to the beginning of the present century.[1] It now remains to sketch its present condition, but before this is done it is desirable to say something about wine in general, to correct some common errors about it, and to explain some points that may need explanation.

Wine is the fermented juice of the grape. That short and simple definition is, like all definitions, not quite true and certainly not adequately comprehensive, but it will serve for all practical purposes.

The fresh juice of the grape is called *must*. It is water, containing in solution so many different things that no one has yet been able to make a complete list of them. Again, for practical purposes, we may say that its main ingredients are various sugars, fruit essences, colouring matter, resins, tannins, fruit and vegetable acids, fatty acids, amino acids, aromatic principles of a most complicated nature, and still more complicated bodies among which are the intricate substances known today as vitamins.

All these substances, which are combined, generally, with many mineral elements such as soda, potash, copper, magnesium and iron in infinitesimal quantities, are derived from the soil and the air. The vine plant is a highly organised chemical laboratory, where the most wonderful splitting up of combinations is constantly being made, and where the simplest elements are as constantly being twisted about in a manner that would have delighted the heart of that Phrygian king whose ingenuity gave us a new adjective. The power for this laboratory is the sun, whose actinic activity both synthesises, that is, puts together and analyses or breaks down chemical combinations. It follows, therefore, that the operations necessary to produce berries that carry fully matured juice must be assisted by sunlight, and that climate, soil and many other conditions may greatly alter the growth of the vine, the production of its grapes, and the quality of their juice. These conditions, so far as South African wine-growing districts are concerned, are on the whole extremely favourable, and it may be interesting to the reader to say something about them here.

The vine depends for its growth on climate and soil. Of these the first is the more important, for while the soil in which the plant grows may be good, containing the necessary moisture and minerals that it needs for development and growth, the climate may be such as to counteract the

---

1 The twentieth century — Eds.

advantage obtained from the soil. Climate includes temperature, humidity, rainfall, frost, amount of sunlight, seasonal variation, and movement of air. The vine needs warmth and sunlight when it is in leaf and flower; it also needs its annual period of rest in the winter months. Climate is therefore an important factor, and must be as favourable as possible if the plants are to grow properly and, when grown, to give a normal yield.

The ideal climate for vines is one where the summer and autumn are long and warm enough, and at the same time moderately dry, to give the grapes time to be fully ripe before the leaves drop. An area with summer rainfall is therefore not the most favourable for vine growing. In South Africa, grapes grown in such areas do not make good wine; an exception to this rule is perhaps the grapes grown at a high altitude in the Transvaal, where on the Lombardy Estate, between Pretoria and Johannesburg, the late Mr Zoccola's vineyards produced very good red wine.

Generally speaking, the vine likes a warm, temperate climate, shelter from cold and dry winds, and a moderate altitude. In tropical and semi-tropical areas it gets no period of rest, and its berries are usually watery and make a very indifferent wine. In the southern hemisphere the conditions, so far as seasonal variations are concerned, are of course reversed from those in the northern; at the Cape vineyards are planted so that the rows run from east to west, preferably on a slope facing the north, so as to avoid extremes of cold. The nearness of the sea, or lakes, has also an influence upon the vines. 'Because of the maritime climate,' remarks Dr Perold in his *Treatise on Viticulture*, 'grapes ripen five to six weeks later in Constantia than in Paarl . . . and our finest dry red table wines are produced in Constantia with its sea climate. Stellenbosch, too, being near enough to the sea to be influenced by it, produces fine dry red table wines. The Paarl district is much warmer, and produces mostly heavy wines . . . its red wines are not so good, but its white wines are quite as good . . . In the Ceres district the grapes ripen about the same time as in Constantia, owing to the influence, not of the sea, but of the altitude, which is 1 500 − 1 600 feet above sea-level.'

Taking all climatic conditions into account, the wine-growing districts of the western part of the Cape Province are ideal for winegrowing. The prevailing winds in summer and autumn do not damage the maturing grapes, and frost is rare in the coastal districts, though further inland it may cause trouble. Strong winds in early summer are also damaging, but less so to wine grapes than to the more delicate table grapes. The rainfall between November and March, when the grapes are growing and ripening, is usually small, although on occasion unseasonable showers in December have been known to injure the grape crop.

The soil in the wine-growing districts varies from the gravelly decomposed granites in the Cape Peninsula to the heavier sweet soils, of shale and clay composition, on the northern slopes of the mountains where the Bokkeveld beds predominate. Individual variations in the soil are of considerable importance, a fact that was well known to the earlier viticulturists. Van der Stel, we are told, was very careful where he planted his vines, and carried basketsful of soil home for examination, although it is certain that he could not have analysed them. Sandy, porous soil, with sufficient underground moisture is stated to be very suitable for vines; the grapes ripen early and are rich in sugar. In the heavier 'sweet' soils formed from decomposed slates and clays, the vineyards produce good crops, with a high sugar content, which makes excellent sweet wines. Farther north, in the Karoo, the soils are exceedingly rich, but need irrigation; little wine is produced there, but some varieties of grapes grow magnificently and are inordinately sweet.

We may now proceed to discuss wine itself. The subject is so alluring, and may be considered from so many aspects, that it can hardly be condensed within the limits of a chapter. There are many exhaustive books on the subject that may be consulted by those readers who are curious to know more about it. Here the discussion must be limited to a consideration of the qualities of wine, with particular reference to the wines produced in South Africa. It must necessarily be elementary, as far as the chemistry and bacteriology of wine are concerned, for those are intricate, and in part yet hermetic riddles that tax the ingenuity of the scientist, but it may sufficiently interest the layman to make him realise that it is well worthwhile to study wines.

The grapes are gathered when they are perfectly ripe, or, if a sweet wine is to be made, when they are overripe. They are nowadays pressed by apparatus that is so constructed that the stalks, and sometimes the pips, of the berries are not crushed and that no part of the liquid must comes in contact with iron. Formerly the grapes were crushed beneath the feet of human pressers, in big pressing vats, and no great care was taken to prevent the must from contact with iron, which was sometimes dissolved and gave to the wine a nasty metallic taste. Contrary to the popular belief, there is little iron in even the most full-bodied red wine such as a Chambertin; its slightly hard astringency is caused by tannin, not by iron, for the grape contains an infinitesimal quantity of organic iron, far too small to be tasted in the wine. There is no doubt that pressing by machinery has done much to improve the quality of wine. The late Mr Merriman, conservative by nature, though extremely liberal in outlook, thought the human foot the best wine press, and was astonished when a wine expert told him that one of the main causes of the inferiority of the Cape wines was the custom of pressing the grapes in the old-fashioned way.

The pressed-out must, usually of a yellowish green colour, is now fermented. If a red wine is wanted, the must is fermented together with the husks of a dark-berried vine; if a white wine is to be made, the husks are not permitted in the fermenting vat. Husks, pips and stalks are now generally dug into the vineyards as manure, a wasteful method, for all three can be

wine

commercially used. From the pips an exceedingly valuable oil can be expressed. Sometimes the husks and the debris left after the must has been pressed out are covered with water and allowed to ferment, producing a thin, watery wine of a very low alcoholic strength which is used to provide the wine ration for the labourers on some farms.

Fermentation of the must is caused by the moulds that are already on the grapes before they are pressed. How they manage to get there, and what becomes of them in winter, no one has yet satisfactorily explained; all that we know is that they are found in every vineyard the world over. There are two of them, one called *Saccharomyces ellipsoideus* and the other *Saccharomyces apiculatus*, and they both have the ability, through peculiar yeasts or enzymes (or, more correctly speaking, substances known as zymase and sucrase, that give yeast its peculiar properties) that are found in their bodies, to split the various sugars in the must into alcohol and carbonic acid gas. This ability they lose through their own efforts, for if the must in which they work attains an alcoholic strength above four per cent, little *S. apiculatus* goes on strike, and if the percentage of alcohol is much increased *S. ellipsoideus* finds it increasingly difficult to continue working. Where the percentage of sugars in the must is high — as is generally the case in South African musts — the stoppage of fermentation may thus happen before most of the sugar has been converted. Not that the two moulds are only concerned with alcohol and carbonic acid production. Their busy activities result in the production of many other kinds of interesting things. Pasteur, the man who first got on nodding terms with them, says that when they have 100 parts of sugar to play with they make it into 48.4 parts alcohol, 46.6 parts carbonic acid gas, 3.2 parts glycerine, 0.6 parts succinic acid, and convert 1.2 parts to their own domestic use. Those with a taste for figures may calculate from this what amounts of alcohol are obtained by the fermentation of our South African musts; I am quite willing to accept the generally stated opinion that to obtain a wine with 10 per cent by volume of alcohol, 'the must should contain 17 per cent of sugar, corresponding to a density of 1.075 at 15 degrees Centigrade' (Hewitt, *Report on Oenological Research*, 1928).

Modern research has discovered that many other substances make their appearance in fermenting must and are later on present in the wine. There are numerous amino acids; there are even fat, phosphorised alcohols, tannin, pectin, that queer substance that causes jellies to set, gums, resins, curious highly scented bodies that are now used in the manufacture of synthetic perfumes, many different kinds of acids, and a lot more about which we know next to nothing. An astonishing feature of the business is that different strains of the moulds seem to have some influence upon the kind of wine that finally emerges when all the turmoil has subsided, and the wine can be drawn off from the lees, or undergo its first 'racking' as the trade calls it. In most wine-producing countries — not, so far as I know, in South Africa — wine makers use different mould strains for their various wines, and claim that they produce better wines by doing so.

There are other moulds that are not so useful. One that was formerly regarded as the viticulturist's friend, *Mycoderma vini*, is now known to damage wine. Its cousin, *Mycoderma aceti*, is definitely a pest; it lives on the surface of the wine and changes the alcohol into acetic acid or vinegar, and causes the wine to turn sour. Another cousin manufactures mannite in the wine. There are many other bacteria that hurt wine. At his laboratory at the KWV headquarters at Paarl, the late Dr Perold studied and photographed, cultured and described scores of them, and every wine merchant has to struggle to keep them in check.

When the fermentation is completed, the wine is drawn off from the lees and fined, that is to say it is cleared and rendered transparent and sparkling by the addition of certain materials that entangle in them whatever insoluble particles there may be in the wine and bring them down as a sediment that can be removed. This process of fining, which in South Africa may only be done with isinglass, gelatine, eggs, albumen, Spanish clay, kaolin or tannin, and not by the more modern and scientific methods now used for the clarification of white wines, may have to be repeated several times. When the wine has been properly fined, it is pure, natural wine, dry when most of its sugar has been used up by the moulds, sweet to a varying degree according to how much sugar remains unconverted. In the latter case it is usually 'fortified' by the addition of alcohol, to prevent the sugar from being again attacked by moulds and another fermentation started. The result is that all sweet Cape wines contain more than 16.6 per cent of alcohol by volume if their sugar content happens to be above 20 grammes per litre.

A pure natural wine, properly made, is thus a blend of water and many other substances of which alcohol never constitutes more than at most a fourth part. The alcoholic content of wine is a difficult matter to discuss, for the terms used are not always precisely defined. A Chancellor of the Exchequer has declared that no one is ingenious enough to give a scientific definition of 'proof spirit', which is an antiquated, empirical way of stating the alcoholic strength of wine. An estimation of alcohol, by distilling the wine, and calculating the percentage of alcohol that it contains, is the only scientific way of measuring its alcoholic strength. In general, it may be stated that our red wines are not much higher in alcoholic strength than their European types, while our white wines are usually somewhat higher, and our fortified wines are on a par with fortified wines made elsewhere. Although the sugar content of our musts is considerably higher than in European musts, there is no valid reason why we should not have natural light wines with a much lower alcoholic strength than those that are on the market today.

The pure, natural wine, when it has been finally refined, may be drunk at once, but it is young, immature, green wine that generally does not possess the virtues that time alone can bring. It may have the fine promise that adolescence sometimes shows, and the connoisseur may foretell that it will blossom into vigorous splendour when it reaches its majority, or that it

wine

575

will never attain to that perfection that is a fine wine. All wines mature and all wines age; they have their period of growth, virile stability and senescence. They reach the zenith of their vigour when they have so changed the harsh chemical compounds that are within them that these have become softened or have altogether vanished and their lingering ghosts have been transformed into volatile esters and soluble aldehydes whose presence imparts dignity and beauty, smoothness and delicacy to their taste. No one, not even the best expert, can tell when that stage will be reached. Some wines, indeed, may never live to see it; they grow grey and hoary before their constituents have had a chance to mellow. Others may take years to attain to it and, having reached it, rapidly decline. There is no rule that we can apply. But all wine should be given the opportunity to show if it can better its youthful promise. It should stay in cask, in wood, for months, and in bottle for some years, to shed whatever it may have to drop, and to be undisturbed by the stimulation of the oxygen in the air around it, resting peacefully to develop those excellencies that only time and the slow, inevitable interaction of its chemical constituents upon themselves, can achieve.

Though wine is proverbially regarded as red, the majority of wines are of a different colour, ranging from almost pure white, like fountain water, through a gamut of lighter to deeper yellow and gold, and ending in green and brown and the tawny tinge of old mahogany. The cabinet of a gem collector, indeed, would afford adequate comparison for the different shades that are to be found among the various wines, and the trade is often at a loss properly to describe the colour of a particular wine. Ports are described as 'ruby,' though few of them possess the intense, living lividity of the pure Burma gem that is more closely paralleled by some of the naturally red wines, like Pontac. Among the Furmint wines are some, like Jerusalemer, whose limpid green reminds one of the peridot, and others, in which the green is blended with a tinge of yellow, that are best likened to a heliodorite. Pure, natural Sherries have the colour of a light topaz, older Sherries approach a brown spinel in colour, while the well-matured Olorosos have an amber tint. Among the red wines the diversities of hue are so great that accurate description sometimes taxes the imagination. The range is from the pale pink, reminiscent of the finest tourmaline, the lighter red, with pink reflections, that recalls the Kuntzite, the deeper yet still flashing red of the spinel, the gorgeous scintillation of the columbine or Alexandrite seen under the lamplight, to the sombre yet transparent richness of the carbuncle and ruby, and finally the dark red, nearing blackness, of the deepest garnet, as seen in the Shiraz wines. In fact, among wines every shade, with the exception of blue, is represented, and there is no reason why, with proper handling, a blue-shaded wine should not be made were it not for the aesthetic sensibility that would abhor such a barbarity. The main thing to remember is that as wine is fermented must, and as there are few wine musts that are naturally red, most wines are without any red colour, and that this distinctive hue must be given to them by proper treatment.

There are few grapes whose juice contains any red colour; even red grapes have greenish or light yellow musts. The few exceptions to this rule are grapes like Isabella and Pontac that are naturally purplish red. Some of the finest light-coloured wines — and especially the sparkling champagne wines — are made from red or purple grapes. Red wines are made by allowing the must to ferment, for a short while at least, together with the husks, that contain the colouring matter in the cells just below the skin; this colour is extracted by the fermenting must, and dissolves in the wine, giving it whatever degree of red that is desired in the final product. Oenologists are not yet agreed as to the nature of this colouring matter, of which five different varieties have so far been described. One is a violet-coloured substance, presumed to be an unstable acid; another is green-tinted, and the other three are reddish pigments that are classed as oenilic acids. They are all made in the leaves, and are passed on to the berries, and they are all oxidised by yeast activity in the presence of air or oxygen. It is therefore self-evident that when they are in solution in wine, and that wine is exposed to the air, they will gradually alter in intensity. The lightest-coloured wine will in time change its colour; it may be very slight, but the change is definite and is caused by the oxidation of its suspended pigments. Where the wine contains much tannin, and the red pigment is in excess, the change will be less apparent even after many years than in yellow or colourless wines with a lower tannic acid content and with merely the yellow or green pigment in solution. Such yellow or colourless wines are made by separating the husks from the must and can afterwards be coloured red only by adding colouring matter to them.

Red wine is made by allowing the must to ferment with the husks, and is naturally, not artificially, coloured, although it may be blended with darker red wines to improve the colour. Fortified red wines are often coloured by extracts, sometimes of darker grapes, sometimes even of things that have no connection whatever with a vineyard, like logwood or elderberries. For legitimate colouring, to produce brown and topaz shades, boiled wine and caramelised sugar are used; the latter is the only colouring ingredient that is permitted to be used in Cape brandy.

Whatever the colour of a wine may be, it must be uniformly distributed throughout the liquid and it must be in solution. If it is merely suspended, the wine lacks that limpidity and sparkle that natural wine always has; it becomes dull, and even when not appreciably cloudy, loses its 'flash' as may easily be observed when a little of it is agitated in a clean wine glass held up against the light. Much of the aesthetic satisfaction derived from drinking a good wine comes from this purity of colour that makes some wines sparkle with an iridescence almost gem-like.

Next we come to the tests that the nose and palate can apply, the smell and taste of good wine. To some extent there is no difference between these, for the one is but a psychological modification of the other.

The smell of wine is the natural odour of the volatile substances in the wine that ascend into the air at the ordinary room temperature and are appreciated by the nose. The taste of the wine is a somewhat more complicated matter. It consists of two things, the appreciation again by the nose of volatile substances in the wine when it is warmed in the mouth, and these volatile substances impinge on the hinder parts of the nose; this is called the *aroma* of the wine; and the effect of the liquid itself upon the taste buds of the tongue and the palate made by the soluble matter in the wine; this is called the *flavour* of the wine.

The fragrance of the wine, technically known as its *bouquet*, is dependent upon certain volatile substances that are formed in the vine-leaves and, like the colouring matter, are conveyed to the grapes. It is easily noticeable in a vineyard that the immediate neighbourhood of the ripening berries is redolent with a fruity odour that, in the case of Muscat or Muscadel, is sometimes overpowering. The volatility of these odorific substances must therefore be great. They are classed as aromatic substances, with a most complicated chemical constitution, and can be extracted from the grapes or from the vine-leaves in the form of pungent-smelling extracts which have on occasion been used to give an artificial virtuosity to vintages that are deficient in bouquet. Some of them are lost in the process of fermentation, but are fully replaced by other bouquet substances that are equally complicated bodies, highly volatile, generated by the action of enzymes upon the innumerable organic constituents of the must. The bouquet of a good natural wine depends largely on these products of fermentation, which are all aromatic, although some are not pleasing to the nose and a few are decidedly rank. But in essentials the characteristic bouquet of a good wine comes from the substances made in the vine-leaves when the grapes have been growing and ripening. These substances are oxidised by too much sunlight and heat, and that is probably why we find that South African light wines, both white and red, are not outstanding as regards their bouquet, especially in districts where the vineyards are much exposed to direct sunlight. Another reason is that the bouquet substances are rendered more volatile by a greater degree of acidity in the wine, and as our light wines are generally far less acid than European light wines, the volatile esters in them are not so apparent. On the other hand our heavier sweet wines compare favourably as regards bouquet with other similar wines, and our heavier table wines from the cooler districts, like Constantia, have no reason to be ashamed of their smell.

The bouquet of a good wine should be distinctive, pleasantly titillating, without being pungent, scented with a clean, dry, aromatic smell. By swirling the wine in a small glass so as to get as much as possible of its surface in contact with the air, the volatile esters can be concentrated within the mouth of the glass and their character better appreciated. Various comparisons have been applied to what is smelled. Raspberry, violet, sorrel and even tuber-rose of all things, have been called upon for a likeness, but the charm of a wine's bouquet lies perhaps in just this inability to classify and describe it. The connoisseur who has imagination and wide knowledge will find comparisons readily enough; the wine lover will content himself in sniffing up the delicate perfume without trying to label it by reference to a herbal.

The aroma of wine is perceived at the back of the palate in what anatomists call 'the posterior nares.' It is the volume of volatile esters released by the greater warmth of the mouth when the wine is drunk, and is a blending of taste and smell. Physiologically, man can only taste sourness, saltness, bitterness and sweetness, but the wine lover confounds the physiologists, for in the combination of aroma and flavour he can detect, beyond these four primary tastes, such impressions as warmth, smoothness, oiliness and a variety of others to which wine enthusiasts have given fantastic names. Perhaps their dithyrambics are birthed from a desire to hide their poverty of experience, for attendance in the compounding room of an old-fashioned apothecary's shop would supply them with infinitely superior comparisons. Again the wine lover has very definite expressions for what he savours when he tastes wine. If he knows French, he has some more than if he has to rely merely on English, but even without a knowledge of French he can manage very well to convey his meaning. Of the characteristic adjectives he uses, *vinous* is probably the most important; it means that the liquid has the characteristic quality of wine, the unique flavour of the grape, that when one has once learnt to appreciate it can never be forgotten, and can hardly ever be successfully imitated. For the taste and flavour of all wines can be mimicked by concoctions that have no drop of real wine in them, and the adulteration and sophistication of wines have been fine arts from the time of the Middle Ages. It is quite true that these surrogates will not deceive the intelligent wine drinker. But he is in a minority. Most people are imitative; they do as others do; they follow conventions, and are influenced by advertisement, by publicity, by what they imagine is authority. A printed label on the bottle gives a virtue of authenticity that they cannot test by their own knowledge or experience. All oenologists know that any type of wine can be imitated in the laboratory. The trade has its special secrets for the manufacture of wines and spirits that, to the untrained taste, are the exact replicas of well-known brands. The best rule for the wine lover, who is not an expert, is to train himself by drinking good wine, to form his own taste, and to judge by it if the wine he drinks is good or bad.

Eye, nose and palate must combine in that judgment, and possibly of these three, the nose is the most discriminating juryman, except, perhaps, when drinking a heavy, sweet, fortified wine. Properly to taste such a wine, the palate must be dry, and that is probably the reason why many good judges smoke a Havana cigar before they test the quality of a port type wine. The convention that port must never be taken when you are smoking tobacco is one of the 'wine fallacies' whose origin no one knows. A delicate, fragrant dry wine is quite another matter; the mere reek of cigarette smoke in its vicinity may mar the purity of its bouquet; a dry cream-cracker, or a morsel of Melba toast, is all that is required to clean the palate for the appreciation of the taste and flavour of such a wine.

The nose will tell you at once if the wine you are about to drink is 'sound'; nothing can hide the distinctive odour of sourness that shows the wine has too much acetic acid in it. It may be that the wine has no special bouquet, no scent reminiscent of something that grows in the flower garden; it is then deficient in bouquet, but not necessarily not a good wine. But it must not have even the suspicion of an odour that is a smell and not a scent; if it has, it is indubitably bad, and there is really no need to find out to what its badness may be ascribed, whether it is 'woody', 'earthy', 'corked', 'rancid', or anything else. All that matters is that it is not a good wine.

The test of smell having been passed, take a sip of the wine, after having twirled the glass round a few times to make the liquid come into closer contact with the air. Let the wine flow gently on the tongue and to the back of the mouth, without consciously pressing it against the roof of the mouth or the sides. Should you unfortunately wear a metal tooth-plate, or have metallic fillings in your teeth, both will interfere with your appreciation of a finely flavoured wine, especially if it is on the acid side, but neither need lessen your liking for it, for the back of the palate and the sides of the tongue will still give enough indication of its excellence. Judge by them the smoothness, the oiliness, the cleanliness, the harmony of the liquid in your mouth, its sensation of warmth, sweetness, tartness, astringency, bitterness or whatever it may have, and then, as you swallow it slowly, its after-taste and what it leaves behind. Too much warmth implies too much alcohol; too much sweetness means an overcharge of sugar; tartness that is more than a tang is evidence of excess of tartrates; unpleasant astringency shows the presence of more tannin than is necessary to balance the wine; a definite bitterness, likeable in some kinds of wine, may be a black mark against others. In a fine wine all these different sensations will blend, harmonising the one with the other in a taste symphony deliciously bland and smooth, above which you will perceive the indescribable but perfectly recognisable vinosity that is the hallmark of a good wine, the proof that it is the perfect product of the grape, and not merely a concoction of alcohol and extracts.

Obviously, to taste wine like that you should not be hampered by sharper and more pungent tastes in your mouth while you are doing so, or immediately before you proceed to do so. That is the reason for selecting table wines with some care. There are some dishes that companion the best wines; there are others — asparagus, for instance, and salads overloaded with vinegar or sour dressings — that ruin even a moderate wine, unless it be fortified and sweet. To choose table wines with success demands knowledge of the various kinds and an understanding of their individual qualities.

Wines are divided into many classes. For practical purposes the classification may be simplified by arranging them into two great groups — Natural Wines and Fortified Wines. This is a better and more simple way than to classify them as Beverage Wines, Dessert Wines and Foaming Wines.

A *natural* wine is a wine that has been properly fermented and blended without the addition of extraneous spirit; a *fortified* wine is a natural wine to which extraneous spirit has been added. Natural wines are consequently of a low alcoholic strength, while fortified wines have a much higher alcoholic content. A *foaming* wine is a fortified wine which holds carbonic acid gas, produced by fermentation, in solution under varying degrees of atmospheric pressure; it is not, and never can be, a pure natural wine. A natural wine into which carbonic acid gas has been introduced forcibly is an *aerated* wine which in this country is not allowed to be sold as a foaming wine. The term 'sparkling wine' is sometimes given to foaming wines, but that is a misnomer; all good wine is sparkling, just as a gem is sparkling, but the presence of bubbles in wine, foaming or creaming wine, is evidence of delayed fermentation.

In the wine trade certain definite types of wine are recognised. Of these the 'Burgundy,' Sherry, Port, Hock, and Madeira types are the best known, and they are made, or blended, to be as close as possible to the wines that are made in the particular districts to which these territorial names apply. As a matter of fact, wines are so individual and vary so much in their characteristics that it is factually impossible for a natural wine grown in South Africa to correspond with one grown, from the same type of grape, in France or California. It is therefore silly and misleading to call a Cape wine a 'Hock' or a 'Burgundy,' when it is no such thing, but merely a wine made from the same kind of grape from which Burgundy wine is made, which may be as good as or even superior to the French wine. It is less misleading to call it 'a Burgundy type,' but even that title should in time make room for a definite local name, descriptive of the wine or the locality where it was grown, that is as distinctively South African as is the French 'Burgundy.' One of the most heartening developments in the wine industry is the increasing consciousness on the part of our winegrowers, of the importance of this desirability.

The title 'claret type' is not so objectionable, for claret has no regional significance, and means a clear light wine. For the present, however, these trade types are useful to demarcate the various kinds of wine that may be bought in this country.

A Burgundy type wine is a red wine, made from Pinot, Gamay or Cabernet grapes, blended with wine from other grapes so as to produce a dark red, dry and, when young, sometimes tart wine, with an alcoholic strength that varies from 18 to 24 per cent. It has, in the best wines now made here, an exquisite bouquet, fully equal to that of the finest French wines, an acid content much below that of the best French wines, and a flavour that is unfortunately not yet as fine as the best French Burgundies. In time it will attain that pitch of high excellence, for it is a matter of blending and selecting. Our 'Burgundy type' wines, especially those made on the Cape Peninsula, are amongst our finest wines. Practically all those on the market are good wines; some are more vinous than others, but all are pure, natural, excellent table wines.

There are those that maintain that our Cape wines are 'too acid.' Never was an accusation made on flimsier grounds. Our wines, made from grapes that have invariably a higher sugar content than those grown in Europe, are never as acid as imported wines. Imported French and German wines are in general far inferior to our own best wines. Even when we do get some of the best brands from Europe, they have invariably been prepared for the long voyage, and have stood the test badly. They need a long rest before they can be drunk here, and they are never — or hardly ever — as good as in their home environment.

That is a point which we should remember when we drink our own wines. They need rest to mature, and rest when they have been agitated. It is unfair to judge them in the restaurant car when they have been shaken for many miles, or to drink them immediately after they have travelled a long distance in a motorcar. The complaint that they have no uniformity, that one bottle out of a dozen may be admirable and the next not so drinkable, is justified at present, but even in regard to this some allowance must be made, especially in these days when good corks are scarce. The best red wines now on our market show a decided improvement in the uniform quality of excellence that they possess, and where that is lacking the wine merchant will readily adjust the discrepancy.

Our claret type wines are red wines, light in alcoholic content, and are pure natural wines with an agreeable, usually not a very pronounced bouquet, and a good aroma and flavour. One or two brands are admirable table or beverage wines, equal to the best clarets that are produced overseas, though there is ample room for further betterment in their manufacture and blending. None of our red wines can be bought sufficiently matured to bring out its sterling quality, but some of our claret type wines will well repay five or six years' undisturbed repose in a cool cellar. One of the finest light dry wines I have ever tasted was a 'claret type' red wine, from a Cape farm, which I drank in 1932; it had been bottled in 1910 and lay in a bin next to a Volnay 1911, with which it inevitably claimed comparison, notwithstanding the intrinsic difference in character. The Volnay, with its magnificent aroma, left to recall its former glory, was indifferent; several bottles had suffered from bad corking, and probably the wine was not to blame for its deterioration. But the Cape wine was at the height of its glory, smooth and silky on the tongue, with a flavour that recalled many pleasant things and an aroma that made up for its want of bouquet. If we laid down our wines and left them in serene tranquillity — this cellar was far too close to the railway, which may have helped to harass the Volnay — undisturbed for 10 or 12 years, we would not be so prone to blazon their inferiority to imported blends.

Our natural white wines are of the 'Hock type,' although none of them can be said to resemble a wine grown along the banks of the Rhine or Moselle. They are now of a low alcoholic strength, and are really light wines in the true sense of the term, pleasant to the taste, but generally, perhaps on account of their low acidity, deficient in bouquet and aroma. Few of them have as yet any distinction, though some are nearing it, especially those in which the main must is from a Riesling grape. They must be served chilled, and some of them when appropriately cold are not as sparkling as they should be. This is because they contain a soluble mineral salt in solution which when the wine is chilled is changed to an insoluble compound that, although present in minute quantity, is sufficient to spoil the limpidity of the wine. It can be rectified almost within a few minutes by placing the bottle where a ray of sunlight falls upon it; the actinic light changes the insoluble compound back to a soluble one, and the wine becomes sparkling again, but it is no longer chilled. All that could be avoided by proper means of fining, for instance, with ferrocyanide, but our wine merchants are not allowed to use ferrocyanide for refining purposes. Another defect of our light white wines is the too-frequent taste of metasulphide that lingers in them, and sometimes spoils their slight bouquet. They have immensely improved during the last decade, and there are now on the market white beverage wines that are sound, wholesome examples of their type.

wine

583

We now come to the fortified wines. The premier among them is our Sherry, which is a peculiar wine, unique in that it has undergone a double fermentation. Not only has the first fermentation changed the sugar in the must into alcohol and carbonic acid gas, but the second fermentation, caused by a mould that is allowed to grow over the surface of the wine as it lies in the fermenting vat and appears like a congeries of oysters, has acted on the alcohol and transformed it into many other complicated substances, chiefly amino acids. Sherry allowed to undergo both fermentations without the addition of extraneous alcohol is a water-like liquid, with practically no bouquet, but with a pronounced aroma and flavour. Such 'natural Sherry' never comes into the market, and it is only since 1932 that 'Flor Sherry,' that is Sherry that has been acted upon by the mould, has been prepared in this country. Before that Sherry was distinctly a 'manufactured wine' prepared by a method in which gypsum was added to the fermenting must and the wine afterwards blended and heavily fortified, while burnt sugar was added to colour it. Today the 'Flor Sherry' is fortified, and its alcoholic content is therefore fairly high. Sherry manufacture is a highly complicated business, and for perfect blending fully matured wines, obtained by the 'Solera' process, are required. The KWV is now building up a Solera from which these matured Sherries will be obtained to prepare high-grade Sherries. Young wines are sold that are very good, and compare favourably with Spanish wines of the same age, and during the last few years South African Sherries have won a deserved reputation on the London market.

Port and Madeira types are heavily fortified wines with distinctive characteristics that, for obvious reasons, are easily imitated. They are both heavy, heady wines that cannot be classed as table or beverage wines. Indeed, no fortified wine can be looked upon as a beverage wine. Real port is a highly sophisticated wine, overloaded with added spirit when the natural wine from which it is made has not yet completed its fermentation. Its excellence depends entirely upon the manner in which this added spirit has been merged into and become part and parcel of the original wine, and that takes many years, during which time the original wine may have completely altered its character. No one who has tasted a sweet highly alcoholised wine that has made its own alcohol — such as the original Constantia, for example, or the 'Nagmaal wine' of the Hugos and Moutons — would care to prefer a port to it. The absurd dithyrambics about Port 'vintages' that are scarcely two decades old are on a par with the inanities that are spoken and written about Napoleon brandies. It is unfortunate that science, with all its advances, is not yet able to tell, by analysis, if the spirit in such a wine is derived from the wine itself or is a distillation spirit. Such a test would be admirable to demonstrate the difference between sweet natural wine and sweet wine that has been so prematurely fortified as Port wine.

Our wines of the Port-Madeira type are made in accordance with the requirements of the trade for the English market. They are not, in my opinion, to be compared with the sweet liqueur wines that have in some measure sustained the reputation of their predecessors in the first half of the past century.[1] Some very excellent liqueur wines of this type are on the market. The late Dr Perold, who was always experimenting with the type, produced two first-class wines that for finesse and velvetiness are hardly likely to be surpassed, one of them a Mataro with a beautiful colour, some bouquet — which these wines generally lack — and a delicious flavour.

Sweet white wines, of the Graves-Sauternes type, should be made here, but winegrowers are hampered by the inept Government regulations that demand that all wines with a sugar content exceeding 20 grammes per litre should be fortified. The KWV, again, has done some useful experimental work in this direction. It has made a blend of Sauvignon blanc and Semillon that is probably one of the best wines of this type that has been manufactured in this country. Privately some winegrowers have made wines of this type for their own consumption and have proved thereby that such wines can be successfully made in South Africa, although there is as yet but a small demand for them.

Very little need be said about foaming wines. They are, for all their popularity, of little interest to the wine lover, who much prefers a 'still' Champagne to the highly sophisticated article that has so huge an appeal to so many. Foaming wine is wine in which the wine is surcharged with carbonic acid gas that comes from added yeast after the original fermentation has ceased. Before this second fermentation has stopped, spirit and certain extracts are introduced into the wine. The great care that is taken in this elaborate process of manufacturing the wine, and the special precautions that are necessary to ensure its uniformity, account for the comparatively high price that is paid for it, a price far in excess of its quality. Foaming wine has special characteristics. It is a very invigorating — and consequently an easily intoxicating — wine. Every bubble is surrounded as it were with a thin film of alcohol, and as a result the alcohol is much more quickly assimilated when the wine is drunk than is the case with a still wine. The carbonic acid gives to such wines a special briskness that is liked by many, but the same effect may be obtained by mixing any fortified white wine with soda water. Champagne should never be taken with food of any kind; it should be drunk, if drunk at all, by itself, as a stimulant and for that purpose it serves very well. Our South African foaming wines are all fortified, sophisticated wines, that have no particular distinction, and our winegrowers would do well to

---

1 The nineteenth century — Eds.

wine

concentrate on preparing a really fine still white wine before they expend their energies on manufacturing foaming wines of the Champagne type.

Chapter 15

Wine Grapes of the Cape

The late Dr A I Perold was South Africa's outstanding ampelographist. His *Treatise on Viticulture*, published as far back as 1927, is still the most authoritative book on the subject. I am indebted to him for all my knowledge of wine grapes, learned by accompanying him on his tours through the vineyards and amplified by long talks over a bottle of the wine that he so much loved. He was himself a lovable man, a great and true student of science, cultured beyond his kind that are often loathe to wander beyond the limits of their own speciality. Like all who appreciate good wine, he had an instinctive good taste for other things that are beautiful and likeable, and with it the simplicity and forthrightness that are the hallmarks of honesty. We owe him much for his services to the wine industry, in which he was a pioneer, a leader, and an admirable research worker. He introduced many new varieties of vines into South Africa. His investigations into the bacterial diseases of wines opened a new field of research that promises, in time, to revolutionise some of our methods of manufacturing wine. For many years he was the recognised wine expert of the KWV, a judge at every yearly wine show, the friend and adviser, often the sharp critic, of the wine farmers. His sudden, unexpected death in the early war years deprived South Africa of one of its foremost scientific minds and the wine industry of one of its ablest and most erudite collaborators.

This textbook on viticulture is an English translation and adaptation of his earlier *Handboek oor Wynbou* that he published at his own expense, in Afrikaans, in 1926, and at which he worked for several years while he was mainly occupied in teaching and research work at Stellenbosch. It was the first attempt to provide the wine farmer in South Africa with a popular treatise on the biology of the vine. It described in detail the various stocks, vine varieties and methods of cultivation, and gave an account of the diseases to which the vine is subject and finally a chapter on the manufacture of raisins, vinegar and grape juice. It was essentially a book on viticulture and said little about the making of wine, a subject with which he proposed to deal exhaustively in a later work for which he had already written several chapters before he died. It is sincerely to be hoped that these remains will in due course be edited and made ready for the press by one or other of his devoted colleagues able and willing to carry on the work from the point where he left off.

Dr Perold was of the opinion that our oldest grapes are the Muscadel, the Frontignac, the Green Grape and the Stein, with the French (that he tells us is 'practically identical with Palomino') and the Hanepoot, or Muscat grape as probably equally old varieties. It is impossible to say what varieties

were first imported, although we know that the first wine was made from Muscadel and French white grapes. The main varieties that are favoured at present by the wine farmers are all accurately described in his book, and what follows is largely derived from his notes.

The most important, and in fact all, of our wine grapes are varieties of the European grape (*Vitis vinifera*), and the most commonly grown are varieties that have proved their worth in the wine-growing parts of France, Germany, Italy and Austria. Among them is one sort that can be regarded more as a table than as a wine grape, although it is very extensively used for wine making.

This is one of the oldest varieties, locally known as Hanepoot, and in the fruit trade generally as Muscat d'Alexandrie. It is one of the heaviest bearers at the Cape, and Perold mentions a plot of vines, 'grafted on Jacquez, planted five by six feet square, 3 000 in number, and trained on wire' that yearly gave a yield of 18 leaguers per 1 000 vines or 380 hectolitres per hectare, which, as he rightly remarks, is probably a world record. Hanepoot makes a pleasant, drinkable dry wine when properly cared for, but very few wine farmers have troubled themselves to produce wine of this type. A more common Hanepoot wine is a golden-coloured, fairly sweet wine, of which several kinds are on the market. Hanepoot is a green grape, thick-skinned and very sweet, but a dark red variety, locally raised, is equally common. It is perhaps the most popular table grape both for export and for local use, and is consequently grown everywhere.

Green Grape, that also has a red equivalent, is probably some European variety that has been modified by culture and climate. Dr Perold was not certain with which European kind it can be properly identified, but considered it one of the oldest grapes in our vineyards. Its musts produce an indifferent sort of wine, sometimes with an unpleasant taste, when they have been fermented in contact with the husks. It was probably the variety that produced the surplus of wine in the early years of the industry, and contributed to the bad reputation that Cape wines then obtained. As it is a quick grower and bears well, it is still favoured. Perold recommends that it should be replaced by better varieties like white French, Stein or Sauvignon blanc.

Stein, another old and favourite variety, is regarded as a modified form of Sauvignon blanc, is very susceptible to oidium, but makes a far better wine than Green Grape. Some of the light wines made from Stein are much improved by a few years in bottle; they develop a pleasant though faint bouquet, and are clean and attractive to the palate.

White French, identified by Perold with Palomino, is a heavy cropper, and one of the most important of the dry wine grape varieties. Its musts vary according to the soil. In districts where the soil is poor in lime, its acidity is slightly higher and its sugar content lower (19 per cent) than in the heavier clay soils where its acidity is very low while its sugar content (27 per cent) approaches that of a Muscadel. Its wine is, as might be expected, singularly low in acidity, and in its natural state is one of the most interesting and pleasant of our light dry wines, although it is deficient in bouquet. It is now used as a basis for Sherry, but appears on the markets most frequently as a light, dry wine, of the 'Hock' type. As such, a great deal is produced in the Tulbagh district, where one particular variety of it is known as Witzenberg.

Canaan grape, the fourth variety listed by Perold in his *Special Ampelography*, is no longer grown, although it was formerly common enough in the outlying districts. Pinot blanc has proved a disappointing wine grape at the Cape, although it grows well and has been well tried. So far I have not tasted a pure Pinot blanc wine that can justly be compared with that made from the musts of Chablis, but no doubt we will in time manage to produce something quite as good.

Sauvignon blanc and Semillon, the two famous wine varieties of Sauternes, are now extensively grown, even though we have not as yet succeeded in making a perfectly blended wine of the Sauternes type. Some of the experiments that have been made have come very near to success. Dr Perold himself made a fine blend of Sauvignon and Semillion with some white Muscadel that had a quality of its own. He called it SS, but it was never marketed, and most of it, I believe, went sick in the cellar of the KWV at Paarl. It had the bland suavity of a fine Sauternes, with a good aroma, and was in every way an outstanding wine of its type, the sort of wine indeed that one would like to see more of made here. Its distinction and liquorosity put it in a class apart, and there is no doubt that if it had been possible to mature it, few connoisseurs would have denied its exquisite individuality. Since then the experts of the KWV have made several other blends, none, however, quite as distinctive as this SS. Their 1936 'Sauternes' is a pleasant-flavoured wine, but lacks the flavour and blandness that one expects in such wines. It is disappointing, too, that at recent wine shows the entries in this class of wine have not been even of a medium standard. This is much to be regretted for we grow as excellent Sauternes grapes here as in France, while there are factors that favour the hope that we should be able to produce quality wines from these grapes that can compare excellently with the best French Sauternes. Here, more perhaps than in any other direction, experimental investigation will be amply repaid by results, because there is an undoubted demand for a good table wine, of the Graves type, that is slightly sweet. Some winegrowers are doing good work in this field, and have put on the market a light sweet wine of this character that is admirably blended and fulfils all the demands that can be made for a wine of this type. Unfortunately the legal compulsion to fortify this kind of wine beyond the 16 per cent mark defeats the object they have in view and prohibits the South African consumer from obtaining a pure, natural, medium sweet wine of this type for use as a table wine. Sweeter liqueur wines, of the SS type, will also find a ready market, and there is a wide field for experiment in blending wines made from the heavily sugared Semillon must with less sweet but more aromatic products of French and Riesling musts.

The Muscadel grape is undoubtedly one of the oldest varieties in South Africa. It is the Muscat blanc of ampelographists, but the red variety is as extensively grown as the white, and the musts of both kinds are similar in possessing a very high sugar content and a very low degree of acidity, calculated as tartaric acid. This grape is a fast, prolific and healthy grower, that seems to flourish as well in decomposed granite soils as in the heavier clay soils away from the coast. It was the favourite grape of the early settlers, for it is both a good eating grape and an excellent wine grape. Allied to it is the Frontignac variety, which is at first sight almost indistinguishable from the true Muscadel; it is classified as the Muscat de Frontignac, and in France yields the renowned Lunel wines whose Muscat bouquet and rich, clinging sweetness are sometimes overpoweringly strong. At the Cape wines made from their musts are not specially aromatic, but their flavour, and when properly made their liqueur-like suavity, especially when they have been allowed to mature, are extraordinarily fine. The original Constantia was probably made from a Frontignac-Muscadel must, and most of the finer sweet wines, of the 'Communion wine' type of today, are blends of such wines, sometimes with Pontac or Hermitage wine, and occasionally with Shiraz. The white Muscadel and the white Frontignac musts give a sweetish white wine that is, by itself, rather insipid, with little body or character. The red wine made from these varieties, even when unblended, is an interesting wine when new, and when matured loses much of its colour, becoming a golden yellow, but gains immeasurably in character and flavour.

Dr Perold lists twelve other white wine grapes that are generally grown. Some of them, like Ugni blanc, Sauvignon blanc, Furmint, Zierfahndler, Catarratto, Inzolia bianca, Codega and Verdelho, are not yet of great importance, although more and more are being planted. The Furmint in particular deserves more attention than has hitherto been paid to it, for it yields a must from which a most delicious wine can be made. It is the variety from which the great Hungarian (Tokay) wines are made, and I see no reason why from its must in South Africa there should not be produced wines fully equal to the best Hungarian types.

There remain Pedro Ximines, Riesling and Clairette blanche, that are all, comparatively speaking, new introductions, although the second has been cultivated here for more than a century. The first, which is supposed to be a modification of a Rhenish vine variety, may have been one of the 'Spanish grapes' that Van Riebeeck imported. It is a common and popular grape, as it grows freely, crops heavily, and is fairly resistant to most diseases. Its wine is now chiefly used for the preparation of Sherry, but when made from overripe grapes is also blended with other wines to make the sweet red wines of the 'Port' type. The Clairette is an interesting grape, one of the oldest French varieties known. Its must makes an excellent, highly aromatic, dry white wine that is, however, for some reason or other — probably bacterial action — merely of temporary excellence, as it rapidly deteriorates. Dr Perold suggests that Clairette should be more commonly grown to enable its wine, with its strong bouquet, to be blended with other dry white wines. That is now being done, and some of these blended wines are admirable.

The Riesling grape, that Perold thinks may be similar to the old Stein, produces in South Africa a must that differs in some respects from that obtained in its native territory, Germany. For climatic reasons, the grapes are rarely allowed to remain unharvested until they have developed *Edelvrot*, as here they are shrivelled by the sun, but where that has been done, by artificial covering, the must has shown an extraordinarily high sugar content of nearly 46 per cent. So far very little of such must has been converted into wine, and I know of no wine farmer that has made, even for home use, anything approaching a high-class *Auslese* wine. The dry wines made from the grapes when not yet overripe are getting better and better every year, as more care is being taken in their manufacture, and some of the 1939 season's wines are of exceptional quality. One or two wine farmers have already established a reputation for their Riesling wines and, indeed, practically all types on the market are sound, natural wines, with a low alcoholic content, very little acidity, and a pleasant, vinous flavour. Unfortunately nearly all of them are deficient in bouquet, a fault which might be overcome by suitable blending, although most probably its cause is to be found in the vigorous growth of the vines and the high yield that they are permitted to give.

The red grape varieties number no fewer than 34 on Perold's list, and since its publication other varieties have been grown. It is probable that for the production of the manufactured trade wine called Port — although that name is sacrosanct to the particular blends made in Portugal — still other varieties will be favoured in the near future, to obtain the qualities that are regarded as essential for that highly overrated wine. Much attention has lately been given to improving the qualities of our wines of this class. The KWV, in close co-operation with the Elsenburg Agricultural College, has established experimental vineyards, where such varieties as Donzellinho do Castello, Mourisco tinto, Souzao, Tinta Roriz and das Barrocas, Cornifesto, Malvasia Rey, Francisca and, above all, Bastardo have been planted, to ascertain their usefulness for making blending wines that can be mixed with wines made from the older varieties already well established here. Similarly, new Italian varieties of red wine grapes have been increasingly cultivated, among the more interesting ones being Montepulciano, Benniolo, Grignolino, Dolcetto nero, Barbera and Kadarka. When the importance of making good local wines, each with its definite characteristics and each with its own individuality, has been fully realised, winegrowers will no doubt find that in certain areas it may pay them best in the future to concentrate their energies upon the making of good table wines from one or more of these promising varieties.

Meanwhile the most popular red grape varieties for wine-making are those that experience has shown to be the best for the South African climate and soil. The two most important of these are the Pinot noir and the Cabernet varieties. The former, justly celebrated as the most important wine grape in France, from which both the choice Burgundy wines and the manufactured foaming Champagne are made, is easily grown in areas where the soil has a sufficiency of lime. Its musts here are richer in sugar than they are in France. It is a wine grape whose cultivation demands particular care, and the reason that our Pinot wines have so far not reached the high standard of excellence that is seen in the finest wines of the Burgundy-Beaujolais is mainly because greater care has not been taken in selecting suitable vineyard sites for the vines and in letting the grapes attain to full maturity before pressing. One of the finest dry red wines ever made in South Africa was the product of Pinot vines planted on decomposed schist soil; it was a wine of the highest quality, excellent in colour, with an agreeable bouquet and a most delicious aroma. The vine is, however, not a heavy cropper, and wine farmers are inclined to rely more on the Gamay noir, which gives a heavier yield and produces an equally saleable dry red wine of the requisite medium quality, although it lacks much of the superior characteristics of the true Pinot wine.

The lighter dry red wines are the product of the well-known Cabernet varieties, from which, in France, the claret type of wine is made. Dr Perold summed up the case for this wine grape with his characteristic bluntness and honesty when he wrote:

> 'In view of the wine conditions here and elsewhere in the world, our wine farmers in the districts of Paarl, Stellenbosch and the Cape Peninsula ought to plant at least one Cabernet vine for every two Hermitage vines, in order to produce a red table wine of good quality that is easily marketable both locally and when exported. This is absolutely necessary and cannot be emphasised too strongly.'

At present the finest dry red table wines produced in the country are Cabernet wines, from the must of grapes grown on decomposed granite soils. Some of them are exquisite wines, fully comparable to the best products of the Medoc *of the same age*. All on the market are comparatively young wines, and for everything earlier than 1930 one has to appeal to private cellars. Where blended with Merlot, Malbec and other musts, an inferior quality wine results, but experience here has shown that with a blend of Hermitage a delightfully pleasant beverage wine, possessing a good bouquet, magnificent colour and the characteristic aroma, can be produced. Some of the Cabernet wines on the market have an exceptionally powerful scent and aroma, but are hardly bland enough to the taste; they are improved by the addition of a few drops of water, but cannot be classed as really satisfying wines. Our vintage wines of the future will undoubtedly come from the Cabernets, and it is encouraging to find that the popular taste for them is growing. The various kinds that may be bought today are among the lightest Cape wines and the least acid of any wine that I know. Indeed, these beverage wines may be said to bear out fully Pasteur's *dictum* that beverage wine is the healthiest and safest drink that mankind can use.

Hermitage, perhaps the most extensively grown wine grape of the country, that owes its popularity not only to the fact that it is an exceedingly pleasant table grape, although it is not suitable for export, but also to its amazingly heavy bearing qualities, is not one of the old varieties. Dr Perold states that it was first planted in 1880 and that it is identical with the Cinsaut of the south of France. It has produced as much as three hundred hectolitres per hectare, a yield that has been surpassed only by the Hanepoot grape. It is therefore hardly surprising that winegrowers who have paid more attention to quantity than quality have given it the preference in their vineyards. As a matter of fact, it produces a thin, characterless wine, dry enough to be rasping on the palate, but generally with the saving grace of a good, dark colour. Such wine can be much improved by suitable blending. It is of low alcoholic content, light and thin, contains very little tartaric acid, and is most commonly used as a wine ration for Coloured workers.

Pontac stands in another class altogether. It is a remarkable grape, whose juice is dark red, staining blotting paper, and of a peculiar sub-acid sweetness when fully ripe, but with a harsh, even acrid after-taste. Its presence in the vineyard in January can always be known by the intense copper red coloration of the leaves; a patch of Pontac vines between acres of Hermitage shows like an island of autumn, set in the green of summer. It is one of the oldest of our wine grapes, and its must contains unusually high amounts of tannin, fruit acids and, for such a sub-acid berry, sugar which sometimes reaches 30 per cent. When, as is usual, it is pressed with the husks, the amount of tannin in its wine is so high that its action on the mucous membrane of the tongue and palate is decidedly unpleasant, and only after fining and maturation does it become drinkable.

Matured Pontac, however, is an extraordinarily interesting and altogether characteristic wine, and when suitably blended with Muscadel or Frontignac wine it becomes a wine of rare and outstanding quality, quite unlike anything else that our vineyards can produce. Such a Pontac wine has an amazingly dark yet absolutely clear and sometimes even sparkling colour, deep garnet red, that after many years in bottle becomes paler and loses its flashing effulgence. The colour is purer, with much less blue in it, than that of Shiraz or Mataro, whose must produces wines that are in some respects similar to Pontac, and the wine is in consequence sometimes used to blend with dry red wines in order to improve the colour. The vine is now rarer than it used to be; it is a sparse cropper, useless as a table or raisin grape, and therefore its yield to the winegrower is unprofitable. But it is nevertheless one of the most useful wine grapes that we possess and it is sincerely to be hoped that its popularity will increase. Suitably blended, it should appeal to all lovers of liqueur wines. A blend of Pontac and Muscadel was formerly considered one of the best kinds of the 'Port' type, and one of these blends was very popular in India in the early years of the last century. Pontac wine is mentioned by several writers from 1760 onwards, and nearly always with appreciation of its intense colouring and its magnificent aroma, but it may be taken that these references were all to blended wines. The oldest Pontac I have tasted was bottled in 1830; it was rich amber-coloured, with a penetrating bouquet, demonstrating the presence of powerful volatile esters, a smooth, somewhat oily taste with no astringency whatsoever, and a remarkably pleasant aroma. It was exceedingly dry, and had evidently not been blended. A Muscadel-Pontac blend, bottled in 1866, still held much of the rich ruby colour, had less bouquet, but was one of the most exquisite liqueur wines I have ever drunk.

In the Tzitzikamma forest grows one of our own wild grapes, with berries that sometimes exceed an inch in diameter. There is no reason why this wild grape should not make a good wine, but I have only once drunk a 'home-made' wine prepared from it. This proved to be a thin, very tart wine, but it had a very pleasant surprising fragrance, quite unlike that of any other South African wine.

Chapter 16

The Wine Districts

The 1881 Vine Diseases Commission published statistics about the number of bearing vines in the Cape Colony in that year. They listed the following districts as wine-producing areas:

Bedford, 1 500 vines; Cape, 265 300; Caledon, 1 318 900; Clanwilliam, 160 500; Calvinia, 150 200; George 211 200; Jansenville, 134 400; Malmesbury, 2 478 000; Paarl, 18 203 300; Piquetberg, 560 000; Prince Albert, 591 200; Robertson, 4 143 900; Riversdale, 280 400; Stellenbosch, 14 651 800; Swellendam, 294 000; Tulbagh, 630 000; Uniondale, 1 000; Willowmore, 174 500; Worcester, 5 548 800. Total of bearing vines, 52 603 400. No returns were available for the districts of Oudtshoorn, Ladismith and Graaff-Reinet, but the Commission estimated that the total number of bearing vines in the Colony exceeded 100 000 000.

Today that number has been almost doubled. The returns for 1937 show that in that year there were 164 705 856 bearing vines on farms, and that approximately 50 000 morgen of land was planted with vines.

The total production of wine from wine farms in the Cape Province for the year 1939 was as follows:

Pure natural wine, red	13 610 000 gallons
Pure natural wine, white	29 210 000 gallons
Fortified wine, red	11 380 000 gallons
Fortified wine, white	9 720 000 gallons
Wine for farm use	930 000 gallons
Total wine production	70 850 000 gallons

The export figures for 1910 to 1939 are as follows:

1910	76 982	value £ 18 423
1920	518 223	value £204 699
1935	1 401 775	value £190 489
1939	2 820 768	value £357 740

The value of wine exported was highest in 1920, when it averaged nearly eight shillings a gallon; since then it has fluctuated between two shillings and two shillings and sixpence a gallon.

Notwithstanding its large production of wine, South Africa still imports considerable quantities of wine and spirits. The imports of wine for the four corresponding years are as follows:

1910	82 246 gals	value £ 65 257
1920	80 963 gals	value £142 411

<pre>
1935   53 102 gals   value £ 51 180
1939   38 564 gals   value £ 38 007
</pre>

During the war practically no wine was imported, while a large quantity of wine and spirit was exported, chiefly to the east and African markets. No statistics about production have as yet been published for the war years, but the available figures for 1945 show that the total production has increased by about 17 per cent, and a progressive increase in production, commensurate with the increasing demand locally and outside the Union, can be looked for in the future. The wine industry is at present more or less stabilised, and winegrowing, in spite of the vexing restrictions laid upon it by inept legislation, is still a lucrative agricultural industry.

The Cape Province, or that part of it, at least, that has a winter rainfall, possesses in certain districts the ideal climate and soil required for successful viticulture. Outside the winter rainfall area, for instance, in the Transvaal and Natal, grapes may be grown, and wine has been successfully made, but the conditions there are not to be compared with those that are to be found in the south-western districts of the Cape Province, where the wine industry is now firmly established. A comparison with the list of winegrowing districts compiled by the Vine Diseases Commission in 1881 and the chief viticultural areas today shows that some of the former wine-growing districts can no longer be regarded as such. The districts of Clanwilliam — where before 1900 excellent wines were made — Calvinia, Bedford, Uniondale, Willowmore and Prince Albert are no longer important wine-growing districts. Their vineyards have been destroyed by Phylloxera, and few farmers have troubled to renew them on pest-proof stocks. It is true excellent grapes are still being grown for local consumption in all these districts. Vineyards have also been established in many other districts, where wine for local use is sometimes made, but their production is but a fraction of the yield of the principal wine-growing areas. Good grapes are grown on the irrigated plots along the banks of the Oliphants and Orange Rivers and in the Karoo uplands. It may be that in time we may get from such outlying districts quality wines of a distinctive character, but as yet there is none. Excellent wine grapes are grown in South-West Africa,[1] where quality wines of a high standard are now manufactured.

The Cape Division, in which lie the wine farms to the southeast of the Table Mountain range that runs across the Peninsula, is the oldest wine-growing area in the British Empire. Three-quarters of its arable surface is still uncultivated; a great deal of the flat lands is overgrown with Australian wattles, and much of its mountainsides are covered with the abominable, alien pine. But a considerable portion of the fertile slopes is planted with vineyards, with Pinot, Hermitage, Hanepoot, Green Grape and other varieties of wine grapes predominating, although on many of the newer farms luscious export grapes are cultivated. Here lie the old, historic

---

1 Present-day Namibia.

domains of Simon van der Stel, now cut up into a number of holdings, some small, others of considerable extent, though there is none today that can compare in size with the original gubernatorial domain. Groot Constantia, its manor house rebuilt after the fire, and stocked with old furniture, prints and objects of antiquarian interest to the many tourists who come daily to rhapsodise over it, its vineyards replanted with grafted vines on Phylloxera-proof stocks, and its fine oak avenue showing traces of decay, is still the first among equals. The original wine cellar, with the beautiful frieze cut by Anreith, serves as both a store and a packing-shed, for the Groot Constantia wines are still made here, although no longer by the government. High Constantia, Klein Constantia, Alphen, Hohenort and many other farms in the vicinity are noted for their products. The red wine from this area has a deserved reputation, ranking among the best dry light and full-bodied wines, and some of them have an aroma and a flavour that lend a distinction to which wines of similar type from other districts can hardly aspire. The most modern methods are used in making and blending these wines, of which a considerable quantity is exported, for of late years the wine lovers in the Congo and in the Far East have learned to appreciate their fine quality. Many of them are farm-bottled, great care being taken to ensure uniformity. Those on the market are without exception sound, wholesome wines, with generally a surprisingly low acidity.

Between the Cape Division and the mountains to the north lies the partly flat and partly undulating country where viticulture is the chief concern of the farmers. Vineyards have enormously increased in this area during the last ten years; co-operative wineries have been established and while here, too, more and more attention is being paid to table grapes, the main concern of the growers is still to make wine. The Stellenbosch, Klapmuts and Somerset West areas are noted for their white wines, and some excellent light dry wines, from Riesling musts, are produced. At Stellenbosch, one of the oldest villages in the Province, there is much to interest and attract the wine lover. The University has a fine oenological laboratory and an experimental wine farm at Elsenburg, the estate that was owned by the Myburgh family whose name is honourably associated with the history of the industry. The KWV has its largest distillery here, and big cellars for the storage of its maturing brandies. A few years ago a disastrous fire burned down the cellars and consumed most of the 1926 stock, but the loss has been compensated by the laying down of many leaguers of brandy of later date from which the well-known export brandy of the Association is made. Under its constitution the Association may not retail its products locally; it disposes of its stocks to wholesale dealers who blend their own brandies according to the private recipes that each individual firm possesses. Here, too, are the offices of *Wine and Spirit*, the enterprising monthly journal of the winegrowers. There are, in addition, several private distilleries and wineries. That at Oude Molen was started by the late Mr Rene Santhagens, whose cellar at one time contained specimens of the oldest brandies, both wine and marc types, in the Union. The products of the

Stellenbosch Farmers' Winery and of the Helderberg Co-operative Winery, and the wines from many private farms, such as Koelenhof, Lanzerac and Stellenrust, are deservedly popular.

Beyond Stellenbosch, on the other side of the Hell's Hoek Pass, one enters into the Paarl, Drakenstein and French Hoek wine region where the Drakenstein Co-operative Winery is a proof of what can be effected by intelligent combination. The Rhodes Fruit Farms produce excellent red and white wines, and there are many private farms whose wines are of superior quality. In the early years of the century, shortly after the end of the Anglo-Boer War, the farm *Plaisir Merle* produced one of the finest light dry wines of the 'claret' type that has ever been made in South Africa; its delicacy, bouquet, velvety softness and fine after-taste were highly commended by the late M Escoffier[1] and his friend Mr Van Andel, at that time the manager of the Grafton Galleries, when they sampled a bottle in London in 1904.

Paarl, the largest wine-growing district in the Province until Worcester surpassed it, is the headquarters of the KWV, whose extensive buildings cover a large acreage, while its underground cellars occupy almost as large an area. Its main depot is here, and a walk through the vaults and the double-storied wine stores gives, perhaps, a better indication of the extent and development of the wine industry at the Cape than any detailed account can supply. Many thousands of casks, some of them of prodigious size, rivalling the giant vats in the German wine stores, are ranged in double and treble tiers; a new store, covering several acres, is now devoted entirely to Sherries, to establish a proper 'Solera' for later blending. All types and kinds of wine can be seen here. The experts are constantly experimenting with different blends, to obtain distinctive wines, true to type. The late Dr Perold was the presiding genius of the place during his lifetime, and his mantle has fallen on Dr Hiehaus, a recognised authority on Sherry, but both were and are helped by young scientists who are encouraged to undertake special research and who have contributed valuable material to wine literature. All the wines bought are carefully and methodically analysed; scientific accuracy, conscientious attention to detail, and methodical recording are characteristic of all the oenological work done in the laboratories. The Association was responsible for starting 'flor yeast' Sherry manufacture, a branch that is now increasingly popular. It manufactures perfumes and cordials, both of which can be bought on the market, although its fine wines cannot be purchased by private clients. Some of these fine wines, such as the Mataro, the lately produced 'Sauternes type' of semi-sweet wine, and the range of 'Port type' wines, are of outstanding quality, but are made to serve as models and are not for sale. In the large underground cement vats are stored immense quantities of wine of all kinds, for the Association has, under its

---

1 Leipoldt worked under Escoffier in London.

constitution, to take over from its members their total yearly production, which it converts either into export wine or distils into brandy.

Farther north, when the Drakenstein Mountains are crossed, we come to Tulbagh and Ceres, where the merits of co-operative vinification have been recognised for many years. Here fine white wine is produced on the farms of the Witzenberg, and some red wine that is of superior quality, though it does not possess the fineness of the red wines made in the Cape and Paarl and Stellenbosch districts.

Worcester, Robertson and Montagu, that now between them produce the largest amount of wine of any area in the Province, differ from the more southern-lying wine-growing areas in their soil and climatic conditions. They are remote from the sea, are sheltered by high mountain ranges, and have a lower rainfall. Their soil is not the decomposed granite, sandy loams of the southern districts, but is much more variegated, with intrusive clays and shales, and on some farms a conglomerate that appears to be particularly favourable for the growth of certain wine grapes. Table grapes for export and for the local market are extensively grown on some farms, but the main business of most farmers is still to grow wine grapes. All three districts have had a reputation for their sweet and full-bodied wines, and Worcester at one time produced a wine of unsurpassed excellence, the magnificent 'sweet Sherry' of Mr Hugo, familiarly known as *Uncle Koos Mostertpotjie*. This was not a Sherry at all, but a wine *sui generis*, a deep amber-coloured fluid with a fragrance of sorrel and Muscat combined into something peculiarly its own, harmonious and velvety on the palate, showing that it had little tannin and a fair amount of pectin substance, a highly vinous aroma, with an after-taste that was faintly reminiscent of many fruits but characteristic of none, and a paucity of free acid that was as surprising as it was pleasant. It was a wine of remarkably low alcoholic content; Dr Hahn's analysis of various bottles shows slight differences, varying between 9.05 and 9.68 vol per cent, which is, I believe, equal to about something between sixteen and seventeen degrees proof. It was a delicious-tasting wine and so much in demand that there was never enough of it, for the vineyard, which was planted among pebbles, was comparatively small and the yield was not large. It was a Green Grape wine, blended with some other must, but its composition was a secret never revealed. A bottle, originally filled in 1864 and recorked in 1888, was opened by the late Dr D de V Hugo in 1927, when the wine was found to be much darker in colour, with a bouquet of almost overpowering strength, far too strong to be pleasant, but it still had its smooth, velvety taste, although its sweetness had almost faded into nothing.

When the ostrich-farming boom agitated the Colony, many farmers rooted out their vineyards to grow lucerne that was supposed to be much more profitable. That happened in the Worcester district, and it was only much later, after the Anglo-Boer War, that wine farming was again in favour. Since then the production of wine in these more northern districts has increased by many thousands of leaguers annually, and today Worcester is perhaps the biggest wine-producing district in the Province. It makes excellent wines, and so do the districts of Robertson and Montagu, though the two latter produce chiefly heavy sweet wines. Dry white wine is made in the Hex River Valley, which, according to Baron Von Babo, is almost as ideally suited for winegrowing as the Cape Peninsula. The sweet wines are nearly all of the 'Port' and Madeira type, but Frontignac, Pontac and Muscadel wines are made in great quantity. The heavy-bodied dry wines are without special distinction and lack fineness; some of them, blended with Pontac, have a bitterness that is unpleasant to the taste. More Port wine type grapes are being grown, and there is no doubt that in time all three districts will produce full-bodied red wines that, while they may not have the smoothness and flavour of the red wines of the Cape Division or the mellowness of the red wines of Stellenbosch and Paarl, will be good, wholesome beverage wines with characteristics of their own.

In the other wine-producing districts the wines are not of such a quality as to merit special mention. Time alone can show if, with proper blending, care in the selection of type grapes and greater attention to fermenting the musts under proper conditions, quality wines will be produced in Oudtshoorn, Swellendam and Riversdale. At present, their wines are of indifferent quality, but there is no reason why they should not be greatly improved. Wines grow in those districts with the same vigour and ease, and produce grapes as grand as in the other wine-growing areas, while there is also no great dissimilarity in soil and climate between them. In twenty years' time, perhaps, George and Oudtshoorn may vie with Worcester so far as wines are concerned, and one, or both, may produce a wine as graceful and distinctive as the old Hugo wine.

The custom, sanctioned by tradition, of calling a locally made wine by the name of a foreign wine with which it is deemed to have some affinity, is still observed in the industry. Cape Burgundy and Cape Champagne were formerly common enough; now the latter title is not allowed to be used, much to the vexation of some winegrowers who make a foaming wine which they would dearly love to market under the name of Champagne. 'Burgundy,' however, we still have with us, which is a pity, for, while our wine is made from the same kind of grape, it has characteristics of its own that differ from those of the wine manufactured in France. Even if it did not possess such peculiarities, it would still be absurd to call a Paarl or Constantia wine 'Burgundy,' just as absurd as it would be to call it 'Assmanshauser' or 'Salerno'. Time after time this has been pointed out by those who have the best interests of the South African industry at heart, but there are winegrowers who still yearn to apply such territorial names to their products. Cape wines can afford to stand on their own merits; some of them are so distinctive, so individual, so excellent, that they would win appreciation for themselves among wine lovers, no matter what names are attached to them. It would be to the advantage of the industry to give them names that are distinctive, either of the farm on which their grapes were grown, or of the grapes from which they were made. Where a heavy-bodied blended wine owes its existence to musts, of Gamay, Hermitage and Pontac, it would surely not overtax the ingenuity of the maker to create a new name, by some combination of the names of these grape varieties, that would in time become associated with that particular kind of wine and assure it the same reputation that a Burgundian wine now bears.

Nothing, indeed, could be more appropriate than to call particular Cape wines, no matter of what type they may be, by the names of the farms on which grow the vineyards that produced them. Many of these farms have names that recall to mind something beautiful in their setting; the knoll on which the vines are planted; the burn that rambles down the kloof, where in late summer the blue psoralea shades the water; the poplar wood carpeted by generations of leaves that have made a springy mould; the marsh land fringed with masses of arum lilies; the high towering, weather-worn ridges of rock, outlines sheer against the skyline; the old white gabled, grass-thatched dwelling house with its guarding screen of poplars; the outbuildings, byres and stables, formerly the slaves' quarters in the days when man still held property in man and thought it no sin to drink good wine; the road winding away into the far distance through untilled fields that in spring are splashed with the flaringly bright colour of innumerable sorrels. Picturesquely framed in an environment that is sometimes imposing and nearly always beautiful, these older wine farms have an appeal that every wine lover understands. The vineyards themselves are part of it, for they too have a charm that changes from season to season but never wholly fades. In winter the stark nakedness of the pruned stems, each twisted and rutted, and all so neatly aligned that nothing breaks the symmetry of their rows, with the bare, chilled earth between, and the whole a pattern of brown and grey, conveys an impression of resting strength. When the leaves appear — and these stark, stubbly stocks are in a few weeks' time so thickly covered with lush green that their stems or the ground between them can hardly be seen — the vineyards from afar are merely large squares of a more vivid colour than the surrounding veld that is already passing from its winter brown into the more lively clothing of spring. But a nearer view shows that the ground between the rows holds a varied range of colours, sprung up 'as at the touch of an enchanter's hand,' for all the vineyards are in districts that are famous for their veld flowers. Later, when the grapes have been gathered, and summer is mellowing into autumn, the vineyard itself shows a surprising variety of colour, for the several varieties have each their individual way of helping the fall of leaves, all eager to effect this by subtle changes in the chemistry of the leaf tissues that have for their object the elaboration of a line of demarcation between the living stock and the dying leaf. These chemical changes bring about sharp and very sudden alterations of colour. Those that occur in the Pontac leaves are of intense vividness, brilliant crimsons, shading into deep reds that veer into maroon and finally into brown; those of the Hanepoot, Green Grape and French, bright yellow, rivalling the autumn tints of the poplars. An autumn vineyard where many kinds of grapes grow is almost like a chequer board, and it is comparatively easy to say, from the appearance of the dying leaves, what are the several varieties of wine grapes that compose it.

With such material for inspiration it should surely be easy to find fitting names for the wines that come from our farms. That we have so far shown so little originality in christening them is simply because, for various reasons, we have succumbed to the temptation to call our wines by the European territorial names. Having done so, we are not warranted to feel aggrieved when strangers complain that we are imitating, or trying to imitate, foreign wines, a charge that has often been brought by those who are best qualified to judge. We should be proud enough of our wines to pilot them into any haven under their own flag, and nothing can harm them more than to try and smuggle them in under one to which they are not legitimately entitled.

The wine industry of the Cape Province is today in a flourishing condition. That is to a large extent the result of the increasing demand for wine and the successful efforts of the Wine Growers' Co-operative Association to control winegrowing and to prevent an unsaleable surplus from over-production. Viticulture gives employment to many thousands of labourers; in the wine districts virtually a third of the population is dependent upon its prosperity and success, while a large amount of capital has been invested in it. It is in the public interest that its development and progress should be unimpeded, and that neither should be hampered and vexed by undue restrictions whose tendency is towards ultimate prohibition or, at least, the imposition of such sanctions as will make winegrowing unprofitable.

Chapter 17

The Future

The history and vicissitudes of the wine industry at the Cape have been traced, for almost 300 years, in the preceding pages. Something has been said about the conditions under which that industry is at present being carried on, the restrictions under which it labours, and the advantages it is blessed with. I may perhaps be permitted to conclude the recital by a brief discussion of the future possibilities of viticulture in South Africa.

There is a consensus among experts that the wine districts of the Cape possess the ideal requirements for the production of good wine, and that such wine, inferior to none made elsewhere in the world, can be manufactured here provided modern methods of vinification are used. Thanks to the experience gained from such co-operation as has existed since 1916, it is now clear that wine farming can be made lucrative, and that the stabilisation of prices, under co-operative methods, relieves the grower from the recurring nightmare of depression caused by over-production. At present the wine farmer, for all the hampering restrictions to which his industry is subject, is still the only agriculturist who does not depend for his existence on outside help, who farms without exhausting the soil or begging from the taxpayer for relief, and who is able, even though he is sadly handicapped by legislation, profitably to dispose of his product.

The question is, how long will he be left in that fortunate state, and what he should do, or attempt to have done, in order to remain in it or to improve his condition.

The first point to be considered is the disposal of his product. There is no sense in growing something for which there is no market, unless it is to supply the grower's own immediate needs. Hitherto, over-production has been the worry and heartache of the winegrower, and he has escaped from its tragic consequences only by timely co-operation. That over-production is, however, far more apparent than real, although under existing conditions even its pretence is economically as disastrous as its actual existence may be. If we may estimate the annual production of wine in the Union at 80 million gallons a year, which is approximately the total yield in 1939-40, and take the population to be 12 million — an estimate that is probably much below the real figure, for we have never yet had an accurate census — the average consumption of wine per head of population is found to be 6½ gallons. If we subtract from the total production the increasingly large quantity of wine that is exported, the total annual consumption of wine per head of population is in the neighbourhood of 6 gallons and a fraction of a gallon. Compared with other wine-producing countries, this is a ludicrous state of affairs. On the figures alone one is entitled to say that there can be no question of a real over-production of wine in this country until the total production has increased to allow for a much greater annual consumption per head of population. Moreover, one is perfectly justified in claiming that, if the public realised that the present attitude towards the wine industry is nationally and economically unsound, and insisted that the existing restrictions on it be removed, there would be no difficulty in finding an ample local market for all the wine that is produced in the Union.

The present unfortunate situation is the result of an ignorance that has engendered a prejudice which for many years has helped to undermine the health and well-being of the population. Through the absurd but insistent propaganda of the prohibitionists, the public has been led to believe that drunkenness is the inevitable effect of wine drinking, wholly overlooking the fact that countries where the consumption of wine per head of population is far in excess of what it is here are invariably more sober than is the Union. A visitor from the Union obtains immediate evidence of this fact when he enters the territory of Mozambique where there is no prohibition of wine drinking, but where spirits and fortified wines are not drunk by the Natives. Many special commissions have from time to time been appointed to consider the question of drunkenness among our Coloured population, but few of them have been able to deal with the matter in a scientific way, and all have been greatly influenced by the opinion of prohibitionists who have had no real experience of the situation. One may instance the recent recommendation of one such commission, namely that the wine ration on the farms in the western districts of the Cape should be summarily abolished. There can be no doubt that the wine ration gives to Coloured labourers, engaged in agricultural work, a *quantum* of food that is of considerable value. That pure natural wine is a food, whose dietetic value is to be measured not so much by the amount of alcohol it contains (which in pure natural wine is comparatively small) as by its amino-acid content, has been shown by more than one investigator. In the wine-producing countries of Europe that fact is now well recognised. The wine ration given to French and Spanish soldiers in Africa was found to be of great dietetic value, and the reasoned report of the committee of French experts who studied the matter has, so far as I am aware, not been invalidated by subsequent investigations. Our forefathers knew this. At the time of Van Riebeeck every sailor was by regulation given his tot of wine. Wheat, wine and oil, after all, are the three basic foods; in combination they make a perfect diet, that needs nothing else, not even the much advertised guava tablets, to improve it. Professor Faure, of the Paris Academy of Medicine, who studied the effects of spirit drinking in urban areas where pure natural wine had largely been displaced by fortified or adulterated wine, stated emphatically that 'nothing is better to combat alcoholism and inebriety than to encourage the moderate use of natural wine, for those who take such wine as their daily drink avoid the invincible need of replacing it with stronger stimulants.'

In order to find out if the tot system on our farms has really any deleterious effect upon the labourers, it would be necessary to institute a series of controlled experiments, and assess the results obtained statistically, with due allowance for errors. That has never been done, and the so-called evidence on the matter is of no scientific value.

One needs no experimental evidence, however, to estimate the appalling evil that results from part prohibition in a wine-producing country, where a fraction of the population is allowed to consume not only natural wine but fortified wine and spirits, while the vast majority is debarred from consuming even natural wine. That total prohibition cannot succeed in making a country sober has been sadly demonstrated in America. That prohibition in part, and applied only to the poorer and intellectually and culturally lower section of the population, must inevitably lead to an increase of drunkenness among that section is a fact that South Africa has learned to know, though hardly yet to appreciate, during the long period in which it has been enforced. The present situation would be as amusing as an insect play if it were not so truly tragic, so amazingly illogical, and so horribly indicative of public ignorance and apathy. A glance at the Liquor Act reveals how fuddled were the minds of the legislators that passed it. In the Cape a Non-European labourer may drink a portion of natural wine if he is over 21 years of age; in the Free State he need be only 18 years of age to get a tot of spirits as well. In the Cape the Native may no longer drink at all, though from the earliest times slaves, who were not Moslems, obtained their daily ration of wine. The qualifications for a Coloured man who wishes to drink a glass of natural wine in the Transkei are defined in a manner worthy of far better purposes. An Asiatic, who may drink natural wine in company with our Union representatives while discussing the future of South-West Africa at a dinner of the United Nations Security Commission, may not be supplied with liquor if he happens to visit the Union. One wonders how it comes about that those who framed this inept legislation have not been stirred to that phrensy of which Latimer speaks in one of his sermons when he declared that there are two things that may raise a just man's anger: 'To be misunderstood and mis-said when his intention is good, and to be blamed for what he has neither encompassed through malignity nor been able to avert through assiduity.' For certainly the colour bar in our liquor legislation was inserted with the best intentions. No efforts on the part of Parliament, however, could have stayed or averted its inevitable consequences. Its repeal, which is imperatively necessary in the interests of all concerned, can only be brought about by educating the public to realise that the proper way to eliminate drunkenness is to promote the consumption of light, natural wine, and to check thereby — and not by prohibition — the consumption of spirituous liquor.

That, then, is one of the first tasks to which the winegrowers and merchants must devote their energies. They should institute vigorous propaganda, by public lectures, through the wireless and press, by advertisement and by pictorial presentation, in the manner in which the Californian winegrowers are tackling the problem today, to educate the public to realise that *natural wine is a food, a valudable dietetic adjunct, and a great national asset.* From such a realisation a change in the existing liquor laws must inevitably follow, for no public that is aware of the food value of light wines will permit them to be classed as semi-poisons whose sale, supply and purchase are hedged round with vexations and arbitrary restrictions.

No less urgent and imperative it is for both the winegrowers and the wine merchants to put on the market light wines of the *vin ordinaire* type whose cheapness should be no indication of their inferiority. The making of 'fine' wines, vintage wines of outstanding quality, need not be neglected; in fact, more attention should be paid to producing such superior quality vintages of which there are at present too few on the market. But if the large local market that will be available in this country if the part-prohibition that now reigns has been removed is to be adequately and properly supplied, it must be with wines that have the merit of cheapness as well as wholesomeness. To many of us one of the amazing features of the wine industry is the variation in the price of wines of the same brand and the same makers at different licensed houses. The late Mr Santhagens made a beautifully balanced light red wine, a wine of individuality and excellent flavour, with a remarkably low alcoholic content. He found that he could not get this wine retailed except at a price per quart bottle double of that at which he was prepared to supply it. That happened some years ago, and the position may have been altered for the better, but it is still a fact that one is sometimes charged two hundred per cent more for a bottle of wine consumed at table than what one would have paid for it to the manufacturer when bought by the case. Unless light wine is moderately cheap, it cannot hope to compete with malt liquors, nor with the many bizarre mixtures that are offered as 'temperance' beverages.

The production of such wines is a matter for co-operative and intelligent combination between winegrower and winery. It would be too much to expect every viticulturist to make such light *vin ordinaire* of a uniform standard and quality, for it needs capital and organisation. When the local market has expanded to demand such wines in quantity, there will be no fear of over-production; on the contrary, a far larger number of tons of grapes will be required each year. That should give a stimulus to the small farmer, the owner of say two or three morgen of ground, who can grow grapes for the winery without the trouble of making wine himself. In France it is pre-eminently the small winegrower who is responsible for the large annual production of beverage wines. 'Of the 18 800 winegrowers of the Cote-d'or,' writes Dr Hewitt, 'more than 14 000 cultivate less than one hectare (2½ acres) apiece, and it is obvious that such small proprietors would not have the capital to procure modern plant or the time to spare to take proper care of the wine when made. Since 1909, seventeen co-operative wineries have been established in the Cote-d'or ... Each makes wine from the produce of 10 to 70 hectares, and on the average each contributor sends in the produce of one and three-quarter acres ... The co-operators agree to send in only grapes of a particular variety.' Co-operative wineries of this character have now been established everywhere in the wine districts in France and also in Algiers, and produce wines that are of standard, uniform quality.

A third matter to which viticulturists might with advantage pay some attention is to obtain such modification of the Wine, Vinegar and Spirits Act as to permit them to apply more modern methods of vinification than those so succinctly detailed in that measure. Chaptalisation, which is permitted in France, is unlawful here; the addition of citric acid to the must, sanctioned by the French law of 1921, is also prohibited with us, although it might be possible to argue that it is allowable under the reservation 'any natural product of the grape'; *platrage* and *tartrage*, and the use of acid calcium phosphate, are also illegal, though allowed in France. Our white wines that are particularly likely to turn turbid (*casse*) cannot be treated by the ferrocyanide process which is now generally employed in Europe. Dr Hewitt's remarks are apposite:

> 'The so-called light wines of South Africa are much higher in alcoholic strength than the average European wines of a similar class, owing to the high specific gravity and sugar content of the must before fermentation. This in itself appears to favour *casse* in the white wines, and certainly detracts from their value as beverages for general table use. There is a commonsense remedy for this which would be simple and efficacious if certain legal enactments were removed.'

The clause in the Wine, Vinegar and Spirits Act prohibiting the sale of wine containing more than 20 grammes of sugar per litre, unless it is fortified, also stands in need of amendment.

The winegrowers have, in the KWV, an admirable organisation that can, and should, take the lead in initiating reforms and educating the public. Already it has ventured to suggest a means whereby the drunkenness among the Coloured population might be attacked. The suggestion will have to be implemented by legislative action, and it is already clear that the whole strength of the prohibition party will be thrown against any attempt to remove the restrictions imposed on the wine industry by the liquor law. The sale of light wines to Coloured and Native citizens of the Union ought not to be a matter for the decision of a group of fanatics; it should be the concern of the whole community. The present situation is an absurdity from whatever point it is looked at. The wine farmer is, by implication, stigmatised as the maker of a food product that three-quarters of the population of the Union is debarred from using; for a Native to use that product is a crime; for a White man to supply him with that product, even in the privacy of his home, is equally a crime. The logical conclusion is that if that product is so frightfully poisonous to everyone who is not fortunate enough to possess a complexion of old red sandstone hue, its makers should be prevented from making it at all. That is a conclusion and an implication which the winegrower and the wine merchant should not submit to, and it is wholly in their interests to expose the fallacy that underlies both.

The public, too, can, and should, do much to help the industry, but here again the profound ignorance about wine, the age-old prejudice against Cape wine, the snobbishness that prefers an indifferent imported wine to a thoroughly sound, wholesome local brand, and the deeply ingrained notion that cheap wine must necessarily be bad wine and a highly priced wine or brandy just as necessarily a far superior article, militate against any progress. In what are supposed to be the most enlightened circles in South Africa, one often hears strong disparagement of local wines. Comparisons, as invidious as they are silly, are made between imported wines and the local product, to the detriment of the latter, simply because those that elect to draw such comparisons do not know anything about wine and are not capable of judging between a good and a bad wine. The annual wine shows that are now regularly held should do something to train the lay public to recognise good wine. The press has in recent years shown a praiseworthy tendency to deal with wine in a practical, commonsense manner, and it is evident to those who can read the signs of the times that the blatant intolerance of the prohibitionists no longer secures from the public that tacit approval and acquiescence that it did in the past. Another encouraging sign is the fact that the Dutch Reformed Church, whose influence in the wine-growing districts is still potent, has expressed itself willing to work in collaboration with the KWV in its efforts to eradicate drunkenness by more scientific and logical means than by a one-sided prohibition. The expression by the Church of that willingness was made in the teeth of violent opposition, which makes the fact that the Synod passed the resolutions in which it was embodied all the more remarkable. The Catholic Church, too, has shown itself tolerant and disinclined to identify itself with the extreme prohibitionists, of whose destructive policies it has had ample experience in America. The Protestant sects, with the exception of the Dutch Reformed, have, however, generally supported the movement for prohibition, largely through ignorance of the facts of the case and under the charitable impression that they are furthering the interests of the Natives.

In the foregoing chapters it has been shown that South Africa has an ideal climate and soil for the production of wine grapes, and that there is no reason why it should not make the best wines in the world. The improvement that has been made during the last 25 years in the wine industry is encouraging, and gives promise of further betterment in all directions. The future of the industry is dependent entirely upon the manner in which the public is prepared to support it, first by recognising that it is an industry of national importance devoted to the production of a foodstuff that is of considerable use to the community, and secondly by admitting that it today labours under restrictions that are odious, vexatious and calculated to strangle any further development that demands capital and labour. We have little reason to be proud of some of the laws that have been placed on our statute book since Union, but there is none so laughably illogical, so flagrantly undemocratic, so ferociously racial and, let it be added, so egregiously inept as that which regulates the sale and purchase of wine. It is an example of attempted prohibition that has not dared, for obvious reasons, to crystallise in it the stupid fallacies that underlie the movement that supported it. 'Prohibition,' remarks Mr A P Herbert's Lord Chancellor, 'is an offence against the customs of the civilised world . . . and the nation guilty of it must be considered an international outlaw.' Without endorsing this sweeping statement, one may point out that the attempt at prohibition in South Africa, which has now been tried since 1851, has been a miserable failure; every year the number of convictions for illicit liquor selling increases, the illicit trade prospers, mainly because the Native population of the large urban areas necessarily grows with the greater demand for domestic and industrial labour, and the consumption of spirits is heavily augmented. The wine farmer and the vintner are presumed to make some noxious thing whose consumption and sale must be surrounded with far more stringent precautions than the state judges sufficient to prevent the misuse of strychnine and arsenic; new offences are created, and all kinds of vexatious and generally utterly useless, so far as the encouragement of sobriety is concerned, restrictions are enforced by law. It is merely because the public so far has not taken sufficient interest in the subject and, because its own interests as a spirit-drinking community have not been seriously attacked, has remained indulgently apathetic about the denial of private rights to three-fourths of the citizens, that this legislation has not met with the protest and repeal that it deserves.

For the development of the wine industry, it is advisable to make an end to this sorry legislation that allows a minority of the population to consume a drink of far greater dietetic value than an infusion of tea or coffee only under certain restrictions, and prohibits the sale and consumption of natural wine to three-fourths of the population under dire penalties. In every wine-producing country every citizen, irrespective of age, class, sex, colour of skin, occupation or standing, is allowed to purchase and drink pure natural wine, and in no wine-producing country except South Africa, where such free purchase and consumption is illegal for ninety per cent of the citizens, is drunkenness and the crimes that drunkenness engenders, alarming or excessive. On our own borders we have the example of such free purchase and consumption of light wines by the Natives, and those of us who have investigated conditions in the territory of Mozambique have returned seriously doubting the efficacy of our own methods of controlling drunkenness within the Union. If the present absurd legislation remains on the statute book, the production of natural light wines will hardly develop sufficiently to counteract the increasing tendency to consume spirits and malt liquors, and the expansion of the wine industry will be confined to the improvement of brandy and fortified wines. No one who

the future

loves South African wine and who has at heart the interests of the industry would like to see that happen in a country whose natural wines should be regarded as a national asset and a communal boon.

Index

bamboo, 87, 88, 165, 349, 394, 472, 505
bananas, 34, 36, 73, 76, 87, 88, 118, 123, 133, 172, 174, 223, 410, 469
Bantry Bay, 36
barbeque, 242
barble fish, 22, 381
Barkly, Sir Henry, 504, 519
barley, 175, 413, 428, 448
Barnato, 545
Barnes, Mrs A R, 22
baroe, 132, 135, 309
Barrow, John, 448
Barry & Co, 548
Barry and Nephew, 517
Barry, JJ, 517
Barry, Sir Edward, 503
barsmielies, 300
basil, 46, 117
Batavia, 19, 394, 412, 414, 415, 421, 424, 427, 430, 436, 437, 439, 441, 442, 483
Batavian rule, 483
Bathurst, Earl, 470
Bathurst, Lord, 483, 485, 486
Baudelaire, 375, 504
bay leaf, 61, 97, 102, 122, 132, 235, 237, 246, 307, 310, 317, 337, 389, 390
Bayonne, 407
bean consommé, 55
bean-herb, 46
beans, dried, 124
beans, green, 124, 125
beans, governor's, 55, 199
beans, stewed dry, 256
bean soup, 54, 55
Beaune, 380, 442
béchamel sauce, 108
Becker, Dr, 532
Beckman, Chaplain Daniel, 426
Bedford, 563, 597, 598
beef at the Cape, 31, 34, 81,
beef biltong, 105
beef bouillon, 52
beer, 52, 61, 209, 264, 329, 360, 361, 411, 425, 426, 474, 527, 569
beer soup, 61
beetroot, 124
beetroot leaves, 49, 214
Belgian sorrel, 46
Bengal, 476
Bengal Hurkaru, 475
Bentinck, Lord William, 503
Berg, Egbertus, 468

Berg, Mrs, 468
Berg River, 462
Bergerac et St Fort wine, 441
Bergh register, the, 501
Bergh, wine merchant, 483
Bergvliet, 426, 442
Berkeley, 531
Berlin Library, 468
Beschreibung des Vorgebirges der Guten Hoffnung, 430
Beulingen, 246
Beyers, JL, 517
Beyers, Mr JC, 517
Bezier of Celte wine, 442
Bezuidenhout, 416
bicarbonate of soda, 93, 177, 202, 296, 302, 333, 373, 374
biltong, 18, 22, 81, 105, 154, 156, 280, 346, 362, 388
bindenfleisch, 280
Bird, C, 473
birds, wild, 258, 261
birds nests from Java, 80
Bishopscourt, 411
Bismarck, Prince, 530
bitter-lemon liqueur, 218
bitterskil, 218
Blaauwbergstrand, 447
Blachang, 19
black moist sugar, 19
black nightshade, 284
black sour braised meat, 93
Blake, Mr Richard, 467, 468
blancmange, 22, 58,
Blankenhorn, Prof A, 537
blatjang, 22, 74, 109, 111, 112, 116, 130
blesbok, 154, 251, 252
blinkblaar, 155, 387
blood sausage, 159
blood soup, 62
bobbejaanuintjies, 132, 277
bobotie, 18, 34, 35, 68, 79, 92, 126, 216, 221, 224, 307, 317, 395
bobotie fruit, 286
bobotie, saffron, 221
boegoe, 234
Boene wine, 442
boerekool, 296
boerewors, 89, 224, 344
boer-meal, 373
Bohemia, 407
boiling, 30
Bokkeveld, 573
bokkoms, 49, 73

bokuintjies, 278
Bols, 209
Bombay, 484
Bombay, Governor of, 503
bonito, 34, 54, 63
Boom, Hendrik, 406, 411
boontjies, katjang, 124
borrie, 44
borrie quince, 95, 113, 288
Borrodiale, 504
Borrowdale, the firm of, 492
bortsch, 337, 352
bossiestroop, 310
Bosheuvel, 409, 410, 412, 414, 420
Bosman, 518
Bosmans, the Paarl, 501
Botanic Gardens, 514
Botha, General, 157
Botma, 416
bouillabaisse, 54, 255
Bourke, Major-General, 469, 484
bowl, 231
brabejum stellatifolium, 132
Bradford, Sir Thomas, 503
Brakfontein, 501, 530
Brakfontein, the Nagmaal wine of, 501
brandy, 264
brandy, old, 217
brains, 102
brawn, 389
Brazil nuts, 353
braaivleis, 242, 370
brain cakes, 159
brain farce, 82
braising, 32
bread, 176, 362
bread, citron, 181
bread, fried, 54, 55, 61, 101, 128, 133, 166, 182
bread mealie, 126, 290
bread soup, 62
bread-and-milk, 175
breakfasts, Cape Town, 35
Breda, Mr Michael, 487
bredie, 38, 81, 94
  bean, 94, 124
  cabbage, 94, 125, 296
  cauliflower, 125
  fish, 72
  hunter's, 152
  lentil, 94
  potato, 94
  pumpkin, 94
  quince, 94, 95, 173

tomato, 94, 95, 130
turnip, 94
vis, 72
Breede River, 524, 539
brick oven, 176
Briers, Mr C J, 475
Brieven der Zendelingen, 1817, 563
Brillat-Savarin, 236, 259, 375
brinjals, 123, 350
brinjal, stuffed, 351
brinjal tart, 351
Brink, Andreas, 410
Brittain, Mr W, 563
Brougham, Mr, 485
brown roux, 49, 58, 92, 93, 97, 108
brown sauce, 108
Bruges, 410
bruin sous, 108
brushwood, 34
Brussels sprouts, 94, 125, 297, 302
buchu, see boegoe
buck, wild, 22, 147, 153
Buckson, Mr A M, 487
buckwheat meal, 238, 239, 240, 252, 258, 262, 312
Buitenzorg, 421
burghers, free, 429, 430
Burgoyne, Cuthbert, Esq, 551
Burgoyne, Messrs, 502
Burgoyne, Mr, 555
Burnett, Sir William, 484
burnt almond sauce, 110
burnt roux, 55
burnt sugar, 55
bush marigolds, 284
bush partridge, 260
bustards, 148
butter, farm, 256, 362, 371
butterfish, 63, 66
buttermilk tripe, 104
butter nuts, 186
button spider, 436

cabbage, red, 125
cabbage, wild, 60, 94, 132, 134,
Cabo, 421, 437
cake, plain, 221
calamus, 39
Calcutta, 11, 476, 483, 517
Caldwell, W, 469
Caledon, the Earl of, 471
calf's-foot soup, 58
calf's-head soup, 58
California, 378, 520, 581, 608

camp sausage, 159
camp food, 369, 372
camp soup, 158, 372
Canaan grapes, 292
Canary wine, 487, 490
candy sugar, 19, 60, 61, 161, 183
Canton, 483, 517
Cape cookery
  characteristics of, 11
  foundations of, 11
Cape gooseberries, 167
Cape gooseberry sauce, 109
Cape Literary Gazette, 475
Cape Monthly Magazine, 520, 532
Cape of Good Hope
  Agricultural Society, 507, 515,
Cape Pittosporum, 307
Cape Town Exhibition, 517
Cape Town fish market, 63
Cape Town Wine and Export
  Syndicate, 545
capers, 39
capsicum paprika, 43
caraway, 45
cardamon, 45, 88,
cardamon seed, 39, 45
Carême, 258, 284, 343, 372
carica papaja, 286
carne secca, 280
Carolina, South, 242
carp, 66, 381
carrots, 125
carrot sambal, 118
caryophyllus aromaticus, 42
Casks, Inspector of, 474,
casse, 377, 609
cassia, 39, 40
cassia quills, 40
cast offings, 99
Castle, the, 117, 189, 468
catmint, 46
Cato, 107
caul, 272, 275
cauliflower, 22, 78, 94, 125
cauliflower, wild, 226
Cavendish, Hon F, 503
Cayenne pepper, 43, 104
Cecil, Lord, 503
celery, 46, 125
celery seed, 45
celery sauce, 109
Ceylon, 40, 218, 405,
Ceylon, Governor of, 503
champagne-cup, 235

Chancellor of the Exchequer, 480, 490, 575
Charente region, 266
Charides, 14
Chartreuse, 218
Chartreux Abbey, 218
Chateau Yquem, 530
Cheap Jack, 35
Cheap John, 468
cheese, chilli, 187
cheese, old ship's, 187
cherries, 167
cherry liqueur, 218
chervil, 227
chestnuts, 60, 134, 239, 300
Chiappini, Mr Charles, 549
Chiappini, E, 517
chicken curry, 89
chicken salad, 116
chicken's eggs, 248
chilli, 39, 43
chilli cheese, 187
China, 117, 161, 171, 341
China, French Commercial
  Mission to, 503
chincherinchee, 226, 278
Chinese, old cookbook, 343
Chinese cooks at the Cape, 11
chlorophyll, 214, 301
chops, 86, 87, 96, 371
  braaied, 370
  cotelette á là Maintenon, 370
  mutton, 86
  Spanish-reed, 347
  tame meat, 370
Christmas drinks, 354
chutney, 112, 113
  Cape, 22
  quince, 113
  rose apple, 113
  sweet, 130
cinnamic aldehyde, 40
cinnamon, 39, 40
citron, 47
citron bread, 181
citron omelet, 182
Citrusdal, 309, 504
Civil Service Supply
  Association, London, 546
clams, 79
Clanwilliam, 171
Clare, Earl, 503
claret-cup, 235
Clarke, General, 446
clay ovens, 34
Cloete, Jacob, the day-book of, 497

Macartney, Earl, 448
mace, 39, 40
macédoine, 167, 293
Mackenzie, Sir Morell, 530
Maclaren, Watson & Co, 504
Macowen, Professor, 534
Madras, 484
Madras, Archdeacon of, 503
Magalakwyn River, 386
Magellanischen Schluckchen, 492
Maitland, 35
maize, 126, 413, 428
maizena, 54, 252, 284, 287, 352, 353
malagas eggs, 36, 137
Malay cookery, characteristics of, 5
Malay trassie, 111
Melbourne, 517
mallemuck, 261
malt vinegar, 47, 348
mandarin orange, 47
Mandelbrote, Professor, 430
mangoes, 174
Mannerschmidt, Dr, 515
manuscripts, 5, 6, 14, 15, 18, 19, 20, 22, 23, 26, 40, 46, 49, 53, 68, 96, 102, 120, 141, 146, 152, 155, 157, 174, 187, 276, 484, 497, 501
maracas, 295
Marais, Mr P, 544,
marakka, 126
maraschino, 207, 218
Marieau, Jean, 418
Marillac Bros, 517
marinade, 35, 66, 74, 87, 88, 154, 251, 252, 381, 387,
marinading, 35
marinading game, 251
marjoram, 46
market, 36
market, fish and vegetable, 207
Marloth, Dr, 206
Marquard, Joachim, 415
Marquard, Tobias, 410
marrow, 97, 104, 183, 272, 275
marrow pudding, 100
Marshal of France, 447
Marsyas, 262
Martin's, Mr, 494, 504
marulas, 258
marzipan, 341,
Mastika, 218
Matthew, Mr R, of New South Wales, 504

Mauritius, 391, 414, 416, 417, 483, 494, 546
Mayer and Co, Bordeaux, 546
Mayer, Mr Clemens, 543
Maynier, Honoratus, 410
Maynier, Honoratus (grandson), 410
mayonnaise, 116,
McGibbon, Mr, 514, 531, 538
meal yeast, 177
meat, black sour braised, 93
meat, curried, 239
meat, frayed, 251
meat frikkadels, 89
meat, salt or pickled, 96
meat, short, 262
meat, stuffed or farced, 96
meat, zebra, 154
medlar, 202, 207, 341
Medulla Destillatoria et Medica, 406
meebos, 166
Meester Cornelis, 447
Melck, 462, 463
melkbos, 206
melk frummeltjies, 312
melk kluitjies, 184
melons, 171
Mentzel, 11, 137, 146, 153,
Mentzel, Otto, 430, 434, 435, 436, 437, 441,
Merklein, 434
Merriman, Mr John X, 309, 527, 536, 537, 543, 557, 573
metachatina kraussi, 283
Mexican pepper, 43
Middelburg, 429, 438
Middle Ages, 14, 92, 224, 341, 579
mielies, 22, 61, 83, 94, 113, 126, 127, 176, 289
mielie and green bean soup, 290
mielie bread, 127, 290, 291
mielie bredie, 94, 127
mielie cakes, 290
mielie chutney, 113
mielies baked, 127
    boiled, 126
    fried green, 127
    green, 22, 61, 83,
    raisin, 176
mignonette, 46
Milbert, the artist, 475
milk, 311
milk and toast, 175
milk and wine, 175

milk brawn, 175
milk dumplings, 184
milk, fat, 175
milk, sago, 175
milk tart, 183, 184, 221
millerandage, 473
Mills, Sir Charles, 537
mincemeat, 297, 344, 351
mint, 46, 125, 296, 307
Mirada, 278
Moddermorgel, 381
moepels, 259
moes, 135
molasses, 47, 529
Moluccas, 40
Montagu, 539, 601, 602
Montagu Dop, 548
Montague, Mr Secretary, 504
Montreal, 484
moorhen, 262
mootjies, 66
moraea edulis, 131, 277
morea edule, 60, 131
moraea family, 278
Morris, Miss, 18
mortadello, 343
mosbolletjies, 266
moskonfyt, 47, 177, 278
moskonfytsous, 110
mossie, 259
Mostert, Wouter Cornelis, 415
Mouille Point, 36
mountain sage, 46
mountain sorrel, 302
Mouton, *Oom* Abram, 530, 584
Moutons, the Clanwilliam, 501
Mowbray, 468
Mozambique, 11, 35, 483, 500, 606, 611
Muir, Dr, 277
Mulberries, 167
mulberry pudding, 170
mulberry drink, 358
Mulders, Martin, 477
mulled wine, 174
mullet, 63, 73
mulligatawny soup, 59
Multatuli, 376
muraltia spinosa, 109
Murray, John, 472
Murray's dictionary, 424
Muscovy duck, 82, 97, 98, 101, 149, 261, 298
Mushrooms, 123
musk, 47
muslin, 44, 53, 59, 455
mussel bobotie, 317

List of scientific names and their modern equivalents

Caryophyllus aromaticus = Syzygium aromaticum
Cinnamomum cassia = Cinnamomum aromaticum
Cyanella capensis = Cyanella hyacintoides
Eugenia acris pimento = Pimenta officinalis
Haliotis capensis = Haliotis midae
Moraea edulis = Moraea fugax
Oxalis lupinifolia = Oxalis flava
Prionium palmita = Prionium serratum

Glossary

baas, master or boss

biltong, dried strips of meat

blatjang, chutney

blits, (in context) spirit

boegoe, *Agathosma* species, usually shrubby with highly aromatic foliage

bredie, stew

dikkop, stone curlew

dop, drink

gogga, insect

grootoom, great uncle

ingelegde fish, pickled or curried fish

kabob, kebab

klip fish, group of rock fish belonging to the Clinidae family

klipkous, abalone or perlemoen

kloof, ravine

koeksister, sweet, syrupy, doughnut-like delicacy

kraal, pen or outdoor enclosure for animals

kraalbossies, bushes forming part of an outdoor enclosure

kreef, crayfish

kukumakranka, *Gethyllis* species

moskonfyt, grape syrup

neef, cousin (male)

niggie, cousin (female)

omie, little uncle (literally), used affectionately

oom, uncle, widely used term of respect, not limited to relatives

oubaas, old master

oupa, grandfather

outa, respected old African or Coloured male gardener or servant

perlemoen, pearl mussel or abalone

platteland, countryside

rhinoceros bush, Renosterbos (*Elytropappus rhinocerotis*)

rose apple, *Syzigium jambos*

salamander, metal plate used for browning or caramelising dishes

sambal, condiment

smoorbraai, braai under and over coals

sosatie, kebab

tannie, aunt, widely used term of respect, not limited to relatives

tassal, biltong cut into small strips

vlei, shallow lake

water hawthorn, floating water plant (*Aponogeton distachyos*) with scented white
    flowers

Measurements

As is evident from the text, Leipoldt was not a stickler for precision of measurement in the kitchen. See, for example, his description of how hot the oven should be when making an *uintjie* soufflé: 'just as warm as that in which you would roast a guinea-fowl'. This is part of the delight of Leipoldt's approach to the culinary art. For the benefit of those who prefer to cling to such exactitude as is to be found in Leipoldt, however, we repeat the somewhat less than extensive guide set out at the end of the first edition of *Leipoldt's Cape Cookery*.

> 'METRICATION: The author did not choose to give specific and detailed lists of ingredients for the recipes in this book. To retain the flavour of the original text it has not been metricated and such terms as "pound" or "ounce" are occasionally found.
>
> (One pound = 453 grams; one ounce = 28 grams)'

Subscribers to the collector's edition of
Leipoldt's Food & Wine

MRD Anderson
GL Ashmead

Dr & Mrs G G Barnett
Nicolas Baumann
Aletta E Bergh
Martin & Yola Bergh
Bobby & Tish Bertrand
Piet Beyers
Mrs A R Bisogno
Hanna Boeke
Desmond Bowes-Taylor, *in memoriam*
John Bridgeman
Keith Bryer
Hugh and Sherry Bush
Anna Butler
Ashley Butler
Michael Craig Buys

Adv Andrew Caiger
Brian Caplen
Anne Chaitman
Delia Chaitman
Patrick Chapman
Sarah Christie
Roger & Glenda Cleaver
JJ Coates
Adv P Coetsee SC
Jan Coetzee
Vivien Cohen
Kristo Conradie
Hugh Corder
John Coulton

Gus Danowski
Henry Danowski
Jane Danowski
Raymond Danowski
Michael de Bliquy
Justina de Jager
Dennis Delahunt
Molteno Library, Diocesan College
Izelle du Plessis
Errieda du Toit
Gillian Durrant

Clare Emslie
David Emslie
James Emslie
Stephen Emslie
Trevor & Anne Emslie

Gwen Fagan
Alan Fergus
John and Vifi Franklin
Glenda Freitag
Isabelle Franzen
Josephine Frater
Paul Frost

Stefano & Tizi Gabba
Andrew & Nancy Gilchrist
Betty L Gillespie
David & Joan Glennie
Janet K Graaff
Tessa Graaff
Verne Grinstead

Alan McA Harvey
CR Haw
Fiona Hayward
Annelize Hennop
Christopher W L Hull
Victor & Thérèse Hulme

Mrs E Jack
FA Joubert

Guy Kern-Martin
Avril Knott-Craig
Peter Knox-Shaw

R le Roux
Frances Liebenberg
Jenny Longworth
Brenda & Nicola Louw
Fred Louw
Nic Louw
Alison Margaret Lowry

Lindsay & Penny Madden
David McLennan

Annatjie Melck
Annie Moag
Anette Molenaar
Kathy Molenaar
Margie Molenaar
Bill Moody
Mary Moore
Beth Murray
Paul Murray

Roy Narunsky
Simphewe Ncwadi
Christo Neethling

Sandra Olivier
Johannes J Oosthuizen
Lesley Osler

Jane and Haydn Parry
Peter N Pentz
Michael Pettit
Dr Bernard Price

Robbie Reddering
Debbie Reinders-Hall
Freda Rens
Marius Retief
William Ritchie
Bruce & Kate Robertson
Antoinette Rossouw
Rozenhof Restaurant
Jim & Elaine Russell

Monica Sandri
Sarietoetskombuis
Mrs Anita Saunders
David Schalkwyk
Thomas Leith Searle
Fraser Shaw
Alice, Frances & Elsie Sholto-Douglas
Simon Sephton
Jessica & Eric Setterberg
Silwood Kitchen
V David Smith
RGL Stelzner

Ethel Steyn
Theuns Steyn
Barry Streek
Retha Swanepoel

Chris Theron
Sheila Thomas
Wendy Toerien-Bristow
Lawrence Tucker

RL Valentine
Brian & Dian van der
  Vijver
Riaan van Heerden
Karin van Rooyen
Rudi van Rooyen
Riaan van Wyk

Cindy Webber
Carin Wiese

John & Marjorie Williams
Jerry Windell
Sarah Winter
John Woodland
Dr E J L Woods
Dr Ian Woods
Steve and Debbie Woods

Christine Zietsman

The publisher thanks the above subscribers, as well as
those who preferred not to be named, for their support.